## Also by Sylvia Ashton-Warner

I PASSED THIS WAY

Sylvia Ashton-Warner

# I PASSED THIS WAY

Alfred A. Knopf · New York · 1979

THIS IS A BORZOI BOOK
PUBLISHED BY ALFRED A. KNOPF, INC.

Library of Congress Cataloging in Publication Data
Ashton-Warner, Sylvia.
I passed this way.
1.  Ashton-Warner, Sylvia—Biography.
2.  Novelists, New Zealand—20th century—
Biography.  I.  Title.
PR9639.3.A8Z47      1979      823 [B]      79-2133
ISBN 0-394-42612-6

Manufactured in the United States of America
First Edition

# Contents

# Preface

A book about a life in New Zealand could be expected to begin in New
Zealand, except that this one doesn't. I happen to be abroad at the moment and have been for some years. So are many other New Zealanders.
Not necessarily for the same reason; not all of us expatriates have been
rejected by our country. Some of us have rejected what was once our
country and we're not short of reasons.

From this country abroad I can say I'm one who's been both rejected by and who has rejected my country, not a world-shattering
statement. What's new about being rejected by one's country? Millions are experiencing this all the time and millions more are doing the
rejecting. Living out here in the wild air of new thought you're soon
cured of thinking you're the only one and self-pity doesn't have a show.

Yet although I've lived and worked in many another place for
many a year now, and still do, I'm putting this on paper for where it
comes from: New Zealand. When expatriates deny the springs of home
the spirit withers and dies. At least you'll know where New Zealand is
and the place-names. Just try writing for foreign reviewers, critics and
editors and your work runs the risk of losing a dimension, unable to
sound the recesses of yourself to mine the common wealth of the
undermind. Rather than make an organic utterance important to you
and everyone else you make only a flat noise.

I too have fallen for this in my time but I've learnt the lesson so
I pick up again the style of my first books written in New Zealand,
about New Zealand and for New Zealand. True, I'm not there now as I
write, but my spirit is. "Spirit" is not an acceptable word out here but
then I'm not writing for "out here."

How can a country be your own when you are no longer her own?

It's like a broken love-affair never again to be mended. Millions of expatriates from other countries well know what I mean, many of whom I'm living with all the time and working with at university. After a while you learn that to be rejected turns out to be not too crucial, since anyone's real "own country" is one's own mind which accompanies us anywhere. Within us as we wander or settle abroad remain the springs of home. The spirit has this way of living on and on wherever you've unpacked your suitcase: in the battlement of an eleventh-century castle in Jerusalem, in a hotel-room in Mauritius populated by cockroaches and lizards for free, in a wide marble-floored room of some past colonial palace in India, a tall-ceilinged apartment in London, in some huge house on the top of the Rockies in the United States, an expansive ground-floor apartment in Canada, in a tight little cabin on an ocean liner, on a seat on some great plane above some great ocean . . . oh hotels, houses, apartments, name it. But to return home is to do no more than look in your heart. "Heart" is another word that is persona non grata.

And now, before I go on, just a word to people out here about where New Zealand is. We get more than sick of hearing it's a province of a large neighbouring continent. You know which.

It is autumn in the northern hemisphere, the fall, and I'm on research semester from the university . . . school they call it here. Rather nice. But it will be spring in New Zealand now. The godwits will have returned from Siberia to the estuaries of those islands; from their breeding grounds to their feeding grounds. Slender birds to a slender country but strong in their native instincts; shooting all weathers, mounting all storms to reach those southernmost beaches, as the Maoris did when they came; man and bird equally unaware of their own genius for navigation.

When the Maoris first saw this place in the exhausted distance it looked like a long white cloud to them and that is what they named it: The Land of the Long White Cloud—which must be how the godwits see it at the close of a long migration, and what we exiles see in mind during our migration; for the tale of New Zealand could be told in terms of long migrations, of expatriates alone.

Frankly I don't know too much about New Zealand myself, for the reason that I lived there. Along with other Long White Clouders I spent my time gazing overseas-ward, living as we did in minor parts of a minor country on a minor planet, one of the least of the planets in the least of the solar systems in a junior universe. How mere of the merest our atom land! Our diffidence abroad can be excused.

In these "lonely latitudes" (Louis Johnson) and unfrequented longitudes, surfed by oceans from every horizon, the New Zealand eye is obliged to turn outward, north-westward back to our first breeding grounds, urgently checking our British origins and tracking our famous exiles, so we don't see much of ourselves at home. "Didn't" I should say. I keep writing as though I were there still. Well, in spirit I am. We saw little more than astronomers see on our dust-speck planet as, gazing away into space, they seek the origins of the Earth.

From a "wilderness of ocean" (Monte Holcroft) New Zealand heaves abruptly to the sky, with no introduction, the tops of her mountains lost in cloud. A slender country as I've said, though a thousand miles long but a hundred miles wide, most of us living within sound of the sea or in sight of the rearing ranges.

A lonely country also: to the east, six thousand miles of pagan Pacific as far as South America; to the south, sixteen hundred empty miles as far as the Antarctic; to the west, twelve hundred turbulent miles as far as Australia; while to the north, six thousand vague equatorial miles to the super-domain of Asia; not to omit that longest mileage to our racial origins: fourteen thousand miles round the world to the United Kingdom. In the eternal ocean the Long White Cloud is the last sizable bastion between the inhabited Earth and the ice-packs of the Pole. Sea-surrounded we burn alone.

Yet accident of dwelling place does not necessarily mean parochialism of the soul. With man balancing nature, people were born and educated with minds larger than size. Isolation is the best condition for procreation as lovers will agree, ostracism the best sperm for conception, silence the best womb for the idea-fetus, persecution the best of incubators, and austerity the best education; all of which the White Cloud supplied with profligacy, tossing up one large mind after another.

Now that I'm far enough and long enough away to look inward on that country, all I can see, still, is the girl spirit of New Zealand standing slight mid-land, her fingers tight on the beginnings of threads, taut from the pull of her ranging birds in the skies overseas. Could she but haul in her exiles, all there together, both buried and living; could she afford her great, the rest of the world might possibly see her and come to learn where she is.

# I

1908 - 1925

TARANAKI  The gale-high hills we walked barefoot, eating the heavy-honey clover, the tough red rose-hips when we were hungry which was often enough and the luscious base of the raupo stalks pulled from the swamp by the lake. Three little girls with wondering eyes, Daphne, Sylvie and Norma. Looming heights of forest giants and sparkling bouldered streams, from which we'd hurry home when darkness chased, home to the yellow windows. Pushing past each other in the narrow doorway to find Puppa there sitting by the stove on his upright chair, his crutches tucked behind him. Stroking potatoes in the pan with a knife in his knotted hand, his mustache proudly curling. Browning the potatoes underneath in the way he knew we liked them. Mumma bathing the babies in the tub by the stove, someone sentimental at the piano, the big ones talking secretly or one of them weeping behind a door on some failed love. These I see when I look inward.

Or I see the miles we walked to school along country roads and the slow miles walked homeward, trailing Mumma ahead of us, a short moving isosceles triangle loaded with grocery parcels and books, forging steadily ahead of us, leading us as we loitered telling stories to each other, glamorous and marvellous about Arab steeds, princely status and dolls as big as ourselves.

These story-laden days reside in mind as I work at this university abroad. As the months and the years count by in my work my adulthood is increasingly bracketed in dream and I am Child again.

Somewhere round Stratford in Taranaki I think was the first school I attended where Mumma took me with her at seven weeks old and where I did my stretch in a pram in the porch. At home I recall standing in my cot boo-hooing in the dark, often, but probably enjoying it. Mumma did confess at ninety, however, "You don't know this, Sylv, but when your father first began to be ill and you were two, I had to leave you home when I went to school, but your father couldn't leave his bed. I used to put some milk on a chair beside him, and some bread, and when I left I shut all the doors. Then when you were hungry or thirsty you would toddle to him and he'd feed you something." She seemed to be regretful about it.

"That's nothing," I said and I meant it. In my travels I see much worse happening to affluent children in the reign of the media. "At least, Mumma, I wasn't alone, I was allowed my *own* thoughts and was allowed to live out my own drama in a two-year-old way." All of which was to say that my mind was free.

"Yes, but Sylv, you did start school at seven weeks."

"So what? One of my own sons started school at thirteen months and the other at two weeks when I taught across him on the school table. What I think, Mumma," I was walking with her, "is that it's not always what we do to our child but what he feels about it. I've felt all right about all that. It's only a sense of injustice that endures and I don't have any." A few more slow steps. "Not about that, anyway."

And that's about all that got through to me about my earliest childhood, but I do recall I was more audience than performer to the rest of the family, manifesting no particular distinction, not even being a boy which went for something those days; neither the eldest nor the youngest, the prettiest nor the wittiest nor the best musician but a freckled nonentity somewhere in the middle of a large sprawling family, thoroughly outshone. But I didn't realise it or mind. It was such fun having Daphne just above me whose fascination and wit and beauty and singing and piano enthralled not only the family but many a gathering for the rest of her life, amusing the doctors on her deathbed. The flower o' the flock, Puppa called her. No one was ever jealous.

I was lucky to be lost in the shadow of Daphne, the one just above me, to be endlessly entertained; it excused me from the spotlight, being shy, ugly and untouchable. After the latest family disaster Mumma would say, "Make us laugh, Daph," at which she would move mid-centre, her brown curls swinging, green eyes flinging and mimic the landlord who'd just tipped over our tank for not paying the rent; then you'd hear Puppa's high falsetto laughter from his chair by the stove, or from his bed in his room.

Hold it. I did have two distinctions: on my own evidence I was the greatest bawler ever not choked. If anything went against me I'd get behind the house and start this boo-hooing, hour after hour, putting everything theatrical I knew into it. To me it was a matter of making a workmanlike job of it, enough pathos to move the devil himself. Real stage practice, except that it didn't work. The only response I recall is Mumma sneaking round the corner, grabbing me, up goes my dress, down come my pants and would I get the weight of Mumma's hand! I knew Mumma's hand well and always on that one bared spot. So did the others in their day. It was only the big ones who boxed your ears.

The other distinction goes like this: the girl who was born just before Daphne was christened Sylvia Ashton but she died. Then there was Daphne. Then me. For some reason never identified Mumma christened me also Sylvia Ashton. It makes a better story to say it was Mumma's absent-mindedness . . . after all, families were very big in those days and each child had several names, so a little confusion can be excused. On the other hand it could have been a legitimate replacement. But this has so messed up my visa that I've got to the place where I myself don't always remember which one I am or what my age is. Daphne had the last word: "No wonder you're frightened of the dark, Sylv: you're named after a ghost."

We played in the wilds, three little girls, telling endless stories. Barefoot, long-haired, talking all the time and making endless houses. That's what I see a world away when I look inward and homeward, to those hardly known South Pacific Islands much of a lifetime away.

The family—
Muriel and
Ashton missing

*School Two*

T O K O   I think my second school was Toko, Taranaki still. I'm sharing an old desk with another little girl and we're both drawing a cup and saucer. The slates in those days before Paper took over were lined in squares on one side so that following the lines our cups and saucers were satisfyingly angular and, since I was copying hers, both exactly the same. But the glow of the moment was not the same; she rubbed hers out almost at once but, to me, that something should appear on that slate of mine, even though strictly copied, that something which had not been there before now was there, and from my own hand, was a thrill which widened the window on fantasy.

Only two other things I see again there at my second school. The teacher was not my mother but some tall faceless lady, and the other is my eldest brother, Ashton, fighting with someone else's eldest brother who roundly defeated him, throwing him face down on the metalled road. To see the hero of our family, our protector, bawling in public defeat, was to be reminded of reality. Yet he related the opposite of this fight to Puppa, sitting on Puppa's bed that night. "And he was so impressed with my strength . . ." and so on. Fantasy and factasy rub shoulders early.

*School Three*

K O R U    School three cannot have been far from the former Toko Road, Toko, Taranaki. I showed Keith that school one day. The old building was still there, heart timber as they all were before our forests went down before fire and axe, and the workmanship enduring, which is more than can be said of the timber and workmanship of modern schools, but there's a reason for everything.

And the pines were still there forty years later. If there were a school built in early days not immediately and automatically surrounded by pines I haven't seen it; less a strong habit of the education department than its authentic signature. And there can be worse signatures. Oh but they're wonderful to climb to the very top, to hide behind, to lie on the pine-needles underneath; to gather cones from for the fire in winter, to kiss a boy behind in autumn . . . you'd get the strap if you were caught. Please Teacher, I didn't. Please Teacher, he did. Please Teacher, I didn't kiss her. Please Teacher, he did . . . to find birds' nests in during spring and to smell on the summer air; though planted no doubt for shelter only. Keith himself planted pines round his schools in a later day and only when he'd got these firmly in would he go the decorative way with trees of grace. His signature is written in trees from one side of the country to the other. He meant to go back over his tracks one day to see how his trees were doing.

And the school "residence" was there still, built of the same heart timber. I'd thought it had been a very big house but now it seemed strangely smaller.

That was the school where Mumma, the teacher, would tie my left hand behind me to leave me no option but to use my right, firmly safety-pinning it to the back of my dress, after which I'd get the strap for bad writing whereas I wrote quite well with the left. Yet I saw no injustice in it, believing Teacher was doing me a service. In some ways she was. I'm very glad to be able to write with my right hand now and pity left-handed writers. Not that anything else went right also; everything else about me stayed left-handed, including my political views, on occasion. Continued playing marbles with the left hand, hopscotch with the left foot and tennis with the left arm. In drawing I use both, alternately or simultaneously, and liked to bemuse the other students at training college, making a blackboard drawing with two hands simultaneously. And I think better on two levels, seeing both sides of a question. It may have been an aid in my later writing, seeing two opposing characters clearly and simultaneously. The only recognisable and enduring disadvantage is the trouble in making up my mind, which my two sons can't stand, though Jasmine can. I'm equally convinced by the two sides of an issue, unless hurled one way by passion, and even then I'll come round later to the other side. Sooner or later anyway. Some people say that my difficulty as a person stems from this favorite hand pinned back. But I was due to be difficult anyway.

My three children don't know how closely I've watched all my grandchildren, their children, for which hand is used most. Even Vincent in Paris now; but I took note in Mauritius and London. As far as I know, none of their children has this left-hand thing. By now, of course, I know what to do about our left-handed child in a right-

Koru—Evadne
not born yet

handed world, scissors designed for right hands, the inkwell on the wrong side in school, the light arranged over the left shoulder and such . . . but these were no more than a built-in nuisance, which you get used to. But this is not a teaching book. Many others know what to do about it. Nevertheless I've always been relieved to see that my children's new babies were not left-handed.

I'm also relieved to get this thing off my chest, especially to my two sons. "You're a very difficult woman, dear." Forget it.

The main thing I learnt in that school from trying to read The Cat Sat on the Mat, Pat Had a Cap, was that reading had nothing to do with living. All I liked about it was drawing the shapes of the letters. Exciting to draw even without meaning. But that didn't matter either. It was *right* to learn to read about Cats and Mats and faceless Pats. We supplied our own living outside school, telling one another daily all the stories we wanted which were endless, from our own living imagery. Daphne's mainly, a prolific story-teller till her last breath. "Just behind those blackberries across the road there's a little girl."

"Yes?" breathlessly from Norma and me.

"Can you see her?"

"Yes," we could in mind, no trouble.

"Isn't she pretty!" from Daph. "She has a frilly green dress on. And she's dancing because she knows she's pretty. Like this."

And the next thing the three of us, Daphne, I and Norma all dance on the grass because we're pretty. As it happens, Daphne *was* pretty, Norma very pretty, big blue eyes and black curls, but it's certain I was not, except that I didn't know it.

Oh school was tough all right—your best hand pinned back, the strap for bad writing or for talking in school, the reading books un-readable—but it was the legitimate place for learning. Fair, justified. Outside was the place for living, and at home, and we didn't get strapped for that.

I think of those times now as I work at a university, training student-teachers, practising teachers, and am in and out of schools in the city, a great overseas city. So many of our new-generation children don't live outside or at home or at school. They fight to live but lose the battle. It's here, right now, that school needs to be a place for living as well as learning. The only chance our new child has before he be-comes a robot. Ah, but I've written a book about all this so we'll leave it now.

Thoroughly living outside school, we three made endless houses in the enveloping fern, down the bank or by the creek, houses which in mind were very grand, like the girl's along the road. Three children towards the end of a family of ten, passionately making houses and passionately playing babies. I recall this when I see our new small children on this vast continent, unable to play house and babies, even with the most expensive equipment. They don't know how. The in-stinct itself is vaporised. One of the more severe casualties of post-industrial civilisation. The students and teachers themselves haven't known how. You people far away in New Zealand are unaware of this. With your sunshine, beaches, bare feet, roaming and boating, how can you realise the non-life of our children over here: to become a robot or to be locked up in an institution of two thousand broken children, classified as "difficult"; I've been to see them. "Disturbed" they're described, because they fight briefly for their right to live, instinctively. Until there's no more life in them to fight for.

And no more instinct either.

Koru, school three I'm at. It's here I pick up the shadowy presences of the big ones of the family: Muriel, Gracie, Ashton, Lionel and a vague consciousness only of the first Sylvia who'd died. Marmie was born there. Also two horses, a foal and a gig. The two big brothers, Ashton and Lionel, riding nine miles on one horse to New Plymouth every Saturday for their violin lessons. The penny doll they brought home to us once, its glamour and wonder to the point of holiness still flashing within me. And I think this is where Puppa first started to be crippled from rheumatoid arthritis. I never knew Puppa whole.

Playing houses, telling stories, making a new song a minute, imagination flaring. Sparks of miracle and marvel aglow on our three fast tongues, in a closed-circuit world of our own . . . oh. But you can get too romantic looking back on your childhood. I'm leaving out too much. Stop me being respectable. What about the smack-bottoms for disobedience from Mumma and the way I'd follow my brothers down the road when they rode off to music on Saturdays, boo-hooing my brains out till the boys were out of sight, wanting them to take me; especially when Mumma drove the gig to New Plymouth and left me behind, though she did take me once and I saw the sea, as well as Puppa in the hospital with the irons over his knees meant to force his legs straight. They didn't. And his shouting sequences from his bed in his room when he finally came home, calling us, every name in the family. "Who am I? Only the father!"

And Ashton's heavyweight boxing bouts up the road after school, to be elaborated in detail to Puppa in the evening, whereas in fact he'd sometimes come home crying. They were big sensational affairs, these appointments up the road after school. And there's a vague memory of Norma being very ill there, so ill that Mumma took her on a sailing ship to Auckland and brought her back, better. She could walk again. And there was a time when, all sitting at table, there was a knock at the back door and Mumma opened it and there was the lady who'd minded somebody at some stage. "What do you want?" says Mumma.

"I want me money."

"What money?"

"The money y'owe me."

"Go and pass Standard Three before you speak to me."

Crash goes the door in her face and she is never seen again. Maybe she's still trying to pass Standard Three.

And the part where Mumma didn't get on with the chairman of the school committee and their encounters at the school door . . . but that's dispensable. As for saying we got no living done at school . . . I'm certainly less than accurate. So much for romantic hindsight.

I don't recall leaving Koru, or why, but I'd say it was chairman trouble, with a dash of inspector trouble maybe, which, along with landlords, tended to recur in Mumma's life. Also there would be, I think, a wistfully youthful desire for a change anyway, a condition that remained with her for the entire length of her life.

This third school, Koru, was quite a place, many years later, to revisit. I saw again these pictures from the past as Keith was talking to the two young teachers in the same old timbered "residence," which now seemed half the size. A rather vivid young man, that teacher, with a slight, pretty, blue-eyed girl-wife in a dress of blue, lying on the couch with encroaching rheumatoid arthritis. This was the house where Puppa too had become permanently crippled. Blue-eyed babies on the floor.

It all came back as I stood in the fragrance of the long-remembering pines.

*School Four*

TE POHUE   My fourth school was Te Pohue on the Napier side of the Taupo Hill. I don't know how we got there. That move was from Taranaki to Hawkes Bay and must have been a train job, easily two days then. Anyone in the North Island must know the Taupo Hill, all forty-seven miles of it, but not as it was during the First World War. At that time it was even more of a scenic masterpiece than it is now but there's a price to beauty. The road was notorious for hairpin bends, hair-raising steeps and drops, and forested clifftops; for coaches keeling over into deep ravines and for bandaged people. Forty-seven miles of accidents and it cornered directly below the bank on which our place stood.

I see Norma and me looking through streaming rain on the window pane, down upon a coach lurching through the mud; the horses gasping, sweating, straining and plunging, the passengers crouching inside as well as standing at the back exposed to the weather, their heads and hands bandaged, and staring fatalistically ahead.

And I hear Daphne at that moment playing on the rattletrap piano a tune, a plaintive melody, which I only need to hear fifty years later to see again the streaming pane, the bandages, the horses and to know again the sensation of that long-past moment.

By this time the older ones of our family were out in the world, standing or falling on their own, backfiring briefly to report to base. Among the ten—nine I mean—were six girls, and among the six girls were three beauties: Gracie near the top and Norma one step below me, both of whom had inherited Puppa's black curly hair, dark blue eyes and the snow-pale English complexion; and Daphne one remove above me who had collected Mumma's auburn curls and green eyes.

Daphne was the eldest of us little ones at home: Daphne, Sylvia, Norma, Marmie and Evadne, who was born here later. When she did bring up the rear, Puppa then had two little ones to mind at home while Mumma was at school: Marmie and Evadne. When the baby was new, the chairman, Mr. Axel, lent Mumma a bad-tempered horse to ride home at noon to feed her, after which she'd ride back to afternoon school. This horse rolled his eyes savagely, whisked his tail fiercely and stamped his feet for nothing, all of which used to frighten Mumma. A far remove from the Arab steed featuring in my fantasy.

Three miles down the valley in the ranges from our place was the school, to and from which we walked most days along that very road, beneath the sentinel cliff rearing to the sky and past the signpost, BEWARE OF THE WIND.

Three little girls trailing Mumma as she forged ahead with her books; Faith, Hope and Charity, Puppa called us. There was no dawdling on the way to school or making up stories; it was more a hurried learning of spelling or something like six-nines-a'-seventy-three.

Inside the school the raftered peaked ceilings in the style of the former century, the sober long-faced windows, the quaint old desks bolted to the floor. Each morning the sing-song tables gusted robustly about quarts and yards, perches and chains and twenty hundredweight one *ton*. Followed by uproarious singing how Britannia rules the waves, We're soldiers of the Queen, my lads, and London's burning, London's burning. Look yonder, Look. Only heart timber could take it.

The poetry chanted in rhythm and unison, you could stamp your feet to the beat: "The Slave's Dream," "We Are Seven," "The Arab's Farewell to His Steed"; "The Charge of the Light Brigade"—"volleyed and thundered, stormed at by shot and shell, while horse and hero fell. Noble Six Hundred." The volume, feeling and punch of it! Unforgettably it entered the bloodstream, pushing the corpuscles out of the way. Remembered for better or worse.

That was *in* school. What I learnt *behind* the school had another dimension, the kind of secret that is uttered gutturally into the recesses of your ear. Little Tell-tit, I told on them. "Please Teacher, they're swearing."

"Where?"

"Behind the school."

"What did they say, what did they say?"

I whisper in her ear the facts of life. But strangely no one gets the strap, or their mouths washed out with soap and water. Mystifying on both fronts. How could babies get born in such a rude way . . . no angels or wings or anything. I remained unconvinced for sixteen years.

. . . and the playground where we played hares and hounds, chasing and jumping, hunting and hiding in the tough fern bracken, and the all-school game called Stones. The whole glebe signed in a flourish of pines by the education board.

There was much living for free in the village after school, living with feet that are free. The old store owned by the chairman, Mr. Axel, where we hung round the door as we followed the action, or peeped over the top of the storied counter carved with names and symbols of Time, to watch when Mumma couldn't pay for the food and the man reached forward a great long arm to sweep back all her parcels. Next door, the billiard saloon owned by Mr. Axel where the men from the mill would herd us out in a burly surly way, along with our curiosity. Across the road from Mr. Axel's store was Mr. Axel's tourist hotel where Mr. Axel's daughter lived, our dream-girl, Bella, who wore patent leather shoes to Sunday School and ribbons on her hair every day of the week whereas Puppa tied ours with string. Also her father could walk whereas our father couldn't. But sometimes Bella Axel asked us in the hotel to see her walking doll or her big sister's brand-new baby. Dream stuff indeed.

Near the hotel was the lake which was said to be bottomless, with its legendary floating island and a cabbage tree like a mast upon it. Undressing in the manuka round the foreshore we'd swim in this lake with Mumma, who called it her "cold water cure." There was a marvellous diving board . . . run the length of it and jump in. Until the day when Marmie, about two, also ran the length and jumped in to sink out of sight like a stone and the next thing here's this picture of Daphne on the end of the diving board she yells out "Mumma!" which is heard as far as the store, then holds her nose and jumps in too, somersaults bottom up and also dives out of sight like another stone to surface a year of moments later with an armful of Marmie and here's this picture of Mumma half-dressed in the scrub she comes plunging down the bank in enormous bloomers reaching to below the knee and charges into the lake and snatches Marmie from Daphne and finally he's on the grass breathing again. After which brief scenario we all get on with our swimming in resumed momentum except that this was one scene which Daph did not re-enact mid-kitchen later for our entertainment. It wasn't mentioned at all.

I was too small to swim to the fairy-tale floating island but the big ones did as it cruised round the lake inconsequently visiting token ports; an image unattainably lovely to me, a symbol of the dream that lures.

Dawdling homeward from the village we pass—try to pass—the slaughter yard where sometimes and awfully we'd compulsively watch throats being cut and bright hot blood spurting. Down on the corner was Mr. Grant's friendly store where we'd spend a penny on lollies about once a year when a penny came our way. Each separate little boiled sugar lolly was examined in detail, its pretty colour admired; fondled in a palm, briefly sucked then taken out again to make it last longer. Next step up the hill the blacksmith where we'd pause at the wide door to watch him shoeing drowsy horses indifferent to the red-hot iron, until again we'd be chased away, we addicted loiterers and peepers in doorways. Inquisitiveness, thy name is children.

Three little girls trailing Mumma along the road homeward, living out our powerful fantasy. Idling the miles on the grass at the roadside there was time to be anything we liked: a princess in a gleaming tower from Puppa's stories, or a rich girl dressed in folds of velvet riding an Arab steed, "With proudly arched and glossy neck, with dark and fiery eye." Sometimes we were carrying expensive dolls that only we could see, or I'd be walking up that hill holding with wonder and care in my outstretched arms a brand-new baby like Bella's big sister's, feeling so much the reality of it.

"When I grow up," Daphne would dream, her green eyes luminous, "I'm going to be an actress on a stage. The curtains pull back like this, see, and I come on like this, you watch." Trailing a frond of fern behind her. "And all the people clap like mad and then I sing like this." As her voice rises and trills, turns corners and swoops in soprano impromptu we forget the shames of our little-girl lives that we're terribly poor and our father can't walk like other children's fathers. Euphoria.

Picking up the billy of milk from Tom King's place across the bridge with no handrails on it, trying not to drink it and not to eat the inside of the loaf we're meant to bring home intact. Past the swamp with the buttercups and the sign, BEWARE OF THE WIND.

Back home at last to the cottage on the bank we'd left years ago in the morning, idling in the back door to Puppa carrying his life on his crutches, sitting by the stove browning the potatoes in the iron pan, smoothing the top of them with a knife. Home to the candle-lit, piano-lit privacy, Mumma bathing the babies in the tin bath by the fire or chopping the wood outside for the morning.

Far-back Te Pohue where most of my imagery came from. Playing with Daphne, Norma and Marmie on the edge of the brooding forest. The day when we penetrated the trees too far and got frighteningly lost. "Follow Daphne," I said. "Puppa said we were to follow the eldest if we got lost." So Daph starts leading us—did we see this tree before with the moss all over the trunk look for things you remember where's that hollow log we played in and we said it had elves in it is this the vine we swung on Sylvs can you see it y'know that stinging nettle Norm that pricked you look up through the tops of the trees Marm and see if you can see the sky or some light keep on looking round for some light anywhere—till from the twilit panic we find some light and follow her out to the bland sweet foxgloves smiling cerise and white. She'd be about eight or nine. How many lives had she saved so far at Te Pohue counting the time she'd dived for Marmie in the bottomless depths of the lake? Yet none could save hers in the end.

Building houses in the manuka, in the fern or up in some spreading tree. We got an old armchair into one, a titoki it was, and here we are playing at entertaining ladies in what to us was an elegant drawing room halfway to the sky, swinging the while undulantly. Single-filing the contoured sheep-tracks, making up pieces of stories and songs as our bare brown feet padded the soft dust.

Tall hills where we flung in the wind shouting great words to the sky: "The Gulf of Carpentaria! The Gulf of Carpentaria!" Deep gullies darkly treed where we crouched and muttered occult words: "Nizhni Novgorod, Nizhni Novgorod," or rolling in the grass's silk in the gale in rhythmic wave motion. The raw banks we carved steps in, caves and roads to play coaches on, Mrs. Greenaway's orchard where we stole apples and strawberries and the time she raged from the bottom of our lane up at us teasing her from the top, "Job-a-jip, job-a-jip," safe on home ground.

A big black earthquake one night and Mumma's shrill calls for help: "Coo-ee, coo-ee!" The jagged red line of bush fires on the range in the evening at bedtime. We saw our first car at Te Pohue one Sunday afternoon; we all rushed to the top of the bank at the unknown bumpy sound and here is this little coach with no horses thumping along proudly, and the ladies with flowers in their hats.

We could hardly be seen as children pinned down by the written word. I remember only four books at our place: Puppa's Bible from which we learnt our lines for Sunday School, texts, verses and chapters; *The Wide Wide World*, which Puppa read to us at night as we clustered round his bed and at which Daphne liked to show a tear; a mysterious book called *Stepping Heavenward*, which no one read at all and a non-existent book, *Yo Ho for the Spanish Main*, which Puppa narrated in serial form since the volume itself was lost. All about this Spanish galleon loaded with ill-gotten treasure, sought by the valiant British sailors who finally found it upon a lake at the bottom of a cliff on an island. "Why, here's a lake right below us and, by thunder, what's that?" Knew the thing by heart.

Really, you'd think, to hear me, recording only the lovely and happy places, that it was heaven all the way, whereas there was the other side. We were so often naughty, riding off on the horses of pupils who came to Mumma on Saturdays for music lessons and not returning till nightfall, and the stinging smack-bottoms for disobedience. What about Mr. Axel, our landlord also, tipping over our tank in summer when Mumma couldn't pay the rent, and taking out our windows in winter. Playing the wag from school when Mumma was away having Evadne in Napier, in spite of an amiable relieving teacher. And there was a minor incident there which has played a major part in my response to children: Bella Axel, our dream-girl, took me into the hotel with her where her mother was entertaining friends, one afternoon after school. They all made much of Bella while I stood unwelcome in the background near the door, my head down in shame for merely being me. That has supplied me with one of the biggest propulsions in my work—to seek the one that's left out.

I know terrible things must have happened to the big ones out in the world: Mumma's silence over their letters and Puppa's solemnity at the table, not shouting to God for mercy. The whispering of the big ones when they came home, their tears behind the door. Also the First World War was on at the time and we three girls would pore over the pages and pages of pictures in the *Auckland Weekly News*, of New Zealanders Killed in Action. Picking out the handsome ones. "That's my father," wishfully, and, "This is *my* father, this one." And the part about Ashton being hauled back off the troopship at sixteen trying to get "over there."

I know. But why resurrect conflict and sorrow. I doubt if anything hurt us three too much, all but unreachable in our secret world. Let this curtain, since it wants to, draw itself across the unbearable places. It's what curtains are for.

Recall only the sources of inspiration. The music most nights round the rickety piano, Mumma at the keyboard and Puppa on his crutches balancing at the back of the group singing to the chorus a tenor obbligato; Mumma quoting poetry at the table and Puppa stirring the porridge. The jokes tossing from morning till night amid the howls of rage and the sudden-spinning laughter. Te Pohue, for some reason, in the pristine beauty of the ranges, enriched my store of imagery with more drama and colour than any other spot we alighted upon. The mind-pictures from here endure as though framed and glassed against erosion, preserved from the wear of time. I see them all here, the family of eleven. Six of their names are on headstones now, but they remain alive at Te Pohue. Mumma would quote prophetically, "They grew in beauty side by side, they filled one home with glee. Their graves are scattered far and wide, by mount and stream and sea." They are.

Three years at Te Pohue until Mumma had had enough of Mr. Axel, or he of her; simultaneously store owner, hotel owner, lake owner, landlord and chairman of the school committee. You ran into him whichever way you turned. I mean you couldn't win. I don't recall any inspector trouble; no overblown shivery word poised over the school and home like a black umbrella, whispered in fear; not as it became later, the bogus villain in Mumma's story. Completely unfounded maybe, I don't know. But one did learn soon enough of her sudden, wilful and passionate impulses to make a change anyway.

We younger children loved the part where she kept on getting up and going somewhere else, willy-nilly, regardless. We *loved* "shifting." New places to find, new things to do, new rivers to swim in, new horses to ride. I was round five, six, seven at the time and I'd already known four schools; now we were off on our way to another. Marvellous. Age and death were for others only. How long and without end life certainly is when we are young and tough. Timelessness is all for us.

I remember one part of that journey. A car came from Napier to get us, a taxi. It was raining all the thirty miles. Puppa was sadly nervous, continually begging the driver not to skid.

It would be about three decades or so later, yes . . . a span of thirty years before a reminder of Te Pohue came. Keith and I were at Fernhill together, about forty miles away down on the Hawkes Bay plain. My schoolroom was that pre-fab I wrote about in *Spinster* with Anna and the little ones in it. I'd described every rafter and nail.

It was after I'd resigned from that job when I saw workmen dismantling the pre-fab and I said, "Where is it going?"

y said, "Te Pohue."

aid, "Te Pohue? Not really. I went to school there when
I w      g."

And they said, "They need another room."

The pre-fab going to Te Pohue? This exciting unlined shed bolted together inconsequently, in which I'd learnt new things, to be casually picked up and lightly put down in the place where I'd learnt first things, side by side with the original building back in the womb of the ranges. Here were all the characters in "the book" returning to join the company of phantoms at Te Pohue, their progenitors. Of all the places they could have taken this particular pre-fab to, and they truck it to Te Pohue . . . I mean, the thing was above coincidence.

A year or two after the pre-fab went I returned to Te Pohue for the first time. Keith was with me and we pulled up on the grass across the road from the school. The pines were gone. Deceased. Phantoms of pines have joined the company.

By now there are modern additional classrooms grouped about cheerfully enough but none with the mystery of age and the classical austerity of the early original sturdily surviving the weather and the years, not to mention forest fires. Standing aloof among them, waves of generation gaps lapping between. Holding her wisdom to herself as she scans past horizons. Long after the casual carpentering, lightweight timber and tea-break labour of the recent rooms have faltered into anonymity the old one keeps her vigil. It takes craftsmanship, roof-height and rafters to support the weight of memory; to house its spirits.

Te Pohue school

It takes time for a spirit to mature to authenticity, and for a memory to recover identity, whereas the new schools don't last long enough.

Astonishingly, however, among these later rooms is the very self-same pre-fab about which I'd written in *Spinster*. So it was true what the workmen had said about bringing it to Te Pohue. With my own eyes I see it. The ghosts of the people in "the book" actually have returned to their own.

Keith and I open our thermos of tea in the car while I try to recover the brilliance of that far-off barefoot life, the source of so much imagery. Later we try the door of the old school but it's locked on a Saturday. We call on the teacher across the road, a young man, whom we disturb watching Rugby on TV, so we visit two old neighbours, not watching football, who remember Mumma.

We tell her about this later. "Aha," eyes alert, "Eva Mackay I taught there who was matron of the New Zealand hospital in Egypt during the war. She used to ride five miles to school. And do you remember Queenie, Sylv?"

Yes I remembered Queenie, the laughing Maori girl who also rode five miles to school and who gave us rides on her horse. Strange that Mumma should mention Queenie, as her attitude towards Maoris was strongly affected by Empire Disease.

We low-gear from the school to the village. "The old store is gone," I say. "This is another one," and go in. "What happened to Mr. Axel's old store?" I ask the man.

"Burnt down," serving a customer.

"And Mr. Axel's hotel?"

"Burnt down too."

"Did you know Tom King?"

"He's still round," serving.

"Don't tell me he's still across the bridge with no handrails?"

"Large as life. Aa . . . can I get something for you?"

"We lived here fifty years ago."

"Did you now."

"My mother was the teacher at that school."

"Tom King would remember. Me I'm a new boy."

Keith and I walk down to the lake. The scrub where we undressed is still here and the raupo with the juicy stalks you eat. "There used to be a floating island on that lake," I say, "with a cabbage tree for a mast. I don't see it now, do you?"

I ask the man in the store, "Where's the floating island?"

He glances at me briefly. "I did hear about that. Some say it grew on to the bank, and some say it sank."

"That lake has no bottom."

But he's busy serving. I don't like it in here.

Listening for them. Looking for signs of them all. This high pointed cliff, plunging above Te Pohue, it must know a lot. Slowly we cruise the three miles along the valleys to find the cottage where I once lived but it's gone too; not burnt down, they say, but moved somewhere else on account of the value of the timber. But the site is still here upon the bank and the place where the woodheap was. The early coach road still corners the hill but as a lane only, heavily overgrown with walloping pines, poplar and unclimbed fruit trees, brittle with age like the bones of the old. A major modern highway sweeps through now, bypassing the route of the past; graded, paved and de-cornered, widened and cambered, sophisticated and sleek. Dozens of superfluous road signs explain every inch of the way like the boring prattle of a compulsive talker, only one of them worth the post it's nailed on, the one that remembers the OLD COACH ROAD. The rest are reach-me-down clichés like WIND GUSTS replacing the storied BEWARE OF THE WIND. Cars swoop through, soft-tyred and swift, their drivers thinking of something else, not knowing the lost population; not seeing the faces when they stop for gas, nor hearing the whispering voices. Not as I who lived here do.

Many times after that we stop at Te Pohue on the through journey. Sometimes we lunch by the school but more often at the opening of the overgrown lane that is now the Old Coach Road. My children were astounded. So often they'd driven through and had never known that their forebears had once lived there. Up through that undergrowth they ploughed on their own, picking their way round swampy water and ducking beneath the pines. The third generation enthralled in the haunts of the first generation. They even found Tom King, who talked to them of their people who'd died before they were born. Well . . . I've remembered enough. That whirring sound you hear is the curtain moving across.

time I needed to draw myself on these horses and slithered into portraiture. The chairman lent us a cow which Mumma milked before and after school, and the committee brought us wood which Mumma chopped though I wasn't so bad on an axe myself. When Ashton came home from time to time he chopped mountains, but Lionel said the axe would spoil his fingers for the violin.

Umataroa

Our true learning was more outside school than inside. The ruler over the knuckles at the keyboard at home which gave me a lifetime of obsessive music, ranging the countryside by horse or on foot, absorbing the drama of the district as well as of the family. And Mumma's sentimental poetry at table. And I remember a Saturday morning with us three little girls on the top of the hedge at the front of the house singing in the sun just like birds in sheer joie de vivre, Daphne, I and Norma.

But why enumerate the joys only, knowing of the tragedy also, untold. My generation knows those big families and all that went on in them. Regardless of Bibles, Life goes on. But I do find even at this early stage how impossible it is to write autobiography. One cannot speak ill of the dead, even less of the living. You can't speak at all of the living, good or ill. Give me fiction any day. Well, I'll get on with the joys at least . . .

Daph with her inventiveness and entertainment value was beginning to find a rapport with one of our older sisters, Gracie, and less with Norma and me. Outgrowing us, sort of peeling off from the team. On the other hand our small brother Marmie, whom Mumma referred to reverently as "the boy," began trailing Norma and me so that it was I who took Daphne's place as leader and story-teller and song-maker of this new little three: I, Norma and Marmie.

*Schools Five and Six*

# CHRISTCHURCH,
# PALMERSTON NORTH

I don't clearly remember what school came next, number five. It's interesting that I don't. During the war we fell on hard times. There was something called Charitable Aid at that time on which we lived. Christchurch told Mumma they had a job for her there, but since she wasn't on the spot she couldn't have it. But she was used to taking bulls by horns and got the Charitable Aid Board to pay our passage there by boat. I don't recall a thing about the boat. Puppa was left in some hospital or old age place which, for him, was inappropriate. Old Age with curly black hair and stories every night and a tenor obbligato.

All that comes back about Christchurch are dark cold corridors like tunnels with steps and stairs and hundreds of children. Nothing about the classrooms or the teachers in them. And the teacher was not Mumma so there were no Latin prefixes and suffixes. But there was no job there for Mumma and I don't know where we lived. Anyway, whatever the school was, it was the fifth.

Charitable Aid must have brought us back to the North Island, what else could have? And we must have stopped at Palmerston North. Here were more dark corridors like tunnels, stairs, hundreds of strange city children and again Mumma not the teacher.

*School Seven*

# UMATAROA

Puppa was with us again when we came out into the clear at Umataroa, school seven, a spread of green out in the country at the foothills of the Ruahine Ranges, about six miles from Dannevirke. It fell little short of Te Pohue and was like coming home again; the fern in the horse-paddock, the tall school with one class-room only, the school "residence" and the lofty pines. Most places where we lived Mumma inadvertently provided us with two kinds of freedom: spiritual and topographical, in the forms of a piano and a horse. We played the horse like a piano and rode the piano like a horse. I drew nothing but horses on my slate until about nine by which

As we grew, a fluid changing grouping in the family. Most of the year the big ones were away: Muriel nursing, Gray at university, Ash making his own tremendous bicepted way and Li at high school. He was fond of Daphne, who learned to play the piano accompaniments to his violin, which was very pretty to hear when we'd gone to bed.

Though it was Gracie's love-affairs every spring that supplied some of the action at home, Daphne was coming along too. Standing in line before school one morning she put up her hand.

"Yes?" from Teacher on the step.

"Please Teacher, Percy Ollerenshaw kissed me."

"Please Teacher," from the line behind, "I did not."

"Please Teacher, he did."

"Please Teacher, I didn't."

"Where?" said Teacher.

"Please Teacher, under the pines."

But although Percy Ollerenshaw had to write a hundred or so lines of "I must not kiss Daphne under the pines," it became known that he did it again.

It's time to move on from Umataroa . . . did I say how Evadne the baby stayed home with Puppa when Mumma was at school and did I mention the snowball tree outside Puppa's window in which we sat to talk with and listen to him? And when Ashton came home he would sit on the end of Puppa's bed and relate to him his adventures and exploits. Puppa did used to laugh. If only we could all have stayed like that . . . But Umataroa, nearly as lovely as Te Pohue, seems to be the very last place I can bring myself to expand on.

A few years only we stayed there; Mumma was feeling restless and ready for change and I'm pretty sure it was inspector trouble this time. I feel like drawing the curtain right here and not going on at all.

Keith and I did call in there one day as we were driving through Dannevirke decades later . . . lured by the ghosts of the past. Instinctively feeling I'd find them all there. The old school still stood heartily with no additions to it and the school residence also. Being holiday time the teachers were away and we were greeted by a cloudburst only. But the snowball tree was still by Puppa's window. We had our lunch in the same old school shed behind a thick curtain of rain, which failed, however, to haze the past. "I can still hear the singing in that school, K."

And the pines were still there.

I had been round about the eight-nine mark, I think, but I'd already attended seven schools.

If I could remember only the happy and funny places I'd get a bit further with this final draft, but the tragic and frightful come back too and are haunting me again. And who wants to live with thoughts like that and who wants to read them anyway. They're best forgotten. Best not to pick them up again. Horror is heavy.

Here in this far American metropolis, remembering at my table, I'll just close this manuscript now. I'll get on with my job of professor and continue preparation for the spring semester of my university. With adulthood bracketed in dream behind me I am a child again. In mind I'm running wild again. As it happens I *like* the alien snow falling outside my window. It's kind, warm snow.

Mangatahi—
the school

*School Eight*

MANGATAHI   So . . . I seem to be going on again. Maybe it was the thought of this chapter that made me grind to a halt.

We left Umataroa. Now we're in a place called Mangatahi, for me school eight. From the green generosity of forested foothills, from the variation in the topography, secret gullies and creeks and forgotten lanes, we land on a dry Hawkes Bay plain as flat as conformity. Mind you, this could well have been my own young reaction exclusively for

I heard Mumma say she liked it. "I can breathe in a place like this," her face at the open window. "There's plenty of fresh air. I like being able to see a long way." There were times when I perceived this vision in Mumma as she led the songs in school with her tuning fork and singing strongly above us. Her grey-green eyes would veer from us through the open windows to the haze of the distant horizon. At this moment now I wonder, What did she seek; the big ones out in the world, the future of us all, or some private dream?

On the other hand it could be that Puppa mourned the seclusion of those foothills we'd left. Though some of the time at Mangatahi he was in hospital at Hastings, when at home he often tried to run away down the metalled road crutching in passionate jerks, we children hurrying with him, but these crises are too sad to describe. He had a plunging spirit, Puppa, up and down, and the exposure on this terrain could have depressed him. It was not till I was much older that I learnt the character of his English lineage back to the Wars of the Roses when his ancestors fought on the king's side; a roving, reckless, innovating, prolific blood to be knighted two centuries later in the reign of the Stuarts for colonising the West Indies. That was Sir Thomas Warner. The coat-of-arms bore the motto "From the king I hold it." Still does. They were people who started things and refused defeat. We were, however, already familiar with Puppa's Black Box which accompanied us wherever we went and which housed his ancestral heirlooms. Many New Zealand families have similar records. That the particular Stuart king who knighted Sir Thomas, Charles I, had lost his head on the block, I was never told, and only found out when I'd picked up some history. I mean how could you put a motto on a coat-of-arms, "From the king who lost his head I hold it?" Neither did I know till later that the king whose side the Warners had got on in the Wars of the Roses, the side of the red roses, was Lancaster who in fact lost the Lancastrian inheritance to York, the white rose. Well, this is enough of this red herring to avoid getting into this chapter. Just one thing, I'd admired till then the red roses on the coat-of-arms. It was not exactly a good luck star from the past . . . nor the image of King Charles' head rolling. Later I was shown the document from the king knighting Sir Thomas, his signature and his royal seal. At least, however, they were fighters for what they believed to be right and surely this could be, not a bad luck star, but an inspiration to me to get on with this record I don't want to do. The royal seal was in Puppa's Black Box.

---

Again a humble cottage among prospering settlers, close to the metalled road. At the front one forlorn lupin tree and a few young pines at the back, the residence. Again the one-roomed school exactly like all the others complete with singing, Latin roots, British Empire poetry and the strap-discipline of silence, the whole signed in pines outside.

Whenever we arrived new in a district the people would start off so good to us, only too willing to make the best of us since a teacher was an indispensable commodity as well as in short supply especially during the war and post-war years when many of the teaching force had either been buried in the influenza epidemic or at the front overseas. Life was short, yet the young had to be taught. They'd give us an initial hoist with a load of wood and someone would lend a cow. They'd even invite one of us young ones to one of their homes hoping for the best, but big families like ours without the need to reach outward for company or the occasion to cultivate tolerance could become self-sufficient. We hardly mixed in any of our districts. Besides, what the Mangatahi farmers didn't seem to like was any visible irregularity, preferring appearances to be as flat as their plain, whereas we were one large highly visible irregularity wrecking the social landscape.

For one thing our father was known to be a cripple, a rank disgrace since nice fathers could not only walk but went out to work on their legs without crutches. Next, our mother was a teacher who went out to work instead, which was ranker still since nice mothers were to be found in their kitchens making cakes all day. Finally we were not only poor but seen to be poor, which was unacceptable so that although the people were not without genuine goodwill, generosity and much patience, we soon, again, came to be titled what in fact we were: the Warner Tribe. I suppose we would have taken all this in our stride had it been the norm for us, but we did have quantities of this blood that was not only hot and red but touchily proud also. In terms of our ancestry it was not the norm.

It may have been this or it may indeed have been the landscape itself that provoked us little ones to a level of naughtiness not achieved till then, though I wouldn't use the word "naughty" now. Nor, in these days, would I like to hold any landscape responsible for our behaviour, though I must say this one did have omissions. The only river a distance away was a mass of great boulders, wide, shallow, swift, noisy and no good at all to swim in, nor was it shaded with trees. No riverbank clay to make things with, no banks to carve your name, cut steps in or hollow out caves, and in summer it all but dried up anyway. We seldom went there and only when Mumma came too. There were no streams to track, no forbidden lanes to explore and no deserted orchards to raid.

Also, although we did acquire a horse, he was the ugliest, laziest shirker, with a backbone as hard and sharp as punishment, a big heavy moronic head with a bottom lip suspended like a basket you could carry parcels in on the way home from the store, six or seven great feet he couldn't himself organise and he'd dash into every gate we came to refusing to take one step further unless we dismounted and led him and whacked his rump. Not that we had to get off; he'd pull up and turn in so suddenly that we'd fall off anyway, the whole four of us. Several removes from an Arab steed "with arched neck and fiery eye." The whole plain itself several removes from our natural habitat.

I try hard not to make excuses and at least I've learnt not to blame. Circumstance is the villain of any human story or the heroine of it if you like. Nevertheless so far we'd grown such wild free creatures of the earth that we couldn't stand restrictions or boredom. Nor did smack-bottoms impress us much. Of necessity Mumma had long since developed as something of a sprinter and could catch us any time. As a chase led over one paddock to another there was always the hazard of a fence where she had ways to corner us, in which case we'd resort to an alternative zig-zagging dodging technique, a rear-guard action, but you'd still get caught at the tape; up with your dress, down with your bloomers and the next thing you'd get Mumma's hand. Bare skin to bare skin. Yet even that failed to remove the cause, whatever that was. My conception of growing up came to be the stage where one could outstrip Mumma.

I was a wretch of a girl at Mangatahi, let's face it, selfish, disobedient, gazing inward on my imagery. Whatever I wanted very much and didn't have I simply supplied it in mind which I now term a kind of theft; taking something that was actually not there. About nine or so. The others were not so bad, Norma was often just plain good, so young yet helping Mumma with her work. For the first time in my life I got the strap in school, for talking. Borrowing a ruler or something, only whispered. I had always been far too careful of my skin to run risks like that. For the first time in my life I cried in the playground, making the most of it of course, wringing out every eke of sensation while trying to keep the tears going.

My behaviour there was disgraceful, though looking back it does appear to have been the desire to see what happened when you did risky things, even dangerous, and I allow they could have been symbolic impulses from deep within the mind like curiosity and maybe resentment also at the flat surfaces of both life and the terrain, for I picked up a lot of guilt from it and still hold regret to this day; the shame of it. I confess to it only now. But it still doesn't qualify to be spoken.


I don't wish to linger in retrospect at Mangatahi. There must have been some happiness, some laughing, music and singing, some stories, wit and fun but they don't surface. A sense of tragedy shadows that place. When the big ones backfired from the world they seemed less likely to elaborate on some triumph than to weep on some failure in work or love. Mumma was very ill there once with miscarriage and was taken away to the hospital and Muriel came home to mind us. But Mumma came back and got on with the job. From hers and Puppa's grief over this loss you'd think it had been the only child whereas it had been number twelve. For us young ones it was an experience too dreadful to relate, as were other similar traumas. Of course those were bad times for most people.

Yes there were some stories. I do know that Norma and I shared secret scenarios ad infinitum when we had to get the cow. We were not trudging along a country road but riding restive Arab steeds "of impatient hoof" and "snuffing the breezy wind," and we were dressed in velvet. Or we were travelling in a mini-train on rails set in the grass on the roadside. It made going to get the cow worthwhile. Our fantasy did not supply the detail of how we managed to drive the cow home if we were riding in a train. In reality we were quite capable of driving the cow right past the home gate forgetting to bring her in. It was only the cow herself wanting to be milked who noticed the gate and paused there in wistful hope and doubt.

I came upon a tiny picture in an advertisement once of a beautiful face which immediately became my own. That this face had no feature whatever in common with mine escaped me. Also in our stories we were steadily affluent and lived in castles with gleaming towers and tall pointed turrets. Trying not to notice the big schoolboys trying not to kiss the big schoolgirls at the store after school in case they got a hundred lines, "I must not kiss Inez at the store after school," added a dimension to the inner scene.

And I did a great deal of drawing horses. I was always drawing. I taught myself to draw horses from every angle, in every posture known to horse. Someone bought me a cheap box of paints along with a blunt brush. I don't know where the paper came from, Gracie's, I think, who sold her charcoal sketches at Otago University; Whatman's paper which I had no idea how to use. Often I've looked back and thought, if only someone had shown me even elementary techniques in working with water-colour, at least the na-ture and function of Whatman's paper, put in my hands suitable brushes and told me a

Norma and Sylvie

bit on perspective. For decades I laboured the impossibly hardest way, I being the last to know I was. Never mind . . .

I'd like to get this chapter over and done with. There was a mysterious girl at Mangatahi called Avis Anderson who unwittingly supplied me with a model of the ideal girl except that no one saw her. She lived in a white homestead behind the trees on the far side of the plain. She was rich and had a governess and was too glorious to appear at all. The more we didn't see her the more we talked of her. In mind I garmented her in all the characteristics desirable to me; she adored me, admired me and followed me round. She thought I was simply wonderful, especially my steed. That I can recall over fifty years the name of a girl I'd never seen says something for the power of mystery.

Muriel, the eldest, is too shadowy for me to remember at that time.

Gracie when home from Dunedin brought names still remembered in New Zealand. She also brought her life-sequences of alternating exultation and disaster . . . it was never nothing. During the epidemic she joined a first-aid team and vanished for months on end. None of us caught this germ now identified as the Swine Virus. Mumma's fresh air didn't give it a chance. Though some in the district did. A little girl across the road behind the trees whom we sometimes played with, a white round face and a dark buster-cut, brown eyes, pretty, she did and later gave us a firsthand run-down on what it was like. "See I started to have convulsions at home so they sent for the doctor and the doctor sent me to the hospital but I had convulsions there so they took me to a private hospital and I had convulsions there so they took me to the nursing home and I had convulsions there so they took me back to the doctor and I turned black there so they brought me home again to die but I stopped having convulsions and came up white again." Talk about impressed! If only I could catch it and win all that attention. Even the glamorous Avis Anderson caught it, we heard.

At least this epidemic gives me a firm date about here. I have a newspaper cutting: ". . . a very deadly immigrant—the Spanish Influenza of 1918 which arrived aboard the RMS *Niagara* and claimed more than 6,000 lives" (in New Zealand). I now know that it came out from Europe on that liner with the returning troops. A plague it was really, patients turned black. Millions of deaths in the world; was it twenty . . . ?

Ashton made a little steam engine which puffed across the floor of the wash-house under its own power. Cotton-reels for wheels, a little furnace and smoke came out of its little tin chimney. I saw it. I watched its first performance. Also he went hunting in the distant ranges and brought home a peacock and peahen. The peahen died the first night in the rain but the peacock became a family pet and liked to keep Puppa company under the lupin tree. We didn't fail to feed this peacock with soft soaked bread, easing it down his long blue throat from the outside of his neck with our fingers when he was new and wouldn't eat. He did eat later. We'd find him up on the kitchen table when no one was about and one time he put his foot in a saucer of golden syrup which stuck, so he hurried outside wearing this saucer for a shoe. On the whole he did not go in for strutting proudly, having no peahen to impress, and seldom spread his tail which is a matter of mood with peacocks.

I don't remember anything about Lionel or Daphne there . . . yes I do. Mumma sent them to Hastings on their bikes one Christmas Eve with her monthly cheque and at the end of the day we went far along the road to meet them. They had on the carriers of their bikes all these strangely shaped parcels which on Christmas morning turned out to be a ball, an orange, some lollies and a book of comics, no Funnycuts, we called them. But no sign of a doll. How to reconcile Father Christmas with the carrier of a bike . . .

Let's leave here. There was a Shetland pony at that school which all able-bodied children had to turn out to catch after school for Inga.

The most bad-tempered form of horse known to God or Man ridden to school by the sweetest-tempered girl. This small pony would bite, kick, buck, growl, sneer and chase you more dangerously than Mumma, bailing you up in a corner, heavens. You should see us get through that fence. All this romance about Shetland ponies, forget it. A zebra would be more civilised.

The idea is to get out of this chapter. I anyway retreated more profoundly into the consolation of imagination. The dreariness I think. I feel like retracting what I said about not holding any landscape responsible for the behaviour of our child; might be wrong there. Let's go now. Did I say how, when we finally left Mangatahi, Ashton sold our peacock to someone in Hastings with a lovely garden? Maybe he spread his tail there. When we finally got to Hastings ourselves we used to look for our peacock.

Thirty years later I did return to Mangatahi, in curiosity and alone . . . no, Keith was with me . . . and twice again to show Daphne and Evadne, but it seemed exactly the same, dreary conformity, the lot. A plain of platitude. The pines had grown bigger, that's all. Yes the lupin tree was there and the ghost of Puppa beneath it along with our pretty peacock. No other ghosts greeted me. There'd been nothing at Mangatahi but concern for us and patience. True, when the cow had calved the owner didn't bring her back and no more loads of wood came our way, but people have their reasons. I like to record their peaceability. I've put down the few joys I knew there; let the sorrows take care of themselves.

It's more merciful on oneself to stay abroad. Better the alien snow.

*School Nine*
HASTINGS   You can see for yourselves the sentimentality of that era in the solitude of these islands.

We'd left Mangatahi. I think it was because the school door suddenly opened one morning, an inspector strode in unannounced and caught Mumma reading a letter from Muriel telling her what had happened and why. It was often the measure of the calibre of an inspector, his

catching-out capacity. Many an able teacher's career stood or fell on
what time the mail-car arrived, usually just after nine a.m.

These were the immediate post-war years and we found ourselves
in the town of Hastings on the same dry plains, a flat town with few
second storeys, being in the earthquake fault, no school or residence
awaited us however humble, and we were on Charitable Aid again
but we children were all agog. We loved shifting.

On the other hand it truly was remarkable how the rest of the
family had vanished without trace. We couldn't know then as I know
now that ours was not the only family after the war wandering the
face of the country, hungry, homeless, jobless, divided. The term
Charitable Aid speaks for itself. That would have been about 1919 or
1920 and don't forget how the world plague had accounted for twenty
million lives. And all the soldiers coming back, what was left of them,
seeking no more reward than work. Married women teachers were
sacked; women were generally denied jobs and had no claim to un-
employment relief. In the depths of the slump essentials overrode
women's issues. Their efforts were turned to the greatest need,
survival.

Daphne, Norma and I were boarded out with a lady called Mrs.
York who lived in a small street cottage. A nice lady as ladies go: fair
hair, blue eyes, not too old, impressively clean, truly sincere with not
one impulse in her other than benign and who did her very earnest
best to make us content. She'd painted the walls of a little back room
to make it pleasant for us three girls, a frighteningly dangerous yellow
bordered in belligerent indigo, not a bit like the lady herself. She'd
been supplied with three camp stretchers and new blankets. Mrs. York
even had a parlour, but there was no piano in it.

No one told stories in this place for some reason and there was
nothing whatever to laugh about or even cry about. Worse, Mrs. York
gave us healthy food at regular times like lettuce and hard-boiled
eggs, she didn't brown the potatoes in the pan at night and expected
us to come to the table when called. And we were not allowed to run
outside when it rained in case we got wet which was incomprehensible
to us and, when we were allowed to go out the door, there were no
hills and gullies nor even distances and far horizons, only the street
right there and other houses close, houses with doors and windows
shut, as well as the gates.

Mrs. York just couldn't make out why we didn't sit on our beds in
our room and be quiet and still or at least share the parlour. Mind you
we did try to at first, but we hadn't known a parlour and didn't know

what they were for. In time she ran into my notorious sulks when I wouldn't leave the little back room at all yet got no smack-bottom for it. I mean I couldn't even get outside under the kitchen window and bawl for an hour or so. Just me alone with the hideous yellow and no audience to convince. As for Daphne you wouldn't believe how subdued she was, she didn't tell one joke. We were no fun for Norma.

There was only one thing to do. We ran away from Mrs. York to find the family, no trouble at all to addicted wanderers. Found Mumma in no time. She was on the other side of town not far from the railway station, she and Marmie and Evadne, boarding with a lady called Mrs. Lawson. The names Lawson and York are authentic because I like putting down names of people with goodness in them. Shakespeare's Mark Antony said, "The evil that men do lives after them; the good is oft interréd with their bones." But I anyway have found the contrary: "The good that men do lives after them; the evil is oft interréd with their bones." The moment Mumma looked up and saw us she said, "Come on, Daph, tell us some jokes." Whereupon Daphne at once comes to life and re-enacts our stay at Mrs. York's.

When the laughing was finally over we learn that Mumma had been given a job, as she put it, "making scones for a sour old man," a job she'd lost in no time because he'd ordered her to clean his stove. "I've never cleaned a stove in my life, I told him. Me, a certificated teacher, cleaning the stove of a sour old wretch, ignorant too, when I'm married to an English gentleman. What did I have to do with his disgraceful stove? I told him to do his own dirty work. But," wistfully, looking out the window upon a factory that developed people's films, "he did like my scones."

Mrs. Lawson had a girl about five or six called Alice whom she kept in a clothes-basket under the kitchen table because, she claimed, li'l Alee-eece was delicate. Mrs. Lawson told us that li'l Alee-eece had a frog in her throat, you could hear it when she coughed, and this frog it snatched all the food li'l Alee-eece swallowed and ate the food itself so that Alee-eece didn't get any of it and that's why she was delicate and had to be kept in a safe place under the table. Hear that cough? That's the frog croaking.

There was no spare room at Mrs. Lawson's but we stayed anyway. Nothing would persuade us to return home to Mrs. York's though to say "home" in this context does put a strain on the word.

The next thing was to find Puppa. It turned out he had again been put away in the same Old People's Home on Green Island out of Napier though his blue eyes were still clear, his complexion fresh, his

mustache romantic and his hair still dark and curly. Green Island was
some miles out of Napier and was indeed an island at that time in the
upper estuary of the Napier harbour, reached by a stony causeway
across the water, though now, since the great Napier earthquake of
the 1930s lifted most of the harbour bed to the daylight, it is no longer
an island, just a mound in extensive green meadows. Thousands and
thousands of brand-new acres.

I don't know how we got to Napier, must have been by service car,
but I remember trudging the raw miles of metalled causeway most
disconsolately with the cool harbour water lapping each side, an occasional passing car hurling dust in our faces and not picking us up.

When we slunk into the ward, dirty, hot and worn out, and when
Puppa saw us three he cried like anything. Until we began telling
him all about Mrs. York's when suddenly he started laughing like
anything instead. We told him all about Mumma's sour old man and
the stove and the scones and "his own dirty work," about Mrs. Lawson
and li'l Alee-eece in the basket under the table and the frog in her
throat till the laughing got out of hand, especially when Daphne started
taking people off. It electrified the sad ward.

Then Puppa recounted to us dark tales of the wicked doctors. "They
keep on hiding my crutches all the time God-damn-it. If only they'd
stop hiding my crutches all the time without stopping, God-curse-it,
I'd have been back with you long ago, confound them."

"But Puppa, you couldn't crutch all that way back along the causeway, the stones, big ones, the dust."

"I'd get as far as that gate and get a lift with someone."

He showed us the ornate picture frames he'd been making from
strips of coloured paper, pretty as anything, and the illuminated addresses he was composing on envelopes in red and blue ink in Old
English printing, bordered and flourished, all of which he'd give to
the nursing staff. Though I do have one envelope right here with me
addressed to one of the family. He'd put stamps on these and actually
send them through the post. You wouldn't believe the beautifully
executed printing done in bed with knotted hands.

But visiting time was suddenly over, a bell rang somewhere and it
was time to go. No one had given us anything to eat and drink. Again
all those miles of stones and dust . . .

Having found both Mumma and Puppa it was time to search for lovely
gardens to see if we could find our peacock.

---

I can see now Mrs. Lawson's point in tucking Alice in a basket under the table: to keep her clear of the traffic. It wasn't exactly a small house but the company tended to foregather in the kitchen. How many altogether: Mumma, Daphne, Sylvie, Norma, Marmie, Vadne, Mrs. Lawson, Alice and the frog. Ten. Wrong. A Mr. Charlie Lawson tended to come home at night. I saw him only once. He could be excused for keeping to his room. That makes eleven. Had Alice been let loose she would not have survived the action, nor the frog either. Pale transparent face, pink and white, silken flowing fair hair like a doll in a shop window and big soft pleading blue eyes peering up from under the table. When Mumma said, "I'd let that child out of that cage and let her stretch her limbs. What she needs is a breath of fresh air," Mrs. Lawson heard and replied with accomplished dolour, "Ai don't think Charl-ee would laike it dear."

When there was a chance Daphne would impersonate the four of them to Mumma: Mrs. Law-sen, li'l Alee-eece, the frog and Charl-ee, which was such a splendidly funny act that she kept it up till the end of her life. Oh no doubt we'd fallen on very hard times but I remember plenty of laughing.

To this day I don't know what Mr. Lawson thought of it all but we settled in together regardless. An easy laconic loose-limbed house a few blocks from the railroad station which I at once found. Marmie relaxed in the back yard at his favorite sport, bawling, a sign he felt at home. He opened his lungs gratuitously to the back windows of surrounding factory offices, delivering his soul undiluted like a spaniel we once had which sang to the piano; its name was Skye. Some of these offices were the film-developing place, the staff of which came to know Marmie. One morning at the height of his performance a man came down and gave Marmie a sackful of spools to play with which the staff had unanimously collected, hoping for a let-up. "Why," said the man, "do you cry every morning?"

Marmie paused mid-holler. "Because we're getting poorer and poorer every day," then completed the interrupted holler. It was Evadne who played with the spools.

We cannot have been attending any school yet because we set about exploring Hastings. Memory lets me down here. I can't see Mumma allowing "any child of mine" to get away with not being at school and I don't think the Charitable Aid Board would either. Also education boards are known to be touchy about children missing school. In our vocabulary the word "truant" was one to be whispered and we ourselves would have resisted it. Maybe that particular fragmented hit-and-miss pillar-to-post sequence which comes up now as years and years was no more than the Christmas holidays.

And though 1919 must have seemed to us a wilderness of a kind it was less lethal than a moral one. Some values had not yet vaporised. That no bitterness took root in the spirit of us younger ones from that time I find interesting. We thought things were all right.

However, to sail airily over that period as one where Mumma, of all people, neglected our schooling would be to provoke her to stand upright in her grave and confront me. Short of money yes, short of food, clothes and books yes, even short of a roof yes, but short of schooling no. What happened I just don't remember.

Whereas those who could have told me, Daphne, Marmie or Vadne, they're dead now, along with their own memories. I'll ask Norma, next time I see her, if she remembers.

I'd soon found the railway station a few blocks along. The express train had a way of passing through Hastings late afternoons and I was enthralled at the drama there. Things happened on the station that didn't happen in the windows of shops. The comings and goings of crowds of people, the glad greetings and kisses when the long train puffed steaming to a stop, the talk and luggage and interaction, the urgent bell ringing to warn the travellers of the train's imminent departure and suddenly the change to partings and tears. I'd sit on a seat on the platform, loiter at the waiting room door and watch and feel it all, indeed become it all hearing in mind the sentimental song Mumma had taught us in school, "Upon a railway station stood a little child one night. The last train was just leaving and the bustle at its height."

This song continued through several verses, every word of which I know, describing how the station-master asks her what she's doing there on her own to which she replies that her mother died when she was born, Sir, and her father had just left for heaven. She's concerned that he might be lonely travelling all that way on his own so, "Give me a ticket to heaven please before the last train has gone."

More than once I risked forfeiting my evening meal in order to be here. I'd come by myself as it didn't draw the others. I was attracted to that station at that time of day as one is pulled to any drama on or off the stage. Long dress, bare feet, severely plaited hair and freckles, I'd lurk, loiter, linger in that place looking up widely about me, intensely agog; absorbing the flashing exposed emotions, compulsively living them through, catching them myself contagiously. In fact the station-master did look upon me but only in curiosity. He didn't say Go away.

Which was all right on warm days but when they were cold there was a price to pay, like a ticket to heaven. Some large red lumps appeared on my legs which the doctor said were rheumatic so I couldn't walk and lay on a bed. They pulled this camp stretcher out in the kitchen at Mrs. Lawson's place. Having at last achieved the distinction of being genuinely ill I found I didn't appreciate it. In mind I kept my appointments at the station whenever I heard the engine's whistle, examining the eyes of these who arrived seeking the eyes of those who met them; the eyes of a young lady upon a young man as he climbed down from the train, thrilling with excitement at their kiss. From my stretcher amid the surrounding hubbub of the household I'd respond to the volcanic life at that station as I heard the fateful trains arrive and depart, actually hearing the engine.

These legs kept me bedded for quite some time, but before the lumps were wholly gone, the moment I could bear my feet on the floor even with the aches still in them I all but crawled along the street towards the railway station, resting on the kerb of the gutter often as the lights turned up around me, coatless in the cold lit street to keep my vigil with the train. "Crawled" is not too far off target either as a word, for I couldn't climb the ramp to the platform itself but again sat on the kerb of the footpath below in the gathering glamorous dusk. "The last train was just leaving and the bustle at its height." Up on the platform lights flashing, people flashing, emotion flashing in the miracle of reality. I felt it all as well as my legs, hearing the clang of the boarding bell, the guard's whistle and the hysterical shriek of the engine. It was some time before I was able to come again.

A vague summer. We are no longer with Mrs. Lawson and Alice but in a two-storey ramshackle house beyond the point of no repair, away from other houses and close to the railway line. It leaned somewhat off-centre, wobbled in the wind and trembled whenever a train went by. A house condemned for habitation, so there cannot have been any rent. Mumma said it would be all right as long as there was no earthquake, and we young ones were vastly impressed to have an upstairs at our place . . . status plus! When a girl at Sunday School boasted to me, "We had a burglar last night. *You* didn't," I replied, "We've got upstairs at home. *You* haven't." Though I must say we all lived downstairs together for various improvised reasons. At least the stove operated.

On the other hand it was in some indeterminate back street in which were to be found no waterfalls to splash under, no trees to climb, no lake or river to swim in, no romantic floating island, no forest to get lost in, no creek to dam up or even a bank to carve your name in; neither was there a horse to ride, a bull to dodge or secret apple trees. Only flat straight colourless paved deserted sidewalks, hot and hard, with boringly repetitive right-angled corners. As a street we rated it low.

Inside it was better. True there was no paper to draw on, no pencil to draw with, or paints, and no rattletrap battletrap piano but you could cluster round the stove waiting for Mumma's scones to come out of the oven or Daphne's rock-cakes except that you couldn't spend all day of every day hanging round the oven. Mumma found a Sunday School deep in the town and saw to it that we went every Sunday. On the other hand it was years between each Sunday. Our fate was like disinheritance.

These long hot dry summer holidays, a Hawkes Bay drought, with no school to mop us up. At Sunday School I had nothing better to do than enter a competition about who was the first to be able to recite the Books of the Bible right through because there was a prize offered. A prize? It would be a doll. The very next Sunday taking my turn I stood up in front of them all and raced off these unintelligible names with a swinging sort of rhythm that substituted for music. Not one mistake. But the prize was only a small dull New Testament with dark green cover and red-edged pages. What waste of memorising; had it only been a doll!

Through the fence from our place was an area where black-currant bushes grew, their sweet pink blossoms heavily scented. We played there, five children: Daphne, Sylvie, Norma, Marmie and Evadne who could walk quite well by now. We'd drowse and dream in the fragrance and shade of all we didn't have. What we didn't have most was a doll. We fashioned houses among the bushes in which new babies were born every five minutes. We pretended we had dolls. From a tuft of grass you could plait long hair and supply the rest in mind. The conversation supplied itself. Yet children do not live by fantasy alone but by reality also. "Mumma, will you buy us a doll?"

"When I get my bonus."

"But you're not teaching to get a bonus."

"Because education boards are simpletons and don't know a good teacher when they see one. They gave my position to a returned serviceman."

"Puppa," we traipse to Green Island, "please buy us a doll, Puppa. All the other children have them."

"When I can walk I'll buy you a lorryload of dolls."

"But you can't walk yet."

"That's because they keep on taking away my crutches all the time, confound them."

Imagery can overflow into reality when it banks up too high. We'd have to think of something else. Through the dream-ridden days we took to roaming the streets again. Apart from the odd loud smack-bottom for giving cheek or for disobedience like dodging Sunday School there was no check to our wandering. Just as free as our minds were our legs. We'd love to stand before some picture theatre, stare at the astonishing posters and long to go inside; also we kept an eye open for our peacock but what drew us most was the dolls in shops, our freckled noses against the windows. We knew every doll in town. "See that one with the green dress," from Daph, "that's mine."

I say, "It's that one with the blue dress for me."

Norma says, "The red-dressed one is the one I like. Look she's got red shoes." The shop was Roach's in Heretaunga Street, a department store which has since been rebuilt after the Napier earthquake and we edge in the door. On the ground floor we find no toys, only men's clothes and things. "They must be upstairs," I say.

We assess ourselves; we're tidy and clean but we agree we don't qualify to go upstairs.

One morning I wander back alone to Roach's, timid and terrified, pad barefoot and nervous across the ground floor, up the forbidding stairs and into this spacious toy department and here within touching range are the dolls. What a shock when dreams materialise. There's no staff in sight and few shoppers. I finger the stiff blue dress of a doll. It's real, incredibly authentic. She's as pretty as anything Puppa had described and I patter back down the stairs, slink across the ground floor and hurry home along the hot hard streets to Daphne and Norma. "Their dresses are all stiff," I report, "and they're fearfully pretty."

"Did you touch them?"

"I touched one. There was no one there. There's a sort of smell of brand-new toys and there's *hundreds* of dolls, Daph."

———

On the top storey of the shaky old house was a narrow hall with small empty rooms each side. The far secret room at the end was asking for ill-gotten treasure, empty as a mail-box when you're yearning for a letter. Imagery overflowed into reality. There came a morning when the doll with the stiff blue dress joined us in this end room and I sat her in the corner where she stared back affrighted at the three of us sitting on the floor before her, ecstasy shooting through us like pains. She was far too holy to play with. I named her Avis Anderson.

By afternoon there were two more sitting there in the corner side by side facing us without a blink. A blue, a green and a red although it had been I who got Norma's for her as she took a different view of this game. Simply terrifying. It took us days to get over it. From being an empty treasure trove or a hollow mail-box the room became a church, a place of devout worship. The two new dolls were christened with ceremony.

Within a week there were several further names to think up. Side by side the line of dolls lengthened. Extremely well-behaved dolls who never changed places or ran away. They sat sedate and circumspect. Beautifully dressed, fearfully pretty and exuding the glamorous smell of the shop. Play with them? Never. We sat and stared at them, endlessly wordlessly enchanted. It was a marvellous business.

Through the somnolent summer one doll added to another until they reached from the first corner along the wall to the second corner so that the naming of them grew to an undertaking in itself. Remembering them anyway. The hot drought became no longer boring. Mumma never came upstairs in case of an earthquake though she did notice that suddenly I no longer protested at wearing Daphne's hand-down dresses, being wider, and that Daphne chose her wider ones. As our technique daily improved our glamorous guests stretched along two walls, something round fifty, I'd say, since we had to make do with small ones and Mumma couldn't make out why we played upstairs and were so much less trouble to handle. But the engagement remained a matter of shivery risks and I can't say we wholly enjoyed it. All Norma did was hostess the arrivals. In that empty room upstairs at home where there'd been in the first place no more than a lightweight nothing, that nothing had now become quite something, bigger than we could deal with, overpoweringly so.

By the time we'd lined three walls with dolls and had begun on the fourth, over a hundred by now . . . I need to insist this is true because who's going to believe we finally scored 144? Talk about bewitching company upstairs! But then Lionel came home from high school for the holidays and was soon looking for some secluded place in which to practise his violin.

I'd like to abridge this red-faced story, this pink-faced story rather. It's only worth telling because of that saleswoman upstairs at Roach's whom we'd feared right through the action. She'd seemed remote, severe and corseted but when confronted with drama she turned out to be one of these rare people who are a great loss to a classroom. Contrary to her spare forbidding appearance her nature was curvaceous, luscious and so forgiving that I'd put her name here if I knew it.

Nor was she without histrionic instinct. Far from disturbing the story-line she was all for bringing it to a rounded conclusion, complete with happy ending, not overlooking every credit to herself. Salespeople don't often have such opportunity. That she might well have lost her employment on account of her own lapse in surveillance escaped us trusting children. In tight conspiracy between accomplices speaking the same language we didn't note that her face was as pink as ours. As for the astonished dolls they found themselves rehabilitated without anyone telling on anyone else. Even so I've told only half this tale.

The fragrant flowers of the black-currant bushes saw a bit more of us children. It's a long time . . . a lifetime since I smelt those particular blooms in that particular summer yet whenever I've seen a currant bush since, wherever I was, and have lowered my face to it, the scent and the pink bring the whole thing back and I'm counting our dolls again.

The scenes come back like separate pictures you find in a forgotten cupboard, framed and with glass, and when you brush off the dust you find them still intact but unconnected one with another. The links between them have gone and you're unsure of their order in Time. But I notice that as I grew older they're becoming clearer and manifest more detail, and relate more one to another.

We're no longer in the shaky two-storeyed wreck but in a dark place like a dungeon; very small, unlined, unpainted, broken panes, they kept their tools and sacks of things there, below the definition of habitation, beyond being condemned at all for any living use, across the back yard of a boarding house called Dean Court. The only access to water was a tap over by the fence, there was a stove inside which did not work and there was no wood anyway.

Those Hawkes Bay frosts . . . no new blankets supplied as there had been at Mrs. York's. Mumma used to go the rounds at night covering us with anything that might keep us warm, even sacks. In the morning she would light a fire on the frost-white grass with scraps of boxes or any piece of wood she could scavenge somewhere, and cook our porridge on it. This fire on the frost-white grass at which we'd warm our night-cold hands.

And the occasional row between Mumma and the proprietor of Dean Court when she went to the back door to ask for more milk. Not that the man was inhumane; one of us must have spilt it or drunk it all or lost the billy or something. It seemed we lived on porridge alone but there must have been other food, bread at least. Only children as tough as we were could have survived all this, though we sometimes cried with toothache, missing the fruit of deserted orchards, and often cried with chilblains, missing the way Puppa would soak them at night in hot soapy water. You didn't hear Mumma in song these days or speaking sentimental poetry, neither did Daphne make us laugh. As for the big ones we didn't see them. It was true what Marmie was saying, "We're getting poorer and poorer every day."

Dean Court was a two-storeyed Victorian boarding house, pretentious with decorative woodwork at the front, fine windows and balconies on which graceful people languished. Lawns, trees and flowers facing the street; in the idiom of the period, elegant. To be seen turning in the front gate to this mansion gave us children a moment of pride, people would think we lived in it. Our dark hovel at the back was no more than a murky impulse hidden at the bottom of a respectable mind. Inadvertently I learnt the true meaning of the word "facade" along with the word "respectability."

That Mumma should have been reduced to this dark impulse for us to live in would undoubtedly be our dire poverty in these nationally dire times, but I'd say she'd picked this particular locality within reach of a school in the same street, five or six blocks along. That street with both the Hastings Main school and Dean Court in it runs parallel with Heretaunga Street. From our hidden ghetto we were at last enrolled at the school, my ninth school, nine or ten I was.

Daphne was in Standard 6, I in Standard 5, Norma about Standard 3 and Marmie in Primer 2. After one week, rather sensationally, each one of us was demoted a class: Daphne down to Standard 5, I down to 4, Norma down to 2 and even Marmie down to Primer 1. There was something so complete, even symmetrical about the action it took on the proportions of classical drama. It was like one of Puppa's exaggerations. Only Mumma took it hard who continued to believe that all her children were supremely gifted, the cream on the milk of society. When she heard what happened she said, "The common creatures. Calling themselves teachers."

"It was because of my sandals, Mumma," I said. "I saw them looking at the hole in the toe of this one and the sole flapping loose on the other." Daphne put on Mrs. Lawson's face and said in Mrs. Lawson's voice, "Ai don't think Charl-ee would laike it, dear," and Mumma came right again.

"The second time I've been in Standard 4," I marvelled.

The teacher in this second Standard 4 was a handsome dark man who oiled his lovely black hair, scented oil too, and who was disposed to press little girls close to him when we brought up our work to be marked. Since I was due to fail this second Standard 4 at the end of the year he cannot have taught me much, not in the curriculum anyway, but I did learn the strange excitement of being pressed to a man's body. His left arm was mostly pressing the pretty Isobel but why he should press me with my freckles and old dress I could not divine. After all he didn't have to, there were plenty of other girls. Perhaps he did teach me something except that it wasn't in the exam at the end of the year. He was picked up years later for this very sort of thing; teaching little girls scented subjects that didn't occur in exams.

I happen to like the story of our blanket demotions, especially the part where, having been demoted from Standard 5 to 4, I failed 4 at the end of the year, so had to stay in 4 for another year which, taking into account the Standard 4 I'd been through already before I'd lifted to Standard 5, it added up to three Standard 4s, whereas I had this thing from Mumma about being the first, best, most and frontest. I was too astounded to grieve about it, too impressed by the story angle. In fact, when Isobel skited to me in the playground, "I've passed into Standard 5. *You* haven't," I replied, "I've been in Standard 4 three times. *You* haven't." But Mumma said to Daphne, "When they want to bring me down, Daph, they get at me through my children."

When the new year came round, the four of us, still living at Dean Dungeon . . . sorry, Dean Court, we settled down at Hastings Main. Fate dropped in my hands two miracles. One was a replacement of the recurring ideal girl in the form of Netta Nye who lived about two blocks from us on the way to school in a large ornate white house on the corner. She was almost the replica of those in the past: a very pretty sweet girl, clever too, a Mummy's darling and only child, patent leather shoes, hair ribbons, the lot. This was her first year in Standard 4, which coincided with my third.

I don't think she registered me whatever until one afternoon after school as she was passing Dean Court on her way to music, carrying her satchel, she saw me playing hopscotch on the drive at the front. She must have assumed I lived at the front for next day at school she actually smiled at me but that's as far as it went. I was too shy to make the slightest response on account of my clothes and because the proprietor at Dean Court had also seen me playing hopscotch in the drive at the front, disgracing the place, and had ordered me to stay at the back. But Netta Nye became even more of an inspiration to me, she being wholly unattainable as a friend and all that I wished to be myself: pretty, rich, clever, adored and with a big well-dressed doll on her verandah visible from the street. An ideal on which to model myself.

The other miracle was a good man teacher. This man's name was Mr. Burns, his real name, and I say it because of the dramatic influence he had on my schooling. For a start he had something to do with his arm other than press little girls and, for another, his intention was obviously to teach. Learn or else, see? The strap swung freely of course but that was right at the time, besides, since I didn't like the strap because it hurt, I saw to it that I didn't get it. Which meant work. As it happens I've always liked work, given something that interested me; as Mumma was, I'm addicted to work.

Mr. Burns had a system of sitting his dunces at the front of the class and I mean just that: dunces. Not underachievers, slow-learners, underprivileged, disadvantaged or "pupils with socio-economic problems" but straight-out frank dunces. According to our performances we graduated towards the desks at the back. Netta Nye shared a desk at the back but I, being a failed Standard 4, sat in the very front. At once I set my sights on a desk at the back and not be too long about it. I had no taste for the word "dunce."

The very first week, just as I would have in the past to Mumma, I took my arithmetic book up to him. "Please Teacher, how do you do this sum?"

Mumma would have said, Multiply that by that and divide by that. But Mr. Burns didn't. "What! Haven't you read it?"

"Please no."

"Then why the devil *don't* you read it?"

Stunned. *Read* a sum?

"Get back to that desk and read it, blockhead."

I note the strap peeping from his coat pocket. I do get back to that desk and read it. I found it interesting. About cows in one paddock, horses in another and sheep in another. How many animals altogether? Moreover if each cow cost this, each horse that and the sheep were so much a dozen, and if the farmer sold out what would his bank balance be? No mention of tax. I saw the light. The thing was a story in disguise. Why hadn't Mumma told me? I mean, I could make up a story like that myself: if each of those 144 dolls cost so much each, how much money in fact had we stolen? Astonishing.

I did the sum, sketching all the animals of course in and out of the figures to make it more intelligible, took it up to him and got it right but nearly got the strap also for the illustrations. "This is a lesson in arithmetic, Idiot, not a drawing lesson. *I'll* say when we have drawing, not you. And another time you read a sum before you come to me."

I couldn't see why drawing shouldn't join forces with arithmetic but mindful of that strap I didn't debate the point. I'd have to do sums without illustrations.

I began working my way back through the desks and not too slowly either, aiming at the back one. When doing our homework at night in the dungeon we took it in our stride having only one candle. But really the chilblains were not fair on our fingers and feet especially when they started itching as the classrooms warmed up in the afternoon. You could have cried over it. I could have got to that back desk sooner. I could beat the others in a lot of things, even Netta Nye, except when it came to reasoning out sums when she left me by a wide margin. What I missed were illustrations whereas she could work without them. Drawing got me nowhere. Only the desk second from the back.

Yet strangely enough, whenever I did relapse into drawing horses the others would risk extinction to watch; turn round, lean across the aisles, fascinated to breathlessness to witness something on paper coming alive from nothing, and when I drew a dashing prince riding one of these steeds or an Arab in robes even Netta Nye herself would peer over my shoulder. Funny thing that. I couldn't reconcile the children's wonder with Mr. Burns' contempt. The family had always praised my drawing.

The formal drawing lessons did occur when Mr. Burns decreed they should and the next thing you'd see this vase on the table with a "Draw me or else" look about it, a school-bag, a box of chalk or "Copy this picture of a tree." I could have drawn better the strap in his pocket or the teacher himself using it. If only I could draw an exact vase like Netta or copy a picture of a tree like her. I did poorly in the drawing exams and Netta got better marks. I'd never make the back desk this way.

Nevertheless I enjoyed profoundly the pacing of that year. I accepted Mr. Burns. How old would he be, in his thirties? He wasn't a big man, not small either, spare in physique. He was dark. He had dark eyes and wore his hair cut severely short with no oil on it. His principles were just as severely short with no oil on them either but they didn't cave in under test. I trusted him, not only because I'd encountered for once in my life a man who was operative . . . don't count the other man who oiled his hair and girls . . . but also because with this one we knew where we were.

We felt secure with him. We soon learnt both Mr. Burns and his principles. He was a yardstick by which to measure our own values and if we didn't have any, by which to assemble some. Dunces were dunces loud and clear, clever meant clever, cheat meant cheat and nothing else, right was right and wrong was wrong, this was this and that was that. Finish. No hair-splitting, no favoritism or compromise. He was intelligible so school was intelligible; in the slipping sliding avalanche of living he was a visible direction-finder.

No schoolgirl crush about it. My crushes were already booked out on Netta Nye in the desk behind me on the girls' side of the room and on a boy called Ellis on the boys' side of the room. There'd be about fifty of us altogether. Speak to either of them, never. This Ellis was the milk-rounds boy who couldn't help being late most mornings from his rounds. A slender tall comely boy with blue eyes, romantic complexion and fair curly hair. In my mind he could have doubled for the story-prince, given a prancing white steed, a flowing velvet cloak bordered with ermine, a crown and a gleaming sword. But Teacher didn't see him this way. To be late was almost as heinous a crime as playing the wag from school. "Hold out your hand," from Mr. Burns each morning.

Crash.

His hands were cold from his early morning round. "Now the other."

Crash. I myself became Ellis.

"The other."

Crash. It was agony to see the noble one humbled.

"Again."

A little tall, a little old for this class having failed Standard 4 last year but fearfully brave. Not wincing, his jaw steady.

Pain in the blue eyes and finally the tears at which Mr. Burns felt

sufficiently accommodated to curl up his strap in his pocket. It could
have been about then when I began to register the whipping of injustice on behalf of someone else even though I was sure the teacher
was right. I'd not so far experienced this on behalf of myself. Not
exactly a clinical compassion but an innate disposition to *become* other
people as I had on the railway station; their feeling became my feeling
contagiously, their strapping my strapping, their pain mine and I
couldn't do anything about it. All of us, including the teacher presumably, believed it was right to be strapped when late, that the
system was all, with no alternative, but honestly we children could
have done without this trauma each morning. Fifty of us suffered
with Ellis.

There came a morning, however, when he walked in late as usual but
there was something different about him. Instead of glancing appre-
hensively, he held his shoulders straight, his romantic head lifted,
his body upright and his blue eyes looked into Mr. Burns' like two
unsheathed knives. His limit had arrived and the teacher was faced
by an animal with its back to the cliff. Warily Mr. Burns rolled up his
strap and curled it back in his pocket, said nothing, turned away
and Ellis went to his desk. And that recurring nightmare was over.

Daphne in Standard 6 made friends at that school though she could
never ask them home to our dungeon. We did have these social un-
acceptabilities: a crippled father, a teacher mother and lived in substandard habitations. But Daphne sailed right over this. For a start who
could resist the shining golden-brown curls to her shoulders, the
sparkling touching long green eyes, her pretty hands and legs. Above
all she made people laugh, even her teachers. She didn't even have
to try. At times she didn't even say anything; she'd just look at you,
that's all, and you'd find yourself beginning to tremble with laughter.
People pay anything, put up with anything for this.

I made no particular or unparticular friend. All I managed was to
idealise Netta Nye in the back desk of excellence in class and to dream
of Ellis. Yet it comes back to me that I was happy enough, even integrated with the company, within the herd. A recognisable normality.
I remember great fun playing marbles or basketball in the playground
and usually got picked on someone's side. I think Mr. Burns respected
me as an impassioned worker and children take their lead from
teachers. I think Netta Nye respected me as a well-documented challenge to her supremacy. My year with Mr. Burns was a turning point
in my education. He was so thorough and detailed and consistent and,

Mumma and Puppa
when they met

in the context of the times, implacably fair. Even though I was mani-
festly poor I was not a marked man.

I played the wag only once and that was to see Charlie Chaplin.
The thing to do was lurk round the corner from the picture theatre
till after half-time then when all was dark and the ticket girl herself
had gone in to see the film you just crept up the stairs and in at the
back, leaning against the wall. There was no other way to see Charlie
Chaplin.

We didn't stay there till the end-of-year exams so I didn't have the
chance to head off Netta Nye and share the back desk with her. But
that's no sob-story. To have been spared that ordeal could have been
a damned good thing. I'd have died sharing a desk with a dream.

When I stayed at my son Ash's home in Hastings those few weeks before I left New Zealand, I went looking for all the old places while
I still had the chance. Mrs. York's little cottage had vanished but I
found Mrs. Lawson's, hard to identify as it looked much smaller. The
railway station nearby was still going strong with not the slightest
difference over fifty years, maybe longer since it wasn't new when
we were there. The quality of the timber again and the precision of
craftsmanship. And there was that same kerbing where I'd sat
when my legs were lumpy, and there the platform where I'd watched
the arriving and departing passengers. Again I heard in mind the song
about the girl asking the station-master for a ticket to heaven.

The condemned wobbly two-storeyed place by the railway line
which had once hosted some dolls, that hadn't survived the earthquake.

Dean Court had, however, but its facade of grandeur had worn off, like an old face that no longer used cosmetics. Its hair was white. I didn't go round the back to . . . yes I did. The dungeon seemed so small, a hut for dwarfs. I couldn't believe a young family had tried to live there once. And further along that same street I found the Hastings Main school; several more modern classrooms added of course but the original building stood. Roof upright, shoulders squared, contemptuous of any old earthquake. You could pick the four-generation room where Mr. Burns had left his mark, an ancestor in the lineage of schoolrooms.

Roach's department store in Heretaunga Street still flourished blandly, having fallen in the earthquake and been entirely rebuilt, a little sadder and wiser. Yes I walked up the stairs to the new showroom replacing the one from which half a century ago 144 dolls had taken a holiday.

And one day I drove across to Napier and out to Green Island where Puppa had been, but now there was no causeway since the 1931 earthquake had lifted the harbour floor 23 feet. Just flat innocent green-grassy meadows as far as the eye could see, and the road out there was paved and Green Island was no longer an island, just an insignificant mound. The building was smaller and the trees were bigger. Seeking the cast of the peopled past. Their ghosts were everywhere and I said goodbye.

*School Ten*

TE WHITI    The last place I was writing about was Hastings, where we attended the main school, my ninth, and lived in a dungeon behind Dean Court. Yet we came out of that. Before the end of the year we were at my tenth school.

A favorite remark of Mumma's when one of us got out of hand was "The world'll take it out of you." Some would say the world already was taking it out of us; if so, it felt all right.

The world was taking it out of our big ones since they'd left home who were finding out for themselves what it was like, their parental support approval only. But standing or falling it made good copy when they rebounded, hurled home from centrifugal action in sudden sorrow or glory. Either way they were right. Mumma and Puppa believed in each one of their children from Muriel down to Evadne. To them we were all marvellous and completely faultless. "She's a wonderful woman," it was said of Mumma, "but she spoils every one of her children."

The world had taken quite a bit out of Gracie but by no means all. A trained teacher by now in a sole charge school, Te Whiti, seven miles out of Masterton. She succeeded socially, which is quite something anywhere. She was beautiful with Puppa's English colouring, like Norma, with thick black curls. Her love-affairs paced the talk at home and you'd see her and Daphne sitting together on the floor, backs on the wall, being short of chairs, talking endlessly as though the subject of love would never run out.

Gracie got on with her chairman and might have stayed longer at Te Whiti but for her inherited desire for change, so although Mr. Trate lent her a fine horse, about one remove from an Arab steed, though she galloped the countryside among the settlers, she'd already begun pulling out an atlas at night to examine other countries. The time came when, mindful of Mumma's travail with the younger ones around her, of our homelessness and of Puppa put aside on Green Island, she applied for and got a job in Wellington, leaving the way clear for Mumma to apply for Te Whiti to which she was appointed in a permanent position.

And here we are, the lower half of the family, all together again with Mumma and Puppa, back in our natural habitat. A small three-roomed cottage in the country with no conveniences whatever but to us, after Dean Court, a wonderful palace. A wood stove in the kitchen that actually operated, a water-tank outside the back door and a W.C. some yards off. What else do you need to be together? True it stood stark mid-paddock, treeless, like a matchbox dropped on a plain, no evidence of its having once being painted and three miles from the school, but we'd known worse. Look, if anyone wants to know what the government really thinks of its teachers take a look at the "residences" it provides. Even today's new ones. Plenty of paint, right; but the cheapest it can get away with.

Chairmen usually start off as guardian angels as any country teacher will verify, which is not to say they can hold the role, no more than the teachers themselves can sustain their role of perfect professionals. It's only fair for teachers not to stay too long, for they're in the position to move on whereas the chairman isn't. Four years is more than plenty. You don't want to let people get to know you too well. When the initial inter-popularity shows signs of thinning that's when you ought to get up and go. No chairman and teacher can be expected to live

side by side in the country and maintain the status quo especially
when one teaches the other's children. If a teacher stays on and on
he'll never get a send-off with a decent present. The perfect solution
to district relations is known to be changing schools regularly; it's a
matter of timing. Though with inspectors it's a matter of changing
provinces. It's poor strategy to let anyone at all get to know you too
well wherever and whoever you are. As Daphne would say if criti-
cised, "We can't *all* be perfect."

In a flourish of quite convincing goodwill Mumma's new chairman,
Mr. Trate, delivered a sledge of wood for someone to chop, lent us a
lame white cow called Lily for someone to milk and, when he killed
a sheep, always left the head in a bucket on a post for someone to
carry home for meat. Ashton appeared long enough to chop a mountain of wood, Norma, about nine, tried to milk the cow and I once
carried home the sheep's head. But in time it came to be Mumma the
sole someone. Well, no, not wholly. Norma wasn't bad on the cow
at all and I liked the rhythm of swinging an axe but the sheep's head
job could not take on.

Puppa was radiant. His narrow iron bed fitted behind the kitchen
door exactly, just made for telling stories from at night, for shouting
to God when necessary or reading his Bible by candlelight. We'd far
rather have him here than not with us at all; he supplied a third dimension. We'd rather have him sitting on his chair by the stove once more,
his crutches at hand, trying to stoke the fire, stirring the porridge in
the morning with Evadne against his knee, boiling the kettle for
Mumma's tea when she came home from school and browning the
evening potatoes. He'd turn over on his tongue the word "perm-a-
nen-cy" as though it were clover honey. Puppa was a great help to
Mumma although I did hear her say, "I wish I'd married a man who
would thrash me with a bridle."

As for us children we took to exploring New Zealand all over again:
hills, paddocks, cliffs, creeks, a sulky temperamental river and a white
pine forest, kahikatea, rearing from shallow water. Enraptured at our
good fortune, joyful as aliens returned to the homeland.

Again we find ourselves trailing Mumma to school and back in all
kinds of weather along three miles of country road with soft barefoot
tracks in the grass at the side. We trailed in what I call the Comet
formation: Mumma the comet, we the tail. Mumma forged rather
than walked, her long skirt swaying. Her head was small, shoulders
not big, middle wide, hips wider and her ankle-length skirt wide
based so that the shape of her cubic content was that of a cone, her

outline that of an isosceles triangle. At the apex the grey-brown hair
knotted in a bun at the nape, at the base her small feet veering outward. Being short she advanced in brief quick steps, head a little
forward, green eyes alert to anything ahead. Always carrying something; seldom speaking.

Mumma streaking ahead through space, I, Norma and Marmie in
diminishing sizes streaming out behind, a familiar pattern of family
action; the oldest leading, the younger following in unquestioning
trust, in the way we'd followed Daphne out of the forest that day when
we'd got lost. Marmie could only just make the distance to school.
You could always tell when Mumma was coming by Marmie's soulful
bawling. "Wait for me, Mumma," from the tip of the tail.

"I never wait," from the comet.

So Marmie would stay home quite often with Puppa, and Evadne
did all the time unless he were in hospital from a heart attack, then
Mumma would bring Evadne with her, holding her small hand. The
two of them leading us, the big and the little, the baby in a bright red
coat. We'd all had our turn holding that hand. A picture enduring the
weathering years.

We'd arrived at Te Whiti towards the end of the year, my tenth school.
Less than twenty-odd in that little school of raw lively children . . .
the same peaked ceilings like all the others and signed by pines. When
at work here at the university and in the schools, in the affluence of
front-line civilisation, I wonder what carpet and chrome have to do
with learning. Out in the backlands of Argentina excited peasants
following my book *Teacher* in its Spanish translation are teaching
each other on the ground itself, doing well enough. They made me a
little magazine and drew themselves and sent it to me the other day.

Daphne was in Standard 6; she'd had enough of country schools
and was bought a second-hand bike somehow on which she rode the
seven miles to Masterton Primary, confronting the stones from necessity and the dust, since you couldn't ride a bike on the grass as you
could a horse. Gracie who was very fond of Daphne planned to take
her away with her when she'd finished primary and be responsible
for her education. By now Daphne had largely separated from Norma
and me, integrating with the big ones when they came home who
all loved her dearly. Growing prettier and funnier every day; the way
she'd re-enact mid-kitchen the latest drama for Mumma and Puppa
till we all laughed like anything. But she did not seem to have dreams
for the future. "My family is my stage," she said. In Masterton she

immediately made friends though she never brought any of them home. None of us did.

The first morning at school Mumma turned from the blackboard to me and said severely, "Ten in Standard 4? The last time you sat before me you were in Standard 5."

"Please Teacher, yes."

Shocked. "Standard 4 still? You would have been in Standard 6 by now."

"Please Teacher, yes."

"A child of mine ten in Standard 4!"

Hang my head in disgrace.

"No child of mine will sit in front of me ten in Standard 4."

"Please Teacher, no. Please Teacher, I could finish Standard 4 by Christmas all over again for the third time, then in the holidays I could take home the Standard 5 books and do Standard 5 by myself at home and next year be in Standard 6. Would eleven in Standard 6 do?"

She turns back to the blackboard. "The common creatures. Calling themselves teachers."

School ten so far, but another school slipped in about here when Muriel had me with her in Taranaki for a month or two. That was Midhirst, and made eleven, though I see Te Whiti as eleven.

Short of an ideal girl to model myself on, a Netta Nye replacement, I made do with Polly Trate, supplying her gratis with extravagant glory enough to meet my requirements, this silent dour daughter of the soil. God, the people I've garmented in glory unrelated to what they were. But life was barren without someone to worship. To be in love with life was to be in love with someone. I tried to look like her. I wore a discarded grey shirt of Lionel's severely buttoned to the chin, a determined tie and somehow got hold of a prim grey skirt like Polly's. The replica also called for grey socks and black shoes but I had to settle for sandals. My naturally bare feet didn't know what struck them. I got Puppa to part my hair like Polly's—part it in the middle as though with a knife, scrape it back behind the ears into two painful plaits—and even assumed the same gestureless posture: head set forward, eyes gazing darkly. This role also called for me to learn to communicate, if at all, in monosyllabic grunts and to try to never smile. Why not double one of the pretty girls in the school? I sheer don't know. Polly's inner mystery maybe. I never knew what she was thinking. As things stood there were now two Polly Trates in the school visibly interchangeable, which must have mystified people. There did exist a group photo of that school in which I'm indistinguishable from Polly Trate herself. What she thought about it or felt I don't know either, not to this day. No clue. Nevertheless there were things in her I could not double: her immaculate big teeth, her glorious brown eyes and her polished black shoes. In all probability that's the point where I began to care seriously for my own teeth under my own power.

At year's end we entered drawings and paintings in the schools section of the Annual Agricultural and Pastoral summer show. Having completed all my own—a painting illustrating a nursery rhyme, I chose The Old Woman in the Shoe, a large painting; a pencil drawing from nature, I chose an ivy leaf, and a map of New Zealand which I painted—I then did all Norma's and all Marmie's under their own names. The morality part escaped me. They took most prizes, possibly all, first, second and third in each of the several classes. I won enough money to buy black velvet material for a dress for Daphne to wear to a friend's end-of-year party in town with a crotched lace collar. Such easily won, joyfully won money confirmed to me I'd be an artist the moment I got out to the world.

At our school prize-giving in a woolshed there was put into my hands the first book I'd ever owned myself, as distinct from school textbooks and journals, or in fact had even seen: *The Legends of Greece and Rome*. A book with green hard covers and no pictures. I didn't need pictures anyway, there were plenty in my mind. Along the dusty roads and down to the white pine swamp I carried it under my arm till I all but knew the thing by heart: maidens, warriors, dragons, the lot. Stunning horses too. Something other than British Empire history. Astonishing . . .

For the Christmas holidays, six weeks of summer, I did bring home the English and arithmetic Standard 5 textbooks and plunged in on Page One on Day One. Outside usually within call of Mumma, sitting on a log if she were chopping wood, sometimes putting down my books to get on the end of a cross-cut saw with her to carve up a log into stove-lengths (not noble, I liked it) or split some up myself, getting them as even as a geometrical drawing. The swing of an axe is a rhythmic business, you could do it in time to music. It would make a forceful ballet, chopping. Or I'd tuck into the seeding grasses as she did the washing outside in the one tin bath, boiling some in a kerosene tin first, to hang them all out on a length of wire spanning from the house to a post, and on the fences too. Or even when she was swimming in the Taura River. Plunging around like a porpoise, gasping at the cold of the water, "Oh this cold is cruel. Oh God is cruel to me. Oh God is cruel!" yet enjoying it like mad. She called it her "cold water cure." She was swimming and taking cold baths late in her eighties. I mean, God didn't exactly force her to do it. Sitting on the bank I'd read out a problem from the arithmetic book. "Mumma, it says, 'If there are 45 head of cattle in one paddock, and 34 in another, and the cost of the cows in the first paddock was . . .' "

"Oh God is cruel to me."

Or when she was milking Lily the cow, her forehead tucked in the flank. To the sound of the squirting of the milk in the bucket, "Mumma, ask me what a metaphor is."

"What's a metaphor?" to Lily.

"Is that when words wear flowery dresses?"

"Learn it again," to the froth on the milk. "Page Twelve, Paragraph Four."

Another day, sitting on the form behind the kitchen table as she was making a suet pudding: "I can't tell the difference between metaphor and rhetoric."

"Ask your father."

When it came to arithmetic I'd dropped the How Do You Do This Sum technique, falling back on Mr. Burns' teaching at Hastings Main and reasoning them out myself, often illustrating them to make them more comprehensible. Teacher never growled at the sketches among the figures. Sometimes for solitude to learn something by rote I'd run off down to the white pine swamp with its romantic islets in green-grassed water, as translucent, reflective as the eye of a horse. By God, a thrilling business, the whole engagement paced, not by Netta Nyes and other idealised girls but by Time itself, looming and towering like the trees above me. It's fair to say that after three goes I was sick of Standard 4. How could I look Mumma in the face at school in the role of dunce? Besides I liked this work and liked work anyway, especially on my own. I meant to be the best, the first, the frontest and be in Standard 6 this year. Those six weeks' work among the wood-pile, the washing, the cow, the river, the white pine swamp and suet puddings in which I'd done a whole class Standard 5 which I'd not really been in before, a year's work in six weeks, was the best class-room I've known in my life.

Mind you, it would bring me to within a year of Daphne schooling in town and I didn't want that, but it wouldn't be the same school, no one would know. It would be sacrilege to compete with Daphne but there was no alternative. When school reopened in early February I *was* in Standard 6 though it had taken me eleven schools to make it.

At school I found a new boy called Rolf Mannington, the same age as me and who rode from across the Taura River on a fat sleek pony, saddle too. A cared-for and handsome boy with clear sunned skin, lovely grey eyes and a frequent friendly smile. From him to us all there emanated a glamour that could not be ignored, a kind of mystery, my downfall. Even his name was interesting.

Yet he was unacceptable. He was too clever by half at his work, too good-looking, too happy and with too pleasant a natural goodwill. Too fortunate altogether. The mob doesn't like the exceptional; it distrusts them to the point where it must destroy them. One lunchtime as we all sat together beneath the pines, as we watched him open a splendid lunch, we judged and convicted him on every count till resentment reached flashpoint.

I don't know who started it but we ganged up and beat him, with our fists first. We had to break the stranger open, expose his inside, kill out that in him which was different from us and which we couldn't understand. Defuse his mystery. The more he smiled as he sat on the grass the more we hit him until, getting up, he struggled as far as the horse-paddock fence to try to escape on his pony. But we held his coat and he stuck in the wires thoroughly at our mercy. Compelled to remove the smile from him we picked up sticks and thrashed him.

We had to witness the fine one broken to see what he was made of, to gloat on his private tears. We did see the fine one broken but not what he was made of. True, the smile left his face and tears took its place but we still could not identify the source of the glamour to eradicate it. As Rolf cried and groaned and sagged in the wires the charisma remained with him so that as we returned to the pines to our lunches, gratified and justified, we only felt just as hungry for the food and anything but satisfied.

Moreover, this new boy not only did not tell Teacher but turned up the next morning exactly the same, his magnetism intact. The perfect answer to persecution.

Three of us now in Standard 6, Rolf Mannington, Polly Trate and I. Polly *must* have had thoughts of her own but she never spoke them. Possibly desires and resentments too but she never showed them. You could call my passing obsession with her (and the earlier ones) a schoolgirl crush but I'm more inclined now to see Polly as what I call the "complement to an artist," a condition reciprocally parasitical, or would have been had the thing been bilateral, but there was no evidence she was even aware of me. She didn't ever, for instance, offer me a ride on her big bay horse. This term about the complement to an artist is my own term and will not be known but it's not too far from the meaning of "amanuensis." Which again is a two-way thing, whereas there were no two ways about Polly Trate. There had not so far occurred in my life the miracle of "fire kindling fire," which is to say that as an artist I did not know company. Nor did I know that I didn't know it.

Terrifically Rolf and I paced each other daily, with Polly the silent minority. "Standard 6," from Teacher every morning, "come out for Mental."

Rolf and I fell over each other coming out for Mental, licking our lips for the contest while Polly took her time, steady about it. Mumma, I mean Teacher, would write our names fatefully on the blackboard as we stood side by side before her. Now, book in hand, she begins snapping out these arithmetical problems, one by one, the first hand to go up gets the chance. Right? You win the mark by your name. "Three-quarters of four hundred."

"Three hundred!" simultaneously from Rolf and me, the hand sequence overlooked. A mark each.

"Three hundred," from Polly soberly.

"How many hundredweight in two tons?"

"Forty," from Polly unflapped. God, a mark to Polly.

A lesson in mental arithmetic equated with a lesson in drama. I suppose I beat Rolf sometimes but he usually beat me. He became an engineer later. At that time, however, I could not but be aware of him, or he of me, the Polly impersonation and all. How I wouldn't know. For a start, to join a mass assault on him as well as play the character of someone else, abandoning my own essential character altogether, is not the prevailing way to get your man, but you've got to allow for chance. In spite of it all, of lifting my hand to him in the playground, of doubling for Polly Trate, we fell slightly in love with each other, or in something with each other. He wasn't the dark prince I knew so well in mind on a fiery white Arab steed—his pony was sleek, placid and fat—but he was the handsomest boy any of us had ever seen. More than that, which I didn't realise, he was company of a kind for me.

Two vigorous elevens ambushed by sex. It crept up behind us like a thief in the night. Rolf began taking an alternative route home after school, coming my road instead of his, crossing the river up past our place and we took to sharing the pony. So-o—slowly along summer roads until one afternoon before I'd got off he suggested with that smile of his that we go right now to that green-shade glade down by the white pine swamp. But I slid off, paused at the heavy farm gate, stammered something then ran inside, setting a basic pattern for future encounters with men: coquetry. Not knowing it was coquetry or that coquetry is cruel. Real love can't play that game. One learns in time but often it's too late to be sorry.

The next afternoon up the road from the school where I loiter for him to catch up he canters right past me. I watch him, incredulous. He gallops up the road after Ofa ambling on her piebald horse, a heavy girl who wore big striped socks and big boots and who milked cows after school. Is this true? It is. He reins in and rides with her side by side as, appalled, I watch the two. No one could say Ofa was pretty but her Norwegian skin is pink and white. I'd left her behind with lessons but she'd left me behind with a boy.

The very next afternoon after school up the road here is Rolf waiting and offers me a ride.

"No."

"Aw come on."

"No."

I give him no second chance, confirming an earlier pattern. Second place is not for me, in school or with men. I'm not Mumma's daughter for nothing. I'm prepared to lose everything. I think now it was Puppa's lineage, the pioneers and knights honoured by royalty. Blood pride.

"Don't you like me now?"

"No."


In Standard 6 at eleven Teacher taught us the analysis of sentences, subject and predicate, all about the verb being part of the predicate, a sentence being not a sentence without a verb. We learnt the nature of clauses and phrases, how to parse words themselves, verbs, nouns, adjectives, adverbs et al.; tense, mood, case, number, person and what contribution they made to a meaning. From the daily Latin roots listed at the back of the book we could not escape the structure itself of a word before it operated at all so that to me words took form as people walking on legs, some lolling round doing practically nothing like little prepositions, others carrying heavy loads of meaning, all of them when together arteried and veined by the rhythm. Sing-song stuff. Obvious in poetry. You could dance to them, which we younger ones in fact did in private during our wilful wanderings; sing to them.

And the strap in school for making mistakes, the prevailing order of that day. If you don't like the strap then don't make mistakes and if you didn't want to stay in the same class next year then pass the exam at the end of this year. School was intelligible. You knew where you were, and why, and what for. A dunce never got lifted by "Social Promotion" up through the standards of school. If you got Proficiency you could get a job in which you could spell, read and write and do sums or else you stayed at school till you could. If you could not, then there were legions of jobs you could get that did not require academic achievement. Whether or not we saw all this to be just, at least we believed it was. On this particular front we picked up no sense of injustice to haunt us through life, echoing; never to be forgotten, forgiven. For the duration, maimed. The fruit of this turned out to be confidence, not only in ourselves but in life.

Only these two others in Standard 6, Polly and Rolf, but I anyway was responding to both, wasting nothing of living in the process. None of us wasted life there; in the austerity and discipline one had no choice. The building itself was a background only rather than a feature, the old desks expecting to be carved with signatures, the gouged-in diary of a school. A legitimate, expected and honoured gouging. It was the "in" thing. I mean, what's a desk without signatures? The desks were to be used in their own right rather than nebulously revered. Starkness tends to be selective, cultivating anything in anyone in whom nests a spark, spitting waste out the window. Many a mind larger than size sprouted in these country schools. Rutherford was one and Barret-Boyes; Alley, Hodgkins and Hillary. Carpet and chrome would not have reared them.

Evenings of homework in the kitchen. The frankness of those old kitchens. Floor bare, spare, thoroughly scrubbed and with sacks at the hearth and the door. Kitchen walls were not papered in those days of anticipated children but panelled halfway up in varnished timber, the token curtain on the one window usually horizontal in the breeze with no more than a flick of wit at the end. The lengths to which our mother went to ensure her supply of fresh air and her "cold water cure" all seasons. I recall no occasion of a cold when young, of the flu or a temperature since no virus could survive the conditions. When it came to virus versus fresh air only we could survive the conditions.

There was nothing in that kitchen you could do without. The only decoration was Puppa himself except that he was also indispensable along with his shouting and heart attacks to follow, his bed behind the back door with a box alongside for his Bible and tea. A stove with the firebox usually open, a piano with the keyboard always open, the tough old cupboard with its food and dishes and the indestructible kitchen table; forms front and back with a chair at each end. The era called for the irreducible.

This private life of a kitchen table; work marks and notches witnessing the past, and grooves where knives had carved. Ink marks where people had signed their names in wistful confirmation of having passed this way, or just plain blots. No scrubbing could erase them. These days they call these blots abstract art to be sold for thousands of dollars and teach children how to make them. I think we make quite enough blots in our lives without being taught how to make them. Given a chance a kitchen table can be a family diary of no uncertain moment for any who know the code. By comparison Formica is pitifully illiterate.

Evenings of arduous study round this table, all heads down to it. The tall kerosene lamp plonked downright mid-centre drawing great moths like zeppelins through the open window and door, scattering their eggs like First War bombs, like fertilised ideas skidding through our wet ink in the hit-and-miss profligacy of nature. Mumma sitting with us, Puppa a human reference library, the feeling of common purpose so contagious that even the baby wanted a pencil till carried off to bed. Most things necessary to life were there, a forcing house of anything in you. An incubator of culture.

This context of austerity, parsimony and discipline of our daily and nightly schooling worked into my being as the ground-soil of security so that in later years when promise betrayed me, when fame and possessions failed to defuse the pain and rubble at heart, it was to these ways I returned.

I tend to linger before these pictures of Te Whiti; moving pictures, coloured and vivid, jumbled on the screen of memory, sound track the lot. Pictures as living as the reality was. They show more of the others than of myself. At that stage I see the family as a faceted unit, the top half harking back to base, not yet dispersed irrevocably.

For many years now the big ones had been looking back over their shoulders to the family at home to try to help with us though we seemed to see least of Muriel the eldest, usually away nursing, who was something of a mystery to us younger ones. My stay with her in Taranaki did nothing to dissolve this. On my return home she'd given me a waist-high, walkie-talkie doll, but it takes more than a doll to establish rapport. To me it was no more than a transient status symbol. Partly she had taken me as company for a boy cousin in her care but mainly it was for Mumma. It was Mumma she loved, whom she returned to see, for whom she did things and brought home presents. At this distance in time her lifelong and full-souled devotion to Mumma not only elucidates and illuminates but exonerates. The ousted first child. But she had been ousted not only nine times over but by the two immediately following her: the flashing Gracie and the worshipped Ashton.

Like others among us, not all, Muriel was irreversibly romantic. No lashes from life could teach her otherwise. She meant to equip herself to be what she wanted to be and that was it. With inspiring and sacrificial determination she saved every penny to buy herself in time a black velvet ball gown, a huge black velvet horse called Jack and a marvellous black velvet piano to force her dreams to come true. This new piano as dark, sleek and ravishing as the horse himself, not to mention the fairyland ball gown, was later delivered to our cringing red-faced kitchen in all its dramatic glory, the old one was dragged away by the hair in disgrace and one afternoon when I came home, alone and late, there it was, gleaming and coy. A miracle. Mumma said proudly, "Let Sylv have a turn."

Whether or not this piano was for Muriel herself to take with her one day when she made a home, this didn't get through to me but in my day it wasn't taken. And although all were allowed to play this piano none was allowed to borrow her gown or to ride her horse, Jack. *Not at all!* It was claimed he was dangerous and disposed to bolt. (Yet I found Jack gentle enough; didn't bolt, bite, buck, kick or anything . . .) And Muriel bought Mumma a few tender songs for her to play and sing; "Two Eyes of Grey" was one which she sang first herself in her haunting soprano.

Gracie, the second in the family, was teaching in Wellington at that time. (I think. You can get vague about these past dates.) She seemed to be often home leaving her presence behind when she went. Though one could not misread the tragedy written in those wide dark-blue eyes, the pathos of beauty and the pleading in them to be spared the foredestined life-break lapping in her soul, she nevertheless had many friends in the outside world and a love-affair every spring. Not that she brought anyone home of course, they didn't qualify. Or home didn't qualify. Daphne was her love in the family, and Norma who was like her. There was a coloured photograph on the wall in my childhood of Gracie and Norma together in their black-haired, tulip-skinned English beauty. The rapport between Daphne and Gracie took the form of secrets and laughter except when you saw the tears. She began talking of rescuing Daphne from the stones and dust of cycling the road, of taking her away the following year to be responsible for her education.

Ashton, about twenty-plus then, would appear, disappear, reappear at will to check on his ancestral origins, after all he was Puppa's eldest son, and to make Puppa laugh. He was very fond of both Puppa and Mumma who both uncritically adored him. He'd report to Puppa his latest victories (never his failures) in wrestling, boxing and Lazy Stick, flexing his Samson muscles to elaborate a point, and in verbal encounter. "And so impressed were they, Puppa, at my shrewdness . . ."

Stride to Puppa on his chair by the stove, "Now listen, young fulla, you wipe your chin," at which Puppa would laugh till his frail bones shook. He'd pick up Puppa and carry him around, admonishing him for ridiculous offences, sit him on a chair outside with a blanket over his locked knees where he could admire Ashton chopping the wood and see his motorbike, a thundering Triumph which by now was the new status symbol of us younger ones. "*My* brother has a motorbike. *Your* brother hasn't."

He still played his violin in powerful sensational tremolo having quite a name among his friends in shearing shed and freezing works circles, though his handling of a delicate bow was hardly improved by his fencing and scrub-cutting contracts. His massive physical strength was his private glory. "Smell the dead men on his fist," to Puppa. To us younger ones our popular saviour. "Tell Ashton," we'd say when crises reared. "Get Ashton to fight them." He was a man of invention also and you never knew what he'd make tomorrow.

Lionel was the next. I remember him for his music, practising alone in a bedroom where the paper peeled from the walls to the scrim, working on his violin for the next exam these strange new and lovely classics objectively, scientifically, and at night in the kitchen when we'd gone to bed. Daphne with all this delighted rapport with him had learnt his accompaniments and played for him with a swing and vigour which spoilt him for routine professionals thereafter. I was aware of her musical attunement to him. These nightly concerts made going to bed indisputably worthwhile whereas bed meant otherwise sharing a lumpy double bed with four . . . sorry, three others.

Next was this mysterious first Sylvia who lived for three days, the one responsible for the messing up of my visas later. Mumma told me she had held her feet in her hands the whole three days to keep them warm. A defective heart valve. I'd wish to forget this but I can't.

Then Daphne; as Puppa defined her, "the flower o' the flock." She remained a year ahead of me in Masterton though I'm vague about this but I'm sure about the friends she made whom she never brought home. She'd arrive at the gate on her bike late afternoon tired, her fascinating face sweaty, dusty and freckled from the headwinds whereas she liked to play delicate with an interesting weak heart though she cannot have been other than the toughest of the tough. I didn't like to see the flower humbled and neither, to more point, did Gracie.

It seemed a long time now since she'd joined the wanderings of us little ones, since she'd led us out of the forest at Te Pohue when we'd got frightfully lost, our secret adventures and risks, having shed her childhood. A year and a half older than I and maturing fast. Essentially different in character we'd passed the fork in the road, she becoming more Daphne, I more me. She looking outward, I absorbed inward. She must have missed the big ones when they went, and joined them when they came.

Anything I could do she could do better which only made me prouder of her, which was the way in this family. There was one big plenty of conflict but little of envy. The word "jealousy" I knew only later. She could draw, swim, act, ride, sing, cook, keep house, tell stories and played the piano with sensation and ear that ensured centre-stage at home. No training and no technique whatever, but Lionel told me when I was older, "There's something in her accompanying I find in no one else. Something that exhilarates, that lifts."

Chronologically I came next but, as for us little ones, I, Norma, Marmie and Evadne in that order, we lived something of a collective life at home watching the big ones come and go, absorbing instinctively, unwittingly, for good or ill the streams of drama they brought, we uncritically receptive. Personally I was no one's favorite in that family, though Norma and Marmie had a place for me for the time being, and I can't say I had a favorite myself but, with solid security and open praise for my drawing and music, I got by all right. Any love I lacked was in my own mind. I was an ugly girl between two beauties,

Daphne above and Norma below, but I wasn't aware of it then if ever. That didn't hurt me. All I wanted in the real world and didn't have I simply supplied in the unreal world of the imagination. No trouble. It was a well-exercised faculty.

Norma was next and was one of Gracie's two favorites as well as being lovely. It was no disadvantage to divide from Daphne since I began to see Norma more as a person. I found behind the pretty face a courage and a generosity new to me. And a quality of sympathy. Marmie, next, had the distinction of being The Boy and was revered by Mumma because of that. Evadne was noticed by Mumma for being the baby, and by Puppa too which guaranteed for her parental attention at least, but I think the big ones overlooked her.

In sum, I was lost somewhere in the middle of a large family and I believe it did me good though I sometimes think now that all my idealising of some girl or other was an intuitive search for a mother which continued most of my years but up till then not one had responded. It is significant to me, however, that much later in life when I was curious to get a line on my babyhood and early years, not one of the older ones remembered a thing.

These pictures on the screen of memory they move like shadows of leaves in the wind patterning on the grass, impermanently fleeting. This one here, now that one there, forming impressionistically yet cohering in a common theme. A theme indigenous to the family nucleus centred in the kitchen.

As I've said, we were known as the Warner Tribe, and no one visited us voluntarily. Only influences from the mystery of the outside world. New music was backfiring all the time per the big ones, some of whom had reached a tutor. From the time that Ashton and Lionel had learned at the convent many schools ago, we younger ones were exposed to the popular classics, registering them inaccurately, irreverently. On one swoop home at Te Whiti, still in the days of the old piano, Gracie brought Paderewski's Minuet in G, delivering it with a flourish which laid us all out so that in the course of time and after she'd gone, the rest of us tried to learn it too, from Daphne through me, through Norma to Marmie in his own way and even the baby had a go. All of which we carefully kept from Gracie, mindful of how uncomfortable it might turn out to be for us did she know that we'd raided her territory or, put it this way, that we'd diluted her musical status at home.

A day when a stranger is unaware enough to knock at our kitchen door, someone lost on the road I think come in to ask the way. I don't think she'd come to Do Good. We all flock to the kitchen to stare as she accepts a shaky chair. Gracie happens to be home and it's Mumma's Golden Moment. "Grace," choosing her showiest card, "will you play the Minuet?"

Gracie obliges heroically while the captive audience measures with her eye the distance to the outside door.

"Now Daphne," from Mumma in a voice of silk, "will you play to us, Daphne, please."

Daphne goes all coy.

The silk in Mumma's voice reveals gritted teeth. "Daphne? Come on, Daphne."

Daphne weighs the pros and cons and opts for the pros. Why she chooses Gracie's Minuet I really don't know. She performs somewhat self-consciously and avoids looking at Gracie.

"Sylvie? Come back, Sylvie." The silk of the cover-up wearing thin. "Where's that girl? Bring that girl! Come on, Sylvs, you play now."

Head down. Face red.

"Sylvia!"

Since I can think of nothing other than the Minuet I too take it on, the sustaining pedal prostrate throughout. Pace . . . you've said it. Mid-stream I cut the cost, crash into Minuet rubble and break up all ways in eternal confusion. The visitor's mouth is opening for breath like the beak of a bird, alarmed and trapped. She keeps on measuring the distance to the door.

"Norma?" the velvet, "Come on, Norma."

To be fair, this Minuet is a lifetime beyond the range of any of us younger ones but in this context that means nothing. We're gripped in some spell. Norma's version of Paderewski, hit-or-miss, she supplies gratuitously, doing us a favour like milking the cow; she was known as the willing one.

Marmie doesn't need to be summoned. So carried away is he by the prevailing idea, accustomed to following the rest of us regardless, that he moves in a cheerful coma to the piano unbidden to rattle off a random selection of phrases from the distraught Minuet that would equal the Way Out new music anywhere. My first encounter with Art in Abstract.

After which the baby, Evadne, who also learns life by doing what we do, offers what she has of the Minuet as seen at three, gratis, the first bar repeating in erratic variations anywhere at all on the keyboard by which time the guest knows the thing. She's got the message. Unsteadily she gropes the distance to the door to vanish dramatically, never knowing how lightly, in fact, she'd got off as several of the family were absent.

As for Gracie she abandoned the Minuet as a status symbol and was never heard to play it again.

A placid Saturday. Puppa sitting at the end of the table relaxed in relative peace, Mumma cutting meat with a terrifying knife and Daphne scrubbing the kitchen floor over by the door. Her dress is tucked in the top of her bloomers exposing her legs from the thighs down. She's near Puppa's bed behind the back door. We younger ones are about, one at the piano I suppose, when out of nowhere sounds a knock. We all look up and see a stranger, no less than a holy minister of the church, clerical collar the lot. So appalled is Daphne she takes one dive beneath Puppa's bed for cover but only the top half of her is hidden; her long, bare legs sprawl out behind her as well-fleshed evidence, beneath the gaze of the man of morality, whereas legs in those days were very rude things especially above the knee. But this time it's Puppa's Golden Moment. With exaggerated elegance, "Come in, Sir."

Sir steps carefully over these thighs, avoids the basin of water and the scrubbing brush and manages to keep his feet on the soapy floor. After which he looks up and around.

Mumma advances smiling to greet him, forgetting the carving knife still in her hand gleaming balefully behind her which the visitor at once takes note of. Puppa adds hospitably and graciously, "Pass the reverend gentleman a chair, someone."

Someone does pass a chair, on which the minister, his eye on the knife, sits in all good faith, except that this chair happens to be the rickety one due to collapse any time. It chooses this particular moment to do it, hurling the gentleman forward on the basin of water and across Daphne's thighs which surprises the remainder of Daphne under the bed who's the last to know what's happening. Mumma shrieks briefly.

The minister reassembles himself as far as his knees, a posture not unfamiliar to a man of the church. Recognising this advantage he clasps his hands, lifts his face and, still covering the knife, prays on our behalf. "Almighty God, let Thy mercy fall on this house."

"Amen," from Puppa and Mumma.

Taking care, the minister gets to his feet, steps back over the thighs to the door and, with one last glance at the knife, takes his departure. Never, for some reason, to return in our time.

The high heat of summer towards Christmas when we'd all gone to the river with Mumma for a swim and to do the Saturday washing, carrying the clothes with us in the tin bath with two handles. Daphne has stayed home for privacy in which to take a bath, I don't know how since we'd taken the bath. It was about the time of year when bands go round singing Christmas carols then come to the door for a donation.

As she tells it later, she's just reached the stage of all-over nudity when a blast of horns and drums crashes round the cottage. The Salvation Army band, working on the analogy of Jericho, had surrounded the walls of this city. Our token curtains did less than service so that in panic, like a startled fawn, she galloped to the bedroom and squeezed in behind the dresser in the corner, trembling suitably, while the brass and the singing crescendoed with many a hopeful Hallelujah. All were in military uniform.

Frequently they'd pause and wait for someone to come out and when no one did they'd knock on both doors, fore and aft, when the heart of the fawn stopped beating, as she said. The siege continued the entire afternoon while the Army sang to her about angels and shepherds, the star of Bethlehem, a manger, a celestial choir and God. "Did you," from Marmie when we returned, "give them any money?"

"That's a bit of a joke, Marm." Evidently the walls of our place had stood up better than the walls of Jericho.

This made three occasions of callers in several years, quite a good score really. Unless the chairman is counted, Mr. Trate, who, intent on keeping this teacher for the school since her own children kept the school roll up, would at times ride to our back door on his impressive horse bringing the rejected sheep's head himself which we regularly left in the bucket on the post. Ungrateful people. Though I can't see that any deceased sheep's head could qualify Mumma's impulses to change, or as they say in America "relocate." But these deliveries of his were hardly social calls. He wouldn't dream of dismounting. No, three it is. Puppa remarked appreciatively, "It's getting more and more like London every day."

Each one of us had a brush with music. Living with Mumma one had no choice. She kept up our lessons doggedly, though "technique" was a word we'd never heard. The piano was seldom quiet and we usually practised if for the wrong reasons. Practising was not without its fringe benefits. To Mumma, anyone at the keyboard was immune from jobs, with the result that, to avoid the dishes after a meal, there was one mad rush to the piano, a thundering stampede. Sudden six-hand improvisations blew up in marathon form because the moment you sagged it was dishes. Not that we were short of other ways of escape; you could miss a meal altogether to sneak in later to pilfer what was left, if any, or on the last mouthful you could up and vanish completely. I had the worst record for dishes. "It's your turn, Sylv."

"No it's not."

"It is."

"It isn't. I didn't use any."

"I saw you eating, though," from Daphne.

"But," from the piano, "I'm practising."

"Mumma, it's Sylvie's turn to do the dishes. She never does them."

Firmly from Mumma, "Never take anyone from the piano."

But often it was Puppa left alone with the dishes. One summer evening after tea when everyone had opted for the vanishing trick leaving Puppa alone again, as I was slipping out through the door I heard him say to Mumma, speaking of meals, "They come in like rats and disappear like smoke." From the doorway I look back at him lurching round the table on one crutch collecting one plate at a time. To my astonishment I hear myself say, "I'll do the dishes, Puppa." I do. I remember it. It stands up to be counted, this strange pleasure.

Another fringe benefit from music at home came through the wall after the candle was out. Daphne singing at the piano her heartfelt love-songs or accompanying Lionel on his violin; a concert a night was routine, and from the rest of the big ones when they were home. Listening in bed in the dark at night you felt the impossible to be easily possible and that any wild dream could be real one day.

One morning in the kitchen I heard mentioned something called the "Moonlight Sonata." No one played it, just said it. The sound of the syllables registered first, then the picture the words carried. Nor did I miss the respect with which the title was spoken. What was a sonata, was it made of moonlight? I don't know who got hold of it for me but I started right in on my own, lured by a swelling wonder, learning more about heaven than the sonata itself. As I laboured from note to note, from bar to bar of the first movement, the octave work beyond my untutored child hands, I was entranced at the unfolding line of the thought, at what I felt it was saying. It wasn't divided into slices like the hymns, the duets and the "Campbells Are Comin'." It

didn't do what Daphne's love-songs did, Gracie's Paderewski and
Lionel's Kreisler. It had a different shape, not cut, dried, predictable.
It wasn't cut or divided at all but flowed in continuity and you
couldn't anticipate what was next, though it didn't stop saying the one
same thing in varying ways all through to the end. The theme came
round corners and down through the hills like a stream seeking peace
in the river. And finding it. It said new things in the language of
music, things that I'd felt but with no skills to say them. To sense
an alternative to the already established was to break cover from conformity, to get out from under the crinoline. It was shattering to
realise there were ways of going about a thing other than what I'd been
taught; that there was a language other than paint that could say the
unsayable things inside you.

The same feeling that came when making a picture, different from
sharing Rolf's pony. Like the effect of the words in poetry. I'd found
my own way to another heaven without asking the station-master for
a ticket like the song on the Hastings railway station. Delirious para-
dises. If this was a sonata, then I'd be a great pianist when I grew up
and spend my life at the keyboard. Once I'd finished this last year
in Standard 6 and went out into the big bright world I'd seek there
the finest teacher and learn like mad. I'd learn this language and be
able to say to others the real things inside me and then people would
love me. In the meantime I'd teach myself, of course, as I'd taught
myself much else. As for what the Beethoven adagio sounded like,
physically and technically beyond my range, plodded through on a
rattletrap piano . . . that part escaped me.

Freedom was our natural state. Though bound hand and foot by
discipline in school the bonds fell off outside the door; then we got
on with our living from where we'd left off. Weekends we'd run outside to the morning, bread and syrup in hand, and take off into whatever the weather in Haley's Comet formation: I, Norma and Marmie
in that order, leaving Evadne behind. "Where shall we go?" in wonder.

"Let's go down to the white pine swamp," and there we'd play for
hour after hour in the limpid water green-grass-carpeted at the foot
of the towering trees, living out our native imagery. These pale trunks
of the kahikatea, nude to the branching crowns, like pillars of the
temples I'd read about in my *Legends of Greece and Rome,* or spires
of castles in fairyland that Puppa told about. In mind you could see
the rippling locks of some princess languishing, waiting for a knight

on a prancing steed to steal her for his own. At the base of each trunk a little green islet softly draped in grass, the water reflecting tall skies of clouds and the tall tree crowns above it. Deeper within it was dark and mysterious like hidden recesses of a mind where we didn't presume to intrude. At once Norma and I would start playing house while Marmie was the boatman, the three of us talking incessantly, prolifically composing scenarios and songs, forgetting the reality we'd left behind.

Beyond this stand of pine was a deserted whare—a small Maori dwelling—where a Maori was said to have died one night, and all his things were in it. It was said his spirit was in there too. We left this whare respectfully alone on account of this spirit in it though honestly we did want to see His Things. Until curiosity began taking over, and we risked creeping nearer. Another day nearer still to dash back and cower in the bullrushes. If only we could get a look at His Things, but we did fear the spirit part.

This spirit must have emanated quite a presence, for the door had remained unforced all this time and the windows unbroken. The day came of course when we had to touch the place, only to scoot off madly all the way home to the safety of the kitchen, gasping in panic. Only there did we turn to see if the spirit were following.

Daphne is ironing her clothes for Monday. "Who's chasing you?" she says.

"The spirit."

"What spirit, whose?"

"The one in the whare behind the swamp."

She puts the iron back on the stove, comes to the door and looks. "Heavens, there it is. Coming out through the swamp. Hoo, what a lovely spirit."

Mumma creeps to the door. "Where, Daph, where?"

Slam the door, we younger three, dive for cover under the table and bed and behind the dresser in the bedroom while Daphne goes on with her ironing and Mumma with her scones. Puppa in bed behind the door absently closes his Bible. "Who did you say is coming?" he says.

In the meantime we had not yet seen His Things. Reconnoitering continued. After all, Mr. Trate sometimes rode that way and so did his brother. The door and window turned out to be locked. In variations of fear one day I broke a window, then back to the cover of the bullrushes. Weeks later before my hand goes in through the hole in the glass to turn the inside catch. Next thing you push up this window then another terrified scuttle home to check on our mortal origins, the spirit puffing behind. Daphne is baking rock-cakes. "Why don't you leave the place alone?"

"We have to see His Things."

"What Things?"

"The dead man's Things."

Puppa says, "Confound it, can't you leave dead men alone?"

"Can't you leave *anything* alone?" from Daphne.

More nervous weeks before we return, as we must, and this time here's the window still open and waiting for us and the next thing we're in. Musty in here. Dim. Only one room and a fireplace. All very clean but far too still, more silent than the grave. And here's his trunk, a ghostly trunk. Taboo, sacrosanct. Open the lid upon His Things which turn out to be *Her* Things. It's a She. A woman's clothes, one dress spangled and some have pretty buttons and beads. Bright hot colours and remembering scent. And what's in this little carved box? "You open it, Sylv."

"No, you."

"Not me."

"Why?"

"She's watching us."

"Who?" from Marmie.

"The dead lady."

"Where?" he asks. "Can you see her?"

"Yes I saw her. Just over there. Now she's gone."

"Where's her body?" from Norma.

"Somewhere. Might be in a cave."

Marmie looks round for the dead lady's body. "Not here," he says. "It must be in a cave. You open the box now, Sylv."

"No."

"I will," from Norma, the brave one. "A ring? Look, a gold ring. *Her* ring . . ."

*You-fulla, you leaves alone my ring ay.*

"Did you hear that?" I breathe.

"Hear what?" they say.

"I heard her say, *You-fulla, you leaves alone my ring ay.*"

They look around and up to the ceiling.

"Put it back," I shriek. "It's alive. Quick!"

Never do we return.

Morning, bread, syrup and wonder. The back road where we lived
continues on through the hills to end at a forlorn gate. A horse grazes
quietly there and lets us approach him, as forgotten as the gate. Tame
as tame as tame. Old maybe. We pull some flax, split it and plait it,
tie the lengths together to loop round his nose for a bridle. Norma
climbs on first, then Marmie, then after they'd proved to me it was
safe, me last and each of us had a pleasant ride. So what? Where
does Sunday School morality come in? To ride somebody else's horses
all round the show, I mean, this was routine. A way of life. The word
"policeman" was no more than an over-romantic term you heard
sometimes. "I wonder," I say, "who rode him before."

"Some people," from Norma profoundly.

"Are they dead?" from Marmie, fascinated with the "Dead" idea.

"Hope so," I say.

"Are their spirits here?"

We look round, wide-eyed. Further into the trees to find out. We're
terribly frightened but we *have to* find out. What's behind in there? A
deserted burnt-down homestead with only the chimney standing. The
ghosts must have lived here when they were people. They once climbed
these fruit trees, untouched now, unpruned. Apples, plums, pears,
peaches, quinces and, "Look, Norm, here's some cherries." Food. We
sit down to a marvellous feast. Where are they now, those who walked
here; just gone away or dead? We sense the presences of their spirits
and furtively back off. We follow the sheep tracks round the hills,
single file. More hills over every horizon never-ending. But what's
over the next hill, can we find out today? Way up high on the wind-
blown crest I note the silk of the drying grass and someone must have
been scrub-cutting here quite a time ago for the cut manuka is withered
and brittle. Wonderful tinder for a fire! With a match what a flame
there'd be. It would run through the grass around the hills, through
the cut scrub down to the gullies and up the other side, maybe to start
some forest fire for which I was intuitively lonely, forest fires being a
part of our youth . . . well . . . when we were younger still. But God
is looking today.

Much later in the hills and ranges of life there did ensue a forest
fire which socially and professionally consumed me. From this distance
of a lifetime I see my thoughts that day of playing with matches as
symbolic, later, of setting alight the national crinoline over the head
of the country, burning it off myself at least so that for the first time I
could see and hear, could breathe more profoundly. But the release of
vision is costly in scars.

Another morning up another lost lane following a devious creek like a line of thought to its source. Where does it come from, how does it start? Past tempting ferny glens designed to lure a looker to loiter, round vertical clay banks you must carve your name on, through undergrowth of difficult bramble confusing the way till we come to a hollow in the hills holding possible answers, even possible fruit. Surely there's some deserted home up here with some deserted orchard. A man-made bridgelet crosses the creek leading up the slope to a little grey hut with the door open. Smoke lifts in loneliness from the iron chimney. Not ghosts this time. Smoke means food to hungry children and certainly something to drink so we cross the low bridge, un-nailed, un-railed, walk up and knock at the door. Not a deserted home but a deserted man; solitary, rough, unshaven. "Come in."

He has no bread so I make some scones, girdle scones on the open fire and the whole time I'm mixing and cooking he lurks at the far corner of the single room staring at the three of us in silence. Norma in her marvellous slap-dash never-mind-what cheerfully makes the tea but he has no milk. No milk, with cattle all round the place? He doesn't speak but drinks the tea, his calculating eyes swerving from one to another of us. "Home," from Marmie with only instinct in him. "Come home," authoritatively, like the Big Man in action round here.

I don't see any danger, only feel it, sharply gruesome in each beat of my pulse. We don't understand but something makes us Must. We drink the tea and eat the scones till suddenly, collectively we panic. Push through the door, rush down the slope, dash back over the bridge and run till we're out of sight. Hurry, cut all over with brambles, till we puff in the kitchen door and gasp out about the man we found. We don't cry. You don't cry in fright, you only go cold and rigid. "Never go there again," they say. "Never trust a lonely man."

"Why?"

"Hunger," from Puppa, "has danger."

"The skunk," from Mumma, and spits.

Daphne says reflectively, "Give me a spirit any day." Then, taking up the broom to the floor, "You little wretches. Can't you leave *anything* or *anyone* alone? One of these days you'll come home dead."

In fact we nearly did, often.

I say, "We should get Ashton to kill him."

Daphne: "Ashton doesn't go round killing people. All you've got to do is leave things alone, leave people alone. Alive or dead. People or spirits or apples."

But Daphne had always been proper when she'd led us. Wouldn't let us steal people's cherries. Even Mrs. Greenaway's strawberries. I mean, how can you live without stealing people's strawberries? We had to survive, didn't we?

All these cuts on us to wash and tie up with rags, and Marmie has two grazed knees. Freedom was our way of life, we knew no other; but freedom, like vision, is costly also. This time there are only physical scars.

The Taura River was half a mile or so from our place. On our side the bank was flat and you could run straight in and swim but the other side was a cliff unscalable. Up and over that cliff was where Rolf Mannington lived and we needed to scout and see his place to find out how rich he was. Standing knee-deep in the water we scan this cliff one day, not being overfamiliar with the thought, "No, I can't." "There's a cave halfway up," I note.

Norma says, "That's easy."

Marmie's content about it.

We swim across in our bloomers which were bulky things, it was far too rude to go naked, and begin to climb. It's not too steep near the base so I lead because it's easy. I reach a shrub jutting out a few yards short of the cave. From the shrub up it's steeper. Anyway the next thing the three of us are in the cave with Rolf completely forgotten. Fun. We explore. Might be some treasure here. In fact there are bones, interesting bones, not like sheep's bones. The skull is quite different, it's round and when you put it over your face it fits as good as a mask; holes for your eyes to see through and a hole for your nose to breathe through. Exciting. "Let's take it home to play with."

My stomach turns over and tells me. "It's the dead lady's skull."

Horror. Terror. We look out the cave opening, it's just one long steep drop to the river. How did we get up? It's easier to ascend than descend, and safer. We're stuck here forever and will die in time. "Go on, Sylv," from Norma, "you go first. You're the biggest."

I no longer lead but baulk and whimper.

So she says with recklessness, "Well I'm going to slide down to that shrub sticking out."

Marmie is all placid faith. After all we'd brought him out alive from everything so far.

"Norma, don't," I say. "Don't . . ."

But she sits, spreads her legs and slides forward and down, hits the shrub, a leg each side, the shrub bends forward under her weight, she topples forward a bit, poised there balancing between life and eternity until the shrub slowly recovers itself and stiffens upright again. "It's all right," she says.

She turns over, face to the cliff, and clambers sideways down the not-so-steep part the way we'd come up and soon she's looking up safely from the riverbank below. "Come on, Sylv, it's easy."

"Norma, get Ashton to save me."

Marmie spreads out his legs too and copies what Norma did except, being smaller, has no crisis on the shrub. A manuka. It holds him, and soon the two of them are down there looking up at me. "Come on, Sylv," from Marmie.

"No. Get Ashton to save me."

I go cold and rigid at the thought of dying up here all by myself with only a skeleton for company, then there'll be two skulls in this cave. Death is all round like an enclosing black cloud, all over the cliff and upon the river and filling up the sky. You can't see a thing.

"Come on, Sylv," they call. "Try it."

Better to die on the way down. I too open my legs and slide down to the shrub which, I being heavier, bends further forward than it had with the others, stays this way longer as I stare down on the rocks below until it recovers erect again. It holds me, the manuka. Turn over, clamber sideways and down and the three of us swim back to the home bank. We don't stop to play anywhere on the way home, don't sing or tell stories as we walk and don't steal any apples.

An adventure which supplied me with the seed of recurring nightmares for about forty years; always falling down steep and crumbling hills, cliffs, caverns, falling, falling, nothing to grasp, finally to awake screaming. Always the same until the time came much later in life when there was something to hang on to and I stopped falling, and didn't wake screaming. They've left me now, the nightmares, but not the emotional scar. It's no fun to me to travel by jet.

There were more safe times, however, than dangers. Playing wild animals on all fours in and out among the rushes; snorting, sniffing, growling, chasing with the sexy undertones. Climbing those pine trees except that only the highest tip would do even in swinging gales . . . oh I did love that. Building houses with manuka, building dams in the creeks, slogging and sweating out the passion of our imagery unhindered. Tobogganing down the sheeny hillsides when the grass was dry on cabbage-tree tops or curved boards from a barrel we found one day; bird-nesting; we knew every egg of every bird in every tree for miles; trotting barefoot in formation along soft-dust sheep-tracks, singing insouciantly; communicating in code that only we knew until our slow tired return homeward, the only time when I told stories.

Children at large like that jeopardise their survival every day of their lives and you wonder how anyone grows up at all, how adults come to be walking round. Maybe because we kept on saving one another's lives all the time. Nonchalantly isn't the word. The thing was casual routine. My own life had been saved at least three times so far: when Daphne led us out of the forest at Te Pohue, when Marmie led the run from the deserted man and when Norma led us down from the cave in the cliff, to name but a few offhand. I don't think we saw it to be any particular favour, it didn't call for sacrifice or anything. Far easier than sharing a stolen peach or giving up the keyboard. I do note that we did in fact grow up, even though I don't know how.

For me, touching eleven, an extended childhood which could well go on forever. Maybe it did. Encapsulated.

Towards the end of this second year at Te Whiti school, my eleventh, when the Pastoral Show came round, again I did all my own drawings and paintings, all Norma's and Marmie's too, and once more won all the prizes, firsts, seconds and thirds, but this time it didn't get by. Someone leaked it. I received the prize money for my own legitimate entries but Norma's and Marmie's were withheld. The judges wouldn't buy this ruse again. Nothing was said overtly, no charges were made, no scandal surfaced but I knew that they knew, at which I was fuzzily alarmed. Their uncanny silence made my blood run backwards. As in the Dolls Operation I'd lost in this second encounter with the world in advance before I got there. Twice was enough. These two exercises didn't leave scars like the other crises but a hard intelligible discipline. I'd never do it again. Nor did I ride someone else's horse again. Not exactly for any moral reason but it was a better idea.

Also at year's end Rolf and Polly and I went to Masterton one day and sat the Proficiency exam conducted severely above board. The one mark that put me ahead of Rolf to make me Dux of the school was a clean genuine mark. Maybe on paper I was about one mark better than Rolf but only on paper. By any other criteria—personality, character, looks, lovability—I'd have come nowhere. It was appropriate that, like the ill-gotten prize money, no Dux medal came my way even though it was fairly gotten.

Eleven years nearer the main encounter, standing at the door. What were my qualifications? To look at, skinny, freckled, insignificant; scholastically I had Latin roots, a little arithmetic and a lot of sentimental British Empire poetry; emotionally I was lawless with an outsized compulsion to dream and a personal morality that barely coincided at any point with the prevailing Victorianism. Far from being ready to graduate from childhood to adolescence, it's disputable if, temperamentally, I'd graduated from babyhood. I'd got away with far too much. Mind you I wasn't too bad with an axe at the woodheap or on the end of a cross-cut saw. At least I was tough, browned and healthy and had never known as much as a cold . . . if any of these qualify one for life.

But whatever I was, it had taken eleven years. "The world'll take it out of you," Mumma had warned me, but so far it had left quite a bit. I was an optimist. It's fortunate we don't know things when young; I thought I was all right. I believed I could achieve anything I chose to set my mind to if I tried hard enough. I'd even get someone to love me one day. I wasn't aware of my untouchability, both inward and physical.

No sense of injustice arose from my childhood to sour me through the life that followed. Punishment hurt but I believed I deserved it. I hated the strap-laden discipline of school, the chilblains in the afternoon, but saw it to be right and fair. I'm sure the family didn't love me, including Mumma and Puppa, but they did praise me lavishly, applaud an achievement, were proud of me and said so. Reward around every corner. There was in me a vague fleeting awareness at times that I had something big to do which to me was not extraordinary . . . just there, that's all. The thing was to get to the world and get going.

Sentimental? You've said it. As I've said, we were reared on "The Charge of the Light Brigade," "The Slave's Dream," "We Are Seven" and "The Arab's Farewell to His Steed." "My beautiful, my beautiful, that standeth meekly by . . ." which leads unerringly back to Mumma quoting at the table with tears in her eyes. Did Life ever scourge the romance from her soul; did she ever grow up? When she was aged and alone, with Puppa gone and her children too, some already dead before her, Muriel, Gracie, Ashton and Daphne, she was still seeking the glamour and stars. Wanting us to take her out for a picnic with a thermos of tea and sandwiches; to take her to town, to a restaurant, to the bright lights of the festival at Christmastime with the merry-go-

rounds, the balloons and the coloured crowds, or begging us pathet-
ically like a child to take her for a swim and buy an ice-cream. She
loved to travel in airplanes to stay with one of us and she watched TV
with delight. With awe she followed "I Love Lucy." Lionel said reflectively, "Mumma never had any youth. She's still trying to find it."

Whenever she was staying with us she wore pretty clothes, colourful
scarves the children had given her, beads we'd given her and the
Maltese Cross on a golden chain, an heirloom from her mother's
Scottish line. Pretty handkerchiefs and her gloves and she liked her
shoes clean. Recovering the early time when she'd once known glamour. And in the evening before our meal she'd come to the piano and
play and sing her favorite songs she'd brought—soft, tender, reminiscent. "Two Eyes of Grey," "I Hear a Thrush at Eve," "I Passed by
Your Window" and some modern favorites too. Her preserved voice at
well after eighty moved me to add my own voice, standing behind
her at the piano to sing a harmony. And all her notes on the piano
were true. A soprano voice that took the high reaches . . .

I was talking about the close of the last school year at Te Whiti, eleven
years nearer the big encounter; about my qualifications if any and
about wanting to get going.

During the following Christmas holidays Gracie swooped home to
get Daphne ready to take her away with her to Wellington and to be
responsible for her education, so I opened up a bawling campaign for
Gracie to take me too. I bawled outside under the kitchen window at
peak listening times, histrionically, putting first-rate pathos into every
howl. Unfortunately, Muriel the first-born repeated every wail after
me a half-tone higher, exaggerating the pathos, which diluted the
dramatic impact, the most infuriating thing. Marmie the ninth-born,
who held exclusive rights to bawling, was more than impressed at this
duet. "What are you crying for, Sylv?"

"I want to get to the wo-o-orld . . ."

Muriel a half-tone up: "I want to get to the wo-o-orld . . ."

"And that," from Mumma, "would be a good thing I tell you. Let
the world take it out of her." She is skimming the cream from the
milk with a saucer for someone to make the butter.

Gracie the second-born reasons defensively, "But I can't afford the
two of them. My salary is for one, not three."

Ashton the third-born: "Sylv, if you stop all that noise and be a
good girl and stay home and go to the Masterton District High School,
I'll see to your education. I'll buy you a bike."

"I don't want a bike. I want a horse."

"All right I'll buy you a horse."

"I don't want a horse *or* a bike. I want to go to Wellington with Gracie and Daphne."

"Want will be your master," quotes Muriel the first.

"Shut-up," from me the seventh.

"How dare she use slang in my presence," from Mumma. "To think how I've slaved for that girl and she can bring herself to debase the King's English in front of me. After all the Latin I've taught her single-handed."

Puppa in his bed behind the door looks up from his Bible.

Lionel the third-born goes off to the front room with his violin and the next thing here's this intricate melody weaving its way back.

Daphne the sixth-born looks wide-eyed out the window over the paddocks of grazing sheep. The thing about Daph, she holds no rancour. "It's a funny thing," reflectively, "how I had to have a year at the District High School and had to keep on riding a bike seven miles twice a day in dust and rain and headwinds all the time without stopping." To the sheep outside, as though seeking from them a solution to one of the more profound of Life's mysteries, "So why can't Sylv take her turn?"

"Because I don't want to, that's why."

"And it's another funny thing," from Muriel the first, "how there was no fearful fuss like this about *my* education. Sylvia Ashton-Warner?" She smiles. "Sylvia Want-Warner."

Another clash blazes which I'd rather leave out; Puppa closes his Bible and clears his throat. Mumma comes up with something like, "Slang *and* blasphemy. She has no respect for God or man. A-ha," gutturally, "a-ha. The world'll take it out of her."

"No world will take it out of me."

Mumma shoots a glance of alert expectation.

I warn, "I'll win."

Mumma to the big ones: "What'd she say, what'd she say? Did she say she'd win?" At last she faces me and looks me over. "Well go and wash your face first and comb that hair."

The big ones survey me briefly. Though they all had every reason to reserve their opinion on my character there did seem to be a residual vein of respect in some of them. I don't know why.

Norma the eighth takes the bowl of cream and a fork and starts beating the cream to bring the butter. Evadne the tenth-born says, "I'm hungry."

Daphne flips the whole engagement out the window to the sheep and tosses back her curls. "Who wants me to make some rock-cakes?"

In the end Gray gave in, which was not a good thing. I should not have been allowed to get away with that. True, I had some awful flaws in my temperament, but I was not beyond the reach of discipline if the lesson were tough enough. It was no preparation to meet the world. Life resists manipulation. Tears get you nowhere.

Never mind, it was fine at the time, the moment of closing childhood. As the summer weeks added up, the finale was more than cheerful; it had a built-in glow, a tremolo. To explore the world to see what was there would be like setting out into the morning with Norma and Marmie to seek the source of another stream, but this expedition would be so much bigger, so very much more unknown. Fancy going soon. My word, I thought, I'm lucky.

Did we . . . yes we did return here once to Te Whiti, Keith and I, but briefly. The stony dusty road I remembered was now widened, paved and cambered. The school was there, not added to, and the pines were immense. It looked forlorn and unused, unused by the living I mean, for Mumma was plain coming from the door in her long tweed skirt. The sole charge school had no doubt consolidated with the city schools with destructive bussing. I don't remember going to see the cottage, or if we did it wasn't there. I don't remember. We didn't have time, Keith being one who, setting out from A to B, meant to reach B with no hold-ups. But I'd wanted to stay the night in Masterton to relive everything else, not least the white pine swamp, that Maori whare behind it, the secret back road up past our place and the cave in the cliff by the river. I could have done with a week there.

What comes back to me from that overshort revisit is, but for Mumma in the door of the school, the absence of ghosts to greet me. Phantoms of those already dead, at least. Why not? Where were they? Had they lived more hotly in other places, were they waiting somewhere else, or were they affronted I didn't stay longer?

WELLINGTON GIRLS COLLEGE    Gracie took both Daphne and me back to Wellington with her and enrolled us at the Wellington Girls College, a large historic public secondary in the

capital city, where I landed in 3C, not 3A as I'd hoped. But I'd get
there, give me time. In the crowded third forms these letters slid down
through the alphabet way below C, somewhere round G or H, I think,
so that this C mark said something for Mumma's teaching. Daphne
was in the Fourth.

There I made two passionately loved and loving friends, Ariadne
and Jean, who chose the role of followers and audience while I played
leader and performer. That these two should be among the pleasantest
girls I'd met before or since says something for the standard of taste
at home whatever it appeared to be to the contrary, and also for my
capacity to behave at least acceptably since they would not have chosen
me otherwise. On these counts the college was a reckoning and my
worst faults fell away. We were devoted to one another and called
ourselves the Three Musketeers.

Even so my new friends did not have for me the inspiration of
dream-girls, the succession of Polly Trates, Netta Nyes and Bella
Axels. Was it because these two were accessible to me whereas it's the
unattainable that lures, or had it something to do with chemistry?
Quite irrelevantly it turned out to be a teacher who supplied the inspiration, the botany lady regally out of reach. This was the first crush
I'd had on a teacher and I must say I did go under. Later on I was
told that a crush on a woman teacher is the quest for a mother. If so
then Miss Pope did nothing to verify it. She was a tall fair circumspect
holy spinster with piled-high hair in golden plaits and eyes as blue
as wonder but the face itself was nothing much and I seldom tried to
draw it. Gracie knew Miss Pope behind the scenes and said she had
Bible leanings.

A schoolgirl crush is an unquiet thing; you fall in love on some
strange plane with everything but physical attraction. You could say
there was physical revulsion. A bewildering set-up for ignorant girls,
and why don't boys catch it? I was so possessed that all I could do
about it was to make a point of securing 100 percent in every botany
test we had, largely on the strength of drawing broad beans through
the stages of germination, sensitively tinted in watercolour. Speechless
in her presence I'd say it with beans. To this day no one can fault me
on the private life of a bean. As a fringe benefit I learnt some lovely
words on that subject like capillaries, osmosis, pith, chlorophyll, photo-
synthesis, transpiration and cambium, which moved me as much as
Miss Pope herself. I still go a-flutter when I see a broad bean, even
when cooked on my plate. Grounded in botany I no longer saw any
future in trying to excel in any other subjects in order to make 3A

since I'd lose Miss Pope and The Musketeers. It was more personally profitable to use the time amusing the rest of them, since Daphne wasn't there to do it and obviously it had to be done.

My word, we had high times there. We were packed into an overflow building round Thorndon way, some kind of army drill hall with rooms joined on and no outside playground. How many hundreds of us third-formers would go rip-roaring round those echoing halls during breaks in the day, bumping into one another with squeals and abandon as though life held nothing else. Often they'd dance in roistering partners which gave me a chance to go to the piano and supply what was required: a tune, a rhythm and volume unlimited which no one could call "music," any more than naming the instrument a "piano." Also there were periods during the week when we had classes at the college proper. We seemed to be always running, tearing from one end of the place to the other; "all for one, one for all."

Sometimes I'd spend weekends with Ariadne or Jean though I was never at ease in their homes. On the whole however, in terms of school and friends, my first encounter with the Wide Wide World was so radiantly happy that dreams themselves were superfluous and the moment was all. That howling under the kitchen window at Te Whiti was plainly paying off.

On the home front though it wasn't. It was soon proved that Gracie's single salary could not support three people, two of them gorging adolescents. Though she had taken a pleasant roomy flat on The Terrace, all harbour view and appearance, she could barely meet the rent; you couldn't pay happiness for tram fares, you couldn't wear a frontage for clothes and you couldn't eat a harbour view. Gracie herself forfeited professional necessities, and besides, Three was never much of a number. Although my behaviour was at least as tolerable as it was at school I was not a sunny presence and as Gracie was not one to be slow in action when a crisis reared she said she would send us both home, which was anything but fair on Daphne. True, I tried a little light bawling but it didn't go down this time. Not with Gray. At the end of this first term in the capital, in a real rare Gracie rage, she did shoot us home and we found ourselves back at Te Whiti.

To be hurled from love in the city back to a vacuum in the country was to learn about the world taking it out of me. It almost got through to me that self didn't pay . . . but not quite. I'm very glad at this moment to recall that discipline, but was less than glad at the time.

I brought home one prize however: that given the circumstance, an adequate field of selection and benign school conditions, I could make dearest friends as fast as the best, which Daphne usually did. But they took it as badly as we did, our new loving friends, and we exchanged impassioned letters.

That was my twelfth school. It was also the beginning as well as the end of my first secondary school.

MASTERTON DISTRICT HIGH   Here were Daphne and I just like the big ones backfired from the world to base in the failure of Te Whiti, as though we had never been to Wellington and had never had dreams. It was our turn to weep behind the door and whisper in the bedroom. Oh yes I was humiliated and sore and all that, too bad, too bad, but Daphne was broken-hearted, not only at leaving her new friends in Wellington, at the seven miles all over again to the Masterton District High School where she'd already done her time, at the sudden demotion from glamour and lights to dust and wind and punctures but at having to part from Gracie. At the time I didn't realise what I'd done to Daphne by evading my own turn on the road and insisting on going with them to Wellington but she must have known herself. When you get a fair distance from a thing like that you can see where it all fits in long after any chance to repair it has passed. I'd seriously disturbed the course of her education mid-stream which could have been the source of the first tremor in her magnificent self-confidence.

From Te Whiti the two of us were enrolled at my thirteenth school and second secondary, Masterton District High, as had been meant in the first place before Gracie set her sights on Daphne. Since the big ones couldn't bear to see the gay one silenced they put together enough money to buy her a new bike, a lovely one too; all shiny and compact with a soft sprung seat, no rattles, punctures and nothing falling off. You should see the tread on the tyres and the beautiful bell on the handle. I had the old shaky bike with everything falling off and we took to the road together sadly dropped in status. She never gave me a turn on the new one. She would ride a few lengths ahead of me and seldom spoke to me. And that seemed as it should be.

Daphne was already known at this school, a cheerful co-ed, for her drawing and singing and merriness, so popularity awaited her. There's no lure like a lovely face when the eyes are green and the curls are brown, no magnet like wit. She took up her class as a second family and went on from there, automatically centre-stage, no less at school than at home the sought-after flower o' the flock. The girls loved her and the boys chased her and the teachers liked her about. I see the correct Miss Cumberland smiling upon her when she submitted her cover design for the school magazine. "You sketch too, Daphne?" she said. Miss Cumberland always used the word "sketch" erroneously.

As for me I was falling for Miss Cumberland as I'd fallen for Miss Pope, whereas Daphne didn't go in for crushes. There was in me a place waiting for people like these. I even tried to knock up some homework for her but for the first time I ran into this road trouble which Daphne had known for a year. Most of the people in our separate classes lived along paved streets whereas we lived seven miles out. In the afternoon the others would be home in time to do homework but, being the winter term, it was often after dark before we were. We'd turn up next day with a low level of work, if any, since you can't hold a book when riding a bike. Daphne could carry this off with a laugh but all I could do was compose excuses to take the place of work. You could say we invented the winter.

Though it was I who was mad on Miss Cumberland, it was Daphne who fascinated her, with or without homework. I was grown with a family before it got through to me that it had been Daphne whom Miss Cumberland loved. Decades later Miss Cumberland asked after her, her face lighting up at the thought. As for whom Daphne loved at that time it was Dorothy Roberts. Many years later when I ran into her, Dorothy was wistful for news of her. Well, look at me right now supposed to be writing a span of my life; it's looking more like Daphne's to me.

In our different ways we got along. On occasion we had a bit of fun together. The time we were stuck in Masterton and couldn't get home, a storm, a flood or something, or our bikes broke down, and we spent the night at a boarding house in a back bedroom upstairs. Daphne, not prepared to hang round and worry and aware of my crush on Miss Cumberland, took the stage between the two beds and played Miss Cumberland sharing the room with me. I nearly died. She was no longer Daphne but Miss Cumberland in the flesh, voice, words, correctness, the lot. How could I share a night with Miss Cumberland in the same bedroom? For a while Daphne would be herself again until I was off guard and said something disparaging about the lady downstairs in the dining room but it was Miss Cumberland who answered: "So you criticise too, Sylvia?" Panic. Settling down to sleep with the light out I felt Miss Cumberland slipping into my bed. God! "Sylvia," from Miss Cumberland, "what on earth are you doing here at this time of night?"

Shrieks . . . and now hammering on the wall from the room next door so that when we were sneaking out next morning we were told firmly by that very lady downstairs not to come back to this place again on account of what she called Skylarking at night. "I can tell," the lady told Daphne, "that it wasn't *your* voice," and glowered at me.

"I'm sorry," I said. "I couldn't help it."

But Daphne was already out on the street thinking of something else. "Daphne, you shouldn't have done that last night."

"We can't *all* be perfect." To her, performance was all, the consequence nil. And that's how you lose a jolly good cheap little hide-out when you're stuck on the road. "All over a bit of fun," she said.

However, we continued to grieve for the capital city, the dramatic street corners, the sparkling of the coloured lights in the rain, the crashing of passing tramcars and the too dear loves we'd forfeited, yet we were not the kind to do nothing about it. Our responses took differing forms. I carved my name on the historied old desk as all were expected to. So ancient were these desks you could hardly find room for a name. Names on desks were the diary of a school, an inadvertent Who's Who. But along with mine I'd found room to add with a flourish my late lamented glory, Wellington Girls College, my credentials for all to see. And when nostalgia took over I'd simply sit there and stare at it, the caption to the picture of the joy I'd known.

But Daphne went about it in a far better way, her style more effective. She kept in touch with Gracie, each writing pages and pages of secrets to the other which she let me see if I chose, so that when this one winter term was over and Gracie had caught up with her bills she made another of her sensational swoops home in August, picked up Daphne like booty all over again and carried her off back to Wellington. All that was left of her at our place of disgrace was her cover design on the school magazine, she called it *Leisure Magazine*, and her name carved not on a desk but on people's everlasting desire for fun in light-hearted images of ridiculousness-es.

I inherited the bike.

As it happens, that Masterton District High was a jolly decent little school, relaxed, with no pretensions to live up to. District highs can't miss. They have cohesion since all children go there from five to seventeen. It makes for a muscular infrastructure. People don't get their growing rhythms segmented all the time. A child can follow his whole education in the stability of one school which with me, already at my thirteenth, was anything but the case. I found it astonishingly unreal. Not even the grounds were demarcated: you could wander from the high school to the primary playground and get to know smaller children. I followed the progress of one little girl who'd been traumatically ill and watched her grow stronger daily. To see her white gaunt face become full, brown and freckled in time was to learn something not in books. From the continuity and integration of such a school one's character maybe could evolve in a flowing pattern rather than zig-zag in jerks. As the twentieth-century New Zealand lurched to its feet after the terrible World War I many a mind larger than size was processed in these schools.

As well as minds lesser than size, my own for instance. There I encountered in Miss Cumberland the second very good teacher in twelve years, in seven years I mean; the first was Mr. Burns in Hastings, making two, which is a pretty good score when you come to reflect what can stand up on two legs in front of a class and call itself a teacher. Two good teachers I found plenty.

Miss Cumberland was an interesting teacher because she was an interesting woman in her own right. She was interesting because she was interested and actually liked her work and it showed. That sparked off vivacity. Yet she was a sedate lady, literate and civilised with an M.A. in languages. I wish I could use her real name as she was too important and influential in too many lives for me to pay short change to, but her people may not like it and besides it would limit me to white-washing her whereas none of us is perfect.

Along with a trim mind was a trim figure, I think, beneath the academic gown. A no-nonsense, I-know-where-I'm-going walk as her gown swung with it. I remember the firm clicking of her heels along scholastic corridors so that you knew when she was coming. As for her face, well . . . faces with distinctive features I could not resist drawing, but hers was not among them; though she actually had an elegantly shaped mouth she was the last to know it. In fact there was one slightly blemished tooth mid-centre, although the rest were orderly enough. That a teacher of manifest correctitude should have to admit to one obvious physical flaw made me ponder on what that proved. Couldn't she have it enamelled white or something . . . but no, there it was, and she couldn't have cared less, apparently. All told, free of extremes, she was sure to keep out of trouble. Bliss.

To a fatuous schoolgirl she was just the thing. Short of Miss Pope to adore with the golden-cloud hair I went down to Miss Cumberland instead. I hadn't truly known the real Miss Pope who'd been something of a creation of my imagination, but Miss Cumberland opted to remain herself and threw off any schoolgirl's haze. She neither ridiculed nor exploited me but saw to it that I knew her exactly as she was, which was healthy and less heady for a girl.

Being a relatively small school there was only one third form with all comers in it. Undeliberately and from an inclination absorbed in the kitchen at home I gravitated towards the few top people who happened to be three smart girls. Among us were some equally smart boys whom Miss Cumberland obviously enjoyed but it was bad to mix with boys. Others would at once start saying things about you. So far my own romantic requirements were supplied by a novel called *The Sheik* which the big ones had left behind. This sheik was to be found under the mattress in a pretty tattered state with the result that no mortal boy could measure up to the image of this immortal desert horseman. Fantasy had not produced any ideal boy but was slanted more to men. So I staked my allegiance to three smart girls: Jessica, Lila, Penelope.

Not that I ever liked that school or did any work there. My drop in status had discredited me to myself and had cut me down to size. A touchy twelve, I didn't relax there as others did. I found stability uncomfortable. I didn't like knowing what was going to come next. To me the place remained no more than an apologia for the Wellington Girls College, a transit camp only from the mourned former joy to a certain future one.

WAIRARAPA HIGH    During this time a large new high school was being built in Masterton to serve the whole Wairarapa province, and Jessica, a tall dark box of brains, took me along to watch it starting. "We ought to sit on the foundation stones."

"What for?" I say.

"So we can tell our grandchildren we did, or even our great-grandchildren." She settles her long bones on the concrete blocks, one straight slender leg crossed accurately over the other, her hands outstretched beside her so that her gold watch picks up the afternoon sun and the after-school hour. Alertly her brown eyes survey the site but I touch the texture of the blocks. This grand new place can never be Wellington but only my fourteenth school. On the other hand the surface of the foundation is inviting. "We ought to carve our names on these."

"What for?" she says.

"So we can prove we did."

In time it became a handsome brick building, two-storeyed, towered in the grand old manner that fosters school traditions, and ivy was started on its way. It was opened in the new year, 1922, under Doctor Roydon M.Sc. with a hand-picked all-male staff but for Miss Winnifred Cumberland M.A. who shared her delight at her appointment with us.

Dr. Roydon turned out to be a short man, heavy of body and features, with a fateful swaying to his walk which swung his gown from side to side as he trod the long corridors. He held his head inclined to the right and his books inclined to the left but if you wanted a decent look at him you'd take it from behind. Who had the temerity to stare from the front?

On the other hand there were occasions when you couldn't avoid this, as in morning assembly when you'd find his face a dramatic piece of work and a gift for one with a pencil. How simple to draw the thick grey hair growing low on the forehead, the black brows overhanging like bush scrub on a bank and the surprisingly beautiful eyes; eyes as blue as cobalt way underneath those brows. As for the double chins, well they'd be easy enough. In fact and in sum the Doctor's face was heavily handsome, but I decided to play safe. The man-of-destiny look suggested risks. Penelope eggs me on with an elbow nudge, "Go on, Sylvie, draw him."

"Not me, Pen. I've too much to lose."

Jessica's chin is cupped in her palm as she examines him like an algebraic equation. "Well yes, he's a bit overpowering."

"Overpowering," echoes Lila.

"Anything but anonymous," I whisper. So I don't draw him, not me.

At the beginning the roll was in hand and the streams were A, B and C. Jessica-and-Lila, Penelope and I, in the fourth form by now, all made 4A in the room at the end of the nearest wing. There was another girl or two, vague in outline, and half the class was boys. Girls sat on one side and boys on the other in case we got talking to one another.

We four girls were much the same age, thirteen or so, ostensibly on the same mark. Jessica Wall was tall, slender, dark and brown-eyed and lanky, I suppose, leggy for certain. I remember her angular joints, her elbows, shoulders and knees with no dimpled padding on them like Penelope's. Her eyes swerved reflectively beneath the lids and her dark hair would have curled had she let it. We knew she was scholarship material straight. Given all things equal I could not have levelled with Jessica though I saw it to be worth a try. After all, she wished she could draw like me, I think, and, though she took piano lessons and I didn't, that she could play like me. Not that she said so. But she was better rated in essay since, knowing what was required to be said, she said it economically with no surplus flesh on her prose whereas my work was wayward and soggy. Moreover paint and keys did not total in end-of-week tests but only homework and brains.

Lila was Jessica's alter ego, shorter, softer, grey-eyed, low-voiced and with marvellously perfect teeth; so pleasant you didn't notice her freckles. Jessica-and-Lila were indivisible and chose desks together back in the room a bit; Jessica alert and erect with Lila soft-shouldered beside her, the two of them forbiddingly self-sufficient. Where I stood with Lila I never knew as I could not identify her but you knew where you were with Jessica.

The third girl was Penelope Donn who could have doubled for Cupid, and did, except that her lips were too thin for kissing class and her nose not love material, but the rest of her face was right: soft brown appealing eyes, flawless white skin and full baby cheeks. She had a whole lot of thick honey-coloured hair which got the exact effect along with a body to match. The curve of her calves came from her ballet. Her collars surpassed white collars anywhere and she was the best-brought-up girl in the world. She put things away neatly in her desk as well as in her head and was seldom stuck for what to say. Strategic is the word that comes to mind. When I'd first met her at the district high she had not already paired with someone else. Preferring the boys to the girls she'd overlooked this.

The fourth girl was me. I don't know how I made 4A and was something of a printer's error. Never mind what I looked like, let's skip it, but I did wish I had brown eyes and night-black hair as in *The Arabian Nights*; in mind I saw it. Like Penelope I'd not paired up either but she saw me to be good for a laugh. "She's a funny kid," she said. Though we were not meant for each other we were thrown together in class so that with less reciprocal allegiance than common intent we chose two desks at the very front, first in from the door in order to be as close as possible to the action, to miss nothing at all and to be sure we ourselves were thoroughly seen.

There was another girl in 4A sitting silently and solo at the back

with Pariah written all over her, by us no doubt. As we read it her
only function was to highlight our own marvellousness. To be seen
walking with her or even talking to her was a mistake we didn't make
in spite of her confounding irregularity of scoring good marks, out of
character with her physical defect, and if I have evaded a description
of my own character here you can see it for yourself in this. The rest
were boys, the funniest who ever wrecked a lesson with laughter.

Maybe I could have paced Penelope and Lila given all things equal,
but whereas their uncluttered minds could think a thing through my
own mechanism was so overcharged with imagery that figment blurred
fact. To find a fact that looked like a fact in what I called my mind
was like rummaging through a jumble stall in some exotic Eastern
bazaar, complete with Arab steeds at hand with brass bells on their
bridles, extravagantly caparisoned.

All things equal? Whereas the rest of them cruised on their bikes
along paved streets or walked round the corner to school, played
tennis in the afternoon or started on their homework it would be
dusk when I got home against a headwind or after dark in the winter,
staggering in the door sweating, disheartened to find something like
Ashton crying to Puppa in his bed behind the door because when
he'd hurried to marry his girl on the Saturday she'd married the other
man on the Friday and had disappeared without trace. Or, on one occasion with Muriel at home, I found her on the back step to meet me
reading aloud my first secret manuscript which I had hidden last night.

All I could rely on was my flashy home-grown wares which were
only too readily available. As it was with Daphne, performance was
all, the answer to all things great and small. It was family status. From
birth we'd been reared to it, the lot of us, so that birth itself was seen
as drama, as death must be in time. And who'd had a better model
than I, the one in the lee of Daphne. But it didn't win marks and I
began slipping behind.

In summer we four did a great deal of swimming at the town baths
and often the other three played tennis at school, Penelope with the
boys. You'd be amazed at how well Cupid plays tennis. In winter,
coached by Miss Cumberland, we played tough basketball which made
me later home still. Penelope made the A team but I could only make
the B, dammit, no matter how arduously I practised. I wasn't quick
enough and nothing could make me that. My canvas basketball shoes
fell off the carrier of my bike one day and I didn't see them again. A
terrible row blew up at home and Muriel emptied her purse to buy

me some more which at once fell off the carrier again, brand-new, same day, so that she put an advertisement in the paper: "Lost: one pair of white canvas shoes. Return to Sylvia Lost-Warner." A story still endures from those times that when Sylvie brought home the mail from the corner they used to send one of the younger children to walk behind her to pick up the letters as she dropped them, so that they'd get their full quota.

By great good fortune our form teacher was Miss Cumberland who loved concerts and music and drama. On account of my freak memory I was useful at the piano and successful with drawings in the class magazine, not sketches and cartoons as Miss Cumberland called them. She and the others loved me drawing them and I took fine care not to ridicule them, and finer care still not to offend Dr. Roydon though I must say he was a cartoonist's dream come true; maybe I did. I remember a drawing I made of him from the back view, swaying along the corridor with a strap swinging in one hand. He may not have liked that. And a poem or two but the boys could beat me there and the girls wrote the articles. But in this area at least my wares marketed and it's a good thing I had *something* to offer.

We were extended to the limit and very happy. There was no doubt in the minds of the four of us that we were excessively excellent, that the new school had been built specifically for us and that if there were anything we didn't know it was obviously not worth knowing. You should have seen us outside our classroom door at morning interval in the crowded corridor talking at top pitch with all stops out and the loud pedal on.

I was not unaware of other people in high school but they had to be stars or I didn't see them; people of charm, breeding and brains. I remember Portia in a form ahead telling me even as far back as that, "I'm going to be an author," to which I replied, "I'm going to be an artist." Not that we friended up, she was already indivisibly united with her Latin suffix Gwen, but we've kept an eye out for each other since. Also included in those out-loud sessions in the corridor were the Mannering girls, a form behind me, Ursula and Madge, whose people had produced a Minister of the Crown, and the new master's sensational step-daughter Jancy, the most beautiful girl in town. I could draw Jancy now with my eyes tight shut.

The nearest I got to actually loving anybody was Ursula Mannering; you often get a pleasant face equalling a pleasant nature, but the real thing whether love or hate, the inspiration, came from a girl I rarely encountered, again from the third form, Veronica Dundonald; a

rather solitary girl, a soprano, who sent word would I play her accompaniment. In the privacy of the schoolroom at home at the weekend I painted, practised and wrote for her my ultimate best. She was
rich, cultivated and authentically exclusive but I avoided her in the
crowded corridors, too shy of the reality to stand it. Exposure to the
source of one's inspiration is a shattering business. Automatically she
took her place in the succession of my ideal girls.

What taxed me was the way people paired off. Once you had chosen
your mate like Jessica-and-Lila, Portia-and-Gwen, the twosome was
unassailable. No third could push in. At best you could be a plus, not
a part. You picked each other at the start and that was it. I'd never
picked a mate at the start of any of my fourteen schools but it concerned me now that people had paired at the district high school before
I'd ever got there, which had something to do with the continuity in
a school like that where a newcomer remained a plus, excepting
Penelope, who also had not paired, yet was never on her own, having
a wonderful gift of integrating with a group. Circumstance alone had
put us together although I liked her very much . . . popular, pretty,
brainy and sporty, though I was not at ease with her. For her part,
she'd visibly weighed the pros and cons in 4A, saw no alternative and
opted to make the best of it. For these first two terms in 4A I was not
alone and I too was popular in a hit-and-miss way. I had no enemies
that I was aware of. I was not a marked man.

Indeed a glamour lit up my living. I had been accustomed to this
in the world of fantasy but now it spilled over into reality like lights
flashing from one mirror to another. A sense of miracle was my companion assuring me I could do anything I set myself to so that, astride
two worlds, one foot in fantasy and the other in reality, I behaved a
bit larger than life. Dazzled and less than responsible. Yet the context
suited one like me and it was my happiest time in any school.

Out of school was another thing. I could not join in their social life
not being in the position to exchange hospitality and I didn't have a
white dress and racquet and all that. However my vanishing after
school without trace was not something they accepted as they couldn't
take readings of my background; in place of a visible respectable home
in an identifiable street was a vacuum of impenetrable mystery, which
I suppose I romanticised and, if I didn't, I should have: you can't
waste good stuff like that.

They tackled this theorem in their own way by organising picnics
halfway home beneath Wardells Bridge where we swam and ran and

climbed the willows and talked about teachers and boys. But all it engendered was an unrest in me. Wardells Bridge was too close to home and their company too close to the bone.

Then they tried inviting me to their homes for weekends but instead of enjoying the elegance and affluence, a language my blood nevertheless understood, these visits were unsettling. The domestic proximity was not for me, besides, since I could not ask them back to my place, I felt I was walking on quicksand and I sensed a trembling at base.

This may well have been the time when the walls of personality began eroding, not only from the traffic between reality and dream but from the wear and tear of feeling. Joy can corrode as much as sorrow; from either you get the battering within as well as the battering without so that the walls which enclose you become thinner as you live along, whereas you need strong walls round your personality to prevent the intrusion of the personalities of others. Feeling is so contagious it can penetrate anything. What was once your own distinct personality becomes a fermenting hotch-potch of everyone else's and you find yourself thinking from so many facets that you don't know what you think yourself.

In my journey through life so far this time spent in 4A with the first and the best was like the highest point on the road where stood an inn with lighted windows. Inside it was crowded where people drank hot fresh tea. To a wayfarer like me the portal was open and I was welcome by right, if not for what I looked like then for the wares I had. In this crisp air I was holding my own within the company, on the inside looking out. The world had stopped taking it out of me and was giving with both hands.

So far none knew of my Te Whiti background of smouldering explosive secrets but there was always the chance they would. At thirteen in that society I believed the dimensions of a person were defined by place and circumstance. I was decades off realising that accident of dwelling place does not necessarily mean parochialism of the soul.

In tracing the course of my schooling in Masterton I am somewhat circumscribed because it took place less in the classrooms than on the roads getting there and back. My real schoolrooms were the countryscapes, my desk the saddle of a bike or a horse and my teachers the wilful weathers. It astounds me how little I remember of what went on in the actual classrooms; I could contain in a few chapters what I learnt in all those schools, whereas about what happened outside of them I could go on ad infinitum without repeating myself.

I had an idea I was missing out. I wanted to do my work. I liked schoolwork but you couldn't hold a book on a bike. Maybe I could on a horse. The high school did have a horse-paddock handy so, as Ashton had once said he'd see to my education if I stayed in Masterton, I asked him for a horse. He and Mumma did succeed in buying me something on four legs but it was hardly an Arab steed. To be fair it had traces of pedigree, cream in colour with white mane and tail and slender flowing bones except that you could see each one. Her head was not such a bad piece of drawing but her "dark and fiery eye" had been quenched somewhat and she "snuffed not the breezy wind." True, her nostrils must have quivered one time but her lower lip by now drooped like a little basket you could carry your homework in, or your lunch.

In the poem you'd get lines like, "Thy proudly arched and glossy neck," but although Creamy's neck was long and shapely it did not arch like poetry. Her head hung down in a disillusioned way till her pendulant lower lip all but scooped up dust. You got the feeling that her dreams had not come true, or as though they had, which is worse. As though some thumping stallion had indeed ravaged the best of her but had got off scot free.

Her movement could have been worse when she moved at all but she seemed so short of energy that you'd think she had a temperature or something and although they bought me a saddle it was only one of those pads with a girth-strap used on fat ponies which did little to nullify her backbone. I could write

Creamy

a strong feature for the editorial page of a newspaper on Backbones I Have Known.

"Fret not to roam the desert now with all thy wingéd speed . . ." Creamy had no speed, much less wingéd. All told, no sheik would have thrown down his gold for this steed.

However, I was not ashamed to be seen on her especially in the spring when the greener grass made her a little frisky when she'd lift her head at least to the level of her shoulders and she was better than the bike. What two wheels could pick their way down a bouldered track under Wardells Bridge to graze among the buttercups? No bike had the amble of a lazy horse like the rhythm of stirring the porridge. Headwinds meant nothing. I could learn my French declensions on Creamy and even tried writing out geometry theorems until the day when Mr. Bee held up this mangy bit of paper to the class like an Exhibit A and said in his lofty upper-class English voice, "Solvia Oshton-Wonner. Do I take this to be your hommwok?" After which I put the time into excuses instead, which called for no writing on horseback, so that when one of the boys had missed his homework too Mr. Bee suggested he ask Solvia to supply his excuse.

The girls liked Creamy though. They saw her to be romance itself and fell over each other to catch her after school to ride her as far as the gate; an unforeseen fringe benefit. Also, ambling on the grass at the side of the road continued to be a good time to learn aloud French and Latin grammar and English figures of speech, to memorise passages of Shakespeare set by Miss Cumberland, as well as passages not set by Miss Cumberland, the pages she skipped in class about Othello throwing his leg over Iago's thigh in bed when dreaming of Desdemona. Had Creamy not known the way home herself we could have ended up anywhere; none of which befell the others when walking on peopled pavements.

One day I met a man on a horse and we got talking he and I. His horse was enviably fat and frisky while mine was shamelessly thin. Why, he said, didn't I leave her home to graze for a few months and ride some of the condition off his fat thing. He said I should start next Thursday and come to school on the service car and meet him after school at the post office at four o'clock. I would ride his horse home and he'd return on the service car.

On Thursday I cut basketball and ran off and on all the way down Renall Street and was at the post office at four. The town clock said so. All I could see in mind was this shiny fat horse to ride to school for months but he wasn't there so I waited. At five I was still waiting on the kerb gazing down the road that came from Te Whiti and feeling a little hungry. It would make a better story to say it was also sleeting and cold but in fact it was a lovely pre-spring afternoon as soft as a note of music.

At six I was waiting. I had no money for food of course and would not have left my vigil if I had. What I remember most about that afternoon is how lovely it was as an afternoon in its own right. Even though it was the main street with traffic and people it was movingly tender, momentous and still as though holding its breath, a feeling unrelated to any fat horse. The cars had a dreamy gliding, the people walked by with less haste it seemed and no one I knew passed by.

The hours turned over into evening, it was seven by the clock and the street lights were on, glamorously unreal to a country girl. The service car had departed long ago and no man brought me a horse. By now a night chill was fingering through my winter uniform though not a breath of air lifted my hair. On the kerb I waited watching. I did not allow it to occur to me that the man may not come. Some dreams are too strong to reject.

"Sylvia," astonished, "what on earth are you doing here at this time of night?" Miss Cumberland with a coat on and carrying a parcel.

A sudden blurt of tears. She stands over me on the kerb. Several good moments of the evening are wasted before I can say a thing. At last I manage to tell my tale upon which she takes me home to her place, the Holy of Holies. This was worse than the boarding house night and what would Daphne say.

The streets give way to a winding lane, unpaved and grassy at the side, named Hope Street. A small cottage shows up, two-storeyed, old-fashioned and narrow, a picket fence set close to the road and the whole painted white. Her mother is inside who sits and smiles with serene compassionate eyes while Miss Cumberland lays a blinding white cloth and gives me a meal which I try not to choke on, then a virgin white bedroom which I try not to die in. Her personality is too close, her composure lethal and my soul exposed to withering point. "Shy" is not the word. Not one single white minute do I sleep all night and by morning I'm ill, unspecifically . . . Dr. Roydon takes me home from school with two of the girls . . .

I never saw the man on the horse again.

About this time Mumma began to show characteristic signs of restlessness, lifting her nose to the breeze scenting fields afar, and Puppa too for all I know. It was not inspector trouble this time and not chairman trouble either. Mr. Trate remained nobly patient though we "little ones" must have tried him to the limit. We deserved to fear him but we didn't.

She must have done quite well at her teaching in Te Whiti because she applied in the open market for and was appointed to another sole charge school with a far better house and glebe, Rangitumau. The district was still within reach of Masterton, it had to be on account of my high school. For her it was a relatively short move as she favoured changing provinces. All we left in Te Whiti were our names carved on desks, banks and cliffs.

It was spring. We'd not seen Mumma so happy about a residence before. For a start it *was* a house, as distinct from a whare, cottage or dungeon; it was modern, equipped with facilities and for the first time we had a bathroom. It was fairly new, freshly painted, near the road with a lawn in front and a stone's throw from the school. No I'd not seen her so uplifted and inspired over her home before. After making the tea for her and Puppa she laid her plans. She bought a few dozen Lawsoniana trees and planted them herself round the fence for a hedge as nice people did and put in a vegetable garden at the side, the whole response unheard of. True, the new chairman and school committee failed to bring us a load of wood, help with our meat or lend us a cow but the service car went right past our place, stopped at the gate with the mail and bread and delivered the big ones when they came. Luxury indeed.

We found ourselves in a house we were not ashamed to say we lived in. When Daphne came home for the holidays she took one dive into that front garden, making paths, planting flowers and ferns and clipping the lawn till it looked, as Ashton said, "like a bloomin' park." Gracie was so relieved that she studied the idea of getting engaged since she could bring a young man home here, I forget which. If for no other reason than to pacify Mumma who would flatly say, "Why don't you get m*a-a-rri*ed." And Puppa too who hinted, "I'm lonely for my grandchildren." It was something the big ones had no answer to, other than do something about it. From her own salary Gracie bought cane mats for the living room floor and two brand-new cane chairs; you wouldn't believe it, we were like other people at last, that elusive desired state. As things were now I could have asked the girls at school to Rangitumau had it not been already a flick of fate too late. Since they'd uncovered my background at Te Whiti when Dr. Roydon drove me home ill I'd been de-registered, de-frocked and dropped. Not that

I would have asked them inside to meet everybody since there'd be no telling what different ones would be doing, or what they'd say in such crisis, but they could have seen it from the top of the road in the distance and said, "So *that's* where she lives. Passable."

Too late. Too bad. Schools as such were overrated as places of important learning. Give me a tree-fern any day to one of your Latin prefixes. In the meantime Rangitumau was a glorious classroom, one of Nature's own; tucked in the foothills of the ranges within sight of the forest fires at night and within smell of the smoke it was a painting of a place like Te Pohue and Umataroa; hills of bush, risky ravines and mysterious lanes all over again leading through the valleys to nowhere and many a fine bank to carve drawings on and sign your name to them. Me and Norma and Marmie and 'Vadne, and in that order, off we'd go into the morning to claim Rangitumau and sign the whole place. Bread we'd carry in a paper bag and we'd drink from a tingling stream. On the lowland was a wistful river with willows gazing at themselves in the water where we'd swim and play an hour away in blank forgetfulness. Talk, sing, laugh and dream like heaven had fallen down.

Singing one evening up some soft glade to an innumerable audience of trees it did not get through to me that this kind of celebration would not qualify a girl for exams or for confrontation with life. By whatever measure ye measured, Rangitumau was a glorious place except for one flaw: my seven miles to school were now eleven.

Heaven had not fallen down at school. We started carving our names into the warm new shining varnish on our desks. I and Penelope and one or two others, I don't know about the boys. How were we to know that Dr. Roydon was on the warpath on the subject of defacing school property? Without announcement he made a tour beginning at the first room of the first wing, which happened to be 4A, and looked at the first desk, which was mine. Penelope's book slides strategically over her name, innocently unnoticeably, but I didn't have time. He opens up his guns in a royal rage about the widespread abuse of new desks in the school and shoots at me specifically, "You go home. Take your books and don't return."

Penelope sharpened her pencil.

I'm expelled. In which case so will Penelope be and some of the others, but no. By now all carved names would be covered with books and Dr. Roydon didn't look further. Besides Penelope's father is on the board of governors whereas who am I? Just a scrap of litter swept up from the roads which he has seen for himself last term when he drove me home. Moreover all the best people need scapegoats; how could you run a good school without them, or without favorites for that matter? "Go," the angry voice and the next thing you hear his steps departing. Mollified.

So I pack up my books in front of them all, fumbling, dropping some, hot red all over and leave the shocked room, and go out and catch my horse and ride home the eleven miles to Rangitumau, recapitulating on the way how it all came from the man not bringing the horse that day. I don't sing one song on the road home and when I've let the horse loose in the paddock I tell Mumma I'm expelled.

After school she does the washing for nothing instead of leaving it till Saturday as usual. I understood that and felt it, having seen it before. As for the other key factor in my schooling, Creamy . . . nice people would say, "Good for Creamy; at least she will have a rest." But take it from me, I had no feeling for that horse, no rapport with her. I felt no obligation to that horse. She was a lazy devil with no ambition. She was a horse who'd failed. She was a bag of bones and a cave of despair because she had not achieved what she'd wanted, being far too slow to make her point. All her stud shaping and slender boning had got her exactly nowhere. She didn't even have any progeny to fight for, to do the washing after school because of. She didn't cry, she didn't laugh, she had no temperament at all. All she had was a lower lip like a swagger's bag to carry her tucker in and how can you respect a fool like that.

After a few days at home I nevertheless saddle the skinny wretch o' the road, ride her back to school, go to Dr. Roydon's intimidating office near the entrance where I've never trod before and knock at the forbidding door. "Come in," I hear.

He is at his desk writing and only his eyes lift. Blue.

"I'm sorry I wrote on the desk, Sir."

He's not angry now. "Don't do it again."

"No Sir."

"You can stay. Go to your room." That's all he says.

In class Penelope and I still sit side by side but the communication between us has vaporised. She had already added herself comfortably to the Jessica-and-Lila axis at school and, out of school, to the Mannering girls' clique. I must say that Penelope had a wonderful gift of accommodating herself to people. That new-moon smile was irresistible and her pretty Cupid cheeks, and no one could sharpen a pencil like Penelope.

When homework time came and I had none I was anything but short of an excuse for Mr. Bee but I didn't make it. Neither did he mention it.

No hope now of keeping up with the others, not at this distance. I really couldn't see what I was going to school for. Gravity, I supposed, of the big body for the particle. Staying home was only fit for a dog.

Sometimes I'd revert to the bike for a change from the horse and on the road I came to know two girls, sisters called Marie and Pru. We saw fit to ride together along that long stretch out of Lansdowne where the racing stables used to be, for collective protection against the obscenities of the jockeys exercising the horses on the road. Not that it worked. Mumma had to complain to the police before that stopped.

Marie and Pru biked eleven or so miles also down another road from the turn-off. They had no mother to call on the police to protect them and their father made them milk the herd of cows in the dark early morning before they set out for school and again when they got home at night, in the dark. It was not their father who made them attend high school, it was they themselves determined to get their education. They too were light on homework and were in a C form I think, though not from lack of brains. You'd see them together in the corridor hesitating as the crowds marched by, late and wet one morning, sweaty and dusty the next, their uniforms weather-beaten. Even I wouldn't be seen conversing with them, not at school, though I had nothing to lose, having lost all. They smiled mostly in a surprising way.

I did no more than brush with them on the road occasionally for, in the community of pariahs, they were lesser than I; they hadn't offended in any way you could pin down whereas I'd been expelled for defacing school property. Even the school's scarlet woman, Dorabella, had not been expelled when caught in the park smoking with the boys, there was only an inquiry and she got away with it. But I had the status of a marked man. Later in life Marie and Pru reappeared as two rather lovely women; Marie became a nursing sister overseas in the war and after that worked for several years in China. Pru smiled her way into a convent and was very happy there. As I bypassed them in the corridors Fate gave me no warning that the day would come when Marie would nurse me through an illness efficiently and generously when there was no one else there to save me.

The hours I spent alone on that road. No, put it this way: the hours I spent on that road. It didn't hurt being alone. "Alone" does not equate with "lonely." You can be quite radiant when alone if your thoughts are, it's only when you're excluded from the company you want to be part of that you know what "lonely" means, being left out. I hadn't known what "lonely" meant till now and it took a big crowded school to teach me . . . funny thing. In my real school, the road, I wasn't lonely, just physically alone. As well as being a hard worker I was also a hard dreamer and you're not lonely when your mind is peopled.

The road was rich in unprofitable ways, in the blood of ideas. My solitary mind was a boundless scape full of the things I wanted. Sometimes they took the form of poems composed when wheeling my bike up hills inside the curtains of rain, and of pictures which shouted for paint, and predatory sentimental melodies, all to be realised per colour and keyboard in Mumma's schoolroom at the weekend, the lot for Veronica Dundonald; wallowing to my soul's content or, since you had to drop to earth in the end, to my soul's discontent, for when hunger and darkness drove me home I'd find it was my turn to do the dishes. "I haven't used any," I'd say.

"You've got to take your turn, Sylvie, and you haven't made your bed."

"And," from Mumma, "she hasn't washed her face or combed her hair or changed her clothes, the heathen." But there was an inflexion of wonder in her voice.

Those profligate times at least exercised the imagery which tends to wither in more fortunate circumstances. You are as alive as your mind is, and your mind as alive as the imagery is. So you couldn't really say it was lonely on the road but you could say it was lonely at school where I'd slid out from the company of the chosen to the sisterhood of the untouchables.

Miss Cumberland, however, was as light-hearted as ever; she loved language, music, drama and action and sports. We felt her to be an accomplice. She and 4A worked out a concert for the Town Hall to be made by our form alone with a few stars from the third and fifth including Veronica to sing. The programme turned out to consist largely of costumed national song-and-dance items, Dutch, Spanish and one Arabian. At practice she played the accompaniments herself. I wasn't included in anything though I was probably the most musically competent on the school roll. They said I lived too far to stay after school for practices but it was they who said it. I would have settled for getting home at midnight had they wanted me. Besides they often rehearsed during afternoon school when, confined to my desk in the near-empty room, chilblains itching, I'd hear the singing from a distant wing. An accurate comment on me. But I got hold of the music of the songs regardless and learnt the lot by heart. Participation by proxy.

In time I heard that the piano would be onstage and that Miss Cumberland was not prepared to go onstage so that as the night drew near so did the crisis draw near of who was going to play onstage. Everything else was ready, material bought, costumes cut out, fitted, sewn and finished in all these vivid colours, their desks and their bags overflowed with them. Suddenly at the eleventh hour I found myself sought again and they chose the one I loved as spokesman, Ursula Mannering. Would I play the accompaniments? she smiled.

"All right then."

Ursula beamed her soft eyes on me. "You'll have to wear costumes, Sylvie. I'll make them."

"I haven't got the material."

"There's enough pieces left over."

I blush.

"You're wanted at practice this afternoon, backstage at the Town Hall. You need to learn the sequences."

"All right then."

When I sat at the keyboard and they stood up the music in front of me the first thing I did was take it down. It's a disgrace to be chained to the music. Backstage at the theatre on the night they made up my face as though I were one of them so that Veronica who was there had no clue that I was anything other. I was terribly happy that night and the concert was a stunning success.

So was the end-of-year class magazine with a poem of mine in it and some drawings. Their poems and their articles, however, were far better than mine so I offered no further writing. But none could do the drawings and illustrations, though Tom Cullen did the cover. On the whole their work was school-taught and they had no home-grown wares. They were plants in a cultivated garden in a park, not roadside weeds. Briefly I was popular again.

I even took up my excuses again when I had no homework. "The paper blew out of my hand, Sir, when I was fording the river, and floated away downstream." In the corridor at break I was part of the out-loud conferences again and took off Mr. Bee's lofty upper-crust voice when he'd rebuked me for no math homework: "Solvia Oshton-Wonner, you're the bost at excuses in the closs."

They oll loffed.

"I'd rather be the bost at math," I added. "The bost ot moth."

But when did popularity ever endure, especially the flashy kind? Flashing doesn't pay as a *modus vivendi*. I've said of Rangitumau that it seemed heaven had fallen down, but little was celestial at school. In the end-of-year examinations I failed to make the required average, which did not cover music and drawing. In the context of that time their reasons were good enough. My only distinction was the grandeur of my third downfall, the first two being the uncovering of my background and the expulsion from school. When the year turned over into the next and the fourth forms graduated into the fifths and 4A glided up to 5A, the matriculation class . . . I was not among them. Years later Miss Cumberland told Miss Pope of Wellington who was a friend of hers behind the scenes, who told Gracie who was a friend of Miss Pope's behind the scenes who finally told me . . . by such devious routes can important knowledge travel . . . "Dr. Roydon did not understand Sylvia." And there we have the meaning of the word "understatement."

The matriculation class where fourth-years sat matric was 5A. Any promising third-years were lifted in there to let them have a go at it too. Jessica-and-Lila, Penelope and Tom Cullen and most of the same boys went up but I was in 5B where you didn't sit matric. We would have to put in an extra year. At this stage of my journey through the teens I'd slithered off the highway down a bank and hit my head on something.

On the road home I worked it out. I'd been far too long in this place. This was my third year in Masterton and I hadn't seen three years in one place in my life. I was fifteen now and you don't want to stay too long in one place when you're fifteen because people get to know your faults and that's a bad risk. You want to break clear just before they find you out when they still think you're all right. No one can *stay* being all right all the time . . . it's ridiculous.

The thing to do was to get through this school as fast as possible and get out of the place again and the way to achieve this was not to waste two good years over matric when one would do—who were they to suppose I were two-year material, second-class?—but to pass *everything* as high as possible: at the end of this first term in the fifth B to come top in every single subject required to the tune of a hundred percent all round, no exceptions, whatever it cost a girl and a horse,

in which case Dr. Roydon would have to promote me to 5A where I'd
sit matric with the others. He couldn't stop me. Even if he didn't promote me I could still sit the outside exam independently if I could
raise the two guinea entrance fee. Of course I wouldn't get the same
grooming for matric in 5B, no former exam papers and such, no selective coaching, but I'd find a way, you watch.

Swept high a-sky with this idea. I'd outstrip them in everything else
while I was at it, outside class too, required or not; basketball, swimming, running, tennis, music, art, singing, riding, eating and sleeping
and I'd beat them all to dust. 5B? Not for me. One term only. A very
fine dream. Even my horse cocked an ear to it; after all she too had
had enough of the road. True, I'd fallen down a bank but I'd climb
up again to the highway. I'd climbed banks before. We'd climbed a
cliff once. Nor would I carve my name on this particular bank to
admit I had fallen this way.

I rode Creamy more often than the bike now on account of the hilly
terrain in the foothills and because you could hold a book on a horse.
I did much work on horseback. I cut the hours of sodden dreaming
and soggy composition to use them in solid study. Corner after corner,
hill upon hill, mile by mile on the drowsy Creamy while the company
in town was playing tennis or trying out the boys I learnt my Latin
and French declensions of regular and irregular verbs, speaking aloud
the definitions of figures of speech: onomatopoeia, alliteration, metaphor, simile, rhetoric, epigram and paradox and memorising Shakespeare blindly: ". . . the multitudinous seas incarnadine, / Making the
green one red . . ." Spoke geometry theorems like Tennysonian verse
and rattled off the dates of the English kings as I had the books of the
Bible, by rote. True I was no longer paced by people better than I,
not in 5B; there was only that nameless girl prone to good marks, the
one with physical defects, but, as Mumma had a way of quoting, God
works in a mysterious way.

For instance in 5B I ran into a young teacher of English called
Mr. Thompson, delicate-looking slender white-skinned amber-eyed
and with soft amber hair. His suits he'd chosen to match his colouring
which had a beneficent effect on me. Did I say soft-voiced? Amber-
voiced. I soon knew he liked my prose for, in an essay, he ticked a
phrase into which I'd put a lot of work. I remember the phrase verbatim. The subject he'd set was A Day in the Country. It was about
riding: "Loping down the sloping glen at a long swinging canter."
So he shared this with me, did he? I got the feeling that he had an

inkling of the essence in me. I allowed the possibility that he'd found in me the secret Someone Else whom only I'd known about. In a way that Miss Cumberland had never achieved I woke up to the latent power in the choice of a word. A stiff new door creaked open on pleasure. I heard later he died young, Mr. Thompson.

I stopped altogether being late for school, not that I had been late much, though I was starting to be late home after dark in the evening as the autumn brought shorter days. But Mumma would have a meal of a kind kept hot on a pot for me and the table laid with a cloth after which I'd sit up late over my written homework, only to get up early in the morning to catch my horse at first light and take to the road again. The exhilaration of challenge kept me in good heart and my country childhood kept me fit; the resilience of youth is a marvel. As for how long I could maintain this pace I was the last to wonder. If there were any disturbance in my work it came less from the accident of circumstances from outside than from the ingredient of dreaming within.

At the end-of-term exams in May I did come top in every subject required, believe it or not in math too, except for second in history. That nameless girl beat me there. None of which is to say that at this point I tolerated being second in anything; to be beaten by anyone in 5B was an affront. On the other hand, I persuaded myself on the road, take a look at the subject concerned . . . *history*. Just dates, dust and death. Creamy could have beaten me in *history*. Some people said history was worse than geography, even as bad as Nature Study which itself was lower than a snake and a snake crawls on its belly. Nevertheless, unsensationally I was indeed promoted to the matric form 5A and finally caught up with the band.

In this inner sanctum of the shining ones the girls were no longer sitting defensively on one side of the room, the boys en bloc on the other, but were peaceably interspersed as though they'd been credited with growing up, fifteen to eighteen. I made no beeline for a desk near the door, not this time, or anywhere near the front. I took a spare one back a bit not anywhere in particular. I'd been longing to be with them again and, true enough, there was Jessica over the aisle with Lila tucked in behind, Jessica's dark eyes mobile beneath the lids, dark hair trying to curl at the tips, slender long arms with angled elbows and her watch high up on her forearm. As I was to see again and re-member five years later when I met her at a Saturday night dance in the Auckland University gymnasium. She was in a loose soft green dress sitting talking with some girls. I left the sheik I was dancing with and went and talked with her, and she was civil enough in her Jessica way, without falling over me, and her watch was still high on her forearm. After that encounter I didn't hear of or see her again. I don't know whether she got her scholarship or not.

. . . and there was Penelope over there beneath the window with a smile like a new moon lying on its back on her Love-me face, her brown eyes luring the boys, "I dare you." Yet twenty years later I was told that Penelope hadn't married but was still in an office in Masterton and that her honey hair was grey. Since then I've heard no more.

I'd been looking forward to being near them again, the girls, but I felt strangely bereft; not because it was plain their fondness of me had gone but because *my* love for *them* had gone. In the place where I'd loved them was now a vacuum and there's no deprivation like ceasing to love. In climbing back and up into 5A with them I'd forced my dream to come true but you want to beware of your dreams *in case* they come true.

When I'd been working with Mr. Thompson in 5B a door on writing had opened to me and now a second one nearly did, a crack ajar only. I met another man outside school but not on a horse on the road. He came in a train from Wellington to enlighten the heathen on pianoforte. There were of course piano teachers in Masterton but Horace Hunt was a Mus.Bac. with his photo in the paper and was gloweringly handsome. To date I had not heard real music except Lionel's violin and had not been taught in depth. I signed myself up for a term as though my people were wealthy landowners and lined up with the heathen. The next thing Norma and I and Marmie were entered for the August Competitions. The motive for this is lost in the mists of time, unless it was Mumma's ambition, or my own. It was as reckless as climbing a cliff we may not be able to climb down from or swimming a horse in a flooded river. Breathtaking.

This Horace Hunt Mus.Bac. was tall dark and intimidating with long strong fingers. Since Mumma's teaching had been the irreducible this was my introduction to technique, interpretation and theory. For the competitions there were set pieces for different age-groups and mine was a Coleridge-Taylor waltz. That Mr. Hunt should set me a further piece for its finger exercise value I saw to be less than fair. I was profoundly moved by the Coleridge-Taylor and all my practice went on it but the exercise piece I left on my plate like porridge with lumps in it. There came a lesson when he took the exercise first; his cold elegance gave way, his white face flushed hot and to my astonishment he shouted, "Can't you get this into your block?" But after the waltz he said softly, "So this is where you put your work."

"Am I as good as that other girl?"

A smile. "You're a natural."

Too natural, however, to win a place in the August Competitions for the same reason I couldn't make the A basketball team in spite of arduous practice: some gap between the idea in the mind and the response in the muscle, the mind-muscle combination. Not quick enough, insufficient intelligence quota. Any good athlete, given a sense of music, would succeed at the keyboard better than I could. At least I no longer called my piano work "music" though it did advance beyond the noise, pace and rhythm stage. The Coleridge-Taylor waltz did inform and stay with me and for the first time in my life Lionel praised me: "That's nice, Sylv."

I had no idea of the extent of my innate limitations then or surely I would have ceased to see music as one of the main routes of my journey through life. Horace Hunt's remark led me astray. Even so a guilt took root right there so that although people sought my piano work for the rest of my life and used it as I did myself, I suspected I was bluffing. I'm held up here on this page talking about music but it is not irrelevant; music became my most desired medium once I found it to be communication, a language by which to say the unsay-ables which pressed increasingly from me, a way of translating the powerful drives in the undermind which determine our action. I was in my late thirties working five hours a day at the piano during the week and seven hours at the weekend before I found my ceiling in music, which was quite low, and had to accept I was not a musician and could never be a concert pianist. Not that this released me but at least it eliminated piano as one of the possible directions, clearing the deck somewhat. On the subject of which road to take from the cross-roads in the thirties the short list was shorter and the decisions easier.

However, one term had to do, for although this man on a train taught me pedal technique my people were not wealthy landowners and he wasn't paid. I'm sorry about that. Pedalling is beyond price and now I owned it. I'd pay him now were he still alive.

Norma was set the Dancing Doll, Poupée Valsante, which she continued to play for years and years so well, she still does. I've an idea that Puppa trained her. I'll drop her a line and ask her. Marmie played a Schubert Moment Musicale which I anyway found the hardest of them on account of the light touch required. Mumma taught him the notes or some of them and onstage he held the sustaining pedal throughout to help him to reach the tape first. He won second place on speed, rhythm and joie de vivre alone, abandoning technique as a factor. The judge said he'd never heard anything like it and would have placed him first had it not been so public. Though he did confide to someone backstage that he wouldn't ride a horse that bolted like Marmaduke. Marmie was paid two shillings prize for that. The story they tell about Marmie's real name is that when Mumma took him to church to be christened she hadn't worked out what to name him. In these big families of the past with several names for each child naming was a matter of logistics. The risk occurred of repeating yourself which Mumma had already done. Absent-mindedness was understood. So anyway the minister said at the baptismal font, "What do you name this child?"

Mumma had no idea. She looked up at the minister and said, "What is your name, Mr. Heavybellie?"

"Marmaduke."

"Ah," from Mumma. "Marmaduke. I name this child Marmaduke."

When Marmaduke reached the high school stage he took to his second name, Maxwell, though he had five names altogether. We still call him Marm.

It's no good looking back on youth and thinking, "If only . . ." With me at that time there was no If Only. Nothing could have made me a pianist so I have no regrets but a new door did open for better or for worse. Horace Hunt so enlightened me I haven't grounded since. I was swept away . . . and so was my homework.

The idea was to get through and out of this school and finish with the road. Move one: get out of 5B and up into the matric class. I'd done that, Tick. Move two: *pass* matric (the equivalent of university entrance today, U.E.). With both third- and fourth-years it was quite a big class but the big fourth-year boys who were nearly men they kept the tone from being too formal since you couldn't help laughing at their tomfoolery. Neither could Miss Cumberland when she came in for language; big Batty Hynds baited her into disarray while as for Tom Cullen he teased her like a girl; blurts of laughter would break her composure and you'd see a pink flush in her sober middle-aged cheeks.

One day our form teacher said he wouldn't stop us making a class concert if we were capable of doing it ourselves, since he couldn't, which was really challenging Miss Cumberland on the concert front.

The takings would be for the library. Because the idea was behind her back it became pleasantly furtive and Miss Cumberland's stock dropped; even her popularity could fluctuate and when the boys said things about her in class, and they were pretty bad, he smiled and changed the subject. Though I didn't think Hek Herickson should have been allowed to get away with it, about putting rat poison in her tea. Nevertheless all of us did get a delicious feeling of being implicated in the underhand, forgetting the great benefits of Miss Cumberland which is the nature of popularity. Mind you, Cullen did hiss across the room at Hek, "Have at thee, varlet!"

There was plenty of talent around. People began preparing their own items in pairs and groups some of which required the piano . . . so I overheard. And I saw Penelope arranging with Batty Hynds to play for her ballet though I knew him to be a slow sight-reader with no memorising and as for pace and dance rhythm . . . his eyes were glued to the music all the time. How on earth could he play *Coppélia*? Portia-and-Gwen who were fourth-years and favorites of Dr. Roydon's they planned an Old English dance duo in costume and there were class choruses to be accompanied. Poor old Batty Hynds staggered round knee-deep in the music till Jessica, who'd had piano lessons, tried to help him out but she was floundering too and all the time they knew I could do it. This had happened before.

Rangitumau

But cracks started showing in their front because Portia-and-Gwen, who had not been in our form last year and had not been conditioned to leave me out, and would not have done so anyway, thought it quite natural to come to me and ask for their accompaniment so away we went off the mark while the others were still running on the spot, getting hotter and hotter under their snow-white collars until Batty and Jessica called it a day and again I was approached at the eleventh

hour. Of course by now I'd learnt all their jolly music and could play
it with my eyes shut and hands tied behind my back. What they
wanted and what I wanted were exactly the same thing.

So this concert comes along in some scouts' hall downtown and I'm
unusually nervous; not over Portia-and-Gwen's dance duo:

> In a quaint old-fashioned garden stands a shepherdess of carven stone,
> And over by the sleeping fountain is a little shepherd all alone;
> But when moonlight floods the alleys and the nightingale sings
>    all night through
> They waken and they meet together in a sentimental rendezvous . . .

Portia-and-Gwen were costumed in white, their faces and hands powdered white and their hair and the lights were low. Portia was the
shepherdess. As they stepped some of the others sang it . . . no I wasn't
nervous over them, it was playing Penelope's *Coppélia*. I fell into my
weakness of gathering pace and ended up far too fast. Behind stage
afterwards she nearly died, collapsed against the wall in her tulle with
Mr. Morice standing over her alarmed. "Too fast," she gasped, "too
fast." I never saw such deep heaving of a thorax. At this moment,
however, her cheeks and lips painted pink, a rose in her hair and the
wonderful line of a girl's body in tulle in the posture of exhaustion
arrested the breath in us all. From the audience, however, the speed
had looked stunning and drew such thunderous applause that she
stopped protesting though she couldn't rise to an encore. Her name
was made over that.

None of these undercurrents and overtones escaped Mr. Morice and
after the concert he had the grace to thank me before them for coming in at the end to salvage the show. Fancy that. For a brief time I'd
been necessary to them again. At this milestone through the teens
once more I was received at the inn where laughter sparkled and wine
ran free. Only for the length of an overnight stay but long enough for
me. "In small proportions we just beauties see; and in short measures
life may perfect be."

The matric form was mostly fourth-year big people who had an extra
year's work under their belt, Portia-and-Gwen among them. The rest
was made up of us third-years, Jessica-and-Lila, Penelope, me and the
boys. Those boys were probably the best the Wairarapa could throw
up and their names are now known both inside and outside New
Zealand. They were very funny. Why were the girls not funny? The

capacity for humour goes hand-in-hand with creativity and creativity belongs to freedom of the mind. And there you have it really: what had this particular society done to its women? At least they supplied the "laughter off-stage." You could almost say the school was male-oriented what with the glorification of the Rugby team and the Territorial Cadets, the all-male staff but one and the fine new hostel for boys, but, if so, it felt all right. No one minded us girls around as long as we didn't rock the boat, or rock the boys if you like.

We third-years had this chance of an early go at matric. Miss Cumberland had a stake in us, a professional involvement close on the personal, having been with us from the start. There's a great deal to be said for unmarried teachers when they're level-headed as well; they're emotionally accessible . . . well, up to a point. So down go all our heads for the haul towards the next stop on the horizon, matriculation, but it grew harder to make the pace, even for scholarship people like Jessica Wall and Tom Cullen. How that effervescent Cullen got anywhere at all, the way he played, joked and sparred with Miss Cumberland, a woman more than twice his age, yet that boy ended up a doctor of divinity and head of a theological college in time.

Uphill all the way on forbidding intellectual terrain yet it did not occur to any of us not to work or to slacken at a corner; you are caught up in a class like that, in the collective ethic. Jessica leaning over my desk trying to clarify an algebraic equation; she didn't have to help me so why did she do it? "I'm going to fail math," I say.

"*This* is nothing," she says. "Wait till you get to the sixth. There's a subject there made up of the whole lot put together—arithmetic, geometry and algebra all rolled into one."

"What's it called?" I panic.

"Trigonometry."

"*Trigonometry?*"

"I'm looking forward to that," she says. She was charitable, Jessica, not that she understood me or I the equation. Some of us were going to fall by the wayside, we knew, though we didn't know who it would be.

These populated years at high school elude being captured step by step; they appear scene by scene rather, or set in some lasting impression. The most comprehensive and enduring of these impressions which qualifies my whole view of that school is the unexpected ostracism which I'd not known before. It was new to me. No one's trying to say I'd been overpopular at home or at school to date but

I had managed to remain integrated with the company, on the inside looking out, but the day Dr. Roydon expelled me in front of the others, rightly or wrongly, for writing my name on my desk was the day I learnt new dimensions: what it was like on the outside looking in. A child hardly thrives in the censure from the head of a school, not the public part. Also the new man on staff, Mr. Sweet, Jancy's step-father, ridiculed my drawing in his art class which no doubt I richly deserved but again it was in front of the others. That was my first art lesson at school and I didn't attend again. I felt a marked man.

It was unnerving. Life had no laurels in hand but wore a leer on its face. It made me feel sick inside, slinking on the fringe of the multitude rather than merging with them. All their cosy twos and threes and groups, their voices lifted in communication or lowered in confidences. I'd think: The world is taking it out of me as Mumma said it would and this is what it's like.

Surprisingly uncomfortable it was, being left out. As for *why* I was, that was because I'd been weighed and found wanting and since so many thought the same, well, they must be right. At fifteen you're not analysing society's values but only the reasons why people like you or don't like you. You could almost say, though not quite, that we're disposed to become what people label us which takes more than discerning teachers to counter. As a reject I was beginning to believe I was persona non grata because of what people thought I was, that I was in truth a freckled road-sweep on the level of the dust. It never occurred to me to remember what I actually was, a descendant of a coloniser knighted by the king, the evidence of which, the coat-of-arms and the heirlooms, was forgotten in Puppa's Black Box at home. I don't know of anyone, man, woman or young person, who can live with public disgrace; it has a force which drives you from your homeland forever.

But there's always a way in the resilience of youth. I settled down to ardent pariahdom. So I'm a pariah? Then I'll be the best pariah. Give it my attention. Do my homework on it. I didn't join the other pariahs for I doubted they were taking their roles seriously and because I found them socially unacceptable. There are strata even among outcasts, like honour among thieves. That two of them, Marie and Pru, were actually among the best of people incognito, escaped me; at the time they were not seen to be so; besides they walked together in self-sufficiency as if they liked it and they were usually smiling. As for that nameless girl in 5B addicted to good marks, well . . . who was I to presume she'd

accept my company, even if I could stand hers which I couldn't. How
could any one of us rejects risk being rejected by the body of the rejected themselves? That I did once painfully speak to her is the measure
of what nadir can be and I richly deserved to be re-rejected. And how
could the "widespread pride of man" survive such as that? It can't,
but in me it did. As for my current ideal girl, standing in for my
inspiration, Veronica Dundonald, she was airily in another circle,
another form, another wing and, above all, in another world, being
largely a figment of my own imagination. Fantasy doesn't mix with
but curdles reality and I anyway saw to it that our paths did not cross.

How to succeed as a pariah. How to get from the school buildings
to the field for sport on Thursday afternoons without being seen to
walk alone when the populace moved out en masse, crossing the wide
green abstractly. Shall I risk trailing the group with Penelope in it . . .
no; she'd notice at once and show it. What about this pair, Jessica-and-
Lila . . . never; two is sacrosanct. Well, that threesome nearby, Portia-
and-Gwen and a new third-former . . . but three is composed of two
and one. True, Portia is tolerant of a third and she's one who answers
me if I speak, strangely, but no subservience for me. What I ought to
do is to walk vaguely near some less specific grouping and if they
suspect then look the other way, as though I'm really looking for my
own friends. But no, this kind of acting is not in my line, not for me,
an apprentice of the gifted Daphne. You just keep on walking, Sylv,
alone regardless, it could be worse. At least your family are not here
to see you, so what have you got to lose. Don't look hangdog, keep
your face up and don't let them guess what's happening inside you.
And another thing: don't you ever sign your name again in celebration of passing this way.


These four formative fateful years. Along with the road and green
were the corridors at school, the highway linking three lengthy wings,
each housing a form, the thirds, fourths and fifths; the holy sixth
were upstairs in the library, most of them prefects and captains and
too exclusive to be on view at all other than passing by which was
seldom. We fifths were in the far wing with 5A at the end, the most
distant spot, and you had to walk miles to get there. When the breaks
from class came here was this up and go all over the show in two
channelled streams, half the school walking one way and half walking the other. No one ran. A continuous collective catalytic encounter.

There were twos and threes and groups but too fluid to matter. Con-
cealing my apartness hardly arose. The sound of my steps was the

sound of theirs and the sound of my voice too had I used it. My direction was their direction, I was part of the great encounter. In the corridors when the great movements came I knew the ease of aloneness with no loneliness, I found the surcease of anonymity.

Ever oversensitive to sound I felt the advancing, passing and departing steps, all kinds of feet going all kinds of ways, you could hear them in muffled unison. Not the beat of one walking alone, no rhythm as when soldiers march in step but a low-key background drumming as though Fate were walking with us. Above it were everybody's voices like water running over stones. Only at your elbow could you distinguish a phrase of talk, from the girls rather than from the boys for the girls revealed themselves as girls in their excitable treble while the boys were an unknown factor who rumbled away deep in their throats, the two together orchestrating one of the loveliest of human sounds, crowded conversation.

Approaching, meeting and passing. We were not supposed to talk to the boys though they arteried among us. Boys were known to be people in trousers which covered mystery and danger. But if you were walking anywhere behind Dorabella you'd know her eyes lifted several times because you'd see the eyes of several boys lift to hers as she passed and you would see them smile. And what a smile can say! How could they so dare in public. And not only Dorabella; whenever we passed a rare group from the Sixth you could count on Penelope's eyes to lift to that terrific dark sheik with a profile that shamed John Barrymore and sure enough his consuming eyes would penetrate hers and the next thing each was smiling.

In military uniform just off Territorial Parade all the boys streamed one way and the girls the other. So close were these soldiers you could reach out and touch them except that none of us did. All those trousers with legs in them and hair on the virile knees. Absolutely shocking. Did then the Sheik of Araby have legs and knees beneath his robes, let alone with hair on them; or his film counterpart, Rudolph Valentino? Studying the face of the Perfect Lover in the film magazine at home the big ones had left I hadn't got past his features; the quivering nostrils, the passionate mouth, the eyes of burning desire since only his face was there. Until I read the passage from Shakespeare that Miss Cumberland skipped in class and made us read to ourselves outside about Cassius and Iago and Desdemona:

> In sleep I heard him say "Sweet Desdemona,
> Let us be wary, let us hide our loves,"

And then, sir, would he gripe and wring my hand,
Cry "O sweet creature!" then kiss me hard,
As if he pluck'd up kisses by the roots,
That grew upon my lips—then laid his leg
Over my thigh—and sigh'd and kissed, and then
Cried "Cursed fate that gave thee to the Moor!"

. . . until then it had not occurred to me that lovers had legs, let alone thighs, but after Shakespeare I was obliged to allow this possibility. As for those hairy-legged boys striding by, however handsome, interesting or funny, none stood a chance against the man of my dreams who so far had only a face and a voice, the face of Valentino and the voice of Caruso, but enough to turn my instincts inside out and my Sunday School morality upside down without any help of legs. Yet he still managed to ride an Arab steed. When Dorabella and Penelope made eyes at the boys in the corridor surely they were not thinking of legs and *thighs. I* wouldn't be. What would Dr. Roydon say if he knew . . . or God for that matter who saw everything in our hearts?

These encounters between boys and girls, between men and women, remained largely a morass of mystery to me like stories interrupted with no conclusion, like saddling a horse and taking to the road with the horizon ever receding, like following barefoot some forest track to be darkly lost in the trees.

The idea was to get through and out of this school somehow in order to be done with the road, but I don't know. That road was not the disadvantage it appeared to be; the break from the race, the winding down and the beneficent refuelling process. Leaving town each day I'd sometimes ride the drowsy Creamy along the grassy lane called Hope Street near Miss Cumberland's place to ford the river there rather than cross the Lansdowne bridge. The horse would like to stand mid-stream with the current eddying round her knees and cooling her slender fetlocks. A pretty mind-picture you could hang on a wall.

Another road-picture persisting here of rain curtaining me as I wheeled my bike with a puncture upon the longest bridge composing a poem called "My Little Bed" in order not to waste good time. Soggily sentimental but I can speak it verbatim. And this watercolour gives place to the next in sequence of the cloak room at school with me standing among the rows of coats and hats well after class is in, irreversibly late, they'd be halfway through math by now. My own coat is dripping, there's a pool round my shoes and I'm wondering what the devil to do. And I hear this down-to-earth click of Miss Cumberland's heels as she steps smartly by, books on arm, gown flowing, then her matter-of-fact voice: "Sylvia. What on *earth* are you doing here at this time of morning? You're wringing wet."

"It's all right, Miss Cumberland." Another *water* picture.

As it happens we'd come to love the rain from a rain-sun life in the country and there's plenty of it near the ranges. We were addicted to homing in exotic foothills and I could write several heavy volumes on the subject and fill folios and galleries with paintings on it and still do on occasion try to get away with it till my metropolitan city-bred editor begs me frankly to stop it and discipline is a factor in all things. But I did love the rain; to hear it clammering on the roof at night was to hear Miss Cumberland's voice in the morning.

Not that it was always raining on the road; some of the mornings were as crisp as the crust of freshly baked scones and the afternoons as sweet as new milk from a cow; white milk frothed in a bucket.

Another poem from the road was about some great vague artist responsible for the dawns I knew and the evening's closing skies. That was pretty awfully romantic too and it didn't win a prize in the poetry competition; Portia won that one and Tom Cullen the other. I didn't ever win a poetry prize on account of sentimentality but I did know the morning's early light and the night's sombre reds. I've forgotten the one about a white road winding away over the hill since I didn't finish it. In mind these pictures are in chalk, crayon and watercolour with captions about the road and they hang on the wall of the past.

In this gallery I pass by the portrait of Mr. Sweet . . . one could think of names for him less inappropriate than Sweet . . . though he must have been a very handsome man one time but now his past was gouged all over his face like cuttings in the clay after a cloudburst. He had about as much art in him as a bull bogged in a swamp and it was said he was given the art class because he was too new to defend himself. Yet he had the most stunningly beautiful new wife whom he often brought to school functions and the most charming and the prettiest step-daughter of all time, our celebrated Jancy . . . now if only he'd been able to deal me a few home truths on perspective, colours and Whatman's paper instead of . . . but "if" is a very weak word.

And one more picture before I leave this winter term in the fifth; "winter" term rather than "wintry" since much good weather reigned within me. It was spring by now with flowers in flood, the kind of impulse in the air that would move Daphne to sing Schubert love-songs she'd inherited from Lionel.

> Ask the spring blossoms laden
> to show me my maiden,
> My love that I long for
> and look for today.

I'm standing at the brick corner of the bikeshed and there are flowers in my hand, freesia and boronia. They must have come from Veronica on account of the power of the accompanying feeling. I don't remember what time of day it was but I do remember the fragrance. It was one of those moments of heightened emotion that leave footprints on the memory.

A good school, I swear it, with some good teachers. It was less bad management than bad luck about people like Mr. Sweet who ridiculed my drawing. In his place Fate could equally well have dealt me another Mr. Thompson who had cultivated my prose. As to that, it was also bad luck about Dr. Roydon; Fate could equally well have dealt me a headmaster with a tolerance for variation in the school. In fact both these men were said to be worthy people and I haven't a doubt they were since their records prove it. Their principles were unassailable and it is I who declare it. I come not to bury but to praise them.

Fifteen in the spring. Matric ahead in the 5A room at the end of the far wing and if you wanted to qualify you had to pass this thing. There was no accrediting then, no social promotion and no passengers either. Anyone who left school with matric had verily proved he could read, write and 'rith, and the professional and business communities knew where they stood.

It was, however, recommended whether or not you should sit, though I can't see what for unless it was to avoid cluttering up the exam rooms to no purpose or to save you from paying the entrance fee of two guineas for nothing, if you failed. You didn't have to be recommended, you could sit the Outside. Schools liked to recommend their A stream third-years whom they had already placed in the matric form; on the one hand they might get it, on the other, if they didn't, they hadn't lost by a rehearsal for next time. Miss Cumberland's initial group were in this bracket, a batch of her boys and we four girls.

Mr. Morice was our form teacher, white-haired, relaxed, amused and amusing with a slant to his running asides. I forget which subjects Messrs. Morice and Bee took, but Miss Cumberland did the languages. A big class it was with fifteens, sixteens, seventeens and an eighteen, boys who meant to matriculate or fall down a ninety-foot precipice trying, and some were very funny about it. You couldn't help laughing at the answers from Cullen, Hynds and Co. especially when Cullen was fencing with Miss Cumberland who continued her resistance valiantly. The merciless wit was like sun in your eyes when rounding a hairpin bend.

A healthy tone in that class from staff who were fair, able, academic and strict and you never want to underrate strictness in a teacher, for discipline is shelter like a roof over you. Democracy can't do without discipline, your own or someone else's, while civilisations collapse into the dust of oblivion when discipline peters out, and our souls can miss the turning.

For us all it was hard and growing harder. The highway through the teens was rising more steeply like a foothill of the ranges, ascending all the way in a three-in-one grade. You needed to travel light with no extra baggage like vanity or envy or dreaming. There were times when you couldn't see a yard ahead of you and could only hear the teachers calling the direction. When you lost sight of the summit altogether you could only concentrate on the next step ahead. You don't let up for the trick was to keep with the others.

What we could see at the summit of the range was a wayside restaurant like the one at the top of the Taupo Hill where you can rest from the wind and wash your hands, have a sandwich or two and a cup of tea while studying the sudden coastline far down below on the other side. Like the Israelites viewing the Promised Land at the end of their journey from Egypt, like Balboa seeing the Pacific from the heights, like the heart-stop pass at the crest of the Rockies in mountainous Colorado. Matric was a ticket like a visa authorising you to glide down the sunny curving descent among the golden poplars to the alluvial plain of the Esk with ivied church and a steeple; into the valley of grapes. Matric was the key word unlatching the gate to the land of the educated.

Near the top we were caught by surprise, ambushed, not realising how close to the finish we were. The word "recommendation" slipped from some tongue. It was a shock. I believed I could pass matric were it not for math. Anything that was not math I could learn by heart or at least make it up, there was always a chance in the hit-or-miss.

My memory would learn anything I wanted it to. In geometry I'd rather learn by heart much of the book of theorems without understanding one line, speaking them like iambic pentameter. It was bad luck you couldn't do algebra that way; you had to understand all the data and work it out. As for arithmetic, well . . . all you could say for arithmetic was that it wasn't algebra. On the other hand, sums were things you could at least see in mind, for instance, all these horses cost so much, if four were sold at such-and-such a price, two got out on the road and were stolen, the man bought three thoroughbreds from the show ring and the fat one was lent to a girl on the road to ride the condition off it and . . . well, you could see the horses and bridles and saddles in the stables down the street, and the chaff in the bags for their feed and the man doing the bargaining. When you made a drawing of it all you couldn't miss. I could smell the sweat from their flanks and hear the chumping of their teeth on the bits. In arithmetic you had a chance. Whereas *algebra* . . . how could you impersonate an *x* or a *y*? Did they have limbs, could they laugh or cry?

Who were recommended and who were not I divined one morning somehow though I don't remember how. But I knew. Among them were Portia-and-Gwen, Jessica-and-Lila, Penelope and most of the boys . . . but not me. It was something I had to confess to Mumma. It was still light when I got home, being summer, before dark for a change. Letting Creamy go and coming in the back door I hang the bridle on the nail there and bring in the saddle from the dew. "I'm not sitting matric," and toss my bag of books in the corner.

"What did y'say, what did y'say?"

I don't say it again. I just sit down.

"Most certainly you're sitting matric."

"Caesar has not recommended me."

"That hound."

"I could sit the Outside but haven't got the two guineas entrance fee."

Mumma had this exclusive instinct of guessing where Ashton was to be found and she obtained these two guineas from him which he borrowed from a mate which the mate owed him anyway, he said, and had done for a year. This mate was notorious for borrowing money and not paying back but this time he had to, see? "Smell the dead men on this fist I said," and gave us a sample right there in the kitchen. Two guineas which should have been used to pay off the top half of the grocery bill in town. It was a precious two guineas, very. I remember it: two pound notes and one silver florin. It gave me the

chance to sit the exam which, if I passed it, would keep me level with
the other three girls, Jessica-and-Lila and Penelope, so they couldn't
leave me behind again. How could I stand being left behind again
downstairs in the same old room with a whole batch of new arrivals
who, so far, had been a year behind me; all over again for a year while
my band would be in the sixth form upstairs in the library, not to
mention being prefects. A good pariah should keep up with people.
Moreover, if I managed to ascend to the sixth form, Miss Cumberland
would say she was proud of me, Caesar would stop despising me and
the family would say, "Sylvie's got brains." So I had to get through
matric.

What I should say here is that I took these two guineas to school in
an envelope or something, tied in the corner of a handkerchief or
safety-pinned into my uniform pocket except that we didn't have
safety-pins or envelopes. What I see quite clearly is carrying it to school
fast in one hand with the reins of the bridle in the other. Even so I
can hardly believe myself. Yet I must have. I see it. Eleven miles in
one hand. Yet I'm jolly sure that if two guineas or its dollar equivalent
mattered as much to me now as those two guineas mattered to me
then . . . yes you'd see me carry it in one hand, the steering wheel in
the other, more than eleven miles; a hundred and eleven.

Anyway I got the money to school without losing it, the notorious
"lost" girl, filled in the application form without recommendation and
handed the form and the fee into the office in as civilised a way as any
other. Only for Mr. Morice to come in one morning soon after and read
out openly the list of names recommended; girls first and mine not
there, boys next and mine not there, which I'd known anyway, until
as he replaced the paper in his folder he added sotto voce my own
astonished name. By itself and in character, you could say.

Don't think I was recommended at the last minute because I'd produced the money; even Caesar was not capable of that. It might have
been Miss Cumberland or Mr. Thompson remembering my performance when left behind in 5B, winning out with all odds against me,
or it could have been Mr. Morice who knew me well enough to per-
ceive the faith I showed in myself by entering against opposition. Someone prevailed against Dr. Roydon. However, whatever happened behind the holy scenes I ended up recommended by the skin of my
teeth, but only just. "Eleventh-hour Solvia," from Mr. Bee. I don't
know what Mr. Bee would have done without me. Blurry-aged like
most of the staff, not quite enough hair to make it across the top, sly
eyes and one of these dead-pan English faces that blot out the shrieking

laughter inside and a ridiculous deep dimple mid-chin as though
someone had just this minute shot him. I think he actually dreaded the
day when I did my homework. But I did wish my recommendation
had been in orderly sequence like other people. At that time I could
have done without all the drama, even I, not unacquainted with it.

Never mind. In the thick of all that I took off to win the junior
swimming championship, with Miss Cumberland who was running
them standing at the end of the baths smiling at me in a fuji silk dress
and her gown off. I hadn't had to be recommended for that. And
when I returned to school with wet hair who should I run into unexpectedly in the fifth-form wing but Veronica Dundonald. Sentimental
encounter. I let her know why my hair was wet. Practically nothing
in the way of words passed between us but a whole lot of something
else and she was wearing scent against the rules. I wished we could
have talked in the medium of the real for I had the feeling she still
thought I was marvellous, *still*. How long can one maintain marvellousness? Uneasy business.

Daphne, a fourth-year, was sitting matric also, in Wellington. Gracie
was in Fiji at this time so who was supervising Daphne? Was it Lionel
or Muriel or Mumma's brother? Inadvertently I'd caught up a year on
Daphne though neither of us seemed to mind. We were not in the
same school or even the same city and I wouldn't pass with math
round my neck. Mumma was proud that two of her children were in
the exam arena together. There's one thing I can say about Mumma:
she was never bored.

The state exams were held in the Masterton Tech downtown, an
old red brick place of faded grandeur which we all knew very well.
In the early days we used to come here for Home Science, cooking
and sewing and buttonhole stitch and Why haven't you brought your
flour? Has anyone seen my recipe book? Please Miss, I've lost my
needle . . . all of which I'd abandoned early, guess why. The scene was
drab, the days were hot and the talk platitudinous, a climate unfavor-
able to artists and felons and dreamy vagabonds. I don't know whether
I was using my bike or my unambitious horse or whether Ashton
had put me in a boarding house, supposing there were any left, but
I know for a fact I was there.

So I'm handed this arithmetic paper with a sum about a train that
came into a station at a given time, stayed a given time and took off
again at what time? There was a station clock in this sum which was
either fast or slow, by how many minutes? So did the train depart

on time? I believe there was a second clock at the next station in fact
the whole railway system was under review. The data did not expose
the emotional condition of the station-master or what the passengers
thought about it though the whole crisis was obviously a human issue
never mind clocks. I've wondered often since how the examiners reacted to pages of drawings of the railway station with anxious people
hanging out windows of the train, tears of sorrow, smiles of delight
registering the arrivals and departures, "Darling-come-back-to-me"
ultimatums and "Where has my luggage got to?" I had the station-
master there playing it cool like "the boy stood on the burning deck"
and was just working out how to imply the clanging of the bell and
the shriek of the guard's whistle . . . yes I had the cowcatcher and the
escaping steam . . . when time was called. Mind you, this sum carried
the bulk of the marks and the best people can be opportunist.

As it turned out later I was the only one in class who attempted
this sum. It was the only one I got right. To be frank it was the only
sum I did at all and a pleasant three hours I had of it. It reminds me
of the time when I was newly married and I won a first prize for baking at the fair. Red ticket, name in paper, five shillings prize, applause and all, but mine was the only entry.

"She was nervous," Ashton told Mumma. "She thought every moment would be her next."


The hot Christmas holidays at Rangitumau with most of the family
home. Gracie was out of the country so that, when Li was practising,
Daphne had more time with us. She was so fond of Rangitumau with
its civilised house that she even roamed a little with us again in the
three-little-girls formation, Daphne, Sylvie and Norma as at Te Pohue
years ago; a barefooted echo. She liked the swimming pool at the river
where one day we took a camera and she volunteered daringly to
swim naked. Norm stood on the bank scanning the paddocks to warn
if anyone were coming while I took the photo and here's this white
mermaid reclining on a rock and all this curly hair. She swam up and
down and round the pool underneath the willows cavorting like
youth itself, trying to convince Norma and me how wonderful it was
to swim without togs but no, not us. The photo remained a classified
secret for years and secret years until it fell to pieces from overuse.

And there was an evening when the sun had gone down at the
intersection where the lane took off from the road leaving a triangle
of soft green grass at the centre and she crossed the stones to this stage
and performed a silent dance. Whenever Daph danced she liked to

trail an invisible gossamer fabric for effect. She'd come on stage trailing this thing looking back over her shoulder upon it. And whirl it and float it, her eyes upon it. You should have seen it. Soon Norm and I joined in since no one was looking and lifted our toes also. That was a solemn performance. But we retired and sat on the side of the road when she decided to impersonate an opera singer with extravagant gestures, impossible treble notes and armfuls of prima donna passion for the hour was no longer solemn. We laughed ourselves to stomach-aches.

There came a morning full of sun and family, even Puppa home from the hospital in his bed in the front room. I'm sitting on the grass at the front of the house when the mail-car brings the mail, an official envelope each for Daphne and me, small and dun-coloured they were with official printing all over them, and a blue lettercard for me also. I find my matric marks and I'd passed by one mark. The blue lettercard was a note of pride from Miss Cumberland: "I'm delighted with you third-year girls." In the middle room Mumma lifted up her skirts and danced like a girl. "Who-oo who-oo!" like a calling bird and Puppa from his bedroom was shouting "Hurray!" But Daphne was crying in the kitchen to Lionel, "I missed the arithmetic exam," she wept, "but I thought my extra subject would get me through. I went along in the afternoon to sit arithmetic at one-thirty and found it had been held at nine in the morning."

I was talking about this only yesterday to my sister Norma who remembered how Mumma had sunk on a chair. "Just cried and cried and cried," she said. And she censured Daphne, her best beloved. "How could you do such a thing? After all we've done for you. After all Gracie has tried." Norma added, "When she was old she told me, 'I wept buckets.'"

I'd forgotten that but I remember how after the drama that summer morning . . . the heartbreak of it for us all right down through Marmie and 'Vadne that Daphne could indeed wilt and fall . . . Mumma rose and turned to do the family washing seeking surcease whereas a household washing with most of the tribe home was not exactly nothing, piles and piles of clothes on the wash-house floor for which she gathered wood and lit the copper. By noon, however, Daphne was telling Lionel, "Let Sylv have her little exams if she wants them, Li. I don't need them."

"You're one of Nature's philosophers."

This matric disaster was the second time I'd knocked Daphne back, the first being when I'd insisted on going to Wellington with her and Gracie, interrupting and diluting Daphne's chances. That had been my own brazen selfishness, but this time, her missing arithmetic, was accident. Her own, yet not quite. Had Gracie been with her she'd have missed no exam. But then Gracie had her own passions to expend. None of which, however, prevents my wondering whether, had it been the first Sylvia who'd lived rather than I the second Sylvia, things might have gone better with Daphne. Daphne called Auckland Unlucky City and I call myself Unlucky Sister. How have the mighty fallen, even our most fragrant flower o' the flock. The next time I look at Rangitumau Daphne's not there, nor did I see her there again.

"Daph," I asked her decades later when she was staying at my home, very ill, "why was it you never did anything with your unique gifts?"

"I had no ambition."

Her eyes are still liquid and her legs like poems. "But," I say, "how could anyone brought up by Mumma have no ambition?"

"It was that summer morning, Sylv. It dated from the time I failed matric. I'd failed in front of the family. You, a year younger, had passed. The worst thing, though, was most of them were there to see it."

"But Daph, everyone knew I'd only scraped through by one mark. They all knew your average . . . even without arithmetic . . . was higher."

The luminous green of her eyes reminiscent. "That summer morn-

Daphne at 18

Later

ing, Sylv. That was the first time I'd let down my audience. Not one flick of ambition have I had since."

"But you have more gifts than the lot of us put together. Wherever you are, whomever you're with, the world becomes your stage."

"My family is my stage," warming up. "I keep my best for my family."

"Others know your best."

"You hear this, Sylv: only the family matters. Until my last breath. And you can take it from me, that last breath itself will be my master-piece."

There can be no such thing as Daphne's last breath. As it happens, my sister Daphne was alone when she died so we missed that particular masterpiece. Lionel told me afterwards, "She asked me to see to it that nobody looked upon her when she was dead. Daphne never liked to be caught at a disadvantage."

When the matriculation results were exposed in the paper for all to see for themselves, Daphne's friend Dorothy had passed all right but Caesar's favorites, Portia-and-Gwen, they'd missed. Conceivably, I'd say, given the quality of Portia's mind, high-loaded with feeling and blazing imagery, while her Latin affix, Gwen, would follow suit even in failure. What price being favorite of Caesar? What price being reliable good clever useful charitable and beautiful in a world made by men for men? Why not? Was this man wrong? Two weeks ago Portia was decorated by the Queen in the New Year Honour List for her services to New Zealand literature and history. I heard later that such was Caesar's disappointment and consternation that far from doing the family washing for surcease he raised the dust from here to there, demanded a recount of their papers, engaged in forceful dia-logue with the education department and obtained for them both partial passes to ensure their promotion to the sixth. It had something to do with a man's ambition but he was in the position to do something about it. Mumma couldn't do a thing about it.

> The noble Brutus
> Hath told you Caesar was ambitious.
> If it were so, it was a grievous fault;
> And grievously hath Caesar answer'd it.

We left Rangitumau. I think Mumma must have been sent to Bideford against her will by the way she wept when we got there. After the nice house at Rangitumau once more she found herself and her family in something not far removed from a hovel, though the word "hovel" needs to be kept for that dungeon behind Dean Court in Hastings. Look, you've got to believe what the education department can get away with in the category of school residence. A teacher is socially condemned before he arrives. Even the Church does better. In his wheelchair Puppa was silent.

Yet Bideford was even lovelier than Rangitumau. Further from civilisation, higher, more isolated in the foothills of the Tararua Range, extravagantly treed. A forsaken garden held up a wistful rose-arch which must have been loved one day. I was touched by the broken-down charm of the place, of the old-time school and the glebe, thickly inhabited by dreaming ghosts of those who'd been happy here.

Between the plateau and the road was a softly painted river carved deep in the gully, overhung by native bush and willows, a swingbridge high above and a ford down below. A sentimental watercolour from a Christmas card that arched with romance. I could have lived alone here forever but for the sharp angular facts that my eleven miles to school were now fifteen and that Mumma wept.

Having matric was a saver though. Here was this most unexpected year in the sixth, could you believe it? Honour and glory for the taking. Even dreaming of being a prefect . . . *mad*. But I'd have to get there first; there's a limit to what a horse can do or a pair of girl's legs. None could afford board.

Perhaps it was time to run away. Stake out my territory in some far-fabled city and start on my real work. It would have to begin with commercial art which paid since the real stuff didn't. And what was to stop me continuing lessons with Horace Hunt to become a concert pianist? Think of it. A studio of my own and sweet new friends. What I would buy first would be a frying pan, a pound of sausages, a teapot, a cup and saucer. Felicity.

But I'd left out Mumma who wanted me to get Higher Leaving Certificate and become another teacher; also Ashton considered me a good bet and worth putting his money on. In truth, he did get me board in Masterton but it lasted one night only which put me back on the road again but a fifteen-mile stretch this time.

The sixth form occupied the library upstairs at the top of the school either way. From this rarefied height prefects were chosen, Rugby tennis and basketball captains and organisational committees but, let's face it, these didn't run in our family as they do in some. You won't find our name in politics or the army, not since the Warners took the side of the king in the Wars of the Roses in the fifteenth century. The red rose of Lancaster on our escutcheon couldn't make me a prefect. People don't give responsibility to artists if they can help it, to wayfarers, wanderers and rejects.

I rather clung to the ostracism. There's much to be said for this condition. You can't go round wasting good ostracism when it's been so expensively earned. Instead of cringing you call their bluff. Sixteen I was now and never been kissed and I had other things to do. Encapsulated in the library my soul germinated like a succulent green broad bean. Veronica had been removed to a posh girls' boarding school.

At interval and lunch when nice people linked up with other nice people downstairs I stayed upstairs rather than go down since crowds got you nowhere. I found a little haven in this library to read in and, it must be owned, to *rest*. Fifteen miles of road was something to be got over in its own right before setting out on the next. I was addressing myself to the unbelievable vacuum in my reading and unearthed in myself a great taste for the French culture until one day I took down from the shelves *Jane Eyre* to find for the first time in my life the story of a woman written by a woman and understood by a woman. The shock was like the crack of a branch splitting. What were women written of by men but men's ideas of a woman dressed up? Jane Eyre had the authenticity of women in the Bible. The Bronte prose I thought was the kind I could write myself given the mind to. True, I was and still am an inordinately slow reader, you could almost say retarded, but what went in stayed in.

In class I ran into trigonometry but didn't run far, baffled from page one. The little math I must have had to squeeze me through matric was burnt up in the fire of imagery. Vaporised into the metaphysical. Instead of working with specific symbols of number I was seeing proportions and related dimensions in terms of emotions and forces. Too bad. During math period I sat busily idle but dear dear me it was boring and I didn't hand in one paper but since it was Mr. Morice on the job there was adequate tolerance there. Homework was out, right out; not even excuses. It was the kind of time when youth turns delinquent, and I probably did in mind, or jumps the fence and runs but I don't remember thinking it. After all, exposed to the drama of vigorous young minds I was making headway of a kind; inadvertently I was flexing a faculty that any art demands, the discipline of observation.

But that came hard to me, observation; being more of the breed of performer, I had no audience value. I didn't follow too avidly the love-affairs of others, the traffic of eyes in the corridor, who partnered whom on the tennis lists, notes changing hands in class, the gentlemanly manoeuvring of Hynds and Buchanan for the favours of Jancy, Penelope exchanging Buchanan for Van den Hoven, the general stampede for Dorabella or the non-stop skirmishing of Cullen and Miss Cumberland. I was not conditioned to live other people's lives. As a matter of fact I'd fallen in love with the botany master, Mr. Evergreen, as we examined the behaviour of cells beneath the microscope. Not that he approached anywhere near my ideal, he was anything but the Sheik of Araby and had no reputation for abducting women and whirling them off to his tent in the desert, but the biology of plants roused extraordinary thoughts in my virgin mind making my blood run backwards; it was beyond me to relate these two concepts of love, biology by day and tents by night. Obviously there were flaws in my thinking could I put my finger on them. In the meantime Mr. Evergreen kept himself to himself as though we were not there with him and spoke only technicalities. His real name was Mr. Bird if you want to know.

The term wheeled by like a bike with a puncture up the hill to the autumn holidays. Oh no doubt I'd learnt a lot of something or other if not what I'd been meant to. "There's only one thing wrong with that school," I told Norm. "I'm still at it."

As the days shortened towards June and winter spread on the snowy ranges, as the frosts whitened up no plans for a cosy future could help my hands and feet. I didn't go in for blaming people or circumstances either but my chilblains were just too unfair, when they warmed up in the afternoon and itched. That was torture. Mr. Morice took pity on me and I stayed at his place for a week but his young girl-wife and twin babies lost their privacy and I myself nearly died. I loved the pretty bedroom and the imaginative meals, lunch cut too, but give me the road any day.

I advertised for board and found myself next in a little innocent cottage with a blue garden and a pink lady with daisy-white hair, the kind you see ladies sewing on tea-clothes with needle and coloured thread; fancywork we called it, dream fare only. In the same street as Jessica's home. I put in one night there and the next day at school I showed Jessica every single one of the flea-bites on my body. Her mother gave aid on behalf of Jessica and the next thing I'd moved in to their place and was sharing Jessica's privacy in a double bed. But oh the lovely food on that white starched cloth, tender mutton chops,

white potato and bright green peas. And, of all things, sitting down
at table in the evening, clean and not tired, doing my homework like
other people.

The miracle of walking round the corner to school on the frosted
morning grass, the wonder of walking home. It was glorious to wander
downtown again as we had when young in Hastings, seeing the display
windows and reflecting on people. Jessica's parents were tall slender and
dark English people and liked me to play each night after tea; Jessica
practised in the morning. But sharing the same bed was awful for us
both, you could play a tennis match in the space we kept between us
and it was a relief when I went home each weekend. But I wasn't in
the position to walk out this time as I had done from the board Ashton
had found in the first place, from Mr. Morice's in the second place and
from the little pink Lady of the Fleas in the third place. I was caged
like the young hare Ashton had caught and over which, when he
rolled upon it in bed, he'd dropped some hard tears. Like the wild bird
he brought home but which flew away. In any case this was costing a
pound a week and had a foreseeable time-limit.

During the winter the school ball came up, programmes and all. I
shortened a dress of Gracie's which was a rose crepe de chine and went
along with Jessica. Sitting at the side wondering many things we
watched the pretty ones dancing with the boys. Jancy was far and away
the belle of the ball, her hair still in two plaits and her figure as supple
as a green twig in spring. Burke Buchanan, alias John Barrymore,
monopolised her but Batty Hynds had an innings too. I don't think
any other boy managed a look-in. That face, all things to all men,
should have brought a monarch down off his throne or at least launched
a thousand ships, yet many years later I was shown a photo in a pro-
vincial magazine of her wedding to someone less than royalty.

Penelope didn't miss a dance but there seemed no one sheik in particular and she only had one with her has-been Buchanan with whom
she shared eyes in the corridor last year. Her honey hair, brown eyes
and Cupid smile combination seemed to knock Van den Hoven for
six but she wasn't rushed like Jancy. One day I saw her downtown
with Van den Hoven, the cricket hero and every girl's dream, much
taller than she and swaggering a bit; both prefects walking side by
side in public and in broad daylight, in uniform too. How did they
get away with that? They both had their hands in their coat pockets
in a show of seeming indifference as though their being together was
obligation rather than choice which was not convincing. Penelope was
seriously playing prefect trying to look severe, her thick hair pinned

down by force with hair-clips like railway lines, as though she needed the severity to deny how she felt.

Those two only I remember after all these years, along with Jessica sitting silent beside me. There must be a moral to all this somewhere but it eludes me; something like How to Be Kind Though Pretty, How to Be Happy Though Careful or Are Men Worth It.

Mr. Evergreen didn't look my way and danced with an unspectacular wife a lot but, after supper, with Jessica and me still holding our empty programmes, Mr. Thompson of 5B English, the pale one of the amber eyes, he crossed the floor and walked our way so Jessica brushed back her hair, smoothed her new dress and prepared to rise while I looked the other way. But it was I he addressed, bowing slightly, "May I have the pleasure of this waltz?"

"Yes Sir."

I found his step in time but it could have been more flowing, yet his beat was unerring. We danced together not too badly and he named the music as we glided, "Three O'clock in the Morning."

"Yes Sir."

"Very pretty song."

"Yes Sir." That was all we said and it was the only dance Mr. Thompson had. Decades ago, let me see . . . forty or fifty years ago and I'm still wondering why he chose me.

At the time I thought my one dance was a very good score.

Jessica's parents were charitable and brainy people, her scholarship did not come from nowhere, but there's a time to come and a time to go. There were nights when I didn't sleep one single solitary wink on my edge of that bed. Both of us were learning the hard way the meanings of, and the shades of difference between the words "proximity" and "propinquity." I stung for the privacy of my real home, the road; equally my real school. You could say the road was my habitat.

I felt it was a shame that Jessica could not avoid being seen actually walking to school with me, I didn't like it myself, but we made the best of it conversing in Latin and French. Never a quarrel split between us. Looking back I marvel at the charity of that girl. I didn't want to dilute her chances for university scholarship as I had (I believed) diluted Daphne's matric chances, not again. Charity and brains must have made a wonderful teacher of Jessica. However, as soon as we got to school her Latin affix, Lila, would be waiting at the gate and we went our separate ways.

This might look bleak but it wasn't; not with youth, physical strength, dreams and with faith in me at home, you couldn't say anything was bleak. The resilience, resources of girls in their teens, *very* much tougher than boys. Put it this way: the endurance. Don't be misled by soft lips and sighs. There's always something new round the corner especially after a run of bleakness and around this corner of winter spring was almost here. Spring is impatient in New Zealand; before their calendar time the immigrant flowers from the seasons of Europe like freesia, japonica and jonquil split the shot and break ahead like runners in a race, leaving the natives behind by months, clematis, rata, pohutukawa and orchid. In the botany class we were already studying the dynamics of rising sap.

Arriving on foot with the crowds at the gates I'd witness scenes I would not have otherwise: here for the looking each morning were Cullen and Miss Cumberland walking side by side wheeling their different bikes, hers a woman's, his a man's, smiling and talking to each other as though there were no generation of years between them, more than twenty . . . thirty? Whatever it was they held in their hands they were decorously frank about it, if anything they delighted to reveal it. As delighted as I was to record it. A loving drawing I made in India ink for the form magazine of these two with their bikes, not overlooking the smiles on their faces or Miss Cumberland's blue-spot blouse. Was she put out? She carried this drawing on her arm from classroom to staffroom for anyone to see, even the caption of a song from Shakespeare she'd taught us: "In the springtime, in the spring-time,/the only pretty pretty ring time . . ."

The road and I again. My habitat.

I doubt if I missed one day at school except for those enforced on me by Caesar for recording on my desk that I'd passed this way, three years ago. I didn't get sick and I didn't wag it, but one morning after a major effort to get there I found the entire school deserted, the buildings locked. Where were they all? No one had told me. I hadn't thought the day would come when I would miss them. It must have been the caretaker who said the Prime Minister, Mr. Massey, had died in the night, that the nation was in mourning. That was 1925.

Instead of a day's rest in the library upstairs I had to turn round and do the whole thing again now. As I watched him furling the flag half-mast it got through to me that I was tired. Right through. Bones, flesh, clothes, hair, bike, shoes, legs, body, brain and soul, the lot. Even with my country toughness I was tired. It seemed I'd not really known till this moment. I mounted my bicycle homeward.

In this last lap of the journey through secondary the terrain was too steep and rough and I sagged from the sweat and dust on my soul. When Ashton took visible form on Friday night I said, "Ash, the road is beating me."

"Eh?" reflectively. He looks out the window to the Tararuas. "And what d'you know about that."

Ashton did not like to be caught short of an idea and this time he acquired for me a small motorbike, a baby Triumph. Unheard of in those days, a girl on a motorbike was of scandal proportions whereas I was anything but after attention: I didn't want Caesar to be reminded I existed. I rode round the back streets to avoid the gasps and stares. As for the big boys at school on their pushbikes they were out to beat me do-or-die down Renall Street, their great hairy bare knees whizzing to starboard but my top speed was 30 m.p.h., and so was theirs but not 31. Talk about touch-and-go but those boys never beat me in spite of many a photo finish. A marvellous little bike that, cheeky and loud-throttled, I loved it. Don't say "horse" to me again. A rapport sprang up between me and that Triumph absent between me and Creamy. I could tell you some tales about that bike on that road, about gear levers, throttles, carburetors and where did that screw fall off from? The uncased carburetor was exposed to dust and weather and sometimes the lid fell off and there was the benzine with no protection. The temptations of the hills . . . that day when Ashton following on his great Harley without my knowing saw me ripping down the hill of Gentle Annie as though the brake had fallen off. "But," when caught, "I had to come down the hill full-speed to get up this other side."

"I feel inclined to box your ears."

"Don't you hit me, Ashton. I'll tell Mumma."

"I'm as like as not to put you back on a horse, you devil."

The trouble was not all with me, however, but with Marmie too who'd sneak the bike out of the shed after school and ride it all over the place, use up the benzine, fiddle with the engine, puncture a tyre or lose the lid of the carburetor so that when it stalled on the road and wouldn't go, *couldn't* go, Ashton had to lend me his own motorbike, a thundering Harley-Davidson, so the thing was to keep it upright for if it fell over it was too heavy to lift up again. Mind you it did have a stand for the back wheel you kick into position to stop it falling. I kept it upright, I dunno how. A very heavy machine but it had a nice character, gentle and pacific like a heavyweight man who nevertheless dances with grace, like the burly Hynds dancing with the china Jancy. And did that Harley-Davidson send the boys at school.

I had plenty of attention if for the wrong reasons. Motorbikes are sensational people.

For the hundredth time Ashton fixed the baby Triumph and screwed a lock on the shed but I never knew a small boy who couldn't find a way and the next thing Marmaduke rode it all the way into Masterton where he had a spectacular accident which joined the canon of family stories elaborated each time it was told. The last time I heard it, one wheel was on top of a shop verandah, the other in the foyer of a distant hotel and the engine in the Lansdowne River. And that was a sad day. I'd felt very close to that little machine which supplied the best excuses for no-homework the class had ever gasped at. But the motorbike answer to the road was proving more expensive than board in town though I be-

Rangitumau—Sylvie, Norma, Marmie, Mumma and Vadne

came good at drawing motorbikes. And that's the end of the story called "My Motorbike" or, as I'd begin in class, "My brother Marmaduke..."

Next thing I'm boarding in town with some more charming English people with my own bed and room; Mr. and Mrs. Staples and their two sons round my age. They were people not glued up with ortho-doxy but who lived flexibly and freely and with feeling. I was softly at ease. Funny thing. How was it that the two homes where I'd felt at ease and had been received with grace were not New Zealand but English people from the heart of civilisation? Work that out. The Staples were full of music and the two boys practised the piano too; the younger of them, Charlie, was a natural and led a fine band later on they say. Overnight I discovered I was quite all right and not a pariah at all, away from school I mean.

I could change my white collars now and keep my shoes clean. I loosened out my hair and wore a ribbon and loitered on street corners to watch and dream. Round that headland on the highway through the teens the rough stuff gave way to a benign plateau with water from the streams and fruit on the trees and shady wayside glades.

In its context the school was a good one, as good as it could be I'll say. No school can outstrip its head-master. No work can be better than the one who does it. Dr. Roydon did his sincerest best as he saw it, playing safe within the letter of the law, in accord with the board of governors and with the society which spawned the school. If some of us came out of it crippled for life, as some of us did, me included, it's futile to blame the Head; or the school, the board or the society: it's the same old vil-lain again—circumstance.

Ashton during the motorbike days

We were encouraged to use some of our sixth-form subjects for Teachers D certificate while we were about it and while we had the chance. The other girls were doing it so I did too. I had a wonderful chance to attend the convent during school hours for lessons in music theory, which raises an interesting issue: young New Zealand teachers were required to cover both music and blackboard drawing in their training, still are I think, which I've not found overseas. In my work at North American universities I've had to budget for large areas of time to acquaint the students and teachers with which end of a brush to hold and how to sing simple tunes and recognise poetry, whereas in New Zealand this goes through automatically. Which makes me think that that country was, is, the real place where my work could have rooted rather than in foreign countries, given one other condition which is missing: an enlightened philosophy.

At the convent the nun herself was severe and cold but she found me an attentive pupil. I was stunned to discover that a written note had a mind and a life of its own, a character with meaning and authority indispensable in the context of a bar. In the ensuing exam I made only 83 percent but that would be the math factor in music theory. To think that from math arose the thrill in the blood when you heard the notes played. Fancy being alive sixteen years before knowing this. It was a tall firm clear direction-finder in the flood which withstood any current. Also we got our Royal Life-saving certificates at the baths up to silver and gold medal standard and that's something you can do with in most societies, especially for an island people.

There was, however, one widespread and tragic omission in the schools those days and that was vocational guidance, which abounds now. It would have saved me, for one; had the curriculum noted and cultivated what strengths I had rather than focus on my weaknesses, for instance got me into a commercial art studio, I'd not have had to pay so self-destructively for the fulfilment of myself and my work. Oh there are many who can tell you of the steel straight-jacket of tradition clamped upon the souls of the wild ones with penalties for variation, the wild ones themselves declare it, and you got a staid, sedated and timid society. Not just New Zealand's; I've known others where the race is less to the swift than to the conforming. I'd rather see education falling down and getting up again in the open-slather of experiment as in the United States than playing it safe within the letter of the law. The concern of New Zealand for safety, its crippling caution.

With Christmas holidays on the nearing horizon as well as the close of our schooling a subtle glamour veined the air. The sixth had its own accumulating excitement of apprehension and anticipation. What was going to happen to us? What would we do, where were we going, where would we be this time next year, this time in two years, five years, twenty? What would we buy with our education in the outside world: success, embraces and kisses or tears behind the door? We were waiting on a station for the train to come in, hearing the whistle of the engine in the distance. All would get on this train and go. Soon would be meetings and partings and traumatic ultimatums along with starry radiances. Too late now to retrace our steps to prepare ourselves better than we had done.

Rather dramatically an essay competition burst upon us for the whole of the Wairarapa secondary schools and the prize was two guineas. With two guineas you could buy material for a dress and still pay your fare to Wellington. In we sprang again, most of the sixth and some of the fifths. From the choice of subjects I settled for Helen Keller myself, the deaf-mute and blind scholar who succeeded against all odds. In-stinctively I understood Helen Keller. I wrote thirteen swift closely lined pages in cramped-up script which I set about learning by heart. The only one, I believed, who could beat me was Portia. Since I couldn't write better I had to write more. This essay was supervised by a new woman on staff called Miss Bethel, a small lady made up of energy and smiles, a change from Miss Cumberland queening it. Being new, Miss Bethel didn't know I was persona non grata and took me the same as the others, as though I were still like other people which astonished me, but Miss Cumberland still hovered round.

A picture unveils here of a sunny morning and a few of us preparing outside. We'd tilted back our chairs against the red brick wall. Penelope is sitting with Jessica-and-Lila, the three of them hearing one another, and I'm on my own apart. Miss Cumberland appears at the top of the steps and takes a look at us. Her black gown has greened a bit on the shoulders, the usual books are on one arm and a strand of grey hair is astray. When she comes down the steps the other three look up expectantly and smile but she passes and comes to me. "And how is it going, Sylvia?"

"It's all right, Miss Cumberland."

"Do you have enough?"

"Too much I think."

"You've chosen well. Helen Keller is certainly a subject you can wax lyrical about."

I wince at the cliché "wax lyrical" but you can hardly correct your teacher. Her dress has repeating stripes, not outrageous in colour but muted like mauve, grey-green, grey-blue and fawn though you can't see much beneath the gown. She returns without addressing the others and I'm left with my thirteen pages of Keller and the haunting bars of the song, "In the springtime, in the springtime, the only pretty pretty ring time, When birds do sing hey ding a ding ding . . ."

Along with the heat was a shimmer in the air above the melting tar in the streets downtown, a sparkling on the top of the water in the baths and a smouldering feeling at school. The days were long-drawn-out violin notes with a built-in tremolo as though telling us news of the future. You sensed tension upstairs when Miss Cumberland was there, preparing Cullen and Jessica for university scholarship though it seemed to be Cullen who was schooling his teacher rather for some other test unspecified. Instead of promoting his scintillating ideas she would juggle with them, trying to quench him as well as herself. Their eyes clasped across the desks, clutched in abrupt encounter. Emotion sweated, you could smell it.

Beneath her sober old gown was another new blouse of white muslin and pink spots linking with the new pink spots in her cheeks, middle-aged platitudinous cheeks, and you noticed the flaw in one front tooth which we took in our stride before.

As the last days biked hairy-kneed up the final grade to the terminal, Caesar came up the stairs one morning, his steps announcing him beforehand like the tramp of Fate. Someone whispered, "Is this a dagger I see before me, the handle towards my hand? Come let me clutch thee!" He brought with him the Higher Leaving results, a deliberately spoken list of names, and mine was not there, not even at the end as an afterthought. It was a box on the ears. In town on Saturday morning when Mumma came in on the service car to buy the family groceries she ambushed Dr. Roydon mid-main-street where the tar was the softest and the traffic going by. I witnessed this. The small tweed-skirted isosceles triangle shaping up to his heavy thicksetness, both of them short, with the cars dodging this way and that. "The overall average of this pupil" versus "You're too blind to see the daylight around you." It was he who disengaged first and when Mumma returned to the pavement she trembled on the kerb and panted, "The skunk."

With no Higher Leaving you'd think I'd see no point in attending the prize-giving evening in the Town Hall but if so you don't know me. Too jolly right I was going. I wouldn't miss for the world one of these large gatherings of the dressed-up populace with flowers in their hair and scent on their ears, not if I could help it. I could always let down the hem of Daphne's black velvet and dig out the white lace collar, I couldn't do anything about shoes though. But no one would see me so it would be all right. You wouldn't see me winning prizes on the stage. As for no one to sit with, what was new about that? True, none of my family would be there, why should they be? The big ones from Daphne up had not yet completed their own year's work out in the world somewhere, at home or abroad. As for Mumma and Puppa and Ashton, well I ask you. In fact I was glad none of them would be there to witness my no Higher Leaving. Mrs. Staples was nursing a sick friend but the boys had to be there. Charlie should get the prize for music.

I walked along through the summer evening towards the converging crowds, the colours of their dresses running into one another, light-heartedly enough though tentatively. Miss Cumberland would be there and maybe Veronica who'd long since been removed to a girls' boarding school which specialised in music and poshness and still didn't know of my exile status. She still only knew of the best in me whereas my previous ideal girls knew only the worst in me. The Town Hall filled and overflowed and I sat in the front row with the sixth just below the platform with the staff upon it in their impressive academic gowns, the audience behind us. Between me and the other girls was an empty seat and there was no one on my other side, which was as much my own choice as theirs I think. The boys were in the row behind us. Sir James Parr was the guest speaker, the minister of education who was good to Gracie when she left New Zealand forever.

I'd forgotten you had to go up to receive your sports certificates; for me the long jump, the ridiculous pole vault and the senior swimming championship and I made three trips to collect them, or two. To reach the steps to the stage I had to walk past the row of black velvet girls each time and, returning, do it again; the only route to the stage short of climbing up through the pot-plants and the flamboyant flowers. To make room they drew in their feet in shiny black patent leather shoes.

The academic lists explored the third forms before climbing through the fourths and fifths to the sixth. It's a long time ago now to be accurate in some things but I might have had a second in one of the three languages, or botany perhaps, then suddenly my name was called for the art prize. The last thing I expected since I hadn't attended Mr. Sweet's classes. Again the passing of this row of black velvet knees, going up and returning, making four times up, eight times passing both ways. I saw their shoes and their velvet knees.

They gave the music to somebody else, I forget who, it wasn't Charlie Staples but should have been. It was time for outside awards like the cup for the Territorial Cadets presented by some big military name, and the inter-school Rugby which won the most sustained applause of the evening, then the Wairarapa Essay and that's the place where the black velvet was smoothed and the patent leather shoes were stilled.

It was my own name spoken. Five. The steps to the stage. Sir James shook my hand and said, "Congratulations," then turning to the people he added, "Here's a girl who excels on both sides: sport and art." I suppose that's what I'm writing this book for, to record that. To me again, "Keep on writing," but my family didn't hear it. Returning to my place I passed for the tenth time the row of black velvet knees and the tucked-back shiny shoes. The Higher Leaving certificates came at the end but Sir James did not select any other for praise. This would make Mumma feel the year had been worth it.

Outside the Town Hall after in the tender summer night, anonymous in the flush of flashing people, I edged to the company of the grey brick wall and leaned my back against it. The heat was as sticky as blood or sap. The occasion had something in common with my first school ball when only one had danced with me but that one meaning more than a programme-ful. Tonight only one had talked to me, Sir James Parr, but what he'd said meant more than anything else. I'd tell Norma when I went home and I'd also tell Norma how they'd changed my two guinea essay prize to a box camera for fifteen shillings.

Engrossed in the crowds as I used to be when nine on the Hastings station, standing by the wall on that soft summer night on the outside looking in, it didn't hurt to know I was a vagabond. I had a feeling for vagabonds, wayfarers and wanderers having lived it as a way of life. Being apart you were less accountable. But Veronica was a long way behind the action and wended through the throng towards me and touched my hand and kissed my face in the most normal way, and with a word of praise like other people. Her dress had a sumptuous flower pattern, blue, green and pink and her scent . . . the scent I reel to it now. Then she rejoined her people waiting for her.

But Miss Cumberland didn't seek me out and say I'm delighted with you sixth-form girls, or she didn't find me. I didn't see her. I didn't see Miss Cumberland for twenty years. On that day in Masterton twenty years on, "Yes," from the dairy lady, "Miss Cumberland still lives in the little white house in Hope Street. Her hair is white now of course and her mother is gone and she's still teaching but . . . oh yes yes. There'd be no Hope Street without Miss Cumberland."

But when I went there to lay at her doorstep as a tribute to her teaching my international fame what she said was not "I'm delighted with your novel *Spinster*," but "Now tell me, Sylvia: where is that wonderful Daphne?"

That's what they all say.

And that was the end of my youth's education to the tune of fourteen schools. All told, I attended eleven primary schools, three secondaries, one teachers training college, one art school (briefly), taught in nine, trained teachers and students in two universities in North America and was funded by the U.S. Office of Education. My subject, guess what? The Variations in Children.

A few days were left up there at school when people sit round and pack up and talk, exchange addresses and squander ardent goodbyes, but I slipped away at that point unsung and must have done the road home for the last time though I don't remember that part. And what shall I write here as I consign this memory back to the darkness it arose from? Nothing really. Only, that was the school where I learnt excuses, and that's it for what it's worth.

Bideford is filling up as the big ones backfire for the Christmas holidays. I must be nearly a big one myself now, almost seventeen and never been kissed. Soon will be the time for me too to look back over my shoulder to the little ones left at home and to help with one of them. Not this year but next I ought to take Norma with me.

In this watercolour of Bideford in summer you see the leaning rose-arch with reminiscent roses, unpruned for many decades but extravagantly scented, rambling absent-mindedly as old folk do. In its shade Puppa sits in his wheelchair with his Bible and pipe as frail as the arch itself and no less romantic, and the spaniel at his feet, Skye. From the arch you can see the seeding grasses, an occasional long-lost bloom and the never-again garden. The house sits squat in the middle of it held up by overgrown bushes and willpower, across the paddock the rheumatic school, and the whole encircled by trees, high-reaching natives. On the isolated plateau the hot air barely circulates; the family a pulse of life in a vacuum.

It becomes crammed, the boxy cottage, with family come back from the world, their clothes new and their faces older. Gracie returns from two years in Fiji with a repertoire of new stories with an alien content, a ukulele, several of the prettiest Fijian songs, a sophisticated love-letter and a case of pineapples and settles down on the floor with Daphne in their favorite corner all over again to their interminable love-affairs; "And you won't believe this, Daph, but you know what he said then?" Whisper, a clap of laughter. Muriel who loved Mumma sang for her Mumma's favorite songs, including "The End of a Perfect Day." Lionel is at the piano most of the time with his M.Sc. and violin letters behind him, composing a piece of music or singing a song for us little ones: "I plays the banjo better now than those who taught me to, for they just plays for all the world but I just plays for you." Ashton, between making Mumma and Puppa laugh, rolls in great logs from the hill and puts in days of chopping them; I'm trying to sew myself a dress of dusk-rose cotton . . . "Sylvie's Paris fashions." Norma is Mumma's right-hand man and usually milks the cow before she gravitates to her soul-mate Gracie to learn the ukulele and the songs while Marmie and Vadne eddy about and the spaniel Skye mopes. Not one of us is missing.

It's time for me to get going on commercial art in some advertising firm in Wellington as an apprentice. A life of painting all the way, wearing bohemian smocks. I dream of a room to myself in the city with just enough for one: a bed, table, stove, an easel and something to wash myself in. I'll loiter as long as I like in the streets in the mysterious shine of the evening when the rain multiplies the lights of the shops and blurs the moving faces. It's time . . .

But dreams cost money. Urgently I start writing a book meant to be like *Jane Eyre*; I do it in pencil in the limited privacy of a back room by candlelight at night or in the historied schoolroom by day but there's an old organ there which I can't leave alone, having found in some torn music the Dead March from *Saul* and Lionel's Rachmaninoff, said to be the hammering of a man nailed alive in his coffin, and I make high thunder of these. Also Daphne comes upon my tattered pages hidden in a box in a tree, reads them aloud to everyone gratis and pronounces them "sentimental piffle" . . . I bet they were . . . so I destroy my juvenilia and when nearly twenty years later my first book, *Spinster*, came out to be acclaimed and filmed, and I sent Daphne a copy, I wrote on the inscription page, "To Daphne, in memory of my sentimental piffle twenty years ago." To which she answered, "You should have put me in it, Sylv." Well, I have in this one, Daph. "Call it," she said, "*I Accuse!*"

But I dodge my turns at the dishes and am frequently chased from the house. The best escape route is from the front door, down the garden path and slip past Puppa beneath the rose-arch since Mumma in full chase can't do the same being of different proportions and by the time she does I am well away, halfway down the lane to the river. But one day when escaping, instead of chasing me full-tilt down the path or hurling rhetoric from the door she drew herself up in awe and pride and told the others at hand, "I've just chased an artist out of the house."

I'd hear them saying that no profession known to God or Man had the advantages of teaching; only six hours a day from nine till three, holidays three times a year with other people slaving and the salary not to be sneezed at. You'd even get paid for these holidays; besides, I heard, "It's the only thing Sylv is qualified for." But the last thing in God's heaven or earth I wanted to be was a teacher. If I had one hate it was the inside of a schoolroom. I'd finished with schools as from now on and forever. Yet I did begin to see "the bloody profesh . . ."

"Don't use that word in my presence," from Mumma.

". . . The profession then," in the meantime at least, as the one sure way of getting to Wellington where I could find the studio work I wanted. Left behind in Bideford moping and hoping would get you nowhere. Just for a little while then, a little, until I climbed on my chosen highway, so I sent my application form to the Wellington education department and startlingly soon I was appointed as a pupil teacher to a school called Wellington South, at which Puppa hurrayed from the rose-arch and Mumma said, "Didn't I tell you?" Then Ashton plonked a straw hat on his father's black curling hair so that he looked like a villainous swagger.

I couldn't believe it myself. Here I was getting to Wellington under my own power and was going to be paid for the effort, seven pounds a month . . . or nine. "Think of it, Norm. No more high school."

Her blue eyes, white face and dark ringlets.

"And Norm," I add, "no more road."

"I've got my turn on the road next year."

"Don't you ever go to *that* dreadful school."

"All right, Sylv, I won't. I wish I could come with you, Sylv."

"Not this year but I'll take you next year." We whisper like Gracie and Daphne. Without question I am one of the big ones now.

Norma says, "I'll pass Standard 6 and come next year."

"You'll have only one year on the road, Norm. In Wellington all you do is walk along the pavement or get on a tram. Next year, Norm eh?"

Mumma laughed a lot these days, sitting on a chair, knees astride, her hands upon them and looking from one face to another; a gay willing laugh with her stomach shaking, vaulting the peaks of disappointments and breaking over bitternesses. She'd become a child at the drop of a joke. A marvellous audience really, on call at all times. Puppa did a lot of laughing too under the frail roses. He only shouted when left alone in bed in his austere room when Mumma would make the tea and pass a cup to the nearest child saying, "Here, take y'father his tea and tell him to stop his shouting." I see an evening that summer as the light encounters the darkness, when suitcases being packed tell of coming departures and a sense of momentousness shooting the shadows before we all disperse. Music, laughing and crying and talk high-pitches over the clatter of dishes, the tears and stars in candlelit eyes. As steps pass to and fro outside Puppa's room his shouting is part of it, calling each name down the spectrum of the entire family: "Muriel, Gracie, Ashton, God-damn-it; can no one hear me? Lionel, Daphne,

Sylvia, God-curse-it; someone come to me. Norma, Marmaduke, Evadne, confound you; who am I? Only the father."

Mumma passes to me his cup of tea. "Here, take y'father his tea and tell him to stop his shouting." So I stop walking past the door and take his tea into his room but already he's stopped his shouting. He's dead. His black hair curling merrily.

Some hours later Mumma makes the tea again in the kitchen and pours two cups as usual, passes one to a child as usual and says the same as usual, "Here, take y'father his tea and tell him to . . ."

I turn seventeen; an unpolished unpainted unkissed seventeen in a dusk-rose dress. Out there in the world a voice is shouting to one of its freckled children. Sylvia, God-damn-it, can you not hear me? Sylvia, God-curse-it, come out to me. Sylvia, confound you, who am I? Only the wide wide world.

First stop Wellington.

# I I

1 9 2 6 - 1 9 3 2

WELLINGTON   It was February 1926 and time for me to go to my first job in Wellington. I'd finished making what I called my dusk-rose dress and I cut off my hair in a buster cut. Surprisingly, once cut, my hair took to curling and I all but changed character. I shed the hangdog feel of the road and my spirit lifted. Mind you, I still had my freckles and did try to diet but I can't say that got me anywhere.

Also Puppa was dead. But I don't recall grief; shock, rather, fear of death and the grave. That any one of us should dramatically vanish from the stage like that, leaving no understudy to play his part, and take on a new role deep in a grave . . . well, it was like too tall a story he himself was telling: "Once upon a time when I was a man with all my family round me, guess what I did?"

"What?"

"I unexpectedly died."

"Oh you did not, Puppa."

I didn't believe it. I don't recall missing Puppa till much later on in life. I didn't visit his grave for forty years, afraid I might find that death was true.

He'd been buried in Masterton. Even with the help of the sexton, and we had to find him first, that took most of the morning only to find that his family coat-of-arms engraved in colour on the slab was all but obliterated and confused by grasses, almost erased by the years. And nothing came to me from beneath the ground. You can't find the spirits of people at their graves; you're far more likely to encounter them in the places where they'd lived and had felt.

Francis Ashton-Warner

1861–1926

Abide With Me.

I felt his presence there plainly and the grief of loss. Now that I'm well acquainted with death, however, and with many a grave, I do at last believe and I have this sadness when I think of him. That new girl of seventeen in Wellington she didn't know how to.

The thing to do then was to get on with my living. I got board at the YWCA hostel in Brougham Street where my sisters had been before me and shared a big room with five shopgirls. Talk about fun in that dorm. As I got to know them better I slipped into an act or two to amuse them till the matron developed a habit after tea of suddenly swinging open the door and demanding, "What's going on in here?" One night, however, after she'd gone I stepped out into the hall then swung open the door on the girls like the matron and demanded, "What's going on in here?" But she'd dodged back and caught me in the act. "So it's you again, Sylvia."

There were shopgirls, office girls and dental clinic nurses in training but no pupil teachers. Among the dental nurses was the best-brought-up girl in the world since Penelope whose mother was sending her new dresses all the time with shoes to match: Deodonné. Every Sunday she dressed up and played the piano in the lounge, at the right time in the right place, though she was tied to her music. I remember her because she beat me at swimming in the baths one Saturday, the first time I'd been beaten in my life in the water. In the dressing shed she admitted she'd come fifth in the national championships, which was not lost on me. I mean, wasn't *I* going to be the national champion, yet here was someone who'd come only fifth leaving me two lengths behind. At the least it brought me down a peg, as Mumma would say, but at most it jeopardised one of my chosen routes. All very quick. Dear dear me.

The matron, Miss Deadline, was small dark sharp-eyed temperamental sensy authoritative and agile and, to hold down sixty-odd girls not long peeled off from home, I must say she needed to be.

And here I was at last out in the wide wide world on my own two feet. True, I didn't mean to be a teacher for long, but I had managed to get to the capital city, hadn't I, under my own power and I was actually earning a salary. I'd see about the studio dream in time.

Wellington South school was on the way to Island Bay. Leaving the Basin Reserve by tram you rattled and crashed through Newtown, turned up the hill to the right, and the school was at the top. I'd say it is still there on account of the native timber and the early workmanship. A large spare muscular building with hard-boned joints and bulging biceps like a bushwhacker who fells forest trees for the mills, you could smell the sweat on it. One of the first things I registered was the history in the outside steps, recording the imprint of passing feet and the half-century of ocean weathers. The cracks in the wood told their tale and the heads of the worn nails shone. It arrested me: the door of a school again, by God.

Inside my fifteenth school I met another headmaster all over again but he was a man I don't mind remembering. No intimidating man-of-destiny like Dr. Roydon but comfortable with the mildness of a good colonial who knew his place in the Empire. A squat man, grey-haired, with a carpenter's shoulders and the lines on his face veering upward. He had this air of easiness you see in people who've given up taking life seriously.

I'd been appointed on my academic record alone with no interview and he told me briefly I'd been placed in the infant department because of my drawing and music, which looked favorable on the face of it, but as I waited a moment in the hall for him with the loud school world encompassing me once more, the lofty ceilings tossing round echoes, the soaring abstract trebles of hundreds of children flooding like water, teachers, intent, darting among them, some with high heels and some with men's shoes, the whole whirling sound obbligatoed by thousands of steps, it didn't look favorable beneath the face of it and I hated teaching on sight.

I walked beside him across the playground to the separate infant block to be delivered to some more grey hair. Here again was the senior single woman whom nice people described as a Maiden Lady and sour ones labelled Spinster. Miss Little was big, a tall elegant person with a large secret bosom and a stomach to match tapering off into the straight long legs of a race-horse. Grey the length and girth of her from hair and eyes to grey silk smock, though her skin had the pale texture of far northern peoples and her lips were a virgin pink.

She was Scotch. She had the clipped haughty accent of imperiousness while slightly forward teeth clipped it even more, so that you didn't follow all she said. A tall grey emblem of authority, regimentation, discipline, efficiency, obedience, order, the Great British Empire and the All-Red Route. It takes a colonial to register this fully. From the first history book I'd ever opened I was familiar with the whole presence: the Soldiers of the Queen, m'lads, Britannia Rules the Waves. Like the headmaster beside me, Mr. Rankinfile, I cogged into position automatically and at once.

Mr. Rankinfile handed me over to her like an offering of homage. Once a colonial always a colonial.

She told me to orpen the windows and t' prepare monning tea at hoff post ton.

"Does she mean," I whisper to the other new pupil teacher, "make the tea *at* half past ten or have it made *by* half past ten?"

Ellen is easy. "Ask her," she smiles.

"No, you ask her."

But Ellen is already spinning round setting out paper and pencils as though born to it. In fact Ellen had come up through this school and through this very infant room. As for the monning tea at or by hoff post ton, that may have been the first of the crises when it was late but I don't really remember.

At playtime I met another pupil teacher who, having already put in a year, had a class of her own and was called Avis or Mavis or something like that and wore anaesthetising scent. By way of opening the conversation I said, "My father died last week."

She heard this and countered, "My boy sailed for England yesterday."

Impressed, "Why?"

"He's been accepted at Sandhurst to train for the army and will be away four years. When he comes back we'll get married."

"Are you engaged to be married, Avis?"

"I am a bit."

Ellen didn't say she had a boy and I didn't either. Avis was well in the lead. She continued immediately to tell us all about this boy of hers at Sandhurst, nor did she, in my time there, ever cease to tell me about him nor fail to bring his letters to school to prove it which she kept under the top of her henna dress where girls also keep their breasts. She remained so full of boy you couldn't get near the real Avis whereas with Ellen you could walk right into her mind and stay there as long as you liked, as long as you needed shelter, put it that way. But neither became my ideal girl, a concept I'd grown out of, and it was plain I was finished with crushes on teachers. A relief to clear the deck. I couldn't see myself falling for Miss Little. Or for Miss Deadline at the hostel for that matter.

A large light hygienic room full of the reception class, fifty or sixty new five-year-olds. Health was the first subject in the morning. On one of the first few mornings it took the form of how to eat an orange. All the little children sat on their chairs with their hands clasped behind them, Miss Little stood tall and grey and certain of herself mid-front-stage holding the orange while Ellen and I, hands clasped on knees, sat either side of her, for symmetry I suppose.

The difficult Scotch accent was not immediately accessible to me never mind the children but as she began peeling the orange I did pick up enough of it to learn that you don't eat the white tissue of an orange, children. See this white part here, the core? That's the part you don't eat. You only eat this juicy part. In fact a drop or two of juice dripped into her palm at which I thought I heard sixty-odd drops of saliva plopping on the floor. Right or wrong I learnt it anyway so presumably the children did also and it must have been Miss Little who ate the orange for lunch as I didn't see it around any more. Since that time whenever I've seen a Maori pick up an orange and eat the thing whole, skin, flesh, core, pips, the lot, I've remembered Miss Little. What price health.

She ran the mornings like clockwork. The high heavy windows had to be opened by something-to-nine each morning with a pole with a hook on the end. I could manage this all right, the thing could be done, but at this time she'd like to take me over the children's songs for the day on the piano while Ellen was doing her preparation like lightning so that I'd still be on the window job while the children were filing in, marching in I mean, and there was no reason to believe Miss Little liked this.

Also there came a day quite soon when I was given a handful of children for story, which I illustrated on the blackboard as I went along, threading in a song, and the next thing I heard it back from Gracie who'd heard it from a colleague that when Miss Little attended an infant mistress meeting in the city she told them she had "a gem" who could both play and draw. No mention of a gem who could teach. Word got round at school and in no time other infant teachers on staff took to borrowing Miss Little's new pupil teacher to take their own class stories, which fooled me into pride briefly, but they'd come to see me about it before school while the windows remained tight shut like grim lips till the bell at nine. None of which was Miss Little's idea of clockwork. It was hard on Miss Little.

Neither was there any joy in doing other teachers' stories; they so valued my drawing they wanted to keep it for another time so that instead of my having the lovely wide firm expanse of blackboard to range about on they'd pin up lengths of flimsy brown paper from the roll which lurched under my chalk and tore from the pins whereas in order to operate successfully anything at all the first imperative is a steady base, a position of strength to negotiate from, like a strong stool at a keyboard; and instead of the dark background on which to dramatise colours and shadows, here I was faced with anaemic brown paper. How can anyone make a point on brown paper? My drawing was dreadful where it could have been marvellous. And you know what they'd do then? When I'd finished they'd roll the whole thing up to use themselves another day in which case the chalk would rub and smudge unrecognisably. As for the infant room music, repeating jingles daily and having to pull up on demand, any ideas I might have

had about school being a place for my home-grown wares, they steadily
lost momentum.

Getting the kettle on in time for morning tea at ten thirty was turning out to be not my strong point either and Miss Little put Ellen on
that in time, in her own interests. Tough on Miss Little all this and
she continued turning more and more to Ellen, who was a simply
marvellous natural; her cool and her smiles and reliability, you should
see it. Some people don't get rattled, can't put a foot wrong and are to
be found in the right place at the right time. It was true that Miss
Little had a gem, though not the one she'd thought.

I didn't turn to Ellen; I could fail just as well on my own two feet.
I didn't want to learn from anyone. But Ellen did live only halfway
down the hill and she used to take me home sometimes after school
and feed the poor thing with cake and I'd play their nice new piano,
the latest love-hits. Ellen had big blue welcoming eyes, long fair hair
which she tied at the back with a ribbon and her main dress was navy
blue serge with a pleated skirt. For some reason I can't put my finger
on she seemed to be fond of me though it might have been hospitality
to one away from home, and maintained me as a friend for as long as
I was in Wellington. She was one of the shining ones, Miss Little's
real gem. And Ellen is her real name.

It would be appropriate here for me to rave on and on about the *dear*
little children, on and on and on, but all I remember of them is a
spread of small heads like a wall-to-wall carpet and no less quiet. Yet
the impression endures they were happy enough and that they enjoyed
their work, for Miss Little was a highly skilled teacher. You'd never
hear a sharp word to them or her voice raised and you'd never see her
hand lifted to them, yet they were obedient attentive and they fitted
into the required pattern of behaviour as though they asked no more.
The way those five-year-olds rolled off the other end of the assembly
line reading, writing, adding up, subtracting and obeying, to supply
in the future good little Soldiers of the Queen m'lads reminds me of
schools in India, which has also been under the British Crown.

It's a long time ago now but I'm grateful to Miss Little for her skill,
which brings up again the issue of the value of domestically unburdened
senior women working with children, I should say maritally un-
trammelled senior women like Miss Cumberland; they have everything
to give, and they give it. Ellen was already revealing these same
qualities. The only vindictive senior women I've found myself under

were night nurses in a hospital and those two were married. Terrifying people.

Yet I have to admit that from Miss Little's infant room I don't recall any one single child as an entity, with a personality of his own. Rather do they come up as a collective duplicate of Miss Little, which in the context of that time could well have been a good thing. At the least it defines a colonial people, at the most it identifies New Zealand; why the nation seems to show only two alternatives in national character— timidity on the one hand, authority on the other. Add the geographical isolation and you've got the picture, for what was there in the first place stays there unchangeably. Most of the best early teachers of this country were from the mother country, Home, busily and happily, sincerely, industriously moulding minds in the image of their origins. A Little Britain more British than Great Britain herself.

Except for Andrew. Yes, I remember one child. Much loved at home, much dressed at school, with a pale clear complexion suggesting his mother was beautiful and big shiny boots he couldn't cope with and who didn't seem to be used to looking after himself and who couldn't for the life of him conform. You'd hear him yelling in protest daily as though someone were taking from him something he valued. "Spoilt" was the word used. There was a freezing day when he wet his trousers and got himself into the boys' lavatory outside and took them off and didn't know what to do next and shrieked and shrieked, while I stood outside shivering not knowing what to do next either since it was immoral to go into the boys' lavatory and it would have shocked me to see a little boy with his trousers down who was not my brother. And the next thing Miss Little is here going for me. "Can't you see the child might get pneumonia?" striding in. She wrapped his over- coat round him and rang up his mother to bring more trousers and I'm grateful for that too now, having had little boys myself. Experi- ence and maturity and the condition to exercise them, you can't buy these at Woolworth's.

Of course Miss Little did finally ease the little chap into conformity but her firm hand was also gentle, I saw it; but it took months, by which time he'd become like the other fifty-nine, indistinguishable from them, and we were spared from any more yelling.

I hope I tried to fit in like Andrew and like Ellen too, not to over- look Avis of the letters in her dress, but if I did I couldn't make it, far from it. Andrew and I were a roadblock before Miss Little's invasion of the self, or put it this way, we were irregularities in the ranks of the regiment spoiling the look of the parade. I ought to be able to say, however fatuously, that I wished to be a credit to her, to be what she wanted me to be in order that she'd like me, but I can't see this from a vagabond of the roads. I had no thought of her liking me, only of how to get away.

Fancy that. From a first-rate infant room my first impressions remain brown paper, oranges, morning tea, windows and a little boy's conformity.

I'd go to the pictures with some of the shopgirls, there being no other pupil teachers in the hostel and the dental clinic nurses closed their ranks. Pupil teachers were drawn from the academic stratum but the dental nurses were hand-picked from the landed gentry so you can see the difference and why they were obliged to close their ranks. They played great ladies in kiss-my-foot style and the matron, Miss Deadline, preserved these social distinctions with finesse. The dental nurses were roomed in single cubicles each or, at a stretch, in double rooms. There were some office girls who, although a rung below dental nurses, were definitely a stratum above shopgirls, which Miss Deadline carefully pointed out by rooming them in threes. That she should room me, the only pupil teacher, with five shopgirls, the lowest on the ladder, showed what she personally thought of teachers or, rather, what she felt about them, not necessarily in the social context but in some more esoteric cupboard of the mind where you pack away fear and revenge. Yet she was not unfair to me, she was completely fair and liked the laughs and, all things considered, handled me like a master.

I did, however, note the lesser status and hoped to climb to a room of three or at least four but in the meantime there was much fun in the dorm. At least two of the girls worked at cosmetic counters and Myrtle wore most of it on her face from which she came up fearfully pretty for most of the twenty-four hours until she creamed it off at night, and Jane it was whispered was *thirty* and had actually been married once. Strangely she was the only unhappy one among us, said we got on her nerves, claimed she should have a cubicle to herself and said awful things about the matron. My bed happened to be next to hers, but we didn't turn out soul-mates.

Whatever your calling, however, the real status symbol was "Has she got a boy?" You don't know what glory is till you've been summoned from the tea-tables of sixty girls at night to answer the telephone. The way the chosen stood up nonchalantly and pushed back their chairs in affected boredom to edge through the multitude to the hall. If a girl were called often you knew she had a Steady, though how anyone

could work up to a Steady on two 9 p.m. leaves a week, one 11 p.m. on
Saturday and special midnight leave once a term . . . well, apparently
it could be done.

I knew a girl who was being called to the telephone every jolly tea-
time (read: every bloody tea-time but don't quote me) which made
her halfway to being married surely. It was Deodonné, the dental
nurse, who had beaten me at swimming so what did she have the
rest of us didn't? Was she slender as a maiden of the moon breathing
elixir, feeding on lotus blossom? Anything but; her body was heavy,
I'd seen it, even though she forfeited her second helping of pudding
every bl— sorry, every jolly night when she went to the phone. In the
dressing rooms at the baths I'd seen it, pulling up her bloomers over
muscular legs and for heaven's sake, look at the biceps. I had reason
to. Not that anyone is trying to say she didn't have good proportions,
I wouldn't have minded drawing them, but she did have as many
freckles as I, and more, masses more and bigger too, and she never
wore make-up. So how does she get rung up every night at tea-time?
Of course she did receive parcels of new clothes in Saturday's post with
delicate kid shoes to match, she did have rather lovely straight hazel
eyes inclined to sparkle, which I'd paint if I had the chance, marvellous
teeth fit for a princess of the kind I'd painted often and a tongue never
stuck for an answer except once: I was pausing at her door one Sunday
morning after the dental clinic ball the night before and she was in
her bed prostrate on her back, her arms flopping all ways and her
breath gasping. "I met such a *stunning* man last night."

"Did he have a car?" the others said.

She closed her eyes and groaned as though she were very ill and
couldn't speak an answer. In due course it turned out she was in fact
ill, unspecifically, and lay on her bed for days. What was it that could
do this to you that had nothing to do with appearances?

If only I could be rung up just once at tea-time by some mysterious
boy like Avis's army officer at Sandhurst who'd return in four years to
marry her, the man who filled up her dress with letters, or like
Deodonné's "*stunning* man last night" . . . hurled flat on her back in
bed for a week ill from love at first sight. To be rung up at tea-time
and to play bored as though it were nothing to me. Mind you, half
the time you'd miss your chance of a second helping of pudding but
it occurred to me it was worth it. What was it that could fall in love
with freckles?

On my first payday I met myself on John Court's Corner on a Friday
shopping night when the crowds jostled and thumped and after first

fortifying myself with a shilling's worth of chocolate roughs I bought some face powder to cover up my freckles if I used enough, and . . . believe it or not . . . some lipstick too; after all, the shopgirls used it and Myrt was never done with talking about her boys. True, the dental clinic nurses didn't use it who declared it was fast and unprofessional. Also a little country plumpness had followed me to the slender swanky city but my hair was curly and silky, people often said so and touched it. As it happened, and I know now, my eyes were very good, but I didn't know it then as no one had said so as it had been the wonderful eyes of some of my sisters which had been celebrated at home, and the hostel, conceivably, was not strong on mirrors. I mean if I'd had a decent mirror and the privacy I could have worked it out for myself. So far on this journey through life no one had said, "Your eyes are lovely," so therefore they were not. As for my clothes, I mean to say . . . I think I was still wearing that dress, the blush pink one, I'd made at home.

One day there was a general invitation tossed compassionately to the hostel about a dance at the YWCA centre in Boulcott Street in town, and there it was on the notice board and anyone going could have eleven o'clock leave. Another girl and I took the plunge and went in on a tram. It was private rather than public and severely supervised. Talk about sterile. A sort of boy danced with me, a bit anonymous, thin dark and inarticulate, and asked to take me home, I didn't know what for. Talk about daring! I said yes. We went home silently on the 10:45 tram and walked up from the tramstop to the hostel gate without one single word. At the gate we tried the silliest first kiss of any seventeen, nothing at all happened, then divided in panic at once. His lips were cold and dull, above all humiliating, and no doubt mine were too. Poor seventeens. He would be seeking too for that thing that threw you on your bed ill for a week.

Within the passionless hostel hall the matron watched me sign the "in" book on eleven before I slipped into the bathroom and washed the whole thing off me. I never set eyes on that boy again and was still not rung up at tea-time.

So, as I've said, I went to the pictures with the shopgirls when we could afford it and if we couldn't we'd walk, until I got to know an office girl or two. There was an office girl there, Gedda, straight and prim in feature and body, correct, courted by her boss, what an honour!, who kept on meeting this man and going out with him. I remember seeing the two of them crossing the street, not touching, not hand in hand or arm in arm, miles apart, both straight and respectable and uncompromising and one night after tea when I was admitted to her room of three she told us all flat and straight she wasn't in love with him. And someone said, "But Gedda, your boss, think of it. Your boss, your position." And she said—she had straight regular features, short straight hair, straight boy figure, straight brown impersonal eyes—she said, "I'm not in love like Deodonné. I'd rather be desperately hopelessly brokenheartedly in love than successfully married with a man I don't love. I want to know what it's like to be in love. I'd give up everything I am and have and know to be in love. Give me a broken heart."

"But . . . to marry your boss, Gedda."

"I want to be in love. I'd rather be in love and lose than never to be in love at all."

I heard later that Gedda had indeed married this boss and that sure enough they fought blue murder. Cat and dog all the way, I was told, even though they'd had a son.

. . . I got to know another office girl or two. Marvellous the difference a little education made to girls. We'd walk through the magic evenings into Courtenay Place or as far as Manners Street in soft vulnerable clusters with the wind throwing our hair, safe enough in the capital city if we kept within the lights. Too wary yet to do more than glance at the boys we encountered and giving nothing of ourselves away, our girl secrets hidden; when Valentino died and a theatre ran his films I'd go on my own after school so no one would know how I felt.

It appears now that society put a value on its girls, as girls, at that time. For a start we had a dragon for a matron who couldn't see a girl without also seeing a clock and some bad man *outside*. We young pupil teachers in the city like Ellen and Avis and me were required to attend occasional lessons after school to prepare for the Teachers D exam in two years' time; we'd meet in some classroom to be taught by some senior teacher: Teaching Method, which was unintelligible mumbo-jumbo to me, History, British History . . . not a word of New Zealand history . . . and Blackboard Drawing, which was a mystery to the others. The blackboards were wide and firm and dark with no brown paper skidding about and the coloured chalk lyrical. I improved in speed, accuracy, economy of line but learnt no more technique. Drawing came up as a new role of performance to an audience and I even had it in me to teach. But it was the hours of singing on a Saturday morning down Thorndon Quay way, the joy of new songs like the "Volga Boatman" and "Who Is Sylvia?" that shine down the years, that lit me to the point of delirium.

During the winter the vicar rounded up a group of us maidens to groom us for Confirmation in the Anglican church nearby for which we dressed in white. I anyway couldn't resist the white drama of the virgin veil and we made our vows to the church. The system could lead us girls anywhere and meant to make of us anything it wanted. Whether in the hostel or at school or out in the city, whichever way we walked, we moved in the shelter of discipline and protection from one senior after another. Schoolrooms, schoolrooms all the way, they supplied our style of life. I suppose it was important that we remained virgins, both boys and girls, till marriage; the Church and the State thought so. To train for teaching, a five-year course, was to be somewhat hallowed and Evil took the form of a Big Bad Man. What are spinsters made of? Sugar and spice and everything that's nice.

For me to break out and away from the system to a solo studio, to make my own way alone at eighteen in commercial art without stability, protection and pay was an idea too fanciful even for me.

Yet dreams die hard. Some. I was ravished by the glamour of the city at night when we went to the pictures or paraded the streets on a Friday night. The lights in the rain doubling up on themselves had the brilliance of coloured chalk and the magic of the songs on a Saturday morning. I'd delight in the din on Perrot's Corner where trams squeezed past each other, the bashing and crashing, clanging and banging of metal on metal, the high cry of a city. It meant I was no longer in the countryside but in the thick of the vortex where everything happened. From a shop doorway I'd watch the people, examining their faces to read what was in their minds, studying how they walked as they jostled by, trying to guess what their bodies were like without any clothes and wondering what their lives were made of. Wishing to penetrate their mystery.

And I'd dream as I walked. I'd find myself one day outside of repeating schoolrooms, out of reach of a watchful matron, clear of an infant mistress, and here was the studio with paint and a piano, the teapot and cup and saucer, the frying pan and sausages, one bed and only me there. It was a dream that increasingly featured austerity and asceticism and there was no man in it.

Yet, prospering side by side with this, was another the very opposite, a new one I hadn't worn before in which I've finally slimmed down, become arrestingly beautiful and wear exotic clothes, I'd meet the man of all men, tall as usual, dark handsome and rich, who'd fall madly in love with me. In a soul-shaking scene he'd propose to me, I'd become engaged with a diamond ring sparkling for all to see and be married in yards of white satin and a veil. Strangely, that was as far as the action went; the wedding was all. I didn't seek any afterwards. Both dreams were doing well though entirely unrelated to each other. The wedding dream flared when I was at the hostel talking love-affairs with the girls but when I was marooned at school I favoured the recluse one.

There's no hope of being accurate about the sequence of events from this distance, but it was during my first year at Wellington South when my sagging at school really showed. There was nothing wrong with the school itself as Ellen and Avis were contented enough and were turning out good teachers, but to me it was no more than a source of income. The infant room was seen to be a very good one. By the standards of those days, and indeed in many places now, Miss Little's department was not much less than flawless. Her grouping and system of promotion were foolproof so that each little child was working to capacity the whole time. Some leapt ahead and some stayed behind till they knew the work where they were. They worked whether they liked it or not and with never a sign of the strap or even a word of reproof. The children were happy, even Andrew in time, and since there was a high level of order it says something for order. Order and happiness went hand in hand, which I think a desirable state. Some people now would take issue, however, with the segmentation of the daily time-table with not a minute's give-or-take either way at any point of changeover. I myself see her teaching to be nearly all input of material foreign to the native content of a mind so that you didn't see personality showing through. The fact alone that I don't remember any one of the children except Andrew. Her regimentation allowed no mind to develop as a personally operating organ in its own right, as an entity, but eliminated it as such. What you came up with was sixty small im-prints of Miss Little, which I think is not desirable. It was the kind of schooling that produced efficient rather than interesting people, promising to supply a fine army one day—and, in fact, did—and a subservient people. No variations of the human theme were encouraged there, as I myself was not. But who at that time was interested in variations on the human theme? She got the results and won high grading.

I remember the morning the grading came out and she'd been graded the highest in town. It was not hard to believe. The small pink lips round the short forward teeth almost achieved a smile and she flushed. The crispness of success crackled through the classrooms. Ellen

and I and Avis capitalised on this exhilarated mood at morning tea-
time to clear up a few things we wanted to know about her private
life but had not risked asking. Did she live with someone or did she
live alone?

She told us she lived on her own.

But surely that wasn't very pleasant to live alone. We thought that
would be awful. We couldn't do it.

It was sufficient. People are adaptable. You got used to it.

But wasn't she lonely?

She said she was far too busy to be lonely.

But she must be frightened at night.

Seldom. Only a bit uneasy when she heard a noise she couldn't
identify, then she couldn't settle until she'd found out what it was.

What did she do to find out what it was?

She said she got up and roamed round till she did find it. Sometimes
it was only some bird in the eaves or some dog on the loose. Or an
outside door rattling in which case she'd stop it rattling and go back
to bed.

I wanted to ask her what her nightgown was like but didn't. I tried
to picture Miss Little's bare feet but couldn't see anything so personal.
And her slippers . . . wanting to sound the inside of her, to discover
that which was hidden.

Avis saw the whole thing from another angle. Was it her own
house?

Yes, she'd bought it when she came out from Scotland. It was up
on the hill in Karori. She hadn't wanted a house on the hill on account
of the Wellington gales. It was the Southerly Busters that rattled the
windows and doors and threw bits of branches on the roof to wake
her up at night.

Did she like Wellington? Ellen asked.

Only up to a point. The people's ways were a bit outlandish. Their
thinking inbred. Though, given the geographical and historical circumstance, she supposed they couldn't help it.

And then the bell rang, and back to severe professionalism and her
impenetrable mystery. To me she remained no more than a grey silk
smock on legs.

Far better would it have been, I thought, for me to have been a shopgirl like Myrtle or a factory hand like May. There came a morning
before the bell went when the grey silk smock sent a message to the
headmaster, a note, I saw someone take it, and the next thing here

was Mr. Rankinfile ambling in the door with a bland don't-blame-me look. Miss Little's face high above me had flushed a dangerous pink as though she were feeling something, a strand of grey hair sprung loose and her hands twitched suddenly. "Take her away from me."

The Head would be about a second- or third-generation New Zealander, I'd say, a colonial in search of an order from the Throne and he obeyed with appropriate deference, though rather automatically as though this specific drama was nothing to what he'd known in schools. With no comment at all he carried me off to the main building into his study where there was already a spare table and chair for emergencies and handed over to me . . . wait for it . . . the holy School Attendances. I'd never been too strong on figures but these I thoroughly enjoyed.

Mid-summer when I'd come to Wellington and in no time I'd found the baths and beaches. One Saturday after lunch I see nothing to stop me from going to Lyall Bay for a swim so I go down to the Basin Reserve to wait for a tram—Number Three it used to be. I haven't bothered to wear powder or lipstick as I'm thinking about men; just the marvel of great ocean waves breaking in thunder and spray. A country daisy on the side of the road.

A car slows down before me, a low-swung sports car with no less than the man of my dreams at the wheel who asks if I'd like a lift. You wouldn't believe it. Black hair swept back from his forehead and a profile like a film star. It can't be true and can't be for me so I don't answer.

He asks me again quite kindly and I tell him I'm going to Lyall Bay for a swim.

He says that's where he's going too. Perhaps he could drive me there.

So I get in, all blushes. He's older than I. He's not a boy but a man with lines on his face which is inclined to be pink. He's not slender either like Deodonné's boy; his body is big and well covered. I don't mean fat but I don't mean thin. I suppose he is tall but can't tell. I can't get over his kindness to me. Me with my freckles and the dress I've made. As we slide out through the hills and the sun to the bay I'm obliged to believe in perfection. He questions me about myself and though I don't say much I have to confess I'm a teacher.

When we get out of the car I'm disappointed he's not tall, his legs are too short for perfection. I would have drawn them much longer than that. What would the girls think? Never mind, he's dark and

handsome and has a car. Apart from
the legs a girl's dream come true.
We run down the beach in our togs
to the water like two happy friends.

As we swim together in the hurling waves, somewhere in the green
of the water beneath the blue of the
sky, somewhere in the frothy white
of the surf I lose my heart to him.
As we run out again together he
takes my hand and when we are
dressed we meet over a table in a
small restaurant at the top of the
rolling beach. How can he gaze at
me with no make-up on with every
freckle flaring and my wet hair flat-
tened in strags, so unnervingly. Yet
our conversation takes a sincere note,
something steady, during which he
tells me he is single, twenty-nine
and a commercial traveller, a term
I've not heard before. He goes to

Sylvie, Muriel and Norma

some length to explain what this is, that he travels for a chemist on
Lambton Quay and that his name is Jake Brownley. It comes up that
his line has a strain of Spanish as if the rest were not enough. After
all, Valentino was Italian. That a dream should materialise with such
near-accuracy is heady stuff for a daisy.

Back in the city he drops me at the street gate for all the girls to see
though I'd rather he walked to the door with me as the other girls' boys
did. As I leave him he says he might be driving past the same tramstop next Saturday at about the same time as he is very fond of swimming and I walk up the lane to the hostel seeing the shapes of things
more sharply and in some kind of glow; the cracked paving underfoot,
the slats of the fence and the tall white virgin hostel itself, the steps
scooped by many feet. A white light flashing like moonlight. I knew
it was love at first sight and for the first time. I was learning love itself
for the first time in seventeen untouched years.

The following Saturday the whole thing happens again and when
we meet on the sand in our togs he takes my hand as he had last time
to run down the beach to the water and fling in the waves together.
We play in the tumultuous surf and lie on the sand afterwards. He told

me that people called him J.B. and called me the Spanish name for baby: Bambino. What astonished me was that he was liking me without my seeking it, with no treacherous popularity. In my vision, although the word "love" had not yet arisen, it could only be a matter of time before I was engaged and after that married in a floating white veil. What else could there possibly be to life but a glorious wedding day?

During tea-times when dozens of girls crowded the long dining tables J.B. began ringing me up; I'd become one of the chosen. As for playing bored as some girls did, anyone could see I wasn't. Over the phone he arranged to pick me up in the evening down at the street gate, which called for leave from the matron, a dark, small, tense person with eyes like waiting volcanoes. "Why hasn't he come to the door?" she says.

"I didn't tell him to."

"You can tell him from me that a man calls for a girl at the door and is not afraid to show himself."

I'd been thinking the same myself. On the other hand it was better the girls didn't see his legs were short.

"Where are you going?" she says.

"For a short drive."

She ponders on this, examining my face. "You've got far too much powder on, Sylvia. And all that lipstick. Much less would do."

"It's only to cover my freckles."

"You'd run less risk *with* your freckles. Safer."

I don't answer because I don't know what she means.

"Anyway you know the rules. You'll report to me at nine tonight."

"Yes, Miss Deadline, yes."

When I tell J.B. about this he's annoyed in a handsome way. "The sour bitch," he says.

This shocks me. I've never heard the word spoken other than behind a school.

Oriental Bay and the lights in the harbour. You don't hear the murmur of the engine as the soft waves lollop the rocks. I've been a habitué of various heavens in my time but this kind I've not known before. Curves and corners till he draws up on a dark solitary promontory favoured by Wellington lovers, turns and looks at me and I hear the hush on the night. In the dark of the car he kisses me circumspectly enough, not too much to alarm me and not too little either. Just right to make his point. The scent of a man so close, the touch of a man's mouth.

When I return home and report to Miss Deadline the powder is still undisturbed on my face and the lipstick intact. My second kiss in the capital city, but this time upstairs I don't wash it off.

At some stage I went home for the holidays to Featherston, a country town at the northern foot of the Rimutaka Range, where Mumma was living in a large very old house called Te Kainga (the dwelling place) to be near Ashton and Lionel. My sister Norma, the next one to me, had been missing the big ones very much and had been carrying the whole weight at home with Mumma alone and Puppa dead, and it was decided to send her with me to the hostel in Wellington to attend the technical college. It was my turn to look after one of the younger ones and her uniform was prepared, a brown gym dress, white blouse and brown blazer. I promised those at home I would look after Norma and keep her from all harm. The two of us stood on the railway platform at Featherston and when we boarded the train for Wellington Mumma wept for us.

Responsibility for another person was new to me but strangely pleasant. At home Norma had always been a companion of mine, my only confidante, and now alone together in the city it was trust and harmony all the way. A very pretty girl with never a freckle, the same English white face as Puppa, the black curly hair and dark blue eyes. As it happened, she was sweet all the way through without my complexities, responsive and reliable, and I liked having this piece of home with me at the hostel very much. To come home and find Norma was wonderful, about fourteen or fifteen she must have been. Outside the hostel she came to no harm but, bewilderingly for us both, it threatened from inside the hostel where Miss Deadline was so touched by her youth and dependence she fell in love with Norma, a condition neither of us could understand. All we could do was avoid the matron, stick together when we could and engage in elaborate dodging and subterfuge. We'd have to get out from here somehow and board somewhere else.

Returning to the scene of my fall from the infant room at my fifteenth school, Wellington South, I found on the very first morning I was to be transferred. I don't think I should let this go undefended here, however late the date, but no doubt I was getting my due. I was poor at teaching anyway, wholly unsuited temperamentally and was a loss to no one.

I was transferred to my sixteenth school up on the heights of Wadestown, on the grounds that whereas there were three pupil teachers at

Wellington South, there was none at Wadestown, and that reason in
itself was charitable. No one can fault the nature of my training, the
authorities were indulgent all the way, looking for the best in us, but
with me they were out of luck.

The infant room at Wadestown at that time was a separate building
a block away from the main school. In place of the elegant antiseptic
Miss Little I found one of these saintly maiden ladies that detective
story writers make up in books. One of these unmarried free untram-
melled people whose lives belong to no man and who dedicate themselves to their work. I'd been through the hands of five by now: Miss
Pope, Miss Cumberland, Miss Deadline, Miss Little and now Miss
Whackington. Her whole name I heard later was Miss Mutch-
Whackington but the Mutch part fell off from embarrassment, though
she signed her name in the original. It's not impossible that our characters were influenced by these ladies; I myself picked up this strain of
asceticism and austerity from somewhere.

Again a tall imposing woman, big body, long legs, yet quite a small
head up top. They were not the proportions I would have drawn in a
woman, not if I were in advertising. From the top she increased down-
wards towards her feet, which were hidden beneath wide tweed skirts.
Sweeping skirts enclosing secrets and limbs and flaring to the ankle
and when they swayed as she moved only two black leather foot-tips
showed. She didn't walk, she moved.

Very beautiful hair, this lady, thick auburn and curly, a centre part
and a bun at the back, the kind of hair women pay fortunes to copy,
her grey eyes still and telling nothing while on her face the weather
had its way. Her voice was retreating and she seemed to be more
involved with the children, as children, than Miss Little.

Yet the strap lifted from time to time. This was a much smaller
room, all infant classes in together. She saw strapping to be indispensable to productive teaching. There was a lot of it too. Yes a lot. Far
too much for young children. I myself felt the severity of the discipline.
I never could stand to see the strap come down on a reluctant hand,
especially a small one, even though I had been schooled likewise. Yet
it was not administered in anger I'm sure; her serene temperament
could not have accommodated wrath. She strapped in sorrow, rather as
though she wished it had not been necessary. She emanated a saintly
patience. The clock and the strap did much of the teaching, successful
teaching too, for their handwriting was copybook standard and no one
talked.

I tried to learn to teach here but once the children saw a girl with no strap in the drawer they relaxed so that the discipline and the silence were wrecked. It must have been seen that I tried, for the headmaster in the other street said that Miss Whackington was pleased with me and that I was doing well, which I told Norma when I got home, but only at the cost of the children. I'd never treated Norma, Marmie or Vadne as I was required to treat these, yet the feeling persisted that Miss Whackington was saintly. It still does.

I did try to fit in to her style and would have done better but for the strapping, which continually turned me over. I thought, if only we could teach young children without having to hit them, without the need to punish them all day. Miss Little had showed it could be done.

Yes, I appeared to be in favour at school for the time being but really that made no difference one way or the other. Get through the five hours somehow, put the week behind me and collect my cheque at the end of the month. It was happenings of the heart that mattered, love, the giving and taking of it, the winning and the holding of it. Looking after Norma was a deep joy to me, she turned to me for everything. And the weather was important as this was the winter term, or maybe the spring term, and Wadestown was a long way from the hostel on the other side of the city on the heights. And money. The recurring crisis was that your season ticket for the tram had finished up.

I was madly in love. Whereas before, all I wanted to see was a studio in the city and me an earning artist, what I saw now was marriage. J. B. had got to the place where he was taking me for occasional drives in the evening. Fancy a big man of twenty-nine taking me for a drive, a handsome man with his own car. Yet there were flaws in the show which puzzled me: why didn't he take me to the pictures on Saturday night like the other boys did and buy me some chocolates, or to the theatre to see the plays, visiting pianists like Paderewski and light opera companies, and it would be wonderful to walk with him through the crowded city streets in the Friday night parade when boys and girls showed each other off. Wasn't it time to meet his friends and people and for him to meet mine? I was disappointed he didn't walk up to the hostel, knock at the front door and ask for me so the girls could see my man; he'd wait in the street at the bottom of the lane by prearrangement and blow his loud horn. It didn't occur to him that I might have wishes and, to be fair, I don't think I believed I had a right to any. Some boys spent money on their girls but you couldn't say he spent a penny on me. His one idea seemed to be to find a corner at a dark bay and give me free lessons in kissing, gratis.

These drives began reaching farther out from the populated city. Sailing along the Hutt Road on a clear frosty night, harbour lights as far as you looked, stars above and the cold air on your face, what joy could touch it. One night we drove as far as a country hotel at Tai Tai where he was friendly with the proprietor and where he gave me a free lesson in drinking, but I turned out a reluctant learner not only because of the shame of it and of what the family would think if they knew but because of the horrible taste of the stuff. How on earth could people drink for pleasure! Until I felt this horrible thing change into an exciting thing as it ran through my simple blood. "I can feel it right down my arms," I said, at which he smiled to himself.

"I can feel it in my fingers," I said. Tea couldn't do this.

"You're cute, Bambino."

However, when he pulled up in a stretch of dark road on the way home drink lost hands down so that he no longer addressed me as a cute Bambino but said I was a stiff little schoolmarm. Yet I still answered the phone at tea-time and dreamed my way home along Lambton Quay.

I don't remember the real reason now but I was moved from the infant department with Miss Whackington to the primary along the streets on the grounds that I needed wider experience. I wonder. A much smaller school than Wellington South and four of us only on staff: two lady teachers, the headmaster and I. My word, I've met nice people on staff. I was in the room with the lady teachers, both unmarried and both sane and sweet, and I don't recall any strap in that room: Standards 2, 3 and 4. You could say it was a sane sweet room.

The headmaster, Mr. Pugmire, taught Standards 5 and 6 in the room across the corridor. His great pride and on which he built his system and reputation was that no one in his school ever failed Proficiency, and you can take my word on this for he boasted of it. He was not a big man, about the same build as Mr. Rankinfile, grey hair and dressed in the same kind of grey suit but in professional outlook you'd never know they were both headmasters.

Everyone in Standard 6 passed every year and I soon learnt why. I often did duty in his room and witnessed the steady strapping and the children's tears and inescapably felt their agonies. Any mistake in anything caught the leather: one sum wrong, one cut; two sums wrong, two cuts; three mistakes in spelling, three cuts; five errors, five cuts. Not only could you hear it from the corridor but from the other room across the way, which seemed worse than seeing it in the room itself. I'd known strapping in class from the start but since I feared it I'd seen to it that I didn't get it; I'd work like mad not to get the strap, hold in my tongue with a wire hook and learn my spelling all night if necessary, but I'd seen it. As a child, believing it was just, I'd managed to take it in my stride, up to a point, but now, growing up in all directions with the responsibility of Norma and a love-affair, with womanly instincts shooting out all ways, I could no longer take it, even though I still believed it was right.

There were twin boys in that room, dressed with love, gracefully boned, delicate of skin, and one was ahead of the other, so it was "the other" who got the strapping. If I were writing fiction I'd put in here how the mother came along in tears one day to plead the cause of the second twin and how she succeeded, but I'm writing document. No mother came because she didn't know I suppose, or maybe she agreed. There was no parental protest that I knew of, that I was told of, which is something I'd noted before. Apparently the parents didn't think it was wrong and neither did the children. What did the inspectors think of it, did they know? Yet as things were, if the other twin failed Proficiency Mr. Pugmire would lose his crown, the only head in town who had never had a failure. From my humble level of pupil teacher, and secretly, I began to shift position on the justice of it. I know that I must have because recalling it, I'm aware of the corrosion from the caustic soda that only injustice leaves.

I've seen schools in other countries since then with differing education philosophies but I've not seen anything like that at all. In my work later in life I've addressed myself to the violence in classrooms, in teachers as well as in children, to find out why; there's a reason for everything. You should hear them now in the media of this country and in the press raving away about the increasing destructiveness in young people up to the vindictiveness in parliament and what'll we do about it sort of thing, the wailing and wringing of hands from the education department in paragraphs of multisyllabic jargon. That my books on the subject are not available in this country now is not because I haven't written them.

Yet outside his classroom, in the staffroom, playground and in his home Mr. Pugmire was the sunniest of men. He was kind to me, too kind. Being a physical force man he had no idea of the inner discipline latent in children, so that according to his ethic I should have been

strapped too when I made a mistake but he wasn't in the position to
do so. His only alternative was to spoil me. The things I said and got
away with. I used to bring my favorite Gramophone record to school
and play it full blast through morning tea, a thing with a tom-tom
beat in it. No one said Don't. Other senior teachers who had trained
me, or tried to, neither punished nor spoiled me but this man spoiled
me to the point where I could be quite cheeky. Never before in any
of my sixteen schools, this was my seventeenth, had I tried out any
of my seniors.

When I answered him back in the staffroom one morning in front
of the others he looked at me in bewilderment, his mouth showing
hurt. So surprised. So was I. I remember a time when I went too far and
he stared at me in astonishment and revelation as though he'd only
just understood. "You're cheeky," he marvelled.

What a disgrace. My own astonishment equalled his. How had this
come about when he was kind to me? I hadn't wanted to be rude to
him or to hurt him. For once I was lost for an answer and I didn't do
it again.

He continued to be kind to me and patient, asking me round to his
home in town for tea on a Sunday, mindful of my position in the city
away from home.

Dates and sequences are beyond recall but pictures and impressions are
clear enough. I'm standing in front of Standard 4 trying to take some
lesson but my body is remembering the kisses last night. Poor awakening body. These pains darting when I'd only been kissed on the lips,
every time I thought of him. And how can you stop thinking of him,
how can you teach when you feel this way? Fancy a man having the
power to do this to you when he's not even here. Any man. No wonder
Deodonné had lain ill for a week when she'd fallen in love at first
sight. I'd believed love was all hearts and kisses and sighs; I'd known
nothing of the physical follow-up.

Yet things were just anyhow on the J.B. front: he continued to fail
to mention marriage and I continued to fail to give one inch.

A summer evening when instead of coming up to the door he sat in
his car in the street and blasted that dreadful horn. Miss Deadline happened to be walking in from town and did she go for him. About his
shocking manners, his horn disturbing the neighbourhood and disgracing the hostel and where was his respect for a girl. She said he'd
certainly come to the door next time or he'd not see me at all. She was
only small but her head was high and her dark eyes shot out bullets.

"The bitch," he muttered when I got in the car, which was the most awful swearing. I could never risk letting my family meet him.

There was a Saturday night after eleven p.m., I was on the upstairs landing and I saw Deodonné come in. Her coat was swinging open, a fur coat, there were diamonds on her ears and a ready-for-anything look on her face. "The car broke down," she warned. "We had to find a place to ring up the garage and then we had to wait for the man." Her eyes were more fiery than Miss Deadline's.

Brave matron who'd take on Deodonné at this moment. This one didn't. She didn't even threaten to write to her mother.

Another Saturday night's eleven o'clock leave and I was late home but only a bit. In the office Miss Deadline's eyes are stormy. "I will not take the responsibility of girls from the country out after eleven. The man's no good."

All I can do is hang my head.

"It's no good, Sylvia. I'll give you a fort-night to find other board and I'll write to your mother."

All I feel is relief. Thank Heaven. Then I lift my head anxiously. "What about Norma?"

"I'll look after Norma here myself."

Gracie was no longer in Wellington and I dealt with my own crisis, I'm glad to say, though following in her footsteps. I got a room in the boarding house, The Gables, where she had been, up a steep hill off Willis Street not far from Perrot's Corner. Being crowded out they put me temporarily in their best front room, which the others couldn't afford, till a cheap one to share was vacant.

Norma in 1938

A room of my own to myself for however short a time. An armchair in a bedroom and a carpet, bow windows looking out over the city and the gale-gusted harbour, the luxury dazzled me. For the moment I was dizzy with glory.

But Norma was so uneasy to be left behind with the matron that we got private board for her with another maiden lady up Wadestown way, Miss Livechook, on my way home from school so we could see each other every day. When I'd call in after school the lady was kind to us both. She'd make afternoon tea on a tray and give us cake in the parlour. We were both more than a little nervous at our sudden growing up outside the shelter of the hostel and it meant a great deal to me to have Norma near. Our reliance on each other called out new dimensions in us both. There had been nothing quite like this reciprocal trust before.

He stopped ringing me up about then because I . . . ah . . . because "the lady refused to yield her favours." But I still got the sting of a broken heart and the worse catastrophe of a broken dream. A dream lost. The pain. A pain no one could help you with, you couldn't go to a doctor. It was like falling ill from love at first sight but in reverse. I'd never known anything like it. Pulling up abruptly in the street when I saw a car like his, panicking in case it was his indeed, flushing and whitening within a short doorway; listening for the phone at dinner time and for the whisper of tyres pulling up outside and maybe the squeal of a brake. So much feeling for him swelling my mind, bloating it, that I didn't know how to deal with. An enormous area of imagery was fouled, the part about the wedding, the lovely home, the status of marriage and the round-the-clock lovemaking. I couldn't tell one day from the next and failed to even wash my hair. I still carry in mind a picture, a miniature like a cameo, of telling Norma in the lavatory about J.B. not coming now. "What did he say?" Norma says.

"He said, 'You don't feel the same as me.' " Sharp crying, short, then stop. One breathful only. I've never cried over a man since. Some grief is beyond it.

"Never mind, Sylv," from Norma. "He's not worth it. His face is pink, he's hardly undernourished and his legs look as though they'd been chopped off at the knees."

By now I was sharing the attic at the boarding house with Miss Hendrickson, a senior shop assistant; I am sitting up in bed writing to J.B. on paper with the crest of my family on it, trying to hide things from Miss Hendrickson, whose bed was half an arm's length from mine, as she didn't go in for men. But I told Jean Beyers, who did, and who boarded here with her mother and who sat at the same table in the dining room. They'd come from South Africa and they took me with them across the street to the hall where the Royal Choral Union was rehearsing *Aida* for a performance in the Town Hall so that I found myself singing on Tuesday nights instead of disintegrating.

Yet I couldn't get over him; the only way I knew to ease my pain was to pretend it wasn't true but then I'd have to take the impact all over again when I found it was true. I was confused, not knowing which way to go, like becoming lost in the bush at Te Pohue when we were very young, when in the twilight of the forest we couldn't see the sky.

When I look round in the past at that time for Norma I don't see her and can't remember what happened to her, so only last week, January 1979, when she and a daughter visited me at Whenua, I asked her where she had been and she told me that after the one term in Wellington she'd been recalled home because Mumma had not been able to pay her board. Miss Livechook had even sued for it but of course never got it. Although Norma saw to it that her own many children became trained professionals—teachers, nurses, a headmaster, a doctor and a music specialist, dispersed round the world as Mumma's had been—she herself had had to return to the country, to "the wop-wops," to be Mumma's right-hand man again. She told me how deeply she mourned this period of her life and that it was written on her heart. So I gave her a pen and asked her to write it on paper for me to use in this narrative, her own words. She sat on a low chair just within the wide open music room, her white curly head lowered, pen in hand, and spoke against the roar of the gale in the trees: "I have a lot to offer this world, Sylv . . ."

"That. Write that, Norm."

". . . but because of the lack of education I've been unable to impart it."

"Write that too."

Norma's nine children and following generations have as many good looks as any other Godzoners but none has equalled that very pretty girl in Wellington half a century ago: white face, black buster cut shining and curling, big eyes deep blue as the ocean; nor will any of her children ever know the beauty their mother was. There's only Lionel and me left to witness.

She continued writing on the paper: "My education is like an unfinished symphony, it haunts me still. However, although I am now sixty-eight, I intend to do something about it. So help me God." Her own words but they still don't make me feel any better about that girl in Wellington falling out of the ranks at fourteen. It haunts me also . . . still. For all that she did rise to public positions under her own power: city councillor and J.P.

When I was a child I was as full of vision as any child can be. There had been no limit to what I believed I could do and what I would be in the world, but I seemed to have gone blind since I came to Wellington. Carried along in the arms of the state, under the authority of education and church and my own arterial morality; matroned in the hostel, even confirmed by the church; passed from one infant mistress to another, disciplined, excused, helped, protected and largely in the orbit of single senior women which gave life the cloisters of a convent. Talk about easy. I'd become dulled. I could not have spelled the word "initiative." I'd forgotten the grandeur of work. No more than just another human organism floating with the current on the surface of the wrong stream.

Or you could say that my vivid vision had been swept away in the floodtide of first love at seventeen. I might even be tempted to say so myself except that I know better. It was those years at the Wairarapa High School which had exorcised my spirit. The dark years I call them, and I don't speak of them any more . . . the pariah days.

Coming home from school one day, dawdling through the swift crowds in Willis Street, I wondered where my future was. Where was the great artist I was going to be? I'd been in the capital over a year and wasn't even being trained. At that time there was no school of art in Wellington; I wasn't doing much drawing at Wadestown, while at the blackboard drawing classes it was I who was doing the teaching, in effect, without trying to, meaning to or even wanting to. In the jostling crowds I stopped short to think until I was pushed to the kerbside, whereas a kerbside with trams thundering by is not a bad place to think. I couldn't just paint gorgeous pictures all day because they wouldn't pay and here again was the familiar solution: commercial art. Advertising. I could draw all those long ladies in the fashion pages, breakfast foods and motorcar tyres. At the very least there would be all kinds of equipment, at the most there'd be other artists for company who could school me on the spot. I'd wear a smock, flowers all over and flared. What heaven that would be after a school-room, away from the drabness, dirty desks, the smell of coats and sweat in the corridor, trying to make children learn things they hated and the swing of the strap all day.

A girl pondering on the kerb in spring. A great green polo-necked jersey on me, inherited, over a pleated serge skirt I'd made from my gym uniform yet within it flushed the impact of vision waking to life again. I turned in the opposite direction, winding through inanimate concrete buildings to the door of Gordon & Gotch and entered the foyer and went to the counter and asked the man if I could see the manager. The following interchange is practically verbatim, like many another passage in this story; though isolated in time these recurring cameos remain as clear as today.

"I'm the manager," he says.

But he doesn't look like an artist: pinstriped suit, paunch, bald head, pink face and glasses. From the foyer I couldn't see any studio, no sign of paint and easels. "I've come to . . . to see . . . if I can be a commercial artist."

"Any experience?"

"I . . . I'm good at drawing and painting."

"So are a lot of girls. What I mean by experience is work in a commercial firm."

"No. Not yet but . . . but I'm always painting."

"What's your age?"

"Seventeen."

"And what are you doing now?"

"I'm a pupil teacher."

"Huh. One of that brainy brood. That won't help you. You should have left school years ago and begun as an apprentice. We've got girls and boys here who've already been years on the job."

"I'd soon catch up."

His eyes take in the length of me as though he didn't agree. "We can't start training you at seventeen," he said. "We'd have to put you on a beginning wage which wouldn't keep you half an hour. No, I . . ."

"I wouldn't mind the beginning wage."

"Listen. You should have come years ago. You're much too late."

Walking back along the street in front of Kirkcaldie's I think I see J.B.'s car drawn up, at which I all but turn inside out and take to a doorway for a better look. No, it's not his. To cheer myself up I buy a shilling's worth of chocolate roughs though it wasn't payday. This shilling happens to be my tramfare to school and back tomorrow.

Back at The Gables over dinner in the evening when I tell the two Beyers about it Jean laughs a bit and says, "There's never a dull moment with you around."

Forget the art escape from teaching and try the piano one. Had enough of being a mediocre nothing. Instead of being first and in the front all the time I was running last in everything. At Wadestown I usually played the piano in the corridor after school for hours when the staff had gone home and the caretaker didn't mind, but I wasn't getting anywhere, just wallowing in the delicious delirium of music, besides it was cold during the winter months and during the spring. What I ought to do was, it was time to take lessons from the best teacher in town whether I could afford it or not. If there was one thing I knew I could do it was work hard as long as the work was what I liked, whereas I hadn't lifted a hand since I'd come to the city. After all, Horace Hunt had liked my Coleridge-Taylor even though he'd sworn at me.

So I made an appointment with the most mentioned teacher for next Saturday morning. As he was also the city organist his studio was in the Town Hall and I walked up the broad stone steps. The last time I'd walked up these steps was to a grand dance for the crews when the Fleet was in port. Four or five dances in a row or, if you like, three. On the first night I'd set a fashion by wearing my diamanté bracelet on my ankle which, apart from laddering my Keyser stockings, had been a sensation. This was different though.

I remember walking that wide high corridor circling the concert chamber, my heels beating in time with my heart. This man didn't know what was coming to him; he'd be astounded when he heard my Rachmaninoff, he'd proclaim a great future for me and shake me by the hand. It was convenient to overlook that I'd had only one term's real teaching in my life, from Horace Hunt who'd failed to shake my hand.

He was the thinnest man I'd ever seen, also the longest, he was steadily chewing something and he didn't stand up and bow. The piano was an enormous concert grand, the first I'd seen off a concert stage, and it had three pedals. "Accustom yourself to the piano first," he said from his chair. "Don't play anything at once."

It was more like a great black stallion than a piano, it might bolt at a moment's notice, and I'd never heard of three pedals before. When I tried one of them I was startled when the whole keyboard lurched to the right, had I broken the thing already? The Rachmaninoff suddenly took off with a leap immediately out of control. When I tried to pull up at the finish it skidded to a stop, skidded on a few bars I think, both I and the horse puffing. The silence of the man I interpreted as homage and in time I stood up.

"Come here a moment."

I stepped forward and waited before him. What did he want, to shake hands, congratulate me and say he was proud to meet me? If so he should be standing whereas he remained sitting and chewing and the next thing he'd pulled me upon his knee. So this was the form that homage took, I wouldn't have believed it. But a thin arm crept round me which was really overdoing the admiration especially about straining me close. "So you come from the country, little girl."

His knees were razor sharp to sit on and I suspected a flaw in the situation without being able to put my finger on it. If this were homage I didn't quite like it and eased myself free.

He chewed on steadily, not disappointed; didn't clutch after me panting or anything like that, as he would have done had I been making this up. He merely crossed one sharp knee upon the other and said, not "You're too late" as the art man had said but, "Buy Czerny's exercises and come back in six weeks."

The Beyers liked this story too. "Is that true," from Jean, "or did you make it up?"

"The best stories don't have to be made up," from her mother.

On payday I bought the Czerny and got to work on practice after school though the days were short and it grew dark too soon; besides the caretaker had no feeling for exercises and wasn't keen on Czerny, and after all he was my audience. Also dinner was at six and girls of eighteen do get terribly hungry. As the weeks worked by, however, I became somewhat enamoured of Czerny and conceded he had a point. On the other hand, exercises wouldn't make people love me. In bed in the dark in the attic I took time off from grieving for that man to reflect on the interview with this new man and the further I saw through the knees part the more I didn't want to return and the dimensions of the music dream dwindled. Perhaps I really was attic fare. Give me a caretaker any day.

Jean Beyers was a pretty laughing girl with a figure that got by my sense of proportions. We called ourselves Pip and Squeak from a popular cartoon at the time. Along with the Royal Choral Union we joined a club that did plays for charity, the Playbox, so we got round quite a bit. Pip was much better on the stage than I. Rehearsals of operas and plays kept us busy and in circulation but we were never short of time for the boys, whom Pip knocked right and left with little effort at all, though some of course. Seldom a Friday night when we didn't paint up and join the evening parade, assessing young men on the spot by the look of them and by the way they spoke, even by the smell of them. My word, we covered a lot of boys, these accidental people in trousers; sampled all kinds, dozens. The year of the mouth we called it. The touch of a man was the true test, that elusive condition of bio-

logical rapport. Seeking the thrill of the magic of a touch and lips
was the quickest way.

We danced at the Town Hall when a British warship was in and
it was there a naval officer fell in love with me, fair, tall, good-looking,
blue-eyed. All the romance a girl could desire throbbed in Jack yet not
a drop of pash did I have for him. Nor was it because J.B. was still
at large in what I called my heart but the thing about touch again.
His kisses repelled me. Yet he was all I wanted in other ways; he was
the kind of young man who came to the door for everyone to see and
he'd come to tea on Sunday night at my Wadestown headmaster's
place who said Jack was just the one for me. He made an impression
on all but me. Boys, boys, boys . . . subject Number One, yet none sent
me looking in jeweller shop windows for the desired engagement
ring.

One Friday night when Daphne was in town and had a cold she
sent me to meet a boy on Perrot's Corner to excuse her and to make
another appointment. This Aden was a young farmer from White-
man's Valley with a big warm car and he took me out that night instead. I was dressing much better by then because Pip could sew and
went in for chic of the highest, and I'd picked up a bit of Daphne's style
I suppose or at least borrowed her clothes and of course I'd drowned
out my freckles with powder; the freckles were fighting a losing battle.

Some friends from the Valley asked me out for the weekend to their
place and they took me to the barn dance where Aden would be and
we danced together all night. Brendon was his name, Aden Brendon.
J.B. had never taken me to a dance or to anything else. Dancing
through the night hour after hour, the touch dead right, his breath on
my face and his cheek to mine. My hosts were kindly waiting at the
side of the hall to take me home again, yawning, and their children
were fast asleep, but we danced to the last note. I would have married
him in the middle of the floor that moment but we had to part at
midnight. My hosts took me home before we could kiss, which was
all we'd been thinking of the entire evening.

In the morning I lived the return of spring. A phone call that morning from Aden, there were flowers somewhere, scented. Waiting to
kiss. Breathless, dizzy, almost sick and the light of magic flashing.
"Let him kiss me with the kisses of his mouth: for thy love is better
than wine." Vibrant hours, shimmering, while the household was
hushed.

At one o'clock I walked down the lane to meet him at the gate but we didn't kiss then. He drove quietly along the winding road of the green valley until we came to a lane turning along a row of poplars in their new spring green and he slowly drew up. At the touch of his mouth I was gone. Only one kiss, light and holy. He'd brought me a soft white rose.

Across the street The Gables ran an overflow annex, a pleasant two-storeyed house, and by this time I had graduated from the attic to the annex, paying a little extra. The place was alive with dental nurses who played status for all they were worth. I shared a large room up-stairs with two of them and we lived in peaceable co-existence. After all, the dental clinic nurses-in-training were a professional rung above pupil teachers-in-training and were even more strictly nurtured. Again there were no other teachers.

At last and once more for me there was the whisper of tyres on the gravel, pulling up on the steep street at the annex door. This sound on a Saturday night, you could hear it from my window. In love again I came to look beautiful and I marvelled at my face in the mirror, at my swinging gleaming waving hair and the texture of my skin. Was this face really mine? I'd made a blue dress of crepe de chine, fitting in at the waist and with folds of lace at the throat.

Aden was the breed of man who more than came to the door, you'd find him halfway up the stairs. Something under fifty years later I hold in mind this tableau on the stairs: I'm descending from the top land-ing, my hand is on the rail and I see on the lower flight Aden coming up. He looks up at me above, his blue eyes ardent, and I look down on him. And we pause. Just long enough for memory's camera to snap a photo. Love wears a biblical dignity in this tableau on the stairs.

Although in the classroom at Wadestown I was making no progress in distinguishing the character of one child from another, in the class-room of downtown life I was learning to tell one man from another and I was drowned in love for Aden. The intensity of feeling gener-ated a lyricism on a level with the Song of Solomon but held within myself. Daphne, whose conquest he was in the first place, dined out with delight on this joke about "Sylvie took my man."

"You're not short of replacements," I said.

Yet the strange thing remained about the men I loved, they didn't take me anywhere as Pip's men took her places; never a picnic, the pictures, Town Hall concerts or to *The Maid of the Mountains* at His Majesty's, nor to their friends and people. All they could think of was

kiss all night. They couldn't wait to get you into their car around
Oriental Bay to park on the darkest headland; they couldn't manage
to get as far as even Evans Bay, let alone farther round to Seatoun . . .
then get to work on my mouth. Not that I minded *too* much.

After a while in the Aden affair I couldn't help noticing it was
taking much the same route as the J.B. affair: all kiss and no marriage.
In his male way Aden also made it plain that kissing alone was not
enough but I made it plain where the frontiers were. There came a
night as we stood embraced in the dark front entrance of the annex,
my body resisting his, when he relaxed and said, "So this is how you
feel about it."

It wasn't. But there was too much in me that wouldn't give way.

He didn't come again. Once more I was left with my two hands full
of falling fragments. It had taken the best part of two years to get
over J.B.; did this mean another two years? I was eighteen, but how
many two years-es did I have to spare?

Learning fast about men and much about music, being in the chorus
of the Royal Choral Union and doing the operas in the Town Hall
dressed in white. With fringe benefits unintended like being close
behind the soloists on stage, within touching distance of the tenor, hearing the astounding audible rush of breath from his lungs, the mechanics of a man's chest challenged to its limit, the behaviour of guest
conductors and the private life of an audience; to be enthralled at *Aida*:
"And in the evening twilight we bless Thee, we praise Thee, adore
Thee . . ."

. . . to sing is a beautiful thing. All the uglinesses in the undermind
of us, the complexities and psychoses, my own at that time included,
cleared out, purified by self-forgetfulness in joy.

Learning fast about men and much about music but nothing of art
and less than nothing about teaching. I think I became worse at teaching itself even though popular with staff and children. If there were
any movement forward or backward in my craft it was certainly not
forward. I found it punitive, the "bloody profesh": the routine, discipline, dreadful workbook, the simply stultifying repetition and the
eroding boredom of children anyway. TGIF? Thank God It's Friday.
I found it a deadly business and the only solution I could see was to
back out of it altogether. *Some* how.

Towards the end of our two years as pupil teachers we sat our Teachers
D exam for which we'd been prepared on Saturday mornings and

after school. I'd already passed singing and music theory in Masterton. I quite forget about the other subjects now but in blackboard drawing I was marked 95 percent, top in New Zealand. I was told soon after that it had really been 100 percent but "we've never given that before so we called it 95 percent which looked better in the records." It possibly still is the top mark in this country.

That was the first time in my life in New Zealand that Precedent raised its head. I'd achieved something that had not been achieved before, *therefore* it could not be accepted for what it was. It was safer and more comfortable for education to show 95; at 100 someone might look at them, the response of officialdom, too timid to give credit where credit was due. I felt that, and still do, for Mumma would have been proud though I was unmoved myself. My main illustration had been of a waterfall in the forest with fern fronds dripping the spray.

The encounter with Wellington was nearly over, for the time being. Of course I was due back after the Christmas holidays. Having passed Teachers D we were enrolled at the training college for Teachers C and I was zoned to Wellington. One night at dinner I was called to the phone but it was not Aden Brendon, it was J.B.'s voice. "I'll be up to see you tonight, Bambino," at which Pip and I nearly fainted. All that obsession I'd had for him. But his kisses no longer said anything important to me; all I noted was that his lips were cold in the evening chill. Over her sewing I told Pip it was lucky I hadn't married him. "Marriage would have died overnight."

"But you did love him, Squeak."

I couldn't exactly deny it.

She knew better than to mention Aden though she was probably thinking it.

I thought but did not say, as you love Ivan Kirkcaldie.

She went on stitching and did not deny it. Her lowered head showed the parting of her freshly washed hair. Ivan was the son of a distinguished family, he drove a whopping car and he was taking her upcountry on Sunday to Pukerua Bay, being the reason she was putting the finishing touches to a white skirt and a diagonally striped top to wear. As it turned out Ivan had taken her there to provoke another girl he was after and Pip took that as hard as anything I had taken, except that it was Pip who threw over Ivan. He never got one more chance.

The two years were closing fast and soon I would be back in the country for six to ten summer weeks with my collection of new stories from the city. Assuring Pip I would be back in February, taking up my suitcase in one hand and the fragments of my heart in the other, I was on the Wellington railway station and I caught the train home to Featherston to Mumma and Norma, Marmie and Vad. At eighteen going on nineteen, on the threshold of teachers training college, although I'd entered seventeen schools I'd not been inside one studio.

There exists a picture which memory painted but did not sign or put the date on and it comes when I think of Featherston. It has the look of a cameo, permanent, strong yet delicate, like that tableau on the stairs in the annex. I believe it was before the time I'm writing of now because of its meaning and because the figures seem younger and new to the district. It must have been when Mumma first came to live at Featherston two years ago when she attended the Anglican church and sang in the choir, for the church is holding a village fair and we three girls are there, Daphne, Sylvia and Norma.

Chronologically it's a non sequitur but on account of its vision-like quality it would fit in anywhere.

A still summer evening with stars in the sky. A stately house with windows aglow set in flower gardens and encircled by trees. The trees are hung with coloured lights. Stalls here and there and many people, some of them dancing on the grass and you can hear the music. On the fringe of the light at the edge of the trees Daphne and I and Norma are watching it all. It's the faces of my sisters I'm thinking of in the shimmering unreality; the beauty upon them and the future within them.

A young man approaches and offers Daphne his arm to dance and she goes with him too, but too soon she returns to us saying the boy is not much and not good enough and that's all there is to this cameo, a symbolic painting of youth in the wings hoping to join the dance. It is their faces I see, faintly brushed with coloured lighting and in their eyes are reflected stars.

Featherston for the summer holidays, a country town at the foot of the Rimutakas. Some of the family were home for Christmas except Muriel and Ashton who'd married and Puppa who had died.

The fire and energy in Mumma might have been quenched a bit for she no longer quoted poetry, but it was a relief for her to be near the shops and the church and she liked to go off on her solitary beat away from the irritations to bring back a little food like a loaf of bread and half a pound of Bell Tea, or a little spiritual food from church like half a pound of St. Matthew's gospel spoken with a certain curtness: "Lay not up for yourselves treasures upon earth, where moth and rust doth corrupt, and where thieves break through and steal." She'd go with that same faraway look in her eyes as when she'd gaze out the window of some country school to seek the hazed horizon, seeming to be moving apart from us who were growing older. Now that she had time and with Puppa gone she'd play and sing at the piano at night, sentimentally, as though she herself were growing younger. "Thinking I hear you, thinking I see you . . . smile."

Unostentatiously I turned nineteen and I was restless indeed. The house was crowded but I no longer roamed the plains, not even the nearby range. Yes, I did go once with Marmie and Evadne as far as Cross Creek but there was nothing in me to send me farther. The country no longer inspired but appalled me and my heart called for Aden. Nevertheless I found plenty to be excited about since there was plenty more future left.

At the back of Te Kainga were buildings which once had been servants' quarters. I spent days scrubbing out these rooms in order to live in them by myself. I was dying to live somewhere by myself. We children had made thousands of little houses in our time but this was the first real place of my own with timbered walls and iron ceiling, a real window and floor and a door that opened and shut. The family called it Sylvie's study but now I see it for what it was: Selah One.

There was already an old table so I put a chair beside it, a pad and a pencil upon it and said I was going to write a book. I didn't consider writing to be in my line but since art and music had fallen through, temporarily, I'd have to try something else and if I failed all the way I'd end up at the Wellington Training College to be a dreary teacher, sufficient reason to make anyone write anything. So I sat there and stared out the window on the range.

I wrote not one word of any book but in time the conditions of silence evoked an idea which all but felled me: instead of writing a book I wrote a letter to the education department in Wellington applying to be zoned at the Auckland Training College. I quoted the 95 percent for blackboard drawing and said I wished to attend the Elam School of Art up there, and I told them I had an elder sister in Auckland. What I avoided telling them was that in this way I might extricate myself from the bloody profesh and move into commercial art. I had an approving letter back zoning me to Auckland. They deserved to get a teacher out of me.

In time the others left to return to their various places of work until there was only me left with Marmie and Vadne. At last the day came for me to depart. My bag was too heavy to carry to the station so Mumma and I held it on the saddle of the horse, one of us walking each side. From the horse the two of us hauled it to the platform and into the carriage. Back again on the platform waiting for the guard's whistle I kissed Mumma's face and said, "Goodbye Mumma."

"Goodbye dear," she said.

I climbed into the carriage in silence and looked back out the window. It was the kind of scene I'd passionately watched on the Hastings railway station when nine, except that I was no longer the audience but one of the cast. As the train bustled out I saw Mumma look away into the distance with two tears filling her eyes.

This time the train was not taking me back to Wellington. How can you return to a place where you have lived for two years? It's best to go somewhere new.

The main gates of the Auckland Teachers Training College

*Elam School of Art*

## AUCKLAND TEACHERS TRAINING COLLEGE

The main trunk to Auckland was the best part of twenty-four hours through the night, seventeen I think. Somebody had put a little money in my purse to see me through till payday and Gracie had arranged my board. I had most carefully studied my clothes; I'd made myself a striped tussore silk dress with a white Byron collar, for what that's worth, and I bought my hat in Featherston, for what *that's* worth; a flesh pink felt with a brief brim with the idea of a colour in harmony with your skin for effect. Yet the first thing Gracie said when she met me in the station crowds was, "Take off that hat."

She took me and my bag per taxi to the Kyle family in Manukau Road in Epsom, a happy and charming couple with three young daughters. Mr. Kyle was a master plumber and the family lived behind and above the shop. Then back to Gleneagles in Carlton Gore Road to dine with her where she produced a man called Leo to take me to a film in the evening, a sophisticated sweet person whom I thoroughly misread, I having been a gauche Wellingtonian in the last two years. What a waste of Leo on me I now see that to be and I wish I could meet him again. All told, though I'd run up a poor record with Gray in Wellington and had never been a personal choice of hers, there was nothing she didn't do for me now, which could be the meaning of family.

On the following Monday morning I found my own way per tram and foot to the new Auckland Teachers Training College in Epsom at the base of Mt. Eden, but recently completed, the grounds, which included a crater or two, not yet laid out; a tall two-storeyed creation in the old architectural tradition with "Learn Here" declared from every brick. I applied for the infant teaching course not only because that's where I'd been appointed in the first place but I believed the smaller the child the easier it would be to control it, though I've found to the contrary since.

The very first thing I did at the ATTC among hundreds of incoming students was to make a lifelong deathlong friendship with Stella Wigmore (Wig). She was dark and I was fair. She was taller than I, black-haired, brown-eyed and with a full-lipped mouth; she had a luscious culpable figure and long legs straight all the way. She turned out to be A class in any sport she chose yet she had this extraordinarily slow manner of moving, you couldn't believe it. Above all she liked to laugh.

I remember the exact morning when we met: on the second day in the women's common room she was standing over there sort of solo and I was over here frankly lost, we inter-gravitated and asked each other our names. Wig was Auckland-bred and sophisticated whereas Wellingtonians are more unworldly. After the courses were grouped we found we were both in Section G, one of the two infant teaching sections, whereupon we at once got down to the serious business of laughing our heads off.

The next marvellous Fresher I met was Gordon T. White, who had been Gracie's pupil teacher. Gray had asked him to look up her sister and see that I had a partner for the Freshers Ball on Saturday. Tall, handsome and dark with gold in his front teeth; a personal built-in polish and his laugh you could hear from one crater to the next. He already had his own partner for the ball but he arranged to introduce me to another man, a friend of his from Wesley College. I was to meet them at the gates in the afternoon.

I was all for Gordon White himself as I walked to the gates after college. The two of them were standing there at ease, the other man not as tall as Gordon, with wavy brown hair on the top, really blue eyes and a rather soft voice, but I barely saw Keith D. Henderson. I was nineteen at the time, he was twenty and it was February 1928.

I walked down Epsom Avenue to the tramstop with these two young men, one on either side, but my attention was for Gordon who was plainly ideal man material. I don't think I addressed Keith Henderson at all unless he spoke to me which he did, about what did I think of college and such. From his loftier level G.T. found all sorts of things to laugh at, out loud too, so that people in the street would glance at him. "What a fearful lot of noise you make," I remarked.

At which he only laughed again. "That's what your sister said."

Keith mentioned something about being my partner for the ball and I do wish I replied with grace though I suppose I said something silly. I hope I wasn't flippant, that's all.

Gray lent me, no gave me, a dress of hers which I shortened and took in at the seams, a salmon-pink figured satin with a frill round the hem but I owned my own silver shoes. On went the powder and lipstick as though my training depended on it and even a breath of rouge. My hair I wore parted in the middle swinging and waving free but it was Gordon who collected me for the ball knowing his way round Auckland, and at the Kyles' his laughter and style ravished the family who foresaw big things to come.

The Freshers Ball was held in that large dance-hall which used to be in Symons Street as the college did not yet have its own hall. Within the foyer, vivid and vibrant with conversation and colour, with lights and scents and the sound of music, I recognised Keith Henderson edging through the crowd and I joined him as his partner though I'd rather it had been Gordon. But I did dance three times with Keith:

the first one-step, the supper waltz and the last, though our steps could have concurred better.

It turned out he was not accustomed to dancing, though he said he intended to be. He told me at supper his father was a Methodist minister and that dancing had not been a feature in his upbringing. I also learnt from Gordon that at Wesley College, a Methodist church boys' boarding school, Henderson had been a prefect and had put in a year on staff there.

On the other hand Gordon's step was a swooping sweeping long-legged free-style highly personal composition which nearly broke my legs keeping up with it. He had a way of dancing with his head held high surveying the surrounding scene and greeting other people all the time so that his partner felt incidental. When the ball was over, however, came the moment of truth: all being impecunious students no one had any car to take anyone home so you fitted in with last trams or went by yourself. I've no idea how I got home . . . but I'm pretty sure I wasn't kissed.

Training college began with balloons, streamers and dancing, with not a child in sight, you never heard the word; with action, laughing and with friends whom you wouldn't dream were teachers. If this were education why hadn't someone told me before? School was never like this, and when I said so to Gordon he laughed loftily all over us and said we were hedonists born, if not unrepentant heathens.

Wig didn't agree. She said we didn't have the chance to be hedonists with last trams at eleven p.m. Besides, students were so bally poor we'd all end up bally saints.

Sections F and G were the infant teaching groups numbering fifty or sixty or so. A few were city-bred but most were from the country, tentative and shy. As the newly opening weeks added up we were selecting one another as personal friends and eddying into cliques: Wig, two Mollys, Lucy, Vignette, Dreda, Maude, Rhoda. Maisie and Violet were secondary people and I think they attended the university. Another advantage of infant teaching—we considered they were so small you didn't need to go to university over them; what you could call the line of least resistance. In these early days at college there was no clue to what we'd become. About ten years ago there was a reunion at my place, Whenua in Tauranga, of Sections F and G, and most of us were there, and from those 1928 Freshers had emerged forty years later a company of breathtaking women, people of poise, presence and polish, nearly all of them still on the job. Keith Henderson was alive then delightedly embracing his old flames and that was a God-given day.

Next year is the fiftieth anniversary of the year we entered ATTC but there are only a few of us left now. The main body has gone . . . and Wig. "Precious friends hid in death's dateless night." Even the brick building itself, I hear, "has, alas, been demolished." I've asked them to hold the reunion here at Whenua again; a few survivors a half-century later.

One day in the first week I took the tram after college by myself to the inner city to find the Elam School of Art. In an area of drab tall buildings round Wellesley Street way I had to concede I'd found it. No great portals and pillars of gleaming white marble as I'd imagined which had lured me to Auckland in the first place but an undistinguished dull harridan building plonked among the warehouses. For a moment I couldn't believe it.

Entering the foyer to enroll I found no spacious studios alive and a-colour with artists in smocks but a rather pinched little woman with sallow skin and glasses peering over a grubby tall counter. As at Gordon & Gotch in Wellington I got the feeling that artists were not exactly sought-after currency for she received me as though I'd come to explain why I hadn't paid some bill. After all, these were the shaky post-war years leading downhill to the Slump. "I want to take commercial art," I said.

"*Commercial* art? All art is commercial basically."

"Oh." Thought.

"We teach art here for art's sake alone. You can do what you like with it later."

"I want to earn my living with it later."

"But you're at training college, aren't you?"

"Yes."

"Well you get paid, don't you?"

"Yes. But I don't want to be a teacher."

"Well what are you there for?"

"I don't know."

She seems to like this answer, someone not knowing why they are somewhere, and she smiles. "My name is Mrs. Reason. Your classes will be from seven till nine on Thursdays. Now," interested for the first time, "I've got to ask for the fee."

"The fee," appalled.

"Two guineas."

"Two guineas?"

"Two. *We* don't pay, you know; *you* pay us."

Blush. "Could you wait till payday?"

"Suppose we'll have to."

I retreat to the street after that, not knowing how to resuscitate my lifelong dream. What harsh places art inhabits out in the wide wide world. My own art had been on a riverbed drawing with a stick on the sand with God's own clouds for a ceiling, carving a clay bank till the daylight dimmed, alone all weekends in solitary schoolrooms with clattering rain on the roof or painting a portrait by candlelight of someone I loved for someone else I loved. But I'd still have to attend Elam or I'd be zoned back to Wellington.

On Thursday evening I turned up at seven and took my place in class, a large slap-dash room full of all kinds of people, men as well as women, but no one wore smocks with flowers on and all were sitting at desks with upright drawing boards. None of the boys was worth looking at twice and I couldn't imagine any of them dancing till dawn. True, there was one rather pretty girl sitting next to me but she seemed depressed. I saw no colour anywhere as we all worked in pencil, circled round a plaster replica of a statue of some obscure defrocked saint dated centuries back, whereas the last thing in my mind was a plaster statue of someone I hadn't met. Moreover, who should turn out to be the teacher but the pinched woman who had enrolled me, Mrs. Reason. A married woman mixed up in art; was this possible or even decent? Never mind, I'd try.

During this first evening the director came in, a man of huge body and face with disgracefully stained clothes and who breathed out loud. He seemed hungry to draw, even ravenous, and from time to time he'd stoop at someone's drawing board and do a line or two himself, including mine, breathing enthusiastically, a great tongue sweeping his jaw. Add the smouldering of his eye and you have the picture.

"So that's art," I tell Keith who meets me outside at nine. "In these terms it looks like work. I can't say I feel inspired or anything."

"Give the place a chance," he smiles as we walk to the tramstop.

I forget what I say then but he could well have said, as he often did in later life, that a hasty decision may not be the answer. His voice is soft without any edges.

Students can't afford supper in town and they don't have cars so that girls looked out and beyond the college for the ideal man with money and a car. In the meantime, however, we filled in with fellow students with whom we walked and trammed a lot, getting to know Auckland from the pavement up.

In bed that night in my room upstairs on top of the plumber's shop I took a look at the theme. I'd simply have to put up some sort of show at attending Elam, otherwise I might be zoned back to Wellington like a counterfeit coin and what would the family think. And imagine returning to Wellington now with its memories of J.B. and Aden. I still had a hot spot inside for Aden, still longed for his mouth and his breath. If Elam had required me to draw Aden by the poplars I'd have managed that all right. In my molten imagery was no room for statues, besides who would *want* my drawing of a statue? You don't just pick up a pencil and draw a statue for no one. Oh well, that other girl had talked of a life class later.

I spent a weekend at Mrs. Reason's place in a suburb where there were trees and solitude, a relaxed unpretentious house with not much paint outside and a homely kitchen inside. I failed to be the centre of attention, however, because that position was already occupied by a young man and a young woman staying at Reasons who were going to be married tomorrow. Art people I suppose. They were going to be married from Mrs. Reason's and all afternoon she was showing the bride how to iron the bridegroom's shirts of which he had dozens; about how you do the yoke first, run the iron round the base of the collar next, then you do the back, then the sleeves, then the front and you do the collar last.

My word, I thought, fancy that. As it happens when I myself ran into men's shirts by the dozen I did them no other way and taught my daughter, who taught her daughter, who no doubt will teach her daughter in time, my first great-granddaughter.

Immediately after dinner the two nuptial people excused themselves casually from the table giving no reason and vanished and I had the chance of asking Mrs. Reason when were we going to work in colour to which she replied that many a great artist had worked for years in pencil before he considered himself qualified to use colour. That I myself had been working in pencil for more than just years, it did not arise. Then the other two came back even more casually and got going on the dishes. How could you do dishes and iron shirts on the very eve of your wedding? Shouldn't you be gazing into each other's eyes in rapture, and why had they absented themselves like that?

I was supposed to go to that wedding on the morrow but I went home instead, unable to recognise artists when I saw them. All I'd recognised was how to iron shirts. So that's all art was—a plaster statue; and that's all marriage was—shirts and dishes. No romance whatever. As bad as teaching.

Wig's home was in Onehunga so we lived in the same direction. In the mornings we'd leave the tram at Greenwood's Corner and wait for each other to stroll up through the craters together to college giggling off and on all about what he'd said last night whoever it had been. Wig was committed to her Steady, Max, and they meant to marry one day when they had trained and had put together some dough whereas I was still at the unsteady stage of not knowing whom I would marry and of course there was only one real unwavering goal for any girl who called herself a girl and that was Holy Matrimony, never mind careers or freedom or anything like that. In marriage all problems would solve themselves automatically; you'd be making love all night and all day too for which no doubt the man would recompense you by having your shoes resoled which were leaking half the time. Talk of love, it never ran out; the subject was inexhaustible. And the private life of the lecturers, that was good for a laugh any time.

Coming home after college often the same except that when I had no tramfare, or a season ticket like Wig, we'd have to walk Manukau Road as far as my corner which was a very long way and Wig would catch her tram from there. Which throws light on the soles of your shoes subject.

Gordon would sometimes join us walking in and out of the craters and did most of our major go-betweening for us between Wig and Max and between me and Keith, why the man had not rung up, what the man had said about it if he had rung up or had the man gone to see Lucy, or to the girl in town who sang "Shine on, Harvest Moon." On the other hand, if we missed Gordon in the morning we'd meet him in the corridor later to find out what happened last night. These encounters had to be in the corridors when changing lecture rooms as the women's common room was discreetly at one end of the college and the men's firmly at the other. What went on in the men's common could not be seen to be believed, only heard about, and I must say it made good copy. Of what went on in the staffroom, however, we heard not one tittle or tattle so we had to make it up.

The words "education," "child" or "school" didn't occur in our vocabulary: to overhear us you'd never dream we were training to be teachers. None of which is to say that our notebooks were not handed in on time and well done too. In Gord's circle they were, for he had this idiosyncracy of keeping faithful notes in lectures, so that when a notice went up that a certain notebook had to be in by Friday and the mad rush was on for Gordon's notebooks we tended to excuse this idiosyncracy, though anyone else known to keep notes was crawling on his belly. It was as unseemly as being liked by a lecturer.

Along with this strange habit of his of keeping his notebooks, dear old Gord was something of a bright lights boy. He'd take me dancing on infrequent occasion to a cabaret on a Saturday night, mainly to the Klick Klack in Newmarket where he liked to try out the latest dance steps or compose new ones of his own. The step he developed to the prevailing tune "Dancing Cheek to Cheek," however, was pretty hard to follow since we failed to dance cheek to cheek, mainly because his cheek was far too high up for mine, but only mainly because. And he collected tennis cups by competing in any tournament within reach and he cared for his cups like people. It was whispered that Gordon was one of the few who received financial help from home since no student salary could have dressed him in style, fed him, boarded him, booked him and danced him so well, but none had met his parents to prove it. It might have been plain good management. But it did look as though he had everything a man could desire, or a girl could desire for that matter. "Except a car," he conceded.

Keith loved to go to the pictures on a Saturday night and he'd take me if I were lucky but I was afraid I was not the only girl in his field. He'd take me to church on a Sunday evening, however, to hear the Reverend Tom Olds at Mt. Eden when I'd borrow my collection from the Kyles. Not that he was religious . . . he joined the Onehunga Bible Class with Wig and Max only because Max wanted a good forward in the Bible Class hockey team . . . but he dearly loved the congregational singing, having a history of it, and usually supplied an alto to the hymns. Until the weekend his elder brother, Elliot called Jim, came to town who did have a car when we borrowed Wig and the four of us danced at the Dixieland cabaret out Point Chevalier way. That was a lovely cabaret with the windows open upon the harbour water. It was the one I've been quoting most of my life on account of the large ball of fragmented mirror revolving from the centre of the ceiling, upon which coloured lights were trained which, as it revolved, flashed back from each mirror piece making rainbow beams, like facets of the kaleidoscopic mind responding to the changing personalities of others.

It was sitting there one night in a cubicle over orange juice I saw for myself the many-faceted mind, and thought for myself of the

Keith
Henderson

many different friends you could accommodate in order to fulfil
yourself. I thought, you can't look to one person for everything. I
also thought the men had whiskey but I could well be mistaken about
that.

Where Wellington had been the year of the kiss, Auckland was becoming the year of the dance. We heard in college of a modern dance
studio in town from six to eight and we managed to find the time and
the two shillings to attend on a Tuesday night to improve our steps.
I think it was Violet who came with me and who was the college's
best-dressed woman. She was secondary teaching and attended university. Wig wasn't there but Keith was and the instructor, Miss
Margaret O'Connell, chose him as her partner for demonstration. To
me, the en-fevering sound of the rhythmic feet on the floor of that
crowded upstairs ballroom . . . oh what life had when you looked for
it; "festive" was the word for Auckland.

Yet, in conditions where all things could have been possible, doors
were closing on my dreams, even on the swimming direction. Two
girls at college beat me. I practised like mad in the city baths but they
still beat me effortlessly, Edna and Dot. I conceived the idea of copying
the magnificent style of Dot and I achieved that too but she still beat
me with a smile; her body and limbs were much longer than mine
and Edna had the same powerful shapely body as Deodonné at the

hostel in Wellington so that it got through to me that my body was too small for a champion. True, I've enjoyed this lovely swimming style of Dot's ever since but it did not stop the door closing at the time.

They were closing this way and that, the doors. Though at Elam in time I made the Life Class, there was no kind of thrill to it; no stir in the deep places where inspiration comes from. Elam came to mean no more than the occasion to meet some man afterwards at nine, Keith Henderson if I were lucky, but sometimes Percy, a man with a car and not in college who lived round Epsom way also and who'd take me to a supper of chicken sandwiches.

As for my piano work the masters were not called for in the common room but light stuff to dance to like "Lucky Me," "Naughty Waltz," "Girl of My Dreams" or "Out Together Dancing Cheek to Cheek" while at home Mr. Kyle's favorite was "Laugh

Keith in his youth

Clown Laugh" and I can see that charming man now, a very big man and dark in his chair after dinner putting down his paper and closing his eyes he loved that song so much. Yet other people in college both boys and girls managed to pursue their music successfully. It shames me to write of this time. When I think of the money and the opportunities squandered by the education department on that girl, all those sound lecturers available in English, education, psychology, philosophy, music, history, science, art and teaching practice, yet all I took seriously was dance and fun. Plenty of friends, oh yes oh yes, but what did that prove? Legend has it that I was the belle of training college but that's only legend. To be the belle of anywhere calls for a certain strength of character. As it happens, there were several belles in that college, girls of beauty and responsibility, but take it from me I was not among them. Life was cutting me down to size: not a gifted girl in several directions but an irresponsible dreamer.

Where was the purpose I'd grown up with, the blazing confidence in some important work to do in the world waiting for me alone when I finally got there; had I lost it in the dark years? Whether or not I had, I was due for a knock-back from life . . . in time, some time. In the meantime, however, three incidents did manage to penetrate to the undermind to influence the course of my thinking; the first slipped by unnoticed by me though it was seen by others.

Nothing could stop exams at term's end. Idling home from college, "Y'know, Wig, there are times when I wish I could fail in every single subject to prove once and for all I'm not a teacher then I'd be forced to do something else."

Wig reminded me you wouldn't have such good hours and good holidays in anything else. She was going to pass in every subject.

Gordon's notebooks helped us all quite a bit but no one else could write for us the essay on teaching method we'd been warned about from the start, which would be written in exam time with no reference books, so it called for much personal study. So far, the only teaching philosophy that had got through to me while dreaming lectures away, gazing out the window at Mt. Eden, I'd found in a page on Rousseau in a slim green book which Mr. Shaw had taken us over in class. With astonishment I'd gathered that I agreed with the views of Rousseau though he was not referred to again. He would take his pupil Emile roaming the countryside for his lessons in the way that we had roamed when young: playing in the creeks, climbing the trees and examining birds' eggs, carving steps in banks, exploring round corners, asking questions, answering them and talking about the creatures on our way.

Now why hadn't I heard about this before? I thought of Miss Little's children packing in the factage and of Miss Whackington's little chicken flushing beneath the strap. If this theory of Rousseau's were valid, you could almost be a teacher. I think Emile must have gone unnoticed by the others as something too fanciful to be serious about.

As this essay was the term's main assignment carrying the most marks, most of the week beforehand was to be given to its preparation but I felt no need to study. Whereas I'd not been able to absorb the formal and standard teaching methods prevailing, the rigid authoritarianism of them, I'd been deeply moved by Rousseau. In the face of the others my mind slammed shut like the door of a vault. "Have you prepared your essay, Squeak?" from Gord.

"How could I when I've been doing your art project?"

"There are still a few days left."

"Then I'll be doing Keith's art project. He hasn't one line in his book."

Wig confesses she doesn't know how the heck to illustrate her nursery rhyme.

"Leave it to me, Wigmore."

"But what about your essay?"

"I'll see to that when the time comes."

The time came one morning at nine a.m. in Room 13. I looked at my blank lined paper, at my blank mind, at the lecturer, Mr. Shaw, a benign man of letters, and at the other students already under way, knowing beforehand what they were going to say. I remembered nothing of teaching method having heard nothing worth remembering. All I remembered was Rousseau. So if I wrote nothing or about Rousseau I'd fail either way. I had nothing to lose. Good. You're in a strong position when you have nothing to lose, like a stag with his back to a cliff facing the hunter's gun, and you usually play well. I started off writing both comfortably and recklessly along the lines of the European master who favoured learning in its natural state, his way being the only way I myself could learn anyway, freely from life itself, within the context of living. For once I was relating this sinful teaching to the imagery within myself, abundant material spanning right back to Te Pohue when three little girls wandered barefoot: the lake with the floating island, the hills, the gulleys, the orchards, the forest and the houses we made for ourselves. The stories we told. It occurred to me that if I were faced with an exam on the subject of the foothills of the ranges of New Zealand I'd come up scholarship material. I only pulled up when time was called three hours later, I think it was called more than once except I didn't hear, to find only I was left in Room 13, that Mr. Shaw was waiting gently for my paper and that I was very hungry.

Marks and assessments began trickling in during the last week on the notice board in the common room. Of course my notebooks came off all right, as did the notebooks of any of Gordon's followers, and I daresay our music and English did too, as we liked these subjects, though we must have crashed in others like history and science, but my art marks topped the college. As for the essay on teaching method, it was one of the others who drew my attention to it, that I'd been marked 95 percent, the only one, but it left me cold and I thought no more about it. It wasn't important. All I remember is Wig before the notice board warning me, "You want to watch it, Warner. You've averaged a pass. You might end up a teacher yet."

Looking back on that morning now I realise the 95 percent could have been another case of the deadly Precedent rearing its head where you don't mark anything 100 percent, but I doubt it. To this day, however, I've not told anyone what I found out about Rousseau, but as the other escape hatches edged shut about me—art, music, swimming and marriage—leaving only the bloody profesh, here was the same skylight inching open again as it had in the dark past: writing.

These were the years leading to the Great Depression, it was 1928— in another year, the Wall Street crash would spawn the Slump of the early 1930s, yet we young teachers in training seemed oblivious of coming doom, continued to be engrossed in personal interchange, talked out our love-affairs non-stop and how to avoid teaching, although all of them forty years later were still teachers and very good ones at that.

As it happens, I think self-absorption has its place in that particular span of the journey through life. It's a good thing to laugh and dance in youth without knowing what's ahead. It's appropriate to gaze in upon yourselves, for in the study of your own mind as well as one another's you're learning Mind Itself regardless, and at the closest quarters. Wig and I and the others were a rapturous nineteen wallowing in the action of the college, well I was anyway; Wig had an innate responsibility with private supplies of common sense.

Plenty of time round thirty, I'd say, to call on what you've learnt of the mind to support you through the non-stop lessons on the road from then on when you need all the knowledge you have to survive; time enough then for the inner eye to turn outward upon the universal, which is my definition of maturity.

At that time I don't think we had one thought on the state of the nation or the country, let alone of the world. Love was forever and was meant for us. Dancing away in the common room with someone at the piano, "I was meant for you; you were meant for me . . ." on a couple of small islands in the South Pacific sixteen hundred miles from the ice packs of the Pole.

First term over and I took the day-and-night train down the main trunk home. Mumma was no longer at Featherston; Ashton, who was married and living in Lower Hutt, had brought her down also to be near to him, but the temporary place I found her in, an urgent transit camp idea only till he could get her something better, was as bad as behind Dean Court in Hastings, it cried aloud the Depression ahead. I don't remember anyone else at home though Evadne must have been there attending school and Marmie too but it seemed just Mumma and me.

It was up on the hill, this place. In the dark dank dinginess we'd sit with each other over silent cups of tea with little to say at all. I suppose there was sympathy, I hope so, but between us was little of the accord she enjoyed with some of the others. As I grow older and become a little more like Mumma in both temperament and appearance, I understand her more and I wish I could restore our earthbound losses.

Sometimes I walked down the hill with her on her solitary beat to buy a loaf of bread and a pound of butter with a half-crown Ashton had given her but no conversation surfaced, though inner monologues tumulted. At least it was an effective warning not to leave training college where I was among dear friends and being paid seven pounds a month. With not a spare job anywhere in the country I'd have to come back here. True, we young seemed to be oblivious of society's trauma but it must have registered somehow for those years then had much the same feel and threat as these years now, 1977 plus.

Never mind, there was always some sweet spot; you could find a cup of tea round at Ashton's place, pretty children, cheerful smiles and a wife with big brown eyes.

Having recorded that I'd met Rousseau I would close this section on training college but for further earthquakes which altered the terrain ahead, in particular one recurring tremor which qualified communication itself: touch. Not only the biological rapport you soon come to recognise but intellectual accord and spiritual fusion or, to put it in

our simple way, you get on with some people and not with others
without knowing why.

G. T. White and K. D. Henderson were far from being exclusively
mine, which did not overthrow me though I knew all about it. I knew
Lucy was in the field who was pretty all the way down, one or two
others in college and there was that girl in town, not a student, who
was a lovely singer and whom Keith used to go and see, but what I
heard was that this girl had a father who chased away every boy who
went there so that highly improper kissing took place in the alleys for
brief moments of time and very seldom also. Because of her favorite
popular song, "Shine on, Harvest Moon," I referred to her as Harvest
Moon.

As for the ones in college you couldn't help knowing who they
were for you'd see them left high and dry in pairs in the corridors between changing lecture rooms. So when K.D.H. did not ring up for
a while I had a fair idea why not. So far, however, share and share
alike was fair enough for us ardent virgins as the first requirement of
a teacher-in-training was unassailable morality. Nor was it hard to be
so, all the girls in college were undisputed virgins, for not only was
drink unheard of but at the time girls put a price on themselves.

So I took my turn with the others. If I were lucky on a Saturday
night I'd be dancing with Gordon at the Klick Klack and if I were
luckier still on a Sunday I'd be going to church with Keith to hear the
Reverend Olds. No one was more surprised than I to find I was
interested in his sermons. I could better understand Tom Olds than I
could the lecturers in college. And that would be a lucky weekend
with young men I knew and liked, but mid-week it was open-slather
sampling new boys, not students, and having a car. But I got through
few of these as I was dropped so quickly, being unprepared to pay with
kisses. All I was after was a story for the girls the next day. I marvelled
at the way Wig kept steady with the one boy, Max, and he only a
student too. Yet girls had to admit we did have much in common with
the men students: all young, all poor, all virgin and most of the girls
and boys paired off though our final goal remained a rich man not a
teacher, good-looking and with a car.

Percy was a rich man not in college with most accessories except
looks who took me to expensive shows in town and bought me Queen
Anne chocolates. But I couldn't stand him. Only good chocolates held
us together and his story value for the Kyles, who knew the family.
This farce went on for some time until one night as I hastily withdrew
from the car he grasped my arm firmly with a thin hand. "I don't

want to shock you, Sylvia, but don't you know that when a man courts a girl as long as I have they . . . well usually they . . . they kiss."

He did shock me but in another way. The touch of his hand. I say nothing and try to squirm free.

"It's your innocence that maddens me," he says.

How dreadful.

"Sylvia, don't you . . . hasn't anyone *told* you what marriage means?"
I fled.

Which relieved the Kyles, but disappointed Wig and Gordon who liked the chocolates though Molly and Lucy nearly fainted with laughing. "He made me ill," I told them in the crater on our way back from Anne's Pantry. "I'll be old before I recover. And I'll have you know, Wig, you can arrange for other supplies of chocolates as from now on."

I had been cruel. Percy's family knew I had been cruel, as had the Kyles and maybe Wig had too. If only it had got through to me that men were not just handy commodities but had feelings inside like women. I seethed with secret shame over this but the issue remained constant: his touch on me.

Though I circulated among several young men I made no headway in any one direction. Though I wished to and I tried. I was still haunted by the memory of Aden, whose physical touch had enslaved me. It was sinking into me slowly that touch was the key factor in affairs with men, something I had no control over whatever. Touch was so selective it made the personal decisions for you. You could say it narrowed the field as it had already done with Wig and Max. Could it possibly be touch which governed the chance of a long and happy marriage . . . or not? The thought had an earthquake quality, rocking the mindscape so that clay banks on the wayside split and crumbled, streams changed course and raw horizons reared.

It was during this first winter when Keith's brother Jim came to town again for the weekend with Keith, and there's little to match a couple of minister's sons veering from the straight and narrow. We managed to gather in Wig again, after all the brother was a charming man wasn't he, not a teacher, not hitched and actually had a car, a Ford New Beauty. On the Saturday night Wig and I sprinkled spangles on our hair and with the boys returned to Dixieland where the sphere of mirrored lights revolved and our favorite jazz band reigned. Really . . . the luxury of sipping orange juice through a straw, talk about sophisticated.

On the Sunday they thought of something else. I'd heard about
these bus rides at night to a terminal on the fringe of the city which
were popular in college, for the round-trip fare was cheaper than the
pictures. The four of us caught a bus at the post office at the bottom
of Queen Street and Keith and I sat in the back. The moment the bus
started and the lights went out and we turned to each other something
lit up between us: for richer for poorer, for better or for worse, in sick-
ness and in health, till death do us part.

College bounced along much as before except that in my mind his
name and my name turned into We and a third dimension changed
incident to drama. Quarrels came, I couldn't believe it. "Wig, this is
no routine difference but a clear-cut case of survival."

"Give the man a chance," Wig said. "He only went to see Lucy because you played hard to get."

"But did he meet me after college as he said he would? He did not."

"That's because someone told him, some woman I might add, you
were still in love with a bloke in Wellington and were only filling in
with him."

"Why should he care?"

"You want me to say, Because he loves you, don't you?"

"He doesn't."

"Who knows?"

On Thursday night he rang up towards nine to say he was coming
round to my place and I rushed upstairs and combed my hair. From
Mt. Eden where he boarded he walked round the back streets to
Manukau Road and I set out to meet him. To see him coming along
the street towards me, my new sweetheart, his arms open to greet me,
was to become as beautiful as any woman on her way to meet her
lover. "You said you were going to swot tonight, Keith."

"I've done a couple of hours."

"Have you?"

"I've been looking forward to Thursday all week."

"I didn't know."

"To being together," he says.

Peace meant being together.

"I say, Gord, why did K.D. turn his back on me at the college social
on Friday night?"

"He said that when he was walking home on Thursday night after

leaving you he saw you going out again with another man in a car.
God you're mad, woman."

"He must have been very hurt to turn his back on me like that."

Soberly, "He was."

"What did he say?"

"He said, What's the use."

"I can't understand why he should care, Gordon."

"Neither can I but he does."

"Will you tell him, Gordon, please, that the man he saw me with
on Thursday night was a friend of Gracie's taking me back to Gleneagles for supper . . . please."

"Liar."

"Please fix it all up at interval, Gord. Don't let it stay like this. I
can't stand it."

"God. The convolutions you women go through to justify yourselves. If only you knew how the men see through it all in the men's
common room you'd save yourselves the trouble. Coquetry doesn't
pay."

"All right, all right then finish. Let it all be over between Henderson
and me."

He laughs upon the moving multitude of students. "Women. You're
all sirens and you're *all mad.*"


"Listen, Molly. I'm going to get on a ship and take off for good." I'll
pack a frying pan and a mug and swag it through foreign lands.
Canada for a start, being Empire, and get a job in a factory painting
china, or designing patterns in a textile firm. Oh for a studio in Italy
where they sit round the wine bowl and talk till dawn.

"Why?" says Lucy dryly.

"To escape the pain of men."

"And all because," says Wig, "one man turned one back one Friday
night. Last week you were for marriage only, now it's a free life. If
you're a sample, Warner, of what it's like to be two people I'm glad
you're not three."

Lucy is a very pretty girl yet she says seriously, looking across campus
to Mt. Eden, "I haven't yet met the man who means enough to me to
get on a ship about or quarrel with or . . . but I want to."


I borrowed three pounds from Ag, the senior woman on staff, and took
off home to Lower Hutt again where I found Mumma in a better

abode, not quite a house but a shelter rather at the bottom of the hill this time. At least the sun came in the door and it was handier to the shops by which I mean the butcher, baker and grocer. Dear old Vad must have been home.

True, the economy of the country was slithering downhill but I can't say we noticed it much. At times we were hungry this spring but we'd been hungry before, having known the post-war years. We'd survived a winter behind Dean Court.

It was quiet at home. Away from the high action on the college front a mind had a chance to look at itself, to find out what, in fact, inhabited the lower stratum. With the candle blown out round midnight I'd find it tumultuous with energy and imagery; all this surplus power released through the cleavages of the last two earthquakes, Rousseau and love. In mind the whole works would start writing with facility yet by morning light all had vanished. Why didn't it stay? What I needed, I thought, was another tough dose of pariahdom since you don't do good work when you're popular.

Back in college I returned to my brushes and paint, my Indian ink, pencil and chalk. I devastated the others in art class with speed, dramatic impact and by drawing with two hands simultaneously, and two different subjects sometimes. Miss Copeland, the art teacher, would stand and watch me and it was she who taught me at this very late date the principles of perspective and the function of the eye-level, but no one so far had taught me the characteristics of Whatman's paper and how to make a simple wash in colour. I was nearly forty when I found this out for myself. I think it was not so much my own art of a remarkably high standard as that everyone else's was of a remarkably low standard because art was considered a second-class subject in schools. It was still like that in Canada when I was there; it was better in the United States.

We were now being placed out in schools on section, harnessed up for weeks with a teacher and class but I'll skip all that . . . my section marks must have lapped round zero. In college also I was running into discipline; I was dying to join Mr. Hollinrake's choir not only for its own sake but because Keith was in it and many of my friends, but I forgot to get my name down by Friday. No pleading would shift Holly. He was only a young man but he was English and No meant No, even though he praised my accompaniments. Exactly the same thing happened the following year when I again missed putting my name down by Friday. I was meeting discipline from K.D.H.

himself over my absurd coquetry, playing off other men against him in the most disgraceful absence of trust in him, trying to prove him in the most amateur way. Afraid my heart would be broken again. For better or for worse it was already. Yet we were able to come together more often and more closely, my mind and my heart were full of my love: it would take just one kiss in the basement downstairs for last week's quarrel to mend.

> —But if the while I think on thee, dear friend,
> All losses are restored, and sorrows end.

The ten weeks' summer holiday took me to my married sister Muriel's place in Nelson's Golden Bay where I got a holiday job at the mental hospital there to see what money looked like. Even casual untrained nursing was well-paid there and Muriel had worked there once so I shut my eyes and . . . went. Here I witnessed the different forms which a breakdown of the personality can take, pieces of it lying round in day-rooms and night dormitories, in the outside yards with high wire fences and in padded cells through the observation slits. I learnt more about the mind as such than any lecturer or any book could teach anyone. To see it in disarray is quite another thing from seeing the mind whole. I'd shut my eyes and brain when I'd come on staff but terror opened them both. In one fortnight I learnt more about the human mind than I've learnt in my entire lifetime since, but when my name went up for night duty I ran off in panic and spent the rest of the ten weeks getting over it, doing less than nothing and lying in the sun on the beach to do it, dreaming of Keith Henderson. He wrote me one sweet letter which I did not answer in case he thought I was chasing him. Trust, I had none.

I spoke to him in my own way which was to practise daily on a neighbour's piano a series of variations on our personal theme song, "Girl of My Dreams," in running scalework and galloping arpeggios. When I returned to Auckland in the new year it took the whole of the first term for us to mend this time.

This second year I came to know a real commercial artist called Pete of very long and slender body and who wore spectacular clothes. He also boarded at Gleneagles and worked a lot in his room. His posters were all over his bedroom walls and one day when he was painting across his bed a ravishing Spanish lady I said, "Pete, how do you get that glow in her skin?"

He showed me how he painted the whole paper a strong yellow first then applied the flesh tints on the top of that and the hint of the warmth came through.

This was the year I looked after my sister Daphne, who had come to Auckland, supporting her through her trauma, walking miles to see her every afternoon after college at willing cost to myself. It was I who secretly cared for Daphne with none of the others knowing, who rescued her and helped her off safely down to Muriel in Golden Bay, and if you want to know the source of her sorrow then spell out that fateful word "love." All she left behind was a name for Auckland: Unlucky City. Love was not being presented to me as the ideal goal for a girl after all, as it seemed inseparable from tears. To put one's faith and hope in love was to put one's life into the hands of another, as I wished to put my own life into the keeping of Keith Henderson, who was by nature human at best and who himself would have to die some time, at worst, though youth never thought of that. I had known three formative upheavals—Rousseau, love and the broken minds in the mental hospital—but I still didn't know what to do about love.

I was still heading for the classroom. I could, however, postpone it by applying for a third year to specialise in art, as Wig was applying for a third year in physical education in Dunedin. Maybe I could stand that since I had to earn my living some bloody how, but I overlooked the fact that the craft of drawing was one thing and the craft of teaching it was another. Our final art assignment had been to make a book illustrating several poems. Having helped Gordon and Keith through theirs I took off three days at home to do my own in order to pass it in on time. Three days of sustained impassioned love in it, working in my bedroom. One verse and picture stays with me:

> And in the orchard there's a place
> Where you can lie and feel the fall
> Of apple blossoms on your face
> And drowsing hear the cuckoo call.

You mightn't believe this but Miss Copeland marked me 99 percent which was worse than the other two 95 percents. She'd withheld the one mark from excellence because, she said with some pride, although it was obviously worth 100 percent there was no precedent for 100. She glowed with satisfaction at the 99 as though she were doing me a favour. Then she asked for my book for the college, which I gave away to her. And I wonder where that is now.

At least Gracie saw it when visiting the college exhibition of work and Miss Copeland told her, "Your sister's work is the high-water mark of art since the college began."

So with a view to a third year in art I asked her for a recommendation and she agreed with some fervour but she didn't tell me what she'd told Gracie. I went along to the principal, a bachelor called Mr. Cousins who was known as Cuz, and said to him where he sat at his desk, "I wish to apply for a third year in art, Mr. Cousins."

"Far from granting you a third year, Miss Warner, we've considered dismissing you for irresponsibility."

Vignette it was who came upon me alone in the cloakroom. "What's the matter, Squeak?"

"Cuz growled at me."

It was the beginnings of the makings of me; I was due for a knock-back from life. The terrain ahead would never be the same again. I was told, however, that when the staff had been discussing dismissing me, Mr. Shaw of the Rousseau essay had protested, "But Miss Warner is a brilliant student."

The end of 1929. Everyone in Sections F and G finished college with Teachers C . . . except me. I failed in one subject . . . guess what? Education II. Wig applied for a third year in physical education and got it and she was going away to Dunedin. Max got a third year in phys. ed. too, I think. They were both going to Dunedin. Apart from that all our year wanted teaching jobs in or near a town but the Slump excelled itself and there was not one job for anyone. Except for two · only of our year, two men who took the plunge into the back country for permanent jobs: sole charge schools on the frontiers of civilisation. One was George Guy and the other Keith Henderson, both of whom got a foot on the bottom rung of the ladder of their chosen profession a year before anyone else and held the advantage as from then on. The rest of us were placed in schools for a probationary assistant (P.A.) year, our fifth year of training, though I was due to sit the outside exam in Education II. They still placed me, however, with the others and at Cornwall Park, which meant at least I was still in Auckland. Our cosy cliques were scattered all directions. But to think that *after all that* I was still not certificated and could not have had a permanent job even with no Slump.

As for Keith Henderson, you couldn't hold the man down in his joy at his first permanent appointment. His own sole charge and he the Head. He'd come out of college with good grading, being a young man who'd kept his notebooks up to date, who had attended the university, done well in practical teaching on section, was on a committee or two, had belonged to the choir and who had made the A hockey team. Neither had he slipped into any showy kind of trouble that I knew of or, put it this way, had not been found out, and was rated responsible. Marvellous word. He'd even joined the superannuation fund and had made me do so also. He was no longer an impecunious student but a trained teacher in employment. The name of his little first school was Whareorino, I forget how many miles out to the coast from Awakino in Taranaki north of New Plymouth, and I heard that his parents, the Reverend and Mrs. Henderson of Rangiora, were overjoyed.

During the last six months or more Keith and I had gone together to the college picnics and peripatetics on the ferry up the Waitemata Harbour to Waiheke and Onetahi, to the pictures in town and the socials and were partners at the end-of-year ball. I made myself a pink dress for that with a full tulle skirt and our dance steps coincided better by now. It was accepted we belonged romantically but there had been no talk of marriage. On his last Sunday night, however, he invited me to tea at the place where he boarded in Mt. Eden to attend church after. Sitting together sedately in his bedroom waiting to be called to the table he showed me photos of his people in the South Island. "This is Mother. This is Dad," as though there were a new dimension between us, and I anyway was all over in love. Happiness painted the room in many colours.

The night before Keith left Auckland for the South we had a meal together in town, the first time he'd been able to afford this, and I wore the blue crepe de chine dress with the lace at the throat because he'd said he liked me in blue. The place was upstairs somewhere in Queen Street and we sat self-consciously opposite each other across a narrow table. The meal could have been better I remember but it made no difference, the hour remained a rapturous one. His hair was long on the top and wavy and his eyes as blue as my dress and a glow, almost tangible, radiated from him, he was so happy at his first permanent position right in the thick of the Slump, the first step in his chosen profession. His thought had the translucence of a young man undivided. His dreams were the same as his needs.

We were shy. In mind we were no closer than hand in hand. Eating together publicly as though we indeed belonged to each other and had a right to be together. I don't know what we talked about but

I suppose it was Whareorino. Later
we took a tram then walked up
Mt. Eden, a warm and cloudy night.
At the very top we chose a small
shallow grassy crater, lay down together and murmured to each other
of the future, as though the future
were for the shaping and the taking.
I was twenty going on twenty-one
and he was nearly twenty-two yet
we'd shared so relatively little privacy we hardly knew each other as
people, much less as man and
woman. Though the grass was our
bed and the clouds our blanket we
had not yet even begun to explore
that territory of the senses known
to lovers alone. In this darkest night
all we knew was an abundance of
stars because of being together and
that we'd rather be kissing than
not. No dream shared my bed that
night, of far lands, art and freedom
of the spirit, like a second lover.

Till death do us part!

I think the heavy word "marriage" intimidated us both, but love
doesn't pause if it can help it, not
in a pillowed crater, and Keith finds
his own way to the future by flank-
ing the word "marriage." "When
I look ahead," he says, "I see you in
a doorway shaking a mat."

I can't see it myself. I don't say a
thing.

The night has a lot to say, however, though muted; you hear a
rumbling in the city throat and it's
not saying anything about mats in
doorways. It's about lights in streets
interweaving intricately, eyes meeting eyes on Friday night and about

spangled tulle in the dawn. The voices crawl up Mt. Eden like an enemy intent on attack, taking cover behind rocks of scoria and in grassy dips of darkness, to rescue one of their own.

I remember every one of Keith's words when he finally asks me to marry him and he does use the word "marry" which I thought was brave. He was sure of life; of his job and of me and his future. He saw it as clearly as I saw the invisible stars . . . and I remember my single-minded answer.

In his orderly way he maps out the journey ahead: in two years' time we'll become engaged, two years after that and we'll marry. Four whole years . . . when I'd have married him tomorrow. He speaks as though youth were for ever and ever and life were never ending. As though Time would wait as long as we wanted, as though Fate were only a pupil teacher and God a passer-by.

Decades later Keith and I drove round the training college. The buildings had been completed long since, the grounds laid out and they'd made a park of the popular crater where Wig and I ate pies from Anne's Pantry, but it still housed the same imagery. We drew up at the original main gates and I said, "This is where we met."

Reflectively he repeated, "So this is where we met." He'd forgotten, I think. Then he smiled to himself at the memoried building.

Keith was well gone when I turned twenty-one. I'd made the mistake of leaving the Kyles' place, a friendly and stable family who'd been good to me. Gracie's friend Bertha Smith who also lived in Epsom asked me to come and board there to keep Gray company who'd been ill. On my birthday Mrs. Smith asked Wig to tea before she went away to Dunedin. Wig must have been saving the whole year through for she gave me a little gold watch. This tender two-girl party marked the end of our training college; Stella Wigmore and I were never to be so long together again. I expected to share the journey ahead with Keith Henderson, as man and woman, but two girls walk separate ways.

CORNWALL PARK    For the first time in my life I didn't go home for Christmas, though Mumma's letters spoke of a better home Ashton had secured for her: painted outside, lined inside, a stove that would go and a garden in front. Instead I applied for a job at John Courts for the eight-week holiday period till school reopened; it was to do the newspaper ads, but they already had an artist drawing clothes all day on elongated bodies so I ended up in the gowns department on the third floor entering addresses of country customers in the biggest book in the world. For the time being I no longer had to admit to people I was a teacher. "I'm a shopgirl," loud and clear. J.B. and Aden had not proposed to a teacher, having had enough of school.

In my fifth and final year of training I'd been placed as Probationary Assistant (P.A.) at Cornwall Park with a class of my own under the supervision of the infant mistress, another serene saintly spinster tall and grey. Miss Pence. About thirty Primer 2 five-year-olds of whom I remember three, one of them a little freckled girl called Polly with straw hair who could not learn the difference between "and" and "the." She'd weep over it. Give me Polly now and she'd read in five minutes in excitement and joy and for good. And that's all I can bear to write of that final year, except for the piano in the corridor and a janitor who liked waltzes.

Suddenly the education board dropped thirty-three pounds into my lap for boarding allowance overlooked in the last two years which I banked at once for an overseas ticket. I'd been in Auckland two years now, which was a long time for me, and I'd been in this country for twenty-one, whereas there's nothing like a change to solve your problems. I tore down to the booking office on the wharf and brought home exotic brochures from other Empire countries. Yet before I lifted a foot from New Zealand soil I'd sit that Education II I'd missed in college, in the outside exam in order to complete my Teachers C and be a qualified something.

A phone call frothed in upon this one evening about nine from a voice which said he'd seen a photo of me on Lucy's wall and could he come round right now. I was wearing the heaven-blue crepe de chine with the lace ruffles at the throat and wrists and I walked to the gate to meet him. A soft summer evening made for lace and lovers at a white picket gate and here I found the rich young man with a sports model Chev and sad dark eyes. He tells me he is a pilot-in-training at Mangere and I had to admit I was a teacher-in-training since he already knew it from Lucy. Even airmen are nervous of teachers; the only people not afraid of teachers are other teachers which is the reason I suppose they marry one another. His name was Floyd Duckmanton.

Soft summer, soft evening, soft lace and soft words, a flawless set of data, yet when he took me for a drive to try his luck every cell in my body turned its back, every gland and neurone, nor was there anything I could do about it. During the following year no amount of first-nights in town, dressed-up drives on a Sunday, sophisticated dances at the Aero Club and the status of being a rich man's girl could bring my hormones to heel. The treachery of chemistry. When he'd completed his flying hours and passed both his written and practical exams he took me up in his Moth as his first passenger, looped the loop, executed the falling leaf, the roll, the suicidal stall turn, landed and took off again several times and skidded back up to the hangar but alas, as the old novels used to say—alas, she loved another.

I spent much time with Floyd Duckmanton, both of whose parents were dead, but we failed to grow closer together other than clocking up common adventures, though I must say these adventures were something. For reasons traumatic, dramatic and sad I left the Smith home in Epsom in a sequence of soap opera action with Floyd in a trail that led to the YWCA hostel in town first, a bleak stage indeed, then to Floyd's own big house in Mt. Albert he'd inherited from his parents where he made me a star guest: bath, meals and school in the morning, ducking down in the car beneath a rug so the neighbours wouldn't see me, and finally to a room of my own *at last* in Manukau Road—a large room at the end of a long cornered verandah with a cubby-hole kitchen in one corner sporting a sink and a bench and shelves. And a gas stove.

Separated by hundreds and hundreds of miles and for months at a time, Keith and I were looking reality in the face. We had to make do with letters which grew so full that sometimes on a Tuesday or a Thursday my little secretive landlady could no longer push them under my door so that I'd have to penetrate the fastnesses of her shadowed private kitchen to openly ask for them. His famous one of thirty-nine pages packed into two laboring envelopes will be felt by all young people in love. So much joy I knew in that room of my own, reading and reading his letters with tea in the pot, dreaming and dreaming when the pot was empty. This thing about belonging to one particular person, exclusively, to be wonderful to someone; to plan ahead with someone else, to share the future whatever it was.

Then Keith bought the little Ford from his brother and he'd come to Auckland in the holidays to see his girl, who was me, no longer an impecunious student with no transport but a fully trained teacher with a job, a car and a future, the kind of man we girls had dreamed about in college miraculously materialised, with more qualifications than we had ever bargained for, a haven in human form, and loving as well, with whom you found accord and company in dreams. You were walking hand in hand with a man along the roads of life, up the hills, down the gulleys and along the flat stretches. In all weathers. You could never be a pariah again when you had a mate. Now who among us would have thought of that when in college? In the world of love we were growing up inadvertently and no longer giggled over silly secrets.

In the room of my own at 589 I had a home of my own in which to receive my sweetheart for once, though he still boarded at Mt. Eden when he came. Most of our friends had vanished from Auckland and we were mainly alone. Tentatively and shyly we began exploring together those exclusive regions of passion known to lovers alone, learning together and from each other the tumescent truths of love. Code language surfaced between us that only we two knew; as the sun spread through the wide bay windows we drank tea together, broke bread together, embraced together and gazed together at a future in which we never grew old and where we were ever in love. In the evening when the curtains were drawn across the wide windows upon the lights of the city, at the touch of his lips the humble moment swelled to eternal proportions yet although our love meant being together it also meant separation, one parting after another so that "goodnight" and "goodbye" were the worst words we knew.

We were so shy with each other. A Sunday afternoon came and we went for a dressed-up drive down the Great South Road where we drew up at a sedate little restaurant and went in for tea. My hat, gloves and bag and he in the same soft grey double-breasted suit I'd known for two years, a meticulous white collar and blue tie. Love is self-conscious in the daylight especially on a Sunday afternoon dressed up in a tea-room, you don't know what to say, it doesn't say itself as it did last night. Trying to live up to what had happened to us, to acknowledge it in public. Relieved to creep back into our car, to drive back through the circumspect city and find each other again in the solitude of my room.

And there was Floyd. I never heard of a woman who could accommodate two men successfully and I was no exception. One bland afternoon Floyd came pounding along the verandah as usual, opened the door, walked right in and the two of them met and I wouldn't like that to happen again.

At times during the year when the term was too long we'd meet down the main trunk somewhere like Te Kuiti, I coming by train and he by car, and you'd get these railway station scenes and really there are none others like them. My new tweed coat and tweed hat, white-flecked pale blue, and Keith with the collar of his coat turned up, the brim of his hat shading his eyes. What I don't know about the stations on that main trunk in the middle of the night between Auckland and Wellington doesn't exist.

And country hotels where the easy-going staff would invariably be enchanted. Sitting silently together in a quiet dining room with nothing to say when there was so much to be said. And the compassionate staff would understand and start off topics for us. Everyone knows how, after separation, there's a necessary period of adjustment. We could talk better when walking strange country roads arm in arm, the gravel crunching under our shoes . . . confiding hesitantly softly. And I'd hear about Whareorino, the single man's quarters of one small room which he was vastly proud of, his own first home, of his little school and the children in it and the settlers in the valley. We simply did not know each other and would meet as strangers all over again. Both being teachers we could have been dismissed for these clandestine lovers' meetings, for romance was no excuse.

The mid-winter of mid-term was far too hard and I trained south to Te Kuiti to meet my love, though as neither of us had any money we spent the night of frost in the car. Love and frost and one rug only. We nearly died. In the morning we drove to Otorohanga and booked in at another warm country hotel to be paid for later where we took hot baths and next a glorious breakfast of porridge, bacon, eggs, tea and toast. The sweet waitress, though younger than we, kept our conversation going. There were some very sweet smiles in that dining room that morning. Oh yes it was professionally unprofessional, deliciously risky, but no price was too high to be together even though paid for later. The only word in our vocabulary: together. Fancy, three and a half years left till marriage . . . God.

And the time Keith's new friend Henry organised the Easter weekend. I disembarked from the train at Te Kuiti in my city tweeds on Easter Friday night, Henry met me in his car, drove miles and hours south to Awakino where Keith was waiting with the horses. In the secret midnight the three of us mounted, rode to the mouth of the Awakino River where the ocean of the Tasman volleyed and thundered, turned north up the beach of black sand, following the white line of the froth of the waves four or five miles, negotiated the hair-raising steep cliff track balancing above the rocks below to the large old farmhouse above where Henry lived with his new wife Lou. On the top of the cliff above the Tasman.

And there by day we picnicked on the rocky beach below, rode horses along the black iron sands, dined by candlelight in the shadowy kitchen with its furtive ghosts, my red satin blouse, Keith's college blazer, with the gales whistling and calling and blustering in from the ocean supplying the music, to sit formally on the couch in the parlour after, side by side, before a mighty log fire. It was a time when I began to suspect that men actually had feelings of their own too and could be hurt and joyed just like women . . . astonishing; when I discovered even tenderness could be excruciating. The preliminaries of communication.

Then the whole journey back to the train in reverse per horse, beach, road and car to Te Kuiti again with Keith this time and the train pulling out at dawn. Parting once more; he southward, I northward. Railway stations . . .

> Trip no further, pretty sweeting,
> Journeys end in lovers' meeting—

The most significant lovers' meeting was when Henry managed to organise me in daylight to see Keith's school at Whareorino in the Waikawau Valley seaward from Awakino. Not close on the coast but in sound of the sea. His sole charge school had no teacher's residence as it had been intended for a bachelor teacher who could rough it. A single man's bach was all, one very small room, with a low iron roof you could reach up and touch and, apart from a stove inside and a rainwater tank outside fed from the corrugated iron roof, there were no facilities whatever: no bench, no sink, no bathroom, no bedroom, no wash-house and you shared the school lavatory. The school was one room too in the historic style and both school and bach were dug into the side of a hill with no track up from the road. This bach was very cold in winter and far too hot in summer, they said, but at least I'd seen it.

Keith was making lasting friends in the valley among the settlers who helped him in working bees to improve the glebe—carving a lane up the bank to the school, planting a shelter belt of pines and decorating the lane with native trees from the bush like five-finger, koromiko and ponga. At that time I did not realise what I was witnessing: Keith's first signature in trees across the New Zealand countryside, the beginning of his getting on with people in his district and his first

zestful school committee. It was mainly lost on me, I hadn't begun to
know Keith Henderson, but decades later I identified the moment
when his attitude to his work first manifested itself; it was a vein
of mission in him inherited from his father who was a minister of the
church, the drive to go out among the people to help, to give and receive, and to lead.

Keith already loved his first little school of about fourteen children,
he loved every one of his children and he even liked teaching . . .
well, he seemed to, but to bring a wife here would be, at least in the
view of the education board, inappropriate in every way. His idea was
to improve his grading so that after the statutory two-year period he
could apply for a bigger school with a residence. When I came down
from Auckland that weekend I stayed with friends of his in the
valley, the Ordishes, and could see all this for myself. Though it was
heaven to be near Keith I had no sense of mission like his, not in that
direction, and found the distance of Whareorino from city life a
matter of emotion as well as of miles. I picked up the heights of the
hills and the horizons all about me but not the dimensions of Keith
himself. Not at all. I measured life from the last kiss only.

The year of journeys, meetings and lovers' partings, 1930. It was
the kind of heart's climate that drew from me many paintings for
K.D.H. which I would post to him and at least I know where these
are; forty years later I found them among his things in his desk, romantic pictures of long-stemmed glasses of bubbling red wine which
I'd never tasted, fantastic flowers and ladies and several impressions
of city streets crowded with bustling people, encounters in Queen
Street on Friday night, eyes of starry intent. Glances in passing. Vivid
colours. And a picture of the wheels of a train grinding out from a
station.

1930 was the year I got Gracie off. When I had been boarding at her
friend Bertha Smith's place to keep my sister company she would sit
up in bed in the morning, reach for the atlas, open it at random, place
a finger on the page without looking and say, "I'm going there." Upon
which we would both look at the place eagerly. She liked this routine
very much, which made her begin to feel better. Gray was about
twenty-nine at the time which is young to arrive at the crossroads of
life. One morning we found her finger on South Africa where Puppa's
brother George of his stories beginning, "One day my brother George
and I . . ." was a judge in Capetown and there her finger stayed.

Sitting up in bed with vision in her blue eyes she resolved her crisis at the crossroads and made her decision. After which she began preparing relatively cheerfully as Mumma had often said, "Once resolved the trouble is over." She borrowed my thirty-three pounds for landing money which she said she'd return the moment she'd landed and one evening—it must have been spring for it was not yet dark and no one was wearing overcoats—I went aboard with her on a great ocean liner. She wore a pale blue suit and hat with a delicate primrose blouse, her black hair was curly and lovely like Puppa's and her blue eyes deep as the sea, and the love of her life came on board to say goodbye to her at which I withdrew and returned to the wharf. Then the lover and I stood side by side on the wharf watching the water widen between the shore and the ship till we could no longer see the ship.

That man was still alive a few years ago and he knows that I know but I doubt if he'd care by now. I'm the only one who knows as Daphne is dead. As it happens he lived a large long and honored life in this country and it would be a shame to put a blemish on it at this late date.

On that fateful night on the Auckland wharf I was the only one of the family there and none of us ever saw Gracie again. She married twice in South Africa, gave birth to a boy named John and a girl named Jill. I believe she had her quota of happiness, I know she worked very hard, too hard, grew rich, helped to buy Mumma a house of her own and sent her a hundred pounds every Christmas until word came to us that she was dying of heart disease at forty-five.

At these tidings my brother Ashton prepared to go to South Africa to see her but he died first himself at forty-four. Soon after, Gracie died, still believing that Ashton was on his way, never knowing he'd predeceased her. Neither did Ashton ever know Gracie had gone, having already departed himself. My brother Ashton was buried in the hill cemetery of Lower Hutt, New Zealand, and my sister Grace was buried in Durban, South Africa, fulfilling in part Mumma's prophecy: "Their graves are scattered far and wide by mount and stream and sea."

My own crisis at the crossroads was coming up too though this kind of crisis doesn't usually come to nice people till the terrible thirties and I was twenty-one. To wait and marry the love of my own life would be to return to the obloquy of the country schools circuit in the foothills of New Zealand's ranges whereas I'd already trodden that track. Nor did the resolution lie in marrying a rich city-bred airman against whom every organ of my body turned its back and who had not even

asked me anyway, but in a repeat of the harbour water widening between a ship and the shore; in some far land where I could finally
extricate myself from the bloody profesh and become the great artist
I'd meant to be. It was not New Zealand as a country I wished to shed
but, as with Gracie, the old villain of every human story: circumstance.
On these little islands in the South Pacific, no matter which way I
wriggled and dodged, I couldn't get clear of the teaching. All of which
narrowed the crisis down to a clear-cut choice: love or freedom. At
twenty-one in the night of the Slump the answer veered strongly towards the glorious image: a great ocean liner at the Auckland wharf.

The first step, however, remained from sheer survival logistics to be
qualified in something before I went anywhere, which spelt out the
Teachers C certificate. So in November I borrowed Gordon's notebooks for the last time and read them up for a week, astounded to
find education the most fascinating subject I'd ever avoided. Now why
hadn't I discovered this in college . . . too busy chasing Keith Henderson, I suppose. It concerned itself with my favorite interest, the minds
of people, a matter in which I was by no means unschooled from my
private thoughts on Rousseau, from the earthquake of love and from
the scenes in the mental hospital. So there was in fact something you
could do about people's minds.

Gordon's notes were in somewhat arresting language. No doubt it
was jargon-ridden but I wasn't in the position to recognise that since
I'd not studied the work in the first place. To me, the defaulter, it
came up new and original, which makes me laugh today. So anyway
I went along on Monday and sat the jolly thing, kept on the straight
and narrow for instance and bypassed Rousseau and got away with it
and the next thing I had Teachers C. As simple as that. *After all that*
I had a trained teacher's certificate which no one could take away
from me. I couldn't even give it away as I'd given my thirty-three
pounds. I carry a replica of this modest document in my visa to this
day. "Why don't you congratulate me, Gordon?" I demand.

"It's the education department I'm congratulating. God, they must
be exhausted after getting *you* through."

Well, well, well. Fancy that. "The funny thing about it is," I said
to Gord, "it's the very last thing in the world I want." Yet I felt such
an exhilarating release about this that I found myself, before the P.A.
year was over, setting up number 589 as an artist's studio—the highest
way I could celebrate. A packing case from somewhere I nailed against
the window for a table near the light and a wide piece of cardboard

The
Henderson
family

from my shadowy landlady to prop upright for an easel upon it. Why hadn't I done this before; had I been paralysed or something? Instead of drooling disconsolately home from school now I could hardly not run. And I plunge into teaching myself from pictures how to draw tyres for sale, the intricacies in drawing the tread. The things you could do with light and dark on a tread. And polish up my printing, DUNLOP TYRES, and when Floyd comes stamping round the verandah to find me waist deep in paint and brushes and says, "What on earth are you doing, dear?"

I say, "Resolving my crisis, master."

"What for? What crisis?"

"It's not love my goal; it's freedom."

At year's end, for the second time in my life, I did not go home for Christmas though my five-year training was over and I had no job. I stayed in my studio in Auckland. Keith came up and took me in his little car down Te Aroha way to meet some of his people, his married sister's family. On the way back to Auckland it was cold and raining and after stopping at some little tea-room we returned to the car to sit a moment. And here is another of those vignettes fashioned in gem-stone that glow down the years unchanged.

He had a big raincoat on belted round the waist and a felt hat with the brim pulled low at the front shading his eyes. One short moment filled right up with him. Outside the car it was bleak and rough with rain attacking the windscreen.

Then we kissed lightly and drove on again, talking about something or other. From Auckland he left for down south to visit his parents leaving me behind high and dry, twenty-two, not engaged and with marriage as elusive as Teachers C had been. Having finished being a teacher-in-training you could say I was now a spinster-in-training.

I was happy painting in my studio. I recalled what Pete had taught me when he'd been living at Gleneagles about economy in the use of colours, decide on two or three only for impact and for the practicalities of colour printing. You can say more with few colours, he'd said, than you can with many. "It's simplicity that has force."

"Like poetry?" I'd said. "Use few words but load the words?"

"Few colours but load each one."

A pity I couldn't go back to Pete now and learn more, but no one knew where he was. It was only known where he wasn't; he was no longer senior artist at Golbergs. What I heard was that, along with some other staff, he'd been laid off in the Slump. As it happens, as I know now but did not then, he was working on a newspaper in another city, on a reduced wage and reduced health and if you want to know any more of that story come along to me and I may tell you . . . if you qualify.

I was very happy at my work and my thoughts moved along with my brush exploring new wide territories.

The year turned the corner from 1930 into 1931 in the most quotable Depression of the century. Of our year all of us were now qualified teachers having completed five years' training but, released at last into the field—how many hundreds of us—we found not a job on the map, except for third-year specialists like Wig and Max who were snapped up smartly. Wig was appointed to a permanent city job in Christchurch where, though young, she was already training students, and I think Max went to Fiji either then or later. They were separated also. Each married someone else.

New Zealand writers have put down on paper what Auckland was like in the Depression years. We new teachers joined the mighty ranks of the unemployed. The government said give it time and it would think of something but that in the meantime we could do worse than think for ourselves. We were not giggly girls and brash boys any longer but were given to making statements on the scene unrelated to love-affairs. To a few of us gathered at 589 Lucy said soberly, "Now it's do or die."

And Gordon said, "For you women it's do which means get a job of some kind, or die which means get married," and laughed it off.

Molly said, "And what if I can do neither, Gord?"

"Get on a ship," I said.

Lucy had delicate bones and features but she'd come out with heavyweight thoughts. "I'm going to marry," she said, "and die."

Gordon stayed after the others had gone, sitting in the old-time armchair with one long elegant leg swinging reflectively over the other. "Women," he said.

"Why don't you up and marry one?"

"*Which* one?" he said.

"*Which* one?" I flare. "You say which one? What about the trail of broken hearts in your wake?"

His foot jigs on. "*What* . . . broken hearts?"

I was only too pleased to be unemployed. In fact I *was* employed in the work of my choice except for the no income part. But I'd kept sufficient money for a few months' rent, ten shillings a week, a pocketful for food and there was always the fish-'n-chip shop on the corner. I settled down with intent to prepare samples of commercial art to hawk round the advertising firms. That a senior artist like Pete had already been laid off—I had to flank that.

I painted all day. Could any life be more dazzling, radiant or rapturous? Here I was in my dearly desired studio and not having to go to school. I forget where I got the paper from but I'd never been without paint and brushes. For models I used illustrations from posh magazines, the latest in advertising, learning so much that was new to me in the area of shading and the effect of dramatic shadows. I'd found out from Miss Copeland about the three basic colours, blue, yellow and red, though I knew nothing yet about complementary colours never having seen a colour chart. You should have seen my ad for Dunlop tyres—who said I couldn't draw a lorry!

At exhaustion point the momentum would sweep me on into modelling in plasticene which brought forth a nude ballet lady whom I swung from the light to watch her pirouette on the string, the fluidity of the changing lights and shadows in a marvellous phenomenon not possible on paper. I can't say I ate well and when I did it was far too much, packing myself to the chin, which sometimes gave me colic and I was forced to sit quite still for an hour or two before it abated.

At exhilaration point, however, the same momentum would sweep me per tramcar to saunter down Queen Street on a Friday night at the thickest concentration of the crowds, to pause on the kerb before John Courts and absorb the glorious din. What a language, the crash and bang and boom of the traffic, assuring me I was no longer entombed in the silence of the country but at large in the vortex of living. Elixir itself.

Floyd Duckmanton, I thought, turned out to be less than generous though considering he knew of the other man he had no obligation to me. There were fine points he overlooked however; arriving well-dressed and well-fed himself to take me to an Aero Club dance, why didn't he feed and dress me too? What about a meal somewhere first and where was the pale blue satin dress he'd promised to buy me which I'd already chosen in Karangahape Road? It recalled an old song from childhood: "He promised to buy me a pair of blue ribbons/ to tie up my bonnie brown hair." Or help me to pay my rent or at least talk of an engagement ring so I could tell the girls. He didn't even play jealous of Keith, making me think he had a girl in reserve. Someone not a teacher.

Besides, I was tired of his choice of entertainment. Instead of a film or a recital he'd choose the motor racing at Western Springs with "the boys." He had fine friends among the other pilots who certainly came before me. What "the boys" wanted he wanted but what I wanted did not arise. I had no time any more for men who were after kisses only so I was seeing less of Floyd Duckmanton and sustained my spirit on letters from Keith.

I stayed so happy, regardless, sitting in my studio for long hours at my packing-case table by the window perfecting my commercial samples. Some of my college friends were still high and dry in town and they'd turn up and praise my drawing like mad. We'd make the tea and play the Gramophone and try to laugh as we used to, except that we had changed by now and had a different view of the scene. After a while, having been given time, the education department thought up something and dealt out to each one of us a few weeks' relieving teaching so that I put in a few terrible weeks at a terrible school in some terrible northern suburb which you had to change trains to get to. But it blew over and we were short on income again. Short on everything. But I've never been short on a supply of dreams and a moving brush nurtures dreams, some of them ranging on wing far beyond the love of a man across great oceans to alien countries even outside the Empire, from wine bowls in Italy to murky dives in risky Latin America. My imagery kept me alive.

This life of a solitary artist gave back to me that which I thought I'd lost in the dark years, something I'd been without since my life on the roads: my self-respect. No amount of favoured care from a patriarchal education department had been able to replace that. Confidence poured over me once more like a stream in flood: of course I could do anything at all that I set my mind to. I felt again I had some work to do awaiting me in the world as I had when a barefoot vagabond. Nothing was beyond me. My role was to be the first, the best and in the front in comet-tail formation; what had happened to me in the meantime?

By now I was making ads for wine which I'd never tasted, Maisie having given me as a parting gift a volume of *Omar Khayyám*, which involved highlighting bottles. Grapevines twined round these bottles and I tossed in a languid lady or two in cabaret scenes, all done in two basic colours only, allowing for the . . . utilising, I mean, the superimposition of the third basic colour during the printing process. And you always had black and white. My word, I was learning fast.

Sometimes to expel extra steam I'd wander alone round the Auckland streets like a genuine absent-minded artist, finding it spacious and fulfilling to walk alone and not missing anyone; peering in the doorways of churchfuls of worshippers and of dance-halls in Freeman's Bay. One afternoon I slipped into a theatre in Newmarket to a film which portrayed a French priest in a starving village in France. The people would come to him with their hunger and he would feed them and teach them but they hated him for it and turned on him in the end and killed him for it, supplying the moral "The Poor hates the hand that gives it bread." It was also the fate of all the saintly spinsters in infant rooms that children hated them for giving them knowledge. The child hates the hand that gives it knowledge. Maybe his congregation hated the Reverend Olds for giving it news of God.

Until one morning I set out into the city on a tram with the samples of my home-grown wares beneath my arm, big sheets, thinking amid the crashing and shrieking of metal on metal it was a good thing there were no teaching positions because I was free at last, or nearly. Vivid dreams reared. When they see my work, I thought, there'll be no talk of lost apprenticeships as it had been in Wellington and why hadn't I come at thirteen or fourteen? One look and they'd appoint me an established artist and on senior pay. And there I would stay until the day I embarked on some mighty ship to escape the doom of my love for a man.

The door of Golbergs was strangely shut so you couldn't walk into the foyer and talk to the man at the counter. Their star artist, Pete, had once worked here. The heavy intimidating door. At least it opened when I knocked, but not wholly, just enough to reveal the form of a man and I stammered my mission. But he replied defensively something like, It's not likely we'll be taking on junior staff when we're sacking our professionals. Anyway, Slump or no Slump, for heaven's sake look at your age. An apprentice at twenty-two, the thing's ridiculous.

I suppose I asked him to look at my work, I hope I did, but I know he wouldn't or didn't. He seemed frightened of it. "You're too late by at least six years." No, he wouldn't look at my work.

I began to starve, I'm proud to say, in true garret style, I couldn't have starved better on the Left Bank of Paris. But the momentum carried me on regardless so that I worked more madly than ever. I couldn't pull up for the life of me until vague elusive pains came licking round, sensations you couldn't catch, so one early afternoon I took them to a pinchy-faced chemist in Newmarket who said if I ate more and worked less I might not die after all, and he'd prepare some medicine for me to take if I came back at six which, having no money, I didn't. But I must say I was relieved to hear there was an alternative to dying young. When Wig came home in May for the holidays she took me home to Onehunga for a while like a loving sister but she had to return to her new job in Christchurch.

Toothache next. The extraction of a mighty molar. I had to take a taxi home with my last two shillings but I still caught a chill in the face, it was winter—avoid at all costs a chill in the face—we'll skip the detail. After that were clutching spasms in my throat which so terrified me that I borrowed one and six from my little landlady and sent a telegram to Mumma: "Ill and starving please send fare."

Mumma plunged out on her beat, as I heard later, found Ashton, borrowed three pounds never to be repaid and wired it. Immediately I bought my ticket, started packing then wrote a short note to Floyd Duckmanton upbraiding him for gross neglect and telling him dramatically what I thought of "his boys" and Western Springs and the sport of motor racing, adding that I never wanted to hear his step on my verandah again. Hell knows no fury etc. like a woman not proposed to. And pinned the thing outside the door with no little vigour and got on the main trunk express that very night telling not one soul except the landlady. Auckland had beaten me. I came, I saw, I did not conquer. Like my two sisters. Yet as the long train gathered its lilting speed I did not look back on Auckland as the place that Daphne had named it: Unlucky City.

Roaring through the rattling night over the mid-island volcanic plateau I had a sudden panicky feeling I'd left something behind. I glanced up at my suitcase on the rack above me and looked in my purse. What was it . . . I seemed to be travelling too light . . .

Te Kuiti round midnight where I'd often hotly met my sweetheart. The express pulled up for a mug of tea and a leathery ham sandwich but I didn't get off this time.

LOWER HUTT    Winter.

Mumma was still in this rather pleasant relaxed little place in Lower Hutt I'd already heard about with a garden in front. Among the wintering flowers she had planted cabbages and carrots along the garden path. I was ill and the doctor came who said I had sub-acute rheumatic fever which sounded more impressive than rheumatic fever straight though now I don't think I had either of these. In any case I lay there at home on a camp stretcher in the kitchen where it was warm and where Ashton came to see me and Marmaduke too, who said to me kindly, "You're crook, Sylv?" I learnt the meaning of home to a prodigal son.

There are months and months or more round here I cannot account for; such a blank on the walls of the gallery of memory there must have been a blank on the walls of life there too. I don't recall mourning over no job, no money, no friends, no Floyd, no clothes, no strength, no hope, no nothing. It is on the cards that I liked it, because they no longer mattered as I had no dreams. All of which maybe is the way the soul heals itself: a black night of surcease. It was the kind of time when in these days of the 1970s young people snatch at drugs or drink or turn into thieves and terrorists—except that none of us did; not among the newly trained teachers.

Only vague dateless images surface: hot porridge with milk and sugar on it, hot scones from the oven with melting butter and hot tea the strength I liked it and a half-page letter from Floyd in the simple script of one who had done little handwriting. It was in ink and it told how sorry he was at his neglect of me in my need and that he regretted the reign of his boys and Western Springs taking his time from me and that he'd see to it about keeping them in their place as from now on whenever I was there. And he wrote of the shock my departing letter had been. It was a missive of simple sweetness and really went home with Mumma as it passed from hand to hand.

I must have been laid up for quite a while since the next scene is on a dry cold morning before the spring, what it pleased Mumma to call "the darkest hour before the dawn." I'm in a big bed in a front room and I'm still in that old green polo-necked jersey Muriel had handed down to me, wearing it in bed to keep me warm. Like the true heathen Mumma saw me to be, I'm not washed or combed and I'm staring at nothing. Suddenly, as in a good detective story, I hear steps on the garden path and, looking through the window, I see no less than Floyd Duckmanton striding through the vegetables and he knocks on the door like the hand of the Law. Mumma opens up and is so charmed, so charmed, to find a young man with a dashing sports car seeking one of her six daughters.

I hear him telling her how he went very early in the morning to the post office, identified the required postman who said yes he knew where Mrs. Ashton-Warner lived and if the gentleman cared to follow him he'd arrive there towards noon. Floyd is jubilant at the success of his sleuthing but admits to being hungry and thirsty though he thinks he would make a good postman; he'd never met such a variety of people in one morning in his life.

Mumma gives me no sort of chance whatever to clean myself up and brings him right into my room—God in heaven; unpowdered unbrushed, even haggard I suppose, green jersey, yet he seems to be as much enamoured as if I were in scarlet tulle on a first-night show all scented and spangled, which says a lot for appearances being unrelated to love. When you think of the fortunes spent on faces.

Mumma kindly held him down in the kitchen with a cup-o-tea and a bit-o-bread while I sneaked to the bathroom to civilise myself and put on a pretty blouse belonging to Daphne though I'd never worn gold in my life and had not intended to; I was not gold like Daphne. I was a brash scarlet or a moody blue. In the meantime Mumma loved the story about the irrepressible lover cunningly following the postman from early morn and whispered falsetto round the bathroom door, "See, see? Didn't I tell you? Sorrow endureth for the night but joy cometh in the morning."

That very afternoon I think he wrapped ailing maiden in blanket and took both Mumma and me for a ride in his marvellous car to Days Bay where we could see the waves of the harbour.

He stayed round making great strides with my mother, I don't know why since he didn't mention love or marriage. Had he done so during this blankness in time there was no telling what a fool might do, though nuptials would not have endured the length of a wedding day much less survived the night. But I was in the vacuous state to consider marriage with a city man against spiritual demise in the country. My cosmic coma was such I might have married anyone for any reason, rich or poor, with both eyes shut—always supposing I was asked. The future had vaporised,

Everybody told me what to do. Mumma said marry Floyd right or wrong though she hadn't met Keith Henderson, besides I think she was impressed by the name Duckmanton. What would the Sergeant of Police think if she had a daughter called Mrs. Duckmanton? The word had style.

Pip said, an hour away in Wellington, "Marry Keith, Squeak, of course. You've loved him for years." But Pip had met him once in Wellington and knew what she was talking about. Lionel said, "Couldn't you produce Keith, Sylv, so we can make up our minds about him?" Muriel wrote from Golden Bay that she'd do all the flowers for the wedding from her own garden single-handed and would start planting them at once whoever the bridegroom was. Ashton said, "Marry the first man prepared to put a ring on your finger. It'll all be the same in a hundred years' time," and Daphne said, "Marry the one who will pass you a cup of tea in bed in the morning."

On the whole, however, there's a glorious vacuum at this time which makes it easy to write about.

We're in the Brick House now at the end of a quiet no-exit street. We live in a brick house with an arch over the porch. Marmie comes here to play deep movements from Beethoven on the piano and, between his bizarre crises, to write profound scientific essays on the solar system, wonderful words rolling over the paper multisyllabically. And Ashton dashed in late one night pulling his wife by the hand who he claimed had been playing up. He slammed her into Mumma who was in bed in the dark and held a candle to her face. "Look at that, Mumma, see? Look at that face. Those eyes. Did you ever see anything more beautiful?" The two great brown eyes like dinner plates swerved and lifted and flashed. In the candlelight the face was so white, the lips so red.

And Daphne more vivid than life itself floating along Willis Street in Wellington in the spring dressed in soft green and the tenderest yellow and an alluring floppy hat. Beneath the wide brim her long floppy green eyes reflect messages in light and a man's head turns. She's laughing and telling me, "And the matron said, 'That loosed-limbed nurse.' I suppose my limbs are loose, Sylv."

And here's Norma consciously radiant visiting the capital briefly, bouncing along Manners Street to meet me in a short hat shaped like a crown, her short black curls springing like Puppa's. Her suit is the last thing in brick red. We three sisters, Daphne, Sylvie and Norma, still favour the colours set for us in Te Pohue when Mumma made us velvet dresses; green for Daph, blue for me and red for Norma. And you hear this story going the rounds which Mumma likes about a beau of Norma's called Hop-along Cassidy who wrote to Norma, "I want to be bandaged to you like a splint to a broken leg." But I'm putting here only the good that men do; the dread is interred with our bones.

At the Brick House I was putting things in my Glory Box, I don't know how with no money; the camphorwood chest Gracie brought from Fiji and which I claimed in lieu of my thirty-three pounds. Floyd Duckmanton sent me three pounds to come to Auckland for an Aero Club dance, to stay with him at his airport bach called Dew Drop Inn, and to dress as a boy in the interests of propriety, but I bought linen for my box instead and paid one pound to Mumma, and told him I paid the doctor's bill with it. Upon which he sent me another three pounds so I actually did go all the way up through the night and the island to the celebrated Dew Drop Inn though I'd rather have been going to Whareorino to a single man's quarters called Don't Drop Inn. But after one awful all-night stand-up showdown in his own boy's clothing I ran away in the morning from the inn and the Dewdrops on my own two legs, over to the Aero Club lounge and was put back on the train that same evening. Perfidy, thy name is Woman.

I still couldn't catch up with the idea that men had feelings like women so the issue of mercy hardly arose. I knew of no Society for the Protection of Men from Women, the S.P.M. Gracie had said that men were no more than providers and lovers. I didn't think you could hurt a man; it was only men who could hurt women. My flimsy apologia. I was overturned with mercy for women.

The new year, 1932, took more shape, and it needed to with me un-employed and twenty-three. A letter from Keith invited me to Christ-

church in May to meet his parents before we became engaged. Having
no clothes I took a live-in housekeeping job in Karori which I'd rather
not talk about. However, living in the city I saw a little more of Pip,
whose mother, Mrs. Beyers, had gone to England. Pip was saving up to
follow her and from London they would both return to Rhodesia.
When I asked her what about Tony who hoped to marry her she said
he'd have to be left behind for no man was going to pin her down in
New Zealand. As it happened, when Pip later sailed I was no longer
in Wellington but she wrote at sea and told me how Tony had wept
openly on the wharf. But I had an idea how Tony must have felt at the
water widening between him and Pip, the ship shrinking till his love
blurred to nothing.

On the journey from London to Africa Pip fell in love again but
this time she didn't have to leave her love weeping on the wharf as
she married the shipboard romance and they went to live in Southern
Rhodesia down Salisbury way. Photos showed their home to be a
compound of separate white buildings like cabins with black servants
at hand, and Pip was pregnant. The way some people could embark
on ships and control their own destiny . . . but then Pip wasn't a
teacher.

Mumma could stand the humiliation of my menial work even less
than I could. "The common creatures," she spat. "Let them do their
own dirty work." I would have too but I was sacked for inefficiency
first. Never mind, I'd managed to put a few pounds down on a blue
hat and coat to wear to meet my sweetheart's parents, the Reverend
Samuel and Mrs. Henderson, and to buy a blue satin linen tablecloth
for my box with four little serviettes. The year did promise a little
shape to it as though I were living a life. At least I was going through
the motions.


Floyd still swept down from Auckland but none of my family had met
Keith at all. Lionel said to me on Perrot's Corner, "Which will you
marry, Sylv?"

"Keith."

"Well take my advice. If you play round much longer you'll lose
the two of them. It has taken years, don't forget, for you and they to
arrive at this stage. You're not growing any younger, Sylv. If you lose
these two it'll take you much longer to arrive at this same stage with
somebody else, if you do at all."

"I'm practically a spinster already, Li."

He turns up the collar of his coat in the wind. "Do you intend to go to Christchurch in May to meet Keith's parents?"

"I would but I have no clothes, Li."

"What do you need most?"

"I've got my hat but I haven't finished paying for my coat."

"How much is owing?"

"Three pounds fifteen."

He gave me the money right there and then in the wind on Perrot's Corner.

On his way through Wellington to Christchurch in May Keith Henderson called on my mother at the Brick House to ask for the hand of her daughter which he could have had gratis years ago, both my hands, feet too. He drove to the gate in his modest Ford which hadn't a show against Floyd's smart Chev but he himself was another matter. Keith was taller than Floyd and where the pilot had black thick straight hair growing low on his forehead the teacher's hair was long on the top and wavy and his eyes a bewitching blue. He wore still his soft grey double-breasted suit that had been his best suit since I had known him but his tie was new and Mumma was nonplussed. True, Floyd was rich and dashing and took her for drives round the bays, but Keith was the second son of a minister of the church and above all a teacher, to her a calling second in holiness only to the church itself. Moreover, my sweetheart was no longer a tentative student but grown in the responsibility of his valley, his committee, his school, his children and their parents. Both young men were twenty-four but where Floyd had flair Keith had poise. Where Floyd Duckmanton would chatter expansively, Keith Henderson measured and weighed his words first. Putting on her very best demeanour Mumma asked, "And how's the teaching profession, Keith?"

He smiles and clears his throat. "I'm responsible for only a very small part of it, Mrs. Ashton-Warner."

"Ah. A-ha. That's a word I like to hear from a teacher: responsible. No Standard 6 boys would jump out the window of *your* school, would they, Keith. Ay?"

"Not so far. Did they jump out of yours?"

"Ha. Haven't you ever seen a big boy jump out a window? They'd think nothing of it in my time. And they'd hide the strap, the Turks, and hide the bell too. But oo-ooh I was good enough for them. *I'd* bring them to heel. The same boy never jumped out the same window twice."

The two of them laugh like anything. It's heaven to hear a man laugh, the whole world rights itself. "Not on the same day, I take it."

"Hoo-hoo," excited, her grey eyes sparking, "I can see we're going to have a good teacher in Mr. Keith Henderson, ay Keith? A man with a future. Ha, a-ha. Here's a disciplinarian coming up. Here's a teacher for you."

Keith was laughing again; he was already a long way ahead of Floyd.

You never saw such propriety in the Brick House before; we were just like other people. The only flaw was when I had to borrow a shilling from Keith for the gas meter in order to boil the water for tea. We'd prepared a formal afternoon tea for my dear and honoured guest and Mumma had made some scones. While I laid the cloth and put out the cups Mumma walked away with romance in her eyes down the path in the back garden patch where she pondered among the vegetables, the carrots she'd planted and the cabbages, until my dearest love followed her and asked for the hand of her daughter Sylvia. He spoke of an engagement this winter and marriage two years later as at present he was housed in a single man's quarters whereas he believed it was inappropriate to take a wife into a place where you could touch the iron roof with your hand and where there were no amenities, not even a bath. He said he wouldn't expect his wife to rough it like him.

"But Sylvie wouldn't mind that," Mumma replied. "A daughter of a long line of pioneers."

When Mumma related this conversation to me later I was glad she had made that point. I'd have married him on the moment without any ceremony or wedding dress and would have dug in at Whareorino since I no longer saw any reason not to. As for no bath I would stand in the rain. We'd done that before.

She said to Keith in the garden, "And where do you bathe, Keith?"

"I go to the homes of my neighbours."

"Neighbours. Another good word from a teacher."

Keith took the ferry to Christchurch the first week and in the interests of propriety I had to go the second week though I'd pictured standing on the deck with him watching the harbour lights. I stayed at the Parsonage in Rangiora, a few hours out of Christchurch, which was a two-storeyed roughcaste white house built for gracious living. Staying in that household was a more profound preparation of the mood for marriage than any wedding itself could have been. Marriage was to be an undertaking into which you put everything of yourself for others, a union for no man to put asunder and anything less would be like riding a horse with four broken legs. Only once I got into trouble when Keith called me into his bedroom upstairs to show me some photos, with the door wide open, and I was strictly reprimanded. Yet Keith's mother did her best to make me welcome though I was more relaxed with his father, a tall man of grace and scholarship approaching something like sainthood.

There came an expedition to Christchurch one day, on our own in Keith's car, to choose an engagement ring, and we stood self-consciously side by side in the jeweller's shop, I trying on rings and Keith asking the price. Miraculously this day had come, unbelievably. He put a deposit on a ring with five tiny diamonds set in platinum to be left with the jeweller and be paid for in instalments, for it cost nine pounds. Then we wandered to the bank of the River Avon and sat on the grass beneath the willows with the sandwiches and the thermos of tea we'd brought, trying to find each other again beneath the damask of holiness. We had lost each other in the Parsonage where desire had been sedated. We were shy in this new dimension where our private and tender love had to take on responsibility and public intention to measure up to some bulky future and was no longer quite our own. It was bearing two families and the church with it. Beside the gliding water we sought to rediscover the other one we'd known, to backtread to the earlier joy with the one who supplied inspiration. Circumspectly we kissed by the river and marriage seemed far away. At this stage two years seemed longer than the earlier four and would be worse before it was better. But we still kissed by the river.

We kissed back the sweetness a little. The touching of lips said we were alive and were sitting side by side. "What I like," he said, "is being together."

"That's what I like," I said.

I travelled on the ferry alone back to Wellington and Keith followed later.

This year was indeed trying to gather some shape and substance to itself and the Wellington education board managed to think of something; it gave each one of its hundreds of idle new teachers one term's work, those girls who had not married. Married women teachers were out all round. I was placed at Eastern Hutt for the winter term within walking distance of the Brick House and where I ran into even another of these excellent senior women made of patience and wisdom of whom New Zealand seemed to have endless supplies, a serene spinster. The only way in which Miss Peterkin differed from the others I'd been

under was that she was tiny. Yet I don't know how they put up with
me, these seniors. When I count over the ones who had trained me—
Miss Pope, Miss Cumberland, Miss Little, Miss Whackington, Ag at
college, Miss Copeland and now Miss Peterkin—I can't recall one harsh
word spoken to me, the most difficult of young teachers. Even Miss
Little had held her tongue. I can be excused for a certain hero-worship
for the senior spinster teacher, and to catch myself out wishing to
model my own life on them. They work in key positions with the
young. But it's teachers I'm thinking of, not night nurses under stress
in a metropolitan hospital who were married with domestic reasons
to be bitter. I wouldn't mind putting it to you that senior women
teachers should be required to be celibate, like priests and that's quite
a good analogy. Well, in fact, New Zealand *was* requiring this since
married women teachers were not, at that time, employed, though for
other reasons. In short, I was trained by priests.

So Miss Peterkin put up with me though it is possible I did a little
better, surely; after all I was a trained teacher, wasn't I? A bit better
here at my eighteenth school than—nineteenth, I mean—than I had at
my eighteenth, I'm going to stop counting schools. Primer 2 again,
forty or fifty little five-year-olds, but I myself could see them slipping
back in their work and their behaviour under my own nose. All right,
I tried and I laboured, but couldn't we stop talking about this? I'd rather
think about the dear and lasting friends I made on that staff, pretty,
fascinating and loving people who put gold stars on the backs of the
little children's hands, so the time was not wasted. Fairey and Dark
in particular and Joanna who was madly in love also and who told us
every day at morning tea why the sleeve of her fur coat was worn out,
driving her man's car with her elbow on the window. At last I had a
new group of friends to circulate among, for friendship and loveship
are a matter of propinquity, seeing one another every day, doing the
same thing side by side, whereas until now I'd belonged to nothing in
Lower Hutt. It made a great difference these new loves in my life. Yet
in spite of a gentle infant mistress, an indulgent headmaster and gorgeous friends on staff I knew I was back in the classroom again.

My pay was seven pounds a month. I paid Mumma some board as
well as serviced my Glory Box, but Daphne was home at the Brick
House now awaiting her baby and I liked to keep her going in wool
and pattern books for she knitted the days away. So I'd go uptown to
do her shopping as she herself was too heavy: wool, knitting needles
or something for the baby's trousseau. In the front bedroom which she
and I shared two trousseaux were blossoming now, one for nuptials

and one for birth, and I must admit we were never stuck for something to say. The way Daph would appear, disappear and reappear in my tracks is another story belonging to itself, and whatever the circumstance I never failed to feel it an honour. The need for money kept me at school as well as habit and the joy of friends, walking the treed secluded streets dreaming of my many loves. I loved so much, so many, so terribly.

Family drama thumped and stamped at the Brick House as the Warners at least got married like other people. Don't forget Ashton lived in Lower Hutt, Marmie came and went, and I remember Norma bouncing around and Vad was growing up, but Mumma stood her ground four-square and had an understanding with the sergeant on his beat when the action surged over her head; not that he ever did anything at all or said anything for sergeants are used to families. The Brick House in Lower Hutt was anything but similar to the Parsonage in Rangiora.

Keith's letters were changing. The strain of our separation was taking on an entity in its own right and began to act of itself. As July frosted up he wrote that he'd finished paying the instalments on the ring, that he'd post it and I'd receive it next Tuesday and that we'd be engaged next week, at a distance.

Floyd happened to be flashing about Wellington at this time and turned up to take me out: not to dine and dance, to a film or to hear Solomon play but for a drive round the stormy bays at night. We ended up on the top of Mt. Victoria in a thundering Wellington gale, what is called a Wellington Special. The well-known place where men expected the maximum of kisses for the minimum expenditure. This routine outing brought the routine conflict and my womanity could not oblige. Not one single kiss could I spare for this man and I admitted I was in love.

"I've always known," he said. Not angry as I'd feared but lifeless and silent like an animal whose spine had snapped, which was more to be feared than anger. He drove me back down the mountain in the screeching wind with screeching brakes, across the floor of the sullen city, along the exposure of the wild Hutt Road where the waves of the harbour beat about it and the lights of cars stabbed upon it, to the gate of the sleeping Brick House. He did not look my way when he stopped but monotoned, "Is there any hope for me at all?"

"No."

He switches off the lights.

"I'm going to be engaged next week," I say.

Sudden and fierce, "I had planned to get engaged to you next Saturday. I was going to buy a diamond ring. We'd marry next week and honeymoon in Sydney."

First I'd heard of it.

He stares ahead into the darkness. Then I'm stunned to see two heavyweight tears bowling down over his cheeks, finding their way in and out of the ridges and crevasses of a man's rugged face. I can't believe it. He must have meant it. I slink out of his car while he still sits there looking into the storm. And I flounder inside where Mumma is awake waiting for the latest news. "What did he say, what did he say?" she whispers in the candlelight.

The engine revs up at the gate. "But he wouldn't have married me, Mumma. He's never ever mentioned it."

Roar of the engine in the street. He must have forgotten to turn on his lights for he's plunged into the ditch. More booming and spurting in jerks and leaps then one helluva zoom up the street.

"Ah, a-ha," from Mumma. "Too late. The early bird catches the worm." Now wistful, "I enjoyed those drives round the bay y'know, Sylv."

I make the tea in the kitchen. Daphne sits up in bed when I take her a cup and reaches for her knitting. "What waste," she mourns, "of a perfectly good man."

"He didn't ever ask me, Daph."

"That's funny, y'know, Solvs. *Why* didn't he?"

"He was frightened of a teacher in his bed."

Spring in New Zealand has a way of co-operating with matters of the heart in a quite primordial fashion; or maybe it's the heart that follows the spring, so when you see the spikes of the koromiko whitening on a bush on the side of a bank some love-affair is perorating. Spring is still a month off as it happens but there are signs of preparation.

Sure enough on the Tuesday of the following week in this term without end a very small registered package for me was delivered in the afternoon mail at school. At *school* mind you. The headmaster, Mr. Benton, brought it in. When he'd gone I turned my back on the little children and opened it and here was my ring. My *ring*, mind you, at school. I mean the thing made me almost like school.

The very same five small diamonds we'd chosen together in May. I edged it on the third finger of my left hand right there and then and when the five-minute afternoon break came I showed it softly to Dark and to Fairey, and when they asked me what Keith was like I said, "I don't know the man. I seldom see him."

Neither did Keith know me for that matter, but I hadn't thought of that.

My winter term at Eastern Hutt would end some time and I'd be unemployed again and who would buy Daphne's wool and how could I pay my board? In the meantime this separation of me and my love was wearing us both down to the bone. Apartness was like eternity whereas we'd thought Together meant eternity. Were there any railway stations in eternity? Since we had first talked of marriage on the top of Mt. Eden two and a half years ago we'd been living apart nearly all of the time when in fact each was a living organ within the other. You could die over it, easily. Just letters we were, mysterious ideas embodied in table linen in a Glory Box and a satin negligée. Would this young man pass me a cup of tea in bed in the morning or chop the wood in winter? Would he resole my shoes? Though time and life were moving so slowly thoughts ran so fast you could not catch them. My mind was inhabited by only one dream now and I must say I found it a rest. All others had lost their substance.

The only images housed in my mind were a man called Keith Henderson, a wedding ring on my finger to show the girls and a white wedding dress with a veil. I couldn't see through this picture of a wedding, not a yard beyond it or an inch either side. All powerful goals which had thrust me since I'd been born, all apprehension of being buried alive in the country once more, vaporised before this white picture which screened off the future like the sun in your eyes.

And this is where spring took a hand. A letter came from my love, not the usual overweight one but something short and urgent. He asked me to marry him not in eighteen months' time but in one month's time in the coming August holidays, *next month*. I lifted from my box the sensational negligée I'd been making with pink satin one side and blue satin the other with an ostrich feather border and sewed on it a design in imitation pearls—not for a wicked dive in Latin America, for the Left Bank in Paris or for the wine bowl in Italy but for . . . Whareorino.

From Whareorino Keith arranged with his brother Elliot who was his best man and who now worked in Wellington to organise a pre-wedding party for the Saturday night before our wedding on the Tuesday. It was held in a cabaret in Cuba Street on the left-hand side going up. The three bridesmaids were there: my sister Evadne, Keith's sister Dorothy and Jean Beyers (Pip); three teachers from the staff of Eastern Hutt school were there: Dark, Fairey and Joanna who'd brought their own partners—no, Dark was Elliot's partner, and then the two Henderson men, Elliot and Keith. The first time anyone had met these two, except Pip, and they hosted the party and you could recognise them now as sons of a church household from their social grace. A first-class band we had and the prevailing tune of the evening was "Can't Help Lovin' That Man o' Mine," and there were real drinks as an alternative to fruit-juice. I think they had whiskey. You should have seen the attention from the girls to the dark horse from the Never-nevers, the man who had come to marry me not later than next Tuesday. The dress was formal, there were low rose lights, flowers everywhere and I wore a long blue gown.

The Henderson men at the wedding breakfast

We married, Keith and I, in the Methodist church in Taranaki Street, Wellington, at seven p.m. on the Tuesday evening of August 23, 1932, with Keith's father, the Reverend Samuel Henderson from Belfast, officiating, my brother Ashton giving me away and Temple White on the wedding music. The reception was held at the Ritz in Manners Street and both of our families were there.

The following morning we called in at the Brick House to say good-bye to Mumma and Daphne and to show them my wedding ring: a slender gold number engraved with fleur-de-lis. I was no longer my own self, Sylvie, but part of someone else, of a man, of a stranger; even my own name had been swept away. I was now Mrs. K. D. Henderson.

Then my husband wrapped a rug round my knees, the spring was cold, and together we drove away northward.

So long as men can breathe, and eyes can see,
So long lives this, and this gives life to thee.

# III

# WHAREORINO
# TO
# TAURANGA

## 1932 - 1969

WHAREORINO   Whareorino is nothing like as lovely as Te Pohue, for the forest giants are jagged carcasses with nothing more to say; not romantic like Rangitumau, for instead of the rolling foothills are the stark ranges of a country geographically young, stripped bare to its backbone like a very thin horse. Nor can you see the Tasman Ocean, only hear it beating the beaches.

The man I've married is a stranger to me and that's one thing I'm sure of. The rest of what I think about him is no more than supposition, half of which I can't believe at that. For a start he is interested in other people and he appears to have motives in life other than pleasing me. How can this be? He doesn't play audience to me yet doesn't take the stage himself and what other relationship is there between people? I think he has inclinations unrelated to mine and I sense he has values of right and wrong; but I only sense it since he hasn't told me. As the new mornings peel off one after another so do the colourful wrappings of marriage—or should. Or *would* if I could believe even the half of it.

He appears to be sincere in his work as though he means it, as though he sees teaching as more than just something to do, as more than a source of income only, whereas what sane man could be sincere about teaching? Although school theoretically is from nine till three, as any new teacher knows, a maxim respected by staffs in town, this one is on the job at 8:30 a.m. and not a minute later, takes less than the hour for lunch and does not return till four; all with no headmaster along a corridor and no inspector round the corner. "Are you," I ask, "your own headmaster and your own inspector?"

"I am my own headmaster." And does not enlighten me further, being brief in word on the subject of himself; if there is wonder for him in his first school it remains muted.

Yet he must have dreams for his tiny little school, his one-room, one-man stand dug into the side of a hill; you can see it in the way he goes about improving the place as though he believes it is worth it, and that he can make something of it to endure forever. His school committee eats out of his hand like horses taking hay and you see them together on a Saturday morning bolstering the bank of the track up the hill with ponga trunks, some of which choose to refoliate, looking rather pretty. They have metalled this track from the road to the glebe, have planted a variety of native trees, have fenced in the buildings from the crowding sheep and have established timeless pines. It was Keith who planted these young pines but less as his signature, I think, than for their incomparable shelter from the ocean winds, and heavens, the children plant flowers.

It's plain he likes his children at school, about fifteen or sixteen of them I think, likes each one from the littlest up and I've seen his hand on a head like his father; he speaks of them and to them with affection as though they were people worthy of respect and important in his life, and not just necessary wretches to be somehow taught, to be forced to learn for the sake of your salary. You could almost say he is proud of them as one is proud of one's family for he doesn't growl or keep a strap in his drawer and you don't see him angry at all.

And I get the idea at Whareorino, but I'm not sure, that he rather likes a hammer and nails and a saw; the happy way he puts a butter-box on legs for a wash-tub outside with a hole in it and a cork for a plug and, as for the no bathroom part, he sets the packing case outside on Saturday mornings which we fill with warm water heated in a kerosene tin on an open fire. The cracks we fill with school plasticene and when the planks bulge as one gets in, the other is on duty replacing the plasticene and darting off to see if anyone is coming. The weather has to be fine, of course. Yes I think he likes planting and carpentering and his broad hands confirm it.

I'm obliged to suppose also that he likes visiting people for he still takes off on his rounds with this marvellous assumption that he's welcome. He's done a lot of it before I came: eating with them, having a bath at their place and sometimes spending the night; in his letters I used to see him walking round the corners of the bluffs and into the gullies between the hills seeking some family in the loneliest lane and giving them enough time to complete their thinking.

One Sunday he takes me walking with him to visit the small-boned district nurse tucked away in a deep-treed valley; she has retired but still goes on with the job, footing the length and breadth of the place with no more salary due; a first-rate mid-day dinner in the true colonial style. A cultivated woman, English, and here we have another priesthood of women in district nurses, people with a purity of intention and action only possible without domestic tumult.

The puzzling disposition of this man to walk out the door of his own home, travel along the road whistling, open a gate, walk up a

Whareorino—
the school

The residence

Inside

The bride

The hill
I ran away
over

path, knock at a door and enter the home of someone other than his own close circle. He can't be doing it in his own interests entirely, for company, with his own wife at home. It's strange to see in a young man and I can't make it out. Nor does he tell me and I don't ask. Only many years later on one of our long car journeys together does he describe to me his life as a boy when the Reverend Henderson was stationed at Te Aroha; how he'd accompany his father in the buggy on his pastoral rounds to open and shut the gates of the farms.

Here in Whareorino, however, it confounds me that Keith has a large life of his own beyond the confines of his life with me and I try out a sulk about it. One afternoon when he is at school and the west wind from the sea calls aloud to me I run away over the hills, not out of sight, but he chases after me and I hear his voice brief and stern and commanding, "Come home."

I stop but don't return. The hills curl on and they rear ahead to the backbone of the range and I hear the roll of the ocean. West Wind pulls my hair and calls, Come away, wild spirit, over the sea.

"Come home at once," from the man behind me. "You're not a child."

You are, from the wind.

"Come home."

I do. I obey the man. It will be thirty-six years before I obey the wind.

But at night when the day faces up to its reckoning I hear his other voice: "I love you, Mijjee."

"Yes."

"Don't run away. The idea is to be together."

"Yes."

"I can't do without you, Lamb."

Keith applied to the Taranaki education board for a transfer to a school with a residence on the grounds that he was married, and with patriarchal indulgence they obliged. After four months at Whareorino during which my sister Norma managed to find her way there with her little baby, we removed the plasticene from the packing case and used it for packing again.

Much further along on the journey through life we two drove back into Whareorino and parked on the road by the hill but there was no school there any more and no bach either. Even the cuttings in the slope where the buildings had been had eroded into shallow hollows and had grassed over into oblivion. A skinny tree-fern proved where the track had been, no sign of any native trees and not one remembering pine. Sheep grazed over all like repatriated exiles. Only the backbones of the ranges remained as they'd been and the sound of the rocking sea. The way nature obliterates what is ours and blandly recovers her own.

MANGAHUME     Early in the Christmas holidays we make this sparkling journey out from Whareorino on a day that is spangled all over, leaving Keith's first school for his second along a road that is metalled in rapture. By now we're quite certain the world is ours and we're praising each other like mad. Mangahume is his second school frolicking in the skirts of Mt. Egmont, whose white cone prays to the sky.

Five years and two babies later I'm saying, "I'm prepared to go teaching again."

"When I was taking choir practice last Tuesday Janet sent her love to you." Then he puts Jasmine and Elliot to bed and plays them to sleep on an old organ he's found while I fold the last pile of nappies.

Later, "We could get a Maori school," I say, "where the wife is allowed to teach. Like some of the others have."

Keith pushes the kettle over the flame. "It will never be said of me that I can't keep my wife and family."

"Well, I've had enough of the Slump, dear. What I used to call my soul has dissolved like soap in hot water and gurgled down the plug in the wash-house."

"It won't be always like this," he says. "I'll move back through bigger schools to the city. What I hope is . . ."

"Hope? Hope for me is a wet nappie dripping on the line after three or four weeks of rain."

"Really, dear. The way your ideas run away with you. These Maori schools are beyond the frontiers of . . ."

"That's just it. That's just it. Two salaries and nowhere to spend it. We could get off the ground."

"I was saying, beyond the frontiers of civilisation. And what about the new baby coming? Come on, Mij, we'll get off to bed. We must sleep while they sleep."

On Saturday morning I try again while my best love is bringing in the wood for the stove and Daddy's girl, Jasmine, is helping him. He has built an excellent woodbox that opens both inside and outside and the two of them are stacking it as neatly as chalk in a chalk box. Elliot is practising his crawling and trying to climb on everything. "K, we could get a Maori school as the others are and we'd both be at school together. Then you wouldn't be walking out in the morning and leaving us behind all the time. You're allowed to take your children with you in Maori schools. They're called Domestic Science."

"But we'd be out of touch with life altogether and I know you, my dear. It's company you like. It'd be much lonelier than Whareorino and you wouldn't find a Janet or a Milly out there having their babies with you. Here you have friends right and . . ."

"We'd only stay a few years, dear; three at the most."

"As I was saying, friends right and left."

". . . and we'd come back with some money, decent car and that; a big one. Rip up and down the country and over the ranges to visit our people and friends and I could make our home lovely."

"I repeat, Mijjee, what about the new baby; the new Domestic Science if you like?"

Good question but the conversation fails through lack of good answers so I pick up our son and give him a kiss then I give our daughter a kiss too and give Keith several; what else is life but kisses and kisses?

As the Great Depression ground on we'd hear of other couples of our year who had dropped out of currency and to hear it whispered of someone we knew, "They've gone Maori teaching," was to hear of their doom and to register the professional stigma on us all. On the other hand there must be something more than kisses and nappies and finding yourself pregnant.

It was early in 1937, I think, with Hitler arming in Europe when a two-teacher Maori school came up in the gazette called Horoera, eight miles by metalled road from Te Araroa, so where was Te Araroa? At the very top of the East Coast, the atlas said, hundreds of miles north of Gisborne, which itself was hundreds of miles north of anywhere. They wanted a male teacher and his wife who didn't need to have been trained and would go on staff as a junior, since all she had to do was teach the primers and train the Maori girls in the home to learn European ways. The thought of living among the Maoris and being lost to the world as well made my blood turn back. Yet, "We could get that one, K, look. Look."

"But dear, you'll have a new baby." He's weeding the garden while I hang out the clothes; he's a captive audience when in the garden. "Do try to see the thing rationally. How can any . . ."

"The new baby will be here in May and we don't have to go till July—and the b-baby will be three months old and—besides wherever we are, K, with three small babies we're out of circulation anyway. With two, we are. I haven't seen a racquet or a basketball or-or a film since . . . since . . . or had a swim or . . . we might as well be earning while we're at it."

". . . and how can anyone teach with three young children? Will you tell me?"

"Oh I'll get round that. I-I could b-bring my class home to the house, the department wants that, or I could take the babies to school. I started school myself at seven weeks and the new baby will be a thumping three months and almost ready to look after itself."

"And you consider this responsible talk?"

"Either that or I could . . . being on salary I could afford a house-keeper and leave the two little ones home."

"There'd be no housekeeper available in a Maori district. I'll be glad when you get over this, Mij."

"Milly called in this morning, K, and Janet in the afternoon. I do love Janet."

"You'd miss your friends dreadfully."

"Yes but . . . I've missed friends before and survived."

"And your family. Do you think they're all going to find their way up to the East Cape lighthouse?"

"You're my family, K. You're my friends, darling, breadwinner, husband, protector . . ."

"Really when you talk like this. I don't know, I'm sure."

We're at the end of a packed-tight day and are both raving tired. He slips some kindling wood over the flame and moves the kettle over and speaks reflectively, "It's a strange thing but you've always been the one to talk of working our way back to the city, to the lights and the action and the life, yet here you are in complete reverse, plunging headlong towards isolation and darkness."

I simply can't deny it.

Keith is no longer a spare young man; he's grown bigger, broader of shoulder and heavier. He wears this tweed coat with a line in the pattern or a white shirt and a tie except when he changes after school into working strides and shirt. His clothes speak protection to me as though they were part of his body. He pours the water in the teapot. "And you've always claimed you have hated teaching yet here you are planning to . . . well I can only say, striding right back into the thick of it. Whichever way you look at it the thing's out of all proportion to the occasion. Dear, you're so prone to hasty decisions, then you come running to me to get you out of the consequences. Now here . . . *here* is a consequence I could not get you out of. These are three-year terms."

I fold a last nappie making a work of art of the pile for no one can fold nappies like me. I see him putting out the cups on the bench, his wide hands with strong knuckles which are gentle with cups and babies and a wife. "I can't help seeing this, Mij, as another of your ideas running away with you."

I put up one foot on a chair. "We've been grounded in the one spot for five years now. It's time to take wing."

He brings in the tea and sits down. "When I contemplate the up-heaval of packing and of trying to travel with babies . . . how do you expect to do it? You couldn't even walk before the other two."

"But this one is going to be small, K. Look, only two months to go and you can hardly see it."

On the other hand, the baby should be moving by now and I suggest to my country doctor my dates may be wrong but, "No, no, no, it's coming in May." So up comes the debate on Horoera again but, "Really," Keith says, "I just can't stand the idea of my wife working. It's a reflection on me as a husband. You'll get over this and see it for what it is."

May came but still no baby. It would be only two months old by July. Never mind, the baby is moving now and, another thing, I'm growing heavy. "We ought to apply, K. There's nothing we can't do together, you've said so. We're not much together now, you at school all day. If we all come to school also then we'll be together all the time, the whole five. Nothing else matters. We ought to apply or we'll lose that school."

"The whole idea disturbs me deeply."

We applied. I'm not sure to this day of the real reason Keith agreed to apply. Money? Pressure from me? Or because he had come to like me in his school doing the art and the concerts? Maybe he saw the oppor-tunity for promotion, elbow-room, the extension of himself . . . I don't know. But I wouldn't answer for Keith at this point; we were polar in temperament and both kept the deepest recesses of our thoughts inviolate.

We applied. The application forms required the names and ages of our children: Jasmine three, Elliot one and a baby expected in June. We ourselves were in our late twenties and both certificated. Maori schools were not under boards but the administration of the Native Schools department which called for special qualifications; music was one and art was another. We both had music and I had art so we were firmly and officially appointed to take up our positions on July 1, 1937, and our present school was advertised. Keith's people in New Plymouth were shocked white and my own people fell silent. Janet and Milly nearly fainted.

"Any day now," from doctor. "Well yes, your dates are a little out."

No baby in June and I was growing very heavy again. God, we had to go next month and couldn't delay packing any longer. I traded in my electric sewing machine for an ancient treadle and Keith was collecting kerosene lamps and was very pleased about a tall benzine lamp that wore mantles. "Any day now, any day."

I could hardly move at all. Keith would have to leave at the end of June to take up his new position on the first of July and I'd have to follow later on my own with the children; a journey of several days by air, road, buggy and horse. We couldn't stay on here for the new teacher was due and our furniture would be gone anyway. What would happen to us?

Janet said on the phone one morning, "If your baby hasn't come, dear, by the time Keith goes you'll stay with us till it does." Keith's people in New Plymouth would take Jasmine and Elliot so July the first found our family not safely settled in our new home at Horoera, all together, but sundered like a pod in the autumn: Jasmine with Keith's parents and his sister Dorothy in New Plymouth, Elliot with Keith's aunties Bern and Bess, I sitting it out at Janet's in Opunake and Keith hundreds of miles off at the tip of the East Coast on the other side of the country. At tea with Janet's family that first night I shuffled myself from the table.

And did any baby emerge in July? The heavy weeks swayed by. Long fat letters flowed back from Horoera in which we learnt that the eight miles by road from Te Araroa as declared in the gazette was a ruse on paper to get the school staffed, even though our application forms told of a very young family. There was no road, metalled or otherwise; only eight miles of rocky beach along the ocean shore and two un-bridged tidal rivers which had to be forded at low tide, notorious among the locals. The idea that had run off with me had not allowed for a doctor's mistake but neither had it allowed for a lie in the gazette.

Vivid stories filled these envelopes: Keith had had to leave his little T-model Ford at Te Araroa, a Maori village with a shop, school, post office and hotel, and supervise the transport of our furniture by wag-gon, he on horseback. He'd followed the waggon across the first river, Awatere, watching all our worldly goods lurching and swaying over the bouldered bed through the swift current rushing to the waves of the sea, a story he often told in later life. Then the rocky beach along the lips of the waves, up and down banks to the second river, Orotua, the villain of the area; deep and treacherous with hidden logs, to be crossed only at the lowest ebb of the tide which shifted the logs anyway so that you couldn't be sure where they were.

He wrote of the school and of the residence in which he'd had to clean the kitchen floor with a knife after the relieving teacher, a single man; of gathering driftwood from the beach to chop into stove-lengths and of his vegetable garden he'd already begun in the sandy soil.

He'd made friends with the Maori neighbours, Hau and Cherry Ruwhiu, who lent him their horse and cart each Saturday to make the journey to Te Araroa for stores and mail between the tides and he told of the school across the paddock with about twenty-five Maori children, of the great Pacific Ocean at the front door and of the steep range behind. The letters came in once a week and Bob Hughson translated the Maori name Horoera to Horror Era and someone else described the advertisement in the gazette as veiled manslaughter. "It tells well anyway," I said.

Yet my waiting was not without joy; at least I was with Janet Hughson and her four small sons and Milly would come with her little baby, being the day of babies. "Why do things happen to you?" she said.

Three whole weeks of July puffed by before my baby saw fit to come; two and a half months after the doctor's date, and after ten days in the Cottage Hospital we returned to the Hughsons' for two and it was time to gather up the others. "Sylvie," said Janet, "I'm not a letter writer. I'll write you one letter and from then on I want you to remember that I'm always the same to my friends." So she was many years later; it was only I who was fickle.

The baby

Then one of the Hughson men drove me and Ashton to New Plymouth and I don't think there is any more hopelessly dependent and vulnerable stage in life than the sequences of birth with a baby at the breast when a mother and her young are as close to death as they are to life.

Like birds with great wings Keith's parents enfolded his family in the Parsonage where Jasmine already was, and the Aunties brought Elliot round, who could walk by now, all too well. Auntie Bern insisted that I had all my teeth seen to before leaving the services of civilisation; Auntie Bess lined one of those rare old cane dress-baskets with blue for Ashton to travel in who was twelve days old; Dorothy helped with the children on all fronts; Mrs. Henderson senior cooked rabbit pies with seasoning in them and the Reverend Henderson christened Keith's son in the drawing room of the Parsonage into the Methodist church before we were to leave on our four-day journey in a single-engined propeller ten-seater at ten a.m. one morning. I was preparing the children's clothes but was corrected for sewing a little pearl button on the baby's cardigan on Sunday, the Lord's day of rest.

The picture I remember most, however, is of the Reverend Henderson sitting at the head of the breakfast table with his library of books behind him, his white hair softly combed, his serenity and grace, saying, "This whole drama has a sweep and a grandeur like a story from the Old Testament dropped into the twentieth century."

*From Mangahume to Horoera*
IN TRANSIT    The morning came and I rose very early to feed Ashton first and bathe him, then wash and dress the other two and give them breakfast. Then washed and dressed myself and completed the packing so we'd all be ready on time. Keith's mother, believe it or not, commended his wife for the "surprising efficiency" of this complex multi-level organisation, then Auntie Bern arrived to drive us all to the New Plymouth airport at Bellblock and both the households of his family were there. But it was not until I had to move away from them that for the first time I realised that although I had three babies I had only two arms; at the steps of the gangway Auntie Bern took a photo of us: Elliot fifteen months on one arm in a hand-knitted blue helmet suit, Jasmine three in a white astrakhan coat by the hand, leaving Ashton, two weeks, in his basket at my feet.

A cold clear spring morning in August and I wore a black fur coat of rabbit skin, a brimless black hat with a half-face veil, high heels and pearl teardrop earrings. I felt glamorous and inspired to be going to Keith, our provider, protector, lover and father, and behind my veil I looked it . . . possibly. Probably, I amend, since there's no radiance like a mother with a newborn baby, whatever else she's like. In four days' time we'd all be together, the whole five of us. A moment of biblical miracle ahead. I couldn't make out why Keith's people in a group apart could shed tears for us.

The Reverend Samuel
and Mrs. Henderson

The Reverend on
his rounds

Elliot, the notorious climber, had to be held down with both arms on my knee, Jasmine had to sit by herself a seat before me, its back to me, and Ashton's basket was on a separate seat across the aisle, out of my reach. How to tend the three when I myself was strapped in? I couldn't even see the top of Jasmine's head who was softly crying. Elliot all but tore off my earrings and veil and Ashton began shrieking at once. Being a small plane it registered the turbulence over New Zealand's moun-tained terrain. There were others in the plane, women too, but only one young man made an effort to help us, had the initiative to undo his belt to pacify Jasmine, but she was not to be comforted, out of sight of Mummy. Neither was Ashton in his lonely basket. As for picking him up and feeding him or anything like that . . . for hours over the mid-island altitudes I was listening to my children crying.

Our first landing was, I think, Ohakea—was it there before the war? —where the inter-island planes changed crews and where we had to change planes, but how? The young man—God will have blessed him by now I'd say—took Jasmine's hand, the pilot himself carried Ashton's basket and I staggered with Elliot reaching for everything he saw. I found myself sitting in a cold comfortless concrete waiting room with no chairs, only benches: Jasmine at knee, Elliot on knee and Ashton at my feet.

I thought of Floyd Duckmanton who I'd heard was captain of an inter-island plane and if I were writing fiction I'd not risk the improb-ability of his being on one of these, but documentary shrugs off im-probabilities. A young very slight woman with a tiny girl by the hand stood at a window watching another plane coming in and I heard her say, "Floyd." And sure enough in ran Floyd himself up the steps in a dashing captain's uniform and cap, only half the weight he'd been in the past and the thick cheeks over which tears for me had run five years ago were strangely lined. He recognised me at once and came at once and I looked up through my veil into his eyes; the same dark eyes, sad and tragic still as they had been on that night of storm when I'd turned him down for Keith. Glancing at my babies, "These yours?" he says.

"Yes."

"Are you happy?" he shoots.

"Yes."

"Mine didn't work out," he says, then joins his wife and daughter and pounds down the steps and away, not helping me from one plane to the next, and leaving no comfort behind him.

The next stop was Palmerston North near which my older sister Daphne lived with a friend in the country and like sunshine they plunged into the plane and scooped us all up in loving concern; the big man taking on Elliot, Daphne taking up Ashton squeaking his new heart out and I taking Jasmine's hand and the next thing they drove us to their country home where I fed the baby and Daph made the tea. Oh what bliss was there. The warm house, the soft bed, the food passed to us and the continuing laughter Daphne brought which obliterated the immediate past, the present crises and the fears for the

unknown future. It was the way the two kept on praising the children all the time, saying they were beautiful, mar-vellous, unique that showed a new dimen-sion to their own con-dition, and the way Ashton calmed down and slept. That gratu-itous heaven; one of those shining cameos you look back on when wondering if life is worth it.

One night we stayed there and in the morn-ing the four of us were kissed upon another plane.

From Palmerston North northward to Napier over one of the coun-try's several backbones, the Ruahines; Jasmine out of sight and reach again, Elliot shredding me to tiny little pieces and Ashton across the aisle practising his screaming, two weeks old now and grow-ing up fast. In writing one's life there is much one forgets but this

At New Plymouth ready to leave for Horoera; the plane we travelled in

transit from one side of the country to the other, alone in the air with my babies, throws up every detail though I'm writing forty years later. Napier about noon where there was not time to unbuckle my belt and feed the baby even if someone in the plane had offered to hold Elliot . . . the crippling timidity of prolonged Victorianism. The planes were smaller by now, however, and even more responsive to turbulence and when we took off again over the coastal ranges northward to Gisborne on the East Coast where Keith would surely be waiting for us, the last lap in the air, one had to reach inward for some courage other than the physical: "Where thou goest, I will go; where thou lodgest, I will lodge. Thy people will be my people and thy God my God."

That last lap must have been the hardest; it was those terrifyingly steep hills below which recurred in my nightmares of falling. Yet radiance found a place in the plane; the thought of reaching Keith at last, that there should actually exist a man strong and loving to lift us out of the frightening sky, gather us all up together and care for each one of us. But would this plane ever land at all so I could do Ashton, put Elliot down and bring back Jasmine's smile? It did land intact at Gisborne, taxied across the bumpy field like a rabbit hopping over tufts and we saw Keith running. "Daddy," said Jasmine.

In the morning of our third day, with tins of food aboard, and drink, the five of us set off in the same little Ford, a box of bones by now yet the means of our survival, on the 112 miles of coastal road through the hills northward. Though spring in New Zealand it was hot on the coast and the road was tortuous, unmetalled and dusty with many a stream to ford. The air was close in the gullies and often we stopped for the sake of the children and whenever Ashton cried, then I could lift the little thing out of his basket and change him and nurse him a little. We lunched on the side of the silent road beneath some casual tree.

Low-gearing through the streams as the hours added up in slow dusty miles, breasting repetitive hills, tiptoeing round hairpin bends above eighty-foot drops, sneaking under cliffs . . . if this were an idea running away with me it had run some distance so far, beyond the point of no return. Yet joy still frothed in us to be together again; nothing mattered too much as long as we were five and at least Keith Henderson was extended to his limit and liked it very much; he was happy all the time.

After leaving European Gisborne we found the colour of the people changing, the population thickening and darkening in an unnerving way as we penetrated Maori territory. To travel beyond civilisation was one thing but to abandon one's race was another. The dream that had lured me had left this out. All those loving arms and kisses, concerned eyes, warm homes and tears of farewell forfeited for three blank years. It had the implacability of iron jaws, like a persistent-occipital-posterior birth unrelated to teardrop earrings, and it was I responsible, not Keith.

Late afternoon with the shadows prostrated across the road like bars, with every face we met brown now and all hair black, we emerged from the hills and soft-geared down a benign slope into Te Araroa ("the long path"), the furthest north village on the coast with the Pacific rolling at it, where we were to stay the night with the teachers, Harry and Bern Black. When the door opened I was struck by the white feet of the girls, slim elegant feet shockingly bare. Private toes exposed to the day. We'd certainly left civilisation behind us. Again the fast rush to tend the children; the girls picked them up at once while I did the baby. Again the arms, smiles and cheer from hospitable people, strangely at peace with themselves and the area as though there were nothing to it.

Any New Zealander knows the pohutukawa tree at Te Araroa in the school playground renowned for its size and age: the biggest in the country, they say, and a thousand years old, and richest in song and legend . . . is it still there? The pohutukawa on that shore are gigantic personages, their lifted roots grasping the rocks like ancestral gods from the ocean.

The breaking waves beat all night like drums of doom and of warning, threatening me and my young, yet Keith was with us, whose first passion we were; our comfort, our safety, our source of love. On this young man we were wholly dependent for our very survival; our eyes followed him wherever he went and when I was tending Ashton in the night and he asked me how I was I said, "As long as you are with us."

"We're together, Mijjee."

The rhythm and thunder of plunging surf ended the third day.

On the morning of the fourth day in transit we prepared to set out to our next school. It wasn't raining or anything and there wasn't any sun but there was a momentousness as though the weather were holding its breath.

Believe it or not I was still the glamour girl from the city in a tight tube skirt, high heels and drop-pearl earrings, but as I minced to the gate carrying Elliot I had a brief view of Te Araroa: a lofty skyscraper bluff overhanging an alluvial lowland, the sea in uproar behind us and the river beyond.

On the road outside Blacks' gate stood a tall giddy buggy with four iron wheels, the seat perched high on top like a nest in a tree and in it sat Hau Ruwhiu, K's neighbour, with the reins relaxed in a hand. In the shafts waited two hefty horses with a ready-for-anything look in the eye yet they seemed quiet enough: sturdy and silent and still like Hau. A saddled horse was hitched to a fence post.

Harry brought the basket full of Ashton, Bern had Jasmine's hand and the two girls helped Keith load our bags. Then someone held Elliot while Keith pushed me up these quite fanciful steps to this precarious seat, put Jasmine between me and Hau, passed Elliot up on my knee and tucked Ashton's basket down at my feet. From this lookout I could see the first river and took time off for a moment of reckoning: taking off the drop-pearl earrings I slipped them out of sight.

Keith mounted his horse, Hau twitched the reins, the horses woke up and, to light-hearted words from the Blacks, we lumbered towards the river.

We began quietly enough along the road as the bluff towered higher, the buggy swaying hardly at all. A few chains through the village and there was the Awatere ("swift water"). You'll find a timber bridge there now but not forty years ago. It is one of these broad-bedded fast-running rivers of clear water common in New Zealand with the round-shouldered boulders I used to draw. A bit swollen from the spring rains, that's all. We used to wade in and float with the current. I wasn't afraid of this river, only of the circumstance. Before we got near the water the buggy began lurching and jerking on the stones with Hau uttering horsetalk. I longed to hold Ashton's basket steady but one hand held Elliot and the other the handrail. Keith rode beside us and as we entered the water he called, "Hang on to the man, Jassie."

Hau was cool, though holding in his hands the lives of our children as well as the reins, as the current flung upon the wheels on its way to meet the up-running battalions of waves at the mouth. Upriver, the wide sparkling water pell-melling down upon us; downriver, the opposing cresting surf. If the buggy overturned, which child should I save? Here I was with my young in the middle of the Awatere River entirely dependent on men and horses. Keith rode on the downstream side of us and Hau only flicked his whip as the horses heaved us up on the farther shore. And I thought, I'll never pass this way again. Goodbye to the world forever.

At last we came to the sand of the beach; hard sand, wet sand, sweet firm sloping sand, with the feeling of a lover's quarrel mended, and we eased our way between the rocks. The towering bluff above us, the turbulent surf below us thrashing at the great pohutukawa roots withstanding the sea for centuries. Although the tide was out waves still reached the wheels, licking in curiosity, whispering to the iron, foam sucking and spitting. Round the bluff we rode to higher ground where the beach was wider, and Jasmine and I relaxed.

The mouth of the Awatere River at low tide in summer

We continued weaving between upthrusting rocks, up a bit on the grass then down again on the sand until we reached the second tidal river: Orotua ("hidden danger"). Not the swift rush of the Awatere but slow deep water, muddy and treacherous. On its floor secret logs may have shifted position in the last high tide. A shudder in the buggy as the wheels hit one, the jolt as the horses jerked it over. Which child should I save if the traces broke, the shaft split, a wheel came off or one of the horses plunged free? Yet there did come a further shore once more, the horses straining up out of the water upon the blessed bank, but never would I cross these rivers again.

Much easier now on a wide flat beach and I recognised the beauty of the rocks upthrusting from the sand, the dramatic shapes of them, and in the design of the heaping driftwood; it was enthralling along the last reach upon the silver sand. Far ahead you could see through the haze the outline of cliffs near the East Cape lighthouse; inland jutted a jagged range and seaward the sounding ocean. Only seagulls greeted us.

As the turning tide began creeping nearer, each wave foaming further,

Keith pointed to a plateau in the foothills, at two red roofs on white buildings: the school and the residence of Horoera. Through an opening in the driftwood he led the way, the buggy squeaking and climbing a steep green slope, horses straining, leather and buckles creaking till we reached the level of the house. To the smell of the sweat of the horses and the steam lifting from their flanks he dismounted, hitched his horse and took down Ashton's basket.

And the next thing I'm sitting on a chair by the stove feeding the baby. On a stool beside me he puts a cup of tea, then goes about feeding the others. The kitchen is spick and span with the dishes reflecting the light while steam whispers from the kettle and the lino is polished bright; picturing the face of the newborn present and erasing the worn-out past.

The end of the fourth day in transit and the last.

By the sea

The sea was right before us, all but at the door, and we lived on a shelf of green above it. Behind us reared the range which intercepted the sun in the afternoon to drop upon us its vast shadow like a cloak upon a body.

The sea never rested; it remained awake each morning, all day, each evening and all night. You always knew when the tide was out by the muted strings of the waves and you also knew when the tide was in by the swelling beat of the drums, orchestrating the hours. You couldn't turn it off when you were sleeping when you couldn't distinguish between the rhythm of your soul and the rock of the rolling ocean for the sea didn't sleep but wave-crashed your mind and took over.

As the tides ebbed and the tides flowed you lived with the heave and the sway of the sea and merged with its moods through season and year, whether twinkling by twilight, moaning by stormlight or dazzling the eye by noon, and though you felt that wisdom lay on the sea you knew of submarines under the sea for war was in the sea.

It called you, the sea. You stole an early morning moment in your nightgown on the verandah to watch the new sun lift from the sea and the wind pull the spray from the surf and you caught a minute of nightmare midnight to read of romance in the moonlight on the sea, for the sea mesmerised, monopolised and hypnotised . . . the sea, the sleepless sea. You were no longer a self apart, independent of the sea. This was the sea, in person.

The first Monday morning when the bell called from the school I rounded up the children obediently enough. Since we'd arrived only on the Saturday I'd hoped the headmaster would have allowed me a week to pull myself together but no; school was school, Monday was Monday, I was the junior appointed to the job and was already six weeks late. The facts were as stark as the rocks on the beach and no less implacable. So we set off from the house across the sand in a caravan: Ash in his pram, El by the hand and Jas helping to push the pram. Three and a half, sixteen months and three weeks into the jaws of school. Yet we were elated; where in fact were we going? To no less than Daddy.

Keith had all the standards in the one main schoolroom and I had a few primers in the porch where he had tacked up cardboard between the coatpegs and had painted it for a blackboard. What with the pram there was not much room and although there was a small window there was not much light so we left the door open for light, not to mention air. Neither was there much English among the small children and I knew no Maori but the open door threw no light on that. Jasmine touched the closed door of the standards' room where Daddy was and, "Mr. Henderson's in there," she said.

A new pattern came to the days at once; at morning interval, a quarter to eleven on the minute, our little caravan set off back over the sandy track to the house for me to see to the little ones and make a hasty cup of tea when a big girl called Moana would come and take one over to Mr. Henderson. Then back on eleven at the call of the bell. At noon the five of us would return for lunch when I fed the baby and Keith fed the other two and gave them a drink. On my stool he'd put my cup and saucer and the loveliest sandwiches except that with the nausea from the rush of milk I couldn't get them down. A bite and a drink for himself, wash the children's hands and faces, clean up the table and return to school at half past twelve while we returned at one.

Often in the afternoon when I was taking a lesson in the big room and Keith was taking the primers Ashton would wake, then I'd lay him on the table and teach across him. As Elliot toddled about, the children would stop him eating chalk, pulling the books out of their desks, climbing where he could and from putting a finger in an ink-well, and Jas would be with Mr. Henderson in the porch. If Ashton cried I'd give the little chap to one of the girls who would hold him on one arm easily enough while doing her work with the other, which is known as Domestic Science. In later years we'd say, "No wonder Ash is a clever boy; he started school at three weeks old."

Since the primers were out by half past two the headmaster would release me then and back we'd trek across the sand, I and my young, when I could see to them: a wash, a drink, something to eat and a sleep, and bring in the clothes from the line, with its load of nappies from two baby boys and start on the dinner till Keith came home at four. There was nothing to stop him coming home at three which was one of the mysteries to me in him that I had not then solved; the man would stay and prepare his work, one of the main things I remember about him: the preparation of his work before and after school.

At four we'd both start on the children to bathe, feed them and put them to bed, we hoped, before sitting down to our own meal, but Ashton was a restless baby, not without reason, and would wake in the night as well as at five in the morning anyway, with the result that quite soon we'd have to take turns with him, sleeping in separate rooms so that at least one of us could have an unbroken night to support the other during the day. Keith liked to tell the story of how he'd position the pram at the end of his bed and rock it with his foot without waking. "You can't help getting fond of the little chap," he said.

Elliot was a boy who was made of sunshine and only talked to himself if he woke and Jas had left waking behind.

But there was now no time for that moment of inspiration on the verandah at sunrise which generated energy, face to face with the sea, nor for the relaxation on a Saturday morning which keeps teachers alive, for K had to harness the horse to the cart and go to Te Araroa for the stores and mail, fitting in with two low tides. On Sunday he'd do the wood for the week, driftwood from the beach, sawing and chopping it, and on Sunday you'd find him in the garden trying to grow things in the lifeless sand; in the afternoon he might be at school if he could make it. And it was he who did the large family washing every single morning and hung it on the line and he'd always get the breakfast; during all of which you'd find me with the two little babies especially the new one, for Jassie would track Daddy.

As it had been in former places Keith was out in the community making friends, but Maoris this time. He bought the cart and horse from Hau Ruwhiu and sold the little car in Te Araroa. Maori people

Bringing driftwood from the beach

I visited families over the range.

would leave a bag of *kumara** on the doorstep, sometimes *puha*, watercress or corn which you had to get to like if you meant to survive. We both visited Maori families on horseback, one staying home with the children, and you should see where some of them lived, though some homes were large and affluent. And the school committee meetings were no longer an evening occasion in the school but took the form of all-day, all-out, district *huis* at the *pa* complete with a *hangi* and speeches, a meeting of the Red Cross of which I was president, for the war, maybe a school concert to end up with a church service.

It was no good Keith trying to plant pines round this school in the unresponsive sand but he did manage to get a fence to stand up to separate the sheep from the children and he did knock up a lawn from the tussock. Having his own clear idea of what a school could be, he followed the lure of it while I followed the lure of wanting to please him.

The reading books I found there for the primers that first Monday morning began with four nouns on the first page: *horse, bed, train* and *can*, briefly illustrated. Horse they could understand as nearly all of them rode to school along the beach or from over the range, but a train they had not even heard of. Some of them had beds at home but some slept on the floor or the earth while a can was straight-out enigma to all; the sketch showed one of those little watering-cans you see stitched in fancywork on old-time tea-cosies which I hadn't seen myself for decades. On the second page, regardless of having used the can as a noun, it suddenly became a verb: I can skip, I can run and such. "It's a funny thing, K, but I can't teach some of these little Maoris to read."

"It's using that noun as a verb," he says.

"But they don't know what a can is anyway, or a bed or a train."

"Give them time, it will come."

In time I remark with rue, "Perhaps I should be stricter."

"Now look, whatever you do, Mij, don't frighten them."

"If only these books supplied by the department had words in them like *sand, beach, sea* or . . . or *fish* or . . . or *cart*, I'd be able to make some headway."

"There's no reason why you shouldn't use those words."

"They didn't say anything about that in training college, K."

---

* *kumara*: sweet potato; *puha*: wild soft thistle with no pricks; *hui*: a Maori gathering; *pa*: Maori village; *hangi*: food cooked in the ground

"Yes, teach them those words . . . as long as they read the set books too."

"But, you see, you get the inspectors and all that."

"As long as they can read the set books too."

"Some of them can."

"So I see."

"The ones with white blood. Y' see, K, what I could do with really is a few Maori words. *Kai* (food), *puha* and—and . . . I mean a word like *corpse* would take on. They'd read it in a minute."

"I think you'll manage to teach them to read without disturbing the dead."

That sounded like his father.

He says, "There's no call for extravagance on this occasion."

Keith coming home
from Te Araroa with
the stores

Both little boys
waiting for Daddy
to come home

And that sounded like his mother.

When Sammy slipped out of the porch one day, picked up a piece of driftwood and smashed the new gold-painted lawn-mower with blow after blow I saw no connection with watering-cans and beds. I just thought he was a very bad boy.

Cheerfully enough I put the local words on small cards, words like *beach, sand, cart, fish* and *bread*—not *lawn-mower*—and sized them over for preservation and taught from them tentatively, though the Dewes children and Jasmine didn't need them who could read the set books by now and, for extras, liked words like *baby, pram, daddy* and *house* while Da went for *truck, car* and *boat.* The other little Maori children, however, began to see daylight with the local words though I still thought they should have done better. As for Sammy no words clicked at all. I know now that *lawn-mower* would have started him off, or Maori words like *kai* and *keha* (ghost), but the key to reading for beginners had not come to me then. All of which complicated my work; how could you teach one small class a whole lot of different words simultaneously? It occurred to me how handy it would be if there were one common vocabulary for small children which suited everybody, and what if we had a whole set of books with their favorite words or even books in Maori? They'd all read in no time. But the main idea in Maori schools was to promote the English culture and it was not so long ago that Maori children were strapped for speaking Maori at school.

I felt there was a risk in the whole operation. What would the inspectors say? On the other hand for an inspector to get here at all he'd have to buy riding jodhpurs, borrow a horse, learn to ride, negotiate the beach at low tide and cross two tidal rivers, by which time the grapevine should have given us fair warning. Not that it made any difference to K, who ran the school as though there were inspectors imminent every day and who, I think, looked forward to them coming anyway.

My blackboard drawing longed to break out and flow over the blackboards as it had in K's other two schools, but the conditions were hardly favorable; also K had an old piano bought for the school and now and again I won an hour on a Sunday afternoon, but although my piano work, like my drawing, wanted to burst out and soar among the rafters of a schoolroom as it had since I'd first known I had fingers, there were some factors missing: time, energy and audience. Besides, these would not make me a better wife and mother or a better teacher either. The only place for them was in my dreaming.

I knew very little about children, they usually bored me. Five years of training hadn't scratched the surface. Children, except for my own, were unnecessary beings with no function other than to make me go to school, who kept on needing to be taught all the time and who cut into the texture of my hidden passions with the scissors of insistence, hacking at my privacy so that I couldn't dream in school. Whereas I did have something new to dream about; we were saving up to buy the biggest car ever seen on New Zealand roads. We'd learnt by now that summer droughts brought the rivers low so that a truck could cross and we could garage the car in Te Araroa. A Gisborne firm had already sent us a large glossy picture of a large glossy model in dark glossy red which K had pinned upon the wall in the living room where we could see it each time we passed even in the middle of the night when taking turns with Ashton. When we'd done our time we would rip up and down the North Island recovering the warmth of communication, kisses kisses all the way.

But tragedy repels. We didn't see our lot as such but others did. Keith was the local postmaster and from Saturday to Saturday he brought back from Te Araroa the faded canvas bag that would surely bring our mail. When he at last returned and the children were in bed we'd tip it out on the carpet by the open fire and down we'd go on our knees looking for the handwriting of those we loved, except for Mumma's and Keith's mother, it was seldom there, though I felt my very breath depended on hearing from Janet.

Yet the resilient spirit of youth is not to be broken or bent, that being the day when imagery flourished in its own right, fuelling thought and action, and as the acute meaning of isolation dug into the heart we'd kiss it out and focus ahead. I kept in weekly touch with the plunker* in Gisborne, supervising the baby's progress, keeping his food right and weighing the little thing, filling in his baby book and posting it back and ringing up sometimes when he wasn't well.

We joined the country library service which sent us all we asked for except Bertrand Russell's *Why I Am Not a Christian*, which was not allowed in the country at that time. Keith enrolled at the correspondence school for music and Maori, trying to study at night; he was succeeding at the music, especially composition, and one of his pieces was praised and accepted at the school for its own use; but carrying as he did the main weight of the school, much of the home and even of survival itself, he finally had to disengage from the correspondence school.

* Sir Truby King's system of scientific baby care

Part of his music programme had been Beethoven's Fifth Symphony and Brahms' Variations on a Theme by Haydn, one or the other of which I'd have running on the Gramophone much of the time and which I couldn't help studying myself on his behalf, thinking that if I knew them he'd know them too. What I learnt from that symphony day in and day out was the concept of shape, or rather the confirmation of the concept of shape as I'd found it in drawing, so that in later years whenever I wrote a book I'd build it on the form of some masterwork in music. The shape of emotion.

A Maori lady taking us to a *hui* (gathering)

His set of music textbooks I studied too, trying to do it for him when he was filling the kerosene lamps for the week and fuelling the benzine lamp, all this inclination to study surfacing which I'd not till that time been aware of, inherited from my lineage; a passion of curiosity about what other people were made of. Along with the mechanics of music was the history of the great masters from Palestrina down on whom I made a time chart through the centuries with pictures in pen and wash of the men and summaries of their work, and it was at about this time when I began inquiring into the nature of genius and its forewarning in childhood.

Neither could I leave his Maori language textbooks alone; in time I enrolled at the correspondence school myself and Cherry Ruwhiu, who had become our off-and-on housekeeper, taught me the pronunciations and corrected my exercises; along with Enoka Potae, rotund, peaceable, who'd sit with me by the stove in the winter with my little ones at knee or on knee, trying to teach me the Maori *nga* (the, plural).

"Nga," from Enoka.

"Ga," from me.

"Nga," from him with a Maori smile.

"Na."

"Nga."

"N-gaa," from me.

"Nga." And that went on for weeks till I got it. Unless you could speak Maori you didn't speak at all. I sent to Gisborne for jodhpurs, borrowed a saddled horse from the Walkers, a Maori family up the beach, two of whose sons were at the war, and with K minding the children, I'd gallop the beaches and explore the valleys, visiting our Maori families, trying out the Maori phrases with them and one thing you had to learn to like was how they laughed at you.

I could not waste these years and I wasn't going to join young wives who went down under marriage and babies, swamped, never to be of any account again, signing their

An hour off

names in down-at-heel slippers. I sent away for astringents and creams for my face, wore gloves on my hands in water and set out to recover the figure I'd lost over three babies: arduous exercises on the floor morning and night and a hopeful effort to diet. Something still waited for me to do in this world, I hardly knew what, but some day we'd return to our kind and I'd get on with my life.

In the meantime I'd have to get ready for it. I'd have to keep well, educate myself, look nice, speak well, walk well, hang on to my natural abilities and, above all, overhaul my dreadful character. Use every hour of these benighted years; rather than to see them as a loss, to see them as a gift.

It was not always easy to see it this way for there were times when the gift blotted out. I think it was our first Christmas there at Horoera with the baby about six months old when Keith's brother was to be married in Wellington and Keith had promised to be his best man since Elliot had been Keith's, and Henderson weddings were holy priorities. Our guardian had to leave us. Three days' travel to get to Wellington, three days of wedding in the capital and three days of travelling back: nine days altogether.

Nine afternoons for the shadow to fall from the range like a cloak upon us, nine overtures to the voices of the night rolling in from sea, eighteen high tides and eighteen ebb tides and nine times twenty-four hours alone with the sea in person.

He stacked up the chopped wood and stocked up the kind of food that would keep through January temperatures with no electrical equipment, only an outside safe for the butter and meat. I helped him get his dear clothes ready and one early morning, after he'd done the family washing and hung the lot on the line, with the tide at the ebb he kissed us all goodbye and went away. From the top of the bank we watched the shape of the horse and cart shrinking along the beach until it disappeared in the haze.

No one came to see us, there was no one to come. Though the Maoris joined us professionally they kept to themselves domestically for the colour bar is not all drawn by *pakehas.** At night on my own with the children our only company was the suck of the sea and the threat of the breaking waves. The perishable food packed up quite soon; I suppose Hau Ruwhiu had been detailed to bring us stores, fresh meat, fresh bread and vegetables and such from Te Araroa on Saturdays, but he cannot have done so though they sent over fresh milk every day by a child. Here's this picture of me sitting in the kitchen with the three little children in a cluster at knee, just sitting there answering their questions which were mainly, "When's Daddy coming back?" from Jassie, "Daddy Daddy," from El and "Ma," from Ashie, "Ma."

Towards the end of those nine days our food almost did run out except for the stable things that kept and I remember that tableau in the kitchen of me and the children in the heat of the day and the boom of the ocean about us when through the door appeared Cherry Ruwhiu, knowing that Hau had not brought our stores; slipping in on slim silent bare feet, finding us there and standing a moment, slight, weightless like a presence only, eyes brown, dramatic. In the way of Maoris she said nothing at all, nothing on her tongue, then vanished again as soundlessly as a wave at ebb tide.

Half a tide later she reappeared, having caught one of the Ruwhiu free-running fowls, stuffed it with kumara, carrot and puha, baked it to

* white people

a turn, garnished it with watercress upon a white platter and she placed it on our table with a smile.

After nine centuries alone with the shadow and the sea, that hallowed cart and horse did reappear in the surf-blurred distance crawling along the sand like a cumbersome insect between the waves and the driftwood, an impression only. Was it true? "Is that Daddy?" from Jas. Was there actually someone in this world of horizons, big skies, "multitudinous seas" who had a concern for us, who knew and cared that we were alone and who had been willing to leave the peopled cities beyond to return to Horoera? In the breeze from the sea at the top of the slope, in silhouette of the family primeval, mother and young, we watched him and waited till he was near enough for us to see him wave and Jasmine said, "Daddy's come back."

"Daddy," from Elliot.

Ashton in my arms was studying my face so I told him, "Daddy's here."

The road
round the
cliff to
the East Cape
lighthouse

Four miles farther along the beach beyond the distant cliffs reigned the East Cape lighthouse, the first point in the British Empire to see the sun rise, when there was an Empire. A community of rather rare people lived nearby: the two young European teachers at the school, Lou and Colin Flavell, the lighthouse keepers, the White family, a

Maori minister of the Anglican church, the Reverend Kohere, and a few other Maori families. Tucked out of sight it held mystery for me but I didn't ride there on account of the hairbreadth track round the cliffs above the Pacific Ocean.

Yet that place drew traffic through Horoera. At long intervals you'd see them riding by on the waterline and if any called at our place they'd be sure to be on their way to the Cape or on their way from the Cape into Te Araroa; the lighthouse had to be attended by people and the people had to stock up from Te Araroa though the lighthouse itself was serviced by ship. It seldom happened I was looking that way when they passed but I must say I was impressed at the way those women got themselves the whole twelve miles from the Cape along the beach on horseback, round those suicidal cliffs and through those hostile rivers as though there were nothing to it. What did they have that I didn't have?

From a distance they seemed to be shadows passing, phantoms drifting but if one stopped and called on us briefly, heavens, we'd be confronted by bodies of real flesh, real voices and living eyes, like visitations from the world of the past. They so rarely came up to the house, however, that when they'd gone they faded into fantasy again. Silhouetted against the sea they looked like shapes only cut out from black paper.

Once in a blue moon the district nurse would ride out from Te Araroa on her rounds to the East Cape and she would call in. The rotundity of Miss Banks and of her horse made them an admirable pair together and they were plainly in accord. Hearty and warm and practical she never failed to have something in her bag for the children, usually oranges and a picture book. A cultivated woman and, given a chance, I'd have tried to make a friend of her but no, she'd throw up this barrier of cheerfulness round her as nurses must to beat off the public who all want her for a friend. Besides I still longed for Janet Hughson, who had only written once.

Harry and Bern Black were fond of Keith, who saw them most Saturdays, and one day they rode out from Te Araroa on such fine whisking horses and up-to-date jodhpurs you'd never know they were teachers, but the cream of the landowners. What touched us about that visit was the attention they afforded our children, whom we'd been dying to show to somebody. As for the children they were confounded at white people. But the Blacks were mainly on their way to the Cape to visit the Flavells in their first school so they had an excuse not to stay.

In fact the Flavells themselves would materialise from the haze now and again, the two of them doubling on the one horse which walked slowly, more slowly and more slowly till they led it up the slope.

Tell you who else called in once and that was Mrs. White from the lighthouse, the most comfortable woman who ever rode the cliffs, sitting in her saddle like reclining in an armchair. An ample lady who tied her cardigan round her waist when charging the sea breezes; a motherly down-to-sand soul with two daughters coming up the same. But only the Flavells would stay, then off again into the mists the others rode leaving only their hoofmarks behind them.

Their visits were exciting indeed but my reaction to white people was changing; no longer nervous of the brown people whose language I was learning, I was becoming shy of the white people now, my children too maybe, and there remained another white visitor yet who was due some time and that was the school inspector.

The house

It was nearing the end of our first summer there, I think, when I decided on something better than taking my little children to school with me, being no longer prepared to disturb the baby like that or to risk having Elliot on the schoolroom floor any more; his little hands got so dirty and his feet and clothes and the things that might go into that mouth or maybe down that throat; a toddler needs the spotless floor of his home. And I would no longer expose Jasmine's chest to an unheated porch, and another thing, I was wearing down myself. So I turned the side bedroom into a classroom for the primers, a few school desks in it, a table and something on the wall for a blackboard where I could simultaneously teach them and stay home with the children, where the baby could sleep his morning out and the toddler was on his own floor.

Not that I liked this; you couldn't avoid the surprising smell of hot bodies issuing from that room, or the primers running in and out all day, not to mention the constant reminder of "teaching" in my sacrosanct home, an unequivocal invasion, and above all, What would the inspector say? If ever one managed to get here.

A Maori action
song at our
back door. Jasmine
is on the left.

It came to pass that one *did* manage to get here and you've got to allow for miracles. Mr. D. G. Ball got here, the new senior inspector of native schools. Believe it or not this man had the unprecedented grace to announce his visit beforehand; no sneaking in behind trees and through swamps intent on catching you out as they were still doing then. You should have heard teachers in native schools swapping stories of their natural enemies dramatically appearing in the doorway or even peeping in the windows first, pipsqueaks whose knowledge of their subject, the Maori, wouldn't fill a cockleshell, whereas the teachers could be excused for knowing their subject. Anyway, so this Mr. Ball not only named the date of his visit but the time of day. How can you name a time of day when you're subject to the tidal system? He must have studied the tides chart. I mean, were Maoris worth this? Talk about electrify the heathen.

He rode out on a mighty-boned horse, ploughing through rivers and signing the beaches like a Viking in the latest jodhpurs. He turned out to be very fair-haired and fair-skinned with extravagantly large blue eyes, all inquiry in them and comprehension, and when he dismounted and hitched his sweating horse, before me and my young,

Ash in arms, two at knee, he was so tall and so big that we nearly broke our necks looking up at his face.

Over at the school proper with Keith he started off by renouncing the favorite word of Empire, "Native," and spoke of Maori schools. His view of Maori education accommodated racial temperament and characteristics and their particular needs in the curriculum and the daily timetable, and he proclaimed there was a Maori culture worth preserving. Heinous thought. He put it to Keith that along with teaching the Maori girls housecraft in our European home, we could, conversely, invite the Maori people to school to teach us the Maori culture: flaxwork, carving, weaving, *taniko,** *tukutuku, waiata* and *haka* and even the discredited Maori language. Who'd ever heard of parents coming to school to teach the holy teachers? He brought an inspiring and powerful presence. Visionary.

On that memorable day in my life at Horoera—I mean the thing was racial charity, wasn't it—our first visit from an inspector when teaching together, he did not find any fault with me whatever but seemed to be looking for something in me to approve of. He did not reject the small surreptitious cards I'd made of local words—*beach,* *fish* and such—and he did not denounce the Maori words I'd included like *kai* and *hoiho* (horse) and he was pleased with the schoolroom in the house. I fell ardently in love with him.

As he was going, standing over six feet on our flowered carpet, looking way way down upon me, his blue eyes wide steady and encompassing, and with me gazing way way up up to them in wonder, he spoke firmly as a man: "I congratulate you on your good heart."

Both Keith and I had good gradings from that visit, K's very good, swinging him up well ahead of his contemporaries. At that time all grading was published dramatically in a supplementary gazette, exposing one teacher to another. It was our first grading teaching together and we praised each other fulsomely.

We were young and we loved to play and that night we were so happy we celebrated with a game of marbles on the floor, sitting with legs outstretched, a row of marbles between us, each with a Tor and laughing for nothing. Over the radio streamed news of the war from a northern station called Voice of America. "That hectic tone, really

* *taniko*: a very close and precise weaving with flax fibre of Maori patterns, in colour; *tukutuku*: they weave these patterns, exclusive to panels in a meeting house, done in reed; *waiata*: Maori songs, as distinct from Maori chants; *haka*: Maori war dance

The parents come
to school

The school
calf club

The children riding
to school

those Americans. Concert pitch. It's your turn, dearest. Hey, that marble over there is mine."

K shoots his Tor and knocks another from the line. "Ah you little beauty," and gathers it up.

The V.O.A. quotes Hitler, "We have wiped the British Army across the face of Flanders."

"Just listen to that," from K. "There's no British Army now."

"We'll have a New Zealand division before long though. It's your turn again, K."

But he doesn't take his second turn. "By gee, just listen to that."

The Voice of America hurtles on, ". . . under heavy enemy bombardment. Everything that floats is on the English Channel picking up soldiers out of the sea . . ."

And that's the end of our play.


My Red Cross was meeting on our verandah or at the Potae meeting house to knit balaclavas, roll bandages and pack food parcels for overseas. Just say Red Cross and they'd meet anywhere though the New Zealand division was not yet in action. But the boys were called up now right and left so play came last in the survival pace and we forgot about grading. There was no time.

Neither was there time to dream but dreaming went on regardless, trying to explode in reality. Unexpectedly the dreams would peer out from their undermind confinement at a line of poetry or the flash of a tune, at a moment in my nightgown on the verandah as the sun flicked the waking ocean, galloping the beach with the wind in my face or at a letter in the mail-bag; dreams of what I had meant to be. Could I return to the twenties again with my hair still silky, my eyes all stars and my body slender like this? They revolted, the dreams, sometimes flooding me out, halting my hands folding the nappies so that I found myself staring at them in the evening and wondering what on earth they were. Surely it was time to return to our own, to return now.

Beginning the second year at Horoera my marvellous native physical energy began ebbing like the tide. Trying to keep up the pace, the moment by moment emergencies of it. Already I'd come to the place where we no longer followed our Daddy to school in the morning, but now I was at the place where I could no longer teach in the house classroom, what next? As the weeks rocked by like one wave after another and added up to months, the little Maoris no longer came to the house and I spent much time lying down, until finally I didn't rise from the bed at all. We hired help in the house, I forget whom, Cherry maybe, but Keith, already taking the full weight of the school, also had to take the main weight of the home, from bathing the children to the cooking and it was here where he had to give up his studies.

I lay on the bed on my back quite still in the dark front bedroom with the window on the sea at my head, and with Ashton pulling himself to his feet at my side saying, "Ma, Ma, Ma," and the other two hovering. Keith believed it was a matter of rest and he saw to it that I got it and my word, those beautiful breakfasts of omelette on toast, and the tasty dinners at night with flawless brown gravies, but although I ate everything I still got thinner and still had palpitation when I sat up, which frightened me mightily. The Maoris whispered I was dying of TB and would leave silent kits of kumara on the doorstep and sometimes fish, but I knew I wasn't. I didn't know what was wrong with me unless it was an impaired heart like Puppa, but Miss Banks said, "No. That's only palpitation from weakness. What you ought to do is start a programme of sitting up, a little longer each day."

"I can't."

"Why not?"

"My dreams are too heavy."

"Well, I hear all sorts of off-beat answers on my rounds but . . ."

As I lay in the darkness at night hearing the thud of the breaking waves my dreams had a chance to surface, trying to surge over my mind, but at least I had the sense to counter them, for I was coming to fear them, as I feared almost everything. During the long days I learnt poem after poem from an English anthology I happened to have in order to recite them in mind at night, some by Alice Meynell:

> As the inhastening tide doth roll,
> Home from the deep, along the whole
> Wide shining strand, and floods the caves
> —your love comes filling with happy waves
> The open sea-shore of my soul.

And Robert Bridges:

> Whither, O splendid ship, thy white sails crowding,
> Leaning across the bosom of the urgent West

That fearest not sea rising, nor sky clouding,
Whither away, fair rover, and what thy quest?

One morning, a Saturday, Nurse Banks turned up on the warpath
on her roly-poly horse, with oranges in her saddle-bag for the children
and her tongue alive with solutions. "Segregation," she pronounced,
"that's what's required. Segregation from all children."

"Ma, Ma," from Ashton.

"The Blacks will take Jasmine and Elliot and the Whites at the
lighthouse will take the baby, and the Mission sisters will take you.
Listen, you have a choice:

"The rivers are so low the truck has got through with stores for the
lighthouse and Bandy will take you in on his way back to the Anglican
Mission and I'll ring Mrs. White to come and get the baby. Keith and
I will take the other two in to the Blacks on the next low tide. If you
don't come today the rivers may rise tomorrow and the truck may not
get through for another few months, if at all, and you'll go on peter-
ing out here, which is not fair to Keith anyway."

I knew that. I hadn't been a teacher, much less a mother for some
time now, but Keith's fourth child.

A no-nonsense tone from Nurse Banks, "So make up your mind
right now, Mrs. Henderson, yes or no. It's now or never."

They're all in the room and I look to my parent, Keith Henderson.
"What shall I do, K?"

"Actually I don't see any alternative but it's for you to say, dear."

From the beach I hear the waves, a lapping only. The tide is still at
the ebb but by the time the truck comes back it'll be on the turn and
after that it'll fill to the flow. Keith has on his favorite old gardening
clothes, the grey shirt open at the neck with the hairs on his chest
showing and a button off, and the worn trousers bulky, and big hob-
nailed boots. We children just love him like that. Then Ashton dashes
off crawling to see Nurse's horse and there's a scatter to catch him and
Jassie carts him back. "Yes or no," from Nurse. "It's now or never."

"All right then I'll go."

"Ma, Ma," from the baby.


Mrs. White was the middle-aged lady, ample, grey-haired, who sat
her horse so comfortably. When she arrived she said, "When I was
young and in trouble someone looked after my baby and I said at the

time, I'll thank you some day by looking after someone else's baby, and here is that day."

And the next thing she had Ashton tied to her with the cardigan on her horse, in the front of her, and I saw Mrs. White riding off with my baby who couldn't walk yet. Ashton, about nine months old at the time, was disappearing along the seashore on a horse with a lady he didn't even know. They'd have to circle the cliffs on the track high above the rocks below before they reached the Cape. I watched till he was out of sight in the haze.

I couldn't find clothes that did not fall off at once and had to use safety-pins in my scarlet skirt. "You *are* thin," reproved Nurse Banks.

So they got me in the truck and Keith kissed me and said, "I'll be in to see you on Saturday, Mij."

"Dearest," I said.

"We'll soon get you right."

"I'm so sorry, K, to be dislocating our family. I . . . I'm . . ."

"Don't apologise, dear. It gets you nowhere."

"I do love you all so much."


I entered the Mission House on the hill overlooking the sea from a circumspect distance, away a bit from Te Araroa, and found myself in the virgin purity of white walls, white ceiling, white curtains, in a white bed and among white people. The white skin of the Sisters astonished me, and after my sojourn with a Polynesian race it seemed their nostrils were too narrow and their lips too thin. More astounding still their language was English.

The two Mission Sisters, sedate, serene, middle-aged and English, diagnosed exhaustion and prescribed complete rest and segregation. That I was by nature an artist, heathen and vagabond, if not an outright child still, I concealed. "I was baptised in the Anglican church, Sister, and confirmed in it."

They were good to me, the Sisters, serving me trays of English food accompanied by stout, and they gave me *Gone With the Wind* to read, which may or may not have been a good thing. So was Nurse Banks good to me, an honest-to-goodness New Zealander who lived next door but although I was delighted to find myself in the care of three maiden ladies, bringing to mind those priestly spinsters who had tried to train me when a girl, all I achieved from the treatment was the loss of what little flesh I had left and a further submersion in an ocean of emotion and undisciplined dreaming, and when the three ladies decided I'd had sufficient of the treatment to try me on my feet all they achieved was a bag of bones prostrate on the floor. And there would I have wilted away decorously down into the grave itself had they not summoned Dr. Grant from Te Puia Springs eighty miles down the coast, a tough customer seasoned by the coast whom no one could hope to fool, middle-aged, middle-sized, dark and sturdy, who dryly questioned the merits of segregation, said it was a trauma of the mind and that I'd have to go to Wellington for treatment.

When Keith came in on Saturday I touched his lovely old cart-and-horse clothes and said, "I'm so sorry to be doing all this to my family."

"Now don't apologise, dear, there's nothing to feel guilty about. Things take their course and we all do our best. There's no place for blame on anyone."

"Dear love."

"I've always looked after you and you know quite well I'll go on doing so."

Our provider—
in the
garden in back of
the house

Lou Flavell from the Cape relieved at our school and Keith took me the long three-day journey to Wellington. On the way in Gisborne we stayed with the Cyril Burtons again where Cyril sat by my bed the entire night, his great fair body folded low, and listened to my fears and where in the morning for some reason I seemed to be walking better. In Wellington we stayed with the Lionel Warners while I was being treated by a neurologist and Keith was appointed temporarily to the correspondence school in order to keep him on the payroll; at least he was occupied there but I can't say he was enamoured for he couldn't see his pupils, and no doubt he was thinking of his own school.

My younger sister Norma threw up her job and came and nursed me and my older sister Daphne walked in one morning in a stunning green swing-back coat, a challenging hat and her legs like twin poems. From the end of my bed, "How are you, Sylv?"

"I'm mad, Daph."

"How do you know?"

"I can't read and big black clouds keep rolling towards me from over that direction."

"Why can't you read, Sylv?"

"I can see the words one at a time and I know what they are but when I get to the next word I've forgotten what the first word was. So I can't read a sentence as a whole."

My eldest brother Ashton came and soon Mumma came to see me looking so smart with a hat on and a nice handbag I hardly recognised her. She asked after every one of the children separately and when Lionel came in she told him, "There's nothing wrong with Sylvie."

He pondered.

I say, "It was the sea, Li. So much water in it. The rivers were full of water too. I didn't like them taking Ashton away round that cliff track on a horse. A very narrow clay track crumbling at the edge and at the bottom of the cliff the waves were crashing over the rocks. And now he's by the water at the lighthouse and I can't see how Ashie can be brought back over that track and I can't get to him. And little Elliot ran down to the beach one day and it was Jassie who found him and brought him back."

Mumma says, "She's quite lucid."

And Lionel says, "She was dying of fear, Mumma."

> But inland from the seaward spaces,
> None knows, not even you, the places
>   Brimmed at your coming, out of sight,
>   —The little solitudes of delight
> This tide constrains in dim embraces.
>               —Alice Meynell

Dr. Allen was another of these big tall men who seemed to be my fate, dramatic with white hair above black eyebrows and enigmatic blue eyes, intimidating really from his soft-footed height, unapproachable within a wall of elegance and brief in word indeed, so that when

I began, "What I want is . . ." he countered, "Now who knows most about this: you or me?"

"You."

"Me. Right. So it's what *I* want that goes."

He kept me sedated on a simple bromide and during my visits, two or three times a week, in the holy quiet blue-carpeted consulting room he began picking up the pieces of my fragmented mind, displaying them for me to see. On his desk he built up a picture of it with whatever was handy: a book, an inkwell, pen and pencil, a cigarette case and a lighter, which took the form of a waggon with two horses, self-preservation and racial preservation; the two heavyweight instincts, fear and sex. One horse was pulling one way and the second horse pulling the other.

Lionel

The idea was that when the horses pulled opposite ways they'd pull the waggon apart, whereas when they pulled in unison the same way, the waggon would move forward. He said I was the driver and had to understand the horses in order to direct them. He showed me how the greatest instinct, fear, was the horse which was out of hand in my waggon, plunging and bucking on its side of the shaft, upsetting the other horse and wrecking everything round it, and unless I took over firm control I'd quite likely get tipped out.

"How are you feeling today, Mrs. Henderson?" from Doctor.

"I cry every morning."

"We like that. It's a very good vent."

Week after week, steadily and methodically, he continued to teach me the nature of the mind as he put the pieces together again in their normal places so that I was obliged to learn about these two great powers in the personality which qualify all living: fear and sex. He showed me other instincts, what they were for, how they worked, their relation to one another and why my mechanism had sprung loose. A simple enough metaphor for me to follow and I must say it needed to be for I was hazed with bromide. But not too bemused to work out for myself that on the East Coast I'd been dying of fear.

The lessons, in the practical language of the mind, not only threw light on what I had seen when nursing in the Nelson mental hospital, but illuminated a lot of what the Reverend Olds used to preach from his pulpit in Mt. Eden in the language of the spirit; I could even see traces of Rousseau's thinking. As one month turned over into another I was assembling quite a fair picture of how things were behind the eyes, which is known by most students today but to me, way back there in the stale air beneath the crinoline over the head of the country, the respectability, righteousness and morality, the revelations came as simply shocking.

For all that, however, I still fell in love with my teacher and was not above buying a very pretty dress: a romantic dusk-rose with a deep white revere collar. Yet the things he'd say to me I couldn't believe: "All that dreaming. You can't get away with living a life in mind you haven't earned. You can't go on dreaming up everything you happen to want. You've got to *win* what you want from reality. It *can* be done since you *managed* to get married. Your dreaming is just common theft."

One morning it came up, "Do you know what you are, Mrs. Henderson?"

"An artist."

He waits and lights a cigarette. "Excuse this smoking, I'm fasting today."

"No, I mean I'm a wife and mother."

"Are you a good mother?"

I wait but I'm not a smoker. "I love them and keep them clean."

And to that he replies nothing and puffs a moment. "Why don't you answer you're a teacher?"

"I forgot."

"You mean you don't want to teach other people but to get away in a corner and do it yourself?"

All too true.

"Do you *want* to know what you are?"

Nothing.

"You're a writer."

I look away from him and tell the blue curtains, "Well I might have been if . . ."

"Don't say *if*; it's the weakest word in the language."

I don't think Doctor likes me so I tell the blue carpet, "I tell you what I'm not, Dr. Allen. I can see for myself that I'm not much of a character."

This time he doesn't answer curtly but looks out between the curtains rather wistfully to the city, turning over a pen in his fingers reflectively. "Maybe humility would be as good a base to build on as anything else. To *re*build on."

It was very cold in Wellington in June and Keith gave me the money to buy a red Stuart tartan skirt, a red polo-necked jersey and a smashing exclusive coat in stripes with a swing-back like Daphne's; none of which I saw to be appropriate for horseback in Horoera though the issue was rather to impress Dr. Allen and it did quite a bit for morale. Home at Lionel's place his wife was learning a Freidmann waltz which I could hear from my bed and the delirium of the beauty of it in my blood also helped to weld my segmented soul. But letters were the best; Lou wrote cheerfully of Keith's school, Bern Black wrote that Jasmine and Elliot were sparking well and a letter from Mrs. White at the lighthouse told of Ashton walking at ten months, that they all loved him dearly and she enclosed photos of the two girls with him. Even Janet wrote a second letter but I've not answered that to this day. The mind which Doctor was putting together began holding in places so that I tried to learn to read again. "I can't get the words to stay in my mind," I told him.

"Reading," he said, "is taking into the mind new images but your mind is too packed with native imagery to allow room for anything else in. You've got to harness those dreams of yours."

"But that wouldn't recover my reading."

"It'll discipline your mind and with discipline you'll have more chance of absorbing the words."

Then I was taken by ambulance to the public hospital with an awful condition called fibrositis and Dr. Allen told me when he came, "Only a symptom. Just another ruse of the body to draw attention to the disturbance in the mind."

"Aren't you going to put something on it?"

"All right, we'll treat it locally, but we continue to treat the cause primarily."

"Doctor Allen. The radio full blast all day. This huge ward, the exposure. I can't stand it."

He's strangely kind. "I understand," and sent a nurse for a screen.

Before we left Wellington I bought a copy of the Freidmann waltz, along with a whole lot of clothes and presents for the children. And my word, did Keith get on that rail-car lightly.

Bringing Ashton
home from
the lighthouse.
A Maori is carrying
him; Mrs. White
and Lena are
riding close by.

How did we get back into Horoera? Maybe we rode in on horse-back. I do know I rode on my own to the lighthouse to get Ashton and stayed the night there because the tides were wrong. I was lying in bed in the morning at Whites' and here was this little chap running into my room in blue rompers with wide blue eyes like pools of water; he'd stand a moment and size me up and smile then dash off back to the girls. In he'd trot again, stare, smile and vanish. "I'm sure he remembers me, Mrs. White."

I'd thought that it had been I who had brought Ashton home but an old old print has surfaced showing a Maori lady bringing him home on her horse, with Mrs. White and Lena riding close by. And that says something for the Maori lady, commissioned to carry the baby on her horse round those cliffs. She's got him wrapped in a blanket.

We had toys in our bags for the little boys but I'd brought my little girl a lovely dress. Pink it was with pretty blue flowers.

And a weighty solid book for Elliot featuring smart white girls.

> You see the happy shore, wave-rimmed,
> But know not of the quiet dimmed
>   Rivers your coming floods and fills,
>   The little pools 'mid happier hills,
> My silent rivulets over-brimmed.
> —Alice Meynell

I'm writing of Horoera only because I must, for it seems to have been an intersection in our journey through life from which each one of us took his future direction, wholly unaware of it. Influences handled the lives of us all, in particular the children's, and stayed with us till now. Otherwise I'd leave the whole place out. I've never written of That Place before.

In any case I'm leaving out a great deal of it which won't bear the telling. We nearly lost Jasmine there from an accident in the playground. It was at lunchtime and she managed to get home and she said to me where I was attending to the baby, "I came home to my Mummy."

But when she slipped into unconsciousness in the big chair Keith rang Nurse Banks but she was away on holiday and the relieving nurse was busy so he rang Dr. Grant eighty miles down the coast at Te Puia Springs, who said he'd come if someone would meet him at Te Araroa. Low tide was about midnight and Hau was there in his cart and together they travelled the beach at midnight, crossing rivers in moonless darkness and arrived about two a.m.

We had the child on a camp stretcher in the living room with the open fire quietly going. Dr. Grant was toughened by the coast, a take-it-or-leave-it character with both feet on the ground and who got on with his nurses; a sturdy man with dark hair and brows who avoided three words if he could do with two. After examining J he talked to us briefly with his back to the fire and a cup of tea in his hand, saying the chances were touch and go as there was a fracture in the skull and that although the case could well become operable the child would not survive the journey out. He gave us some directions then Hau took him back on the same low tide.

Keith kept the school open while I nursed Jassie, keeping a chart of the temperatures rising and falling and bathing her temples and wrists with cold water from a bucket. Cherry took over the house till Keith came home, feeding and washing the little boys and putting the clothes on the line. Other Maoris came and sat with us silent picturesque on the mat by the fire, taking turns to change the water in the bucket to keep it cold. In the evening Keith would take his turn at the bedside so I could sleep but since I couldn't I'd return again.

On the second day the relieving nurse, about my age, she rode out on her rounds to the lighthouse and surveyed our scene on the way, casually enough. "What else can we do?" I asked her.

"Nothing," lightly.

I followed as she went out and mounted her horse and looking up with the sun in my eyes I said, "Will she live?"

"I don't know," and rode off down the slope. Relievers.

Lionel telegraphed me he would ring up at seven in the evening and the rest of the family were at the phone, Mumma too, and each had a word with me. The Reverend Kohere at the Cape sent his daughter, Mrs. Poi, who took turns with the cold water bathing while I kept the charts, watching the temperature climb higher at each swing. More Maoris gathered and sat outside but you never heard their voices. On the third day Keith closed the school.

After three days and three nights I noticed towards dawn that the temperature peak was the same high as the previous peak and had not risen further. I continued the readings right down to zero and back up again to find the new peak level lower than the former reading before it descended. The tide had turned. And that's how it went for the rest of the night, a little lower each time and her limbs ceased flailing. At about eight o'clock that morning her open eyes recognised me and she said, "Where have you been, Mummie?"

She took pneumonia after that. She'd already had it once.

Since Ashie could walk now Mrs. Poi agreed to mind him when I went to school and I took young El with me. She was slender and soft-voiced and had dignity, spoke excellent English and was lovely with Ash but he still knew when I had gone and I couldn't do anything about that. Jas was in Keith's room by now and that was better and El cruised from one of us to the other.

In the meantime K held down his job though we no longer had the car to look forward to. On the other hand he was rising in his profession the hard way, staying a headmaster on every rung. Having had the taste of running his own school, expanding at the challenge by the hour, he had no intention of going on a staff though he didn't say so. The people called Keith the Master and me the Teacher which amused Col Flavell at the Cape very much. "There's a subtle distinction there, Keith," he said.

I tried to be the headmaster's good wife. I see a group of us, a Maori kuia and some Maori girls sitting in the shade of a solo cabbage tree near the school learning to weave kits* in flax, to plait taniko and we even made a whole piupiu; how to cut the flax strips, how to cut the pattern on them while still green, how to dry them till they rattled and clicked and how to attach them to a taniko waistband; result, a Maori skirt. We used the black mud for dye and the traditional red.

Riding on my own I visited the Maori parents far and wide up and

* kit: a hand-woven bag

down the beach and under the range, and over the range once to visit
a child who was said to be very ill; the horse climbed the height one
side to the top and slithered in the mud down the other side on its
haunches to pull up before a one-roomed hut with an earthen floor.
So astounded were they to see no less than the white Teacher walk in,
all who were mobile vanished like smoke leaving only the kuia sitting
before the open fire smoking fish and a little boy panting unconscious
on a mattress. In time, however, Hine crept back in and made me
strong tea in a mug sweetened with condensed milk and I tried out
my faltering Maori, and attended to the very ill little boy. Pneumonia.

Getting back over the range was another thing which I can only
accredit to the horse.

I even rode into Te Araroa about twice when the rivers were low
and the tide right, and to the Cape twice round the cliff track, but
nowhere did I find what I called a friend, brown or white. I think
I had changed too much. Living so close to survival values, to crises
of life and death, I found the trappings of society peeling off, face to
face with my essential self, and the rest was pantomime.

Jas was six or seven by now and sometimes Keith took her with
him in the cart on Saturday to Te Araroa for the stores and mail and
to see the Blacks, who had harboured her and El. One Saturday afternoon they had not returned before the shadow was cast from the range
though I and El and Ash were waiting at the top of the hill, and when
they did appear they told me a log had shifted position in the Orotua
River and the horse had scrambled over it but the wheels had stuck;
they had been pinned mid-stream with the tide advancing and the
plunging horse had threatened to burst the traces. The water, they
said, had been on the cart floor and lapping round their feet, then
suddenly a young Maori on horseback had dropped from nowhere.
He rode straight in, the water saddle-high, picked up Jasmine, rode
out and put her down on the bank, then he led the cart-horse another
way out extricating the wheels.

Horoera was not the place for Jas. Ashie had had a rocky babyhood
at the start but was on an even keel now, Elliot was the sunniest thing
on two legs with a gift for survival, but the sooner Jasmine returned
to her own the better.

I even tried to be an artist one Christmas; it was Keith teaching the
schoolchildren the Christmas carols through the wall, so indivisibly
part of our bloodstream, that started me off painting dozens of Christmas cards for Keith to take to Te Araroa to sell. They were pretty little

cards in watercolour as I recall them, delicate allusive and sentimental, into which I put all of myself without signature, to send away into unknown hands for reasons other than loving someone, never to be seen again. He put them in the grocer's shop and they did sell too at a shilling a go. Who were my buyers? A few landowners I supposed, maybe the grocer's own wife, the policeman's wife, the postmaster's wife, the butcher's and the two English mission ladies on the hill. The Blacks and Nurse Banks had already gone off for Christmas to their own. Who on earth and in Te Araroa thought my paintings worth one shilling? But it did feel exhilarating to do commercial art.

And I tried to be a writer. I wrote a poem for Dr. Allen, with whom I was still in love, called "Hands," just what I felt about his hands, a very personal thing, and sent it to him. As for music Keith did have an old piano plonked in the school as he had in Mangahume, I still read, studied the music textbooks he'd had to abandon and the lives of the composers which led me into European history, into Russell and Murdoch and people like Coleridge; an enlightening, boundless, ever expanding domain with no ceiling on the thinking awakened. Plainly I'd go to Freud one day. All of which helped to discipline dreaming, but only discipline it.

Music, art, philosophy, the mind and Maori mythology but nothing on teaching. And I learnt a lot more poetry by heart to recite in mind when I couldn't sleep for how could you sleep when the ocean didn't sleep but kept up its chant of the tides? No, you couldn't waste the isolation. I tried to be everything: a good wife, mother and teacher as well, trying to salvage my life simultaneously, and I must say I knew great joy and a lot of it too . . . simply in having a purpose.

Our third year in Horoera, however, I began to decline again, to sag. After the spring holidays in August I could no longer trek across the sand with my young to the school, nor teach in a room in the house either. As the third term of the third year resumed I was not with Keith at school; I found myself instead sinking on a bed in the living room all over again, in the corner by the window; in a room done in blue to join the blue of the sky and the sea outside, the thrilling un-attainable outside, and me in a blue flowered smock.

The bell called but I didn't answer. Keith was father, mother, family and friends, husband, lover and provider, headmaster, protector, doctor and saviour and above all he interested me. I never knew what I'd find next in the man I'd married. "When the inspector comes," he said, "I'll apply for a transfer, on the grounds that this locality does not suit my wife. In the meantime I'll teach the school and Ashton can come with me. After all he's a great boy over two. Now have you got everything, dear? There's your thermos of tea. You rest, Mijjee."

"But I'm still drawing my salary, K."

"We'll see about that. Come on, Ash, want to come to school? Elliot, got your book? Jas, you bring Elliot. Say goodbye to Mummie. See you soon."

Mr. Connor came. More of the Viking breed. I hadn't encountered inspectors like these two, Messrs. Ball and Connor, before or since; larger than size, plunging about on Viking horses, "leaning across the bosom of the urgent west." Mr. Connor rode out about mid-term, fair like Mr. Ball with whom I was still in love also, six feet of vigour, inspired and brisk from his morning ride on the beach and terribly kind along with it. Did he have in mind the lie in the gazette that had tricked us here? A mighty horse he rode.

All ready to
leave Horoera

Keith brought him over from school and there was nothing I could do about being caught out. "How are you, Mrs. Henderson?" from way up high. I'm prostrate on the bed by the window.

"I'm getting weaker every day."

"I'm very sorry to hear it. What can I do for you?"

I don't answer. There's far too much.

"What do you need?"

"My people."

"I understand. I'll talk to Mr. Henderson about it."

When he'd gone back on the same low tide Keith came in and told me, "He's arranging a transfer to some other school. He said he'd see to it the moment, the *very* moment he got back to Wellington. By gee, he's a nice chap."

"What about my salary, K?"

"They're not even docking your pay for being away. He said, Oh the less who know about that the better."

"He might be making up for their secretary."

"Now steady, Mij. Give Mr. Connor credit for his own motives."

"Oh dear, I wish I'd put up a better show."

"You're doing all right. Don't expend yourself on being sorry for things. All will be well as long as you're with *me*." He looks through the open window upon the Pacific in high good humour, his eyes full of the future. Plainly he's delighted about a new school and things must have gone well over there today. "By gee, he's a nice chap." The little ones are curling round his legs.

"That was a stunning horse he had. Mighty."

"Now I'll put on the dinner and start on the children. Do you want some more tea, small Midget?"

"Ye-es," quavering, tragedy-queening it.

"Ye-e-es," he quavers, taking me off, at which we both laugh like anything and the little ones too.

Again we are both well graded, Keith very well. Fancy, fancy, *after all that*. But secretly then, and still do, I suspected they had given me anyway a lot of benefit of a lot of doubt, that they'd given me a sympathy vote. What I'd rather have thought then, however, and still do, was that, being the rather rare men of vision they both were, they'd seen something in me worth cultivating and promoting, like courage to the limit, for instance; beyond the limit. I'll never know. But one thing I know: professionally together we'd made a fine start and I suppose K.D. knew it too.

> What, I have secrets from you? Yes.
> But, visiting Sea, your love doth press
>     And reach in further than you know,
>     And fills all these; and when you go,
> There's loneliness in loneliness.
>                     —Alice Meynell

PIPIRIKI    Transferred to another Maori school on account of the health of the headmaster's wife; from one Maori fastness at the

Pipiriki—
the school

East Cape to another Maori fastness to the west, a week of arduous travel in reverse but all five together this time and we were terribly happy.

I don't remember arriving in Wanganui at the end of the fifth day when the children were tiring of cities, pavements and shoes on; of hotels, electric lights and railway stations; of trains and many white people, but I do recall taking the notorious bus the next morning up the notorious Wanganui River road, legend-heavy, beauty-burdened and forested; eighteen miles of dramatic gorge, thick rain and the Maoris again. On the other hand it *was* a road and it *was* metalled and you didn't have to cross the river.

We arrived late afternoon at Pipiriki* in pouring rain, crowded into Pipiriki House and up the stairs, keeping a non-stop watch on the little boys on the high white balcony. A Friday it was. The end of the sixth day.

From oblivion, through the lights of civilisation briefly, to oblivion again yet no rain could quench the flames of our joy. After all, this was our new job, wasn't it, and what could be more exhilarating than that? Moreover, we were together, the whole five, and even though the rain was perpendicular, permanent and all but impenetrable, on went our coats, up went umbrellas and out into it we forged, up the

* *pipiriki*: bush-wren

hill through the rivulets on the road to explore Daddy's new school: his fourth.


The school and the residence are carved out of the top of a hill over-looking the valley, the grounds laid out in lawns and flowering shrubs, all the blooms white, and the whole glebe enclosed in fruit trees and thundering forest giants trailing with moss.

I think the little boys must be relieved to feel the soles of their bare feet on the true ground again, and in a home that remains constant, by the way they trail Daddy round but although Jassie trails him too I don't think she is carried away by the River; I think she would have preferred to be a little white lady among her own colour and kind, I can't speak for her really. But there does happen to be another white family in the River valley with a little girl of her own age at school.

On the first new morning when I follow Keith over to school I carry Ashton in my arms, who is unusually nervous, his arms tight round my neck; Elliot is at my side but Jas has already found the other little girl, called Lois. On this first morning we are dumfounded at the schoolchildren saluting us, clicking their heels together in atten-tion in unmistakably military style, something they'd learnt from the teacher before us from the Indian colonial army. My word, the Maoris we've just left at Horoera would never salute to pakehas and I wonder what link there may be between this pukkha-sahib from India and all the white blooms prevailing.

This school is twice the size at forty. I'm still the junior whether I'm qualified or not, an automatic rating in a two-teacher Maori school. Keith teaches the standards and I have the infant room and he apportions to me the much larger room, whereas he has more children and his room is so poky you can hardly get round between the desks; and I must say I find this room of lofty ceilings and tall windows a recuperating place after the porch among the coathooks; you can think and feel in space like this.

Henderson likes order. For a start, the bells go on time, the first at eight a.m., a carry-on from the pukkha-sahib, to wake everyone down the hill in the pa who don't go in for clocks, and the second at five to nine for the children to line up for health inspection when sometimes the district nurse comes up from her cottage across the road. You've got to respect education when it comes your way by being in time for it and clean for it. Learning is not mocked.

Don't think there are fringe benefits for the headmaster's wife; I have to write my own scheme somehow, plan my own daily time-table and I'm required to present to him each Monday morning my workbook, the teachers' cross, and fully done too as though we were in the heart of Auckland. There's no playing on my position: a kiss in the kitchen in the morning, "Lamb, I love you," and half an hour later at school, "Your workbook please, Mrs. Henderson."

Jas is in my room now and the little boys run in and out but when Ashie falls down the outside steps and cuts his little lip I drop my bat, carry him to the house to mend the little chap, dry his tears, give him a mug of cocoa and nurse him, and when Elliot sits in a desk and writes wonderfully I call in his father to see it; such excellent work for a little boy of four.

But Keith does have to help me a lot with my teaching, organisation mainly, and I also fall back on him in matters of control and disci-pline. "Mr. Henderson, this boy comes late every morning of his life."

"Why are you late, Henare?"

Henare has eyes as deep as the River and a bottom lip like a kit. He salutes. Click. "Plissir, there's no rooms for me on the firs' canoe. Plissir they makes me come on the las'. Plissir I gets late."

"Look at that now. I'll have a word with Wingo about it, Henare. You cheer up. You'll be in the first canoe tomorrow."

Salute. "Please yes," which economises down to "Plishess," which ends up universally as " 'shess."

"So you'll be the first at school tomorrow, Henare?"

" 'Shess." Salute.

Before tea this night Keith says to El, "Righto, little man. You slip along and bring your pyjamas and we'll get you into your bath."

"Yissir." Salute. Click.


The issue of whether or not I continue teaching is fast vaporising for you can't throw away a whole salary with the Slump and the war on; moreover, it is becoming daylight clear that he likes me with him. I think he even values my art and music in the school, if not my temperament; the acting work and the school concerts, together on which we claim to be masters. Not that he's one to rave, but you pick up clues when you're married to a man. Also, what with our whole family trekking over there five mornings a week the school is be-coming a part of the home, which doesn't seem to hurt either school or home; all it hurts is my secret self, my other artist self. However, since I'm a teacher in Keith's school he is the mother of us all at home and I one of the children. "Keith has four children," I tell Opal, the district nurse across the road.

The only way I see of extricating myself from the bloody profesh at this late date is to change my occupation for another that pays sufficiently to replace my teacher's salary, that leaves me at home to be a mother to the children and gives me time to be an artist, and this spells writing. Not a marvellous writer, famous and all that, just a working writer, functional. In turn this requires that I learn to write and under the present conditions at that; deep and widespread study, a secluded place to work in and . . . and the *time*. To all of which there is no alternative, for I must escape from teaching.

Keith has this inspiring way of falling two-square on his feet and taking a grip with both broad hands; home on two legs for the rest of us, the place to which we gravitate whether he's filling the lamps, tending the fowls or milking the cow, whether chopping the wood, digging the garden or harvesting the prolific fruit. I seem to be something like that to him for as the seasons turn over he brings

The residence

all produce back into the house to me: eggs, milk, wood, fruit, vegetables and the very first radish every spring as though I were the reason for his being at all, and he'd lay his hand on my head and say, "Lamb." And this is one thing he did in fact tell me, "Everything I do is for you. In the garden I think, I wonder if she'll like this . . . or these."

Until Pearl Harbor when we no longer have the American Fleet to save us in the Pacific and we begin learning to preserve the food and to grow more of it.

He appears to be too engrossed in what is at hand to gaze wistfully back beyond the forested rim to the pakeha life he's left behind; he sets his sights on the actual and the possible, whether he likes it or not, and if he doesn't like it you don't hear him say so. He makes friends of the Maoris whether he finds them good company or not; you see his parents trailing from the pa up the hill to sit on a step, a bank or a log to confer with the master, relieved to have professional teachers in place of the Indian Army. And the way he can stand and listen and smile a bit or laugh is something I can't do. Working bees with them upriver cutting manuka for the school's winter fires, committee meetings in the school ending with supper at the house and digging trenches on a Saturday morning in the school playground against the coming of the Japs, who are drawing uncomfortably closer to Singapore.

Two or three evenings a week he makes a trip down to the store to collect the mail, buy groceries and sit and talk with the Templetons a moment. For the wet stony road he wears these great hob-nailed boots and a haversack he has made from a sugar bag. For the rain he wears a bulky oilskin and a dripping sou'wester and when he sets off you'd never recognise him as the sprucely dressed teacher leaving for school in the morning, hair brushed, shirt collar immaculate, tie straight, shoes polished, walking across the grass with one hand in the front of his coat like his father; peaceable, approachable.

And we hear him returning, Jas and I, his great boots squelching the sodden ground and his bag full for the rest of us, and he peels off and kisses us and sits with us and tells us all the news as he did at Horoera: what the Templetons said, what was going on in the pa, the latest scandal at The House about Wingo and the proprietor's daughter, Willow. Bringing her in too late at night and pushing her into the office, "There's your daughter, Mr. Boss-man. Keep her for the Japs."

"But Daddy," says Jas, "his name is Mr. Boxman."

He laughs. "Not to Wingo," he says.

Bringing the world back to us through his eyes, by his ears and on his tongue like the male bird feeding its young.

> Whether I live, or whether I die,
> Whatever the worlds I see,
> I shall come to you by and by,
> And you will come to me.
> —Mary Coleridge

Pipiriki is a hollow in the ranges shaped like a heart with a high brim forested to the top. No wind can get in and no moisture gets out so the climate is as heady as the skullsplitter Old Mai brews in her copper. The rain drops straight down most of the year.

Only the River can get in and get out, lying on her back on the floor of the valley like a woman besottedly in love, forever desiring the forest above her reflected in her eyes. With no movement of air the yellow leaves stay on the breathless poplars, repeated upside down in the water, week after week after week; unmoving, unfalling, hypnotising.

The valley is a cauldron of steaming passions irregularly stirred by Fate; a place where quite orderly, usually routine people, tourists included, drop their guards like clothes on a riverbank before entering turbulent waters; to act themselves out for once in a lifetime with no accounting to God, man, past or future, babbling in tongues of the red rata worn in the hair of the forest, of the yellow of the kowhai in spring and of the profligate roadside flowers, to the point of inebriation which honest souls seldom dry out from.

There are so many dells and grassy nooks calling for people to fling themselves down in to kiss and kiss, that love-affairs flame with forbidden lovers and hate-affairs deepen unto death and guests are never the same again; an incomparable place for army deserters until they're hunted through the forest by police and dogs. You hear of drowning accidents and of suicides of romance, and burial grounds tell lurid tales on the wooden headstones. I never saw such drama at gravesides in my life or so many tears of grief. Nor have I myself known such rarities; a goodbye kiss at the bus stop one morning radiates to this day. This barefoot, bare-brain, bare-heart place is where I first learnt to play "Night and Day."

> Whoever was foolish, we were wise,
> We crossed the boundary line,
> I saw my soul look out of your eyes,
> You saw your soul in mine.
> —Mary Coleridge

I have my pre-war chalks I bought in Auckland years ago at a colour merchant's near the waterfront and I've kept them in a wooden box all this time. Hefty sticks like mini-logs about two fingers thick which you can't buy in the shops, by the name of demonstration chalk.

There's a purple among them like the berries on the hawthorne and a

yellow like the poplars marking the graves of those who have long
departed to greet illustrious ancestors; here and there in the forest, on
the riverbank and upside down in the water. I've a scarlet as lurid as
the rata blossom garlanding the hair of the forest, and another shade
of red as livid as blood when Whistle took the life of Mai Mai, and
took his own too for good measure. "All for a love," they say.

This green will do for the Maori brew you can drink from Old
Mai's copper which seldom gets the chance to mature to a mellow
amber, and you drink it from a mug at a party at the pa till the dawn
chorus of the birds. There are inquiries at the store when malt and
sugar are rationed because of the war. "You got a malt an' a sugar,
Bill?"

This turquoise I'll use for the mood of the river voluptuous on her
back, and this bewitching blue of the sky when it's dry for about six
weeks of the year I'll use if I make a portrait of Opal, her enigmatic
eyes; the all-purpose black for the twilight in the forest at the height
of noon or for shading the blackest night of the soul when some dear
love is forsaken.

I send for seven more small cardboard boxes of Johnson's chalk of
the standard size before it runs out in the shops which is quite as vivid
as the heftier chalk; with the finer tips you can pick out smaller things
like buttercups beneath a willow, or daisies wet from a waterfall. A
rich brown for smouldering eyes of the Maoris shadowed by long
black hair and their bare feet in the rain. For the finer things like the
features of a child or the iridescent feathers of the tui you need a special kind of razor blade to sharpen the chalk to a point, a special kind
of love-affair to sharpen your senses and a special passion to fuel you.
Colour is love and love is colour and there's any amount of both.

When I come upon an abandoned Maori whare a mile up the forest
road as I'm walking with the children I claim it at once as a studio
to learn to write in, clean up the back room and K fixes the open
fireplace, rebuilds the tiny window, makes a little table attached to
the wall and puts a strong new lock on the door; and when I have
repapered the whole small room and when Opal has finished fumi-
gating it I print its name on the door in charcoal and lipstick: Selah
Two.

I cover a large area of the inner wall with black chalk-board paint
and the next time I trek up here on a morning off with a kit of equipment to learn to write, like paper and a pencil and a book, I bring my
pre-war coloured chalk too and the first thing I do in Selah is to begin

drawing an Egyptian water-carrier holding her vessel upon her head, and I caption it "Moon of My Delight." But Opal doesn't call in on her way home after her rounds and I hear her car buzzing past down the road home to the nurse's cottage. She's very late and I suppose she is tired so I don't tell her anything about it on my own way home for she doesn't know I can draw.

When she does see it one day she no more than glances at my water-carrier before she discusses the Japs, so I suppose it is sentimental.

Me

Keith

Before I start learning to write, however, I just have to put one more drawing on that wall, high in the remaining space: a great bird with wide-stretched wings and iridescent feathers, the whole of the colours in its eyes, and caption it "My soul, there is a country/far beyond the stars . . ." For, at the risk of being sentimental and fatuous, this bird is my hidden spirit. Opal doesn't mention this either other than to remark dryly of the two of them, "After *all*, no one can exactly steal them."

"No. You won't see them auctioned at Sotheby's."

So the bird must be sentimental too. It's I who am sentimental, my spirit, and what I should do is change myself somehow, educate myself

out of this weakness till my mind is as clean as Opal's and she'll come
to approve of me. If only I could stop feeling that the water-carrier
and the bird with flying wings and searching eyes are lovely master-
pieces I'd have a better chance of changing myself.

Very few people ever see these drawings in the secluded Maori
whare, avoided since Whistle and Mai Mai died here, except the man
of four kisses whom we call Pan while he's staying with us briefly.
And my youngest sister Evadne sees them when she and her baby
girl are evacuated from the capital city because her home is between
two targets, the aerodrome and the gasworks, who announces firmly
that the soul-bird inspires her, which she has sorely needed since her
young husband was killed in Crete. She gets to work at once with my
poster colours and paints through six months of rain till she puts down
her brushes to return, saying she prefers her two targets to the mud
and the Maoris. She knew the drawings in Selah Two but she died
last September.

Some years after we had left the River, K's Auntie Bess sent me a
cutting from a women's journal about how these drawings had been
discovered by a tourist who was told they'd been done by a local Maori
who had since "passed on." Before Elliot left for England he visited
the River and said they were gone by then. There was no sign of anything when I revisited the River before I left New Zealand, not even
paper on the walls, let alone drawing.

High on the back wall of my schoolroom I make a huge picture
for Keith, more than twelve feet by ten, executed from a ladder at the
weekends, and you get the required viewing distance from outside the
porch down the steps. For models I have a photograph from a long-
past magazine of the people in the town of Hamelin in Germany
enacting the story of the Pied Piper leading away the children. The
school wall is lined with lino which has too rough a surface for chalk
but youth and fever have no choice. The ancient photo is in black
and white so the glories of colour are left to me and my hoarded chalks
are alight like lamps.

Keith and Jas keep me going with thermoses of tea and sandwiches
up the ladder and Opal brings me a mug of soup she's made with
everything that's healthy in it. It is only half done when Pan is here
who, pulling up short in the porch, says, "I can walk right into that."
It is well finished, however, when Mr. Vicarage, the senior inspector of
Maori schools, is halted in the porch also, and who wants to take it
away to preserve it. "But who wants it preserved?" I say.

"Far more people would see it in an art gallery." He's an elegant handsome and cultivated man with whom, for some reason, I fail to fall in love. It's Opal who does.

"But I only did it for us here and for now. We often do the play, Mr. Vicarage, the whole school outside in the grounds, in and out and under the trees; round the school, across the grass and even down the bank. Piper, Mayor, Councillors, rats, the lot. We use that picture."

"But the colours of the chalk will fade," he says.

"And we use some of the passages of Browning's poem for choral speaking."

"I'm concerned about those colours, Mrs. Henderson. I've never seen such brilliance in chalk. They won't last. There's no permanency for chalk on the wall of a school."

"They'll last for our time here."

He turns to Keith. "Look, Mr. Henderson, if you agree to it being moved I'll spend the weekend taking it down myself and repapering the area."

But I'm getting worked up. "Then we'll have no picture of the Pied Piper with the children and we'll never do the play or the choral speaking again."

"Now steady, dear," from K. "That's the last thing Mr. Vicarage would want. He's concerned with another issue."

"The alternative is," from Mr. Vicarage, "when I get back to Wellington to send a supply of size and the equipment for you to spray the whole picture to preserve the colours. The only hope of any permanency."

I've never considered permanency.

We do try the size when it comes, on a sample, but it dulls the colours by several degrees, and forget it. I've never heard what happened to that picture, "and ended all the splendid dream."


Within our schoolroom when I draw on my blackboard something like a sentimental daisy, its petals lovingly serrated and shaded where they curl, the children all draw them too on black paper with school chalk which is still bright at this time, or with vivid crayons, or sometimes they paint with the school tempera which is quite sophisticated; and up they all go on the walls and the room is a meadow in summer. Birds we draw too, the voluble magpies or a duck skimming the river, and many a nursery rhyme character lives it up on the walls so that one of the tourist attractions for the guests at The House is a walk up the hill to the school to see the children's art and to hear them sing or to watch them toss off the plays they write.

One day with the tremolo of a sonata to it when I accompany Opal
on the boat upriver on her rounds, after visiting the homes in the
upriver pa, we are waiting on the bank for the boat to return downriver and pick us up again and we lunch on a log beneath the willows;
but there is very little talk between us, for I think Opal is put out by
the way that Maori mother goes about having her baby, refusing an
induction, which does not coincide with modern methods, whereas
Opal is a highly modern nurse with post-graduate qualifications in
obstetrics and who believes Maoris should be modern too, even in the
upper reaches of the Wanganui River.

So maybe it is inappropriate for me to pick up a willow stick and,
to use the silence and endure the waiting, begin drawing in the damp
sand the profile of a lovely lady for, with a gesture of impatience, she
turns to her book of verse. But seeing no good reason why I should
not draw on a riverbank, on a wall or anywhere else, I proceed to
mould it up with my hands to a third dimension, developing the
original outline into a head and shoulders, as human as anything in
damp sand can be; though Opal's unmistakable indifference reminds
me that my work is sentimental and representational for the sheer reason, as I see it, that it *looks* like what I mean, a lovely lady; whereas she
likes abstract and obscure art in which the meaning of the artist is
inaccessible.

So I get the old feeling once more that I'm in the 99 percent syndrome, not allowed 100 percent, where it is not discreet to excel,
which irritates me all over again as it did in the past but which nevertheless does not stop me from adding dark twigs to delineate the eyes
and brows, with moss and bark to dramatise the hair and, although
in the closing stages Opal has closed her book and is watching intently, I feel unforgiving. It's finished by the time the boat returns
when once more I have to leave my work where it is, whatever it is,
impermanently in the damp sand of the upper Wanganui River for
no one to see except Opal, the sole witness.

Maybe she has changed her mind for, standing at the rail together
as the boat cleaves the mirror water, she senses accurately I have shut
her out and says quite kindly, "Do you feel exhausted, dear, after that
intense concentration?"

I do but I don't answer, upon which she opens her book of verse
again which is T. S. Eliot's *The Wasteland*; "The dry old stick," she
murmurs. "He has no juice."

What I hear later about that model is the local Maoris build a
stockade round it to keep off sheep, cattle and guests but it can't keep

off the weather, falling leaves, the next flood or the doubts of my neighbour, Opal.

In my whare studio up the road where Whistle and Mai Mai chose to die "all over a love, Sylv, all over a love," from our Maori house-keeper, Ruth, leaving their phantoms behind them, I secretly paint for Opal at times instead of learning to write; when I'm too happy or too sad about something that's happened. Maybe I've hurt her by not going down there last night, finding it impossible sometimes to meet the requirements of two homes across the road from each other, or maybe she's hurt me by revealing there do exist people in her life important to her other than I. Heinous indeed. On the other hand, I might be overjoyed at some word or act showing that she knows me for what I am inside and approves of what she knows. And people like this don't come by every day.

There's a day I spend in Selah painting for her a watercolour of the face of Beethoven to celebrate the symphonies and concertos on her Gramophone we have shared by lamplight and firelight; I do it in one sitting in a fever of obsession not entirely arisen from the thought of Opal but as much from the delirium of painting anyway, and when I pass her cottage on my way home and her car is not there I slip in the gate, down the path through the heavy scent of the old-time roses, into her bedroom and hide the portrait in the book she is reading which is D. H. Lawrence's *The Rainbow* so that when she returns from a heavy day on her rounds and sinks wearily into bed she'll suddenly come upon it in private and I won't be there to get the knock-back. Furtive tribute.

If anyone knows where Opal is now, if she's still alive, you'll find that portrait framed on her wall. I am learning the hard way that praise from Opal seldom takes the form of words.

A row of brilliant yellow poplars spearing the forest across-river calls aloud for a piece of black paper and bright crayon and one afternoon I and the children sit on the hill outside our house and we make a very quick light-fingered record of them, the fronds of the tree-fern gracing them, the whole reflected upside down in the green eyes of the River. It takes us no time, no more than the flick of a fantail's wing, but in the context of our concentration it is all of eternity. With more joy than I can walk with I pin mine on the wall of Opal's bedroom and when she returns from a long day's rounds up Raetihi way we trail into her bedroom where she goes to get out of her uniform and put on her blue-green smock and suddenly sees it. And these poplars are framed on her wall, or were the last time I saw her.

I am standing at the school gate one morning in the bitter mist lifting from the River as she leaves for Wanganui for a few days, after a deep division yesterday over something unnecessary, irresponsible and inexplicable, which is to say it was my offence, and she looks back over her shoulder at me, her face saying everything I've wanted her to say, but which she has not said in words: a look that must be engraved on time.

I send to Christchurch for a special white sculpting clay and begin modelling this look of Opal's, her face looking back at me. I use the large sturdy table in my schoolroom to work on and Keith makes me a stand with a supporting rod to hold the weight of the head on the shoulders. So Opal finds herself obliged to sit for me in the schoolroom after work which she hates doing, being tired as well as hungry, and she speaks words that upset me about her days being quite as full as mine and that other people besides me have a right to their lives, and I reply that art claims prior right before everything, before everyone, that it *is* everything, the speech of life and when she doesn't come for her sitting I weep to Keith about it as he sows the spring carrots. "Really," he says, "I've not seen you quarrelling with a friend like this before. There must be some reason. Just hold that stake over there dear, pull the string taut."

"It's different, K, that's why. It's not just being friends. It's . . . I . . . living across the road from Opal I . . . it's my sentimentality peeling off. Layers of it. It's like being skinned alive."

"Now, right . . . stick the stake in the ground just there, no to the right a bit. Really. To think how you continually call for your own kind. I don't know I'm sure. Take this trowel, Mij."

When Opal appears at the door in the evening for her milk she looks rather lovely and her voice is kind. "What have you been crying for?"

"Just feeling sentimental, that's all."

"But that's why I love you."

When Keith comes in later from milking the cow with the bucket of frothing milk, and begins filling Opal's billy, he's laughing to himself so much he spills a bit. "By gee," he tells us, "I'm glad *I'm* not Sylvie's own kind. I don't know where we'd be if I were."

"If I were," echoes Ashton.

And we all collapse laughing.

———————

In order that I can work when she doesn't come I snatch a few pencil sketches of her in Selah on Sunday, with a 4B pencil, soft and black and sharp, and she doesn't like sitting for these either so I don't show them. We sit talking for a while till she gets up to go and suddenly sees them accidentally and gasps upon them. I think I gave these away to her friend Sophie years later when I no longer wanted to see them.

It is while this model of Opal's head is in progress, covered with a wet cloth on the schoolroom table—this is the weekend when Pan accompanies us home from a teachers' refresher course in Raetihi. He's somebody big from the department, they say, though I haven't met a humbler man in my life, and he does a little lecturing which I don't attend; he's so not anything in a man that electrifies me I would not notice him at all except that whenever I turn and glance somewhere I see these over-big blue eyes behind big dark-rimmed glasses and tailored city suit at which the teachers laugh lightly and say, "He's like a successful American businessman."

The Catholic sister from the convent on the River says, "Do you think we should be laughing at America when their Pacific Fleet is only up in the Coral Sea trying to head off the Japanese from New Zealand?"

"But," says the art specialist whose philosophy is known as anthromoposity, "his conversation is that of a schoolboy."

"That's not the point," from Sister Auberne.

He seems to be with our family all the time and takes our children by the hand as though they are people in their own right rather than offshoots from adults only. And when we lunch I find him with us and when we are waiting for a bus on the kerb. As men go he could be slimmer, so could his face and so could his mouth which seems unnecessarily full for its purpose, whatever the purpose of a mouth might be. After a week in Raetihi as we set off back to the River in a hired car he is with us on the footpath and Keith says, "Would you like to come with us, Mr. Morris?"

So he smiles all over himself and says, "I'm perfectly certain I would like to. It is frowned upon to socialise on a professional errand but I do have a few days due to me."

It is this weekend staying with us when, walking into the school on Saturday, he pulls up short in the porch at the view of the Pied Piper and says, "I could walk right into that," and, entering my infant room, he encounters the clay model on the table and it is he who enlightens us how to cast it in plaster later.

We take him for a walk in the afternoon to Selah, cutting across

the paddocks, the children and I running ahead jumping over thistles
and he chases me in his city suit roaring with laughter behind me,
leaving Opal in the rearguard, till we all burst into the silence of death
in Selah laughing and gasping, affronting the phantoms lurking here:
"These clothes of officialdom," he rues.

In the intense privacy of Selah he is transfixed by my glamorous
water-carrier with the glow through her skin of the East, and the wide-
winged soul-bird in paua colours, musing, "And to carry that off is to
carry off the whole wall."

This is a milestone, a
landmark, on the jour-
ney through life.
Strange how the first
thing people think of
when they see my work
in its impermanent con-
dition is how to "carry
it off. To preserve the
colours and so on."
When my life has been
a matter of spontaneity,
from this moment to
the next. The moment,
itself, rounded, com-
plete.

In the evening I play
the piano disgracefully

The children ready for school

and clumsily, lightweight stuff, with no hint of the term on pianoforte
I am taking in Wanganui on the "singing tone," to interpret Beethoven more respectfully, so Opal will interpret me more respectfully,
and mainly for exhibition only, for I sense by now that Hilton Morris
has divined quite profoundly enough into the hidden recesses of me
without my exposing any more. But when he is drying the dishes for
me the subject arises of the lives of the musicians I've been trying to
read and the nature of genius. "Some people," I'm saying, "don't go in
for a string of verified facts before a flash of vision. There's just the
flash, right or wrong."

"But that flash," he says so quietly, "can be full of inaccuracies. It's
when you build up fact on fact, first, that they flash in a sudden vision
which is far more likely to be accurate. That's my theory of genius."

There's a crowd in the house this evening. Our family, Opal's family which consists of her and a young nurse staying with her by the name of Joan, and Mr. Hilton Morris. The rest of them are in the music room but at this point my dear Opal joins us and says, "What are you two up to?" Which I read to be her own particular oblique way of saying she loves me, or this is what I like to think; I don't always know what she means. This very Saturday morning when the four of us, Pan, Opal, Joan and I, were swimming mildly back across the River towards the home bank I, unable to resist such an audience, suddenly lower my head and shoot into my racing sprint cultivated over a lifetime, leave them all behind and sit on the bank and wait for them. To hear Opal protest, "She's a killer."

And I don't think that was saying she loved me but when they finally arrive and climb out of the water Hilton Morris says, "What a beautiful style."

It is Dot Croker's from training college. But I still don't see why I should not exercise the racing crawl I've practised all my life, because the others don't have it. Is it not in accordance with her brand of socialism for one to go faster than another? A desperate row on this subject could last all evening and she would win it for certain on account of the veiled slogans. Is this why she's reserved about my work, because the masses don't have it too? Echoing another culture. When I risked once, "You were born in the wrong country," I received the worst answer of all: silence.

Passionately, "Is one not allowed to excel in your ideology?"

Silence.

"My experience in this bloody country supports you."

I still don't really know what she means by "What are you two up to?" but it remains with me. Our little children are still kicking up their heels playing with Joan and Keith and there's quite an exciting company of us and I feel there is a great deal of hot feeling banking up in the evening, cross-currents of emotion discreetly unspoken, most of it flooding love, and the hot juices of passion interflowing that lubricate the works, inspire ideas and fertilise blind action; fuel for great things. Here is the stranger from afar, the right-hand man of the director general of education cohabiting in our home, with the strength to see me as I am, the molten inside me, approving of and loving what he sees, almost adoring me for it, from no performance on my part; which is surcease from trying to win it from my sole audience, Opal.

In this brief close hot time at our place and amid talk and whispering, hilarity, music, children's voices and the clicking of dishes, far from the centres of sophistication and "my own kind" I've longed for, it occurs to me that I am, after all, still what I believed myself to be when a girl on the long long roads to school, a vagabond and an artist; a catalytic impact on one buried alive in the New Zealand forests. "We'd love you to come and stay with us in Wellington," he says.

"Who, me?"

"When we do come upon a lovely teacher," using the royal "we," "we like to show her off, to let them see what a teacher can be," and returns to the music room to the others.

Opal is still sitting on my favorite stool by the stove where I usually nurse babies. "Really," she says unexpectedly, "you do look beautiful tonight."

Later he is teaching us all this marvellous Maori hand-game called Hautama tutama at which we laugh like mad.

The young nurse staying with Opal, a dark lissome pretty girl called Joan with long eyes and long legs, joins us in a cruise upriver on the Sunday afternoon while Keith minds the children, and when we pair off in the forest both Opal and I see to it that our guest walks with the youngest and prettiest of us, for what that's worth, while we two get to work on our quarrelling. Probably it's waste, for Joan tells on the boat downstream that she talked the whole time about her fiancé Joom in a POW camp in Germany whom she'll marry the moment he steps off the troopship when the war is over. What with the beat of the engine it's terribly noisy on the riverboat

The sculpture of Opal

but we've brought the ukulele and take turns doing the hula on the deck and you should see the guest doing the hula in his clothes "of officialdom" as we sing the tune and clap the rhythm, and that was worth it.

> Oh going down the river in the old steamboat
> Yippai, yippai, yippai, yippai
> Yippai pai day . . .

In the morning when we all go down to the bus stop by the store to say goodbye to Pan he takes his leave of the others first then comes to me last, and kisses me in front of the Templetons, the tourists, the Maoris, the fowls, dogs and children, and on the mouth too for all to see; his big blue eyes steady behind the large glasses and his full gentle lips on mine telling me how wasteful that paired walk had indeed been in the twilight of the noon forest.

I've later written three books about Pipiriki, or the River as we called it—*Myself, Greenstone* and *Rangatira*—and several short stories, but even though here is another go there's still a great deal left out. It's no good even starting to try to put on paper my love for Hilton Morris, by the name of Pan; there'd be no end to it and I'd squander all the poetry I'd ever learnt.

It takes a long time this thing, the model of Opal's head, but when I come to the place to set it in plaster the three of us face up to it, Ruth too I think; Keith and Opal and Ruth holding the two halves together while I glue the edges and tie the whole. Crises plus on plus but we make it and here is that look of Opal's, back over her shoulder, caught at last for me to be held for the duration of plaster.

Fascinating about sculpture, the variations in its lighting, not fixed as in drawing: turn it a little and here's another set of shadows, another expression on the face. I choose one of these sets of shadows, the one with the optimum of concern in it and take a photo of it with our inadequate camera, amateurishly off focus which turns out to be an advantage, supplying the mystery which Opal is made of. I get it printed and enlarged in Wanganui by post and pick it up next time I go for my piano lesson, and it's no time before I see it framed on the drawing room wall of her cottage, as though she values it; about the only clue to what she thinks of it. She doesn't squander words on her profoundest feelings unless in a line of poetry from W. H. Auden, or in a wonderful verse she has written herself. To encounter someone like Pan and to find a neighbour like Opal says a lot for the back of beyond.

In the cave studio Keith helped me make in the bush down the bank from the nurse's cottage when the white landowner reclaimed the whare studio to dock his sheep in—some men can do such to a woman, his wife has left him— I carve in the clay bank over the dug-out fireplace a replica of Opal's bronze Buddha and I am here when she comes to the door and sees it, so I know what she feels about it . . . this time.

———————

And when her friend Sophie is staying with her and I beat it to Selah one Saturday, all day, and make in vivid coloured pencil four abstract pictures of the minds of us four in the metaphor of the ground—the normality of Keith's, green growth above and the strata below; Sophie's normality but with rifts and crevasses from topographical strains; my own a black cavern full of ravaging flames with no surface coverage at all, and Opal's a strange composition in turquoise greens and blues, a fluid compromise and with little relation to standard topography—and slink into the cottage on my way home at twilight, they both give these abstracts their total attention for the rest of the evening so that I realise I have at last learnt from my living near Opal to peel off sentimentality however sore the process, to escape from the representational and to speak in uncluttered symbol. Nor does she resent my portrayal of her as something out of the ordinary, like the inscrutable heart of the gemstone opal itself. By this reception of it you'd think my work has authority, which tosses me to the crest of such a high wave of confidence that the following day when they're both sitting at the back of our table sharing our Christmas dinner I take centre-stage mid-kitchen like Daphne and play Sophie till they're holding their stomachs with laughter and can't eat their leg of mutton. "That's the first time," Opal says to Sophie later, "I've ever felt real pain from laughter. I didn't know what emotion was till I came here."

"It's the first time," from Sophie, "I've cried from laughter." I didn't risk playing Opal though. And here I am on the boards with an admirable audience over the road until Daphne herself sweeps up from Wellington with her young son Vern to avoid the Japs, her hair trimmed short and swept up in natural curls silken and brown, her long eyes—there are none like them except her son Vern's—and she's wearing a tube frock with vertical stripes in black and white which change the green eyes to grey.

Wholly unintentionally she's at once centre-stage and Opal and Sophie have left me in the wings; though Daph, engrossed in her own series of drama, barely registers them at all. "Don't let her bring you down like that all the time, Sylv. Depressing you. It's like shooting a bird out of the sky. Warners always fly. I never let anyone shoot me down."

She and Vern stay for some lovely time until she decides, as Evadne had, the Japs are preferable to Maoris and mud and as we carry her suitcases down to the bus stop early morning she remarks of Opal, "I don't know what you see in her, Sylv."

"It's because she doesn't keep on giving me aprons and tea-towels and oven cloths for my birthdays all the time . . . as my in-laws do."

This very same evening I drift down to the gate of the nurse's cottage in a powder blue ground-length housecoat to talk to Opal and see if it's true. The night is like a Schubert song and we stand at her gate in silence. Then we walk a little way up the road through the moonlit trees but return again defeated. Yes it's true; there's no longer an Opal to inspire the flowering of my home-grown wares, though she murmurs "Sylvia Moonlight."

"That wonderful Daphne," in Sophie's letter.

> We were not made for refuges of lies,
> And false embattled bulwarks will not screen us.
> We mocked the careful shieldings of the wise,
> And only utter truth can be between us.
> —Mary Coleridge

In the school grounds there's an enthralling bank of papa* rock crying out for someone to carve in it so I do begin carving a life-sized horse with a spatula and the carving knife. You have to do something to discharge and relieve the weight of love on the River, to balance the noons and the nights of the soul like a man kissing your mouth in the morning then getting on the bus. Living with another man of a thousand kisses you'd think this is enough but all I can do about it is carve a horse, thinking about the long beautiful letter from Pan addressing each separate one of us in turn. It takes me weeks of weekends this horse for there's no time with three little children, a school, a husband and a home, and what about the rain? The papa rock seems to be affronted to be disturbed and often breaks away so that I'm unable to fully finish it. "What's that, Mummie?" from El.

"An Arab steed. Its master has just sold it to a horse dealer for a bag of gold."

My drawings and paintings and sculptings leap and call from one end of Pipiriki to the other on banks and in sand, on walls and on blackboards, on paper and in plaster, impermanent as kisses; as a first kiss at the bus stop in front of the store, as a morning kiss when he brings in my tea when I am staying at Pan's place, as a last kiss on a

---

* papa: a hard grey clay

train. All of them, drawings and kisses, the froth foam and spray from my cascading love for people and from their dear love for me.

When Opal leaves for her new appointment on the coast—the East Coast of all places—she bequeaths to me more experience with the music and art of the masters, a taste for modern poetry and, most of all, an alternative philosophy; whereas all she has from me is a water-colour of the face of Beethoven, a crayon portrait of the yellow poplars remembering across the water, an off-focus photo of the model of her own head, abstracts of four types of mind and, least of all, an introduction to emotion. Or, in a wider perspective, you could say, all these are gifts from the River itself.

Including the exquisite powerful poems she wrote, for the first and last time in her life. The stream of health department people, district nurses mainly, who followed each other through that nurse's cottage, all startlingly unmarried. There was not one in our time who failed to succumb to the rarefied climate of the River, both emotional and topographical; the kind of light-headedness you get eight thousand feet up the Rockies in Colorado where there's not enough oxygen. My word, that cottage with its white picket gate, the rosemary, lavender and old-time roses dreaming in its bland front garden—it could tell a tale . . . and has.

The poor are always with us, and so are inspectors; and by this criterion they get away with a lot. They can be excused, for instance, for liking to rest on their rounds at The House for a weekend; sleeping well, dining well, trying the whiskey and cruising on the beautiful River and God knows we're glad enough of their company; amiable urbane pragmatic men with an eye to promotion, even to the point of getting on with teachers, whereas any departmental official, professional or office staff who can achieve this is a superman and should be appointed to the next space probe.

And here are three of them stretching their legs before one of Keith's famous open fires one rainy Sunday afternoon since there's no cruise on the River except that Keith is at Home Guard. But Opal is here, her lovely hair piled up on top of her patrician features, who is always on hand when Mr. Vicarage is. So is Mr. Albert Flake, secretary to the Maori Schools department, a small man of sandy grey hair and clothes and sandy grey eyes which are hard to catch.

My neck flushes as I ask him, "Why did you advertise Horoera in the gazette as being eight miles by metalled road from Te Araroa when there was no road, a rocky beach and two tidal rivers?"

His sandy eyes slip sideways. "We get our information from the locals."

In galloping terror, "When you knew from the application forms we had three young babies, one just born."

His eyes slide the other way and his voice has an edge of defensiveness, "We got our information from the locals."

"The locals said they didn't give you false information."

Repetitiveness is an effective technique. "We got our information from the locals."

I'm too young to pursue this; what would go on my files? Mr. Flake has the whole of the department behind him and it's best for a young teacher to keep on side.*

There's every reason why they should relax at The House, they can be excused for it, but not for examining the school on a Saturday morning to fit in with their itinerary. To call children back on a Saturday morning, let alone the teachers, is to upend the rhythm of the week, of the village, of the school, unbalance the entire cosmos. All right, do it, but not when a teacher's report depends on the school's performance. But these men, the senior inspector, Mr. Vicarage and Mr. Bletcher, get away with its because we are young and because one of them, Bob Bletcher, is a high-rise footballer appointed for reasons known only to the department itself, so big and tall you could build apartments in him with up-shooting lifts. Teachers tell the story of how Bob Bletcher was required to deliver an address on choral speaking at a refresher course—and you can take it from there. In our kitchen early on the following Monday morning, "But," from Keith, "they haven't spoken to me about my school."

"It's not like Mr. Vicarage, K."

"They haven't said what they thought about it. They'll be driving out soon and in silence." Seldom indeed that Henderson reveals anger but his eyes spit blue fire and the children at our knees can't get over it. But he doesn't give way where his teaching is concerned. His voice lifts. "They've said nothing. A year's work and they drive out saying nothing. A disrupted, an overturned Saturday morning with only half the children here, to grade me on an unsatisfactory, a simply dreadful condition which they themselves have created to suit their itinerary. A morning which they themselves have turned upside down.

* on side: a Rugby football term meaning in favour

No verbal report. Of course there's no verbal report. And they think they're going to get away with it. Slink out and away to the stronghold of the city and write a report on something they've forgotten anyway, and if they do it's dreadful. And me not there to defend my school. Why don't they face up to me?"

"Face up to me?" from Ashton.

"And take what's coming?" Strides round the kitchen and Elliot falls into step behind him.

Jasmine is part of Daddy. "Daddy, what are you angry for?"

More than I will ever be. "It's not like Mr. Vicarage, K. It's that high-rise footballer, Bob Bletcher, throwing his weight round, thinking he's still on a football field."

"I won't have it," roars our protector and provider, "I insist they speak. And so will *I* speak, by God."

"K, they said they were driving out at eight o'clock."

The next thing here's Henderson striding out and across the school grounds and down the steep steps to the school gate to ambush them and from what I hear later from both him and Opal, who is backing her car out across the road, these three middle-aged men, Vicarage, Bletcher and Flake, are crammed together in the front seat shivering in the river mist. The car lurches to a stop and here is the young head in school clothes shooting away point blank at his seniors. Well *I* wouldn't have done it. Mr. Vicarage admits the omission gracefully, agrees he should have conferred with the headmaster and does make a verbal report right there in the mist, his lips blue with the cold, to which the teacher has the right of reply, before they low-gear off through the bush. It is quite some rumbling volcanic time before my headmaster cools down and once and for all both I and the children learn the place his teaching holds in the priorities of his life.

We have no more Saturday morning inspections.

You never want to stay too long in a place, even Pipiriki. You use up the people. They get to know you and no poor human can survive being known. Towards the end of our fourth year here, with Opal gone and someone else from the health department in the nurse's cottage, with Singapore fallen, with the war blazing away in the South Pacific and the Tories downed, and the Japanese in the Coral Sea and the Americans taking Rest and Recreation in New Zealand, Henderson is called up, but the education department appeals for its teachers married with three children, all the rest have gone, and he is very disappointed.

They are very short of teachers and he's not allowed to go, though he's already been to camp, and I've already started to try to milk the cow, the wretch. Keith milks her in the middle of the paddock without any bale but when I come near her—bucket this way, I the other— Susie her name is and he strokes her under the chin and calls her Darling. My rival dammit.

I can't speak for his motives, but what it looks like is that to counter his disappointment, to pacify his soul, he applies for this much bigger school in the gazette as his grading is good, taking the precaution to ascertain first the truth of the access. Waiomatatini has a roll of about two hundred and a sizable Maori staff and they were calling for Maori school experience, art and music but, "I couldn't ever go back to the East Coast again, K, I . . ."

No reply but his eyes are alight like sapphires.

"K, we can't possibly take the children back to the East Coast."

"It might be better to have the children out of the way with the Japs at the door."

"I love you, K. I love you. I want to lie on the floor and let you kick me to prove how much I love you. I . . ."

He can't help laughing.

"But I had been hoping to get back to town: films, concerts, friends . . . to my own kind."

Well we both have to laugh at the "my own kind" thing.

"Mij, that's a little way off. I'd have to go on a staff and I'm jolly sure that won't happen. To get a headship in town I'd need much higher grading and be much older. Those jobs go high. And a woman wouldn't be appointed anyway, not a married woman. So that's not yet, dear." He's in the old clothes he milks the cow in and does the garden, big boots and no tie, you can get close to him and we love him passionately like this. But he's still gazing somewhere else. "In a school that size both our salaries would be up and you'd be an assistant, not a junior; you'd have a junior of your own. By gee, I'd like the experience of a staff to work with. A man could do much more."

"But K, with a bigger job I'd have much less time for my own work."

"I'd see you had time to do your own work. I have so far, haven't I? Is there anything I haven't done to give you a measure of freedom? I'm jolly sure there's not another wife in the whole profession with the free time you have."

"That's not quite my point. It's not . . . not how much time I have. It's what I am. I'm not a teacher; I'm an artist."

"I'm an artist," echoes Ashton.

"What's an artist?" from El.

Jas wraps her arms round his legs. "Daddy, I want you to go."

"I could earn as much as a teacher could. If I could free myself I'd prove it." I'm laying the table for five for tea.

"You don't want to talk like that, Mij, about freeing yourself. It's not all money. I like you at school with me. I can do anything when you are with me. I'd try even harder to give you time." What is he seeing over the forested rim?

I sink on my stool by the stove and both little boys climb on my knee. Keith lays his hand on my head. "Fear not, Lamb, it's well above me. I won't get it."

Six of my family—me, Daphne, Mumma, Lionel, Muriel, Evadne

I wouldn't like to leave this further account of the River without mention of Mumma when she was evacuated here; with her burdens put down there was no more tension, only the enemy at the door. About the scones she baked, her interest in the children and the school, in her white apron in the garden where she'd talk to Keith. "Sylvie's an artist, Keith," she told him.

"I know," he said. "She should not have married."

A gentle peaceable presence.

And Lionel came up the River in the uniform of a squadron leader which lifted my status with Opal Owen; he was selecting and programming cadets for the air force, seeking the brainy daredevils of the country in order to save the country.

The Reverend Henderson died in New Plymouth while we were here, that was 1942. My own father had long since gone and Mumma wrote to me later, "If you want to see your brother Ashton alive again you'd better come soon." A big widespread family beginning to crumble down into the ground it had come from. You couldn't believe all that vivacity and passion and love on the wing could ever crumble away. But the three major formative loves of my life, Keith, Hilton and Opal, were under way simultaneously in Pipiriki and I had no thoughts of crumbling away.

> Long suns and moons have wrought this day at length,
>    The heavens in native majesty have told thee.
> To see me as I am have thou the strength;
>    And, even as thou art, I dare behold thee.
>                                    —Mary Coleridge

Waiomatatini—
the residence

WAIOMATATINI    Waiomatatini was near the Pacific again; Fate did seem to be tossing us from one side of the country to the other—from Mangahume in the west to Horoera at the tip of the east; back to Pipiriki in the west again, and now the extreme east to Waiomatatini—bouncing us like rubber in a match ball game. Only in transit did we see our own culture.

A flat riverbed of stones only lightly soiled over so that the grass was dried to whiteness. A scattering of black tree-manuka on the bleached grass gave the scene the blenched face of a nightmare when the artery of love is severed. True, there was a river there, but one of these bouldered swift noisy extroverts which reflect nothing at all.

The only manifest life was the hysterical skylarks shrieking from the sky. After the lush of Pipiriki the mouth felt dry.

The residence was no more than a matchbox dropped on the plain by someone in a hurry, exposed to every gale, but the school delighted Keith, modern for a change; a row of three large open-air rooms in the latest style of that time, a staffroom and a headmaster's office, can you believe it, and detached at one end a smart home science block with kitchen and laundry facilities much better than the residence itself, for Waiomatatini was the home ground of Sir Apirana Ngata, "my own dunghill," a cabinet minister and acting prime minister at one stage during the war, and you're not going to find the Maori girls of his tribe, the Ngati Porou, doing the servants' work in the white teachers' home under the guise of housecraft.

I think the roll was about two hundred Maori children with no Europeans till our three came and there were no white people in the district except Jim Griffin, the roadman. It was our Daddy's—let me see: Whareorino, Mangahume, Horoera, Pipiriki and now Waiomatatini—his fifth school. But I'd rather count kisses than schools.

Whom in heaven's heart did I find visiting Ruatoria, the cowboy town six miles away, the very weekend after our arrival, but the man of four kisses, Hilton Morris, on an errand from the department to speak to the teachers. A strain on the word "coincidence." At least it's a chance to meet the other teachers, and who can say that was not his intention. And here's our benighted little family standing apart, our young clustered round us, with Pan standing before us still in "the clothes of officialdom." It must have been spring for I'm wearing a warm wine suit, a wine felt hat with a wide floppy brim and high-heeled wine suede shoes. A word with Keith, with each little child, then his big eyes cover me all over. My shy head is so low it nearly falls off while the pause fills up to the brim. The last time I saw Pan he kissed me goodbye on the Wellington station and the "Night and Day" theme recharges my blood and every bumping corpuscle. Will he ever stop looking at my face so I can lift my head, yet all he can say is "Sylvia."

In time I do look up at the large horn-rimmed glasses. I look through them to find the man himself.

In his talk to the teachers I don't really hear what he says for I'm seeing his smooth dark parted hair, his tailored city suit, the bird-like movements of his hands in action, his big glasses flashing, his full face and mouth, and I'm remembering Pipiriki when he sang one evening

"Who Is Sylvia?" in a voice thumping with volume and man-ness, and I'm counting our kisses to date: the goodbye one at the bus stop, the good morning one on the pillow at his place and the farewell kiss on the train, adding up to only three.

But the other teachers heard what he said which they complained was nothing and that they'd have been better off at home gathering wood. We hear he is only the director general, Dr. Bellamy Gully, on the prowl by proxy and that he's a bit of a pufter.

"What's a pufter?" I say.

One says, "It's someone called the director of visual and audio aids when a debutante could do the job."

"His wife probably does it at home," says another.

As it happens Megan and I did review a couple of films for him one evening when he'd fallen asleep exhausted but I don't say so.

It's Keith, not me, who again asks Pan to our place on the Sunday afternoon before he returns to Wellington, for Keith is tirelessly amused at what he calls my soul-mates: S.M., a company which includes all my ideal girls, best friends and conquests since we were married. "Your S.M. wants to see the school," he says.

"Oh . . . *you* . . ."

And he laughs like anything. Somehow he gets hold of two horses, one with a saddle and which canters for me and the other with no saddle which only trots for my S.M. for Pan and me to ride out to Awarua beach, by which time the night is dark. He dismounts, so I do too, and immediately we kiss in the greatest relief, standing on the wet sand by the waves, communicating the tumult you find in music. Until we hear the steps of a solitary horseman and we divide as he passes, a dark shadow in the night. But there's a chance to recover myself and I mount my horse, so he mounts his, and I lead the way from surrender by the sea till we reach the grass and the trees, where once more he dismounts and tries to draw me down from my saddle but I stay where I am. Pan doesn't say one word and soon we are riding back along the treed track. "I accept every experience," he says.

I'm thinking, It's different from Keith and me, "For better, for worse, till death do us part"; it's the other violent variety "under the hide of me . . . a hungry yearning burning inside of me." But we chat of surface things. "What kind of a man is Dr. Gully?" I say.

There is a moment before he replies, "He's a man who is able to examine life without cutting it up."

When Pan is in bed in a back room I go in like a good hostess to see

to his needs and he gathers my hand and pulls me to him in the
dearest way but I'm far too shy to respond; I blow out his lamp and go.

Next day, Monday, he shares with us the first day at our large new
school, in strict professionalism, visiting the rooms of all the teachers,
who are mostly Maori. Having no idea what to do with so many
dozens of little Maori children I spend most of the day on all those
marching and dancing and singing games which infant teachers know
back to front, introducing the musical commands from the piano so
you don't have to raise your voice and when Pan comes in, "I'm trying to establish some kind of communication, some common feeling,
as a point of departure," and of course we both like rhythm.

At lunchtime I race him across the broad bleached paddock back
to the house, he laughing and puffing and squawking behind his tie
of officialdom flying. Before we return after lunch I play "Night and
Day" and then a Beethoven adagio. "You didn't play like that in
Pipiriki," he says.

At the keyboard I hang my head.

"Why didn't you?"

I'm so shy of white people.

"You didn't want to," he says.

True.

Even with the perfect opportunity offering we don't kiss. Both of
us are in professional hours, he values his marriage and I value mine
and neither of us can stomach deceit. This, after all, is the home where
I live with my husband, but the point is made: we know. As I pass
him, however, to return to school our shoulders accidentally collide
but neither apologises. We've touched. But no man is going to walk
this earth to look back and say, Her? Huh . . . I've had *her*. Not outside a marriage. To hold his love I must deny it.

After school he kisses me goodbye on the front porch, legitimately,
in bright broad daylight before everyone. When he closes the gate behind him and turns to me on the porch I open my arms wide to him
and he opens his to me then he gets in someone's car and goes. We part
again with arms wide open.

Astonishingly Opal comes the next weekend, but her heart is
troubled about other things and I'm no longer first with her. Her
whole self is in tumult but not because of me. I also am in tumult but
not because of Opal and we can't recapture that which we'd had;
standing back to back neither is able to calm the other as it had been
on the River. But she remains ineradicable from me and I get the idea
that this is how Waiomatatini is going to be, not searing isolation all

over again but recurring celebration: a place where people come to me. As a first new week ... explosive.

The school and the domestic block

There were hills in the distance with sheep on them and kowhai amid the manuka but too far away to dig a cave in, whereas for a wife who teaches with children at home and hundreds at school silence is a matter of priority and of wrecking your hands over. K afforded me many of his indispensable Saturday mornings helping to build a hut of sods dug from the meagre turf, sited some distance from the house. An iron roof he puts on it, a little stove in it, a marvellous tube chimney and the sweetest door with leather hinges but it takes a long time. On this unpainted timber door I printed the key words, Selah Four; for me to study, learn to write, paint, dance and consult my instincts in, for unless I created for myself under my own power an alternative source of income to teaching, unless I exercised my homespun function of an artist, I'd decompose from the spirit outward.

The roll grew during our time there to over two hundred, I think, and the staff expanded to about nine, maybe more, all Maoris except K and me. Each February I'd start off with about forty-five Maori infants, startling warriors to be accurate, which swelled during the year's intake to sixty or so until by spring it lapped round seventy. True I had a junior, a tough attractive and able girl and she needed to be, but the job was very heavy when you meant it and even when you didn't. To be frank it was heavier when you didn't than when you did and I found myself in time meaning it. Another thing making it unnecessarily heavy was the silly supply of American reading books, the ubiquitous Janets and Johns, jerkily joltingly unrelated to a people like the Ngati Porou, a proud and brainy crowd who spawned scholars, politicians and Victoria Crosses and ran their own Red Cross.

As I've said, our three were the only white children at school: Jas in K's senior room, El with a white teacher from Ruatoria for a while who upset him very much—"She's kinda angry all the time"—and Ash in the infant room with me, the only fair head there. White children are the casualties in the Maori school context. You still hear about the arrogant pakehas drawing the colour line but you want to see who draws the colour line when the Maoris are in the majority, from the Maori teachers down. At basketball practice one afternoon I had to witness from the open-air door Jasmine standing for the whole two hours on the sideline without one game, and when I asked the teacher later how this came about she replied, "Aw they were picking their own teams, see, and she didn't get picked, like." Nor was I in the position to suggest an alternative, being the Head's wife; it would have looked like privilege.

On the football field they'd target in on Ash and he'd come into class with blood and bruises, but they'd mistaken their man. Ash still played football each year regardless. As for El, he summed up his own situation and withdrew socially, being one with an eye to his own survival. A common circumstance in this country is to see Maori children hurled to the periphery of the action, their culture ignored and their human rights, but you'd find the story written in reverse with white children in a Maori school, so that fatuous talk about "my brown brother" has two sides. "Jimmy," I asked a Maori man on the River, "all this about the bad pakehas making the colour bar. I get the feeling it's you Maoris who don't want us. True or false?"

"True." He smiled.

A noted teacher at Ratana Pa once told me, "Sylvia, when I see that one fair head in the line of black ones walking into school I curse God."

Among the white teachers in Maori schools on the East Coast it was said that the attitude came from Sir Apirana himself, who mistrusted the motives of the white teachers: "They're only in it for the money." But whatever the racial climate at that time, Keith Henderson strode ahead through his work in a way the district respected and the department also, even, as the years turned over, The Sir himself who, being our neighbour round the corner, loved to come round to school on sports days when he was home from Parliament to watch the team games and laugh for an hour at the yelling and the impromptu humour, and learnt for himself the motives of that particular head-master. He allowed me access to his priceless library.

The district even came to accept me in time, not only on account of my work in the infant room or because of the marvellous concerts I prepared in my room of an afternoon, to which white people from Ruatoria would trickle out—white culture all the way through, for the Maori staff did the Maori concerts; it was there at Waiomatatini where I saw the best waiata, *karakia** and haka ever, though I took no part in them—but because I did as usual attempt some token local visiting among the tribe like a real Head's wife.

No doubt Keith had his blank spots, it's just that I don't recall them. I hadn't married the perfect man; but it was good to see a young man extended and in action with his gift of welding a district and school into one strong unit.

The pattern on the coast was for teachers, brown and white, to hold the institute meeting on a Saturday afternoon after which the white teachers with all our various children would group off to some of our homes, aware of our need for interchange. All of us, I think, would have returned to our own culture in the populated areas had there been jobs for married women there, for the sake of our children at least. To meet the rare Leslie in the street of Ruatoria, a cowboy town, with her two little girls by each hand—"This bloody hole. What a place to walk with your children"—was to see our condition at its blackest. On the other hand, to visit her and John in their private wilderness, at the ultimate end of an unbridged riverbed near the ocean, Leslie's face and grace, her degrees and legs, John's philosophy and boogie-woogie was to see our fate as worthwhile.

But however we tried to bolster ourselves, regularly one of the wives would fall sick to the soul and collapse for a week or so, applying to the department for sick leave with a medical certificate from that same Dr. Grant at Te Puia who still, single-handed, held the coast together.

At Leslie and John Shaw's or at our place we'd drink nights-ful of beer, eat, talk and laugh and reinvigorate one another. A huge man John was, six foot something and dark, who'd had a classical music training which, along with his strong forearms and hands, made him

---

* *karakia*: chants

a master of boogie-woogie, reading it from the book. I'd go clean through one sonata after another, the Waldstein was one, No. 10 was another and the poor old Pathétique and Moonlight, and between us the piano would sing all night till breakfast. Cascades of music in some poky little residence to the domed silence of the night. Philosophy in and out of the hours, metaphysics on the beach and sensational tales of inspectors. You could talk into the eyes of Leslie, walk right in. "Leslie, Leslie. Listen. Our terrible thirties. We can't waste our thirties, I can't *waste*. Not a moment, let alone a decade. I refuse to accept such an awful decree. Do you have any taste for mediocrity, for-for anonymity and oblivion? We ought to capitalise on this incarceration so when we return to the world, if ever, we'll not have slithered back down the slope into purposelessness; at least be level with our own year. We could even be ahead of the main body. Look at the advantages of isolation: with no social uproar siphoning me off I can study, practise, paint, write, think and consult my instincts. Instinct being all I've got. I don't have any brain."

She's low in a chair in their kitchen, her long legs flowing together. "But one's thought would tend to the ultra-individualistic. John's is already."

I stand, a beer in hand. "At least I know each idea is my own, not a reach-me-down. Your own native thought is the strongest thought wherever you happen to be."

John is making the toast for breakfast, for our children are waking, "Am I to take it, Sylvia, that you're the only one on the coast with an original idea?"

"Sarcasm belongs to the twenties."

Leslie laughs out loud. "Whoo . . . down comes John."

From John with the toast, "There remain flaws in your argument, Sylvia."

Finish off the last beer. "Oh well—it made a good story."

"Ye-e-es?"

"It tells well."


We Hendersons at least had a metal road access but the Shaws had a riverbed with several separate streams which changed course arbitrarily after a storm. Unless you went there in daylight on a Saturday and returned by daylight on the Sunday you wouldn't be going at all, or returning either. Except for the time the storm came at night and continued all Sunday and the streams joined in one high torrent, like your skills channelling into one in the thirties, and none could get back to the firm main road. Well, we all *did* get back for school on Monday. In time too.

But these gatherings were too rare.

I was still beyond the world of my own kind, my work and my looks unsung. A man told Sophie some years later, "When Sylvia looks at me with those eyes my knees turn to water." I saw life as an arbitrary gift; a flick of mind between two eternities; between the eternity gone by and the eternity to follow and only one turn. Sheer chance to have a turn at all, to be alive. To give the journey a point you could aim to give back to life what life had given you; pick up any gems in the grass by the wayside, polish them up and hand them back when your turn is over. You could even leave more in life than you found, and there was a design I could live with. At least you'd have standards to live by other than the old ones. And not next week either, or even tomorrow but now this very moment. I'd not be passing this way again.

You need to be certain of your direction, which route to choose at the complex intersections and detours, then channel everything into the one stream to become a current with force like the riverbed to Shaws' in a storm. If only I . . . if only there were not all this music in my head, if only I didn't love so much. I could have been a very fine spinster coming up like Miss Cumberland and Miss Little and the others had it not been for the beat, beat, beat of the tom-tom. Juices flowed like sap in the spring, and the spring pushed on and on, round corner after corner, up steep hills and down the gullies, beneath overhanging cliffs. You forded frequent floods of passion or they'd swallow and sweep you away.

Nor was there endless time any more: my eldest brother Ashton died in Lower Hutt while we were at Waiomatatini and soon after Ashton my sister Gracie died in South Africa; they rang me from Wellington and told me. Also the Americans dropped the atom bomb when thousands died in one blast. You had to believe that life was finite, that the journey did come to an end some time.

The loss of Opal I couldn't stand, even though we intervisited and tried to write letters; all the ideal girls since childhood embodied in one, the woman I'd sought and had found at last and her face was turned from me. I was no longer wonderful to her, or first with her since she'd fallen in love on VJ Day with a romantic young man. All she wanted from me now was ordinary dry friendship, not inspiration or love or anything vital. The agony of the ousted child was beyond definition.

In the evenings after towering days I'd go to the big kitchen table the housekeeper scrubbed each morning, with my dear paper and paints to make a book of pictures for Opal, to somehow tell her, explain to her by imagery, to communicate with her, to try to share with her again what we'd shared on the River with barely a word spoken; to try to recapture that peace I'd known. So that she'd love me again. Two cups of tea in warm ambers and browns and a whiff of yellow steam captioned Sympathy; a study in greys, whites and blacks of one cup overturned in its saucer, the tea spilt, titled in my best printing, Loneliness; the group of tender tossing daisies beneath the great dark pine at Awarua I'd done in coloured pencils on the spot when the pain was too hard, and called it Wind Rising; a branch of gumtree leaves clicketting staccato against the sky and that caption had something about music in it; and I illustrated the nightmare I'd had of her pulling away from me, trying to free herself from my ferocious demands in a great storm, and I'm desperately holding her hands, the hair of us both streaking in the gale and that one had a verse on the opposite page:

> I dreamt that the dearest I ever knew
> Had died and been entombed;
> I know it's a dream and cannot be true
> Yet stays the nightmare too appalling
> And like a tempest shakes me
> But no one wakes me.

Nor did I stop doing these until I found myself making a self-portrait, breaking out of the sentimentality I knew offended her; a long face with features out of alignment like a French abstract; small staring eyes too close together, crooked nose, uncombed straggy hair; not beautiful whatever. I think I captioned that just Me.

I posted this book to her but either she found it too fatuous or she was too engrossed in her passion to acknowledge it nor, when I called in at her place for a night on my way across to Wanganui to my former piano teacher—three days there, one lesson only, three days back—did she even mention them, except for the abstract self-portrait which she liked and praised and had pinned on the wall; pinned, not framed.

On my way back I did not call in but she came to the evening station with her young lover and with a thermos of tea for me but she did not meet my eyes.

During my study of Herbert Read later, the sentimentality began peeling off in rolls like torn wallpaper, but by then Opal was lost and only the void left.

That memory surfaces from a clear forty years ago and I've never told it till now. "Really, Sylvia," she said years later when I was staying with Sophie, "these tantrums of yours—"

"You tease me and bring them on."

Three loves: my husband, a woman, a lover. Plenty of room. By my reckoning there was a place for two men in a woman's life simultaneously and most certainly for a woman too. Each love differed from the other two; rather than overlapping they complemented one another. From what I could read from the other white teachers, most marital rows in the thirties blew up from the wife's cry, "He doesn't understand me," and as it happened we hadn't had the company of other married couples till now. No man understands a woman, only thinks he does. All the big books they write about women whereas only a woman understands a woman, and by instinct mainly.

I've thrown a complete volume of Beethoven's sonatas not just out the window but across the lawn, over the fence into the stony road at two o'clock in the morning because my husband didn't understand me, and another night I've taken off in my nightgown down that same road towards the unbridged river at three o'clock in the morning because, in trying to say the right thing, he said the wrong thing. Mind you, I didn't run too fast in case he couldn't catch me. Possibly these collisions would not have occurred had Opal been round one corner and Pan round the other, but only *might* not. "All that's required of a man," Gracie had said, "is a provider and lover."

There can be many facets of the kaleidoscopically revolving mind which call for many counterparts and you can't demand from one man to play them all. At one of the gatherings down at Shaws' John said, "Keith, do you understand your wife?"

"No John, I don't. But I'm jolly sure of what to expect."

I can't recall any contretemps because Keith complained *I* didn't understand *him*. The subject did not arise. In fact, however, I don't think I did. Though many women do claim they understand all men as they understand all their children.

———

The department of Maori education kept the Maori infant rooms faith-fully supplied with stacks of those alien reading books which had originated in America, Janet and John, though it took small Maori children with their bilingual burden three years to get through the primers where it took white children only two. It's an arduous under-taking trying to turn one race into another, involving both force and failure, so for little other reason than to make teaching easier I plunged in and made hundreds of Maori infant reading books. Since the little dark maidens were always drawing houses and mothers and babies I made a set of four on this subject, in sequence and graded, and with a Maori content; illustrated exuberantly. Four of each on account of the numbers in the room. At least the J and J gave me a lead in techniques like word recurrence, sentence length, page size and gradation, though, on examination, they often erred by their own criteria and had no line of thought, not having been made by a writer.

The little dark warriors were forever drawing trucks and men, we never saw an airplane, so I made a sequence of four on that, four of each, and at that time there was no duplicating machine or Xerox; all by my own hand. But those only came to thirty-two whereas my roll swung from forty-five to near seventy. So I made dozens and dozens more, every week, to accompany the weekly themes. Songs and verses so far for the Maori infant room—about 1945 to 1949—were still En-glish, all about squirrels and their nut problems, red robins in the snow —I didn't see a robin till 1970 in Colorado—and skinny little English boys in long trousers whereas shorts are worn in this country from small boys to big men—"It took me hours," from a lady visitor, "to get through customs. I had never seen men's knees in such abundance"— and about falling leaves, whereas all New Zealand trees are evergreen. I made some relevant local songs by lifting a simple and short passage from the masters and writing words to it, like the drama of the manuka bloom in the spring, the scandalous private life of a tui and the skylark who forgot his way down to the ground.

There was still not nearly enough reading material, local or foreign, for the crowds and crowds of erupting young Maoris. Strange thing about this school committee, it would pass money for school equipment or sports trips but didn't believe in schoolroom libraries. The depart-ment supplied the textbooks but any further books the committee con-sidered waste of funds. At Keith's first meeting with them he had to employ persuasion, persistence and even guile to extract from them twenty-five pounds for school books.

I took to the large rolls of brown paper and made huge books to lay

on the floor which several children at once could read together down
on their knees. Back in Pipiriki I'd made reading cards in three-ply to
withstand the kind of use they met from small Maoris, used builder's
paint for the printing, varnished them over and they were washed every
Friday in hot water and soap. How to teach warriors and maidens to
read. I considered, or hoped, that after having picked up the actual
craft of reading per books of their own culture, they would pick up the
J and Js later under their own power; sort of move out automatically
to the dominant culture under their own power.

During my training I'd learnt that a teacher should hear a small
child read solo every day but this was logistically impossible for Kara
and me. I acquired permission from the head teacher to second two
local mothers to help with the reading, Daisy and Mrs. Tuhi, from
eleven till twelve, who were only too delighted to follow their children
to school, dressed up, black hair shining and shoes on. They more than
heard them read; I taught them how to take reading lessons proper,
making four streams under way with me, Kara and them. Some little
Maoris in time were doing the primers in two years, but not enough of
them for me to make my point. I couldn't divine why more didn't do
so. I surmised there was some fine step I'd overlooked. There were large
numbers of young Maoris, almost primitive, doomed to the intellectual
level of the infant room for the rest of their days, ending up illiterate—
unnecessarily, for the tribe of the coast, the Ngati Porou, was an academic breed. I had made the point sufficiently, however, to show that it
could be done.

Keith kept his eye and hand on the number work, teaching me and
also taking my room while I took his for art, acting and choral speaking. He took his own music in the form of a choir. All the Maoritanga*
came from the Maori teachers and in time the whole staff was Maori
but for us two.

The whole large new Maori reading concept was registering in my
workbook and soon I was keeping two workbooks: one indicating
specifically the hour-to-hour plan and the other holding the content of
what we were going to do, in order that I couldn't possibly miss it or
forget. No inspector any more would be able to report that my workbook was too brief. Apart from the dimensions of the labour of preparation, teaching itself was at least easier because clearer, with recognisable goals, and even at times enjoyable. It had this characteristic of
calling on all my home-grown wares as nothing else could that I knew.

* Maoritanga: Maori culture

I think it would not be too extravagant to say that I was no longer going through the motions of teaching only, but was actually and effectively teaching. At long long last after years of training, and seven years of teaching—after twelve years, there was coming to me that desirable condition where teacher and children understood and trusted each other, became at ease with each other in classroom rapport so that discipline came of itself.

I still felt, however, that more young Maoris could be going through the infant room in two years, easily and comfortably like white children, like Ashton who used the white books, but I couldn't put my finger on the missing step and the inspectors when I asked them didn't know what I was talking about. They thought the work should continue to be entirely of the English culture and that the more you hammered it, the better the Maoris should progress, whereas the reverse was the case. I thought it should be even more Maori initially than I already had it and it was the word "initially" that counted. It was not a matter of native intelligence. I just wasn't a good thinker, that's all, and knew I had no brain. All I could do was *see*, and what I could see was that to try to teach the Maori children the white reading was to impose force, whereas to use force for any reason was what made teaching exhausting and tired the children too maybe. Presumably, to teach white children brown reading would equally call for imposition but no one tried that since there was no Maori reading material anyway, till now in my room. And it was here, right in this area of culture and force, where I sensed the vital link was hidden. To try to turn a whole native race into correct English people was to try to turn night into day or day into night.

When the new Tentative Art Scheme came from the department for teachers to try out, based on the latest from Sir Herbert Read, *Education Through Art*, it so answered every question I'd ever asked myself that I sent to London for the book to study it and didn't put it down for about ten years. Along with the scheme a man by the name of Tovey was appointed as an art supervisor with a hand-picked team who went on the schools beat teaching us how to apply it. My own traditional style of teaching art turned a spectacular somersault and blew into the fresh winds of the modern style so that Keith's senior children began producing the most moving work while in the infant room I learnt for the first time to respect the schematic drawing of young children for what it was, captions of the imagery, and how to interpret its meaning.

Flourishing
in the
wilderness

Inspectors came and went, mainly tall men with soft voices, nice people as such if slightly forgettable; not the vibrant people you fall in love with, if that's a criterion. Grey souls in a grey area as are usually found in Cogdom. The brilliant Mr. Ball had left us to take over the army education at Trentham. The inspectors were nonplussed at the new Maori reading scheme and said nothing, just doggedly heard the children on the J and Js, as though no one in Wellington had schooled them in what their response should be to an alternative thesis; a circumstance which still baffles me to this day for we were all aware of the new thinking at the top. The Maori schools service had been trembling and trying not to wake up ever since the new director general, Dr. Gully, had surveyed the scene, a man determined to haul the whole system of education in New Zealand out from the mouldy air beneath the crinoline and plonk it in the twentieth century. As it was, all the inspectors appeared to do was to take word back to Wellington that Mrs. Henderson was not conforming; you could tell by my grading which, instead of improving as my performance improved, deteriorated year by year in a way that a teacher would appeal against or resign over but I couldn't care about it and forgot what my mark was after five minutes. Besides, by now my teaching had so merged with the current of creativity that no man's assessment of me by a number lifted a whiff of spray.

One day a small man in a pale grey suit walked mildly up the path to the school in the morning; a fair-skinned man, pink and white, golden curls, blue eyes and soft voice, all the features of Gabriel except wings. Over lunch in the home science block he smiled across the table into my eyes and I was a goner. That day he did the upper school and had me down for the following morning. I'd picked up the distant beat of the tom-tom and looked forward to his coming like mad, dying to show my work to someone, and laid the roll and the two workbooks on table for inspection.

Quite soon he's on the reading, sitting meekly on a low chair. He doesn't lift one of the hundred-odd Maori books or look at the large floor books with groups of young Maoris reading en bloc but goes straight for the Janets and Johns as though none other existed. He calls little Katy to him first who's returned only today after considerable absence, puts down her Maori book and holds the Janet and John for her, and she stumbles a lot. "She doesn't know this book," he says to me.

"Katy's been away ill for six weeks."

He rises and takes up the roll from the table to check on me and finds the six-week absence a fact, but he doesn't apologise. Then he hears a little boy by the name of Cairo on the same book who reads it right through without fault. "But he knows this book," from Mr. Scagg. "He shouldn't be on it."

"I didn't put him on it. He put himself on it. He learns on the Maori set."

He turns to Cairo to check on me. "Why are you reading this book?"

"Tha's why, me I likes the read."

"But why this particular book, Cairo? You know it. You've finished it."

"Tha's why, you tol' me."

He smiles then calls other little children and holds the J and J, but

Jasmine

they've been learning on the Maori books. For some it's sight reading; some do well and some don't but logistically he can't get round more than a dozen or so as it takes four of us flat out to hear them all.

Soon he leaves the reading and addresses himself to my records on the table. The scheme is still no more than a breakdown of Keith's master scheme and not my own, I don't know whether he looked at it or not, but he examined the roll which Keith watches over, and my two workbooks. Then he did the most unforgivable thing from any inspector, he called me from the children, engaged me in conversation and the classes were left unattended. Kara did her best and did it very well but ...

"Your workbook," he says "is far too full. You don't need two, you only need one and that one should be more condensed."

You can't win. By the time the morning is over I'm no longer in love. The quickest and most effective recovery of all time. As he's opening the door to go at noon I tackle him with heat; uncharacteristically. "You haven't seen my work, Mr. Scagg. You haven't looked at the Maori reading scheme."

He's delighted. "The department has supplied the reading scheme, Mrs. Henderson." So much for the angel Gabriel.

Word filtered up from Wellington over teachers institute grapevines that the man Scagg had been sent to "get" the wives teaching with their husbands, with special reference to the East Coast. We heard he'd been a high school teacher down Christchurch way where Maoris did not frequent at that time, and that he had boasted about having known only one Maori boy. We heard he had been appointed an inspector to shake up the Maori schools and wrench the scholastic level up to that of white schools. Several of the married women had been suspected and insulted and were very upset, as the man knew nothing of the Maoris and less than nothing of their temperament and culture. One said, "If he wants me to turn my Maori infant room into a European high school form, well I'd like to see him do it himself first."

"Ladies, oh ladies," from John above the boogie-woogie, "aren't you giving this cog undue attention?"

Inspectors' reports come in quite soon after a visit while the encounter is still fresh in mind but no report came for me. Months turned over and by the time they had grown to the best part of a year I'd forgotten about it.

Until October. The mail-car came before school and Keith brought my report along to my room before the bell and waited while I opened and read it. It didn't take long, about seven lines on a large sheet of official paper with a letterhead like a subtropical forest. "Not one child in the room recognised one word. The workbook was sketchy and incomplete." Keith read it and stared at it as though he too couldn't recognise one word.

"But K, he complained that Cairo knew his book too well, and others read to him. How cannot one child in the room recognise one word when several read to him? He complained that my workbook was too full and that I didn't need two. How can he say it was sketchy and incomplete? Why does he do this?"

My grading was *nil*. Some on staff scored better than others and the headmaster's was high and even my junior had some marks but we had to wait till lunchtime at the house to talk of it in privacy. "If I'm as bad a teacher as that, K, I shouldn't be on a staff. Not *any* staff."

Keith is unusually grave about it. He's standing by the table in the soft tweeds we love and still holds the report. "Every teacher," he says, "is legally entitled to one service mark a year, regardless. For being on deck at all."

I'm moving about. I'm wearing a dark red crepe de chine smock with a pattern of small bows, black and white, a white tube skirt below and a white satin collar above. "I'll put my resignation on paper tonight and post it in the morning."

"Now hold it, Mij. Don't let it upset you. Don't be carried away. There's . . ."

"Do you expect me to accept a report all lies?"

"It's better to use the word 'error.' Lies have a malicious intent."

"But it has a malicious intent. Would you allow this for any other of your teachers? They've . . . he's . . ."

"Don't talk like that. It's not relevant. There's a reason for everything and a solution. I'll—"

"You can't do anything. I'm your wife. It would be seen as favoritism. And you can't be discredited by a wife who won't accept a report. They've gone too far. They've come right out into the open and exposed themselves. And I don't even know why. Tonight I'll—"

"The first thing to consider, dear, is not to let it upset you. Don't give him the satisfaction of *knowing* he's upset you. After all, that's what Scagg wanted. I'll see to it. I've always stood by you, haven't I? And protected you. I'll—"

"Fancy the department encouraging an inspector to lie like that to bring down a teacher. What for?"

"Will you let me speak? I'll ring George Ashbridge this afternoon." Moves into the hall. "I'll put in my call to Wellington now."

"But he can't do anything. You can't say, Come up and see for yourself whether or not one child can recognise one word because that was ten months ago. There's been time to teach one child one word, if not me then someone else. Kara. You can't win."

He folds the paper. "George is not there for nothing. He's the secretary of the teachers institute on a jolly decent salary." Top-pockets the report and lifts the phone. "I'll ask George to go to the department and have it corrected. No one has to prove a thing like that is wrong."

I pace into the music room and back again. "You can ring George. It's your school. I'm your teacher. But I'm not a wrangler. I'm not wrangling with any department. This is where I stop teaching. Right on this moment."

"I wonder if George will be in this afternoon."

I don't say, The job's not worth it. I don't want to hurt my love, but I would have with some other headmaster. For me the long farce is over. "I don't fight; I retreat."

He doesn't come to my room during the afternoon but after school when the other teachers have gone he follows me to the house and I hear that George was in. "George said it was not possible in a room of fifty-five children that not one child could recognise one word. Some have been there for two or three years; some must have picked up at least two words, even inadvertently."

George rang Keith in the evening. He'd gone to the department, asked for a copy of the report, the man Scagg had been hauled into the presence of senior officers, faced with the report and had been required to rewrite it; it now read something like, "Not one word was recognised by *some* of the children." I can't remember whether the one legal grading mark for service was returned to me or not, it didn't matter enough, but I suppose it was. As for the "error" on my two workbooks, they just stayed in the report which itself went into my files for their future reference, which is the blood-chilling thing about files. We don't have access to theirs.

In the music room in the evening we sit down together and his hand covers his eyes. "Don't leave me, Mijjee."

"How can I stay?"

"I can't do without you. With you at school it's all worth while."

"All I do is disgrace you."

"You bring something to a school that others don't. You draw people to a school. Don't leave me."

"I'm not leaving you, dearest; I'm leaving the school."

"I am the school. Leaving the school is leaving me."

Up again to thrash about. "How can I go on teaching as a marked man, K? I've been a marked man once before at high school. I can't drop back in time to the Janet and John monstrosities now that I've got this far with the Maori reading. I can't let inspectors qualify how I work. It's *my* work."

"Don't leave me. With you there I can do anything, without you I could do nothing. I can't do without you. We need to be together to be effective. We can sail over the top of this crisis if we're together. We've surmounted worse in the past."

"K, if only I—I could earn just as much from writing if I had a clear run at it."

"I'll see to it that you get to your work more often."

"But I feel hunted."

"That's extravagant talk, dear." He lifts his face from his hand and on it is the light of solution, his eyes very blue in vision as they had been when I first met him. "And note this, my lady: *you* can't do without *me*." He stands and puts more wood on the fire. "Where would you be without the school? It thoroughly extends you in every direction, your paint and your piano, and I'm jolly sure it'll pick up your writing in time. Right apart from salary. School doesn't hinder your work; school engages it."

Fact.

His arms around me and the glorious man-scent, the rough of a man's face. "Now I'll make the tea, my Midget. You get into bed and I'll bring it to you. You're far too overtired. In the morning we'll go to school together and we'll ride over this thing."

"Darling, I love you."

"I love you, Mijjee. In the morning we'll—"

In the morning I'm back on the job. In the morning also when the mail comes to the school it brings word of my first publication, a short story in *The Listener* about a little blind Maori girl called Kata on the River titled, "And See, No Longer Blinded by Our Eyes."

Keith was growing in stature as a man and there was not a grey hair on his head. He was growing in stature as a teacher too; it's a profitable idea for young men to be in big positions. By now he had special qualifications in Maori schools and knew how to work with staff who ate out of his hand, both men and women. He was genuinely fond of his Maori staff because, he said, they could take correction; when he gave them a blast for taking it too easy they'd not only laugh but pull up their socks as well, and didn't brood and sulk like some Europeans who resist correction on principle. Some. Except for the morning when arriving at school he was faced with a wire clothesline strung between the domestic block and the main building flying an entire household washing which a married couple on staff had brought to school and put through the school laundry; tea-towels, sheets and trousers flapping away in the breeze; dresses, nightgowns, pyjamas and shirts confessing all that had happened; singlets and underpants wrecking academia, at which Mr. Henderson was not amused. They had to recall the clothes and take down the line and there was not much laughing that morning, though it did make a story which Keith told later.

And he frankly loved his Maori parents, who'd do anything under heaven for him, bar nothing; from a district show at the school with entries for cooking, handcraft, handwriting, art, Maoritanga and sewing, a class which Ashton entered because he liked using the sewing machine, inadvertently winning the prize with forty pairs of girls' shorts—to a signature of new pines planted round the boundaries of the wide bleached glebe, for shelter, for heaven's sake. Though I think that particular school committee was one of the tougher ones with its resistance to expenditure on books; it thought the department should see to the books. But I'd say that was Keith's good gift; his relations with his districts were love-affairs.

The roll was over two hundred by now—I think, I could be wrong—and the department was generous, from powdered milk to classroom equipment and extra staff. He was at peace with the Maori schools department and clocked up grading marks as En-Zedders gathered toheroa on the seashore. Yet he never visited the department for any reason and he didn't say why not.

The way this man had grown and expanded and fruited from the slender tentative boy I'd met two decades ago, yet one Sunday afternoon with the wind rushing at the house and the black and white plain at its bleakest, I had to witness his tears: "I'm lonely for white men." Oh yes, he knew loneliness too but to the point where it paid a dividend in wisdom, intelligible wisdom and earthy. It would be too easy at this point to slip into saying he had a sense of mission; I don't think he did, but I don't know. Not in his thirties anyway.

What I did know, he was simply a kind man who went the extra mile and turned the other cheek; not only to his school and district but he was kind to us at home, but you had to know him a long time, outside the family I mean, before you found this out as he was not a man to sell himself but something of a man of mystery. In speech he could put his hand on the words he wanted but only on a subject removed from himself. You only knew what he really meant and felt by what he did; you could read it in the famous wood fires in winter, in the Saturdays he gave to splitting and cross-sawing logs on the riverbed with Jim Griffin, the roadman, in the breakfasts he'd cook for us all in the morning and in the time he gave to the children. He could even live with me and I don't know what other man could have. He'd bring me tea after I'd gone to bed with a buttered maltmeal biscuit, and a cup of tea in the morning to get over the night and can any wife ask more than that? My lover, provider, protector and head-master and I loved the man madly.

There came a year with the war over when Madame Lili Kraus, a celebrated Hungarian concert pianist, was released from a Japanese prison camp in Java. Before the war when she'd been on tour in Japan a Japanese officer had attended her concerts and when he found her in the Java prison of which he was commandant he had a piano delivered to her compound. Now, she came to New Zealand to collect herself, upon which the government granted her New Zealand citizen-ship. In joyful response to the welcome and four years in an Asian prison she travelled from one end of the country to the other giving concerts, into the furthermost recesses of the backblocks on any con-traption with a keyboard, opening up Schubert, Mozart, Brahms and Bartók to the heathen. Everywhere but to the East Coast largely popu-lated by Maoris. But for one trip to Gisborne with the Shaws we heard her only on radio.

 Along with other teaching wives on the coast I usually had to take a week off mid-term some time during the year from exhaustion, flu or nervous strain, though I never had flu, when you applied for a week's sick leave with a certificate from Dr. Grant, and pulled yourself together again. Faced with the routine mid-term sag I applied as usual but in a marvellous moment of suspended responsibility I told the department I wished to take the leave in Wellington during the winter season of Madame Kraus, giving them the real reason that as music was one of my subjects I wanted to meet her, and I named the dates. I'd send the certificate nearer the date. Then I got to work on the bookings; three days and nights to Wellington by service car, railcar, train and hotels and the same back, if you could call that rest. But no reply came.

 It would also be a chance to see the director. What I'd do, I'd take examples of the children's art arisen from the Herbert Read scheme

and Mr. Tovey's in-service to show him, whose controversial new education policy was enraging the country. I might even tell him about
the new Maori infant reading; after all, whose word did he have?

I made two gorgeous books of the school work—one large with big
pictures and one small one of sparkling gems—mounted and bound. I
had no intention of seeing Hilton Morris, called Pan, as I'd never
pursued a man in my life, and left insolubles like love to Fate.

As my dates approached and still no reply I obtained the medical
certificate from Dr. Grant, who knew me well from Horoera days,
prescribing a week's rest or more, wrote again and sent it, but still no
answer. I and the children trailed over to school on Sunday to Keith
who was in his office doing his letters. "Why don't they reply, K?"

"I don't know that you're going the right way about it. They mightn't
like it."

"It's for them to say yes or no, isn't it?"

"You can't go, Mij, without their permission."

"I must go. I need to go. I've applied twice in three months. I can't
have my life de-railed by the vagaries of men."

There came the eve of my departure and late at night the telephone
shrieked; a telegram from the director general himself. "Do not leave
your post. Gully."

We are standing in the hall by the phone, my travelling bags near
the door for the early morning bus. "You can't possibly go," from K.

"Not go?"

He takes the paper from my hand and examines it. "I don't like the
look of it."

"Not go, did you say?"

"We'll talk about the rights and wrongs and reasons later but don't
you go. You can't possibly defy a directive from Dr. Gully. It's not
safe. You stay and I'll see you have a rest. You can go to Selah all day
every day and I'll see to the children. Piri makes the mid-day meal and
I'll give them their breakfast and tea. You don't need to return to the
house at all. You're always so happy at your work you'll forget it in
no time. The children . . ."

"Not go at all? My clothes ready, the books, my bookings and
tickets and the reliever arranged?"

"Dear, you need to take a careful view of this. There's a great deal
at stake. You're tired enough. Now you get into bed and I'll . . . and
in the morning we'll . . ."

"K, how is it I can take sick leave in Waiomatatini but not be allowed to take it in Wellington? I need to see and to hear this great artist who'll be gone soon. It's inspiration in my work to brush with the great. If one man is in the position to hold dominion over my soul, arbitrarily, then the job's not worth it. That's one of the old values: obey unconditionally. I don't go along with it. I have new values and that's the old."

His blue eyes upon my face.

"Life wouldn't be worth it," I say.

"You're talking in extremes."

I take back the paper with the message on it: Do not leave your post. Gully. "Why didn't he say so before?"

"An oversight I suppose."

"No, it's autocracy. Intimidation."

"I'm going to bed anyway."

In the morning he puts me on the eight o'clock bus for Ruatoria.

In Wellington to hear Lili Kraus

I stay with my youngest sister, Evadne, in her apartment on the Terrace and tell her nothing. Her young husband has been killed in Crete and her little girl is at Marsden.* Next morning at nine I take a tram to the Maori schools department in Government Buildings with the sample work from our school. Upstairs I'm closeted in a dull panelled waiting room with the football star inspector, Bob Bletcher, even larger in girth and voice than before, and the secretary half his size, Mr. Albert Flake. "What are you doing here?" from Mr. Bletcher.

"I'm on sick leave, Mr. Bletcher, as you know."

"No you're not. We've granted you no sick leave. You came to see Lili Kraus."

"Yes. I told you."

"You're going to be dismissed," sepulchrally.

"What for?"

"Disobedience."

My nerve's not too good with white people. "But I'm on sick leave. You have my doctor's certificate."

Mr. Flake leans back, his face aside, but his eyes slurred towards me. "We don't accept the doctor's certificate. You came to see Lili Kraus."

---

* a girls' boarding school of reputation

"Yes. I also came to s-see Dr. Gully to show him samples of our children's work. We've been operating the Tentative Art Scheme up there. I've been studying Herbert Read's—"

"That's got nothing to do with it."

"I'd like to see Dr. Gully please."

"He's not going to see ya." A hint of the football field diction. A trace of snarl in it. "You're going to be dismissed. Ya cime ta see Lili Kraus."

I stand to go, Fluke Flake shifts the position of his feet and big Bob Bletcher says, "Come back here tamorra mornin' at noine o'clock."

I tram back along Lambton Quay to the *Evening Post* building where the office of the teachers institute is on the third floor, to see George Ashbridge. George is our secretary, a man easily as big as Bob Bletcher and who's never been known to be downed when defending teachers at the department. But he's not there; only the editor of *National Education* is there, a very small slight soft-spoken man who'd never be picked for a football team or for a school inspector, who says George is doing the rounds of the island territories. He agrees to go to the department on my behalf in the afternoon but as he admitted later he'd been carried from the field. Descending in the lift I reflected that in the education game, apparently physique was all.

Nine a.m. next morning at the department finds an exact repeat of the former scenario: big Bob and Fluke Flake with their lines word-perfect but Bob's diction is reverting to type. The two of them fast qualifying for a role from Dickens set in the slums of London. "Ya cime to soy Lili Kraus."

I've brought the samples along again. "Will you p-please tell Dr. Gully I'd like to see him."

"He's nokkuna soy ya. He's gunna dismiss ya."

"But you have my certificate."

Fluke Flake flares for once, his diction adapted to his role. "We've mide an appointment with a Wellington doctor of our arn choice. Dr. Bowen will soy ya on Thursday afternoon at two o'clock."

The thing's an inquisition in the Spanish style of the Middle Ages, right in the heart of the twentieth century. "Ya cime ta soy Lili Kree-ows." Yet both these men had good English before. Bob's snarl has a grating in it now. "Come back here tamorra mornin' at noine o'clock."

It's true I'd come to see Lili Kraus but I should have been devious about it. I walked round the street corners to the Broadcasting Building where Madame practised in their studio all morning and sure enough

there she was through the glass doors at a marvellous six-foot concert
grand playing Stravinsky, running trilling cascades of broken chords in
the minor tumbling over one another and she turned and smiled. A
handsome amber-skinned woman about my age with thick heavy
black hair to her waist which she wore in two hefty plaits. Her husband
was on guard outside the door, much older than Madame, with grey
hair and grey shaped beard and a face where smiles lived, who chatted
away merrily about life in Vienna and about the conservatorium there.
You wouldn't believe he was of the same human race as the inquisitors
at the department. The climate here was kind to the soul, serene and
beneficent. Music's version of education.

Next morning at "noine," the chamber. This effective technique
they'd cultivated in holding down teachers, like the Japanese drip-drip
of a tap on the same exposed spot. Was I really one of their teachers:
a wife, mother and . . . and what? Nothing else. What would they
put on my files this time?

Round at the broadcasting studio again Madame invited me to turn
the pages of the Stravinsky, which I bungled as I could not keep up
with her. At noon on Perrot's Corner I watched her return on foot
along the Terrace with a male companion to the St. George Hotel where
they said she ran everywhere along the corridors being one who practised yoga. Watching her crossing the street carrying her music satchel
I reflected on her desirable manner of life; the wandering musician
selling her wares, singing for her supper. My own desired manner of
life which I'd not so far achieved. All kinds of people, places, adventures, one country after another. But where were my wares? The department didn't want them. All they wanted was an obedient civil
servant, not even a good one, and for me "not to leave my post."

In the evening I attended her recital in the concert chamber where
she ran across the stage in plaits and slacks, where I heard a mainly
Schubert programme and once again the Schubert Impromptu in G-
flat Major. Afterwards I went up backstage and found her sitting on a
chair with others standing about her and she said to me, "Vat iss zor
broblem?"

How did she know? I could only smile.

Next morning the department, same men, same routine and same
directive to return next day. Why? To make sure I didn't relax and
rest, that I didn't enjoy Madame, to make me feel I was still at school?
I wouldn't like this disgrace of mine to affect Keith Henderson professionally but I wished there were someone to save me. The depart-

ment technique was softening me up. The second time they'd censured me to the point of persecution whereas the only thing a teacher could be dismissed for was immorality. What was at the back of it?

At the studio I confessed to Madame's husband vot my broblem voss: that after travelling three days and three nights over the volcanic plateau to hear Madame I was on the point of being sacked from the profession, and he invited me to attend wherever Madame was playing, and also to join their family and entourage next Sunday afternoon, which tidings I wired back to the coast, so they'd think all was well with me, knowing nothing of the reality. They couldn't do anything from the wilderness.

In the afternoon I sought out another studio at Broadcasting where the symphony orchestra was in rehearsal and Léon de Mauny who was conducting allowed me to sit in with them.

At this distance I can't sort out those days, one from another, but towards the end of the week my will and my courage had so eroded that my heart was turning to porridge. I didn't tell Vad a thing. I didn't want my shame to be seen. Pan should have been looking after me, he and his wife Meg. Did he, a close friend and colleague of the director, know what was happening? His offices were only on the Terrace, a block or two from Government Buildings, and at night he'd be at his home on the hill. One twilight I stood in the shadows across the street for a cold while, not to accost him but merely to see him leave at five for home. Waiting in the Wellington winter I thought of him and pondered on the meaning in the kisses of men. I didn't see him but when I reached home at Evadne's place I wrote him a note, every word of which I remember: "Dear Hilton: I'm in Wellington at my sister Evadne's place. Will you come and get me and take me home to Meg? Sylvia."

To which I had no reply for thirty years. Until a long letter to me when we were both in the United States saying, "Wherever I go in educational areas I hear your name. Sylvia, where are you?" As I read it I saw again that half-hour in the shadows across the street from his offices and the note I wrote later calling him, Hilton, where are you? And I thought to myself, I'd rather have had a short note then, Hilton, than a long letter thirty years later. I supposed Pan had been faced with a choice of loyalties, his career and his director versus me, and he'd stood by his boss and his job. It would not be fair to say that his kisses had been invalid or that his love had failed the test. It had lasted all this time. Holding his long, impassioned letter I could at last see in hindsight that the whole long-drawn-out shady drama had not been a matter of Maori reading or of seeing Lili Kraus at all, but of a rather juicy jealousy in the rare air at the top; a personal contretemps between two men, one of whom had adored the other since boyhood. Pan must have praised me to the director as a teacher and innovator, let slip his feeling for me, and the higher man hadn't liked it. That letter from Pan in the States seven or eight years ago still exists and I haven't answered it yet. As our Maori housekeeper on the River, Ruth, would say, "All over a love, Sylv; all over a love."

But I didn't see these things in Wellington that nightmare week; I was all love and longing for Hilton, expecting to see him round every corner. I was wearing a wonderful white polo-necked jersey, self-designed, and hand-knitted by a lady in Ruatoria, with a knitted-in smocked yoke, a black tube skirt and high-heeled shoes and many other men looked at me. It was not Hilton who looked after me but Madame Kraus and her husband who were neither civil servants nor native New Zealanders. But I still hear Pan calling, Sylvia, where are you? Thirty years too late.

By the time Thursday came and the appointment in the afternoon with the department's Dr. Bowen, I clearly needed it. In the morning I could hardly mount the stairs for the rack-session with Messrs. Bletcher and Flake. I couldn't believe the director general, aware and brilliant, was only upstairs and wouldn't save me from them. I'd practically lost trace of what my offences were: something about Maori reading and a Hungarian pianist. Yet they still said, "Come back here at noine in the mornin'. You're gunna be dismissed."

Dr. Bowen was only across Lambton Quay, a dark good-looking and amiable man with none of the cog-marks of the civil service, and the next thing I was telling him everything, not leaving out the part where the certificate of a fellow doctor had been rejected without referring to the doctor concerned. No doubt he had his own thoughts on the whole show and he was professionally discreet but I did pick up a strong sense of understanding and sympathy. At least he conveyed to me that all would be well and that he'd send his certificate over to the department that afternoon. He seemed so concerned about me that he prescribed me medication to calm me down. Talk about a friend at court.

I still kept everything from Vad and in the morning, Friday, I went up the stairs like a delinquent on probation reporting to the police, where it was apparent at once they'd heard from Dr. Bowen, for their diction had come back on the rails. The "agents" dispensed with any more drip-drip treatment, they admitted in quite good English that their own doctor had exonerated me and, far from dishonoring my week's sick leave, had increased it to a month or more. He'd also recommended that on no account should this teacher be dismissed. Then they excused me from reporting again on Monday morning and "gave me permission" to return to the coast or to stay on in Wellington as I chose. But their new attitude warned me that the director general had lost face before his department, whatever this might cost me professionally in the future; the reckoning from Flake's mistake.

And that was the morning, after descending those terrifying stairs for the last time with all my poor nerve-ends still in disarray but still a shining morning, that I swept back along Lambton Quay with the walk I'd learnt from our pregnant Maori housekeeper in Horoera, and bought presents for the beloved at home: a simply marvellous with-it outfit for Jas, an electrifying book for El, an engineering kit-set for Ash and a shirt and tie for K.

Vadne said in the evening when she'd heard it all, "Whenever I see a woman in trouble I bet my bottom dollar there's a man at the back of it." She stretches her legs before the fire and her arms go behind her head. "By God, Sylv, I'm glad there's none of them here at this moment."

Another sherry.

"You ought to wake up about men, Sylv. You can't play honorable with men."

"Who the hell said I was honorable?"

"Daphne."

We attended together the Kraus concert on Saturday evening in the Town Hall where I'd danced my youth away in spangles and diamantés with every naval officer who came into port but where I still looked among the glittering audience for a man called Pan. Madame was no longer in plaits and slacks; her epic black hair was piled high on top, there was so much of it, she was gleaming all over in white soft satin and she skipped across the stage to the piano. But I forfeited the Sunday afternoon with the Kraus family and company to get on the train at the Wellington station, back to my desired wilderness; to the cluster of people out there who loved me.

I dealt with the sample pictures, of course, when I got home. In that infant room was a very fine tall wood stove asking for exotic fuel, but

I didn't let Kara see it. Burn as you go is my new motto: bonfire every two years. The Czechoslovakian corsetière in Wellington had said when fitting me for a bra, "If I had a bust like that I'd go places."

"I do."

You want to travel light when you're going places.

Selah Five among the sentient sods. The travails of my spirit drove me to Gerard Manley Hopkins, who is very good company when consulting your instincts. Why, I challenge God in mind, have you apportioned me gifts when you won't let me use them?

He replies willingly enough, Because I like my tools sharp.

But I'm no tool of yours.

It's not, He says, for you mortals to say. It's I who chooses the steel I want, and I who tempers it in the furnace.

But I spend half my time in the furnace, God. What for?

Because, He says, you're such substandard metal.

Then why bother with me?

There's work to be done, of course.

Well, can't you pick on somebody else?

Many are called but few are chosen.

Occasionally on a Friday night after shopping in Ruatoria other teachers' families might come back to our place to eat and drink and talk and generally get over the week and there's a scene here in our kitchen with the Shaw family and another family at our large scrubbed table and I'm at the stove browning the potatoes as Puppa used to do. The dialogue is lifting with the wine until John halts his knife and fork and says squarely, sanely, "Sylvia, are you an artist?"

I go on browning and I think. A pseudo-artist would giggle, evade the point and play coy, but I've got to be true to myself. Cost what it may. "Yes."

It's the other family who giggle and smirk. Philistines. But not John and not Leslie either. Their knives and forks remain poised. "How do you know?" from John.

"My mother told me."

It's marvellous the thinking one can cover when looking the other way, like practising on the very good English piano in the infant room which has oversized acoustics with its echoes. Or with Keith helping me to put up a brush fence between the house and the plain on account of the unkind wind. He cut and brought the manuka while I stood it up and bound it. In our late thirties then, the terrible thirties, I looked the whole thing in the face and tried to work it out, for I wanted to be sure that life was worth living so that I could live it. At this intersection in the journey, detours lured all ways; art, music, writing or teaching and a big road sign with an arrow pointed to FEARFUL FORTIES AHEAD, and another read DECISIONS HERE. A road patrol on a horse advised briskly, And don't be too long about it. And get it right first time. You pass this way but once.

There were crowds of other young people in their thirties at the crossroads but they were less disposed to examine the road signs than to forge ahead along the highway nearest at hand. By the wayside was a long open shed with the words CHECK EQUIPMENT HERE so I went in. Any number of others sat thinking on the benches so I did too. I took things out of my haversack, a sugar bag with a strap like the one Keith had made on the River.

Any brains? Not a grain. Well, what did I have to replace it? Instinct. Right, so I'd cultivate this to serve as a compass. What next? Art. Plenty there but functional only. Home-brewed. Music? Having met Lili Kraus face to face I'd soon learnt that an effective pianist is a transmitter really between the composer and the listener, like the seemingly cold piano star Solomon, whom I'd seen playing as though preoccupied with the veracity of his visa more than with the message of the music, or like the Austrian Artur Schnabel, delivering the composer intact through the keyboard in "the way of most resistance" as even Madame had not wholly achieved, her woman's emotion having too much to say; whereas I was the most flagrant interceptor ever loosed on a piano, wearing the glory for my own adornment. All I had was the fever of the passion, unable to control the momentum of practice. Also, in the complete absence of any musical interchange I'd developed a personal interpretation and a rogue style that no professional would ever accept. "I don't know," from Sophie years later, "that Sylvia has any technique, but it's very exciting when she plays."

As for the poor old teaching, an excellent source of income no doubt but not my chosen work. On the other hand, it called on and mopped up everything I had: any art, music, writing, language, walking, dancing, study, responsibility, people, appearance, clothes and even falling in love. A marvellously comprehensive medium on an incomparable stage if only you had the aptitude and desire. Well, my record at the department supported what I'd always known myself, that I'd never be a good teacher, though you'd think I'd not been able to avoid picking up something about it after all these years of training and in classrooms, wouldn't you; but even though I'd thought I was doing well, after the inquisition with Bletcher and Flake, it was obvious that I wasn't. I was some kind of monstrosity lost its way in schools. Temperament trouble.

Which left only writing, the last in the running, with its accompaniment, study. From Herbert Read I'd become acquainted with the nature of the mind of a child, any child, including me. True, I'd had but one short story actually published but I'd got the message. In my non-stop novel, unruly native imagery found a channel through which to surface, clearing out on its way the delirium of both music and paint to enrich the main stream. Writing siphoned off the effervescence of dreaming, the constant opposition party, and there was discipline required for that. You can't think at all with a heart in uproar over longing for Opal and Pan, neither of whom I'd heard from in years. You learnt what mail was when you knew what no mail was. When you're in love with life your vision becomes blurred with dreaming and the solutions were to be found right down in the lower caverns of the mind where emotion combusted. Coleridge: "Touch the true voice of feeling and it will supply . . ." the answers.

Checking my equipment in the wayside depot I could at least see that for the journey not to be boring I myself had to be not bored, me the most profligate hedon who had ever squandered her inheritance. What was the operative condition then? "And the greatest of these is charity." Without that you'd be drier than the boulders beneath the soil of the plain. Juice had to rise like sap in the spring, the lubricant in making love. You'd have to be lightweight as the birds in the kowhai on the unreachable hills in order to lift up high in the sky above the white-lipped plain and to see like a morning skylark.

Replacing my gear in the haversack I returned to the crossroads. After all, one did have a choice and I'd take the writing road. The decision was no weight, it was water to drink for anyone going places.


When the polio epidemic ripped round the country in the summer holidays so that all schools were to remain closed indefinitely, we thought we'd find casual jobs, for getting a break from Waiomatatini at Christmas was an axiomatic priority. Usually Keith took the children over to New Plymouth to his people while I camped by some romantic lake like Okataina, went south to my own people or stayed home alone to work; none of which was a good idea as we all missed one another too much. At Lake Okataina I left my tent and moved into the Fishing

Lodge where I helped serve tea to the tourists and played the piano to the guests in the evening and kept on side with the proprietor till my family returned and took me.

From the Labour bureau in Gisborne Keith obtained the last job they had on their books, manager of the motor camp at the government tourist resort at Lake Waikaremoana in the heart of the forest. The catch was that it was a dual job and the wife had to do the laundry at Lake House. "K, the thing's too silly. Me doing the laundry when I run a housekeeper at home to do our own. What would Piri say?"

"Piri doesn't have to know," from Jas.

"But," from El, "if you don't take the job, Mummie, Daddy can't take his and that means us staying home all the Christmas holidays and a long time after."

Keith: "It would be a jolly good place to keep the children away from the polio. I don't know I'm sure."

"Wouldn't it be terrible if the staff found out: the headmaster's wife a laundress?"

Ash said, "Would there be boats on the lake, Dad?"

I drew out my superannuation, twenty-five pounds, with which we bought two new tents and a second-hand trailer and I told only Leslie, "I have to do it for the children. A holiday and safety in one hit."

We had a daughter of my sister Norma in our household that year to keep Jasmine company so we were six and the next thing we were all at Lake Waikaremoana in the heart of the deepest forest. A heaven of a place. Other children arriving at the camp had to be turned away by law so our four had the lake and the boats to themselves. When we walked into the foyer of Lake House we were received with respect as guests until I registered at the desk as the new laundress, a moment which pointed up the difference between a profession and domestic service. That was terrible.

Keith took over the camp and the shop and I woke up in the laundry at the back of Lake House at the top of the bluff above us. The hotel was up a very steep track through the towering trees with a postcard view out over the lake, entirely surrounded by forest. The managers, on the payroll of the government, were Mr. and Mrs. Foggo and this is one of the tales I need to prefix with "This is true," if you don't believe it. I might add this is not to be found in my files at the education department and has not been told to this day.

"By the way, Mrs. Henderson," from Mrs. Foggo, "you eat with the staff."

"But I eat with the family at the camp."

"You're on the staff and you eat with the staff and you should be sleeping in the servants' quarters." I didn't.

Two things solve most problems with me: tea and a piano. One afternoon between showers with the laundry on the line I drove five miles round the lake to Tuai, a hydroelectric station settlement where I excavated an embattled rattletrap in the YMCA hall and yes I could use it if I didn't lose the hall key. That road down the gorge into Tuai . . . Before gathering in the laundry from the lines at four I'd duck round there each afternoon and practise. One day, however, as I wandered out of bounds round the front of Lake House I heard a piano in the lounge and while the guests were at dinner in another wing I took to using that one also.

When Mrs. Foggo finally caught up with me she didn't blast but surveyed me speculatively. "We could do with you in the lounge after dinner, Mrs. Henderson, for the guests."

Music draws all kinds. Fortunately for my dual identity most guests stayed less than a week, but two European men there who knew their classics were disposed to linger; how to keep from them that I was in fact the laundress and that, after playing to them in the evening, all glamour and scent and earrings, I was doing their sheets and towels in the morning? I'd changed my name in the lounge to Lotus until I all but forgot who I was myself. Risks accumulate in a double life. The near-misses of being unmasked belonged to a whodunit. "Where are you all day, Lotus? I've tried to trace you for a week but you only surface at night. Could you spare me an afternoon on the lake?"

Mrs. Foggo had me helping in the kitchen on Christmas Eve making date savories, if you want to know, for the holy guests . . . among the four cooks and kitchen boys. Then she spin-bowled me from the kitchen to the crowded lounge to get the guests going on Christmas carols which is child's play to any teacher. As the drinks whizzed around, the singing lifted and soared out over the water and echoed through the listening trees until when they'd sung themselves empty and limp I took a header into a formal recital of the masters to the most marvellous audience in the world, and when I too finally petered out towards midnight and rose from the keyboard what should I meet but a crash of applause and you bow this way and you bow that way just like Lili Kraus and the two European refugees took me by the arm to their table for coffee—and what about a cruise on the lake and where was I to be found during the day? But I couldn't stay any later on account of the laundry early morning—*theirs*.

Well there's no time or room here for the rest of the stories at this time—what about the Hastings couple who actually *did* track me down to the laundry lighting the fire under the copper at seven, and kept the secret, and what about the stag party in the lounge when the hunters and fishermen hired Lotus from the Foggos to supply the pianowork—at least I know now what a stag party is. I'm afraid I was caught out twice by people whom I desired and who dropped me overnight but I'll leave that out and try to forget it. But it had to happen. So much for the fortunes of war. Men of course; the bloody New Zealanders.

I didn't see that job out to the finish on account of what the concrete laundry floor was doing to my feet and on account of the extra help they sent from the Bad Girls' Home who brought her chewing gum with her. That mouth action was like the crack of a whip on a straining horse or the split of a branch in a storm.

Waiomatatini with the polio over, sitting with Leslie in her car on Saturday morning in Ruatoria. "At last, Sylvia! I think you were wonderful to do it. Now tell me what it was *really* like."

"I can't talk about it. The humiliation left a scar on my soul. But," remembering, "I gave eleven recitals at Waikaremoana and found another source of income. As hotel entertainer."

Mr. Woodley came, a friendly thoughtful man whom we'd known for years, big like most inspectors and well acquainted with the Maori people, including me. He took a long comprehensive look at all the new Maori reading, heard many children read from both Maori and white books and was down on his knees with them on the big floor books and seemed to be relaxed and pleased. He said so in his report, mentioned the wholesome tone in the room and hoisted me back on the grading rails as though I were really a teacher. On the other hand, being due to retire, he was in the position to make his own judgment, having nothing professional to lose.

A rolling teacher gathers no moss. After four years at Waiomatatini soft winds whispered of other places, other faces, new skies to explore. Moreover it was time to return to our own. With the teaching ranks depleted by the war and the post-war birth rate swelling, married women teachers were wanted on the job outside of Maori schools and the Shaws had already gone. More partings. The lure of change, but you pay for it.

Before I leave this scene of the married women teachers in Maori schools I'm moved to put down this word: the husband and wife were a team and the school became part of the home; an extension beneficent on the children. Our children didn't come out of it too well but I'm speaking of Maoris. Except for the effect on white children and on the health of the wife it was profitable from whichever other angle you look at it. Whatever either did, it was for the other. Everything had point. For a start you were together all day and that's lovely in marriage. Then you had this common interest; there was always something to talk about, however polar your natures, which interested you both so that the lines in the old-time church marriage service flowered in minute-by-minute fructification. The common work, especially the "for-others" nature of it, turned both minds outward, bound the marriage together, however inadvertently, all of which made not only a fertile home but a fertile school and brought out and up the best in both home and school. When they returned to the white schools, they brought with them the tolerance of temperament they'd learnt when working with the Maori people, and a flexibility in the timetable that was new and humane.

Jas had been at boarding school in Gisborne for about two years now; we sent her there at about twelve to give her a chance to adjust to her own culture, so imagine how we felt when for her first holidays she brought home with her not a European but a Maori. Well, we nearly fainted from surprise. But she was a beautiful girl who trained as a dental nurse later and was probably better adjusted to the white race than Jasmine herself. Poised and brainy, from Whakatane way. After that Jas chose her first sister from the world, and she went on doing it all her life, supplying her own sisters.

By now it was time to give the boys priority, who were entitled to live some of their own lives among their own kind: a matter of the English language at least, as well as of values. Ash had managed to wrench from the Maori community a token friend for himself, a charming boy, but Elliot didn't know what a friend was. He'd be in Standard 6 next year and Ash in Standard 5.

We applied for a small two-teacher school six miles from Hastings, a job known as a plum on account of the town and the high school. Although Fernhill was administered by the Hawkes Bay education board who ran European schools, this roll was largely Maori and the board was calling for teachers with Maori school experience and music and art. It would be a drop for Keith of course, professionally, but it had to come some time for a man not prepared to go on staff. Returning to our own culture after an abysmal absence it was a time of reckoning. Keith sailed in on high grading and I was part of the deal. Waiomatatini had cut me down to size but Keith had increased and prospered.

I have this picture here in mind of Waiomatatini: the long modern open-air school with its supporting buildings at nine a.m. in the morning; the hundreds of children assembled before it, staff among them, and the young headmaster up on the verandah trying to say goodbye. The school grounds spread over a large area of the burnt white plain and around the boundaries grow Keith's signature in pines. He looks so young up there. He'd known great success here and much good love from the Ngati Porou who'd extended him to his limits in professional levels. But as he begins his farewell there arise signs and sounds of weeping in the ranks, one here, two there, and one of the women staff breaks down. Suddenly Keith himself covers his face and the next thing here's a true Maori *tangi** at school. And that's what I'd believed to be the end of the Waiomatatini story until another old old photo surfaced from the past reminding me of how the whole school, teachers, little ones and all, followed K to the gate, lined up along the fence and watched him drive away.

It was miles and miles south on the main road before we two recovered but Ash and El were full of delighted talk. There still remains nothing more exciting than changing schools and soon you couldn't hold any of us down. Our last trip down this coast. Exhilarating, inebriating to the point of wings. Four skylarks in a car. Picking up Jas from her high school in Gisborne pro tem we lunched en famille, the five of us together, at the Gisborne Masonic where in the dining room who should come over to our table and sit with us a moment but The Sir himself: Sir Apirana Ngata. "So you're taking your children out for their education."

He thanked us for all we'd done for his people and said to Keith, "Well done."

* *tangi*: weep

# Fragments

FERNHILL   Only two on staff, Keith and I. Somehow I was to substitute for his former full staff. We were still at the hotel in Hastings when we took over on Monday morning, and two Maori girls of about twelve, Hilda and Mere, at once picked up Keith's mood of dismay and tended the two of us as though we were the original babes in the wood. As there was nowhere on the school glebe to make the tea—no staffroom, no office, no power point, teapot, cups, no nothing—they brought trays from the Karena home across the road with white starched traycloths, silver teapot, dainty china cups and they baked sweet cakes for us, morning, noon and after school until the residence was ready, speaking to us in tremolo voices of apology accompanied by soft bare feet until their desired new headmaster finally smiled.

I've already written three books on Fernhill so I'm brief this time round. Two of them, *Spinster* and *Teacher*, about my work there with small children, are still available in the U.S.A. in hardcover and numerous paperbacks, and in translation in a few countries, though no longer in New Zealand and London. In them I have recorded in detail the surfacing of the key vocabulary in the context of organic teaching, to ease problems of reading and of race and personality and to lessen delinquency; not only for young Maoris and not only for young pakehas but for people of any colour and age, including myself, outside the area of brain damage of course; a key of universal dimension.

   I can't go back into all that again now but I can put down here the formula of teaching by the key vocabulary which I perfected when working overseas:

"Touch the true voice of feeling and it will create its own vocabulary and style," its own power and peace.

Supply the conditions where life comes in the door: let it.

Supply the conditions where the native, inborn imagery of our child can surface under its own power to be captioned or named, harnessed, put to work and to make its contribution to society.

Supply the conditions where the impulse to kill can surface to be isolated and defused.

Children were reading the very first day effervescently and the inspectors saw for themselves.

Fernhill school

*Teacher* was written first, which was my version of a scheme. In fact it was a thesis though I was the last to know it. I had, after all, studied a great deal since Horoera: Rousseau, Herbert Read, comparative religions, the Bible, Gerard Manley Hopkins, Blake and Coleridge; the English poets, French literature, history and poetry; Russell, Freud, Jung, Adler, and Fromm; Maori mythology, history, culture and the language; the lives of the musicians, music textbooks, and even ploughed through Havelock Ellis, believe it or not. Everything except education. My level of learning, experiment and engagement as I see it now, but did not then, probably could not have been too far below a doctorate, with *Teacher* my inadvertent thesis, though it hadn't crossed my mind.

Inspectors borrowed this "scheme" to help other schools working with Maoris and visitors came to the school, mainly from the education department, so that one day, in fact, I submitted the scheme to the department but they lost it and didn't answer till I wrote for it and it came back without comment. However, since I myself recognised it for what it was I sent it to three New Zealand publishers, one of whom said the style was inappropriate, the second said it was before its time and the third after nine months still hadn't read it when I recalled it. Neither would London have it, though for different reasons, while New York was not so far mapped on my reality at that time, so the scheme, my thesis which was *Teacher* in disguise, waited on the shelf in two Selahs for nine years.

In the meantime, still at Fernhill, and since I believed in *Teacher*, I rewrote the whole story of the key vocabulary in the form of a novel so it might sell, employing drama, suspense, love, disaster, unrequited passion and dialogue and created a new character in place of myself, a spinster; not only remembering the priesthood of senior unmarried women who had tried to train me when young but also because of the circumstances of my life at that time: a molten infant room in experiment, a household of seven, and the artist in me holding her ground. How wonderful to be a spinster: it was a job of wishful thinking and I loved it. But no; New Zealand with a population at that time of about two million had not yet staged a major novel, and with good reason, and the leading houses again turned it down in these "lonely latitudes." So it wandered London for two forgotten years looking for a home until it came to rest at Secker and Warburg, the house which had reared George Orwell, and where I met a good editor called John Patterson.

The Fernhill residence. The shed at the back is Selah Five, where I wrote *Spinster* and *Teacher*.

When the proofs came out I sent a copy to Opal whom I hadn't seen for two schools—foolish euphoria. I deserved what I got: a laconic remark that it might help the Maoris a bit, and when the published copy arrived, an underground stream of hostility swirled round from N.Z. men educators and teachers from the director down, who told a friend of mine, a journalist and poet, "I can't stand that book"; all of whom I've privately named the PSBMEH—the Permanent Solid Block of Male Educational Hostility.

On the publication of *Spinster*, 1958

London took *Spinster* over to New York where it fell into the hands of a young editor by the name of Bob Gottlieb at Simon and Schuster (then, not now), and within a year *Time* magazine described it as a "major literary masterpiece." At the end of that year *Time* chose *Spinster* as one of the five best novels for 1959 in the English language. Although it was on the best-seller list in New York, none of this got back to the New Zealand press, until MGM bought it and was almost in N.Z. to film it when it sure *did* reach the Godzone* press. The director general, however, had no trouble in keeping MGM out of Godzone—I was told all this by a member of the Maori National Executive—which turned out to be a good thing in time when we saw for ourselves the Hollywood travesty they made of the book. By which time New York *was* mapped on my reality. The third book arising from Fernhill, though written later, was of the eternal conflict between religion and physical desire called *Incense to Idols*, a shocking business which weeded out my fans overnight but which nevertheless managed to get sold to Twentieth Century-Fox. What I heard was that the leading executive bought it for his French mistress to star in but that after a sensational row in Paris in which the American film man sued the French actress for "intellectual and physical cruelty" (I heard there were other reasons) that story never reached the screen, an ideal fate for your work: you are paid for the film sale but escape the public mutilation of your book. Yet *Incense to Idols* also was named by *Time* as one of the five best books for the year, and again failed to make the Godzone press. It's past the time to take a look at the New Zealand

* Godzone: abbreviation of God's Own Country

Press Association agent in New York and to ask him what he's there for.

The fourth piece of work from Fernhill was the set of four Maori reading books, graded and disciplined and with 123 original illustrations in watercolour and line, but I've already covered that subject in *Spinster*, though thoroughly soft-pedalled. Until Fernhill the education department had held in its hands the fate only of my teaching, which could not matter too much, for my own true work, my home-grown wares, was out of their reach, but there at Fernhill my work fused with the bloody profesh at all levels so that its fate too came to be at the mercy of Cogland: the Bletchers, Flakes, Gabriels, inspectors, the director and right-hand men. As it happens, the inspectors at Fernhill were civilised peaceable men, all very tall again for some reason I can't put my finger on, who approved of my teaching, helped me with the reading books by lending me a historic typewriter and supplying me with a junior. Their later performance only throws up another insoluble.

I had the books beautifully bound in hardcover by a printer in Hastings, made an appointment with a publisher well known for its school publications and its interest in Maoritanga, took them to Wellington myself and passed them over the desk to the editor, from my hand to his, without one word as I simply could not speak, he being the first and only editor I've ever met right up until this day. I told Vad in the evening with whom I was staying, "He loved them. The missing link, he called them, in Maori education. He's calling a meeting of directors at once and asked me to wait till Thursday."

Evadne quoted Puppa, "By Jove, Frank, that's a caution." She was already a practising artist. "But I still say, Sylv, you ought to back out of that teaching." She's a small dainty woman, being the last of a crowd, but is much bigger than I in vision. "Look, Sylv, even me; my work coincides with my income but I don't have to be a teacher about it, thank God. You run the risk of being shot out of the sky."

Another red sherry. "I can't get Henderson to see it, Vad."

On the memorable Thursday I visited the editor-publisher again in the flesh unbelievably, to be told that the directors were delighted to the point of jubilation and planned to put them through at once "but first we need to obtain an advance order of ten thousand from the education department and if you agree we'd like to take them there this afternoon."

And that day the fateful step was taken: my work was put into the hands of Cogland, "the soldiers of the Queen my lads," to adjudicate on and to judge, which looked all right to me. They went to the Maori schools department for the word of the senior inspector, and who was that? No less than our Mr. Vicarage who knew Keith and me and our work inside out. Presumably he also knew the Maoris inside out having been on that beat for years. Mr. Vicarage had known the picture of the Pied Piper on the school wall at Pipiriki and had pressed to preserve it. Nor had there ever been any hazardous emotional complications between us since I'd never fallen in love with the man. I called them the Transition Books for the young Maoris to learn to read on first, and from there move into the white culture books.

But what did our Mr. Vicarage do? He didn't make the decision himself, the man most qualified to do so, but submitted them to a white senior infant mistress in Auckland who'd never taught a Maori in her life and was saturated in Janets and Johns. Why didn't he submit them to the teachers on the East Coast or in other Maori strongholds who'd learnt the hard way? Insoluble.

Mr. Vicarage sent me her letter at Fernhill, the original, not a copy, a foolscap page in handwriting, green ink, and I read it in Selah Five, the shed at the back of the residence, with the frost squeezing in through the cracks in the walls and the cold sophisticated spiders. Who was this pronouncing on my holy work? A stiffie in the heart of a city. She disapproved of the schematic style of the illustrations, watercolour and line, was horrified at the real life drama in the *pa** in the text, and denounced the whole idea of Maori reading books. After all, she argued, what point was there in teaching Maoris at all other than to instill the British culture? The books were suspect on all counts. Any more of this deliberate subversion and the British Empire would disintegrate. (It would anyway.)

And that's the last I heard from Mr. Vicarage; they said he had a bad heart and that you should see him trying to mount stairs in hotels on his rounds, stopping and resting on every step to preserve his breath. He retired after that and went to Spain.

So the Transition Books came back to me by registered post with a letter of regret from the editor and took up their new position on a corner shelf in Selah Five, somewhat humiliated after having thrilled to the spotlight, where a spider reflectively read them. Read them very well too. A Maori spider, I'd say, with emotional problems. In *Spinster* I had the teacher, Anna, bury the books but that was only fiction

* *pa*: Maori settlement

We are seven
now.

protecting the real life performers with whom I was still working at that time, and I was far too timid to take them on and show them up. A scandal would have damaged Keith.

Some time later for various devious reasons I gave the Transition Books, *gave*, to the senior teacher as a present saying with disgraceful subservience that I thought they'd be more useful with him than with me but really, I think now, as a cover-up action to hide from any of them my defeat in disaster; don't expose yourself to the philistine again but in fact, as it turned out, there was no evidence that he ever used them and I never set eyes on the books again.

When Keith and I were moving from Fernhill, however, I rang the senior and told him I couldn't bear to leave them behind and would he lend them back to me for a while to

take with me. Yes, he said he would, but he couldn't at the moment
put his hand on them. He'd look for them, he said. So I had to leave
them behind.

At the new place I wrote to him quietly enough inquiring after the
books but he didn't reply. A colleague of his wrote on his behalf to
say that the senior had inadvertently burnt them while cleaning out
his office. The colleague said he regretted it. And I'm not writing cover-
up fiction now. And that's the true story of the Maori reading books.

We were both round forty and more at the time: a blazing age, a
do-or-die stretch of life and the momentum was a bush fire. These
were high hot days at Fernhill. Jasmine had finished high school in
Gisborne a year too young to go to training college so she took a year
at home with a job at a bank in Hastings, her chosen sister André came
to live with us, Elliot and Ashton were still at home attending high
school in Hastings and Daphne's son came to live with us, making
five great ravenous teenagers; with Keith and me we were seven. A
comprehensive two-tier dinner every night, a large bowl of rhubarb
Keith kept full in the attempt to keep the holes in the boys filled, and
homework everywhere. As well as teaching I was writing *Spinster*.

With the peak birth rate from the war years then hitting the schools
the board had planted a pre-fab in the playground which I and my
junior commandeered at once, and two more European teachers were
appointed, one with a class in the porch, making five, so that Henderson
was finding himself extended again. School called on everything he
had and was too, and I think he was another of the lucky ones with
work and income from the same source. From him the school had
found an identity and a new spirit arose in the tribe, the Ngati Hau
subtribe of the Ngati Aotea. Keith and I and the school were in full
bloom to the point where my private work actually fused with teaching,
believe it or not. My capacity to get over and forget recurring disasters
and betrayals rated as another craft again. I could even conceive the
idea of a future as a teacher side by side with Keith provided the
department let me progress and not keep me treading water, and if the
artist in me would sign the deal.

But that artist was no romantic wraith feeding on dreams any more;
he was a monster from outer space inhabiting the mind, a ruthless
invader, demanding, fierce, bumping round knocking things over,
jealous of the school and not prepared to accommodate either the wife
or the teacher. The monster was the other man in the home whom I
knew Keith resented, however consistently he helped to supply the

conditions for my work, from support at school to fires in Selah and to giving me time. A man could be expected to be able to contain a physical rival whom he could see and fight and rout, which in fact had already occurred at Fernhill over a man in a pulpit, but what chance had any human husband of shaping up to a lover intangible, invisible, yet voracious and permanent? If Keith also feared him he had good reason. Very seldom would Keith mention my work or praise me for it but I knew why and I'd learnt not to bring up the subject. In the interest of domestic harmony I'd keep the monster out of the home, lock him up in some Selah apart from the house, a Maori whare, a cave, a sod hut or in the shed in this back yard where I could go to him like a secret paramour and let him have his way with me, then return home again as a wife. Two distinct lives.

It was the woman whom Keith loved, the wife and mother under his feet at home with a homely apron on. We were never so happy as in the kitchen preparing dinner together, both with aprons, talking about our children intimately, about the jokes at the Gala Day at school on Saturday, the marvellous concert in the pa last night or an inspector's funny visit, praising each other gratuitously, generously and grandly. I think he liked the teacher at school as a lively mate, up to a point, but it was the woman at home he loved.

Divisions only came when something made me want to break away from the school when our voices became formal and tea grew cold in the cups, but even then we avoided the real issue, the other man in the home, skirmishing harmlessly on the surface. My line was usually in his interests: ". . . but I'd be replaced by someone much younger, K, who'd keep her records without your help and who wouldn't make mistakes. She'd do her own Attendances at end of term, get all of those massive totals right first go by herself and keep a workbook that wouldn't baffle inspectors. And she'd write the kind of scheme that everyone else does that's not lofty philosophy and she wouldn't be tired all the time. And if she were it wouldn't be you having to look after her at home, putting up her feet and passing her tea. You'd end up with the normal rights of any other headmaster to be looked after himself when he comes home from school. You wouldn't be preparing half the dinner in the morning before school. A new and a young infant mistress, not married to you, would make much easier going all round. Someone with brains and common sense and a mind of her own. No temperament. Temperament doesn't make a teacher; it wrecks a teacher. I'm fearfully sorry about it."

And Keith would usually support my interests: "If only you'd be calm and not apologise all the time. Now listen, dear, we both know about your ideas running away with you. A hasty decision is not the answer at this point. Bear in mind that all you've achieved has arisen in the setting of the school itself. You'd miss it dreadfully. You like people. It's not all a question of two salaries; surely I can support my family. I don't know I'm sure . . . You can be a writer but you can still be a teacher. You've proved it and I've proved it. And you've been saying for years now that you've come to like teaching, you've often said it. You've been happy at school, you've said so and I've seen it. If I haven't helped you enough I'll help you more. Have you ever gone into Selah early morning and not found your woodbox filled and your fire set? We've had these crises before and in the morning you've changed your mind.

"I am the school. For you to leave teaching would be a divorce in the school. We've always agreed we can do anything together."

Skirmishing only, for neither stirred the real issue, not in words: the other man in our marriage. The artist locked up in Selah. That was a matter of living and of dying involving us both when I'd book my cabin on an overseas ship, of knives and blood to the death between the headmaster and the monster, which he knew all right and I knew but which remained unspoken till death did us part.

The disconcerting factor was that since my work had fused with teaching, its fate was now at the mercy of the philistine. By now I was not only a good teacher and knew it but also our inspectors said so to Keith by word and in our reports. With the idea of staying with Keith I even set my sights on training young teachers in the organic teaching right there on the spot in Fernhill as an extension of training college, but of course that didn't come off; one idea that didn't get away with me. But to stay teaching with him I had to advance and not mark time. On the road I had arrived on a very high promontory of fulfilment where the air was rarefied and exhilarating, where there were great views of the intellectual countryside, of many stars in the emotional sky with miles to the clear horizons, where your spirit spread wide on the wing trusting tricky fate; nothing was hopeless and everything possible.

Until the mail-car passed one Saturday morning when Keith was in bed with the flu, leaving our grading in the mail-box; Keith's headily high as usual but mine punitive beyond any teacher's professional recovery. Where had it come from? Not from our local inspectors but from someone faceless. But why? What for? As I sat on the end of

Keith's bed in my long scarlet housecoat pearl-buttoned from chin to toe my resilient spirit snapped clean in half once and for all and I groaned and held my stomach.

That afternoon when Daphne blew in all fun and news and we were sitting under the tree at the back she said, "What's the matter, Sylv; sick or something?"

"No, just tired."

I did not at once leave my love at school until an advance royalty for *Spinster* of one hundred pounds flopped on the table between us—a moment to clasp my sad breasts about, to hold my heart together. Then the knives were drawn at last by my headmaster and my monster and the two of them fought it out to the finish: seven days and seven nights of combat. To all appearances the monster won, I'd stop teaching, but only because, as was revealed later, the headmaster held forces in reserve; that in time he'd be in the position to apply for a bigger and more desirable school where, after a year or two's rest, I'd surely return to him. Not that he told me so in words but you're not married to a man for nothing.

The students

I wrote a short correct letter of resignation to the Hawkes Bay education board, not trusting them any more with what I really felt, but saying platitudinously I was finding the school and the home together a bit tough and that I would like a rest, and they wrote a brief formal reply releasing me in December but I wished they had expressed regret. It must have been about then I gave the Transition Books to the senior as I'd no longer be in class to use them.

The Maoris gave me a farewell in the pa; astonishing to be honoured as a teacher in my own right independently of any headmaster . . . fancy that. I couldn't believe it. True, it was I who supplied the dazzling children's programme for the evening, but it was they who laid Maori gifts on the stage. How was it that the Maori people themselves saw me to be adequate as a teacher? I replied to their tributes in Maori.

But when the new school year opened in February I no longer followed Keith to school in the morning.

This part of my story is finished, me no longer with Keith all night and all day. I was in the wilderness myself, having fallen into the hands of the philistine who, on that high plateau of boundless horizons, had ambushed me and hurled me over a cliff upon the rocks below where I'd broken every bone in my heart. A matter of survival alone now, of groping my way where no road was. Seeking some stream for water to drink and food like rose-hips and raupo. If ever I found the highway again I'd travel differently, except that I no longer sought the highway; I liked it where I was and had already reverted to type. From being the life of the party I'd become reclusive. My adulthood was bracketed in dream and I was a child again.

So there's no need to close Fernhill on a downbeat, and in fact it rose to an upbeat. Keith worked there eight years piling up grading marks, not only to see the boys undisturbed through high school but also to be in the position to survey the scene and pluck a professional plum, which turned out to be a large Maori school under the administration again of the Maori schools department which he was still nostalgic about; Bethlehem was only four miles from Tauranga on the most beautiful harbour in the South Pacific up Bay of Plenty way. Most reluctantly I agreed to put in eight weeks relieving there in Standard 4 to please, to mollify him, which he hoped would lure me into a permanent position but which turned out to be beyond telling about at all. But after *Spinster* he told Vad, not me, that he regretted it and that he wished he'd freed me much earlier. Well at least he *said* that.

Jasmine had finished training college, had married and we had our first grandgirl, Corinne. Elliot was at university in Wellington and Ashton was having it out on his own in Hastings and we had come full circle; on our own again. It was spring in Godzone. With a choice school upcountry for Keith and the prospect of me back on staff with him did the sun come out on that face. Nine years to go and he said we'd . . . he'd retire in Tauranga. Second honeymoon time. The shining morning arose when we two set out to drive up through the heartland of the North Island over the volcanic plateau to the promised land by the sea.

During the time at Bethlehem other books came: that long first novel I'd learnt to write on, *Rangatira*, in all sorts of Selahs, which emerged as a stormy saga of brown versus white in several parts: Greenstone 1 appeared in serial form in a N.Z. journal; Greenstone 2 found its way to New York in 1966, but Greenstone 3, which I called "Tenth Heaven," the most impassioned and turbulent of the lot, I've not been able to get published to this day. They all say the characters are not credible and since they were all portrayed live from the River, of course they weren't. No one was credible there and I couldn't make them so.

Then came a minor local story, *Bell Call*, followed by a good book, *Myself*, the diary I'd kept on the River. All came from Simon and Schuster with the hand of Bob G upon them, except for "Tenth Heaven" which did not convince Bob either. I still might rewrite "Tenth Heaven."

BETHLEHEM    I'm writing in Colorado this piece about Keith, while I'm in my romantic grey and white house on the corner, opposite the Aspen meadow, across from the Aspen Institute. The meadow is feet deep in snow at this time like my unsophisticated heart, but I remember the wildflowers in the summer.

He liked working with the Maori schools department again which had a history of partiality for its Maori children and which gave him anything he asked for: equipment and funds through more staff to extra classrooms, though he had never crossed their doorstep. He thought the education boards who ran white schools made insufficient effort to humanise the condition of Maori children in their schools; the way their culture was put aside and their language forgotten and they lost their pride of race to become periphery pupils whereas Henderson believed the priority for Maori children was to attend a

Maori school until at least twelve in order to confirm their racial and spiritual strength; a condition from which to venture out into the dominant culture with more confidence in themselves. "The day Maori schools go over to the boards," he'd say, and there was growing talk of it, "will be the day I retire." As it turned out that day coincided with the very day of his formal retirement.

By now he'd come to like the Maori people very much; their personal warmth, their laughing, their cultural gifts, their distinctive temperament and above all, I think, their increasing need of him, arising from their racial minority status making them second-class citizens, which touched his compassion and drew from him the spirit he'd inherited from his father so that over the many years with them had grown a rapport between the Maoris and Keith Henderson; in his last two districts he'd made the dearest friends among them whose names were often spoken in our home. "Why don't you," white teachers would ask him, "take on something your own weight, Keith? A European school in town?"

"Because," he'd laugh, "they are ulcer factories."

"But you'd have a bigger salary, man, and a house in town."

"I can't see my wife in a street."

What I thought was that he felt extended.

Keith had to learn that he *could* do things without his wife at school. True, he kept me in and out of all the concerts, running prose and poetry and oratory competitions and receiving weighty guests, but I was not on staff. He'd had stylish young infant teachers in my place, at Fernhill when I resigned and now at Bethlehem, who could stand on their feet till midnight at large school functions as well as hold down a class; also there were Europeans, but the staff was mainly Maori. No doubt good teachers are drawn to a good school, but this was a particularly good school in the first place on account of Eric and Jay Naumann whom Keith had followed. He found the tone like clover honey and the energy innersprung.

With Keith the school continued to spring as I had seen before; the roll grew with both Maori and white children, the staff grew, both Maori and white, more modern classrooms were built and a lovely new administration block, the delight of his life, including a library and above all an office measuring up to his dreams, light and airy with flowered curtains, not to mention a new secretary, Joan, and in time he became a walking headmaster with no obligation to teach. At Bethlehem he planted many trees but not pines this time; they were

Bethlehem—
the school

carefully selected English and native trees including a few kowhai. Visitors were always coming and he trained a few children, both races, to run out to the gate to meet them, converse with them and welcome them, strangers in particular, and there were plenty of them; local and overseas people like the Commonwealth scholars from Central and South America, all night-black, North American observers, Rotary exchange scholars from around the world including young men from Malaysia and Indonesia, Polynesian teachers from the Island Territories, the Prime Minister Mr. Nash and above all no less than Sir Herbert Read from England who, with Lady Margaret, stayed with us at the school residence; all of whom were joyfully entertained by the children with oratory and waiata (songs) so that those receptions were something to buy new clothes about. Of course the school, though bi-racial, still ran into the usual European hostility—"the terrible Maoris" sort of thing—but you can live with that. The cameo I hold most from Bethlehem shows Keith crossing the road to school in the morning and here are all these little Maori primers running and taking his hands, four or five a side, and you'd see him lay a hand on a head.

For all that, however, being in his fifties now, he was looking forward to retirement for although he held to his own values he was conscious of his old-time training and not prepared to grind through the new, which he felt to be a fault in himself and he'd tell me it was

The residence

time he gave way to a modern young head. On the other hand, a school can still keep up-to-date provided your first assistant and infant mistress (supervisor of junior classes they call it now) attend frequent in-service training and provided you give young teachers fresh from training their head with the new ways; when the new math exploded he had Abel go to town and learn it to return and teach the others. But he still thought it was time to move over.

His own way of life, however, was beyond any new curricula or modern math. In Keith the practicalities of teaching had matured into spiritual dimensions, manifest in his actions if not in words. As he had done since his first tiny school at Whareorino he would move out from his home into the people about him, child or adult, brown or white, except that now the field was much wider; he took his turn as president of the headmasters' association, an office he happened to be holding when the governor general, Lord Cobham, was visiting the Bay of Plenty, which called for a speech at the assembly of children in the Memorial Park, and I'm not mentioning that speech for nothing, he would be secretary of two or three committees at any given time and he even attended the rate-payers' meetings. Wide enough.

Until Rotary picked him up to represent primary education and opened the field much wider still and where, against all rules, he was secretary for three years running and from which he helped establish the Maori Education Foundation to further the education of teenage Maoris. From there he would organise teams of Rotary cars to take old people out on a Sunday afternoon for a drive round the beauties of Tauranga, bringing them back to the school for tea and a few songs from the children, and he'd join Rotary working bees on a Saturday morning chopping and delivering firewood to the aged in the winter. Many a sad widow he'd call on to listen to her loneliness: coming home late for dinner, "By gee, it's a shame. There she was standing at the bus stop so

Visit by the governor general, Lord Cobham

I picked her up and she said, 'Mr. Henderson I'm not used to bus stops. My husband always drove me to town but he didn't teach me to drive the car and now it's sold. I'm so bewildered. Fancy catching a bus, *me*. To think such a thing has come to me.' I don't know I'm sure."

Along with school and Rotary there was the entertaining at home. After parsonages and residences all his life and school residences the whole of my life we built our large home, Whenua, on the harbour front: a long stone house on a long high bank overlooking the long blue sea, designed for full-scale gatherings and to house overseas guests, mine as well as his, with a music room half the size of a hall opening out upon a deck to the water and I remember him standing out there looking at the harbour entrance and saying, "Look, Jas, a ship coming in. That's my good luck sign."

Sometimes the staff came to Whenua and often Keith held his Rotary meetings there. After his time in the wilderness he loved his friends in that club, more than I'd known him to love before, with something like adoration, and although he had always liked teaching it was Rotary which opened the biggest door of all into the life of the people. "Service before Self" was their motto. I have found reason

since to believe that Keith was heading for public life when he had
finished teaching. On the other hand, Rotary itself found Keith a
useful member and in time he was invited to form his own branch
club in our home suburb of Otumoetai as charter president; to take
his first meeting in December and to be inaugurated the following
year. His nine-year peroration to retirement.

Keith's last day at school was to be December 19, 1968, a Thursday,
which, believe it or not, was the very day Maori schools as such were
to be abolished and put under the administration of the white boards,
so you've got to allow for miracles. But Keith had been sickening for
the last two years and during his term in Bethlehem I'd had occasion
to sit at his bedside in hospital more than once while we learnt the
languages of X rays and surgery, subsequently to nurse him back on
to his feet again and to his work.

A year before retirement, however, found me sitting at his bedside
in Auckland three times a day for six weeks which still didn't stop
him from returning to school the next year or from completing the
fencing on our lower land to graze a soft Jersey heifer on it and you'd
see him on a Saturday morning conferring with Susie and stroking
her throat as he'd conferred with his Jersey cow at Pipiriki. In hospital he'd ask, "How's Susie?"

Only the family knew how ill Keith was and one or two Rotarians,
but as he entered the last fortnight before retirement his physician and
his surgeon were pressing to get him into hospital again but he was
determined to see out his time.

"They want you to go in now, K."

"Wild horses won't make me."

End-of-year and farewell functions were banking up at school but
his interest was muted by his love for Rotary. What concerned him
most was his first meeting of his own Otumoetai club as charter president on the last Monday; whether or not he could make it. The first
of the functions was the Maori farewell at the Judea pa. Ashton had
been abroad for a while and he came up from Hastings for his father's
farewell, and as the three of us walked on to the *marae** early evening
the sun was setting redly, mercilessly, blinding us briefly to the festive
crowds.

Within the meeting house later they presented a superb Maori programme of waiata, haka and *poi*†—songs, war dances and other danc-

---

* *marae*: meeting area in front of the meeting house
† *poi*: a Maori dance with pois

ing inspired by Maori singing and rhythm. Then they gave their headmaster a set of Maori lintels carved by Toni Te Kaokao of Rotorua for the outside door at Whenua, and a Maori mat plaited in flax by a *kuia** on which they said Keith's spirit would forever abide. And it was there that night where he was appointed a *rangatira*—Maori chief—of Ngati Te Hangarau, Ranganui, one of the few white men, to my knowledge, to become a Maori chief. An air of celebration effervesced but along with Ash and me sitting with Keith, only Jas and her husband David in the audience with four of their five children, Corinne, Grant, Adrian and Kirstine knew how ill Keith was. He was all smiles himself and the photos next day in the paper told nothing.

At home that night he did wonder if he actually would get through to his last day the next week. In any case, he spent the whole of the weekend at school trying to tie things up for his successor next year, but what I wondered was whether he would get through only to the following Monday to initiate his new Club; there were three functions on that day. In fact I rang his physician, Dr. H, and asked him to take Keith to hospital at once and he said he would get in touch with his surgeon, Dr. G, and get things organised, but when I told Keith this he said, "I mean to finish off what I started. I'll see my time out and retire on Thursday."

In the meantime there was the schoolchildren's farewell on Monday morning where they gave him a red leather swivel chair for his desk and we had a few jokes on stage about who was going to sit in it first, and at five he actually succeeded in opening his precious Otumoetai Rotary Club after all as charter president, but from there he had to dash back to school at seven for a major school end-of-year break-up with its speeches, the heaviest function of any year. And that was the night when we got home when he first said, "I made it." But I knew which of the three ceremonies he meant: opening his own Rotary club at five.

During this last week journalists and photographers were on the job and the papers were full of him. Photos and reports in the local press, the Auckland *Herald* ran an editorial about his dedication and stature and about what a relief to see a man of integrity and ability directing his work towards others. The Auckland *Star* covered the whole editorial page with an account of his life and work, but when he'd return

---

* *kuia*: old Maori woman

late from school and I'd show him he could only say, "How I wish I were well enough to enjoy all this."

Tuesday was the junior school break-up involving Jasmine, who was on his staff, but his surgeon rang me. "We've seen the X rays, Mrs. Henderson. We don't like the look of it."

"Is this it?"

"This is it."

It was my birthday but no one remembered.

I told Keith when he came home but he said, "They don't know what they're talking about." To Keith it was only a matter of hanging on till Thursday, having another operation Friday, after which all would be well. I told him to go in now but he'd have nothing of it. Then realising these next two days would be his last at Whenua I sent a telegram to his physician saying I would keep Keith till Thursday.

Early Wednesday morning I drove up and met David at his road gate and told him Keith's number was up but he didn't believe it and I left it to him to break it to Jasmine. At home I rang Ashton in Hastings and then I rang Elliot in London, who'd been away six years. "If you want to see your father again, El, you'd better come soon."

A blood test in town after school for Keith, home before five, then

The farewell

Challenging
the visitor

A Maori *haka*
(war dance)

straight off to take two of Jasmine's children to the Rotary Christmas
party and I went to walk in the garden.

A summer evening after dark with the sea at full tide and the
lights of Mt. Maunganui. I walked beneath the towering trees and

the scents of the quiet flowers and consulted the harbour in which a high pale shocked moon gazed at her own reflection. Out in the great world I'd sought as a child I was a celebrated writer and educationist, but that was no anodyne now. Over the lawn through the shadows and moonlight, round the camelia, under the karaka, back over the lawns through the shadows and moonlight waiting for him to come home again for the last sweet time. Yet when he did return in his suave sleek car he seemed so happy about the children's party and he told me much about it, but I still sat with him through the relentless night nursing him through the last hours at his own first home; a man of smiles by day but not at night. Yet there was never such a dawn at Whenua; the birds tuning up from four a.m. on, the dark tide excelling itself, tree trunks black against the sky and a ship coming in, all to witness a big star falling from the southern Pacific sky.

When morning came it was Thursday at last with only the staff luncheon left, after which I could take him away.

A large staff now, all Maori but for his secretary Joan and Jasmine. They sat Keith at the head of the table with me on his left then got down to feasting and drinking hilariously, spinning with laughter, and they sang to him with their guitars for over an hour into the afternoon, all these tender and tragic love-songs about meetings and partings in Maori and in English, harmonising with abandon; a heady recapitulation of all the joy he'd known working with a passionate people as the sun flowered through the curtains, all these brown Maori eyes full to the brim of him. And he sang too, I couldn't believe it, when he must have known he was soon to die and when he was presented with a leather executive case with his name on it in gold for his future Rotary work and when he stood to reply he still managed not to reveal his fate in his speech. It was only when they sang, "Some day, my love, there will be songs to sing; although the snow covers the hope of spring . . . You'll come to me out of the long ago . . ." that he suddenly clenched a fist and hit the air.

It was still he who drove the car home and when we were collecting his things for hospital he told me for the second time, "Anyway I made it." And he told me, "When I was in town this morning people were stopping me in the street. They were coming up to me and shaking my hand." But when I showed him the paper with more word of him he could only glance at it. "I'll read that another day."

So he walked out on the deck and remembered the harbour— "There's a ship coming in; my good luck sign." Then down the steps to the car where instead of taking the driver's seat he at last got in the passenger side and leaned wearily back. "I got to the tape," he said.

Driving towards the Otumoetai causeway he noticed the petunias in the triangle, a celebration in bridal white, and a hand lifted. "Look, the flowers."

I take a room at Norfolk hospital and when Keith comes out of the anaesthetic on Friday I have good news for him. "Elliot's coming," I say. "He has compassionate leave from his university and he'll be here in January."

After a while he remembers. "That beautiful letter he wrote to me on my retirement." Another wait. "I don't know I'm sure . . ."

I'm sitting in his room keeping vigil while he is sedated and looking out over the sloping lawns in the high summer sunshine when his physician, Dr. H, comes in. "Doctor, I'm going to need a trained nurse when he comes home and a . . ."

Doctor's voice reproves, "He's not coming home, Mrs. Henderson."

"Who'll go and bring me a newspaper from the desk?"

Jas and I cringe, "Those Sisters . . ."

"Are you brave?" he says.

We both know what he means. He's trying to tell us he knows.

"I'm brave," from Jas.

"I can take anything," from me.

We all three know what we're talking about and Jas goes and brings the paper.

His room at Norfolk hospital is too beautiful to be dying in; white French doors open out upon curving lawns with scarlet rhododendra and through the tall trees the water is hushed in summer introspection. From my low chair by the door I see most people, his most loved friends from Rotary. So quiet they are, more tender than women, with men's capacity to look out from themselves, without the demands from women; and when they come I absent myself to allow them their final communion: men who drew from him more joy than any other men in his life. I'm not there when he talks to Lionel, and when Ashton comes I go. But I frequently remind him, "Elliot is coming." "Your sister is an angel," he told Lionel; his last word on me.

On Christmas Eve with the late sun farewelling the rhododendra, the scents from the garden inebriating and the blue harbour water thinking it over, his surgeon, Dr. G, comes; elegant, courteous and with the poise from long arduous years of the life-death confrontation and he tells us together that Keith has no future.

"Is there no place for hope at all?" from Keith.

"I myself never abandon hope," he says, adding, "Wait and see."

After he has gone, whether by his design or by chance, we both hear the Christmas carols from across the lawns with all the weight that carols carry and Keith says to me, "Oh well . . . I've had my life and I've had my honours. We've taken our knocks and we've had much joy. He said wait and see and there's a measure of joy in that. We've accepted this blow together and we'll face it together." Then he adds with force, "*By God* I'm glad I went through the process of retirement."

Before sinking into sedation later, "As for that other thing, forget it. We'll live from week to week." But it's only from day to day, from night to night; when Keith wakes they wake me.

On Christmas Day they bring us our very last Christmas dinner together and set it on the bed table with one red rose. Chicken and champagne. He tries the chicken and I have to see him sip the champagne but what could we be celebrating? "Elliot is coming," I remind him. Our Christmas present from God is the rain.

All these nuances of greys on the harbour, dark grey The Mount. The flowers, the trees, the lawns and the scents absorb our grey mood of life's ending. As he is sleeping I'm writing:

> January 6, 1969:
>
> It is better for it to be raining
> while my love lies dying
> better than hot sun on his pain
>
> > the rain
> > has harsh grey loud appreciation
> > of life-long lovers parting
>
> > > but the sun on the harbour water
> > > on the slope of the delicate lawns
> > > on the sedated rhododendra
>
> > > > the sun
> > > > knows nothing of us two parting
> > > > knows not the pain of death
>
> > > > > it is better for it to be raining

Elliot runs into Whenua terribly happy to be home but pale from the London skies; with black hair curly upon his forehead and dark blue eyes like Puppa's he's a wan Romeo straight from Shakespeare. But it's late in the day and Ash and I hurry him to Norfolk where I rouse his father. "Elliot is here, K. Here's Elliot, K."

Keith opens his eyes upon Elliot.

"Here I am, Dad. Can you see me? Do you know me?"

His father smiles and speaks his last word, "Wonderful." Then closes his eyes again.

Keith died the following afternoon, Tuesday, January 7, 1969, at twenty to three, nineteen days after his retirement. In the night a prophetic storm rose in which a mighty macrocarpa in the city was split by lightning and felled to the ground asunder so that in the morning Maoris rang one another saying, "Some chief has gone in the night; who was it?"

The afternoon papers told them, with a photo of Keith Henderson on the front page, captioned, "Friend of the Maoris." Above that was a full-scale picture of the macrocarpa tree in its final prostrate form and I heard there was much white shock in the city as few had known he'd been going.

The first funeral service was in the morning on the Judea marae. Three weeks after Keith and I had walked on to this marae one evening for the Maori farewell in the meeting house we arrived again together but this time not side by side. He was carried in first through long lines of his schoolchildren to the shrill of a kuia's lament, to be lowered on the verandah of the meeting house where a chieftain's cloak of kiwi feathers was laid upon him, while I followed with Elliot.

The second ceremony was held in the afternoon at a European church in the city with the kiwi cloak still laid upon him and where the oration was themed with the motto of Rotary, Service before Self. Capacity crowds attended both occasions, Maori and pakeha, and later in the afternoon Keith was buried with the rings he'd given me long ago; he sleeps in Tauranga now, New Zealand, his promised land by the sea . . .

. . . while the snow falls outside my window in the mountains of Colorado.

# I V

# WEST WIND

1969 - 1973

*March 30, 1969*

MAURITIUS    From the sky above the Indian Ocean, after a night and day flight from the South Pacific, you see a drop of green paint upon the blue—Mauritius. On that island of sugar cane down there, eight hundred miles east of Southern Africa, the family of Elliot's French wife have been domiciled since the French Revolution. Elliot himself landed there two weeks ago on his way back to London to meet his people-in-law. I might be able to live there myself. "You could do worse," Elliot has said, "than settle near Jacquemine's people."

The island had belonged to the French up till the Napoleonic wars when the British took it from them, though the culture has remained French; Baudelaire once visited Mauritius. It's an independent state now. The brush drop of green is spreading on the blue like wet paint running.

At the Hotel Le Morne where Elliot and Jacquemine first take me I don't see any place for me to live; all I see here, along with the glossy tourists, are the cockroaches zipping between the sheets, the lizards sprinting on the walls and the many African servants. Moreover, with no air-conditioning, the heat swells my feet up to one last pair of shoes, sequinned sandals, and serves me a bout of food poisoning so that E and J decide to move me up to what they are pleased to call "the highlands" of Curepipe. "The best hotel please, El."

"There's only one."

The Hotel Vatel turns out to be Dickens material or, since the culture is French, Balzacian. Fewer cockroaches maybe but the lizards are swifter and although I open my typewriter it won't be here where I live. Nor do I see anywhere else in Curepipe though I do wander into residential areas. Many of the shops are run by Chinese, the post office and civil service by Indians, the bank staffed by Jews and the menial work done by Africans while each nation, I'm told, runs its own schools. But although I've not yet seen any of the white European French, other than Jacquemine, the language and the spirit of Mauritius remain embeddedly French.

Articulate, picturesque population as I return to the main street and walk among the multi-racial crowds; Indian, Chinese, Jewish and African with no sign of the European French until I see ahead a wan Romeo with English colouring and in a white shirt, head and shoulders above the Asians; my own race, my son. He sees me too and I quicken my step and embrace him in the street, "Elliot."

"You were not at the hotel so I worked it out. Have you heard from Tel Aviv?"

"No. El, if I don't go to Israel I might go to a friend in California. I don't know that I could live with insects the size they are here. Look at my legs. As for the *heat*—look at the size of my feet."

"I need a drink of water."

"Hotel, come on, hotel. I'll give you a drink of water."

We walk side by side through the alien crowds and he says, "I've been having visions at night of water; cold bubbling streams as I knew in New Zealand. Waterfalls and springs."

"I'll put ice in your water."

Plenty of communication between us three, E and J and me; Jacquemine, slender-boned, olive-skinned, dark-haired, Paris-educated with Sorbonne degrees in psychology and sociology and with very good English as a second language, and Elliot who speaks French with the facility of a first language. I've hired a car for El since I've arrived and one day the two of them take me into the country, E and J, to show me a cottage they've already chosen for me but it's Lilliputian: pocket rooms, porthole windows, low ceilings, musty and with a thatched roof—*thatched*. What about the insects? And what about no hurricane shutters? I've got to say it, "There's not enough light, El." And they both seem disappointed. I'd thought Elliot knew me better.

I continue to ask E and J to show me a school, but the time is never quite right. But I do come upon a less frequented street, a family group of little Chinese children on their way somewhere, thoughtfully dressed, smiling and happy. What would their key vocabulary be? What would surface from that national serenity? Ancestors? Rice? Family? Shrine? I happen to know the first drawings of children in mainland China are flowers. What would the fear words be; do they have the hidden impulse to kill? I'm inclined to doubt it; they seem so happy. They all seem to be first with one another.

Driving in the country with my African taxi, Jojo, I see a dark slender child walking behind her mother, the two of them carrying firewood, and I think she should be at school. What would be the impulses in the undermind there governing her behaviour: food, firewood, family? If so she could read these words. Mother, for sure. One afternoon Elliot takes me to visit the psychiatric hospital in the heart of the Mauritian forest where J's qualifications could win her a job and within which many Indian families live; you see dark people standing white-robed among the trees like phantoms taken body, motionless like trees, only their eyes following the car. Still white trees that are people: the sugar cane workers awaiting the harvest. Some are sapling children in white. Are they really alive or are they images only in the forest undermind of Mauritius—a physical picture of the unconscious? On the road one day on the way to Tamarin where the Latham-Koenings, J's parents, live, "There's a school. What's that school?"

Jacquemine says, "That is Catholic."

It looks all right to me; just little children running and calling, black-haired children. "Can we stop?"

E says, "We've got to relieve Madame of the baby; she tires."

I don't see the children in the streets; where are they? And I don't hear children crying.

My own Kirstine is the first to get a letter to me in Mauritius but to collect it I step over the mess of sour food on the pavement where a man is cooking in front of the post office door. The Jasmine-David family is living in Whenua now and there is news of them. So it's Kirstine to be sent the first present from Mauritius: a pack of cards with the dodo bird on them, extinct, of the Dead-as-a-Dodo legend. The intricate double-crossing with the shadiest character on the street to get hold of these dodo cards for which he charges easily treble. But in my letter it makes good telling.

During the last years since *Teacher* came out I had many invitations from abroad, mainly from North America, travelling expenses, honorariums and such, until they'd find I lived at the bottom of the world in which case education was no longer good business, and they'd fade out strategically. On the other hand, I'd come to learn that all they wanted was talk, talk, talk, whereas my philosophy was how *not* to talk; after years of work on the key vocabulary with its vital technique of listening I no longer sought centre-stage. Let only those talk who needed to.

One day, however, the mail had brought me an invitation that I read twice: from a man by the name of Major Aron in Tel Aviv, on

behalf of Rotary International, asking me to come to Israel to form a
peace school in the Hebrew University in Jerusalem with the children
of the lecturers as pupils. After which the nucleus of trained children
could divide out into the city and then into the country, a job which
appeared to me to be about my size. Plainly Rotary International had
not been concerned with what my New Zealand grading might be.

Since this letter came after the 1967 war and after some Israeli
teachers had put their hands in their own pockets to bring out *Teacher*
in Hebrew—would it be for the kibbutzim I wondered?—and even
paid me an advance royalty, I read the letter a third time and replied
that I would come in two years. Early in 1969, however, I wrote to
Major Aron and asked him if, on account of my bereavement, I
could come a year earlier and this was the issue at that time in
Mauritius: whether Rotary would be ready for me or not. "But if you
don't hear from Israel," from Elliot, "why not come on to London?"

Jacquemine was with us at Hotel Vatel and E was lying prone on
my bed, uncharacteristically; the heat, he supposed.

"London? I hadn't thought of going to London. I haven't been
asked there. Mauritius, California, Israel and now London. I don't
know my fate."

Jacquemine says, "I do not know mine either."

Only Elliot claimed to know his fate.

You come upon Tamarin at the end of a long winding one-track road
through the sugar cane, opening out upon a flawless bay of the kind
I used to draw as a child where the waves file in from an Indian
Ocean as languid as the dark blue heat itself, where the trees reach
their arms in dimensions of eternity and where the only architectural
answer could possibly be a cluster of log cabins, which it is. Before the
verandah of the central cabin are body-high boulders on which people
sit, and down the bank are families of African servants, and here live
the Latham-Koenigs on their own personal terms with nature.

"How do you do," from Elliot's mother.

"Enchantée," from Jacquemine's mother.

Though Monsieur is a man of sun and sea his skin has the paleness
of a city-dweller, dramatised by dark hair and eyes like a sketch in
charcoal, and his tall tapering build belongs to a walker-on at court
in the days of Louis XIV. Fortunately for me his English has the
correctness of a second language though Madame has no English at
all. J and E sit on the boulders at the front while their son Vincent,
my grandson, is looped round Monsieur's neck, the living image of

his grandfather; except that he's as dark as his mother and all he wears is a nappie. Le petit monsieur.

Standing upon the bank later with me Elliot says, looking down upon the bay, "You could do worse you know, dear, than settle here near the Koenigs."

I look down upon the exotic vale. "What I'd do, El, I'd—I could build another cabin down there. Make another Selah. I don't want much, you know."

"What do you want?"

"Anonymity. Just a little safe place where I can settle down and go on earning my living. Be independent. A table, a bed and a place to make the tea."

Through the branches the waves rock white. I have memories of the swing of the sea and I chatter to escape. "And—and then when you come to think of the rest of your nights under mosquito nets— though I-I must say it remains an idea to be near your people. Ashton would feel easier if . . . and I don't know about being grounded in Mauritius after you've returned to London. I may never get out. So much depends on hearing from Israel."

"That's still the war zone. Ashton doesn't like it."


There's a picture in mind of two women sitting side by side on a white wrought-iron seat beneath a tree at Tamarin Bay: Madame Latham-Koenig of Mauritius and Mrs. Henderson of indeterminate address, the maternal and paternal grandmothers of le petit monsieur. Madame wears a frock of the grey-blue of her eyes with a tier of pleats from the hipline and I wear a white silk model printed with orange flowers, a bit loose on me from grief. I'm not tall myself but Madame is a miniature on an ivory brooch who could have been lifted this minute from the pages of Chateaubriand. It is boning that endures in a face so that the years uncovering Madame's features only increase her indestructible beauty. From her inborn elegance you'd think she was Parisian, whereas, in fact, as Monsieur has told me, she'd been born and reared on an island off Madagascar, five hundred miles east of Southern Africa. As it happens, Madagascar has been renamed since, except that I'm unable to relinquish that glamorous word which oc-curred in a song my father would sing about a character called Little Jimmee: "I see Jerusalem and Madagascar . . . I see Jerusalem and Madagascar. And North and South Americee, and North and South Americee-ee-ee . . ." and that she has not travelled beyond Mauritius. As Monsieur translated to me, she had been brought up in a family of

thirteen(?) by a French grandmother and had had no formal education as such, which is not always a disadvantage; it was Madame
Latham-Koenig herself I was sitting with rather than a carbon copy
of some educational system imposed by a government.

But although I had only forgotten high school French and a snatch
of correspondence course I'd taken when Jacquemine had first begun
writing to me, from which I'd gathered she wanted to marry my son,
and though Madame had not one hint of English, French women
don't sit side by side for nothing, as I'd discovered when studying the
French culture long before Elliot had gone to France. I'd written a
book on a French courtesan.

Monsieur is serving tea from a white garden table while an African
boy is holding the baby, and for a while Monsieur graciously acts as
interpreter until he is moved to take le petit monsieur for a swim in
the overpainted waves, leaving the two of us trying to communicate
as best we can. For instance, Was Elliot going to take Jacquemine and
the baby back to London with him?

"Kahore au mohio." Wrong, that's Maori. "Je ne sais pas." In some
way I get it through to her that I think that Elliot thinks the baby who
is a sunny brown little islander should not be locked up in a London
apartment for the winter but should stay longer in his natural habitat,
the sun, the sea and open cabins.

Madame thinks it would be hard on Jacquemine to be pinned down on
Mauritius when she is used to Paris and London.

I say Elliot thinks she could get a job here with her Sorbonne degrees.

Madame says, Let no one think she is going to mind the baby if
Jacquemine gets the job at the psychiatric hospital. He tires her.

I say, "Mais oui."

With impassioned gesticulation to replace words, Will Elliot come
back for them some day?

I indicate that Elliot is a bird with wide wings who likes to fly
high in the sky but no doubt the bird will alight in Mauritius from
time to time, according to the law of birds.

The very beautiful mouth agitates a little, then blue hope comes
to her eyes. Where then was I going?

"Je ne sais pas." Who knows? Israel, California, London . . . I
might even get a job myself in Mauritius. I do not know my Fate.

Why not then, from Madame, take Jacquemine and Vincent with
me? Wherever it was. Jacquemine could get a job there.

I say, How can I take anyone anywhere until I myself am settled?

The three of us could end up in some transit camp starving. On the other hand, if I do come to rest somewhere I could send for them.

Suddenly Madame weeps like a girl. Mauritius is a place everyone keeps departing from.

It is also a place to which people keep returning.

She replies she's not weeping because people go away. It's because everyone keeps on leaving her behind. She says she's always going to the airport but only to see other people off.

When I settle down somewhere, I tell her, I could just as easily send for her as for anyone else.

We understand each other and she sends the boy to boil more water for more tea.

When the wonderful cable comes to the Hotel Vatel asking me to come to Israel next week, offering me a home and a job in Jerusalem, I engage Jojo to take me to Tamarin Bay and he is so excited and happy that his job will let him buy rice for his family that he sits forward on the seat mile after mile, leaning over the wheel to encourage the car. Winding through the sugar cane, field after field, I arrive at the Koenigs unannounced. They see me at once and come out to the road in the most homely way. I'm wearing a Chinese style dress just finished by the tailor, sprays of white flowers on diaphanous green voile.

Monsieur takes me round the headland through the breathless heat and beneath the eternal branches to his own separate cabin, its eyes wide upon the sea, where E and J are centred, to show them the cable, and where they are still languidly debating J's fate as E is taking flight on Saturday. Since Vincent is with them I go into the cooking room to make a drink for him and open a drawer for a spoon, only to disturb a colony of insects, all rushing intent in the same direction from the light, shocking me to a vision of the PSBMEH (Permanent Solid Block of Male Educational Hostility) moving in the same direction, when "Everyone went to your files." I slam the drawer shut and hurry back to the others and when Monsieur asks me, "Will you return to New Zealand, Mrs. Henderson, some day?"

I reply, "Mais non, Monsieur."

"I have not travelled myself," he says, "though once," with pride, "I had a trip on a sailing ship to Madagascar."

He shows me his shell collection displayed on a wide table in row after row, subtle colours and delicate shapes, and selects one for me to hold in my hand: white inside, brown outside, clustered with white spots. "When you are away in that great world I have not seen will you take up this shell and think of me: of a man, solitary on an island at the end of the Indian Ocean? A Frenchman who has never seen France."

I look at the pretty shell in terms of the key vocabulary. Monsieur has put in my palm a tangible caption of an image surfaced from deep within him: a key word symbolising the Tamarin seashore.

Back at the central cabin Madame has already begun early on a grand supper with a base of rice in a capacious wooden bowl and Jacquemine's sister, Marie-Ange, arrives covered in her mother's beauty with the long bones of Monsieur as well, encircled by her husband-in-love. She is also sparkling with glory for she brings news she is enceinte. Yet, as we lunch and drink wine on the verandah for hours, Jacquemine tells me they have a brother too who ran away to Spain and Elliot tells me of another sister who was lost at sea off the coast of Mauritius and who has never been found to this day.

The large cosy family gathering of Koenigs and Hendersons when we dine deep in the night, with Monsieur and le petit monsieur at the head of the table, celebrates the fusion of two bloods, French and English, but we are enmeshed in the mosquito net of the illusion of happiness only; behind the low lamplight and beneath the high laughter Fate is the unseen guest, sharing the old soft wine from France.

Wandering round Curepipe, waiting for E and J to come in from Le Barachois at Tamarin, I come to know a deserted Catholic cathedral near the Hotel Vatel with all its doors open to mortals and phantoms. There's a place and a function for deserted churches here and there in the world in which the wayfarer can enter and think things over, and more than once I sit in this one, slightly cooler inside than outside. In a church I like to think and reflect rather than to kneel and pray; to take readings of my position and get my bearings. An overdue reckoning.

I find much difference in churches, especially between the modern with flat roofs from Woolworth's and the others with peaked exalted ceilings which have inspired the past; the distinction to be found mainly in the architecture of the walls and ceilings reaching heavenward like two hands in prayer, in continuous worship; the fingertips pointing upward and touching in the consummation of Man and God.

In this cathedral are a minimum of statues and icons competing with a traveller's thoughts; height is featured, space and distances; shadows and silence and coolnesses, a condition much favoured by phantoms. The young have little traffic with phantoms when in the throes of creating them for their futures, but with me, now and here, I'm aware of their presence, a picturesque parade: Puppa, Mumma, Muriel, Gracie, Ashton, the first Sylvia and Daphne and the newcomer, Keith Henderson. Beneath the timbered consummation overhead, I open up my memories and here are my dead.

It turns out I have status in these parts; not as a teacher, thank God, and not even as a writer, but as the wife of a late charter president of Rotary with evidence to prove it. In my passport wallet I carry my major credential: the programme of the March service in Tauranga when Keith had been inaugurated posthumously, though none of his family had attended. Some families can do that and some can't. A glossy white card with dark blue lettering and his name featured in capitals at the top. Also I never part from the leather executive case given to him by his staff on retirement with his name on it in gold: K. D. Henderson.

Through Jacquemine, a Koenig cousin in Port Louis handles my bookings to Tel Aviv and, noting my peace mission for Rotary International, copies the VIP from my N.Z. ticket onto my new one. "You'll be better looked after this way," he says; which is true of some airports only. Furthermore, when I'm in Port Louis for my cholera injection, he presents me and my credential to Rotary Mauritius who cable Rotary Bombay where I hope to spend a few days on my way through to Israel. And the next thing Rotary Bombay has undertaken to have me met, hotelled and hosted there by the Rotary Inner Wheel.

There are many things in Mauritius I'm leaving out as I'm travelling fast and light; for instance the whole of the Latham-Koenig branch at the airport to farewell Elliot at six o'clock, the banquet I treated them all to at the Hotel Le Chaland where I'm waiting for my own plane the next day, with Monsieur taking the head of my table, writing to Ashton till five a.m. under the mosquito net after his cable of permission to go to Israel, the boys on the staff dealing with the insects and the drawings I was doing in coloured pencil when time was too pendulous—the mountain view through the hurricane shutters, but there's one thing I'll not leave out.

It is not until I'm on my own at Le Chaland the next day that I'm able to catch up on the country's children: "Take me to a school, please, Jojo."

At Mahebourg we walk together through the gate of a state primary into hundreds of children playing and running and calling like other children elsewhere, and up to the school building: a refreshing variant of architecture in concrete with curved rising ramps linking the separate sections and the classrooms upstairs and down; an innovative design. The roll, according to Jojo, is largely Indian with a small colony of Africans. And who ever heard of a headmaster delightedly embracing two visitors? Fancy *me* being welcome in a school.

It's the little ones I ask to see and here's this roomful of tiny wee Indians in orderly rows of old-time desks with the Indian teacher barely up to my shoulder, the voice of a canary. Yes yes they spik Eenglish. "Jansee?"

Jansee stands erect in his little old desk, his fingers stiff as sticks of chalk. Solemn as Krishnamurti.

"Fhat ees dor nem?"

"May nem ees Jansee."

"Goot."

Oh the dear little chap. These are my true friends. Mates.

Good heavens, they've still got slates, some with large holes, but the writing on the wall blackboards is jolly good. Some peoples put the cultural before the material. Suddenly I ask to see their reading books upon which the little bird-teacher all but falls over herself bringing them. Beautiful little reading books in French, illustrated brightly and full of the local vocabulary: (in French) mother, father, brother, sister, baby, sugar cane, rice, firewood, hurricane, cart, fish, airplane . . . you wouldn't believe it, with New Zealand still on Janet and John. "I think they're just *lovely*. Ces livres . . . ils . . . sont . . . beaux?"

"Très beaux."

"Where are they written? Where are they printed?"

"Frunce."

Madame and Jacquemine come across to Le Chaland airport to see off Elliot's mother and we have a great deal of fun playing VIPs. Parade with stateliness and sit in the special lounge. We've never laughed so much.

Another unnerving flight up the Indian Ocean with the trade winds from the west shaking the plane; the Roaring Forties we called them;

that very same West Wind which called to me when a girl and first
married to my love: Come away, wild spirit, come over the sea.

Here I am, West Wind; what have you for me?

*April 16, 1969*

B O M B A Y    Black-high above the Indian Ocean in the middle of
the night, another eight-hour flight, wondering what was at the end of
the wind, but when the lights of Bombay appeared below from horizon
to horizon in every direction merging into the stars themselves I could
see for myself. Ideas running away were the order of the day.

Indians in white on the drive in, sleeping beneath the sky. The West
End Hotel. A large earthenware pitcher of water on the central table
told some tale which I did not read at once but I soon did; it was talking
about the heat of India and the sting of the Indian curry downstairs in
the starched dining room; a crystal jug of water on that table too.
Water flowed willingly, both hot and cold, in the roomy tiled bathroom with a bath large enough to please the longest man with inches
to spare. Water, water everywhere with the supercity parched outside.

Tall cool ceilings in my room, cool marble floor, spacious enough to
house several families rather than just one me. Air-conditioning revolving and humming, moving cool air. Below my windows in the shade
of a tree, a never-ending reaching tree, a family of small children, one
holding a baby, on the pavement outside. By what right am I the one
inside?

When Dr. Rane calls and we sit together drinking water the first issue
is mutual identification. He himself is the president of Rotary Bombay,
a dark-skinned man; scholarly, gentle and with eyes that seem sad.
"I'm a Hindu," he tells me.

"I'm a Christian." And show him my credential, pathetic yet unique:
the posthumous inauguration programme of a charter president of
Rotary in the South Pacific, presenting the glossy white card with dark
blue printing like a pass at a frontier. "Mr. Henderson died three
months ago."

He holds the card and reads it and tells me, "My wife died a year
ago."

Not unlike the Maoris we think on our dead before proceeding further, our eyes lowered, Hindu and Christian. Each knows of the four-inch nail of grief embedded in the heart of the other, curtailing its maneuverability, until I look up and out the windows upon the centuried trees shading the hot streets outside, eternal branches inhabited by ravens. "Do we ever get over it?"

"Some grief is too deep to get over."

"We are Parsees," from Purviz Banaji when she and Homi come to get me. Her English is the Indo derivative of the home language, whereas Dr. Rane's had been English itself. Taller than I, Purviz, and older; articulate, lean with a sober sari. That look in her eyes, is it hunted, haunted or . . . when she tells me of her only son in Israel I think it is mourning. Homi, swiftly spoken, obliging, confident and wiry, is the kind of man who drives his own car in Bombay and you need to know the traffic to appreciate that. European suit, no children of his own. They're taking me to the Tower of Silence.

On the way Purviz tells me the Parsees, a fair-skinned race emigrated in the past from Persia, are concentrated in the Bombay area where they hold administrative posts as a rule. "That monument, do you see it? He is one of us." In the Tower of Silence, I hear, the Parsees expose the bodies of their dead to the vultures which clean up the flesh in a matter of minutes when the bones are dropped down a central well. "Our solution to the pollution of the soil of India." From outside the burial grounds you can see through the trees the tall white circular tower, the sketches of birds on the wing above and a group of mourners leaving. "We believe," from Purviz, "the soul emigrated from the Sun in the first place and returns to the Sun in the last place. The souls of our dead enter the vultures which fly them up near the Sun. We do not worship any god; it is that we worship the Sun as the giver and taker of all life and we worship in the Temple of Flame."

On the way back she points out this Temple of Flame, not a big edifice, crammed between other buildings which makes me ask the size of the Parsee population, at which I learn there are no more than a few hundred thousand Parsees in India which provokes inbreeding, which in turn is the reason why they don't breed well. To correct this cycle they'd tried to implant another branch of the Parsees in the south of India where they built another Tower of Silence and where they transferred a colony of vultures for the anti-pollution work but the vultures all flew home again so the new branch failed. I'm trying to leave things out to keep this short in order to travel fast and light, but how could I leave out the Tower of Silence?

I can't leave out the women either; these flashing forceful professionals who take me on in their stride. Vivid saris, sleek hair, bangles on their arms and jewels in their ears, their own cars, own drivers—where have they been all my life? When the Banajis take me to a Parsee wedding reception, a numerous company sitting on the grass in the open air, you should have seen the silks on them; saris and sandals of gold and of silver and gleaming gems in their hair; older, heavy-bodied women, grey hair matched by grey saris and pendulous diamond earrings; the widow nearby to whom others were paying homage, she'd salvaged everything from her disaster: wealth, health, dignity, prestige, her limousine and her driver; and I suppose that's the way to do it. You could see why she didn't speak to me; the only white face in Bombay so far, the only woman at this ceremony revealing her legs in a knee-length dress, with her hair trimmed foolishly short. Moreover I further discredited myself by not being able to eat one single dish served on banana leaves on account of the alien flavours though none could have cared less. In the meantime, look at the bride and bridegroom returned for their wedding from a holiday alone together, required *before* they were married, for a change.

On the other hand, the women featured less than the men at a Hindi reception in the Taj Mahal Hotel facing the Gateway to India by the sea; here it was the patriarch of the family welcoming home the bride and the bridegroom from a holiday alone together, this time *after* marriage. In the bride, standing like a figurine beside the groom, greeting everyone, was truly the Kashmiri Song in person; the original "Pale Hands I Loved . . ." dripping with laces and love and wealth.

I'll have to leave out Bachan Gobhai I think, or I'll never get out of India. After my first half-century, "woman" was a word with new meaning. Handsome, vivacious, energetic, childless . . . Parsee again . . . and with a built-in purpose. About my age whatever that was. At their home Burjor Gobhai ran an advertising art service which was more than I'd ever achieved. Startling paintings and designs in ink on the spacious walls; among his tables of paint a soft-mannered man who declined to accompany us. I'll have to leave out the Hindu Temple on the summit of an abrupt hill, the puffing ascent . . . the little children in caves by a malodorous well of water . . . cholera talk. Did I have to believe Dr. Rane himself worshipped a plaster goddess like this, her eyes lit from within by electric bulbs, red . . . and in a temple like this with the priests chanting absently. Bachan's crowded workrooms of small Indian women bent over rows of sewing machines, room after room of them: "It is a tenet of our faith to find these women, rescue them from idleness and employ them profitably. We even pay them too. What else would you like to see, Sylviar?"

There's much I wanted to relate here but there's no way of writing successfully of India and getting out again; it's all been said since the beginning of India. The shops in Mahatma Gandhi Street, the touching and beautiful department store there of Indian Industries, brass, ivory, ebony . . . the sandals over the street, the old man playing a violin on the kerb, the vivid rapturously sequinned stalls . . . the romance, the horror too. But I do have one firm fact to hang on to with both hands, before and after, which is recorded in my diary: "Adverse telegram from Major Aron." Saying, I think, they were not ready yet for me and not to come for a while. A direction-finder I'll come back to.

Mrs. Antony on duty to show me some schools; own car, own driver, like Bachan Gobhai. Her own identity. A fair-skinned Indian of the Church of England which, since I was christened Church of England, baptised and confirmed, should have engendered a rapport between us, had it meant much to me; that we were both on our way, however, to a Montessori school in a Buddhist temple was more productive. And here are these tiny little Indian children, all dressed in brilliant yellow, yellow ribbons on their black hair, yellow pants on the little boys; the yellow upon the shiny black hair and the eyes like night. Happiness written all over them, teachers too. None more than five, some were younger, and most could read and write, I saw it for myself. I couldn't believe it. The dainty live Indian teachers enchanted that someone should come to see their work.

True, the style of teaching was proudly authoritarian, the content of their work was what the teachers chose to implant, no sign of the children's own vocabulary, but children can be happy whatever the style as long as their teachers are happy. There was discipline in my own classroom for the Family of Man yearns for it. The key vocabulary can thrive just as well in the context of benign discipline and most American profs work it that way also. I myself give no quarter to license and anarchy because that's not freedom at all; freedom has an ingredient of responsibility. The issue remains inherently the same: does a government want carbon copies of its teachers, or people in the image of their own separate selves?

For the first time in my life I understood the Montessori sensitivity exercises, though it took a Buddhist temple in the thick of India to show me; the very last nation needing them. The first nation to need them is a country in the South Pacific which is still on the soldier-boy bang-bang syndrome. I saw a Montessori school in a Buddhist temple and all these really dear little Indian children, so tiny, so pretty and dressed in yellow, from about three to five, reading and writing, in English too, and so gay and happy. And I was shown a Catholic convent and an English boarding school; the same orderliness plus laughter. Mind you, the teachers were cheerful, it seemed, because they had confidence in themselves. Efficiency without tears; it can be done and the key is the teacher. *No wonder* the key vocabulary was persona non grata in the country I once called my own; I'd come a long way to find out why. Mrs. Dolat, the head, says, "Do you know the Montessori, Mrs. Henderson?"

"We did have it in college but I haven't seen it operating. But how do you come to have the Italian Montessori in India?"

"It has been here for the best part of a century. Dr. Montessori came here with her son and settled in Madras. There are several centres in India now."

I should have incorporated these sense-training exercises in my own work. "They're absolutely beautiful."

A touching encounter.

Mrs. Antony took me to other schools, Catholic, Anglican and Buddhist, there were more Montessori, rich spacious and lovely buildings, fun in some, dolour in others, but they were all private schools orientated to religions. I wanted to see the schools that picked up little children from caves in cholera conditions or who kept vigil at a mausoleum in the street. Could Mrs. Antony take me to a state school?

"Oh—they are closed today. A religious holiday." Like Mauritius.

"Bachan," when I next saw her, "could you slip me into a state school?"

"Today—no. They're closed today."

"What for?"

"It is they commemorate the birthday of a saint."

In Mauritius you could take your favorite African taxi and go and find a school for yourself, but Bombay—forget it.

Outside my windows the tree shading the whole street for the length of the block, its roots penetrating deep strata to bring up water to the foliage and the air, like a mother cathedral to succour and protect us all—a sanctuary. I know where this tree would have been had it grown in a Godzone street; an electric cross-cut saw would have severed its great trunk decades ago to prove man's dominion over nature. A paternal oak I've seen come down at the gate in Bethlehem to make way for the power lines and a royal gum tree soaring at the corner. The New Zealand male is uneasy at anything growing above his shoulder level, a timid soul. Where's the axe, bring it down—ah now I'm bigger than you.

I once grew a great tree in Godzone, the organic teaching, its bloom the key vocabulary; a tree whose branches reached right out beyond into countries overseas where its seed fell on fertile ground to nurture children in other places. But that tree came down too . . .

There were many huge Indian trees in that street, the Marine Lines it's called, and I'd walk there on a Sunday in their shade and rest in the American Cultural Center at the other end where there were books and films and many young Indian people.

Now that "Adverse telegram from Major Aron," recorded in my diary, which they gave to me at the desk; one look at that, about not coming just yet, one look and I was up and out and after a job. You need to earn in the currency of the country you're in. The *Times of India* would be the place for me, a heady cynical paper, as a feature writer. The reporters' room was the biggest and highest I'd seen that was not a mosque, a museum or the domed central post office; typewriters and men as far as the eye could see. Appointment with the editor next Tuesday morning, tomorrow, but when I went there the man said, "Tuesday morning? No one sees the editor on a Tuesday morning. It is that he writes his editorial on a Tuesday morning. No one would dare to go near him."

"Wednesday morning then."

"He meets the board on Wednesday."

"Thursday?"

"So come along anyway at ten o'clock on Thursday."

My eye to a job. It's Bachan who takes me miles across Bombay, in a taxi this time, to a publisher she knows at the Asia Publishing House and drops me there to return myself. Lili Jayasinghe, another of these flashing forceful professionals—where have they been all my life or, more to the point, where have *I* been all my life? Mrs. Jayasinghe was a dark woman, very warm as though she were well acquainted with the hazards of personal love, not unacquainted with passion, in a way I hadn't felt it to be with the Indian women, Purviz Banaji, Bachan Gobhai and Mrs. Antony. In fact I thought she was Jewish. Delighted, she was, to hear about editors in other parts of the world, in London and New York, and to meet a living writer; as I was to meet a living editor. Called in her husband, made the coffee and I told her a bit of the ways of Bob G, as compared with John P, and she tells me of the writer of the main book she is editing at this moment, by an Indian writer in the Indian language. "I'd like to live in Bombay and write a book about India," I say.

"We don't publish in English. We don't have the reading public in English."

"Oh I see. Well I suppose I'd have to send it to London or New York, like other writers in English, writing of India, and hope for the best."

"Or to your own country."

I let that one pass and lift the subject from me to her husband who's not saying much. He's the kind of man, I think, who would not be driving his own car in Bombay and who wouldn't be a man to dominate his wife. The deep brown eyes I see everywhere in Asia beneath bushy black eyebrows. "Alipur, do you write?"

"N-no. No—not yet. Well, some day I may. I have not yet ascertained where my—where—"

"Where his soul abides," finishes his wife. "Alipur thinks his soul is waiting to find a place where it can say, This is my home."

Years ago I would have crashed in with "I understand exactly what you mean," all grandly patronising, but much work on the key vocabulary engenders humility and anonymity when listening with care to children so that I stand back instead and am quiet. This powerful private image Alipur exposes to us is the vulnerable thing in conversation; one word from me would intercept its passage. Don't interrupt the surfacing of an image. I try my strong coffee and wait.

Alipur is not a lightweight man but fairly full in face and in body, with the gentle movements of a furry feline. "So far," he says, "I am no more than a foot-loose citizen of Asia. When, if I ever come to rest somewhere, even here, then . . . well I might . . ."

"Alipur," supplies his wife, "believes any work of value can only arise from still waters."

Under the mind. Jung's action in non-action; let things happen in the psyche. But I don't say it. Between them the Jayasinghes have delivered part of Alipur's key vocabulary, words captioning some of his deepest instincts which to me appears as a privilege: *soul, home, world, rest* and *still waters*. Had Alipur been a child at school on the first day these would have been his self-chosen first words and he would have read them next day from one look only. He would have loved them too for they are serviced by the bloodstream of his mind, living images which are an organic part of him; unforgettable. He would have loved reading from the first word onward. Now I understand a good deal more of Alipur and maybe I was not wrong in thinking they were of Jewish origin.

He moves in his chair and crosses the other leg. "I think, but I don't know ... what I am trying to say is I would probably be a poor writer because I don't read much. I did not like reading as a child."

Lili confirms, "He did not like reading."

Lili Jayasinghe would have made a marvellous teacher; interesting, lovable and intellectually charitable, as a good editor should be also.

Eyes and hands flash, white teeth too in a smile. Everything talks in Lili's face except her tongue.

"Have you had a good day, Dr. Rane?"

"From one patient to another." We sit by the windows with glasses of water. "Not all physical patients. The soul of India is not always calm. The agitations. It seeks to escape its fate but Fate treads with steady step; none escapes." *Fate, soul, treads, escapes*, he's used these words before. Is this Hinduism?

The keys turn in the double lock, the strong door opens and this time it is the polished smiling attendant from the desk with a telegram on a brass platter. It is from Major Aron. A telegram of welcome this time and he'll meet me at Tel Aviv airport at nine on Thursday morning. It burns like curry, I drink more water.

Thursday morning? But that was my appointment with the editor. I drink lager instead of water when I go down to dinner. You can get very good beers in Asia, German or Dutch—a Steinekker. You need something to confront the curry when it's the real thing. Have I said about the three uniformed waiters all to myself? About all the guests in the dining room being men, none white, no women? How it's the men in Asia who handle and serve all food and all guests, you never see a woman on staff except for the cleaning? Ah there's much I've got to leave out—the lovely nuns at that big Catholic school in pure white robes and smiles, how happy all those little children were, how they sang to us ... about how they could read and write at five, saw it for myself? Travel fast, travel light. The journey is shortening and death is for real.

Excess baggage; cram it into the rubbish bin: prose, grammar, punctuation, cross-reference and line of thought—don't forget the cable to Ashton.

*April 23, 1969*

ISRAEL    There's nothing like a hurried diary for brevity of word:
"Took off for Tel Aviv at 1:30 a.m. Overshot Tel Aviv on account of
fog and landed at Cyprus for four hours. Returned to Tel Aviv about
9 and Major Aron met me. Took me to hotel. Slept till 8 p.m."

I awake from a Librium blackout to the sound of a woman's running
voice. "See, I told you so. It took me to guess where she was; asleep
with the door locked." I open my eyes upon strangers round the bed.
She's small and dark-haired, the one who's talking. "So you're awake.
You've been asleep since morning; don't you remember we were calling for you at six to take you home for dinner? We've knocked on
your door. Everyone's been looking for you all over town, on the point
of calling the police. But I guessed; I said to the proprietor, You come
upstairs with your master key and that's where we'll find her; asleep."
    Two women, two men; one the proprietor and the other very tall
with features I faintly recall. I smile foolishly.
    The eloquent woman, "I don't think she knows who we are. Do
you know who we are? Do you recognise that man there?"
    "No."
    "I'm Rose Aron. That's Major Aron, this is our daughter and he's
the proprietor."
    Major Aron in a good bass voice, "Does she know who she is herself?"
    My eyes almost close again, and the young woman says, "Jet-lag."
    Major Aron in reproach, "I was at that airport at five this morning,
and the plane was four hours late. No breakfast."
    My reply a fatuous smile.
    Rose Aron on stream again. "And no dinner either. A beautiful
New Zealand meal of lamb and mint sauce especially for you, wasting
away for the last two hours. Do you know *where* you are?"
    Suddenly I sit up in panic. "I'm in Tel Aviv."
    "That's right."
    "Oh dear, dear, dear. I'm so . . . I . . ."
    "Well you'd better go back to sleep now," from Rose Aron. "We'll
pick you up tomorrow for dinner at six. You ought to be awake by
then."
    They all smile, thank heaven, no, not the proprietor.

Major Aron had this most reassuring way of always making his big self broadly *visible* whenever he came to the hotel, either to pick me up or to put me back; walk right into the lounge in view of the desk and other guests there drinking coffee and wait for me in silence, making it quite clear in the war zone that here was no adventuress on the prowl. I sure could do with it. Sometimes with Rose. In town he would sit with me in a coffee shop on the corner for all to see from the street and I'd be seen in his car in the Square.

Also I was frequently to be seen with him and his family in the vast lounge of the Intercontinental on the hill behind the Old City, feasting or drinking and talking, so that his care

The twenty-first birthday of Israel

on this particular point, establishing an *identity* for me, was something I would have called Christian had he not been a Jew. Since, however, I had never met Jews before he was simultaneously introducing his race to me. I called his thoughtfulness Jewish.

It was during my second night at that hotel on the waterfront at Tel Aviv that I awoke to the long eerie shriek of the murdered; striking high and shrill on the hour then tailing off into silence. My God I was in the war zone. At daybreak I rang Major Aron and asked him to take me away; he was gruff and reproachful on the line, upbraiding me for ungratefulness and such, but only, as I guessed later, because he suspected the call was being intercepted, for when he arrived he was concerned enough. As I booked out at the desk the proprietor gave me a shady look straight out of a spy thriller and said, "Did you sleep well?"

But I knew what he meant: So you heard that in the night.

"Yes I slept well, thanks."

Major Aron picked up my bag. As well as being my Rotary host and someone to wear my stunning clothes for—the white linen skirt tailored in Mauritius, doing up down the front with black buttons, the white

muslin blouse with black spots to match and the black-and-white
sandals from Bombay with rosettes on them—he was becoming something more: an impromptu personal bodyguard. As it happens, he was
also a seasoned soldier who had formed and led the only Jewish bat-
talion in a recent war and had written a book about it in Hebrew.
Just too bad my heart was nailed down.

Centuries ago in the time of the Crusades Christian churches in Europe
used to build fortresses in Palestine in the form of castles to harbour
crusaders and pilgrims visiting the Holy Land, protecting them from
the "infidel." This Hospice belonged to the Church of Scotland dating
from about the eleventh century, a tall imposing white fort, a church
attached to one end and a battlement at the front in the form of a tower.
A regal marble staircase commanded mid-centre while the entrance
door was forbidding and powerful enough to repulse any horde of
infidels, if not Fate himself. Norman-Moorish architecture. The whole
was surrounded by cypress trees, melancholy witnesses mourning the
centuries away. Beneath the Hospice rested bones from the eleventh
century.

Mine was a double room upstairs in the battlement tower with narrow barred windows all round, overlooking both the Old City of
Jerusalem and the new. Oddly yet pleasantly enough it took a Jew to
bring me here, Major Aron. "You Christians," he said from his height,
"still thinking that Jesus was someone. At that time the Jewish intellec-
tuals in Jerusalem had no respect for Jesus at all; they saw right through
Him." But he still brought me to the Christian Hospice. His first name
was Wellesley.

The Reverend Gardiner-Scott was a tough resilient and versatile
Scot who, after leaving school at fourteen, had been everything from
a hallboy and footman, restaurateur, university graduate and theological student to a ship's steward on a world circuit; from an ordained
minister, pastor, chaplain to the forces in the Middle East during the
war and at Victoria University (N.Z.) later to minister and warden of
the church and hospice in Jerusalem . . . from the gardening to the
Sunday sermons, while his wife and alter ego, Darinka of Serbian-
Yugoslav parentage and reared in America, was the most alert spirit
who ever conferred with Jesus on the moment—at the family table or
in the stable at Bethlehem—or who ever gathered lost sheep to tend.
The two of them were finely sophisticated and expansively cosmopoli-
tan, had met and married in—wait for it—Godzone, had survived the
'67 war only just and were so acquainted with death it made you feel

better about it. So it was no surprise to hear they meant to see out their time there, to retire in Jerusalem.

Tania was their daughter of eleven who joined me at the piano and in drawing the Hospice and in hilarious games of marbles in my room; a soldier on leave from the border sleeping in the room next to mine as though he'd never wake again was one of the sheep to be tended, and I was the latest, while the staff consisted of one Arab woman ceaselessly mopping the marble floors and murmuring to herself devoutly, "Jesus loves me."

Various sounds of life echoed through the Hospice all day but the sweetest was the grind of metal on metal as Mr. Scott went on his evening rounds turning his keys in the locks.

The Rotary people were nowhere near ready for me, I'd crashed in a year early, but I set to equipping Selah Eight anyway to get down to work. My Arab taxi knew where to find everything from the best table lamp in Asia to a foam rubber sheet for my bed and two more pillows, though I did have a bit to learn about Mediterranean gallantry; having carried everything up to my room he very kindly made up my bed and turned back the sheets then opened his arms to me. "Just one kiss."

I can't help laughing.

A softly spoken man in his thirties with eyes like hot coffee.

"Just one." Sophistication, to put it mildly.

"But, Acida, I'm a grandma."

Tenderly, "Only one."

I can't see "only one" with the bed laid open. "I'm nearly twice your age, Acida. What about the pretty young girls in town?"

His arms wide, "One kiss, one."

Mrs. Scott when I speak of it says, "The Mediterranean men become very excited at fair women; the white skin, the blue eyes. To be middle-aged as well and a grandma only heightens the lustre: more to be won."

Neither of us sees fit to mention Wellesley Aron's Mediterranean style.

In Jerusalem when they heard I'd been asked there, "You can come to see *me. I'll* welcome you to Israel. Anyone who comes to help our country. *I'll* be your friend." Far more passion in Israel than in any country yet; smiles on the touch, tears on the spot with the only issue survival. Though abrupt in the street at a stranger. Across the desk at

Barclay's Bank where the woman accountant had lost a son at the front and the second had been called up, the two of us wept together on our dead. I became accustomed to the armed soldier patrolling the front of the King David Hotel where the Americans were known to hang out, to my bag being searched in the supermarket, the bank and the post office, so when the Scotts asked me to speak to a group of ministers' wives, all of whom turned out to be American, I took them instead for a key vocabulary lesson on how to defuse the impulse to kill, with brown paper cut up for key vocabulary cards and I heard the word "wonderful" for some time after.

I wrote a long letter to Ashton telling him I wished to live here and earn in the currency of the country. My family were all right; the boys were on their feet, Jasmine and David and five children were living in Whenua, the most beautiful home in the world so far, and my work was looking after itself, so I was free to wander as a child, to answer the call of the wild west wind. So although a bomb went off in the supermarket killing nine people and Ashton begged me to come home, he couldn't look after me in the war zone and when things were bad a family should stay together, I replied that the Scotts were looking after me as well as the Arons, people in the city and my taxi, Acida. Where else would I see the rising sun gleam on the dome of the Church of the Holy Sepulchre, and dawn on the Garden of Gethsemane?

If I got killed, so what? My work was done, was it not? I'd completed what I'd set out to do, paid life back, put something in that had not been here when I came; that my country didn't want it was the luck of the draw. But for two things immovably wrong, the nail through my heart and a sense that Fate was shadowing me, my soul might have said: this is my home.

So down went my head to the work at hand: a review for some U.S. publisher of A. S. Neill's *Summerhill* which I didn't approve of and said so since he couldn't see the difference between freedom and license; a request from the *New York Times* Op-Ed page for an account of Israel's twenty-first birthday as a state, that very day in May, for American Jews to read and ponder on—for this I climbed up to the ramparts on the roof of the Hospice to watch all day the country's defence forces arriving from various parts of the countryside to converge on the Old City; Air, Navy and ground forces, girls in uniform, Red Cross, hospital staffs, transport, to march round the ancient walls in all the colours of Jacob's coat with white and blue flags tossing; the sound of their singing as they passed with passion beneath the Hospice ramparts . . .

until a suspicious helicopter dropped low above me to take a closer look and I took off down out of sight . . . when that too was done there was yet the new curriculum to write for the proposed Rotary peace school at the Hebrew University.

The terrain of my journey through life, no longer the trodden highway, had become, since *Spinster* had been published bearing the key vocabulary, like the jagged fragmented lines drawn by a child when first given a piece of chalk: completely unpredictable and without design, until one heavily sleeping midnight the telephone cried out like murder in the night and Mrs. Scott came to my bedside; I'd been summoned to London where Elliot was dangerously ill, and the war zone could have been no more than the grassy crag beneath my battlement windows where the Arab shepherd was watching his flock. Then the way descended again into the valley of the shadow of death from which, five months ago, my love had never returned.

*May 8, 1978*
L O N D O N    Several places in this narrative I've had to leave out and London will be another. As it happens I've already written a book on London, I don't know how; I couldn't do it now. The priority I suppose of keeping my mind disciplined in the interest of survival at that time, as well as the part about earning my living since I was a spinster now. Coming events, etc.

Though overshooting London I can still record, however, a few people whose Samaritan qualities would be good for my book, shedding a glow on a vale which was otherwise shade: my London agent for a start, Ursula Winant, who strode to action stations the moment I arrived and helped me to call Ashton from New Zealand to help me with his brother. Also, in the crush of the tourist season, she somehow got me a room in the hospital area on two odd days—I spent the nights at the hospital—and contacted Rotary Inner London, the president of which, a huge gentle Reverend with a still small voice, caught up with me on Friday evening at the hospital where several of Elliot's friends were sitting round his cubicle looking at him in the silence of hopeless grief. He appeared among us like a rotund Gabriel and I asked him for

living space in the hospital area. As all members lived out of London
he handed me over to his Rotary secretary who lived in an attic at the
dizzy top of a high city building wearing the garb of the centuries.
After three flights of stairs there followed two sets of steep steps which
I anyway had to climb per hand and foot and descend backwards.
Moya was much younger than I, very pretty, ultra mod with a flared
red mini-skirt which looked its best on the steps. The attic had every
comfort, it was terribly pretty up there, you wouldn't believe it, a
red-and-white heaven hard to get up to, and she could not have been
kinder. Until Ashton arrived from New Zealand and Jacquemine from
Mauritius and Ash opened up Elliot's apartment at Nightingale Lane
and put us all down there. From which time he and Jacquemine took
over from me the nights at the hospital. But I remember Moya.

Ashton was immediately lent a car by a New Zealand poet living
in England. A very small car which went very well though there were
parts to be found which, if they were not a carburetor, plug or points
may have been a fan belt, muffler or tools to work with, but I'm sure
about the door handle which took some finding. In our position to be
lent a car . . .

From New Zealand again, Elliot's friend of university days, David
Halley, was the impromptu co-ordinator, the sender of cables, meeter
of planes and the man on the telephone; and Elliot's physician and
surgeon who himself went out into the streets to obtain fresh blood
for the drip, Professor Wolfe; all sprang into instant action as though
it had been arranged for years. The only one who didn't was the Queen's
secretary whom I'd met in Godzone and who had invited me to let
him know if I ever came to London. When I asked him by letter later
on for living space in London he replied by letter that their Grace and
Favour Residences were all full, by which time, however, I was equipping another Selah at Nightingale Lane.

But it was Ursula's hand in the first place. A tall young woman with
the exquisite face of classical chinaware which did you good to look
at, from a family bearing an illustrious name; a senior Winant had
been the American Ambassador to the Court of St. James's. She and her
mother were extravagant royalists and lived on the ground floor of a
gracious house in Kensington where I'd dine sometimes and stay the
night. The two Winants had a genuine concern for writers whose
books Ursula handled from New Zealand to South Africa, built-in
from the days of Empire. But they also knew from a story I'd written
that I'd lunched with Queen Elizabeth II in Godzone which raised me

from the tolerated level of a former colonial to the pinnacle of Kensington circles where conversations tended to be about the ambassadors
in a nearby street and how that character from deepest Africa allowed
his front garden to grow shoulder high with weeds discrediting the
whole area. There came a pre-supper cocktail party at Winants' one
night when several stately devotees of royalty gathered to exchange
stories of the Queen with me, a pastime not of my choice. You never
knew where your next status was coming from.

During my time in London, however, it was not social status the
Winants were thinking of, or even of having a writer at base; there
were times when my only distinction was a personal nadir when I'd
sleep on a bed in Mrs. Winant's dressing room and share their breakfast table. It was Ursula who made the appointment for me with my
distinguished London publisher, Fred Warburg of Secker and Warburg, who had brought out *Spinster*, the first man to recognise and
publish my work. Simultaneously, however, advising me not to keep it.
"You never know how he'll receive you," she warned. "I'll ring up
and say you've been called to the country."


I'd barely alighted at Heathrow when my American agent, Monica
McCall, miraculously took body on the scene, a New Yorker of Scottish origin, "a canny Scot," Bob G said, thoroughly in command of
herself, the situation and her tongue, and to see Monica hail a taxi or
a waiter was worth being in London for. About my size and age; my
missing business sense in person. She took me to supper in high American style at an exclusive English restaurant where we exchanged some
overdue confidences over wine of her choosing. What I told Monica
was that I intended to drop everything and everyone from my past life,
like changing the colours of the clothes I'd worn and the subjects I'd
written about, as well as my publishers on both sides of the Atlantic—
I had none to change in Godzone. "Everything new," I told her trekking through the menu jungle and losing my way, working backwards
at times. "A new country too."

None of which qualified her enjoyment of the steak and she only
protested when I included Bob Gottlieb.

"I've been long enough with the one man there. It's not my style."

Monica summoned the wine waiter again and told me that Bob
usually visited London in June on business which would be a good
chance for us to meet, but I insisted I would not meet him. Then went
on to qualify: "Our two-step by letter has been so pleasant that any

personal encounter could only impair it. I'll meet him when my writing is over and it no longer matters."

From Bob when he heard, "Don't you think you're going to fire me, because I won't *be* fired!"

I began equipping a rather lovely Selah Eight under Elliot's roof— no that would have been Selah Nine; the Hospice was Selah Eight— and started another book with Bob at hand whenever I stalled. "There's got to be another conclusive section on the end. As it stands the book's not finished. From a publishing point of view it would never sell and artistically it lacks balance. But you *are* working and that's the main thing."

I don't think he was yet forty at the time, still wading through the terrible thirties—we've had more than one disconsolate smile over them —and he was no longer editor-in-chief at Simon and Schuster. He was now editor-in-chief at Knopf and I woke one morning in Godzone to find myself at Knopf. The London book—*Three*—was my first from Knopf.

He's still a generation younger than I, twenty-two years, a workable pas de deux as I've found elsewhere, reminding me of Acida in Jerusalem. He rang up from New York when Keith died but I did not go to the phone; the stakes were too high. Elliot spoke with him but Bob has recently written, "I was an offstage presence." His letters always spark affection and he sends his love freely but to me the whole minuet is beyond the beat of emotion; love was too seasonal with me to be trusted and far too disrupting. He was my work, itself inviolate. "I know you," he wrote, "better than any other man walking this earth because I have read not only all your published work but all your *unpublished* work." A benign presence offstage who sometimes took lodgings in my mind, on speaking terms with the monster.

He's a man who's diluted my appreciation of many another. I know a little more about Bob: his origins, his childhood, his family; his tastes and travails, his passions and weaknesses and the ambitions of his youth—you don't have letters from a man over two decades without picking up something—but its place is not here.

So it was strange in that June of 1969, fiction fare, that both he and I should be in London at the same time yet neither made a move to meet. It reminds me of Tchaikovsky and that woman behind the scenes, in reverse.

These Samaritans by the wayside in London, and there was another: who should be Dean of St. Paul's Cathedral but the Very Reverend

Martin Sullivan of Christchurch, New Zealand, who ten years ago had been the first New Zealander to review *Spinster*. "I don't know what I've been reading," he spoke on radio. "I've just put the book down and all I can see is crowds of children and all I hear is their chorus of voices. How can I think in this racket?"

I more than frequented St. Paul's, more than haunted; I sometimes attended his services there by day beneath the translucent dome and one at six on a Sunday evening. He refused to take this service in the great auditorium itself. "It's too big," he said. "We're too far away from one another." He took us all down to the vault, or the crypt beneath the Cathedral among the tombs of the honoured departed where you could see every feature of the choirboys' faces and hear every word Dean Sullivan spoke. About the distances between people, the vacuums where interchange should be. A beautiful service among the dead.

That was the time, I think, when I anyway spanned the vacuum and introduced myself to him and told him who I was; with the result that on the following Tuesday I went for coffee in the morning with him and his wife at St. Paul's vicarage across the street from the Cathedral, the vicarage also from Sir Christopher Wren. They'd asked a dark young artist too, a Jew, and the conversation was about his work, though it was Martin Sullivan who led it, adding extra dimensions to the thinking, and it was in this setting of Sir Christopher Wren's where I perceived a further dimension to the Dean: a "poor artist." An expatriate of Godzone, like me.

This brief section on London is not irrelevant to the line of this narrative, for the people I've mentioned bring relief to me now as they did then. In the midst of death they helped us.

I nursed Elliot through that summer at Nightingale Lane until he rose to his feet and, with the help of the staff, shuffled back to his university. There came a day when, returning from Oxford Street with heavy parcels, by underground at the peak hour, I heard that wonderful song in my head: "I'm not in New Zealand. I'm not in New Zealand." But I found Elliot in his favorite chair in his lounge holding a blue aerogramme. A lovely old lounge with the trees in full leaf through the window and the Common across the street. "I've had a letter from Ashton," he said. "Sit down while I read it to you."

My parcels . . . "No I'll stand up to hear it."

Ashton wrote of how Jasmine's young husband, David, had died suddenly on Sunday, had been buried on Tuesday and he himself was only able to sit down and write on Wednesday. He thought a telegram would have been inappropriate. That Jas was expecting a new baby at Christmas, but not to come home. They'd manage. "You stay with El," they said.

I left for that country on Saturday.

IN   TRANSIT
The picture of Whenua endures "like a retinal image after the lights are turned off, at once romantic and classical" —a phrase I've read somewhere. Whenua is a long block house lying upon a long high bank overlooking the long blue harbour. Great trees reach for the sky, thundering when

Inside the music room at Whenua

gales rush in from the sea, whispering on soft summer days, spreading their wide arms over all to protect, embrace and cool. To come in from the hard heat of the city and beneath the shaded canopy is to know green heaven.

From one end to the other the roofs are peaked like those of old-time schoolrooms, complete with bolted rafters, the entire length is windowed on the water, picturing the trees and the harbour, letting in the sun for solar heat, and from upstairs to downstairs, through foyer, music room, hall and guest wing white peaked ceilings with dark brown rafters, pale-painted block walls dark-panelled, and bare floors varnished amber; one high spacious music room mid-centre like a Maori meeting house, two studies, two kitchens and laundries, three bathrooms, six patios, ten outside doors and up to fifty windows while the cloister leads from the main house past the guest wing to Selah. The garage is off a covered walkway and, monitoring all, a tall purple chimney.

Beneath the lofty ceilings are spaces and distances with vistas repeating through windows when you turn a corner inside; scenes exploding
through the low ones like freshly framed paintings of close-up tree
trunks, feathery tree-ferns and arbours, flowers and panoramic seascape,
while through the high ones you get the skyscape so that inside includes
the outside, even the boats on the water with coloured sails and ships
moving in and out. I know places where you can look right through
that house to the other side like houses in the islands.

Whereas before only two of us had lived at Whenua, now it's a
habitation packed with children using all the doors, with their joys and
crises, voices and faces, sudden exhilarations; alive with coming and
going. A home only a decade old even now, yet Whenua has known
arrivals and departures, weddings, births and deaths; the union of two
families and a growing company of phantoms. So young in time, so
old in story.

She looks her best overflowing with people celebrating some occasion;
the doors all open by day or the lights all on by night. The best place
to see her comprehensively, however, is from the beach below the bank
looking up at her lines above.

So profound the architecture, it has art's own power to absorb emotion and though I work oceans and continents distant it still exercises
that power. When I turn out the light in some far country my spirit
joins the phantoms there to walk among the sleeping living and the
remembered dead, the birds and the cats and the hedgehogs rustling
the autumn leaves; stoops to the flowers, touches the tree trunks, loiters
in the cloister in the moving shadows patterned by the moon and looks
up to the cathedral of branches. In the night I lurk on the patio, see if
the tide is coming in or if it is going out or if a ship slips out through
the entrance; whether the horizon warns of a storm by morn or the
night-sky foretells sunshine.

I wander the spaces and heights of Whenua while the household lies
sleeping, open the keyboard of the grand piano to talk to them in their
dreams, visit the large picture of the galloping horses hoofing the dust
from the plain, of St. Francis feeding the birds from the eleventh
century, glance at the books and the Maori carvings; I confer with
the portrait of the gold-framed woman, with the nude in Selah Seven.
At night I take back my expatriate life to be absorbed in the architecture and shed. When walking by day in an alien land, and at night
when the great jet voices roll down from the dark . . . I remember
Whenua.

Jasmine's family

*October 1, 1969*

NEW ZEALAND    "Ashton met me in Auckland and brought
me home. Desperately happy. Spent morning not dressed and talked.
Went to town in afternoon with Jasmine and Martin. Went to the
bank, reopened account. Very tired. It is so quiet and beautiful here.
I feel now I'll stay for ever." (Diary)

A star above Whenua. In the western sky in the early evening after
the sun had gone, down a bit from the moon. When I'd left the big
part of the house after helping Jas with the children and walked along
the cloister to Selah where my bed was I'd see that star up there which
Lionel said was Venus. I'd loiter in the cloister in the romantic dark
and look up at the star.

There needed to be a star. Death had struck three times at the men
of our family and only one survived. Mine and Jasmine's men, the loves
of our two lives, had died within eight months of each other and were
buried within eight graves of each other. I had lost Keith but Jasmine
had lost both her Daddy and her young husband, had been left with
five children and another to come. We had a family to rear but no men
to earn, though we agreed when we talked over tea in the night when
neither of us could sleep, that we did have some assets: the children

and Whenua. And we did have Ashton who could be counted on to fill up our doorway with his height and bulk, travelling the hours and miles from Hastings to feel the pulse of Whenua.

Sometimes I'd stop altogether in the cloister on my way back to Selah after dark, lean on a pillar and look at the star but it responded in no way; it said not a thing to me and cast no comfort; offered no apologies, explanations or solutions and promised nothing whatever. A truly cool customer. But it did do one small thing; I found myself looking upward. It did give me one thing; it tossed me down a cosmic perspective.

At least it *came* every evening in the western sky whereas very few humans managed that. Not many of us are able to function in the presence of tragedy and most of us flee it affrighted; it's easier when you're part of it. You've got to have a gift for grief. I've not had that gift myself but I was still astonished that nobody came. I'd been the grand look-after-er of all time. Some of J's friends visited but of my own former friends from our days of grandeur, of high-powered entertaining, about three at the most made their way to me. My former secretary Kit was one, "all things to all men," and Keith's secretary was another, Joan Trotter; both people brilliant in responding to need. About two men from Keith's own Rotary Club which he'd founded showed brief colour but only to vanish without trace. How was it that in other countries of other cultures and colours arms had opened wherever I'd been: the French in Mauritius, Indians in Bombay, Israelis and Londoners and two Americans? You had to remember this when slipping back into the old national concept that there was something wrong with you, what is called the Kiwi* Kringe, picking up again the old established feeling I'd had before, the Kiwi Kloak of timidity. "What do we fear?" I've been asked on film.

"One another." Was it I or the country? Abroad I'd believed it was the country, not me; but here it's easier to believe it is I—oh forget this thing.

What Jas and I had to learn was that we were *widows* now, a word I'd not heard overseas; I'd been just a someone in my own right who'd happened to be passing that way. What *was* a widow? as we talked in the night. A clear-cut label printed in New Zealand; look out for a widow; she might want help with something she can't manage herself, and look out for your husband; she'll be after him too. When

---

*kiwi: a flightless bird indigenous to New Zealand which favours the darkness of the forest

I thought of the men I'd enjoyed overseas; men friends in this city had usually been a matter of suspicion and scandal and their wives had turned sour over-moment. A dimension of God's Own Country from the receiving end.

But the star was there in the after-dark, down a bit from the moon, unconcerned with our status; it reminded me of Fate in human form; something like the gaunt figure of Time but without the scythe, with garb of an operatic green. A presence walking on and off stage arbitrarily. I doubted if Fate had malice in him, only a craving to amuse and to be amused and with a gift for theatre; a cynic who found the human race the most comic of subjects as well as the most responsive of audiences. A great one, Fate was, to manipulate people with a view to his own entertainment and who only became vengeful when omitted from the script; he'd dash on stage unwritten. A ubiquitous character with a sense of humour. I could have sat down and made a portrait of the wretch in expensive coloured pencils I'd bought in London, or in vivid pre-war chalk I'd bought in Godzone all over the music room blackboard—ears, eyes, fingers, feet.

This was Selah Seven. Eight I'd left behind at the Hospice in Jerusalem and Nine at Nightingale Lane in London. Seven· had been built into Whenua with style but in it endured the poetry of the first; the back room at Featherston when I was still a girl; and of the Maori whare where two lovers had died, the cave in the bush and the sod hut later.

I settled down at once, a grandma, to help earn the living of the seven of us, to be eight of us by December. For this family I was the only grandparent left standing, there was no one else. Before David died Jas had been teaching but now she picked up his cane work from where he had put it down in his garage studio, but in order to stay with the children she used the wide music room as a studio which opened through sliding landscape doors upon the front deck where she could work in the sheltered sun—though it would have to stop when the new baby came. The cane in its raw state, the baskets both finished and unfinished in David's several designs, they looked lovely spread about; the cane art did grace Whenua.

I began another book but though Bob gave me much help—"Now you have the sequence of events; it remains for you to point up the dramatic situations"—no hot imagery flared. The story was called Five Women, I think, but the whole five bored me. So I left that and wrote a second book through eight drafts in a string of dramatic situations all the way, but whereas before my books wrote themselves, not· me,

I was now only going through the motions of writing a book. The monster had vacated or was comatose. No selfish artist rampaged round the house of my mind demanding to be first all the time. Where was he? Was he not liking our groping through the valley of the shadow of death, one after another? How could any person or circumstance down that monster, my rapturous dangerous companion-in-mind since I first drew a horse on a bank? I couldn't believe it.

Maybe Bob too was missing the monster with whom he alone had been on working terms, missing the excitement of combat, détente. Don't tell me Bob was finding now an ordinary woman's unfired mind, content to be offstage; a mind of no contentiousness, of the kind to go on the rate-payers' committee, play bridge or join the gold club; to integrate with society and get on with my neighbours. He didn't even criticise the second book. Only good writing could get past Bob, who has been quoted as saying, "Good writing pays."

Neither book got by him. I jerked to a halt. How then had I written that book in London? Momentum, or the magic of Elliot's roof? With six children and two adults to help to support my capital was coming down like *that*—like the woodpile in winter. What I needed was a miracle, but I saw none on the harbour when I sought one there. I ought to apply for a job at the dry-cleaners in town, in the city laundry, go out charring for my former friends or borrow a bike and deliver the mail. At least the PSBMEH wouldn't mind, which was alive and well and flourishing in God's Own Country. Young New Zealand teachers following *Teacher* were still sending letters to me about being warned and threatened by headmasters and inspectors: "If you go on with that work you'll have no future." "The book salesman was in last week," from the bookseller in town where I was buying Christmas presents for the children. "He said the education department had warned him not to carry *Spinster* and *Teacher*; they didn't want those books in the country."

Rigidity, timidity, beneath the crinoline; stale mouldy air. Inbred thinking. And that goes for me too when I'm here.

That morning as I sat at my table in a green silk padded housecoat with pockets and silver buttons from chin to toe, looking in the garden for a miracle, I got up, walked back along the cloister to the big house and found Jas tending the new baby and said, "I can't write now, Jas."

"Why?"

"The artist in me is sedated. I'll do the new baby if you earn the living."

"I'd be able to give more time to the old baby."

So Jas picked up the cane work again and I picked up the new baby and here I was near sixty with a brand-new baby boy called Daniel. We moved his crib into Selah by my bed, along with his nappies and bottles and gear and that very first night after I'd washed him and changed him and fed him his milk in his bottle I sang him to sleep with a brand-new lullaby never heard before till that minute. "By-bye for Daniel."

Jasmine's cane

Bringing up Daniel

I'd forgotten how to bring up a baby so I sang Dan up instead. I'd sung to the others in babyhood and already had a repertoire of lullabies, but with Dan-dan the songs fell like mercy from the heaven above upon the place beneath; songs in the minor for the bathroom to keep his hands still so as not to get the soap in his eyes, a dozen or so verses; songs in the major for the kitchen to keep him from snatching the spoon—just one first bar and he became spellbound—songs for midnight if he woke and cried to dance with him in my arms, songs I'd made for Co and for Kirstine and had sung to the boys as well and songs I'd made in the pre-fab infant room to sing to the little Maoris. After tea with the children ready for bed Jas never failed to take us all to the music room to sing with the piano for Dan-dan; we'd sing and sing to Dan on his mother's knee, enthralled . . . Whenua absorbed it all.

A bereaved and shaken household, each one of us manifesting his own particular shock, but Jas remained her father's daughter: before Daniel was born, I think it was, her spirit dried its eyes long enough to think of others in her own condition, now that she knew what it was like. She began organising the first solo parents' group in Tauranga and there came an evening with the children in bed as I was retiring to Selah with Dan when I saw one slight sad young woman sitting by the fire with her. Another Saturday night two came, then more.

The whole six children were casualties from David's dramatic death though their pain showed up in personal ways. Most of them looked like David, inheriting his dark good looks, except Grant, the eldest boy, who'd inherited Jasmine's, but all were lovely to look at, brown eyes and blue, dark hair and fair. Co was at high school, Grant at intermediate, Adrian and Kirstine at primary, Martin the old baby of three at his mother's knee and Daniel the new baby at crib level. Two babies, the old and the new. And it was no joke getting the top four to school in the morning, homework done, lunches cut, where's my bag, I can't find my socks, four bikes operating; especially when it rained and supplying enough coats, or taking them by car with two babies at home. And don't forget the family washing every single morning, every line full up, and the nappies to be folded.

For the first time since I'd had my own children I couldn't afford a housekeeper but that worked out all right for Jas wouldn't hear of one anyway, believing that children should learn to clean up after themselves, make their own beds, do their own rooms and take their turns at the dishes. Besides, I wasn't writing so I needed no housekeeper myself, and needed no secretary either. But we seldom had time to talk things over except at the clothesline hanging out the clothes or in the middle of the night when neither could sleep and we drank tea with the phantoms of our dead. "Jas, I loved that man so much I wanted to lie on the kitchen floor and for him to kick me to prove how much I loved him."

It was the old baby, Martin, who'd been the toddler round David's feet, who'd shadowed him, hung round his neck, spent his waking hours in the garage studio amid the cane with his father and who'd accompanied him to the railway yards to freight the completed baskets. Now, when not demanding his mother's attention, he'd developed a lethal passion for electric points and plugs and connections: "We're going to lose that boy one of these days, Mummie." He took to lighting secret matches, he'd light fires in his bedroom early morning before the rest of us woke up and, "You boys, you must hide that axe. Put it on top of the garden shed." That he was marvellously handsome with his father's face alleviated nothing. One morning when he accompanied me to the woodheap he stopped and patted the ground, "Daddy's down there. Unner the ground."
      Wait.
      "He's in a box."
      "Yes."
      "He can't walk."
      "No."
      At the door of Selah, "I've got to go and write now, Mart," and he cried. "I can write, Grandma."
      On my left side at the table and a big white card. "Well what are you going to write?"
      "Daddy."
      So in my old way of the pre-fab I take the little chap's key vocabulary each morning and when I didn't he'd cry at my door.
      Over some weeks each school morning when the others have gone to school he comes to my door for what he calls his writing and the words surface, the captions of the imagery within: words like *box, ground, plug, points, Mummie, Daniel, goods shed, car, railway, matches* and *axe*, but he's not always sure of them the next morning, from which I suppose there is some other image blocking the channel, jamming the mechanism. The words he doesn't recognise I withdraw

so that instead of his vocabulary accumulating it remains but a few. To Jas at her cane, "I don't know what the image is holding things up. I never do."

In the sun on the patio with Jas weaving, Martin writing and Daniel asleep, I give Mart stiff white cards to write on and my own big black crayon and he makes these jagged strokes all ways, like mod pop art or the sounds of the new music; abstract. No curves yet. I hold up his own card to him, "What's that word, Marto?"

"That's Daddy. Now *I* do it, *I* do it," and snatches the card, and holds it up to me. "What's this word, Grandma?"

"Daddy."

One morning he comes in from the garage and tells us, "Daddy's out there. He can walk."

And Jasmine says, "Yes."

"That's the eidetic image, Jas. He's actually seen David. It occurs with some children and with adult artists. I've seen Keith come to my window in Selah, from the vegetable garden, and in his old clothes. Smiling."

Excitedly, "I've seen David come in the door. That door, there."

When Jas has a load of cane baskets ready to put on the train we all go to the railway yards, she, I and the two babies, but as we don't know the way it is Martin who directs us. He runs away into the goods shed and disappears behind piled-up cases and when he comes back, "Daddy's in there."

"What's he doing?" from his mother.

"Oh he's just packing the baskets in the van."

Now that I was doing the new baby Jas could give the old baby priority to counter the ousted child syndrome, holding him on her knee and talking with him. But his recognition of his words remained inaccurate and his behaviour saddening. Jas got the man out to fit covers over the electric points, but Martin made short work of those. And she hid every match in the house and the boys kept the axe out of reach on top of the garden shed until the day he managed to climb up there. Some day, I hoped, the damaging rogue image would surface. So much crying from the little chap.

On the patio one morning with the witnessing trees spreading a roof above us, and with Martin doing his writing, his mother stepped back from the pitcher basket to judge its symmetry. "Is that right, Mummie, do you think? Doesn't the left shoulder bulge a bit?"

I don't answer at once. "That boy should have a vocabulary of about thirty by now, the other children did, but there's only a few. I still think there's an image there seizing up the whole show. Like that basket, it has a bulge on one side, so it can't slide through the exit. But look, Jas, at his writing this morning; there are curves coming among those strokes."

She says, "What's that writing, Martin?"

"That's the ammulance taking Daddy away."

So *that* was it and he'd written it himself.

Next morning I hold up to him his own writing from the patio, jagged erratic marks and curves, "What's this word you wrote, Marto?"

"Ammulance." And from then on he recognised the rest. A very beautiful-looking boy, Mart. A rest to see fewer tears on his face.

With Whenua to maintain on my own, a big family for Jas to support and me not earning, by the time one year was out, my capital was at ground level and Jas and I had to stop smoking. At an impassioned address from Corinne one night on the evils of smoking she'd learnt at school her mother reached over and put out her cigarette so I had to do the same. Where was our living coming from now? About this time it was when I noticed an excellent line drawing ad in the newspaper of a bulky jetliner covering half a page. On the wall blackboard in the music room I copied the plane several sizes larger, taking the whole area, and when the children piled in from school, "What did you draw that for, Grandma?"

"I just felt like drawing a jet."

A few days later another miracle was in the mail-box, an aerogramme in handscript from Aspen on top of the Rockies in Colorado inviting me to come and take over a new breakaway community school, all round-trip travelling expenses; they'd meet me, house me and put me on salary. I read this letter in Selah on my own first, then trekked along the cloister to find Jasmine at her cane with Martin, and put it in her hand. "You ought to go, Mummie, for your own sake."

A few days later Kit breezed in and I gave her the letter.

"It means teaching again, my girl," she warns.

"There's always the faint chance, Kit, that I might find the ideal conditions to repeat my work—you never know."

"I told her she has to go," from Jas.

"Well who wants a drink?"

Kit calls for whiskey, Jas has sherry and I drink a whole bottle of lager.

Kit says, "That's a very fine plane on the blackboard, Sylvia."

Jas, "It flew in just before the letter."
Martin, "Grandma's going to Ameri-go-round."

Aspen sent my round-trip fare, second-class, at which I cabled back, "I don't travel second-class. Send first-class fare." It came at once, by return cable. It was for Aspen to do the spadework about the work permit to admit me to the United States on the grounds that they wanted me. You can wait eighteen months otherwise. A year they said. Rip down the island in the Chrysler to Ash and Marg to say goodbye; "Ash, if anything else happens out here, don't call me. I've *made* Jasmine get her visa—in case of Elliot. Or in case of me. *She* can go."

"How can I look after you?"

And to say goodbye to Wig in Wanganui, the friend of my youth, only to find she'd been buried the day before. Called on the Shaws too in Te Awamutu, our friends of Waiomatatini; we had wine and roast lamb and I stayed the night and we talked about Keith Henderson. "I'm not coming back," I told them. That was all; slip out like a thief in the night as I had done last time.

It was Jas who drove me to Auckland and put me on the plane. I forget who minded the children. Just one sniff of that international terminal and off peeled the Kiwi Kringe. I tell you, I walked off to that plane with my head up, with a determined steady step. I'd done it before. I'm always at my best when leaving New Zealand—though Jasmine wept for me. What I didn't tell anyone except the Shaws was . . . I preferred to be buried in a foreign land.

ASPEN   Beyond the blue Pacific, arms opened again. No longer a second-class citizen of Godzone I was becoming a world citizen, my philosophy well known ahead of me. Outside of New Zealand, people liked me like anything; they didn't seem to mind having artists around and gave you 100 percent when it was due, with no skirting coyly about 99, complaining, "It hasn't been done before." In place of the label "widow" I was an ordinary person in my own right. "This is Sylvia. What'll you have to drink?"

"I drink lager."

I must be all right after all, but it was hard to believe. With half a lifetime as a recluse behind me and established fame ahead I wondered in the plane towards Hawaii if it were too late to shed the past even though I'd already changed everything possible; clothes bought in London, the colours wholly inspired by the paua shell: turquoise greens with a vein of purple, a thread of scarlet and maybe a point of orange, while the paua earrings to match my eyes I'd bought in Tauranga. Paua was the very last thing you'd think I'd cultivate but something deeper than reason warned me.

I'd changed all the music I used to play; dropped the old masters with too much overhead of memory and tried to understand the twentieth-century music, abandoned the old poets too. During our sleepless nights at Whenua, Jas and I had worked out what to do about grief: only one thing—forget. But my old-time heart was still nailed down in something like rigor mortis so how could I love again? Except for Dan-dan I'd loved no one new since Keith had died over a year ago, which is no condition in which to respond to people. I couldn't change my heart like clothes and music.

Loving fans in Hawaii, the Leibs, flicking me off between planes; in San Francisco two professors of education who had stayed at Whenua and had known Keith, to meet me, and the next thing I was neck-deep in fame at close quarters for the first time: an American reception, suppers, restaurants, wines, people, shopping (trying to find a teapot), telegrams to both my sons and phone calls to and from Aspen. "Yes she's arrived. Yes we'll put her on the plane on Saturday." The personality of the country was something new, unrelated to Asia and Europe. I sure arrive in different countries in different ways.

Cruising by air over state after state, hard blue above, deserts below with the Rockies snow-clad ahead. Cities, canyons, mountains—no end to this land. What was beyond this new horizon? In the mind new dimensions exploded, broad new perspectives hit me, a child from the foothills of Godzone. Panic leapt white as light yet I could still hear that song within me, brilliant, rapturous, "I'm not in New Zealand." Let the plane fall into the heat below, let it crash on cliffs, let it crack into a thousand fragments on the snowy peaks and that would be better than home.

DIARY: October 3, 1970. "Saturday. Travelled by plane to Salt Lake City—then Grand Junction. Planes both smooth. Roby and Margaret Albouy met me, also Wanda. Drove me up to Aspen about five to the Ickies home lent to me. Many parents came with food. Very kindly received. Slept well alone in big house."

Aspen—the
residence

In Aspen a large elegant unoccupied two-storeyed house full of staircase, bathrooms and affluence with a fine grand piano downstairs. In the kitchen were gentle people, soft voices, courtesy and attention. Exotic food prepared, casseroles for several days ahead. They'd sent for me having a use for me but I was so exhausted I could hardly speak, hardly keep my head upright. Did I need a maid? Yes. Did I need a secretary? Yes. Did I want a car? No thanks. You've not brought your typewriter." No. "Have some wine, Miss Ashton-Warner."

"I'd rather have lager please," and someone dashed uptown. I drank a lot of Colorado Coors, elixir itself, until I was able to say something. "I'd like you to call me Mrs. Henderson or, for short, Mrs. H."

October is the fall and well before daylight I haunt the windows to see what the day is going to be, to watch the mountains appear in the sky and the aspen trees on the ground in amber. I find the world is full of flakes erasing all outline.

> When I wake in the morning
> it is snowing
> I hadn't known
> I'd been awake during the night
> but hadn't heard
>
>                     when it is light
>                     the scape is white.

In the big suite upstairs on my own with snow on the ground below. Eight thousand feet up, oxygen-short, light-headed, jet-lagged, culture-shocked. Every night while the broad central staircase creaked from nocturnal contraction like phantom robbers raiding, with snow-slides from the roof booming on the ground I wrote to Elliot who I reckoned was closer geographically than Ashton, but I'd not told El in the first place that I was leaving New Zealand. "Where exactly *is* our mother?" he wrote to Ash.

"Why don't I ask Mrs. H to supper on Saturday?" from a parent to Margaret. "Other people want to meet her."
    "She's booked out for the season."
    "During the week then?"
    Margaret appears to have appointed herself as my guardian angel; it had been she who had written to me in Godzone, after Kate's aerogramme. "She doesn't go out at night during the week. She goes to bed early and gets up early to work."
    "What about Sunday?"
    "She doesn't go to parties the night before school."
    "Uh-uh. So why don't I get in on the end and start another season, okay? What's she like?"
    "Charming to distraction."

> The hour is alive with floating flakes
> the new morning full of them
> they have no sound
> as they fly
> on every whim of air
> as they flip
> inconsequently.

I didn't know what had happened to my mind. I must have known about jet-lag before but I hadn't heard of culture shock though I must have had it several times. No one had warned me of light-headedness in high altitudes, even in the young who soon adjusted. Dr. Whitcomb told me over supper at his mountain mansion, "Any islander with sixty years of sea-level behind her is bound to overreact to eight thousand feet." Ignorant as a snowflake.
    The first time in my life I'd lived entirely alone in a building, at the very stage when I needed to be living with others. Faced with the evening in this empty house, empty but for the phantoms of the family

who owned it—the senator had taken his life when young—I turned
to my solution to all problems: work. But settling down with my papers
at seven at the long family dining table in the cornered shadowy
lounge, my imagery took over in uproar. The events of the day, people
on staff, the unleashed children; what they'd said and done, what I'd
said and done, what I should have said and done. Conversations
repeating themselves to the point of rote memory. Feeling spinning and
plunging—control shocked away. By nine I'd find myself still sitting
there on a hard dining chair staring unseeing at the paper with
nothing on it at all; every night except Saturday when I'd be taken out
to dine. And even then when bathing and dressing the imagery would
grip and I'd become mesmerised. Why hadn't I known these things?

I don't know how long it lasted like that till it stabilised. And then
it was only because there was no master design at school on paper for
new staff to refer to in the interests of co-ordination, and no reading
books for the children either; just arbitrary commercial stuff from toy
shops. The school wouldn't countenance the standard reading books
put out by monopolies which provided headmasters with more than
one car and holidays to Europe, and not without reason. I started on
a set of graded reading books, twelve of them, specifically for the
children I was with; swift roughs arising from the locality—raccoons,
snowplows and skiing, using the material at hand and the local dialect.
Strictly transitional, as I'd not yet assembled sufficient collective key
vocabulary to divine what was really there in the lower regions of the
instinctive mind, or to employ its miraculous therapy. Painting fast
illustrations of American children in American clothes with American
talk. It turned out to be this work, especially the painting, which
enabled me to hold my mind together in the bewildered evenings.

The theme story featured a small guy who wanted to go to school
with the other kids but cried when he finally got there. I made a set
of twelve with all the technique which was second nature to me of
word choice, word recurrence, sentence length, page length, careful
grading of difficulty and the erupting drama of home and school.
Above all I had the rhythm of cadence and the line of thought and
cross-reference known only to a writer. And one extra for Halloween,
my favorite, with devils, witches, spooks, the lot. And four copies of
each one to go round—no, two copies of each one, making twenty-
four little books and laid my home-grown wares before the little
Americans—until I myself had trained the teacher or the graduates
how to teach the children to write their own books. On these the
children were learning to read though no one said thank you for the

books. I thought they could have said "At least they're workable," but it was reward enough to see the little books becoming progressively dogeared.

Nor did I know what was happening to my body; not enough oxygen in the air at this altitude made you puff and gasp, even in young people newly arrived for the skiing, though they adjusted in time. Also because Aspen on top of the Rockies is surrounded by deserts, the air when it arrived had a minimum of moisture and your respiratory passages dried out. Again, air-conditioning at 70 degrees during eight months of snow makes hothouse conditions, which I think influences North American academic thinking in a major way; the same even temperature at home, in the car and at work does not promote metaphor in terms of nature so that speech levels out into monotone and jargon and multisyllabic platitudes with a depreciation in cadence of delivery and in facial expression. I used to think it very funny the way North American faces remained flat still when they spoke, while the lips galloped along. It's like going through the motions of speaking rather than communicating thought and feeling—their writing like that too. It takes an islander whose physical mechanisms are accustomed to swinging in response to heat and cold to miss the rhythm of the seasons and I walked a lot to replace it.

But you don't adjust at sixty. I'd hardly had a headache in my life but now a persistent pain in one temple was found by Dr. Whitcomb to be incipient high blood pressure. I'd seldom had a cold in my life but later in the corner house some winter affliction entered my chest and I couldn't breathe enough. I had to buy a moisturiser for the big downstairs room where my table and bed were. I'd have it going all night of every night. Even so, after a week in bed, Margaret slept on the couch all night, nursing me, until by morning I was begging her to take me down to lower altitudes, but since for me to go away was for the school funding to go away, understandably she rang Dr. Whitcomb instead, whose own children were at our school, and the next thing I was in the Cottage Hospital halfway up a mountain and even higher still, for ten days of oxygen. Outside it was about 28 degrees below, inside crammed with broken bones from the several skiing fields. "Nurse, please take me to some door where I can breathe some air."

"It's too cold. It'll kill you."

"You take me to a door, Nurse. Let me *see* the air."

Edging through the beds packed in the corridors, limbs on pulleys sticking up all ways like radio aerials, and foreign languages, but when she finally opened the front door a crack, in slashed an icy dagger of cold slicing up your face and slam it went again. And that was *air*. I tell you I lost no time learning to operate the oxygen tubes.

Much goodwill in that hospital and care and the school looked after me like its own, which in truth I was. The only factor which spoils this story is that whereas in Godzone you could go into public hospital for as long as required, with the best medical treatment available, all for free, here these ten days of oxygen mopped up my entire N.Z. medical insurance and more and I had to take out another. In North America health is business.

Mind and body were plainly not Aspen material but I was not here for nothing and I'd see out my year somehow. The problems of an islander at the dizzy top of the world at the heart of a major continent. I lurked round art shops uptown looking for a picture of the sea. Had I owned the house I was in I'd have painted a glorious mural on the walls with waves washing from ceiling to floor; in the kitchen too and on the ceilings. A gleaming heaving ocean.

> The air is breathing
> spinning flakes
> often colliding
> the careless flakes
> to fall
> regretfully.

Adapt and survive, my motto. Well I suppose I did to a point. To achieve it I walked a great deal in the snow. With no mail delivery or collection or taxis I'd walk the mile and a half or so each day to the post office and I'd like to explore the base of the mountain where the skiing was, watching the thousands of brilliantly hued visitors chairing up to the summit and gliding down and to see the multi-national multi-condominiums and hotels put up by developers. A gaudy microcosm of the outside world. On Sunday I'd be drawn to the Aspen Institute across the snow-deep meadow where world seminars were held in the summer on any major subject agitating humanity. Yet Aspen was only a small town, village-like, with no fences in the streets like country lanes, fewer kerbs and the houses were either marvellous survivors of the Victorian best or dreams of originality, most of them log-built in style.

I was in love with the snow. Kit had written, "It is not unknown, this mystical response to the snow when you first meet it." I liked it best when thickly falling. I'd brought my fur coat, blue Siberian squirrel from Arctic winters, bought fur snow boots at once, leather mittens, woollen balaclava and borrowed Mrs. Ickies' walking stick, she the owner of the big yellow house where I lived, who only returned for the skiing at Christmas. I loved walking in the snow, a spinster alone, hearing my song, "I'm not in Godzone."

Especially when spring walked in the door like the return of a lifelong friend, a member of the family you could say, when the aspens began confessing themselves, explaining what they meant to do, green touching overhead along the streets like the beams of cathedral cloisters, when I'd put away the fur coat and wear the cape and a scarf round my head. Or when wildflowers arrived in summer like exotic young girls, their skirts colouring the rocky meadow and the abruptly tall mountains, in purple through cerise to ochre and red. A long walk for the mail would end in a picturesque restaurant open to the street in which starry tourists strolled, where I'd rest and read a letter from home. Daniel had been crawling when I'd left and now they wrote he could walk. Through the hot noons I'd like to wear white touched with turquoise or cream backgrounded in brown, wearing soft sandals I'd bought in Bombay. I'd rest there over a coffee.

But when autumn painted the aspens yellow to graduate through amber to sepia and the cloisters in the streets had stained-glass windows I'd swing my stick in reflection; recalling some long-past picture which had arrested me when young, of a solitary cloaked wanderer; some artist, musician or poet I think, a philosopher or absent-minded professor; an image which either took me over or which I took over to myself, feeling instinctive accord with him; a feeling which placated my turbulence as though I'd recognised myself, but whereas before I'd wondered what had been in his mind and what had made him like that, I now knew, for I was that solo wanderer. I now knew he'd been engrossed in thoughts of other people of many kinds and colours and that some destructive sorrow had made him like that. The picture had taken form in romantic reality. When walking alone I was full of good company and I fondled my solitude.

> What I love about the snow
> it is so soft
> to touch
> and to be touched by
> it ravishes me
> when it brushes my face
> sentimentally.

I've already written a book on the Community School, *Spearpoint*, so I don't have to retrace my tracks. The school was in the physics building, a long narrow flat double row of very small rooms divided by a tunnel-like corridor. There were three double rooms and a foyer, though I never occupied any of the rooms, small or double, but tried to work in the open corridor; Judy was in our double room where she worked on the key vocabulary and needed it most. The building had been designed for offices for quiet studious physicists but now it was a crowded rocket halfway to space.

A breakaway school in its embryonic stage, rejecting the public education system and funded, for a start, by the parents themselves. No facilities whatever other than adult furniture; no one in charge, no equipment, no discipline, no rules, no authority, no responsibility and above all no central design—no written constitution, you could say; or, what I'd say, no master scheme; the only philosophy apparent being that all were equal and that all were free. It had been open only a few days by the time I arrived; bang in all together and hope for the best.

Only three trained teachers on staff: Wanda with the seniors, Judy with the juniors—and me; the balance were mainly unarmed adventurers come to Aspen for the skiing who had somehow been accepted on their own recommendations. Several held contracts from publishers to write a book about me, whether they could write or not, and one elongated student from California had been allowed on staff not to teach but to follow me round with a notebook and pencil as material for her thesis. Not that I minded—a change from Godzone, and Mary was exuberant company.

Letters and phone calls poured in from the States for me to speak at universities, banquets and conferences which the office staff handled on my behalf, I didn't read them. I'd supplied them with a sample reply: "Thank you for your kind invitation but the nature of my work requires that I forfeit these professional pleasures," which I'd used for ten years to all comers. Also they put notices at the school entrance directing visitors to the office rather than allowing them free access to the infant end which had become indistinguishable from a crowded street fair. There was an average of nine new applicants for jobs per day.


The rooms were matchbox size except for the one double matchbox at our end which had to be for Judy and the key vocabulary children;

one matchbox for painting, one for clay, one for math, one for the
seven-year-olds and the double one for Judy, which left the corridor
for me cluttered with coats, lunches and snacks, parkas, skis and
"Where's my other glove?" No light of course except electric, but the
particular thing about this corridor was its being the highway to the
one exit at our end, two toilets for the whole school, staff included,
the one storeroom where everyone snatched coffee standing and the
intersection for the traffic between all the rooms, clay, paint, math, the
sevens and Judy. So I sat on a low chair there with a group of fives
and sixes amid a haze of moving legs about us, stepping over, through
and round us. It did get through to me, however, that in fact I needed
to sit here mid-centre as a unifying focus of the several segments, and
whenever anyone closed a door, by God I opened it, I tell you.

As for the desired ideal conditions to demonstrate my work, well
I had to lift my sights and see it as an excellent exercise in vision, the
challenge of all time and the luck of the draw. There was no alternative other than to return to Godzone and I sat this out for five months,
mentioning it to none, before I called it a day. Only Mike S on staff
appreciated the situation as it was and he didn't talk for a year.

As I've noted in *Spearpoint* I found in the minds of the small children
a redistribution of the instincts with some absent altogether. Parent
love was replaced by dog love, while workaday fear was mostly not
there. Was this latest stage American, a throw-up of the post-industrial
society, the avant-garde of the race heading for space? I made my set
of reading books all over again—began to make them I mean—with
more time and more thought, introducing dogs to the theme, give or
take a cat or raccoon, and still mean to put in a dinosaurus, and played
down family love which I'd featured in the first place; illustrated them
more abstractly in the twentieth-century style, and called them the
*Aspen Books*. By which time I'd brought my own little group of fives
and sixes to write their own little books as the En-Zedders had done
twenty years ago; which is the magic of the key vocabulary—it ac-
commodates itself to any state of mind, any variant of the mind, any
culture, any race; in a cave or on its way to space.

This new dimension of responsibility in a school for a "poor artist."
What I needed most was to get to know the children, and the office
staff drew up a programme for me to meet the parents of each child
in the junior department, one couple at a time, twice a week after
school at my house to talk to me about their children. "I need this

more than most teachers," I told Margaret, "being an alien and a brand-new one at that."

And there in that big yellow home of Mrs. Ickies, in the vast cornered white and black lounge with touches of red and a grand piano, the snow thickening and whitening towards mid-winter, I'd brush my hair after school, make up my face, put on some Chinese gown of black satin and gold dragons and receive the new parents. Cultivated people of European origin, desperate to rescue their children from the bolted system which could bulldoze the identity out of a child and into anonymity as a person. "The battle against mediocrity," said one. I felt quite equal to honouring their faith in me and the money they'd put into the school, for I'd never been without respect for, and confidence in, my own work.

I'd already met some of them in their own original log-built homes, panelled in spruce, in the valleys of the mountains. Most spoke very good American and even the Queen's English. From years in the key vocabulary listening to the faltering or impassioned captions of the innermost instincts I learnt more about these residents in that congressional lounge than I had at their evening tables. With a notebook in hand, "What would you like me to enter here about your children for me to refer to later?" And I'd suggest to them they join the staff

in the afternoons to give us a hand with the many skills which no one
teacher could know.

You'd never recognise me as that girl from the past habitually playing the limelight, talking too much, throwing round my music gratis
and flaunting my art; I was becoming that someone I'd always been
interested in—a contained impenetrable spinster, an indispensable
unit of society. At times Judy or Wanda would join me in these conferences and sometimes Margaret would come in later. "Glorious
creature," she said.

Though Aspen was a small fabled and famed town, I found most
stages of Americans there—I'd known them in the past from my fan
mail—with the exception of orthodox criminals. The magistrate's
court had little to do at that time, though it has had since. The battles
took place between mind and mind rather, the knives were unsheathed in words, for the recognised sin was dissemblance while good
equated with frankness—right or left, right or wrong. The mupersons
were the spearpoint of civilisation so far, and since several mupeople
had seats on the Community School board there resulted power politics on it which recurringly made front-row drama: "Who's the new
director now?" A species not easy to work with and uneven to love
with, but dangerously innovative to fight with.

> The snow
> does not hit like sleet
> or sudden memory
> unexpectedly.

Dr. Jan Veatch, professor of education at the university in Tempe,
Arizona, had stayed at Whenua and known Keith. She was mindful
of me in my first Christmas in the States, and since I would not fly
any more she asked a doctoral student of hers, Florence, to drive to
Aspen and get me. As it happened I had to vacate the Ickies mansion,
for the family was returning for Christmas and the skiing, and Kate
had arranged for me to take over another house at five hundred dollars
a month. In the meantime I'd go to Jan.

The new house was nearly the prettiest in Aspen: old-time, grey and
white, two-storeyed and surrounded by flouncing verandahs. Nearer
to the school, on a corner in the same street, across the road from the

Aspen meadow in which stood the world-famous Aspen Institute frequented in summer by leading orchestras, world seminars on global issues, radio, TV, science, physics and even education. The music would wave over the meadow into my house gratis. You should hear the voice of a coloratura soprano lifting among the mountains in rehearsal, soaring among the peaks like a voice calling, This Is My Home. I'd wend across the meadow through the wildflowers to sit in on some rehearsals in the vast music tent, attend the concerts in the afternoon four times a week—the music tent held thousands of people. On Sunday afternoons at two o'clock everyone alive was there, pretty dresses frothing among the flowers as on some ancient village green.

My second
Aspen residence

A few of the stars I met at parties whose contracts included a clause about circulating among the people: physicists, violinists—the Institute building itself was a star. I myself spoke twice at that Institute, running into an interchange with Bill Moyers.

"Now tell me, Miss Ashton-Warner, what do you think of Aspen?"

"I don't want to be run out of town."

At a cocktail party at Pomegranate Inn Mr. McNamara said, "We like new blood in this country."

But that was in the summer, later. Right now in mid-winter the day I moved into the corner house was one of the days when I cancelled my berth on a Pacific liner home, a booking which changed

as often as the director on our school board. Aspen was a tangible
visible representation of what my journey through life was like:
knives and wine; blizzards and flowers. Yet I could live in Aspen.

Whenever I contemplated going home I remembered our plight at
Whenua; only Jas and me to bring up that family of six, educate
them, feed and clothe them, supply them with bikes for school, rain-
coats, rainhats, gumboots for the rain and promote opportunities for
them and not only for the present but right up through their secondary
schools into university and their futures, till they got jobs and married,
with Ashton our only man who had his own family hundreds of
miles away—Elliot was still in London. Those moments when I
wrote out a cheque for an envelope home, whenever I was paid,
justified this arbitrary life so that my walk to the post office among
the dogs to post it rose to the level of a pilgrimage. Those moments
sent me to school in the morning, plodding through the snow at
daybreak at sixty, fending off the dogs.

> It does not soak like rain
> the snow
> it does not push me
> like the wind of circumstance
> or pull
> demandingly.

Three colleges were bidding for me at that time: Pasadena, the University of Colorado at Boulder, and the University of Denver, which
wanted me for both literature and education. Two men from that
faculty came to Aspen to see me. Soon after Christmas the dean rang
me and actually welcomed me there. Neither I nor the Community
School board quite knew how to work it, for to be affiliated with a
university would be a route for grants. Half a term here, half a term
there, we wondered.

Another thing on the mind of the school was the local election
coming up. Maybe there can be no fiercer elections than in a town with
its beauty at stake; in the spring and the fall with the visitors gone
Aspen belonged to itself with little more traffic than bikes and dogs.
You could cross a street backwards and make the other side, and most
residents wished Aspen to remain like that, small and village-like.

Speculators, however, saw fortunes in development to accommodate
the high tides of skiers in season. Some businesses made their year's
income from the winter alone so there was every reason to plant your

own man on the town council and other public bodies. The Community School was concerned to put its man on the Aspen board of education with survival in mind in the form of tax support and the use of the public schoolbuses, all of which split the people down the middle.

I soon picked up which side I was paid to be on, if only by shopping in the markets where some people kissed me and others cut me which I didn't like much. It was unnerving to find how the school was hated, even feared, whereas taking sides is not the philosophy of a writer; I'd rather see the whole. So I took to crossing the picket lines some afternoons, having put in the morning at the Community School, to visit the state primary, the middle school of hundreds of children where there was at least a central principle for co-ordination, and I'd spend an hour sitting in a desk in a straight row among the children and doing what they did, being still and quiet. One day the headmaster, Mr. Harvey, ran into me strolling along one of his own corridors, the official foe. He was stunned. "Fancy meeting *you* here."

In time I was dining in the homes of some of his staff and in his home too, hilariously; they said it wasn't fair for me to be kept inaccessible to the rest of the schools. I invited Mr. Harvey to lunch at Toro's where you could get these incomparable Mexican tacos and the Coors lager, in full view of friend and foe. A quiet firm friendly man, Mr. Harvey, whom you felt you could turn to, who knew where he was going and why and who valued a joke. And you'd think that after the deprivation I'd felt at the Community School with no hand of a headmaster I'd have felt nostalgia for the old order, but no, not wholly. I hadn't enjoyed sitting in straight rows and having trouble borrowing a pencil. I was one for the teaching freedoms myself. What I missed most at the C.S. was responsibility.

My community family took this crossing of the boundary equably enough, seeing it, I suppose, as an extension of free movement, or that's what I hoped. Wanda said she'd accompany me one day, also Mike S, but as it happened they didn't, though some teachers from the middle school came to visit us. I felt my function to be more natural as a both-sides job for I understood both schools. I saw Aspen as a family and you can't have a family divided like that, not so bitterly. I'd visit other schools too from about two p.m.: the high school out of town, the junior school, pre-school, Catholic and Montessori and looked in on a kindergarten. I wasn't keen on it and didn't enjoy myself but I meant to do my job as I saw it whether I liked it or not, whether I was paid or not for that matter. In the meantime I got away with working astride the border until the elections came up. It was spring in March and the snow was fast.

So was the pace; we were expecting Washington next week who were coming to look us over, a team from the Office of Education. Diary: "Wed. Revised paper for Washington people. Shampoo, manicure uptown. At 4 Margaret grabbed me and took me to the airport to meet the Feds: Don Davies, large, good-looking, dark and young; Bob Leasme who was small and smiling, and a senior woman judge of the children's court in New York who was seventy. Then to a hard welcome cocktail party which nearly killed me. I slept ten hours till seven in the morning."

The school

That night I gave a smashing dinner party in a private room at the Paragon for the Washington people. Thirteen present. I didn't drink. Some wore evening dress, some in jeans and one still in his skiing suit. I wore black sequins myself and sat at the end of my table, inviting Don Davies to take the other end. I'd expected to bring down Don in the interests of an education grant for the school, but Margaret, who'd been a model in New York in her youth, she sat at his right and saved me the trouble. From Don to me later, "She's a very beautiful woman, isn't she?"

Everyone had their say in the American way, gowns, jeans and suits from D.C., and when it came to my turn I welcomed them in both

English and Maori then limbered up and performed a Maori action song, Tamariki, complete with swaying hips and fluttering fingers, earrings, sequins and all. Godzone entertaining Washington, D.C. From Don later, "The most extraordinary dinner party I've ever attended."

Next morning the Feds were at school at eight-thirty. I wasn't there, I came at eleven. I wanted the young teachers to have them to themselves for a couple of hours. Later I gave a paper at the Aspen Institute across the meadow, on the place of responsibility in freedom, and the occasion for discipline when working with small children, though I didn't actually believe in the effectiveness of talking, as such. "Without responsibility freedom becomes license and anarchy."

After that Don Davies and Bob Leasme lunched with me at my corner house where the talk was of a Washington grant in the fall to keep the Community School afloat, if I agreed to stay another year in Aspen to train U.S. professors in my work, the school as a centre. The way you go about it, they said, was to affiliate with some university and the grant could come through that way. But all next day when the visitors were skiing I was irresolute as I hadn't heard from Jasmine for four weeks, alone with six children, and had been thinking of going home in the summer.

In the evening, however, as I heard later, at a critical meeting of our school board and Aspen headmasters with the Washington people another terrible row over money, reverberating all over town. Out came the Aspen knives, they said, slashing at one another and splashing blood in pre-election fever. The fearing versus the feared. What a disgrace, a bloody one at that, unleashing their tongues in the presence of the Office of Education from HEW in Washington, D.C.; before a man of goodwill his pockets full of grants. I disassociated myself. I told Margaret to tell our board I'd release my salary and would continue to do what they wanted of me but on my own terms, without obligation or dictation. Then spent many wakeful nights wondering what my Fate would be: remain in Aspen to train profs in the fall or go home in the summer to that star over Whenua. These intersections in the journey through life, unsure of which turning to take. Fate was the most flagrant wanna-dowanna of all.

In spite of the big row, however, there was much joyful excited talk of the Washington grant in the fall and even some of the opposition teachers were looking our way for a job. I found in my house some of the big education administrators in town, people like a commissioner, superintendent and chairmen. With a view to reconciliation I asked the antagonists to tea at my place: the state commissioner for education from Denver, Mr. Hansford; the superintendent of education in Aspen, Richard Lee; the chairman of the education board in Aspen, Mr. Guy, and our own director, Bruce Le Favour. But for Bruce, what huge men. Like in Godzone. What was education trying to prove by requiring administrators to be minor giants? You should have seen them trying to fit into the low canvas chairs. One of them had a silhouette mighty from any angle and his chair was never the same again. Delightful people. Tea and many laughs. The diary is always recording laughs. "Great success in reconciliation all round."

All sorts of people would bring my mail, even Denver *Post* reporters, and bring me gifts of food like wine, nuts and home-made jam, but it was Bruce Le Favour who brought me the news that the school had *agreed* to my new terms of work, could you believe it? "Allowed to follow my own course, my salary intact." Judy to run the infant department, me keep in touch with the school daily and get down to research and writing in the afternoon for the school. I went to the keyboard after that for an hour or so of Schubert.

But as March grew into April and the snow began melting, handing us gratis the heavenly spring days, the elections were growing in reality. Judy must have been on leave at that time in New York to see her mother, for going to school for an hour in the mornings, I'd come home bewildered and dismayed at the shambles in the infant end. The para-teachers who'd been with us for six or seven months, you'd think they'd have managed better for the few weeks Judy was away but the wanna-dowannas reigned. There's no substitute for many years' training of a teacher. There came a noon when I went up to school to find, as usual, the little ones banqueting on the carpet in the foyer deep in lunch paper, cartons, bottles, cans and butter, yelling and fighting and one little chap walking on the piano keyboard in ski boots. I went into the side room to three wanna-dowannas who called themselves teachers sitting on the table swinging their legs smiling and chatting comfortably. "Why are you not supervising the children?" I said.

"We're too tired," they said.

"You don't like authority," I said, "and you've had none so far but now you'll get it: *GO*."

They did. I heard later they went up to the office and wept all day but the diary is briefer: "Went to school and fired the entire infant staff and engaged mature parents."

That afternoon and evening many people, including Bruce, stopped
by at my house, some bringing food, and the phone was going all the
time. The way these people reacted to happenings by getting up and
eddying about like water disturbed. The way they'd say it with food
I'd not seen in other peoples. Or they'd take you out for food, and we
dined at the Copper Kettle that night.

I was of the eddying water myself and I needed to be. In the morning I heard the board had reinstated the wanna-dowannas and had
fired the replacements. I cared all right, up to a point, but not enough
to defend myself. You'd have to have a heart to defend yourself whereas
my heart was too frozen over to even have dreams on the pillow.

Election day was moving in and the Community School had to get its
candidate onto the Aspen education board to fight for its share of the
education grant, with survival the stakes. I hear the clash of steel to
this day, and tighten to the tensions. I found myself in the thick of
the crossfire from both sides, having been seen on both sides, but when
the local press misquoted me on our school I became the star of a
witch hunt, our own staff too. "We don't want your work," the
candidate of our board told me in private. "All we want is your name
and the money your presence brings."

The scenes and the drama at this time are best left unwritten. Being
the goose that laid the golden egg, as well as the foreign traitor, I
featured in some of these and at one stage was foolish enough to defend myself, but most passions blow themselves out and after the elections the Community School board passed a motion of confidence in
me, acknowledged my contribution to education and appointed me as
consultant; Farnum, Wanda's husband, as director. Happy—Wanda
and Farnum and I—we were stunned. We all took off uptown and
dined at the Foc'sle. "The night of the long knives," I said.

Then the snow returned like the final curtain in a packed-out
theatre.

> The snow
> when I walk uptown
> decorates my cape
> or my hair maybe
> and kisses my mouth
> reminiscently.

I'd written the central design of teaching, what we'd called in the
past a master scheme for the infant department, including the tests,

results, conclusion and a working philosophy, bound it in a large green hard cover and laid it on the office table for all comers to read. Believe it or not, two whole people read it, Karline Keyes on the board and Wanda, which I considered a very high score, then got going on a book for Knopf. When it was ready I sent it to Bob, with whom I was now in the same country, no longer tucked away "Behind the Woollen Curtain" as he termed New Zealand. Books from Godzone were one thing and a book from the U.S. was another, but I was working with only half my mind as the other half had to be on guard and Bob didn't call it a book.

He could have dropped the manuscript with no debate as he had done with others of mine in the past, but he seemed to be intent on a book from the States. He seemed to know what I wished to say but either couldn't or wouldn't. After the action of the elections I was not disposed to expose myself to any public again. But he didn't drop it. He made it clear that I should identify the flaws in U.S. education and then supply the alternative, but I claimed I could not criticise my host country.

It was he who was agitated . . . or seemed to be. I think he was missing the artist in me—the rampaging monster flaring with ideas and spurting jets of inspiration—and now it was Bob himself taking its place, striding about the house of my mind trying to raise life, for none knew more of what had been. But even Bob could not resuscitate him. Several drafts went to New York but could not get by. "There's another section to come," he wrote. "The book is not finished without a conclusion."

"Bob, the book is finished. I *know* it's finished. There can be nothing more."

"It's only a textbook," I told Wanda and Farnum after school, "for U.S. teachers. Something to pick up and put down in the classroom, showing the mistakes I made, what to do about them and how to supply the conditions of work. It's not a personal statement. It can't be another *Teacher* in an American setting."

In the end Bob decided to take it, but that was a sad passage between us. He has not called *Spearpoint* "my book," as he has often called *Teacher*. I still had never admitted to Bob that I hated teaching and I've wondered if he ever guessed my deepest and darkest secret.

"My last book, Bob," I wrote, which he had heard before, "except my life." I'd already done a lot of my childhood whenever round the world I'd found myself grounded; I'd done quite a bit in Aspen and it seemed to anchor me.

But Bob had a way of saying after any break in my writing, "At least you are well and are working and that's the main thing."

From Jan Veatch's review of *Spearpoint*: "As for *Spearpoint* . . . it's a tombstone . . . this really rather sad log of what might have been."

Summer holidays, the wildflowers dressed up in the meadow where men were erecting the music tent. Above in the soft blue the hum of distant airliners. Young people eddying and flocking instinctively in my white picket gate not knowing the reason why, that I was a child myself. They sensed I was on their side, right or left, right or wrong, a wanna-dowanna in disguise.

I was at my table making reading books for the Aspen children when two of the young materialised at my door, the girl in a long full skirt with an Indian border, her hair in a soft plait, and the boy in jeans and beard, and they said, "Would you like to teach us what you know?"

"Fair enough. Come in."

So I gave them an hour on the key vocabulary with a song or two and a dance. I made a strong point of keeping infant room material at my house, everything from paper and blocks through paints to clay, and when they went they said, "Do you mind if we come next Tuesday and bring two friends?"

Each Tuesday and Thursday they came, growing in numbers, boys and girls, till I was running what I called my impromptu workshops. They were not interested in "your name, and the money your presence brings" but wanted my work. In fact through the whole summer no money changed hands, but the diary records, "Uptown Ned Vare kissed me on the forehead with respect and reverence." I'd been crossing an open area with new trees and water and he'd approached me with simplicity, kissed me, and withdrew with no word spoken between us. He was the man who'd lost his seat on the town council, known for his care of the young.

With the Vietnam war at its worst they were the young of America seeking an alternative way of life, preparing for the time when the bomb went off. For the first time outside Godzone I taught the Maori action songs, one haka—"Kamate, Kamate"—and the poi dance for which they learned to make their own pois, and from the start I got them on to making little children's books, illustrating them and incorporating their own key words, which revealed to me anything within them I had not already known. What I had not known was that their guiding thought was cosmic love. I still have these books with me.

I had a technique for teaching adults; I required they returned to childhood, became threes, fours and fives again, and I simply took the normal sequences of the organic programme as I'd done in the distant pre-fab, no different. I'd come upon this way back at Whenua in Tauranga when busloads of people used to come to me from high schools and training colleges, people I'd taught at Whenua in the big room gratis. Down on the floor everybody, up to eighty a go, everyone back to childhood again and out would come the key vocabulary cards. What I'd discovered in no time was that whereas the young had difficulty initially in becoming children again, giggling self-consciously, the grandmas were marvellous at it, and very funny about it.

On the other hand, one of the very best workshops I'd ever had turned out to be a group of young local mothers intent on qualifying for duty at pre-schools and who were required to meet me as part of their training. They'd brought some of their toddlers and babies with them and I never saw such understanding of the key vocabulary. The worst failures were the upper forms from the high schools who sat as silent, still, wary and speechless as Maori carvings from the past; I'd rather have had the Maori carvings, at least their paua eyes would have flashed. A comment on the teaching in the high schools. I'd never take one of those classes again; there's too much to undo.

The same style I'd used in Jerusalem when the wives of ministers had come to me at the castle Hospice, when again it had been the young wives who had giggled and blushed to become children again and the grandmas who'd become children on the turn of a moment and fearfully funny about it. So accurate and true. Why I don't know. My theory has been all along that, generally speaking, one learns less from someone talking than from living the situation through, so, with the increasing numbers of the young in Aspen, I swung into the living situation though it took them a few days to return to childhood. The thing was to supply the conditions.

It was this style of teaching and these truths I'd uncovered which gave me such unshakable confidence in taking on big seminar jobs at universities because it never failed. The key vocabulary never does. I knew exactly what I was going to do and exactly how. Throughout that summer I laid before my impromptu workshops my enduring home-grown wares like a wandering peddler of joys, and the key vocabulary accommodated them all.

I had found I was too old to work with young children themselves directly, and too theoretic, and it was at this point I came upon another valuable maxim though not unknown: I was the right age to train young people, even liked it. My impromptus were picking up the principles of teaching without former training though they had years to go yet of experience. It was from Judy's brilliance on the key vocabulary that I realised this; I'd train the Judys and it was they who worked directly with the children. Teach them the theory and style and they would interpret it according to their own personalities. It was more than a stroke of luck that my first trainee should be a Judy; it looked as though Fate was waking up to his mystic responsibilities. From all of which I had not the slightest apprehension about taking on U.S. professors in the fall.

Twice a week with the American young. I went to their fair in the meadow, spoke to their Golden Boys, bought their own home-produced wares, went to their homes and parties in the mountains where some young player from a visiting orchestra would get up from the floor in jeans, lift his violin and deliver Mozart, or one with an oboe, a French horn or a flute, and where you could ask a young physicist from the physics seminar about chances of life in outer space. "There are many planets in the universe with conditions for life." And straight-out old-time hippies would come in the door, men mainly whom you'd see sitting on the kerbs in town, or steps, who bedded in teepees or geo-desic domes and lived on nothing visible. When they got too hungry they'd meditate. None cared which side I was on, which school paid me or whether I was paid at all.

At one stage a New York rock band performed in the vast music tent which was packed to the flaps with the young from far and wide, from mount and stream and sea. Several of us went over early to make sure of a seat near the exit so we could duck out when the hysteria blew, but apart from the brain-shattering amplification of the electric instruments they were more silent than the dead. "I thought," to Cassandra who was doing my housework, "I thought they'd love all that."

"They were all high," she said.

Another world of young people I came to know were girls come for a housekeeping job who told me themselves; skilled and educated they'd arrive in Aspen in the spring or early summer to compete for employment, any employment, and for living space in order that by the time the men arrived for the winter skiing they'd be sufficiently established to receive them; any men. The men had an easy time: a roof, a bed, someone else's money to live on and plenty to eat, all for the simple price of serving a girl; a price they didn't mind too much. From these girls I drew my housekeepers more educated than I. Alicia was from a lawyer's office in Boston with degrees in law and psychology. Vacuuming the floor, "I just *hate* doing this. Only the law is worse," with the result that before Alicia came, or Lucinda or Dotty, I'd hastily do much of it myself. They'd be pooled in together in twos and threes in back rooms and attics and if one couldn't come, another would, for on these few dollars a week their survival depended. I let one of them sleep upstairs for weeks, a well-nurtured girl from Los Angeles, otherwise she'd have been on the streets. But, "No, Bev, you cannot take your men upstairs at night."

"I didn't, Mrs. H."

"I thought I heard steps on the stairs last night."

It was nothing to be told that the waitress in town was currently doing her doctorate. From one on the C.S. staff, "I met a wonderful man yesterday on the chair-lift. *Rich*. He's coming to supper tonight." But I'm leaving out most of it, for it's impossible to write about Aspen; even *Time*'s journalists can't do it.

All that passionate sustained work on my wares in the foothills of Godzone you'd think was intended for a place like Aspen, but only the impromptus wanted it here. No blackboard drawing of mine you'd have seen on the walls at the Community School, and you'd never hear me tell a story. You seldom saw me dancing or laughing with the children for the conditions failed to call on the best in me; it was true they hadn't wanted my work.

But I'd finished with that months ago. There came an exquisite summer morning when the voice of a coloratura soprano who was rehearsing in the tent lifted to the summits like a skylark on the wing; a soul's voice calling, This is my home. I ought to buy this house some day; maybe this is the sanctuary I'd been seeking all the long way through life. I could live with the drama of the mountains even with the knives unsheathed and the snowfall in my heart. My love-affair was with the snow.

> The white cold
> of the snow
> is less than
> the white cold
> of the frozen place
> where once I'd kept my heart.

I'd taken the precaution of accepting one invitation from the many flowing in to speak at a conference of teachers at a university, so that when I was old I wouldn't have to look back and reflect with regret, "Fancy, I've never spoken at an American university in spite of all those opportunities." It was at the University of Colorado in Boulder, a day's journey over the Rockies away. "It's my home state," I'd told Bruce Le Favour, "and I owe it to them."

Margaret had decided to drive me down there —well—but the very day before the trip, Farnum, the new director, came in and suggested it would be far more appropriate for Wanda to take me since it was an academic

Walking in the snow

occasion for teachers only. So next day Wanda drove me over the enthralling timeless Rockies following the Colorado River through two hundred and twenty miles of canyons through the mountains, and over a twelve-thousand-foot pass where I nearly died of fright but I really saw my home state of Colorado. Down on the plains at last Wanda said, thinking of the engagement ahead, "Aren't you nervous?"

"Oh, I know a few things they don't."

I could have said, "The key vocabulary never fails," but I didn't. It was she who said something like it: "I suppose it's a matter of being sure of yourself."

The only thing I was nervous of was the return trip over that pass.

Two hundred teachers in the hall and a hundred outside unable to get in. Entering the door with Dean Carline I was very happy. I walked among the teachers first and talked with them to get the feel of them, my fans by letter in the flesh, then, on the stage, remembering

the ministers' wives at Jerusalem, invited five grandmas to come up onstage with me; down on the floor and return to early childhood. And
simply took a key vocabulary lesson as though we'd been in the distant
prefab, with no equipment at all, miming the K.V. cards and the small
blackboards. And what does the diary say about that? "June 28:
Lectured and demonstrated twice at University of Colorado in morning
and afternoon. 100 extra teachers turned away. I have been *greatly*
praised and appreciated. Honorarium paid of $275, expenses added."

Wanda spoke too, and very well, as Margaret could not have done,
and that day Dean Carline offered me a job on faculty at the University of Colorado, even showing me the building available. My only
nervousness reared from another quarter altogether—that twelve-
thousand-foot pass again on the way home. But the way these American girls can drive big cars . . .

The important step forward in my work was that I'd tried myself
out to confirm what I'd thought, that numbers meant nothing and
that I was quite at home on the stage; it meant that I was ready to
take on any university job training young people with no preparation
or equipment at all. As long as somebody else did the organisation.
Just put the people in front of me and I'd do the rest.

So is this what life required of me: not just uncover and prove the
K.V., but get out into the world and follow it through? And I not even
a teacher? God . . . be good and spare me.

The snow came back in September like a lover to my arms but no grant
from Washington for the school as promised last spring, though
Farnum had composed a contract for me; a young handsome dare-
devil journalist, Farnum, who would dare to compose anything required and do it well too. Judy had gone since they couldn't pay her,
so there was no longer any trace of my work at school. True, a new
young teacher was there, trained, skilled and polished in the traditional British style, but the signature was that of the wanna-dowannas.
Aspen had not supplied the ideal conditions for my work to repeat
itself.

I'd been working flat out all summer on workshops, reading books
and writing with no salary, though paying five hundred dollars a
month on rent, so whatever lyrical thoughts I'd had about staying here
had given place to a berth on a ship, for November, though no one
else knew that. I told no one. I never do when I'm leaving a country.

One day when Wanda and I were in my kitchen making tea, a

member of the school office came in the open door, a fair pleasant real girl, and held out to me a cheque for three thousand dollars. "Where has this come from?" I said.

"The school."

"But that's parents' money. Washington is to pay me. If they don't pay me I don't work, do I? I'm not accepting school money. The school needs it," and guided the hand with the cheque back to her, at which she groaned aloud in relief.

"Does your country," to Wanda when Fay had gone, "really expect me to train its profs for free?"

Wanda replied that she had no salary either, a family of four, and that they might have to go also like Judy, "but we'd rather stay here."

"You know what, Wanda? It's time to call their bluff."

In October with the snowplows at work again, we thought the trainees might be held up with the blizzard in the mountains, for they had to come by road or in a paper dart, but no they arrived on time and Farnum came and told me. There was a man in his fifties called Tom Turbyfill from the university in Silver City, New Mexico; Pat Spitzmiller from Denver, a young slight girl radiantly in love with her husband; Bill Cliett, blond and tall and twenty-six from Gainesville down Florida way, and Dr. Selma Wassermann from Vancouver whose husband Jack had accompanied her. Later she told me that on the first morning of the seminar she'd come to my house before nine and had stood outside my gate in order to "savour the wonder" of being near Ashton-Warner at last, on her own before she came in—and there she had been on that white fall morning listening to me practising Schubert.

In the grey and white house on the corner I worked with the four every morning in the original authentic style as I'd done it in the prefab: on the floor except Tom, who had a sore knee, and back to childhood again. The large ground-floor room had long since been a model infant room with all the equipment, even water and sand and a blackboard on the wall. I took them through the key vocabulary: cards, writing, reading, clay, dance, singing, stories, all of it, and they also attended the impromptu workshops, at a high level by now, which was a very good thing. My work was no longer a book to be followed or a matter of talking but of living the style through. Last week, September 1978, Bill Cliett rang me in Godzone from Florida and I asked him if he could remember anything he had said, verbatim, in

Aspen and his letter came this morning, enclosing his impressions of
Aspen as he had put them down on arriving home.

There was snow on the summits, and the super-chargers which brought
us over them were disengaged. I was in Aspen.

Eight thousand feet with my feet on the ground. It was autumn, and
also Aspen, while the mountains, fortresses of time as well as space,
locked the world out. Breathing was made difficult by both altitude and
view.

I was in Aspen to study under Sylvia Ashton-Warner, author and educator. I knew her only through her book *Teacher* which I found exciting.
I was to find its author much more exciting.

Three others also came. Selma, Pat, Tom and I arrived from our re-
spective universities. Together on a clear, cold Monday morning, we
approached the charcoal house with the white picket fence for our first
meeting with Sylvia Ashton-Warner (Mrs. Henderson). Red Mountain
at our backs, we knocked.

As Mrs. Henderson told us sometime later, "Four people walked up to
my door one morning, and I said, 'Good.' " That was the beginning, and
it was good.

We were told only to come as five-year-old children. So four five-year-
olds stepped inside. "Come in, little ones," she said, and we sat at her
feet and learned what only the heart can teach from a woman who main-
tains she is not a teacher.

And she does not teach in the usual meaning of that word. She *does*.
And in her doing she sets an example from which others may learn. We
were never told how to teach by her organic style; she took us through
it as children, and we learned from the doing. She never said be warm
and loving with children; she hugged each of us as we came in each
day, and the first one in received a kiss. She did not tell us to be accepting
of children's work, but every morning we found our paintings of the day
before on the walls and received a kind word of thanks for them. No
preaching—only practice.

The living room was arranged like a small infant room. Paints, paper
and easel were at the window, clay on a low table, blocks on the floor, a
water play area in the corner, and a sandbox near the water.

An atmosphere of love and complete acceptance touched each organic
element in the room. No plastic here. No man-made products for the
young. Only natural objects from which a child's imagination can create
an infinity of fun and learning. Elements that do not dictate to young
minds. Elements that ask only for a creative touch. "And that's just what
organic teaching is," she wrote in *Teacher*, "all subjects in the creative
vent."

"Sit close to me, little ones," she said. "I want to put my hand on everyone's head." We gather closer as she gently lays her hand on each head.

"Let me see everyone's eyes," she said. And we all turn our eyes in her direction. She does not talk without our attention, and she does not repeat.

She explains the materials in the room and sets some limits. We are encouraged to create something for her, and, one-at-a-time, we may come, if we wish, to sit by her and begin our key vocabulary.

Nothing is demanded, nothing forced. Freedom pervades, yet there is discipline. "For the spirit to live its freest," she wrote in *Teacher*, "the mind must acknowledge discipline." It is there, understood and integral, yet gentle.

The output period began. Selma sat on the floor beside Mrs. Henderson to begin her key vocabulary while Pat, Tom and I began to explore the creative possibilities of our infant room.

We adjusted well to the age of five for Tom was soon making fun of my clay sculpture. In retaliation I threw some clay at his block building. He yelled to Mrs. Henderson that I was bothering him for no reason. Back came the first of many unexpected responses. "How lucky you are, Tom. Now you have some clay to play with." She had seen and understood. We all returned to our work.

The time came for my key vocabulary to be taken. I sat on the floor on the left side of her low stool as she directed. She asked for my name and talked with me as though I were the most important person in the world and my every word a revelation.

She wrote my name on a large white card and took my finger to trace over the letters when they were written. She made up stories about each letter, and I learned their personal histories. L is a thin, lazy boy who never brings in water or wood for his mother.

We talked about my loves and fears, my life, my friends. Soon I had my key vocabulary on the white cards. This procedure would take many weeks with children, but we capsuled it into one morning.

Only one word is normally taken each morning. These are words of intense, personal meaning. Words that are tied to the heart and the soul. From them I learned that the written word is important. That it can speak directly to me. That words can express my world.

"Are you afraid of anything, little one?" she asks. My adult mind reaches back to the age of five. I stand paralyzed with fear in the shallows of the Atlantic. The surf is heavy, the clouds dark. And there, surging toward me . . . "Wave!" I say. "I'm afraid of the big wave." Calmly and slowly she writes the letters on my card, saying them as she writes. Together we trace the letters and continue our talk, sharing our feelings.

I return to my clay knowing someone understands, and somehow, the fear is less.

These are instant recognition words. One look and they are mine forever. No picture can convey them. The picture is already deeply etched into the mind.

At the end of this first session she knew more about us than many who had known us for years. Yet she never seemed to ask anything of us. We confided so freely in her friendly manner, and we left as a family rather than the most recent of friends.

We walked the road home together in the cool, thin air, and I was short of breath, not from the altitude or view this time, but from the morning's workshop.

The next morning all the key vocabulary cards were on the floor, and we had to find our words among them. We sat on the floor with a partner and taught each other our words. We could write them if we liked or create from the materials around us while Mrs. Henderson worked with individuals. At this time we would read our words to her while any un-recognized words were discarded, those not being true key vocabulary.

Finishing this first movement we continued to the second, which con-sisted of smaller yellow cards with two-word phrases. These two words were drawn from our individual conference discussions. She wrote what seemed to be most important to us at that moment. My first was "golden leaves."

During the next two days we covered the third and fourth movements. In the third we had small blue books, first unlined, later lined, in which we began by writing three-word phrases and ended by writing sentences. The fourth movement saw us in larger green books where we could write stories about anything we wished. When we needed a word spelled for our own stories she would write it in the back of our books. That became our personal dictionary. These four movements, in her Maori infant room, would take the children from the age of five to seven.

We were always required to fill each page on each side so as not to waste paper. "Those are forests you are throwing away," Mrs. Henderson would say of wasted paper.

At recess we would revert to adults to help make the tea, talk and walk. On one of these mornings Mrs. Henderson and I took teacups in hand and walked toward Red Mountain. The sky was bluer than blue and we were showered with the golden aspen leaves as though a pros-pector, dizzy from the height, had spilled his whole year's pannings from the mountain above us. We silently drank in this beauty until we reached a mountain stream. "This," said Mrs. Henderson, "is the Roaring Fork. But it doesn't roar and it doesn't fork." We laughed together at this and walked to the house to refill our cups and begin the intake period.

She is very like the Roaring Fork, I thought at the time. She never roars and does not fork from her organic work. But, with the exception of the key vocabulary, she does encourage us to vary it to fit ourselves. As she said, "You cannot write a variation on a theme you do not know."

The intake period followed our break, and it was at this time that we five-year-olds grouped in pairs and read our words or stories to each other. There were also little books that she had written for us using words from our key vocabulary. For after we had a chance to express ourselves fully in the output period it was time for us to share our work and talents and put something new inside. As we learned about each other, we learned from each other. We were regaining the glorious feeling of being five.

Mrs. Henderson not only maintained that she was not a teacher, she also insisted that she was only five years old. "I am a child of five," she once told us. "I was an adult once, but that time is bracketed in dream." Her open, trusting and beautiful nature confirmed it.

There was always music in our mornings. We took turns with the piano or guitar. We danced, we sang, and we learned from it. For there was a rhythm to our days, a perfect balance and blending of the intake and output. A balance necessary for life itself. And each day became a symphony.

I may have come to Aspen for what I thought to be a method, but I left with a philosophy of life. A philosophy whose poetic formula she quotes from Coleridge: "Touch the true voice of feeling and it will create its own style and vocabulary": its own power and pace.

She translated the poetic into her professional formula: "Release the native imagery of our child and use it for working material." And this must be the primary concern. Preserving the native imagery of the child; using it as the foundation for learning; preventing its systematic destruction through the years.

It was time for my return, and, as the plane lifted me eastward over Aspen, I realized that I had added a new word to my key vocabulary—Sylvia Ashton-Warner.

> September 18, 1978
> The Secret River,
> responding to our needs,
> I found it once in Aspen.
> Perhaps again in N.Z.?
> —Bill

I let the four of them visit the school on their own because though I'd not been there for seven months I knew what was there—let them see for themselves. I had nothing to say, not one syllable, and did not inquire of their thoughts.

But recently I wrote to Selma in the interests of this narrative and asked her, eight years later, what in fact had been their thoughts and I received her letter this morning. It's certainly a letter that should be on this page, but it's impossible for me to be disloyal to that school regardless of what I know. If her letter is ever to appear let it come from Selma herself. The parents were the most enlightened and able body a teacher could hope for, the office staff was irreproachable, while the board—well, the board. At least the mupersons on it were articulate and active, never boring, and supplied Aspen with more drama in one year than you'd be likely to find in a century. Their false step was the unarmed untrained wanna-dowannas they allowed on their precious staff, and those I have less loyalty to in the interests of education.

In retrospect, however, seeing Aspen at a distance in its place in my life, it was that Community School only, embattled—mupeople, parents, board, wanna-dowannas; elections, knives, snow and dogs—that had had the enterprise, the will, the desperation and the vision to get Ashton-Warner before it was too late out from under the crinoline over the head of Godzone and plonk her into the heart of America. It had been Bob Gottlieb who had injected me into the bloodstream of America, but Aspen who injected America into mine. I'll never be the same again, but neither will America.

I can, however, put here the beginning and the end of Selma's letter: "What we said about the school to ourselves was considerably softened in our translation of it to you. But Tom was the only one who could say it to you as we had felt it. We were shocked and appalled."

Then the observations on the school, bracketing, however, twice: "with one or two notable exceptions." That would be Wanda and the new teacher, Angela.

A page of it then:

> We left the school and went to the small house which Bill and Tom had rented, and talked among ourselves to ventilate our feelings of outrage. . . . I find that even after all these years, remembering about that time, to write about it still stirs up some of the old feelings of outrage. I can only then begin to guess, those feelings multiplied many times, what it must have been like for you and what kinds of physical and emotional consequences were its toll.

It was not as though Dr. Wassermann was a stranger walking in uninformed, for she'd been with me for a week in the seminar taking part in the organic work as I saw it, and had attended the impromptu

workshops too, and she knew. She wanted to take me back with her
to her own university in Vancouver, Simon Fraser, and during that
time she had several long-distance conversations with her dean about
appointing me to that faculty. "Selma, I'll be doing one of two things:
go to Vancouver or sail home to Godzone on November 29. My only
problem is how to get to my ship in San Francisco. I can't imagine
anyone here helping me to *get away*."

The six of us dined together most nights and that evening we dined
in Selma and Jack's apartment was the first time I realised the Wassermanns; in a low chair with a glass in my hand I had this feeling
that I'd managed to find a spare seat on a crowded railway station before the next train came in and could put down my bags and rest.
We also had a meal with Tom and Bill in the little house they had
rented when I asked Bill, "What was that you said in class this morning about the effect of white carpets on the vision?"

"I forget," he said. "I make a habit of not listening to myself."

Dressed up on Saturday night at the Steak Pit and Tom saying to
me, ". . . and a bit of an actress too."

"I'm a great loss to the stage."

They laughed so hard at that I added, "I asked a sister of mine
once, 'Daph, why don't you take your acting on to the stage?' And
she said, 'My family is my stage.' Me, I find the infant room sufficient
stage."

"Right," from Selma, "*exactly*."

Three weeks was far too long for these people; by Friday they knew
the lot and we veered to philosophy; I wanted to learn from them.
Friday morning I set the subject for debate: What does America worship? By noon they'd admitted they worshipped the dollar because
they had no alternative. When I went to the kitchen to make them
coffee and Tom followed me, "Tom, I'm looking for the words to
sum up the morning's work," so he went back to the others. I brought
the coffee then stood and said, "You say you worship the dollar. You
say you have no alternative. But is it *wise* to worship the dollar?"

The four were not prepared to see out the three weeks with the
school centre as it was—as it wasn't, I mean, and I'd told them I was
going. Selma and I walked along the lane to the stream where the
leaves of the cottonwood lay amber on the water. "Selma, it's bad
enough with no salary when you're in your own country; Judy and
Wanda and Farnum can go home, or to friends, or get another job,
but I can't stay in an alien land and not earn anything."

"My country is your country, dearest."

The warmth
of the outer snow
melts the inner snow
where once I'd kept my love
its purity informs me.        Strange
                             what I've found about the snow
                             its coldness
                             thaws
                             and warms me.

They were leaving the second week. By God, here was a chance to get
to San Francisco. On Monday several came in to see me, among them
Farnum, who told me the next intake were all blacks—God, how
wonderful—and Wanda, neither of whom had any idea of my November bookings. Over the year together Wanda had got to that place
where she believed in me and my work and she was living in the glow
of it. After the others had gone we got out the lager at the low coffee
table and got down to basics. Wanda began talking, not a girl to talk
of herself. She was excited and inspired at the prospect of the black
intake coming next. For the first time she began telling me about herself, trusting me to the point where she exposed her central recesses in
a moment in my work which I call holy, when I become someone
else's self on the instant. Revealing her own instinctive imagery in
low-spoken captions, wide open. About her childhood, her happy
home life, her sister and the love between her and her father and
how she rang him—called him—last night and he wanted her to leave
Aspen. We drank and I listened in my long-disciplined way, her long
slender purple legs crossed one upon the other, her long flaxen hair
flowing round the wide brown eyes lost in ". . . the obscure reveries
of the inward gaze" (Ezra Pound).

Mike S breezed over the verandah and in the door as he often did
after school with snow on his hair and shoulders, a bachelor and the
brother of the millionaire who owned the physics buildings that
housed the school. Bringing a glass from the kitchen he joined us and
relaxed in a canvas chair. "Beer and faculty, that's my life. And how's
things with you, Mrs. H?"

Off guard, "I'm booked on a ship for November 29."

Wanda cried out.

My impromptus were making their books next day, I was sitting at
my table, and Selma came in the door, kissed me and whispered they

were all leaving Aspen tomorrow. Tom had already gone, being lonely for his wife and saying that if he went home early enough he and his wife might take me to San Francisco. The four had witnessed my crisis and I'd told them I was going. But I whispered to Selma to take me with them tomorrow, that I'd hire a car and one of them could drive it.

She whispered I could wait a week in San Francisco while she returned to Vancouver to confirm my appointment to the faculty at Simon Fraser University. She had friends in San Francisco who would care for me.

We told no one. Bill Cliett offered to drive me, though he lived in the other direction, and hired a big new car uptown on my behalf— the latest Oldsmobile 88 sedan, the biggest they make, same model as his own at home—and that night Selma and Bill and Pat came to my house with the car full of cartons and helped me pack while Selma played through my Schuberts . . . though I regretted missing the black intake and grieved for Wanda. Near midnight, all lights off, we loaded the car in the darkness like practised robbers to depart before daylight. The snow had paused. Then remembering Keith Henderson's courtesies, I wrote a brief note to Farnum, told him where I was going and why and with whom and that my forwarding address would be the Hotel Clift in San Francisco, and included my school keys. And put the month's rent and the house keys in another envelope for my landlord's agents in town.

Before dawn Pat knocked on the bathroom window to say goodbye and I let her in the back door. My last act in that house was to turn off the moisturiser. In the darkness before dawn Bill came and we drove uptown through the sleeping streets, put the two letters in the post office, linked up with Jack and Selma in their little Triumph Spitfire sports car, the big and the little, and slipped out of Aspen in an outright American kidnapping. Bill driving the groundliner, Jack and Selma following; sailing down the mountain valleys as day revealed the Rockies. Great dawns I'd seen in my travels but none was ever like this. Swooping down the highway to Glenwood Springs, the altitude diminishing, then out on the desert spaces. How I sang—"Beyond the blue horizon waits a beautiful day . . ." It was not until we'd crossed the border into Utah that we stopped at a desert café for breakfast. "The Great Escape," someone said.

Bill said he would hold me to ransom.

"My departures from countries," I mused.

Selma, "We loved you and wanted to protect you."

Four days and four nights across the deserts of Colorado, Utah, Arizona, Nevada, staying in Holiday Inns at night. Bill Cliett was twenty-six, I was sixty-two, an improbable harmonious duo. Several times the Wassermanns offered to take a turn at the wheel of the Oldsmobile but no he said he meant to do the whole thing all by himself though at night Selma would give him therapy on the back of his neck and shoulders.

Through the Indian reserves of dozens of tribes, Navajo, Apache, Hopi, Pima . . . past the tall gates of the nuclear testing stations. KEEP OUT, pause at the intersection of the four states, travelling about fifty miles per hour on account of my Aspen nerves and dining together at night. Kidnapping de luxe. The deserts were divided by unexpected ranges of mountains snowed at the top, then down to the plains again . . . canyons, buttresses, salt lakes, blue horizons—"Goodbye to things that bore me; life is waiting for me . . ."

At Reno, Dr. Rosella Linskie, professor of education at the University of Nevada, who had stayed at Whenua and had known Keith Henderson, a very beautiful woman with Italian boning, she slid into the inn in a glamorous white car, "What are you guys up to?"

But she didn't believe a word. She took me for the night to her place and I gave Bill money for my throw at the casino.

The Hotel Clift in San Francisco where Jack sent telegrams to both my sons informing them where their mother was now and in the morning the Wassermanns left for Vancouver where Selma was to complete negotiations for me to go on faculty at Simon Fraser. She'd call me at the end of the week to confirm it. "One of two things, Selma; here I stay till the first one happens; a car to Vancouver or the ship to Godzone."

The intersections in life were like a U.S. highway. Which way was I heading now? I was anybody's property, like mislaid luggage. As it had been in Aspen, people picked me up, put me down and picked me up again, and I was the last to mind it. Wassermann friends in San Francisco picked me up, put me back, took me out. Saw a doctor about the blood pressure, up another few points, wrote to Elliot every night, being the son geographically nearest, and wrote for the local press. A real jam-up with my tax clearance when trying to leave the country—said they'd stop me at the border. Wandered the streets, sent presents to the children, bought clothes for my new job—what was my fate: New Zealand or Canada?

Selma called on Friday to confirm that I was now a professor of education at Simon Fraser University and that no less than Tony Vogt and his wife Birgitta would pick me up on Sunday morning and put me down in Vancouver. Tony was of Norwegian birth, European education, New Zealand adoption and a poet. On the phone from downstairs his magnificent bass voice and glorious British speech. Could you believe it? A straight-out theft. How the British succeed.

Three more days, three nights up the California coast, a story of gas stations and motels to the simple border between the U.S.A. and Canada. The customs was a modest building with a low-spoken modest staff but oh to hear the English language. On the moment the tone was completely different and the pace slowed down. Unflappability. True, there was a spot of delicate play about the tax, but Tony handled that. It felt like coming home. The train had come in and I walked off the station.

Vancouver—
the school

VANCOUVER   No one at the new university on the hill, Simon Fraser, minded my working at home at the foot of the hill, Montecito, rather than at the university itself where in fact there was not sufficient spare floor space for my programme, coming in on faculty as I had mid-semester. A spacious super-mod apartment on the ground floor at the corner of the block which Jack and Selma had ready for me. Montecito was a community-style complex of apartments and townhouses off the street, landscaped, hillocked and treed; and before the week was out I had a Blüthner grand piano delivered after which I bought a teapot.

It was said at SFU that Dr. Wassermann had pulled off a coup in picking up Ashton-Warner from Aspen and putting her down at Simon Fraser and there was nothing they didn't do to supply my conditions, even to a work permit from immigration, where Dr. Ian Allen, an Australian on faculty who also lived at Montecito, took me down on the waterfront. "The computer doesn't like an immigrant over forty-five," the immigration man said.

"You need to be well over forty-five to lead the education in a city," I replied and showed him the dean's letter.

"I'll have to write to the computer," he said.

First thing I asked for was a carpenter who, with sincere craftsmanship, built all I wanted in equipment for an infant room in the very large cornered living room—to my own measurements, varnished and lidded, to be used as furniture when not in class. Dr. Allen and two other Australians, also in Montecito, Lawrie and Diana Kendall, brought carloads of material from the top of the hill—name it, here it is—a stand-up two-sided blackboard while the carpenter screwed up a central blackboard on the wall. In a matter of ten minutes a domestic living room could switch to a model infant room of the kind I'd known in Godzone, and back again into a home—flick.

My only nervousness came from a quarter other than my work, as it had done when I'd spoken at the University of Colorado where it had been the twelve-thousand-foot pass that had laid me out: the first time I followed Selma into a faculty meeting my head hung down on my chest, my lower lip all but scooping the ground like a horse I'd once owned and I couldn't lift my face to look at anybody for the entire meeting. Poor old Godzone faced with consequences. Shy . . . my God, my God. Speechless, sightless. How had I come to wander upon this lofty stage? Though I did tell Tony and Selma later in the cafeteria, "The academic language was like distant music."

As for the work itself: "Just put them in front of me and I'll give you teachers." Which the dean and Selma and Ian did with smooth organisation. They had me working with students first, sixteen the first intake, increasing through the fall and winter semesters to thirties and forties and fifties. I just simply took the organic morning as I had done in the pre-fab years ago, they all became four and five again, though for a start it was in the afternoons: Tuesdays and Thursdays twice a week, six weeks a go, making twelve workshops a semester. I chose my assistants from the students and I changed my name to a Maori word, Mere; nothing before, nothing after. Mere. Finish.

Here is a Tuesday covered in snow and many young people with me, packed knee to knee on the turquoise carpet in my wide room; no furniture except the Blüthner and one long coffee table. I own sixty coffee mugs so far. That there should be no room at the university on the hill is a blessing not in disguise. Through the glass of the frontage the falling whiteness of snow, within are the colours of their clothes and faces. Outside the fantasy, inside the reality of people I've not met before. In mind I see a picture in the snow of a figure at the door peddling forgotten wares and I hear his voice, snow-muted. "Who will buy my pretty magic? Specially composed for the young and tragic."

I'm on a little low chair before them. What are they thinking about—money, men, girls, rent, assignments, evaluations, examinations and grading? When I was a student all I thought of was men, how to avoid work and how not to hear the lecturer. There's one thing I'm certain they're not thinking of—teaching, and there's one thing I'm certain they are thinking of: does anyone here like them? I know what I'm thinking: here I am, an inadvertent wanderer, a "poor artist" plonked amid thousands and thousands of people, no less than a modern university and what for, by God—to *teach*. How *did* this come about? So sudden.

Into the trap of silence, "My name is Mere and I am five."

No answer but a sea of eyes all colours. I'm wearing the cream fugi silk shepherd's smock I made myself in Waiomatatini, with hand-done smocking on the shoulders and cuffs, full and billowing. You can't buy these things.

"If I were a teacher I'd explain first all we are going to do and you'd be taking pages and pages of notes . . . if you were students."

More trap, more eyes.

"But I'm not a teacher and you're not students; you're five-year-old children on the receiving end. Getting a child's-eye view of teachers."

No tongues yet so I get up, step over the crossed legs, holding shoulders and head-tops for balance till I reach my solution to most problems, the keyboard, which supplies any amount of answers gratis . . . after which we get to work on the key vocabulary and away goes the workshop. Plenty of tongues now, asking for words lodged deep in the mind to be printed on their word cards, and conversations over the paints, clay and water, white fingers tracing in the silvery sand; in time there's a song and awkward dance. Live first, teach after. Life is short.

From my chair, again to the snow and the darkening day . . . this

work should be in the morning. Settled together again on the floor
at the close, a young man with beard and drooping hands speaks to
me; hands which have never held a cross-cut saw gathering wood on
a riverbank or wrested driftwood from the beach. "Mere, why do
you say you aren't a teacher?"

"Good question, Joel."

"What are you then?"

"A 'poor artist.'"

"Good answer, Mere."

As the afternoons snow the fall away and then the winter through,
as the key words add up on big white cards, one intake after another,
I take to sorting these words out between workshops, according to the
instincts they have surfaced from, to print them on charts on the
wall; Fear Words on one chart, Love Words on the next, Sex Words,
Hate Words, Food, Family, Animals, Occult and Media, Play and
Others, from which one can stand back and take a good look at the
nature of the collective mind of British Columbia, and as I watch this
mind turning kaleidoscopically, its facets flashing arbitrarily or dim-
ming reflectionlessly, I'm looking for some cultural variation specifically of this country, some definitive characteristic.

No villain in the story so far; no madness incipient, no genius unfolding that I can see, and practically no sign of the impulse to kill.
But there is a chilly cavern where fantasy should be, a feeling for
magic should be, whereas everything from madness to genius nests
in fantasy. It is as though these dozens upon dozens of young adults
had never inhabited the world of childhood, pinned to desks by
determined factage, the sum of their culture the three straight Rs.
Where's the inspiration in the minds of the young, the dream that
lures? Where's the vision that makes men go? If the national mind
is mutating, as it had been in Aspen, it is discreet about it. Drying
up. Have these people already been carpet-bombed by baby-sitters
and the man-made imagery on the TV screens, manipulated into
stereotype by jargon-tongued teachers, sedated beyond awakening
by the TV opiate? It's only I, two generations before them, who still
knows magic, who sees the shape outside the door peddling living
wares.

I visit many schools in the city and suburbs at the invitation of headmasters and supervisors not only because of the main criterion of a
prof's job, "impact on the community," but also because, working with
young adults, I'm curious to see what is actually happening to the

children on the scene who become passive later on. I don't like going,
I almost hate it; finding myself *still* going to school over sixty—
could I not have managed my life better? But I've got to do the job
I've fallen backwards into, as I see it, as well as how my university
sees it; since I've somehow become a professor of education then I'll
be the best professor of education or fall dead trying. So I go along on
my own per taxi and sit with children on the receiving end and do
what they are doing, as I had done in Aspen, to get a first-sight picture
from the child's-eye view. Floor? I sit on the floor. Desks? I squeeze
in a desk. Scooting across Vancouver towards nine through the icy
brittle morning, dodging traffic, banking up at intersections, huddling
in my squirrel coat I'm reminded of how I used to feel as a child when
facing a day of internment. My psychotic compassion is the one illness
I've never recovered from.

Nearing the school I examine the environment; variations of boxes
in right-angled streets, no trees or open spaces; no hillocks, hollows
or hiding places; an area where children spend the day in a very big
box, the school, walk out upon the paved straight street, turn a right-
angled corner, follow another sterile street, mount some steps into
another smaller box, the home, and sit before a smaller box still, the
TV screen. If school is not a place for living, then children get no
living . . . until suddenly the taxi drops me quite mercilessly at a high
iron gate. Fancy leaving a new girl on her own without any sign of
a mate. Levelled playground beneath the snow with tall brick walls
around it while the school itself is a centuried fortress called the General Somebody School.

. . . shown into a room peopled by five-year-olds and not too many
of them, a well-dressed company. Teacher on chair in smart-cut frock
and the latest in shoes, not young but smiling in a fixed plastic way.
The door is closed behind me and the windows too high to see
through, to see life passing by outside. Walls covered with the teacher's
work but no equipment in the room relating to nature. A pretty respectable and colourful scene like a two-dimensional illustration in an
advertisement from a glossy magazine with soft background conversation. I'd rather have Aspen any day.

By the time half an hour is up on the floor with the children I cannot deny that they are already sedated from the simple loss of living;
imagination dulled, impulses blunted. No sign of the mind itself of a
child excepting on two orderly easels with two lovely paintings and
no one smiles except the teacher. No footprints of the personality on
today; tomorrow I'll remember not one of them.

I recall other classrooms I have known explosive with the excitement of a marketplace with fantasy and factage jumbled on the stalls, food for the leaping mind for sale, drinks to steal and dangerous dancing girls; someone piping on the inner ear and the pulsing of strings; where the hatted peddler barters his wares of magic and miracle vociferously, but only facts reign here. Never mind, kids; you'll all fit fine into the computer to serve King Dollar one day; the only real evidence you have passed this way.

Teaching

Another morning, a pleasant new school, the wings spoking out upon the snow and plenty of money around. The headmaster's hand on the doorknob. "These pupils are disturbed, professor. They're having special curative treatment. They can't concentrate."

No sound from within. Are they unconscious?

Another tall polished room, high windows again, the teacher's work marauding over the walls. Sixes and sevens, I'd say, known as Grade Two whatever that means in terms of living tissue, whereas

education is forever fluid. Screens jut from the walls forming separate cubicles in which each child sits alone at his separate bench facing the wall unable to see any other. About nine or ten children, backs to the room, to the teacher and to life. The silence of a mausoleum. Why does the teacher whisper? I move to a boy, slender and vital in the end cubicle, "Do you mind if I join him?" I whisper.

Whisper, "You must excuse him, professor. He's the brat of the class."

It's the brat who brings me a low chair and I sit beside him. "What's your name?" whisper.

"Duthie," breathed.

"My name's Mere. How old are you, Duthie?"

"Seven."

"I'm five."

His doubts he keeps to himself.

"I could do one of those puzzles," I whisper, but without my glasses I bungle it and stall.

"I'll help you. Look, it goes like this, okay? I know all these puzzles. We do them every morning. I can do them without even looking. You watch."

From the teacher, "Duthie, will you keep your voice down please."

With his eyes on the wall he tosses off the whole puzzle, then, "How come you can't do a puzzle?" he whispers.

"Tha's why I'm only five."

"If you're only five, Mere, how come you've got a grown-up skin and you're big?"

"Ah," whisper, "tha's just it. You can't tell by people's skins and how big they are. Sometimes people are not what they look. They might be something else. What happened was my body it grew up but the little girl inside me just stayed five."

"I can't see her."

"Duthie," long-suffering from the teacher, "remember. Try to remember. Concentrate on remembering to keep your voice down, not to talk." No hostility, kindly enough. "Try to *concentrate* on your puzzles."

I breathe in Duthie's ear, "You can't see me inside and I can't see you inside. You might be an old man inside who grew up suddenly but you still look like a boy outside. You can do puzzles without even looking. A boy of seven couldn't do that."

He looks at his hands and knees and feels his face. "Do I look like an old man?"

"No. It's just doing the puzzles not looking."

He stares at his private blank wall. "I might be an old man inside."

"You might. Where does this bit go?"

He places it, staring at the wall.

"Now this bit?"

Irascible as any old man, "Here I'll do it all for you."

"Duthie," whisper, "if only you would speak more softly. The other children can't concentrate on their puzzles. Try to think of other people." To me, "He comes from a very bad background, professor."

He leans to me, concentrating, "You know what, Mere? Know what's happening soon?"

"What?"

"We're going to gym."

"Not really."

"We go every Thursday morning," whispers Bad Background, "when we've done our puzzles and then our letters. Do come and see us in the gym, will you?"

"I'd like to but you're a bit old for me, Duthie. I want to go and play with someone who's five."

"No don't go."

"I'll try to get back."

Bad Background clings to my hand as far as the door, "Will you come back, Mere, please?"

"I'll try."

"You've got to understand Duthie, professor. Strange," baffled, "he always behaves like this with visitors."

I escape from the foyer of hell.

Another morning, the Earl of Something school, an impregnable brick pile. But a gentle principal, hand on doorknob. "I'm afraid these pupils are a little disturbed, professor. Troubled backgrounds. Grades Two and Three. They're having individual treatment. The one-to-one therapy."

Door opens on one-to-one. Not even the teacher's work on the walls. Ah . . . they're in cubicles again, not side by side but two to a wall with teacher screened at a table mid-centre with a boy. "Now watch this card, Derek."

His eyes lift to us then lower again.

"C-ar," from Teacher.

"C-ar," from Derek.

"C-ar," from her.

"C-ar," from him.

"Now which comes first, the *C* or the *ar*?"

"*Ar.*"

"No, *C* comes first. You go back now, Derek, and write it."

Offstage again to his one-boy cell in the holiness of hell proper, where souls and cells are dying by the minute. I'd like to have seen Derek let loose at the school in Aspen. I'd seen nothing like this in Asia, Mauritius or Colorado and unheard of in Godzone. Hell is a new place now; there's no eternal fire, for it is quiet and cold and solitary. Not as hygienic as a mausoleum where bodies have been dead for years but it has the smell of decomposition, the sickly sweet stench of the not-yet-dead.

Surface from that past to this alien present. What I need is a walk round the university on the hill. I love doing that. I'll go up this morning, I think. In myself it gives me brief status in life, besides it's a lovely place, dramatic, memorable. And I'd better get round the city a bit, have a break from my table before I prepare for the summer semester.

Outside the snow no longer falls. The spring bulbs I've managed to get to grow in my patio garden are something to walk outside to see. I planted them last fall before the ground froze too hard. At that time I just couldn't believe they'd survive the ice and snow. Marvellous. Tulips they're pretty and the pansies were already here in boxes when I came. There was already the slender maple mid-patio and one of the young men planted for me a beech, quite big now.

My friends are mostly academic people who live a lot in the mind; they seem to wonder that I should squander time, money and back-power planting. To them I must appear an anachronism to give flowers priority. It baffles me when people who love me, coming gaily across the patio to my door, don't notice and examine the garden first as one does in New Zealand. Neither do they stoop to smell the scents and I wonder how they can understand, if they can fully understand the conditions for, and stages of growth in the mind of our child when they don't see Nature's child at their feet.

So the snow has gone and the crisp sharp spring air is here. I'd thought the flowers would have been company for me but what I've found about flowers is that people plant them only when they're happy and hopeful, which makes it look as though I planted these because I was happy and hopeful. So I am half the time. But being loved as I am here does not necessarily mean that therefore I become happy and hopeful and therefore plant flowers about it. Being loved is no reason on its own to get going planting flowers, for joy emanates not so much from the love one receives as from the love one gives, whereas nothing much emanates from a heart in deepfreeze . . . unless it is like a bulb.

I'm learning the hard way of the poverty of being loved when oneself is unable to love in return. Since the thaw to love anyone new at all has not yet returned to me I can hardly be wholly happy and hopeful. Better I had not done that planting. The blooms are too reminiscent for comfort. I'm thinking I was premature. How can I have escaped the lesson over the years behind that it's richer to love than be loved.

This school is hospitable enough, not brick and of a homely age and principals are all very nice men. "Here's a class you might like to see, professor, pupils ranging from six to nine; a composite class of disturbed pupils drawn from other rooms," but a regretful hand on the door handle. "Except that Mrs. Breen has come late to teaching, very late, only a few years ago. She brought up her family first and then trained, but she has all kinds of wisdom; she knows things."

A comfortable grandma standing four-square, feet apart in a ready-for-anything attitude, I-can't-help-it, and children are up and down like in a marketplace, hands up for questions and answers, in and out of their desks, so like children you can't tell the difference. I squeeze into a desk. Children's work all over the place and a large picture of winter on the blackboard and the children have adhesive silhouettes. From Mrs. Breen, "Who's got something to stick on this picture?"

Someone runs up and on goes a cut-out of a boy with woollen clothing.

"I don't have a picture," I say.

A few turn.

"My name's Mere and I'm six."

"Who's got a picture for Mere?" from Mrs. Breen. "We're the Friendly Class."

I've just been told you're the Disturbed Class.

"She can have mine," the boy in front though not too keen about it.

"Thanks so much. What's your name?"

"Dopey."

"Thanks, Dopey; that's alert of you."

"What's a Lert?"

"Aa . . . this what you gave me. A strange animal, it lives in trees."

"No, Mere, that's a zebra."

"Who said?"

"I know."

"How?"

"Because it has stripes."

"Lerts have stripes too and are just this shape."

The adhesive zebra looks confused, though it allows it might be a Lert in disguise. Teacher says to me, "Can you put your picture on this big one, Mere?"

I walk up and stick my Lert on a branch high in the tree. "This is a Lert and it lives in trees."

Chorus, "No it's a zebra."

"No it's not."

"What is it then?" from the kids.

"What I said: a Lert."

" 'Course it isn't," from the chorus. "It's a zebra."

"Why," from Teacher, "do you think it is not a Lert?"

"Because it has stripes and it can't climb a tree."

"All right then," I amend, "it's not a Lert; it's a monkey."

Uproar. "Not a monkey, not a monkey, it's a zebra."

"Yes, yes," from me, "it *is* a monkey. I can prove it. I heard the zebra and the monkey and the Lert talking and the Lert told the monkey and the zebra to change skins just to fool us. The zebra put on the monkey's skin and the monkey put on the zebra's skin; this very monkey on this very tree is wearing a zebra's skin. I know because I was there. That's only a monkey in a zebra's skin."

They accept this thesis gravely with no editorial arrogance. Magic supplies silence until the teacher ruminates, "You can't always tell an animal by its skin, and you can't tell a person by her skin either. They might be something else inside." Surveying me speculatively, "For all we know Mere herself may be someone else inside."

"That's just it," returning to base, "I just might be too. I look like an Old Lert with a wrinkled skin and I'm big but all the time inside I'm a little girl of six who didn't grow up, by the name of Mere."

Dopey, "Can you climb a tree too, Mere?"

"At least as well as an elephant."

"But elephants can't climb a tree."

"Neither can a wheelbarrow."

"I didn't say it could, right?"

"Neither did I."

"So now you know," from Teacher.

"Know what?" from Dopey.

"Why an elephant is like a wheelbarrow; because neither can climb a tree, okay?"

"Why," from Juniper, "doesn't Mere take off the Old Lert's skin so we can see the little girl?"

"Why ask me?" from Teacher. "Ask her."

"*She* heard."

"*It* heard," I correct. A Lert sure has to be alert. "Why doesn't the Lert take off its skin? Because the zip down the back is jammed."

"I'll fix it," crowds. "We're the Friendly Class."

"Listen, listen," from Teacher, "why don't we open these big new boxes and see what's . . ."

"Mere said Lerts have stripes. I can't see them."

"Underneath its clothes. On its skin."

From Teacher, "Who wants to open these boxes and see what's inside them? They only look like boxes outside but inside they . . ."

At the door from Grandma, "They didn't learn much from that lesson on winter, professor."

"Didn't they?"

"Well, not about winter."

"No."

"Maybe they learnt not to go by appearances."

"Think so?"

"Well *I did*."

"Oh."

"But," she reflects dubiously, "maybe it's true I've come in too late."

"Maybe just in time."

I stood outside many schoolroom doors and sat with many children on the receiving end, including the extensive home for two thousand broken children fed from some city schools. In most was the decay of fantasy which I call the third dimension of the mind, less attributable to the teachers than to society itself. Astonishingly, however, the teachers appeared to be the kindliest people delivering what they considered to be their best, but give me Aspen any day: wanna-dowannas, mupeople, license, the lot. I understand now the Aspen Community School and why they broke away.

There are two main ways a child can go: sedated early to set finally into copies of the screen adults or, in the tougher ones not ready to die but geared to stand and fight, the impulse to kill takes root. Better for jail prisoners to be let loose in some classrooms who at least would let the children out for one brief chance of life.

The spring semester came up with a large enrollment of practising city teachers down on my carpet, senior people mostly, full of outrageous fun to be five again on the receiving end, imitating their own small children, and I could talk over with them the causes of what I had seen in the schools. After which I was ready to take on a summer session with allcomers from anywhere.

*Spearpoint* came out at this time. I know because I remember the stack of complimentary copies available in class. Also London Heinemann brought out a paperback of *Spinster* for New Zealand and sent me some so I had plenty on hand which was lucky indeed. As it happens another of the requirements from a full professor is to be published, so that part was mopped up all right.

Knopf made a lovely job of the American book in binding, cover and format and when Bob sent me the first copy off the press, I set out in a letter to somehow share his pleasure, to appear appreciative of a third book about teaching, until I noticed on the cover the words, "One of the great teachers of the world," when the letter leapt the rails and I wrote with rage and blindness of how I hated teaching always. Goodbye to the other man in my life. It was such a ferocious impassioned revelation that after I had posted it I had to write another the next morning to excuse myself.

But he replied:

> Your letter undid me. Your next letter—which came *with* the other—did me up again. But it's good that you said it all; then it's both real and gone. Only the part about reading the future of the little ones is truly terrible, but I believe you. And yet even bad, sad lives have goodness, and most people are glad that they have lived. . . .
>
> As for hating to teach: that I believe. Writers hate to write too. The hardest and most painful thing is always the thing that means to oneself Truth; when you have to express your most inner meaning, and express it directly. You hate to teach because you are Teacher; because being Teacher, you can't teach from the surface. *I* could teach without pain, because Teacher I am none. . . .

I heard up at the university that *Saturday Review* had featured *Spearpoint*, but it was only later when a copy was sent to me that I saw for myself the illustration all over the cover: a dramatic painting in scarlet, indigo, white and black of a rocket on its way to space. If only Godzone could see it, but nothing about me in America ever reaches Down Under. Oh to be praised in the country of my youth, as my family had always praised me. At least I learn the hard way what it

The new intake of allcomers for the summer session, fifty to sixty I believe in this enrollment, none of whom I've met before or know anything at all about, but I often look at them as I play and smile as they flock in upon the green, noting many leggy summer beauties, at least two in white shorts, scarlet tops and swinging black hair to the waist—teachers?—and young men with beards and drooping hands like the helpless fins of fish, hands which could never have reconditioned a Maori whare or built a cave Selah in the forest.

Filling up from corner to corner with crowding talk and colour and coffee mugs, with legs, beards and hands to the under-running obbligato of the piano until silence finally comes of itself and the company has become an audience instead, so I make my way through them, stepping over limbs, touching shoulders and heads for balance to my low chair before them. I'm wearing, if you want to know, the fugi silk hand-done shepherd's smock I'd composed and sewn in Waiomatatini; a garment which ensures you are right outside and beyond any passing fashion whatever, except that of an artist. A garment of experience with some seams frayed and an ink spot or two on it.

Directly before me at my feet is one of the girls in short white shorts, legs and hands demurely folded, black hair flowing and brown eyes lifted like a doe in a glade unblinking on my face. Every nuance of the soul of the young exposed in this stance: trust, faith, hope, joy and the radiance of a girl in love. Like a child I engage her in the brand-new greeting song I composed the words for last week from the melody of Schubert, and chance has arranged she is marvellously musical with an ear like my own, or better, following the tune as though she'd composed it herself. "And what is your name?" begins the song.

"And what is *your* name?" she sings with me.

"I'm Mere," I sing.

"I'm Paula," she sings.

"Hi Paula."

"Hi Mere."

"Hi-i," together, hands meeting, embrace.

A moan of delight from the company.

A picture which takes precedence over the many other crowding pictures from Vancouver; a bloom on the lifetime that led this way.

This summer school I called Mornings with Young Children and it was advertised as such: twelve mornings played twice a week on Tuesdays and Thursdays covering six weeks. I was vaguely aware that is like for a child not to be loved at home. Success can be hollow and lonely sometimes.

As for the increased mail it had, from my arrival here, all been answered per computer up at the university according to the well-tried formula. They'd say no to nothing at SFU.

When I think of Vancouver at that time I see a picture in the fore-front of my mind of a row of white charts on the central wall of my living room when changed to an infant room, oh about ten or so; each a hand and a half wide and half a body long but there's nothing printed on them so far and they wait there like a set of as-yet-unfilled glasses as though you were expecting a party, or you could say like an empty stage anticipating the star. Above them in my very best print-ing is the name of the star: The Mind Of Our Child.

The room is ready: white walls and ceiling, white counter and coloured bar stools and the turquoise green carpet, with no furniture but the grand piano. The landscape glass frontage there is no longer snow piled up but you can see the pocket patio with flowers round it and an adolescent maple straightened up mid-centre like a solo actor. An appropriate setting for a model infant room and a flawless setting when changed to a home. Half a year after my arrival here in the snows of November the time is now May in summer between eight and nine on Tuesday morning.

All my preparation is complete. Written in my handwriting on another blackboard is the formula for teaching which had evolved in the far-distant pre-fab; the one about "Supply the conditions . . ." Tested for decades in many a setting and no weak link in it yet.

Dozens upon dozens of young people, men and women, eddy across the patio and in the door where my American assistants, Frank and Ann, whom I'd drawn from former SFU workshops, intercepted them to check on enrollments and forestall gate-crashers while I con-tinue at the keyboard. I usually do practise at this time in the morning and have for the last forty years and, in any case, have a habit of sheltering at the piano when waiting for someone important, the masters being very good company, and I see no reason this particular morning to up-end my routine for I too am a cell of life, not dead yet; I happen to be practising, that's all, Schubert if you want to know, featuring a tune from him I mean to use this morning to familiarise them with it beforehand; a brief tune to which I've written my own words of greeting as between one child and another, and for dance . . . if they can.

among the allcomers were to be nine hand-picked teachers but I didn't think twice about it; they were gifted young people chosen by Selma in an arduous and widespread search, to put before me with a view to demonstrating the organic mornings back in class but I declined to know who they were. "Adamant" is a word I seldom use but I was adamant that I be told nothing of anyone in any of my workshops, wishing to encounter them on their own terms with no pre-organised attitudes. My own thought had always been completely unfettered since the days on the roads to schools—I was freer that way and so were they, though Frank and Ann knew who they were.

Even afterwards it was not important that I should know, for the organic style needs no help from me once I have established it; a self-sowing plant repeating itself with the endurance of the toughest weed: "Touch the true voice of feeling and it will create its own style and vocabulary," its own power and pace, in my handwriting at the top of the central blackboard.

The only blight which I thought might halt its self-propagation would be for it to fall into the jaws of academic analysis in unintelligible multisyllabic jargon by which so much living on this continent is programmed to die from verbose manhandling—the growing tissue of the mind can't stand it. I don't think I had even heard the term Vancouver Project in which had been chosen the nine young teachers, I tried not to know and talked to no one of it. There was a late afternoon with Selma sitting on a bar stool across the counter from me, she in the latest suit from New York; I drinking tea, she sipping water. In her early forties at the time, I think, she was on that turbulent stretch of the road through life where a woman is at the mercy of buffeting passions and was something of a talked-about professor. "I'd thought, dearest," she said, her wide eyes steady, "that we would have been having long talks on education and philosophy as it had been in the Aspen workshops."

But I had long years since shed talking as a means of communication, as a habit; I never teach by talking or live by it either. I finish my tea then touch her hand and say only, reflectively, "Oh?"

At which she laughs full throat like Lionel or Daphne, then the two of us go to the piano and play four-hand Schubert—education and philosophy enough for me.

The design of work I followed was the pre-fab design all over again with the teachers all back to four and five. They too wrote their own little books to read to each other so that you could never say their books were unsuitable, since they'd come from themselves. If I had thought my work had been completed in the distant pre-fab, at SFU it rose to its all-time zenith. With so much love towards me, such excellent conditions and scintillating young people the artist in me who had been in a coma for years since my love had died . . . he stirred again and stretched. After having been in deep freeze through the perma-winter he woke in the Vancouver spring like the bulbs I'd planted before the ground froze to crack up painfully to the northern light and breathe the sharp spring air. He found things to his taste: no competition; no husband, no family, no lover, no ideal girl, no PSBMEH and no Godzone hostility for and suspicion of an artist. I'd known the artist in me to fuse with teaching once before with Keith Henderson on guard but now the two became like one tree grafted upon another until there

The Maori *tiki*

was no more conflict. Now I knew at last what it was like to be an artist only, as well as discovering the private life of a spinster.

Between workshops the preparation overflowed like Heidelberg frothing in a glass. Not one story or song or dance did I use in that summer that had not been composed only the week before, except for the lullabies I'd written at home. Believe it or not, for the first time since Keith's day out came my old pre-war blackboard chalk to make two full-scale drawings on the stand-up blackboard; on one side, a Maori tiki in red and black with flaring occult paua eyes in greens and blues, and on the other side an erupting Godzone volcano shooting out flames of key words on white cards from its underground molten caverns. The paintings of the sixty five-year-olds on the walls changed from week to week, there were magic shapes in the silver sand, sculpture in the laundry and guitars on the lawns outside.

Several Maori action songs I taught them, yes—bodily rhythms, swaying hips, quivering fingers, hands clapping and feet tapping, I showed them how to make their own pois and then the poi dance itself which I must say they found hard. All this should have been North American Indian culture but, in the way that Bombay would not show me its state schools, British Columbia wouldn't show me its Indians. "Never mind, my dear people," I told them, "you make jolly good Maoris."

That was the summer I took the primitive media, thinking of Third World countries and of the fields of UNESCO; we collected bark from the groves of trees nearby and charcoal left from open fires out there, writing on the bark with the charcoal or on protruding rocks or hard dry clay, as though paper had never happened. The mornings were like wide open craters of blowing energy, like steam from the ground on the volcanic plateau back in far Godzone; as the pre-fab had been, identically.

Towards the close, the waiting white charts we'd started with were now alive with the words of the key vocabulary, a microcosm of the mind of the Canadian child for all to see and use.

The last three mornings they made children's books, using the native vocabulary from the charts, their collective own, in as many languages as they knew; all of which were photocopied three times each and added up to a sudden new library. A juicy crowd, this intake, better cultivated, not media-opiated, with endless supplies of imagery and energy.

At the close of the last morning I sat on the carpet among them and told them three things: "Congratulations on the six hundred books you've made in ten languages in three mornings.

"When you return to the system and if you find it rigid and sterile do not attack it; inspire it," and

"Keep close to the great; but you've got to go back for them."

A faultless workshop, the summer of '72, like a ray of sun picking up the peak of a snowy mountain, or like a top note from Galli-Curci. Only one thing wrong: it was not in Godzone.

I had anticipated doom for the key vocabulary when it faced the audience, exposed onstage, but it liked the spotlight and, with Selma as the gardener, thrived like a native plant in its own environment; by which time I had come to know the chosen nine in the Vancouver Project who took the organic mornings back to their classrooms for demonstration before daily streams of observers. Their principals allowed the project, and the Vancouver Board of Education supported it to the point where some of the members visited the girls and even came to see me together. Who had ever heard of such a thing in Godzone? Even I visited the girls on occasion: glamorous, brainy, leggy people forging the new style with such brilliance at the spearpoint of sophisticated education that I named them The Spears: Joan, Maureen, Sheila, Sheryl, Marion, Margaret, Betty, Saioko and Ariane. They'd turn up at my place on a Friday after school with their own meals and wine and fun and love for me, my acknowledged family, and I'd get out my Heidelberg. "But couldn't we keep all those visitors off you Spears so it would be just you and the children?"

"No way, Mere. I like it."

"I work all right with them there."

"The kids would miss them."

Selma was often with us. "They're part of the scene, dearest."

It looked as though my work was tougher than I was myself; you could almost say it was leaving me behind. Nine demonstration rooms in Vancouver. Sitting with the children on the floor it occurred to me how more appropriate it would have been for them to have been planted in the country in which it arose, wholly organic that would have been. I had no doubt they could have been found in Godzone like scintillating leggy sophisticates, even in the bloody profesh, but I couldn't see departmental support of them or education boards visiting a young teacher's room, other than to hold an inquiry over some misdemeanour. No . . . this was the only place. But I kept all this to myself as I'd come to keep most things.

Often, however, among these happy children, active and productive, writing their own books, teaching one another, singing and dancing and talking, I thought of Duthie in his incarceration, whom I'd promised I'd try to come back to; and of Derek in his little boy cell in hell.

It's hard to come back to the present, it's so far from then to the now. Distances by air, by sea, by countries and peoples and differing climates and by the gathering years. I've used up some of my research semester working on this manuscript, four months from September. I'd better get on to preparation now, I'd better visit our demonstration rooms and I ought to show up on campus.

There are trees at Montecito where I live, a new-made townlet within the city, and now in the fall the dogwood is blooming for the second time this season and the maples are crooning through their colours from yellow through orange and red and burnish to close in the final browns; as brilliant as showrooms up escalators. The maples give everything they have, are and know to the job in hand, taking their own good time about it while the audience of the city holds its breath as though witnessing the performance of celebrities. You walk along the streets and stop all the time . . .

There were letters from my three children this week. Pages and pages from Jas, swiftly intently written, telling me about the children, the heaving dramas, and about my home, Whenua. And one from El, in London, saying he'll be over again at Christmas to share the thrilling snow. I remember saying to him last Christmas, "Have you noticed no presences in this apartment, how sort of un-memoried it seems?"

"So that's what it is," he said. And one from Ash, saying again the thing that is never absent from any of their letters: "I think of you all the time, dear. Please come home."

I've been out a lot this fall into and around Vancouver with all sorts of lovely people, to their homes and to vivid restaurants. I'm permanently astonished at how people here love me. But what I love best is to wander alone around strange corners, into downstairs import shops among exotic people, selling their foreign wares; to wait at thundering intersections, anonymous in the crowds. In the thick of it. And all the time this song in me, "I'm not in New Zealand, I'm not in New Zealand," the sweetest song I ever heard. From the moment my plane lifted from the Wellington tarmac that evening when I left those islands, from that moment when the shaky old DC3 ploughed out over the Tasman and I looked back over the receding lights thinking never, never and never again, from that moment, even with the weapon of grief in my heart, this song began singing itself: "I'm no longer in New Zealand." In the postcard streets of Curepipe on the uplands of Mauritius, among the wonders and squeezing heats of India from beggars to marble floors, in the mouldering history of modern Israel, in the heavy-laden streets and undergrounds of London, in the six-months' snow on top of the Rockies in the United States and now where I work in Canada . . . this brilliant song revivifies me: "I am not in New Zealand." Though pain can be as white as the snow, this song is red like wine. Come back, winter, with your snow. The kind, warm snow.

The fall brought my research semester. One morning Selma gave me a lift up to university in her little Spitfire for a faculty meeting. There was already a return of the snow. "I'm starting to dream again, Selma, after a blank of four years. When the mind is frozen it doesn't dream. Did you know that?"

"Yes," that's all. She never does talk on her way to work, only when she stops by on her way home to Jack.

When I first came I had been appointed as a visiting professor for six months, then when that was up, appointed for another six months, but now after a year at SFU there came a party at my place when Tony Vogt said, "Do you wish to be reappointed, Sylvia?"

"Doesn't matter either way." The wine is French white dry.

"But you like the university, you've said so, and you've said you like the country." His bass cello voice and his immaculate English diction.

"The climate suits me." I'm sitting with him and Selma. I don't think either of them follows; a professor is expected to desire more than anything else an appointment to a university but I've got to untangle with teaching some time, yet, after all they have done for me, I can't admit it. "I'm not interested in education."

They stare. Jack is playing Mozart precisely.

I continue, "Education has so discredited itself I don't want my name associated with it," not the whole truth. I'm dissembling. Yet all they mean is to do me a good turn by letting me know it's the time to reapply and that they would see to it themselves on my behalf.

Below the Mozart the cello voice again, "You could help children better through a university."

"In or out of a university it remains a lost cause."

"It wouldn't hurt you to go on."

"I'm not crusader material, Tony."

I shouldn't drink wine and I know it, but even in my cups I can't reveal how I've always hated teaching and that no success or acclaim could make it otherwise; that rather than be known as a teacher I'd choose to be accused of a felony or of dissembling. Selma doesn't speak but much is taking place behind the thoughtful eyes upon me so I join Jack at the keyboard where we play together the dance movement from the Beethoven Seventh. All Selma says when she kisses me goodnight later is, "Another famous Henderson party."

As it turned out I found myself appointed permanently on faculty as a professor of education until retiring age about two years hence.

And I meant it too for I felt I could live in Vancouver. I could always resign and continue to live at Montecito as a writer and artist only. I'd said to Elliot when he'd come over from London for Christmas, "Do you notice about Montecito, El, how there are no memories here?"

He'd been reading in his favorite armchair and he had looked up and around. Inside it was warm and domestic, through the glass the piled-up snow. As I passed him coffee he murmured agreement; we were both thinking of his father.

Selma was all that I was not: a brilliant thinker, gifted organiser with a New York background and a continental reputation, and I was just about all that she was not, yet her canvas of the Vancouver Project. told me of a strong artist, involving as it did the whole of the province and the world of children beyond. She was a real teacher; dedicated, committed, thorough, wide-ranging, sacrificial, crusading and, above all, was proud to be. "The university is my life," she told me one morning when she'd come to me in the nadir of "a love." On the floor with head on my knee. "I don't advise people," I answered. "I can only say what I do. I'd pack up my tent and go. That way the pain is hard, but short. If I stayed the pain would perpetuate. You can't win either way. But when I go, as I always have, the pain at least has an end."

"But the university is my life . . . my *life*."

So I choose an easier word. "You can at least disengage."

"Disengage. Yes." She can take this idea. "I will disengage."

One late afternoon in my low chair with Heidelberg lager at hand, my steak in the oven and some of The Spears on the carpet with the wine and food

With Selma

they've brought, my new steady family, talking out with one another the week behind them or helping each other with their

love-affairs . . . the whole scene and its cast a canvas of Selma's . . .
though she drinks only water, Selma stops by on her way home to
Jack after a thundery day on the hill and sits on the carpet near me,
her long legs in black silk stockings, folded. Plainly she needs cheer-
ing up.

"You know what, Selma?" I say. "I've got my university pension
all fixed up. I've now got a work permit, social security number and
government health insurance. I'm a legal landed immigrant now, a
Canadian citizen."

"I love you very much, dearest." Apart from her brain she's a child
like me . . . I think. I don't know.

Gwenda drops in sometimes, my sister Norma's second-marriage
daughter, his, if you know what I mean, and she's playing the Mozart
she learnt from the nuns; accurate sophisticated touch. There are all
sorts of fringe benefits from housing a good piano.

Heidelberg, "I've noticed, Selma, a very fine cemetery in West
Vancouver, over that big bridge on the way to your place, Eagleridge,
on a green slope with trees. I ought to buy a plot there. Do you think
it's full up? I don't want to die in Godzone."

"That's what you wrote in *Teacher*. Jack and I are only twenty
minutes away."

"Half an hour by my taxis. Selma, you're the cleverest best friend
I've ever had." I recall Opal on the River to whom I had given access to
myself, and I thought of Kit who could quote anything on the moment
and I thought of beautiful Leslie Shaw in the wilderness of Waiomatatini who had been reading *Dark Son* and of all the former ideal girls
on my way through schools on whom I'd tried to model myself . . .
but none of them had been Ph.D. material and could have created the
Vancouver Project. And I don't think any of them had called me
Dearest all the time and liked to take my hand, and could play with
me four-hand Schubert; had worn New York fashions and had come
to me with life's own love-affairs; put it this way: who had—forget it.
So I say, "I've never had a friend before who was a Ph.D. and a tenure
professor and whose favorite sport was Clothes."

Only now, six years later, is it coming to me through Selma's letters
how much my presence there meant to her for the completion of the
Vancouver Project, that I had been a major colour on her massive
canvas, though, had I known, it would have made no difference. There
was a great deal on that subject unspoken between us, and even more
behind those wide still eyes.

To be permanent on faculty turned out to mean that the next year was to follow the pattern of the first and my dean ran into the problem of how to get an artist to repeat herself. Dan had started off his life in China, through the revolution too and all which that meant, had become an ordained minister of the church and now, Dean of Education at Simon Fraser, was a master of sensitive response and a master of consensus, but though I tried to my limit to do what he wanted the year came out another way. He told Elliot, who had come over from London again for Christmas, "Your mother worked obsessionally until she reached perfection and then she lost interest."

"My mother is the most difficult woman in the world."

Which Dan told me on the phone. "Don't forget," I defended, "it was a son who said it."

"Elliot, I can't do the same thing twice."

"You might as well do it, dear. You're among friends, you have a lovely home here, you're on a high salary and your work is recognised," which sounded like his father; trying to save me by reason.

"Both you and Dan are men."

"Well, put up with it."

"But you both want me to repeat myself."

"It's the least you can do for Selma."

"All right then. I'll see out this second time round. That'll make two years. But a *third* year, man . . . that's far too long in one country."

Jasmine wrote, "You stop work if you want to, Mummie. You keep both hands tight on your own life," while Ashton wrote, "Please come home, dear. I can't look after you when you're overseas. I'll build you a house in Havelock North, or next door to me; if only you'd come home."

It was after Jasmine married again, a tall older man with three older children, making nine in their family, eleven altogether living at Whenua, and there were exhilarating photos all over the piano of the wedding of two families at Whenua, when a new thought came to me: "I've only lately realised, Selma, that I'm no longer first with anyone."

"But many love you."

"Not the same thing."

It did astonish me, however, that with so much love and so many friends as well as a ready-made family in The Spears, not to mention several charming men in my orbit, accomplished, sophisticated, poetic, at least two of whom were handsome, I had not been able to love anyone new since my own true love had died. "Yes," to Selma and Jack over dinner at Eagleridge, "I was attracted to him but six hours was as long as I could hold it. Then I lost interest. He's handsome up to a point but he didn't have the face of Valentino or the voice of Enrico Caruso." Also, I did not add, as I was speaking of a colleague on the faculty, when you sank beneath the surface of what appeared in his poetry to be a mind of beauty, you hit hard edges and distortions and the water was muddy, not beautiful at all. And he had no idea of what I myself was like inside as had the long-lost man of four kisses in my youth, who had loved what he'd seen and who had sung "Who Is Sylvia?" Drinking wine with him over my counter I had felt none of the uproar of response to a letter recently from that same distant Pan calling "Where are you, Sylvia?" Yes, he'd betrayed me but it didn't matter now. Not that I'd even con-

Wandering the streets

sidered answering the letter though he was in the U.S.A. Godzone bloody pride I suppose.

But Selma never lost hope of a love-affair for me, seeing it, she'd say, as a further means of keeping me grounded at Simon Fraser and she took alert note of the men who passed my way. True, it had been I who had invited the Vancouver education board to come and see me but only because of her canvas; all six foot plus except Charlie, but what about Charlie? Nor had it been on account of the parade of accessible suitable men that I had had that lower half of the face-lift: "Why do you want this?" the surgeon had said.

I'd had the answer memorised. "Because I am a professor of education and my work is with very young children. When I was young

I was terrified of an old face and it makes me reluctant to sit near them. I've not seen any terror in them so far but it's I who feels the reluctance. It concerns my work." My word, The Spears were excited about that. I remember the unveiling before Selma came; Joan was there and I think Sheila. It took place after four in my green chair with the rest of them on the carpet. The severe grief-turned mouth had gone.

These pictures I have of the happiest years I knew abroad, at Simon Fraser University. In the forefront the Montecito ground-floor apartment and I'm sitting in my low green chair at four, my steak in the oven (New Zealand steak) and the Heidelberg lager on a round cane Chinese table, all these people, mostly young, spreading out on the carpet and someone like Selma or Jack or Gwenda playing Mozart on the Blüthner grand. People clustered on the floor about me as though I were dropping bright words of wisdom, whereas I had given up speaking as a medium of communication; it was they conferring with one another; supply the conditions and they will ease one another. You'd see my dean there sometimes, cross-legged nearby, not tall, quite short, the humblest man I'd met. I asked him to change places with me one day and yes, at once, whatever I wished and I sat at his younger knee. He drank water. "Dan," I confided, "I avoid doing things I know someone else can do. I think that's a waste of time. I concentrate on doing what I know no one else can do, and then it's very important."

No one played that grand who couldn't play. The masters present at these four o'clock end-of-days were Beethoven, Schubert and Mozart. You should have heard Norma's Gwenda on Mozart and I'd see again how Norma sent all the children, his, hers and theirs, to the N.Z. nuns for music, and here was Gwenda half a lifetime later dispensing Mozart in a foreign land, holding down a big music job in the city. It's all a matter of housing a fine piano; my parties at Montecito were ceiling high with the masters. By now I owned three grand pianos round the world: one at Whenua, one at Montecito and one I helped Elliot to buy in London.

A foremind picture, the scenes at four o'clock at Montecito. Different ones would bring a psycho-sick friend to sit at my knee; "His girl was killed on the road last week." Diana Kendall, my Australian right-hand man, brought the wife whose husband took his life from drugs, a brilliant and celebrated scholar he'd been and there were two little girls. At least two Spears revealed a feeling for Elliot, but Joan said, "Mere, I don't have to marry Elliot to be one of your family. I *am* one of your family."

They were all my family, whoever came. You can find a family anywhere.

The second year turned round the corner of December and into the Canadian spring, my flowers appeared on the patio and a flowered umbrella table and chairs and here was a second summer. I still had a third year to go after this—wouldn't you think I could have settled and stayed, but no I was lifting my nose to the breeze from the ocean like Mumma scenting new pastures. There was everything in that life I'd dreamed of in the past—home, job, friends, security, loving arms and thousands of kisses—but my face still lifted to the mountaintops and the wind from over the water, still listened to the stories it told. Two years was more than enough in one country.

And thawing is a painful thing. It seemed as though bulbs planted deep within the long winter of my heart were pushing up in the spring and cracking the ice and I'd dream of Whenua at night. I remember lying on my bed resting one afternoon in a loneliness I couldn't bear, "and Selma, I saw Jasmine and Ashton standing there at the bottom of the bed and they said, It's all right, Mummie. We're here. You're all right now."

"Jack and I want you to come to Eagleridge on Saturday, dearest, and we'll make a New Zealand meal: roast lamb and mint sauce and an apple pie with cream that runs."

"My spirit must drink from the springs of home or it will wither away."

My second open summer session was arranged, but privately I didn't know how I could do it. Repeat myself . . . *impossible*. The Spears were flourishing in the city with Selma and the point had been made. Though I told nobody at all how I felt I heard later they'd been reading the signs, remembering how I'd thrown over an entire session on the first day last fall semester (there *had been* sound reasons). "We couldn't be sure you'd do it," they said. "We kept our fingers crossed."

Oh yes, oh yes I meant to do it all right, but the day did come when I had to confess to Selma I had finally booked my passage home on *Arcadia* for when the session was over, with the result that in the evening Jack brought Selma over from Eagleridge and stood her up in my kitchen for me to see for myself: wan and drenched. "Look at that," he said. "She's been crying all day."

Jasmine and Bill sent two of their daughters over to Vancouver "to bring Grandma home"; my own eldest grandgirl, Corinne, and Jasmine's new eldest daughter, older than Co, Robyn, both of whom enrolled for the summer sessions at SFU, Selma's first and then mine, along with other subjects . . . Co took music and Robyn took art. As it happened, Robyn was already training as a teacher in Godzone though Co was not, being too terribly in love with a man back home. Rob was fair and taller than Co and I, and Co was dark and petite. My household was now three and I told Jack at the piano, "I've finished living alone forever."

Whichever way you looked at it the summer session conditions were excellent, not the least the choosing of my own assistants again; the qualifications I required being (1) happily married to each other, (2) no previous teaching experience, (3) it would have to be they who made the approach and (4) New Zealanders. So when two young Godzoners wrote to me from somewhere in the States and met all criteria, the next thing the two Kirklands were on my patio, as well as on salary from SFU. John was tall, fair, sophisticated and maybe circumspect, maybe not, and warming up at that time for his Ph.D., while Cheryl was a physiotherapist with memorable legs. Nothing to undo in either of them and they both were fond of a joke. Though the Kirklands lived elsewhere, my household was now five Godzoners, and when Gwenda dropped in it was six.

The conditions supplied, and allowed, by Simon Fraser University were enough for any artist, however temperamental, to repeat himself, but although I started off as well as I possibly could, I began to fragment about halfway through, by which time the Kirklands had learnt the work and John ran the show. The workshops had no chance to break in half. Cheryl took over the nine Indians from the Arctic Circle as though she'd been born to it—and probably was. Also, as well as the Kirklands on staff, The Spears would take turns giving a hand with the core teaching towards the close, though I continued to do all the music.

As well as the Indian culture blazing away, up came the Maori culture again and Cheryl introduced the Maori stick game, the most popular musical ever seen in class—whites and browns all in together. I've seen it start up at parties at my place or on Friday nights when The Spears came in.

But no ideal conditions could hold me; the day came . . . at noon on the last Thursday, the goodbyes all over and the last of the company departed, and only we five Godzoners left—John, Cheryl, Rob, Co

and me—all exhausted to the last cell and corpuscle in our bodies, to
the last hair on our heads, when we gathered on bar stools at the
counter gasping. The two Kirklands had successfully run an open
summer school at the spearpoint of education, Rob had got three
straight As for her university work and Co had been granted a scholarship. All of which said quite something to me of the quality of New
Zealand education, in a way that nothing else could have. As for me,
I'd finished teaching at sixty-three, the one thing I'd not wanted to do
along the whole journey through life. How had that come about?
John Kirkland had his own definition of me; as one of the girls
made the tea he filled a glass of bubbling lager and passed it to
me gravely with a courtly bow: "Madame Heidelberg."

They stayed on to clean up, the girls were shopping, and the moment came when I had to wheel the tall stand-up blackboard out upon
the patio for its chalk to be rubbed off, then the blackboards washed;
on one side the full-sized Maori tiki with its fierce visionary eyes
which had been there two years and on the other the New Zealand
volcano of the key vocabulary, both in the brilliant pre-war chalk.
You couldn't leave them on for chalk does not endure and they'd soon
be defaced, a fate worse than erasure. A case of the Pied Piper of
Hamelin on the school wall at Pipiriki in my youth and of all my
other drawings and carvings and sculpting on walls and banks and
riverbeds in the valley of the River. Transient.

Well I couldn't quite clean them off deliberately myself so I walked
back into the room and left it to the Kirklands whereupon they took
a rubber each on either side and lifted their arms but their hands fell
to their sides. So I returned to the patio and rubbed off both sides
myself, then they washed the boards. But only New Zealanders, compatriots, could have felt like that. All that was left of Godzone was
the chalk dust on the patio in scarlet and indigo, orange and green
with the shading of white and black. As impermanent as passion. The
three of us have never spoken of it. When all this was over, however,
and they remained standing side by side at the cleaned blackboard, in
silent sadness, even horror, that only compatriots could feel, I went
to my bedroom and picked up a framed colour photo of the tiki they
hadn't known about, returned to the patio and gave it to them. Not one
word passed between us, then or since. The whole drama was played
in silence.

The Kirklands were returning to the U.S.A., but our three berths
were booked on *Arcadia* for September 10 though I had resigned five

times before I was heard: in prose, verse, jargon, cartoon and code. Then my dean sent a message down to Montecito inviting me to name my salary if I would stay on, or at least return for a semester next year, but I deliberately named the impossible and priced myself out. Dr. Ian Allen paled when he heard the figure.

Some other universities made bids for me, first among them Cornell which, at that time, was receiving nominations for the position of Professor at Large, left vacant by the sudden death of Dr. Leakey, the archaeologist in Central Africa; so far three schools at Cornell were promoting my nomination—education, sociology and psychology. And Calgary in Canada for the position of working with North American Indians. There were others like New York City, I forget what for. I valued them all and can only hope they were answered. (Later: They were answered. I answered them myself, the Cornell letters. I wanted the job, but I didn't get it.)

Rob and Co now had two new big projects on hand: organising the packing or selling of my furniture and buying presents for the family at home. As for me, I could only sit in my low chair at four o'clocks among people widespread on the carpet around me and perched on the tall bar stools.

After all, I had done what I'd set out to do; safely established the key vocabulary. True, it had already been established in countries other than the U.S.A. and Canada, but by other people. In the Vancouver Project I'd planted it with my own hand and had witnessed Selma and The Spears at work, with the backing of the Vancouver education board and SFU: to defuse the impulse to kill. And so were the girls doing what they'd set out to do: to bring Grandma home.

The Kirklands departed first, then our Australian bodyguards, Lawrie and Diana Kendall, took over my little household of three and if ever you're in a hopeless spot call an Australian. Somehow they got us to *Arcadia* at the wharf. To the shipping company lady on the phone I asked, "Could I have some more boarding passes please?"

"Any more, professor, and *Arcadia* will sink."

At last it was *I* on the ship drawing away from the shore . . . streamers, flowers, tears, kisses, but a whole lifetime late. On deck I heard the West Wind which had called me when a girl, when I'd run away over the hills from marriage: "Come away, wild spirit, come away with me. Come with me over the sea."

I left the girls to it and climbed to the Lookout.

# V

# EPILOGUE—
# HOME

1973 - 1978

*October 31, 1978*

WHENUA  Yesterday I posted to Bob Gottlieb the end of this manuscript, *I Passed This Way*. There's only this epilogue on God-zone to write, and it's going to be brief, bringing the narrative from 1908 to 1978, spanning five generations and seventy years. The pace and the distance and the tensions are over and I'll not pass this way again. I'll write my last word and last fullstop on my birthday in December.

The girls and I arrived home five years ago and joined the large family at Whenua, making a household of twelve. Both are married now with new children; Co's little girl Adèle, my first great-grandchild, is already two and a half. Later, Jasmine's large Beveridge family moved to their own home a mile away and I live on my own at Whenua, along with the phantoms and occasional prowlers on moon-lit summer nights; also the birds, stray cats in the shadows of the trees, the voice of the pheasant down the bank and the gulls patrolling the harbour. And when I take a lager at four no crowds of young people spread on the carpet.

You might say I live with my memories, but since I sent the manuscript to Bob they've been receding hourly. The boundless area of imagery housing all those overseas people is moving away like a day that is over. In the past, each single one had been my reality but now that entire company populating the mind is departing from the stage. I've said before in this narrative that my adulthood was bracketed in dream and now my life out in the big world I'd so desired as a girl is also bracketed in dream, leaving me with reality only and the swiftly running present.

I have felt bereft and I thought I might write to them all now that I have the time, but you can't stamp and post a letter to disappearing people; you can't address the envelope "To You Who Loved Me, c/o Fantasy." True, the present is pressing but there remain vast vacuums which it cannot yet fill in; neither a walk to Cherrywood market nor a visit to Co and Dearheart; neither a moment in the garden nor an hour on the beach. Such a no-man's-land only a writer knows. Not even the monster lashing his tail or my travelling companion, Fate. I do not even hear within me my favorite song, "I'm not in New Zealand," because I am, though I do speak the other often enough when wandering the spaces and heights of Whenua, "This is my home," along with the final masterpiece, "I don't have to teach any more." Only the phantoms remain unbracketed and the star in the southern sky.

Another lap that is fading is the onslaught of Kiwi Kringe when I returned to God's Own Country; years of culture shock manifesting itself psychosomatically in weeks of public hospital at the mercy of night nurses who knew who I was . . . other patients didn't get it . . . when I walked again the valley of the shadow but on my own account this time; of traction, sedation, crutches and walking sticks. Yet I recovered from all that

Four generations

as Puppa never had, so well that I'm thinking of returning to work in the garden for the first time since Keith died; to plant more native bush along the paths down the bank, first carved there twelve years ago to re-create the forests of my childhood, for me to walk again in the third age. Grant and Adrian are re-forming these paths like the sheep-tracks round the hills we'd padded barefoot; Sylvie, Norma, Marmie and Vad, and sure enough I walk in trees again while the new present spills over to fill in the vacuums of the departing past.

Returning to work in the garden did I say? But only in the garden, not the classroom, though the ever-treacherous heart is still good for a trick or two. Over the years I've been home it has been secretly looking for Godzone to say, Well, you've proved yourself and your work overseas so *now* we'll consider it ourselves. Here's a fine job for you, professor; training young teachers for the infant rooms. Good salary, staff, building, equipment and with the support of the education department. I'd hear my heart whispering that when I woke in the night though in the morning I'd say *NEVER*. It's not teaching you want, dearest; it's the approval of your nation family; for them to see your work and say, That's good, Sylvia.

For that I'd go into the freezing works chambers, go scrub-cutting or shovel gravel on the side of the road. And that's how you spell the word Pain.

But the heart's bluff was not called, the choice did not come. You'd read of these grand-scale, country-wide, year-long and desperate conferences filling up the newspapers and journals on how to solve the education but no word came to me. You'd have to witness them floundering round with symptoms, symptoms and symptoms with not one glance at the causes; bewailing the uproar and indiscipline of youth, and why are the teachers so upset, leaving the profession and the country itself, and what shall we do about it? Yet here I was accessible among them but growing older and older.

Until one day a man came along to me, an enlightened benign educator, though lacking the fire that vision needs, and we sat together in Selah Seven. As it happens I knew this man, he'd reviewed *Myself* and had seen me in hospital and he said, "I can't get over how well you are. You're better every time I see you," and we kissed.

Then he said he'd been commissioned by Broadcasting to make a tape with me "so that when you're gone, Sylvia, we'll know what you said. When you're gone we're going to revere you. What do you wish to be remembered by?"

"You're too late, New Zealand. You've missed your chance."

He groans and covers his eyes. "I know, I know."

"I've been here all my life."

"But now there are young teachers in the country longing to meet you. Some have come from abroad to find you. Would you agree to see them?"

"What for?" I'm in a ground-length suit of deep purple and my hair was, is, a long curl down my back. "I know about them, Birk, they've written, but they've told me that whenever they start my work they're threatened and hounded by headmasters and inspectors—'If you continue with this work you'll have no future.'"

Groan. "I know, I know." A hand covers his face . . . on behalf of Godzone I'd say.

"One had a breakdown and applied for another school. Another and her husband sold up their home, left the province and finally got a job in a convent school where she has all the freedom to work with the children. Found all the classroom joy she'd sought. Both these girls had made their own way to me." Advanced like The Spears, Spear-point people. Brains, looks, vision, legs, energy. New Zealand Spears.

He kisses me. "Sylvia, couldn't you try again? They've begged me. Just . . . just to meet you. Just see one or two others?"

Fierce flare. "But I'm first-class."

His Godzone breath stopped. Shocked.

"You're asking me to do something second-class. All this back-door, hand-to-mouth furtiveness like a thief, like a failure. That's not my style, man. My work calls for tall halls, tall salary, friendly col-leagues and the goodwill of the department. I'm not an international saboteur. I'm not sacrificial or a mediaeval crusader. (I'm not even a teacher.) I'm an artist."

"But when you're gone . . . ?"

Really, the man's preoccupation with the "when I'm gone" part—it has a ghoulish quality like eerie music in the minor. It reminds me of the vultures in India employed by the Parsis to clean up their dead. Does he have a death wish? But that was my only encounter with the PSBMEH, sepulchrally apt. Silly . . . that's the word. So much for tricks of the heart. Better to work in the garden and get my hands dirty some other way.

Whenua is an inn by the wayside for people who come to stay, a place where they put down their bags for a while and think them-selves over. I maintain Whenua in the best condition expensively; windows, garden, plumbing, beds, towels at the ready, the water hot in the cylinder and the log fire set in the winter and since none of this does itself I employ a housekeeper, a garden in season and a man for the windows after a storm. Then I leave guests alone to cook for themselves, fend for themselves while I get on with my work in Selah where I also sleep. None needs help from me; all you do is supply the conditions for the mind to take care of itself, and the body too half the time, while the traveller unwinds his tight knots to see ahead more clearly, for Whenua has this secret healing quality which has nothing to do with me.

As it happens Whenua will fill up again in January when the film people foregather here from Los Angeles and Godzone, all agog to get going on the filming of my book *Teacher* in New Zealand. She's at her best when overflowing with people with lights on and all doors open.

I like to say light-tongued that Whenua has seceded from Godzone, socially and professionally, a token principality of which John Kirkland loves to call me the Chief Denizen and addresses his letters that way, but only because it tells well when the Kirklands come who've returned to N.Z. But people do cross this frontier, usually from overseas, so that briefly I'm of the international community again. Americans come in our winter which is their summer in the northern hemisphere and, God, you want to try keeping these people warm accustomed to an unwavering seventy degrees from central heating, this inability to adjust to the swinging temperatures of Whenua, the backlogs in the open fire they go through . . . huddling by the fire, drinking wine and talking non-stop and obsessively of North America . . . never mind; they sure keep my wits up to date, the debate. Five days and nights a go. But the Australian Kendalls who share the same summer have crossed the Tasman three times.

And people like the Gardiner-Scotts from Jerusalem, Bill and Darinka, visiting their parish astride both hemispheres, discounting borders and seasons to negotiate the more nebulous frontiers between past and present so that when they materialised unexpectedly at Whenua I was back in that worst moment of my wandering in the Hospice at Jerusalem, when I'd been summoned to London at midnight, the last time I'd seen them ten years ago. Yet they remained real and inspiring people who held me and kissed me all over again.

Mainly, however, Whenua is the only life I lead. As it happens three of my families live within a mile or two. Jasmine's, Co's and Grant's, while Ashton and family come from Hastings to stay and Elliot ducks out from London, air fares permitting, bringing my French grandson from Paris to see me, Vincent. In the meantime, with everyone at work or at school through the week, or away at university it's Co and Adèle my travelling companions along this last lane of life; great-grandma, Co and Dearheart hand-in-hand.

But this is enough writing for today. I'll walk to market now and buy some animals for Dearheart, colourful, plastic little things.

I found Dearheart on her swing yesterday at home. "Bape grandma," she called, "my fwing."

White frock with blue flowers. I get out the plastic animals I've bought and hold up the fat red frog. "What's this, Dearheart?"

"F-f-fwokk."

Hold up the sleek black horse. "What's this, Dearheart?"

"F-fworse."

Keith Henderson would have loved to see her.

---

Goodbye, Marmie and Evadne. Only three left now: Lionel and I and Norma.

Exactly three weeks till my birthday but I've already slid into seventy when I sent the manuscript away holding my life as I saw it; the journey behind me is vanishing swiftly, leaving only reverberations of a turbulent symphony in a world diminishing to the size of Dearheart's. The past is becoming no more than a sudden touch of tears at unexpected music, something I cannot recall but which I had not had time to weep on then; or a thrill of magic and romance at scent when whole scenes flash intact.

The season now of examinations, birthdays, weddings in the family and another Christmas tree though it is not easy with the carols filling the air in the shops in town and at home. It takes music to knock on the doors of the past to rouse what is sleeping there so that it was a rest in other cultures when you did not have to hear them. Enough for today.

On Sunday I woke and said, "I'm seventy." The time to do what I've long desired; instead of going at once to my table as I have for thirty years, I open the door of Selah, walk out on the grass beneath the trees to the dawn chorus of the birds and sit on the tree stump there. Very still on the harbour it was with no subversive west wind luring the spirit away. Just me solo, and I remembered something from Russell about the soul being alone on a raft on the great wild ocean of the night.

At the afternoon party at Jas and Bill's most of the four generations were there except Elliot and Vincent but Ashton gave the toast for his mother and I called the toast for absent friends and I did not sting any more. All the food was homemade and exquisite from the hands of Jas and Co while Kirsto had iced the cake and had arranged the candles in the number 70.

You should see the music room at Whenua now, full of flowers, some from beyond Godzone, bouquets heaping, colours leaping, and all for me this time. Not unlike the days following Keith Henderson's funeral except that there had been far more then ... everywhere they'd been; covering up the wide fireplace and frothing into the foyer but most of those had been wreaths. Keith never knew about his flowers, nor about mine either, but Whenua absorbs them all; knows and registers all. When the early light arrives next morning my great

Ashton and
his family

loves revisit me. By star**light** and by stormlight, by noonlight and
dawnlight they rem**ember me**.

And now . . . to s*urf*ace again to the breezy present where the your
are coming and *going* and the voices are real. The morning is wide

the sky is new and I'll take a walk with the great-grandbaby and we'll go down by the water. I've been longing for this, to forget the past, though I'm very pleased to have done what I set out to do, to speak of Keith on paper.

From my Lookout at the peak of seventy I can see back to the generations at the beginning of the century and ahead to the generations after me to the end of the twentieth century, a story of continuity. The inner eye ranges up and down the years in gratuitous perspective and in child-wide wonder so that I understand my country and forgive her all . . . yet with no famous last words to deliver. I spoke my words thirty years ago in the pre-fab at Fernhill, on the subject of the releasing cooling key vocabulary that eases violence, treats illiteracy and defuses the impulse to kill. At the time, swung by passion, it seemed to take years to say, mountaintops and miles, but against the backdrop of a lifetime . . . a moment only. They *were spoken*, however, whatever the cost, and I am not cursed with regret.

This epilogue should take a light-hearted look at Godzone but when I try to turn my mind out upon this sovereign nation the hinges tend to grind and the screws fall out and my vision becomes myopic. Not that I feel any call to either praise or blame the country, for New Zealand habitually de-rates herself much more severely than I ever could; it's her sport, her way of life.

Elliot's son, Vincent

When you think of the brilliance come from this country; talk about brain drain and what about skill drain and youth drain. I could write pages of explanations and excuses about our social, racial, historical and geographical isolation; from our markets on the other side of the world and shipping costs to our inbred thinking and island size, mesmerised by our own land's beauty: as a people we're a problem child but we're too tiny to be heard. It's enough to say that the population is falling steadily and that speaks for itself. "Where is New Zealand?" they'd ask overseas.

"As far as you can go."

neighbours in Southeast Asia say they doubt if New Zealand has ome to terms with her geographical situation. "Does she wish to remain an outpost of European civilisation? A delightful country but they're loath to work and afraid of competition."

Our other major Pacific neighbours, South Korea, Japan and China, envy the openness of our country and our small population, often expressed to New Zealand visitors; understanding why we wish to preserve what we have, but in Southeast Asia's historic millions there is evidence of a growing resentment that N.Z. does not take a greater number of refugees from Indochina. "We hear she could do with an infusion of new blood."

On occasion they attribute our reluctance to racial motives and not infrequently to our fear that hard-working Asians would ginger up productivity to levels unacceptable to the New Zealand work force; from a N.Z. official in Asia recently, "My God, let too many of them in and they'd take over all the milk bars. We've got to be careful about this one. They're very hard workers."

"Besides," from the government, "high migration inflow could be inflationary because of the large government expenditure required before a migrant family becomes productive."

"Nonsense," from the multi-millions of Asia, pointing to our steadily falling population. "There's a clear availability of space to absorb more people. My God, what a beautiful country . . . but you don't deserve it."

I don't know what North America thinks

of Godzone, for largely she doesn't know where we are, what we are, or even *that* we are, except for the military heads. On the other side of the world, however, the place of our origins and major markets, Jean Monnet, identified with the creation of the European Economic Community, wrote at ninety in his memoirs, "The sovereign nations of the past can no longer solve the problems of the present; they cannot ensure their own progress or control their own future. The European Community is not an end in itself but a process of change, continuing that same process which in an earlier period of history produced our national forms of life. It is only a stage on the way to the organised world of tomorrow."

With Godzone still apronned to the skirts of Europe, when can we create our own South Pacific Community? Monnet warned, "We cannot stop when the whole world around is on the move."

True, my home and families are here but somewhere over the continents and oceans, in and out of the valley of the shadow of death, I graduated into a world citizen. And what I learnt out there was that a wide-flung company of expatriate New Zealanders, along with Elliot, would wish to return and live quietly in Godzone but precious few have "because most of them know they would not be welcome; their experience has been that the very skills they exercise to such an advanced degree in the most sophisticated environments of the world are not wanted, no matter how desperately they may be needed, in their own country."*

On the other hand, I'd rather go on record as saying something in praise of the islands I was born in; I find a very fine coverage of world events in the papers and magazines, better than most and much better than America, almost as comprehensive as the *Times of India*; not only because we plainly need it but because so many of our greats are overseas or have been buried there. It reminds me of the very first pages in this book where I was talking about the godwits which ply from Siberia to New Zealand each spring, from their breeding grounds to their feeding grounds in the estuaries of our coasts. "In these lonely latitudes and unfrequented longitudes, surfed by oceans from every horizon, the New Zealand eye is obliged to turn outward, north-westward back to our own first breeding grounds, urgently checking our British origins and tracking our famous exiles...

". . . the girl spirit of New Zealand standing slight mid-land, her fingers tight on the beginnings of threads, taut from the pull of her ranging birds in the skies overseas. Could she but haul in her exiles all there together both buried and living, could she afford her great,

* Tony Simpson, N.Z. *Listener*, October 14, 1978.

the rest of the world might possibly see her and come to learn where she is."

On the journey through life I'd often come upon some inn by the way-side which gave me shelter from the Pacific cyclones, but none had been quite the haven I'd sought, though sweet and bountiful enough, yet all the time the ideal, the perfect had been waiting for me in my own-built home in Godzone. Whatever my disasters in this country, surrounded by a wilderness of ocean, these islands turn out to be the one place where I would wish to be, and Whenua the one inn I desire.

> And I have asked to be
> Where no storms come,
> Where the green swell is in the havens dumb,
> And out of the swing of the sea.
>                     —Gerard Manley Hopkins

A NOTE ON THE TYPE

This book was set on the Linotype in Granjon, a type named
in compliment to Robert Granjon, but neither a copy of
a classic face nor an entirely original creation. George W.
Jones based his designs for this type on that used by
Claude Garamond (1510–61) in his beautiful French books,
and Granjon more closely resembles Garamond's own
type than does any of the various modern types
that bear his name.
Robert Granjon began his career as typecutter in 1523.
The boldest and most original designer of his time, he
was one of the first to practice the trade of typefounder
apart from that of printer. Between 1557 and 1562 Granjon
printed about twenty books in types designed by himself,
following, after the fashion, the cursive handwriting of
the time. These types, usually known as *caractères de
civilité*, he himself called *lettres françaises*, as especially
appropriate to his own country.
Composed by Maryland Linotype Composition Co.,
Inc., Baltimore, Maryland.
Printed by The Murray Printing Company,
Forge Village, Massachusetts.
Bound by The Haddon Craftsmen,
Scranton, Pennsylvania.
Book design by Margaret M. Wagner.

LEARNING RESOURCES

CENTER

ILLINOIS CENTRAL COLLEGE

MCMLXVI

**East Peoria, Illinois**

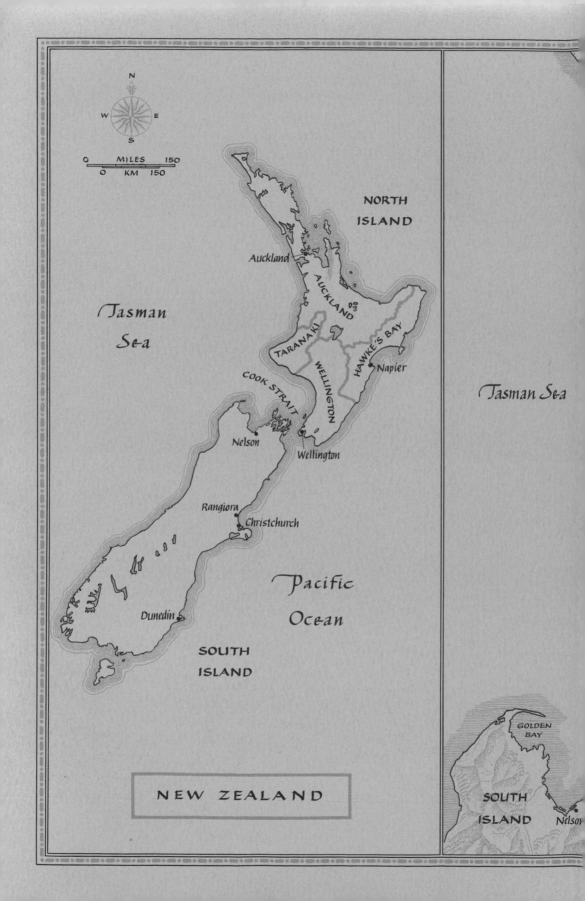

NEW ZEALAND